OXFORD SHAKESPEARE CONCORDANCES

OXFORD SHAKESPEARE CONCORDANCES

HENRY VIII

A CONCORDANCE TO THE TEXT
OF THE FIRST FOLIO

OXFORD
AT THE CLARENDON PRESS
1971

Oxford University Press, Ely House, London W. 1

GLASGOW NEW YORK TORONTO MELBOURNE WELLINGTON
CAPE TOWN SALISBURY IBADAN NAIROBI DAR ES SALAAM LUSAKA ADDIS ABABA
BOMBAY CALCUTTA MADRAS KARACHI LAHORE DACCA
KUALA LUMPUR SINGAPORE HONG KONG TOKYO

FILMSET BY COMPUTAPRINT LIMITED
AND PRINTED IN GREAT BRITAIN
AT THE UNIVERSITY PRESS, OXFORD
BY VIVIAN RIDLER
PRINTER TO THE UNIVERSITY

GENERAL INTRODUCTION

In this series of Oxford Shakespeare Concordances, a separate volume is devoted to each of the plays. The text for each concordance is the one chosen as copy-text by Dr. Alice Walker for the Oxford Old Spelling Shakespeare now in preparation.

Each concordance takes account of every word in the text, and represents their occurrence by frequency counts, line numbers, and reference lines, or a selection of these according to the interest of the particular word. The number of words which have frequency counts only has been kept as low as possible. The introduction to each volume records the facsimile copy of the text from which the concordance was prepared, a table of Folio through line numbers and Globe edition act and scene numbers, a list of the misprints corrected in the text, and an account of the order of printing, and the proof-reading, abstracted from Professor Charlton Hinman's *The Printing and Proof-Reading of the First Folio of Shakespeare* (Oxford, 1963).

The following notes on the main features of the concordances may be helpful.[1]

A. *The Text*

The most obvious misprints have been corrected, on conservative principles, and have been listed for each play in the introduction to the corresponding concordance. Wrong-fount letters have been silently corrected.

Obvious irregularities on the part of the original compositor—for example the anomalous absence of full stops after speech prefixes—have been normalized and noted. Colons, semicolons, exclamation and interrogation marks after italicized words have been modernized to roman fount after current practice, since this aspect of

---

[1] An account of the principles and methods by which the concordances were edited appears in *Studies in Bibliography*, vol. 22, 1969.

compositorial practice would not normally be studied from a concordance. The spacing of words in the original printed texts, particularly in 'justified' lines, is extremely variable; spacing has been normalized on the basis of the compositor's practice as revealed in the particular column or page.

For ease of reference, the contractions *S.*, *L.*, *M.*, and forms such as *Mist.* and tildes, have been expanded when the compositor's own preferred practice is clear, and the expansion has been noted in the text. For M^r, the superior character has been lowered silently. Superior characters like the circumflex in *baâ* and those in $\overset{\iota}{y}$, $\overset{e}{y}$, $\overset{u}{y}$, and $\overset{c}{w}$, have been ignored. The reader should find little difficulty in distinguishing the original form of the pronominal contractions when they are encountered in the text. They are listed under Y and W respectively.

B. *Arrangement of entries*

The words in the text are arranged alphabetically, with numerals and & and &c listed at the end. Words starting with I and J, and U and V, will be found together under I and V respectively. The reader should note that the use of U for the medial V (and I for J) leads in some cases to an unfamiliar order of entry. For example, ADUISED is listed before ADULTERY. The reader will usually find the word he wants if he starts his inquiry at the modern spelling, for when the old spelling differs considerably from the modern spelling, a reference such as 'ENFORCE *see* inforce' will direct the reader to the entry in the concordance.

In hyphenated compounds where the hyphen is the second or third character of the heading-word (as in A-BOORD), the hyphenated form may be listed some distance from other occurrences of the same word in un-hyphenated form. In significant cases, references are given to alert the user.

Under the heading-word, the line numbers or lines of context are in the order of the text. The heading-word is followed by a frequency count of the words in short and long (that is, marked with an asterisk) lines, and the reference lines. When a word has been treated as one to have a frequency count only, or a list of the line numbers and count, any further count which follows will refer to the reference lines listed under the same heading. Where there are two counts but no reference lines (as with AN), the first count refers to the speech prefix.

C. *Special Forms*

(*a*) The following words have not been given context lines and line references but are dealt with only by the counting of their frequency:

A AM AND ARE AT BE BY HE I IN IS IT OF ON SHE THE THEY TO WAS WE WITH YOU

These forms occur so often in most texts that the reader can locate them more easily by examining the text of the play than he could by referring to an extensive listing in the concordance.

Homographs of these words (for example I = *ay*) have been listed in full and are given separate counts under the same heading-word.

(*b*) A larger number of words, consisting mainly of variant spellings, have been given line references as well as frequency counts.

These words are: ACTUS AN AR ART ATT AU BEE BEEING BEEN BEENE BEING BENE BIN BUT CAN CANST CE COULD COULDST DE DECIMA DES DID DIDD DIDDEST DIDDST DO DOE DOES DOEST DOETH DONE DOO DOOE DOOES DOOEST DOOING DOON DOONE DOOS DOOST DOOTH DOS DOST DOTH DU E EN EST ET ETC FINIS FOR FROM HA HAD HADST HAH HAS HAST HATH HAUE HEE HEEL HEELE HEL HELL HER HIM HIR HIS IE IF IL ILL ILLE INTO LA LE LES MA MAIE MAIEST MAIST MAY ME MEE MIGHT MIGHTEST MIGHTST MINE MOI MOY MY NE NO NOE NON NONA NOR NOT O OCTAUA OFF OH OR OU OUR OUT PRIMA PRIMUS QUARTA QUARTUS QUE QUINTA QUINTUS SCAENA SCENA SCOENA SECUNDA SECUNDUS SEPTIMA SEPTIMUS SEXTA SHAL SHALL SHALT SHEE SHOLD SHOLDE SHOLDST SHOULD SHOULDE SHOULDST SIR SO SOE TE TERTIA TERTIUS THAT THEE THEIR THEIRE THEM THEN THER THERE THESE THEYR THIS THOSE THOU THY TIS TU VN VNE VOS VOSTRE VOUS VS WAST WEE WER WERE WERT WHAT WHEN WHER WHERE WHICH WHO WHOM WHOME WHY WIL WILL WILT WILTE WOLD WOLDE WOLDST WOULD WOULDE WOULDEST WOULDST YE YEE YF YOUE YOUR YT & &C 1 2 3 4.

Homographs of words on this list (e.g. *bee* = n.) have been listed in full, and also have separate counts.

(*c*) All speech prefixes, other than *All.*, *Both.*, and those which represent the names of actors, have been treated as count-only words. In some cases, however, where a speech prefix corresponds to a form already on the count-only list (e.g. *Is.*), a full entry has been given. In some other cases, when two counts are given for the same heading-word for no apparent reason, the count which does not correspond to the following full references or to the list of line references is that of the speech prefix form (for example AN in *The Tempest*).

(*d*) Hyphenated compounds such as *all-building-law* have been listed under the full form, and also under each main constituent after the first. In this example there are entries under ALL-BUILDING-LAW, BUILDING, and LAW. When, however, one of the constituents of the compound is a word on the count- or location-only list ((*a*) or (*b*) above), it is dealt with in whichever of these two lists applies. References such as 'AT *see also* bemock't-at-stabs' are given to assist the reader in such cases.

Simple or non-hyphenated compounds such as *o'th'King* have been listed only under the constituent parts—in this example under OTH and KING.

(*e*) 'Justified' lines where the spellings *may* have been affected by the compositor's need to fit the text to his measure are distinguished by an asterisk at the beginning of the reference line. If only location is being given, the asterisk occurs before the line reference. If only frequency counts are being given, the number *after* the asterisk records the frequency of forms occurring in 'justified' lines. Lines which do not extend to the full width of the compositor's measure have not been distinguished as 'justified' lines, even though in many cases the shorter line may have affected the spelling.

D. *Line Numbers*

The lines in each text have been numbered from the first *Actus Primus* or stage direction and thereafter in normal reading order, including all stage directions and act and scene divisions. Each typographical line has been counted as a unit when it contains matter for inclusion in the concordance. Catchwords are not included in the count. The only general exception is that turn-overs are regarded as belonging to their base-lines; where a turn-over occurs on a line by itself, it has been reckoned as part of the base-line, and the line containing only the turn-over has not been counted as a separate line. Turn-overs may readily be distinguished by vertical stroke and single bracket after the last word of the base-line; for example *brought with* | (*child,*.

When two or more lines have been joined in order to provide a fuller context, the line-endings are indicated by a vertical stroke |, and the line reference applies to that part of the line before the vertical stroke. For the true line-numbers of words in the following part of the context line, the stated line-number should be increased by one each time a vertical stroke occurs, save when the next word is a turn-over.

The numbering of the quarto texts has been fitted to that of the corresponding Folio texts; lines in the Quarto which do not occur in the Folio are prefixed by +. The line references are similarly specified. The line references of these concordances therefore provide a consistent permanent numbering of each typographical line of text, based on the First Folio.

PROGRAM CHANGES

Preparation of concordances to the first few texts, and the especial complexity of *Wiv.*, have enabled some improvements to be made to the main concordance program. For texts other than *Tmp.*, *TGV*, *MM*, and *Err.*, the concordances have been prepared with the improved program.

Speech-prefixes now have separate entries under the appropriate heading-word and follow any other entry under the same heading-word. Entries under AN in *Wiv.*, AND and TO in *TN*, and AD in *AYL* offer examples. This alteration provides a clearer record of the total number of occurrences of words which occur both as speech-prefixes and also as forms on the 'count only' or 'locations only' lists.

Another modification supplies a more precise reference to the location of words such as BEENE for which line numbers but no full lines are given. When a 'location only' word is encountered to the right of the 'end-of-line' bar (which shows that lines of text have been joined together in order to provide a sufficient context), the line number is now adjusted to supply the exact reference. In the concordances to the texts listed above, users will find that in some instances the particular occurrence of a 'location only' word which they wish to consult in the text is to be found in the line after the one specified in the concordance; this depends on whether lines have been joined in the computer-readable version of the text from which the concordance was made. It is not expected that readers will be seriously inconvenienced by this. Should a concordance to the First Folio be published, it will, of course, incorporate all improvements.

HENRY VIII

The Lee facsimile of the First Folio (Oxford, 1902) from which the concordance to *H8* was prepared, contains the corrected states of pages for which Professor Charlton Hinman (*Printing and Proof-Reading*, 1963, v. 1, p. 278–80) records variants. The order in which this section was printed, according to Hinman (v. 2, p. 517), runs:

By C*x	By C*x	By C*x	By C*x	Ex Ex	By C*x	By C*x	C*x By
t3ᵛ:4	t3:4ᵛ	t2ᵛ:5	t2:5ᵛ	ff1ᵛ:6	t1ᵛ:6	t1:6ᵛ	v3ᵛ:4

C*x By	By By	C*x By	Ex Ey	C*x By	C*x By	Ey Ey	By C*x
v3:4ᵛ	v2ᵛ:5	v2:5ᵛ	ff1:6ᵛ	v1ᵛ:6	v1:6ᵛ	*gg3ᵛ:4	x2ᵛ:3

By C*x	Ey Eyx	Ex Ex	By C*x	By C*x
x2:3ᵛ	*gg4ᵛ:3	*gg2ᵛ:5	x1ᵛ:4	x1:4ᵛ

TABLE OF LINE AND ACT/SCENE NUMBERS

Page	Col.	Comp.	F line nos.	Globe act/scene nos.
t3	a	B	1–17; 34–56	1.Prol.1–16; 1.1.1–13
	b	B	18–33; 57–79	1.Prol.17–32; 1.1.13–25
t3ᵛ	a	B	80–145	–1.1.90
	b	B	146–209	1.1.137
t4	a	C*	210–75	1.1.197
	b	C*	276–336	1.2.11
t4ᵛ	a	C*	337–402	1.2.68
	b	C*	403–67	1.2.128
t5	a	C*	468–533	1.2.185
	b	C*	534–93	1.3.18
t5ᵛ	a	C*	594–659	1.3.67
	b	C*	660–718	1.4.40
t6	a	C*	719–82	1.4.82
	b	C*	783–843	2.1.16
t6ᵛ	a	Cᵛ	844–907	2.1.66
	b	C*	908–73	2.1.127
v1	a	C*	974–1033	2.2.8
	b	C*	1034–98	2.2.62
v1ᵛ	a	C*	1099–164	2.2.117
	b	C*	1165–224	2.3.19
v2	a	C*	1225–89	2.3.73
	b	C*	1290–349	2.3.107
v2ᵛ	a	B	1350–415	2.4.61
	b	B	1416–81	2.4.121

HENRY VIII

Page	Col.	Comp.	F line nos.	Globe act/scene nos.
v3	a	C*	1482–547	2.4.181
	b	C*	1548–613	2.4.241
v3ᵛ	a	C*	1614–73	3.1.50
	b	C*	1674–739	3.1.108
v4	a	B	1740–805	3.1.168
	b	B	1806–64	3.2.30
v4ᵛ	a	B	1865–930	3.2.78
	b	B	1931–94	3.2.130
v5	a	B	1995–2060	3.2.186
	b	B	2061–124	3.2.240
v5ᵛ	a	B	2125–90	3.2.298
	b	B	2191–256	3.2.356
v6	a	B	2257–322	3.2.409
	b	B	2323–81	4.1.3
v6ᵛ	a	B	2382–445	4.1.36 SD
	b	B	2446–511	4.1.90
x1	a	B	2512–71	4.2.17
	b	B	2572–637	4.2.79
x1ᵛ	a	B	2638–701	4.2.114
	b	B	2702–67	4.2.173
x2	a	B	2768–828	5.1.49
	b	B	2829–94	5.1.98
x2ᵛ	a	B	2895–960	5.1.157
	b	B	2961–3017	5.2.20
x3	a	C*	3018–82	5.3.34
	b	C*	3083–148	5.3.91
x3ᵛ	a	C*	3149–213	5.3.143
	b	C*	3214–74	5.4.17
x4	a	C*	3275–339	5.4.82
	b	C*	3340–98	5.5.29
x4ᵛ	a	C*	3399–423; 3450–6	–5.5.53; Epil. 1–7
	b	C*	3424–49; 3457–64	–5.5.77; Epil. 8–14
			(Finis)	

Obvious misprints and other features of the text which have been corrected are:

t3ᵛ	173	ir	t6	779	aud
	177–8	Buck-|ham,	t6ᵛ	854	couldnot;
t4	228	Inly,		896	Buck˄
	277	theee	vlᵛ	1180	Camp˄
	286	practise:	v2ᵛ	1466	eunning.
	331	Snffolke:	v3	1487	Qſ
t4ᵛ	382	er	v3	1599	World˄
t5	541	Blumer.	v3ᵛ	1674	shoul
t5ᵛ	612	Pruiilegio,		1715	affllictions,
	616	L. Cham˄		1730	Iudge.
	705	Gntlemen,	v4	1757	Qu˄

v5	2010	gald			2581	Repentanee
	2028	kcpt (?)	x2^v		2895	greeuous.
v5^v	2238	Legatiue			2981	*Lady,*
	2248	os	x3		3124	faultly,
v6^v	2474	crow'd	x3^v		3167	'Ts
xl	2559	thanke	x4^v		3453	*Tumpets:*

T. H. H.

July, 1970

HENRY VIII

A = 404*47, 10

ABOUE *cont.*
My Lords, I care not (so much I am happy | Aboue a number) if my
actions   1657
Heauen is aboue all yet; there sits a Iudge, | That no King can corrupt.   1731
To me, aboue this wretchednesse? All your Studies | Make me a Curse,
like this.   1755
His Contemplation were aboue the earth,   1996
A peace aboue all earthly Dignities,   2285
Enter the King, and Buts, at a Windowe | aboue.   3014
'Tis well there's one aboue 'em yet; I had thought   3026
＊Seate being left void aboue him, as for Canterburies Seate.   3038
ABOUND = 2
They shall abound as formerly.   135
Abound, as thicke as thought could make 'em, and   2071
ABOUT = 15＊4
What 'tis you go about: to climbe steepe hilles   202
Sur. Being at *Greenwich,* | After your Highnesse had reprou'd the
Duke | About Sir *William Bulmer.*   539
Or some about him neere, haue out of malice   1010
About his necke, yet neuer lost her lustre;   1065
There ye shall meete about this waighty busines.   1195
Attendants stand in conuenient order about the Stage.   1350
*＊goes about the Court, comes to the King, and kneeles at | his Feete.
Then speakes.*   1365
Qu. Sir, I am about to weepe; but thinking that   1427
Suf. No, no: | There be moe Waspes that buz about his Nose,   1898
About the giuing backe the Great Seale to vs,   2247
Going to Chappell: and the voyce is now | Onely about her
Corronation.   2318
But 'tis so lately alter'd, that the old name | Is fresh about me.   2521
About the houre of eight, which he himselfe   2580
Lou. This is about that, which the Byshop spake, | I am happily come
hither.   2874
*＊now reigne in's Nose; all that stand about him are   3301
＊ The Troope passe once about the Stage, and Gar-| ter speakes.   3362
This Royall Infant, Heauen still moue about her;   3387
God shall be truely knowne, and those about her,   3407
*＊To all the Plaines about him: Our Childrens Children | Shall see this,
and blesse Heauen.   3425
ABROAD = 1
Card. Is he ready to come abroad? | *Crom.* I thinke by this he is.   1937
ABROAD = 2
One care abroad: hee would haue all as merry: 671
What Newes abroad? | *Crom.* The heauiest, and the worst,   2299
ABSENCE = 1
In our long absence: pray doe not deliuer,   1329
ABSENT = 1
Camp. So please your Highnes, | The Queene being absent, 'tis a
needfull fitnesse,   1601
ABSOLUD = 2
The willing'st sinne I euer yet committed, | May be absolu'd in English.   1672
Whil'st your great Goodnesse, out of holy pitty, | Absolu'd him with an
Axe.   2151
ABUR = 5
ABURGANY = 2
O my Lord *Aburgany*: Fare you well.   295

ABURGANY *cont.*
  Lord *Aburgany,* to whom by oth he menac'd | Reuenge vpon the
  Cardinall.   477
ABURGAUENNY see also Abur. = 1
  the Duke of Buckingham, and the Lord | Aburgauenny.   36
ABUSD = 1
  Abus'd extreamly, and to cry that's witty,   3455
ABUSING = 1
  Abusing better men then they can be   606
ACCESSE = 1
  Barre his accesse to'th'King, neuer attempt   1846
ACCOMPANIED = 1*1
  **side, accompanied with Sir Thomas Louell, Sir Nicholas*   891
  Of Canterbury, accompanied with other   2407
ACCOMPANYED = *1
  **accompanyed with a Sergeant at Armes, bearing a*   1341
ACCOMPT = 1
  This paper ha's vndone me: 'Tis th' Accompt   2090
ACCUMULATED = 1
  King. What piles of wealth hath he accumulated   1968
ACCUSATION = 1
  We come not by the way of Accusation,   1678
ACCUSATIONS = 1
  Came to the Bar; where, to his accusations   839
ACCUSD = 1
  1. The same, | All these accus'd him strongly, which he faine   852
ACCUSE = 3
  Stubborne to Iustice, apt to accuse it, and   1484
  And by that vertue no man dare accuse you.   3099
  You shall know many dare accuse you boldly,   3105
ACCUSERS = 3
  Yet I am richer then my base Accusers,   950
  Your selfe, and your Accusers, and to haue heard you | Without
  indurance further.   2919
  That in this case of Iustice, my Accusers,   3094
ACHE *see* ake
ACQUAINTANCE = 1*1
  Perforce be their acquaintance. These exactions   378
  *Grow from the Kings Acquaintance, by this Carriage.   1798
ACQUAINTED = 1*1
  **Kin.* Two equall men: The Queene shall be acquain- | (ted   1155
  Acquainted with this stranger; 'tis as like you, | As Cherry, is to Cherry.   2975
ACQUIRE = 1
  'Tis sweet at first t'acquire. After this Processe.   1210
ACT = 4
  For our best Act: if we shall stand still,   420
  The Part my Father meant to act vpon   546
  Does pay the Act of it, as i'th'contrary   2057
  And sleepe an Act or two; but those we feare   3452
ACTION = 1
  The action of good women, there is hope | All will be well.   1270
ACTIONS = 4
  Which Actions selfe, was tongue too.   87
  Our necessary actions, in the feare   412
  My Lords, I care not (so much I am happy | Aboue a number) if my
  actions   1657
  No other speaker of my liuing Actions,   2628

ACTUS *I*.34 819 1615 2377 2768 = 5
ADDE = 2
    Yet will I adde an Honor; a great Patience.   1770
    And to adde greater Honors to his Age   2625
ADDES = 1
    A Thousand pound a yeare, Annuall support, | Out of his Grace, he
    addes.   1280
ADDING = 1
    It can do me no damage; adding further,   531
ADIOURNE = 1
    That we adiourne this Court till further day;   1603
ADMIRATION = 1
    As great in admiration as her selfe.   3413
ADMIRER = 1
    Healthfull, and euer since a fresh Admirer | Of what I saw there.   42
ADMIT = *1
    Kath. Admit him entrance *Griffith.* But this Fellow   2690
ADOE = 1
    Make me no more adoe, but all embrace him;   3230
ADORNED = *1
    the Queene in her Robe, in her haire, richly adorned with   2438
ADUANCE = 1
    What, and how true thou art; he will aduance thee: 2330
ADUANTAGE = 1
    And for his owne aduantage. | *Norf.* I am sorry   269
ADUERTISE = 1
    Wherein he might the King his Lord aduertise,   1545
ADUICE = 1
    That I aduice your shunning.   174
ADUISD = 3
    Norf. Be aduis'd; | Heat not a Furnace for your foe so hot   212
    In seeming to augment it, wasts it: be aduis'd;   218
    Be by my Friends in Spaine, aduis'd; whose Counsaile   1409
ADUISE = 3
    Betwixt you, and the Cardinall. I aduise you   162
    Can aduise me like you: Be to your selfe,   206
    And pardon comes: I shall anon aduise you   444
AFFAIRES = 5
    Looke into these affaires, see this maine end,   1073
    Is this an howre for temporall affaires? Ha?   1114
    They should bee good men, their affaires as righteous: 1643
    Some touch of your late businesse: Affaires that walke   2786
    And we must root him out. From your Affaires   2832
AFFECT = 1
    Nor. As I belong to worship, and affect   84
AFFECTED = 1
    Affected Eminence, Wealth, Soueraignty;   1237
AFFECTION = 1
    My King is tangled in affection, to | A Creature of the Queenes, Lady
    Anne Bullen.   1870
AFFECTIONS = 1
    Haue I, with all my full Affections   1762
AFFLICTED = 1
    Suff. How sad he lookes; sure he is much afflicted.   1102
AFFLICTIONS = 1
    They that must weigh out my afflictions,   1716

AFFOORD = 1
   San. As easie as a downe bed would affoord it.   689
AFFRAID = 1
   Dwell in his Musings, but I am affraid   1998
AFTER = 6*3
   L.Ch. Death my Lord, | Their cloathes are after such a Pagan cut too't,   586
   She neuer knew harme-doing: Oh, now after   1206
   'Tis sweet at first t'acquire. After this Processe.   1210
   *Scribes in the habite of Doctors; after them, the Bishop of   1335
   *Canterbury alone; after him, the Bishops of Lincolne, Ely,   1336
   *Siluer Pillers: After them, side by side, the two Cardinals,   1343
   Or di'de where they were made, or shortly after   1559
   And after this, and then to Breakfast with | What appetite you haue.   2079
   'Tis like a Pardon after Execution;   2709
AFTER = 1
   After his Patients death; the King already | Hath married the faire
   Lady. | *Sur.* Would he had.   1878
AFTER = 9*1
   Buc. Euery man, | After the hideous storme that follow'd, was   144
   Whom after vnder the Commissions Seale,   510
   Sur. Being at *Greenwich,* | After your Highnesse had reprou'd the
   Duke | About Sir *William Bulmer.*   539
   Sur. After the Duke his Father, with the knife   556
   2. After all this, how did he beare himselfe?   859
   Exit King, frowning vpon the Cardinall, the Nobles | *throng after him*
   smiling, and whispering.   2081
   For after the stout Earle Northumberland | Arrested him at Yorke, and
   brought him forward   2565
   Pursu'd him still, and three nights after this,   2579
   Kath. After my death, I wish no other Herald,   2627
   The Vision. | **Enter solemnely tripping one after another, sixe*
   Personages,   2642
AGAINE = 22
   I say againe there is no English Soule   219
   And point by point the Treasons of his Maister, | He shall againe relate.   327
   And vnderstand againe like honest men,   610
   To lead 'em once againe, and then let's dreame   816
   But he fell to himselfe againe, and sweetly,   864
   Like water from ye, neuer found againe   976
   Old L. Alas poore Lady, | Shee's a stranger now againe.   1220
   I sweare againe, I would not be a Queene, | For all the world.   1256
   (Which Gods dew quench) therefore, I say againe,   1438
   Shee's going away. | *Kin.* Call her againe.   1486
   Our hard rul'd King. Againe, there is sprung vp   1959
   Springs out into fast gate, then stops againe,   1978
   Will bring me off againe. What's this? *To th' Pope?*   2100
   And when he falles, he falles like Lucifer, | Neuer to hope againe.   2272
   Or gilde againe the Noble Troopes that waighted   2325
   1 Y'are well met once againe. | 2 So are you.   2379
   Then rose againe, and bow'd her to the people: 2506
   And with the same full State pac'd backe againe   2514
   Let me ne're see againe. *Exit Messeng.*   2691
   Where being but a priuate man againe,   3104
   Win straying Soules with modesty againe,   3113
   Let me ne're hope to see a Chine againe,   3284
AGAINST *see also* gainst = 27*1
   Buc. I read in's looks | Matter against me, and his eye reuil'd   195

AGAINST *cont.*

Kin. By my life, | This is against our pleasure.	401
At which appear'd against him, his Surueyor	846
For then, my guiltlesse blood must cry against 'em.	909
Were hid against me, now to forgiue me frankly.	924
Who first rais'd head against Vsurping *Richard,*	954
And proue it too, against mine Honor, aught;	1393
Against your Sacred Person; in Gods name	1395
I haue no Spleene against you, nor iniustice	1448
For no dislike i'th' world against the person	1593
(I would be all) against the worst may happen:	1648
Enuy and base opinion set against 'em,	1660
The way of our Profession is against it;	1794
Matter against him, that for euer marres | The Hony of his Language. No, he's setled	1851
His eye against the Moone: in most strange Postures	1980
As doth a Rocke against the chiding Flood,	2073
You writ to'th Pope, against the King: your goodnesse	2180
But that I am bound in Charitie against it.	2191
That therefore such a Writ be sued against you,	2241
Is the Kings hand, and tongue, and who dare speak | One syllable against him?	2816
It fits we thus proceed, or else no witnesse | Would come against you.	2904
Being of those Vertues vacant. I feare nothing | What can be said against me.	2925
To sweare against you: Such things haue bene done.	2934
A man that more detests, more stirres against,	3087
And freely vrge against me.	3096
Against this man, whose honesty the Diuell	3178
We may as well push against Powles as stirre 'em.	3273
*was his Nose discharged against mee; hee stands there	3304

AGE = 2

I seru'd my King: he would not in mine Age	2371
And to adde greater Honors to his Age	2625

AGED = 1

An aged Princesse; many dayes shall see her,	3429

AGEN = 5

1. When he was brought agen to th' Bar, to heare	860
2. But that slander Sir, | Is found a truth now: for it growes agen	1006
Your high profession Spirituall. That agen	1477
King. 'Tis well said agen,	2024
He gaue his Honors to the world agen,	2583

AGENT = 1

Is posted as the Agent of our Cardinall, | To second all his plot. I do assure you,	1903

AGO = 1

His Loue, too long ago. I am old my Lords,	1752

AGOING *see* going

AGONY = 1

With such an Agony, he sweat extreamly,	862

AGREE = 1

Onely a show or two, and so agree,	11

AGREED = 1*1

**Cham.* Then thus for you my Lord, it stands agreed	3144
Be knowne vnto vs: are you all agreed Lords.	3148

AGUE = 1

Buck. An vntimely Ague | Staid me a Prisoner in my Chamber, when	44

AH = 2*1
  Kin. Ha? What, so rancke? Ah, ha,   535
  Ah my good Lord, I greeue at what I speake,   2892
  *Cran. Ah my good Lord of *Winchester*: I thanke you,   3107
AID *see* ayd
AIME *see* ayme
AIMST *see* aym'st
AIRD *see* ay'rd
AIRE *see* ayre
AKE = 1
  Man. You great fellow, | Stand close vp, or Ile make your head ake.   3349
ALANSON = 1
  It shall be to the Dutches of Alanson,   1940
ALAS = 10
  Old L. Alas poore Lady, | Shee's a stranger now againe.   1220
  Of equall Friendship and Proceeding. Alas Sir: 1372
  Alas, I am a Woman frendlesse, hopelesse.   1706
  Alas, ha's banish'd me his Bed already,   1751
  Alas (poore Wenches) where are now your Fortunes?   1784
  Vpon what cause wrong you? Alas, our Places,   1793
  Where she remaines now sicke. | 2 Alas good Lady.   2417
  Kath. Alas poore man. | *Grif.* At last, with easie Rodes, he came to
  Leicester,   2570
  Almost each pang, a death. | *King.* Alas good Lady.   2851
  Man. Alas I know not, how gets the Tide in?   3275
ALDERMEN = *1
  *Enter Trumpets sounding: Then two Aldermen, L.(ord) Maior,   3354
ALE = *1
  *Do you looke for Ale, and Cakes heere, you rude | Raskalls?   3267
ALIGHTED *see* lighted
ALIKE = 3
  You that are blam'd for it alike with vs,   368
  Things that are knowne alike, which are not wholsome   376
  Touch me alike: th'are breath I not beleeue in.   1088
ALIUE = 1
  Cran. The greatest Monarch now aliue may glory   3235
ALL = 153*7
  Buck. All the whole time | I was my Chambers Prisoner.   55
  All Clinquant all in Gold, like Heathen Gods   63
  As Cherubins, all gilt: the Madams too,   67
  Buc. All was Royall, | To the disposing of it nought rebell'd,   88
  Nor. All this was ordred by the good Discretion   98
  Or ha's giuen all before, and he begins | A new Hell in himselfe.   121
  Of all the Gentry; for the most part such   127
  Buc. Why all this Businesse | Our Reuerend Cardinall carried.   158
  Be done in this and all things: I obey.   294
  Of all their Loyalties; wherein, although | My good Lord Cardinall,
  they vent reproches   349
  The Clothiers all not able to maintaine   359
  Daring th'euent too th'teeth, are all in vprore, | And danger serues
  among them.   364
  Queen. My learn'd Lord *Cardinall,* | Deliuer all with Charity.   484
  Queen. God mend all.   554
  L.Ch. As farre as I see, all the good our English   576
  L.San. They haue all new legs,   582
  With all their honourable points of ignorance   604
  Salutes ye all; This Night he dedicates   668

ALL *cont.*

In all this Noble Beuy, has brought with her	670
One care abroad: hee would haue all as merry:	671
And to you all good health.	714
By all the lawes of Warre y'are priuiledg'd.	737
Shall shine at full vpon them. Some attend him. | *All rise, and Tables*	
remou'd.	748
A good digestion to you all; and once more	751
I showre a welcome on yee: welcome all.	752
Cham. Such a one, they all confesse	783
By all your good leaues Gentlemen; heere Ile make | My royall choyce.	787
1. The same, | All these accus'd him strongly, which he faine	852
He spoke, and learnedly for life: But all	857
2. After all this, how did he beare himselfe?	859
In all the rest shew'd a most Noble patience.	865
1. Tis likely, | By all coniectures: First *Kildares* Attendure;	872
2. All the Commons | Hate him perniciously, and o' my Conscience	884
*They loue and doate on: call him bounteous *Buckingham,* | The Mirror	
of all courtesie.	887
Buck. All good people, | You that thus farre haue come to pitty me;	896
As I would be forgiuen: I forgiue all.	926
Henry the Eight, Life, Honour, Name and all	962
Heauen ha's an end in all: yet, you that heare me,	970
But where they meane to sinke ye: all good people	977
Cardinall *Campeius* is arriu'd, and lately, | As all thinke for this busines.	1013
**My Lord, the Horses your Lordship sent for, with all the*	1028
*I feare he will indeede; well, let him haue them; hee | will haue all I	
thinke.	1036
Norf. How holily he workes in all his businesse,	1056
Feares, and despaires, and all these for his Marriage.	1061
And out of all these, to restore the King,	1062
And euery true heart weepes for't. All that dare	1072
Or this imperious man will worke vs all	1080
From Princes into Pages: all mens honours	1081
Norff. A gracious King, that pardons all offences	1108
Aboue all Princes, in committing freely	1134
The Tryall, iust and Noble. All the Clerkes,	1139
Cam. Your Grace must needs deserue all strangers loues,	1149
For all this spice of your Hipocrisie:	1234
Anne. No, not for all the riches vnder Heauen.	1244
I sweare againe, I would not be a Queene, | For all the world.	1256
The action of good women, there is hope | All will be well.	1270
More then my All, is Nothing: Nor my Prayers	1284
Are all I can returne. 'Beseech your Lordship,	1287
To lighten all this Ile. I'le to the King,	1297
For all the mud in Egypt; haue you heard it?	1313
And on all sides th'Authority allow'd,	1355
At all times to your will conformable:	1378
I hold my most malicious Foe, and thinke not | At all a Friend to truth.	1441
Before you all, Appeale vnto the Pope,	1479
Of all these eares (for where I am rob'd and bound,	1511
By all the Reuerend Fathers of the Land,	1572
But all Hoods, make not Monkes.	1644
(I would be all) against the worst may happen:	1648
Deserues a Corner: would all other Women	1655
So deepe suspition, where all faith was meant;	1677

8

ALL *cont.*

They are (as all my other comforts) far hence | In mine owne Countrey
Lords.   1718

Heauen is aboue all yet; there sits a Iudge, | That no King can corrupt.   1731
And all such false Professors. Would you haue me   1747
And all the Fellowship I hold now with him   1753
To me, aboue this wretchednesse? All your Studies | Make me a Curse,
like this.   1755
Haue I, with all my full Affections   1762
In the Diuorce, his contrarie proceedings | Are all vnfolded: wherein he
appeares,   1858
All his trickes founder, and he brings his Physicke   1877
Sur. Now all my ioy | Trace the Coniunction.   1883
Suf. My Amen too't. | *Nor.* All mens.   1885
Is posted as the Agent of our Cardinall, | To second all his plot. I do
assure you,   1903
Together with all famous Colledges   1912
Beyond all mans endeauors. My endeauors,   2043
(Though all the world should cracke their duty to you,   2069
Of all that world of Wealth I haue drawne together   2091
The Letter (as I liue) with all the Businesse   2101
I haue touch'd the highest point of all my Greatnesse,   2103
The heads of all thy Brother-Cardinals,   2145
(With thee, and all thy best parts bound together)   2146
Farre from his succour; from the King, from all   2149
Wol. This, and all else | This talking Lord can lay vpon my credit,   2153
Dare mate a sounder man then Surrie can be, | And all that loue his
follies.   2163
Card. All Goodnesse | Is poyson to thy Stomacke.   2174
Sur. Yes, that goodnesse | Of gleaning all the Lands wealth into one, 2176
You maim'd the Iurisdiction of all Bishops.   2209
Nor. Then, That in all you writ to Rome, or else | To Forraigne
Princes, *Ego & Rex meus*   2210
Of all the Kingdome. Many more there are,   2228
Because all those things you haue done of late   2238
To forfeit all your Goods, Lands, Tenements, | Castles, and whatsoeuer,
and to be   2242
So fare you well, my little good Lord Cardinall. | *Exeunt all but Wolsey.* 2249
Farewell? A long farewell to all my Greatnesse.   2252
A peace aboue all earthly Dignities,   2285
O *Cromwell,* | The King ha's gone beyond me: All my Glories   2321
Beare witnesse, all that haue not hearts of Iron,   2339
In all my Miseries: But thou hast forc'd me   2344
And sounded all the Depths, and Shoales of Honor,   2351
Let all the ends thou aym'st at, be thy Countries,   2362
There take an Inuentory of all I haue,   2366
And my Integrity to Heauen, is all,   2368
2 'Tis all my businesse. At our last encounter,   2383
Of all these Learned men, she was diuorc'd,   2414
Our King ha's all the Indies in his Armes,   2459
2 Those men are happy, | And so are all, are neere her.   2464
1 It is, and all the rest are Countesses.   2468
Could say this is my wife there, all were wouen | So strangely in one
peece.   2500
She had all the Royall makings of a Queene;   2508
The Rod, and Bird of Peace, and all such Emblemes   2510
With all the choysest Musicke of the Kingdome,   2512

9

ALL *cont.*
3 All the Land knowes that: 2531
2 He will deserue more. | 3 Yes without all doubt. 2540
With all his Couent, honourably receiu'd him; 2573
Ty'de all the Kingdome. Symonie, was faire play, 2591
Kath. Spirits of peace, where are ye? Are ye all gone? 2658
But now I am past all Comforts heere, but Prayers. 2711
Kath. I thanke you honest Lord. Remember me | In all humilitie vnto
his Highnesse: 2753
With Maiden Flowers, that all the world may know 2762
To make great hast. All fast? What meanes this? Hoa? 2991
That Chayre stand empty: But we all are men 3058
Farewell all Physicke: and what followes then? 3075
Cran. My good Lords; Hitherto, in all the Progresse 3080
Lay all the weight ye can vpon my patience, 3115
Gard. Good M.(aster) Secretary, | I cry your Honour mercie; you may
worst | Of all this Table say so. 3127
I take it, by all voyces: That forthwith, 3145
Be knowne vnto vs: are you all agreed Lords. 3148
All. We are. | *Cran.* Is there no other way of mercy, 3149
Suff. 'Tis the right Ring, by Heau'n: I told ye all, 3167
One that in all obedience, makes the Church 3186
By all that's holy, he had better starue, 3201
To let my tongue excuse all. What was purpos'd 3220
Make me no more adoe, but all embrace him; 3230
*thousand, here will bee Father, God-father, and all to-|gether. 3296
*now reigne in's Nose; all that stand about him are 3301
They grow still too; from all Parts they are comming, 3327
Theres a trim rabble let in: are all these 3330
Cham. As I liue, | If the King blame me fo't; Ile lay ye all 3338
All comfort, ioy in this most gracious Lady, 3371
A Patterne to all Princes liuing with her, 3392
And all that shall succeed: *Saba* was neuer 3393
Then this pure Soule shall be. All Princely Graces 3395
With all the Vertues that attend the good, 3397
The merry Songs of Peace to all his Neighbours. 3406
*To all the Plaines about him: Our Childrens Children | Shall see this,
and blesse Heauen. 3425
To th' ground, and all the World shall mourne her. 3434
I thanke ye all. To you my good Lord Maior, 3441
Ye must all see the Queene, and she must thanke ye, 3445
'Has businesse at his house; for all shall stay: 3447
All that are heere: Some come to take their ease, 3451
All the expected good w'are like to heare. 3457
All the best men are ours; for 'tis ill hap, 3462
ALLAY = 2
Or but allay the fire of passion. 222
To stop the rumor; and allay those tongues | That durst disperse it. 1004
ALLEADGED = 2
He pleaded still not guilty, and alleadged 840
Of my alleadged reasons, driues this forward: 1595
ALLEGEANCE = 2
Allegeance in them; their curses now 395
With lesse Allegeance in it. Men that make 3091
ALLEGIANT = 1
Can nothing render but Allegiant thankes, 2050

ALLIED = 1
  For high feats done to'th'Crowne; neither Allied   110
ALLOWANCE = 1
  Without the Kings will, or the States allowance,   2220
ALLOWD = 5
  A full hot Horse, who being allow'd his way   204
  Not ours, or not allow'd; what worst, as oft   418
  Schollers allow'd freely to argue for her.   1160
  And on all sides th'Authority allow'd,   1355
  Almost no Graue allow'd me? Like the Lilly   1787
ALLS = 2
  1. Ile saue you | That labour Sir. All's now done but the Ceremony   825
  'Tis his Aspect of Terror. All's not well.   2881
ALMOST = 8
  Not vs'd to toyle, did almost sweat to beare   68
  The sides of loyalty, and almost appeares | In lowd Rebellion.   355
  Norf. Not almost appeares, | It doth appeare; for, vpon these Taxations,   357
  Almost with rauish'd listning, could not finde   459
  Almost forgot my Prayres to content him?   1765
  Almost no Graue allow'd me? Like the Lilly   1787
  Almost in Christendome: shortly (I beleeue)   1913
  Almost each pang, a death. | *King.* Alas good Lady.   2851
ALONE = 6*1
  San. For my little Cure, | Let me alone.   708
  Buck. Nay, Sir *Nicholas*, | Let it alone; my State now will but mocke
  me.   946
  Canterbury alone; after him, the Bishops of Lincolne, Ely,   1336
  For speaking false in that; thou art alone   1500
  I haue kept you next my Heart, haue not alone   2029
  Th'estate of my poore Queene. Leaue me alone,   2858
  Let 'em alone, and draw the Curtaine close: 3033
ALONG = 2
  My Barge stayes; | Your Lordship shall along: Come, good Sir *Thomas*,   654
  Cran. 'Tis *Buts.* | The Kings Physitian, as he past along   3003
ALONG = 1
  My comfort comes along: breake vp the Court;   1612
ALONG = 1
  Buck. Sir, | I am thankfull to you, and Ile goe along   223
ALREADIE = 1
  But that you shall sustaine moe new disgraces, | With these you beare
  alreadie.   1831
ALREADY = 6
  Hath shew'd him gold; my life is spand already: 312
  King. What's the need? | It hath already publiquely bene read,   1353
  Alas, ha's banish'd me his Bed already,   1751
  After his Patients death; the King already | Hath married the faire
  Lady. | *Sur.* Would he had.   1878
  And one already of the Priuy Councell.   2539
  Th'are come already from the Christening,   3344
ALTAR = 1
  Came to the Altar, where she kneel'd, and Saint-like   2504
ALTER = 1
  That he would please to alter the Kings course,   265
ALTERD = 3
  But 'tis so lately alter'd, that the old name | Is fresh about me. 2521
  Pati. Do you note | How much her Grace is alter'd on the sodaine? 2674
  Kath. O my Lord, | The Times and Titles now are alter'd strangely 2697

ALTHOUGH = 6
   Of all their Loyalties; wherein, although | My good Lord Cardinall,
   they vent reproches   349
   Nor will I sue, although the King haue mercies   911
   Would for *Carnaruanshire*, although there long'd   1260
   Haue I not stroue to loue, although I knew   1384
   There must I be vnloos'd, although not there   1512
   Then lay me forth (although vnqueen'd) yet like   2764
ALWAYES = 2
   Wol. I know your Maiesty, ha's alwayes lou'd her   1157
   You are alwayes my good Friend, if your will passe, 3108
AM *see also* I'm = 65*1
AMAZD = 1
   Crom. I haue no power to speake Sir. | *Car.* What, amaz'd | At my
   misfortunes? Can thy Spirit wonder   2276
AMAZED = 1
   Enter Cromwell, standing amazed.   2274
AMBASSADOR *see also* embassador = 3
   Abur. Is it therefore | Th'Ambassador is silenc'd? | *Nor.* Marry is't.   153
   Ambassador to the Emperor, you made bold | To carry into Flanders,
   the Great Seale.   2216
   If my sight faile not, | You should be Lord Ambassador from the
   Emperor,   2693
AMBASSADORS *see* embassadors
AMBITION = 4
   Sur. Thy Ambition | (Thou Scarlet sinne) robb'd this bewailing Land 2142
   Suf. That out of meere Ambition, you haue caus'd 2222
   Cromwel, I charge thee, fling away Ambition,   2355
   Become a Churchman, better then Ambition: 3112
AMBITIOUS = 1
   From his Ambitious finger. What had he   101
AMEN = 5
   An. Now I pray God, *Amen.*   1272
   Suf. My Amen too't. | *Nor.* All mens.   1885
   The Lord forbid. | *Nor.* Marry Amen.   1896
   Lou. Me thinkes I could | Cry the Amen, and yet my Conscience sayes 2799
   Into whose hand, I giue thy Life. | *Cran. Amen.*   3379
AMITY = 1
   England and France, might through their amity   257
AMONG *see also* 'mong = 10
   Sent downe among 'em, which hath flaw'd the heart   348
   Daring th'euent too th'teeth, are all in vprore, | And danger serues
   among them.   364
   What was the speech among the Londoners,   500
   A Spring-halt rain'd among 'em.   585
   Among my Maids, full little (God knowes) looking   1701
   A woman lost among ye, laugh't at, scornd?   1739
   3 Among the crowd i'th'Abbey, where a finger   2474
   Is come to lay his weary bones among ye: 2576
   They had parted so much honesty among 'em,   3027
   Go breake among the preasse, and finde away out   3345
AMONGST *see also* 'mongst = 3
   There should be one amongst'em by his person   777
   I her fraile sonne, among'st my Brethren mortall, | Must giue my
   tendance to.   2018

AMONGST *cont.*
Diuell was amongst 'em I thinke surely.   3317
AMPTHILL = 1
From Ampthill, where the Princesse lay, to which   2410
AN *1.*23 44 383 562 599 625 627 664 765 862 970 989 1114 1123 *1177
1197 1201 1259 1311 1400 1604 1696 1770 1922 1960 1987 2011 2152
2366 *2431 2458 2486 2575 2589 2607 2630 2677 2855 2979 *2981 2982
3052 3236 3337 3429 3452 = 44*3, 1
Choose Ladies, King and An Bullen.   770
AN = 11*1
ANB = 2
ANBUL = 1
ANCESTRY *see* auncestry
AND *see also* &. = 662*51, 3
And if I haue a Conscience, let it sincke me,   901
A great man should decline. Nay, and you weep | I am falne indeed.   2279
It seemes you are in hast: and if there be   2784
ANDREN = 1
Those Sunnes of Glory, those two Lights of Men | Met in the vale of
Andren.   46
ANDT = 3*1
Hath a sharpe edge: It's long, and't may be saide   170
Gent. And't please your Grace, the two great Cardinals | Wait in the
presence.   1635
Mes. And't like your Grace ---| *Kath.* You are a sawcy Fellow,   2681
Por. And't please your Honour, | We are but men; and what so many
may doe,   3334
ANGELL = 1
Sir, as I haue a Soule, she is an Angell;   2458
ANGELS = 6*1
Goe with me like good Angels to my end,   917
1. Good Angels keepe it from vs: 991
That Angels loue good men with: Euen of her,   1067
*Ye haue Angels Faces; but Heauen knowes your hearts.   1781
By that sinne fell the Angels: how can man then   2356
Will make my boldnesse, manners. Now good Angels   2964
Of our flesh, few are Angels; out of which frailty   3060
ANGER = 6
Requires slow pace at first. Anger is like   203
For when the King once heard it, out of anger   1002
That had to him deriu'd your Anger, did I   1386
The Queene is put in anger; y'are excus'd: 1527
Suf. Maybe he heares the King | Does whet his Anger to him.   1947
I feare the Story of his Anger. 'Tis so: 2089
ANGERS = 1
What sodaine Anger's this? How haue I reap'd it?   2084
ANGRY = 2
Kin. Who's there? Ha? | *Norff.* Pray God he be not angry.   1103
Who can be angry now? What Enuy reach you?   1136
ANNE see also An., An.B., An.Bul. = 7
longer Table for the Guests. Then Enter Anne Bullen,   662
Enter Anne Bullen, and an old Lady.   1201
My King is tangled in affection, to | A Creature of the Queenes, Lady
Anne Bullen.   1870
Anne Bullen? No: Ile no *Anne Bullens* for him,   1942
Crom. Last, that the Lady *Anne,* | Whom the King hath in secrecie long
married,   2315

ANNE cont.
The Lady *Anne*, passe from her Corronation. 2382
ANNE = 3
ANNUALL = 1
A Thousand pound a yeare, Annuall support, | Out of his Grace, he
addes. 1280
ANON = 4*1
And pardon comes: I shall anon aduise you 444
San. I told your Grace, they would talke anon. 732
Strikes his brest hard, and anon, he casts 1979
We shall heare more anon. 3034
**Port.* You'l leaue your noyse anon ye Rascals: doe 3259
ANOTHER *see also* other = 7*1
Infecting one another, yea reciprocally, 237
Another spread on's breast, mounting his eyes, 558
Suff. No, his Conscience | Ha's crept too neere another Ladie. 1048
Norff. If it doe, Ile venture one; haue at him. | *Suff.* I another. 1130
Enter two Gentlemen, meeting one another. 2378
The Vision. | *Enter solemnely tripping one after another, sixe
Personages,* 2642
Is this the Honour they doe one another? 3025
Her Ashes new create another Heyre, 3412
ANSWER = 5*1
**The Queene makes no answer, rises out of her Chaire,* 1364
To make a seemely answer to such persons. 1817
I answer, is most false. The Duke by Law 2155
How to liue better. For your stubborne answer 2246
As a man sorely tainted, to his Answer, 2567
Which will require your Answer, you must take 2901
ANSWERD = 2
It was much like to doe: He answer'd, Tush, 530
King. Fairely answer'd: | A Loyall, and obedient Subiect is 2054
ANSWERE = 2
But how to make ye sodainly an Answere 1696
You must be Godfather, and answere for her. 3234
ANT = 1
Cham. An't please your Grace, 797
ANTHONY = 1
Enter Sir Anthony Denny. 2866
ANY = 20
Of this Commission? I beleeue, not any. 428
Vpon our faile; to this poynt hast thou heard him, | At any time speake
ought? 488
If euer any malice in your heart 923
Must now confesse, if they haue any goodnesse, 1138
For any suit of pounds: and you, (oh fate) 1305
For you, or any: how farre I haue proceeded, 1449
Vpon this businesse my appearance make, | In any of their Courts. 1494
Laid any scruple in your way, which might 1515
Nor to betray you any way to sorrow; 1680
That any English man dare giue me Councell? 1712
(If you haue any Iustice, any Pitty, 1748
If ye be any thing but Churchmens habits) 1749
The stampe of Noblenesse in any person | Out of himselfe? 1840
Any thing on him: for he hath a Witchcraft | Ouer the King in's
Tongue. 1847
On you, then any: So your Hand, and Heart, 2061

14

ANY *cont.*
As 'twer in Loues particular, be more | To me your Friend, then any.	2064
From any priuate malice in his end,	2157
To mow 'em downe before me: but if I spar'd any	3281
This happy Child, did I get any thing.	3437

ANYTHING *see* thing
APPEALE = 3
Before you all, Appeale vnto the Pope,	1479
Made to the Queene to call backe her Appeale | She intends vnto his Holinesse.	1605
Deliuer them, and your Appeale to vs	2954

APPEARANCE = 2
Vpon this businesse my appearance make, | In any of their Courts.	1494
And to be short, for not Appearance, and	2412

APPEARD = 2
At which appear'd against him, his Surueyor	846
She was often cyted by them, but appear'd not:	2411

APPEARE = 5
He shall appeare in proofe.	275
Norf. Not almost appeares, | It doth appeare; for, vpon these Taxations,	357
Appeare in formes more horrid) yet my Duty,	2072
Ye appeare in euery thing may bring my ruine?	2127
You do appeare before them. If they shall chance	2948

APPEARES = 3
The sides of loyalty, and almost appeares | In lowd Rebellion.	355
Norf. Not almost appeares, | It doth appeare; for, vpon these Taxations,	357
In the Diuorce, his contrarie proceedings | Are all vnfolded: wherein he appeares,	1858

APPETITE = 1
And after this, and then to Breakfast with | What appetite you haue.	2079

APPLES = *1
*and fight for bitten Apples, that no Audience but the	3319

APPLIANCE = 1
Aske God for Temp'rance, that's th'appliance onely | Which your disease requires.	193

APPOINT = 1
(Without the priuity o'th'King) t'appoint	125

APPOINTMENT = 1
If I command him followes my appointment,	1188

APPROACH = 1
Should the approach of this wilde Riuer breake, | And stand vnshaken yours.	2074

APPROBATION = 1
By learned approbation of the Iudges: If I am	406

APPROCH = 1
Prethee returne, with thy approch: I know,	1611

APPROCHES = 1
Cranmer approches the Councell Table.	3055

APPROUE = 1
Cham. Lady; | I shall not faile t'approue the faire conceit	1291

APT = 1
Stubborne to Iustice, apt to accuse it, and	1484

ARCHBISHOP = 5
1 That I can tell you too. The Archbishop	2406
Keep. My Lord Archbishop: | And ha's done halfe an houre to know your pleasures.	3051
Chan. My good Lord Archbishop, I'm very sorry	3056

ARCHBISHOP *cont.*

 Kin. Thanke you good Lord Archbishop: 3374
 Kin. O Lord Archbishop | Thou hast made me now a man, neuer before   3435
ARCHBISHOPRICKE = 1
 The Archbishopricke of *Toledo*, this is purpos'd.   1018
ARCHBISHOPS = 1
 2 He of Winchester | Is held no great good louer of the Archbishops, |
 The vertuous *Cranmer*.   2528
ARCHBYSHOP = 2
 With which the Lime will loade him. Th'Archbyshop   2815
 Enter Cranmer, Archbyshop of Canterbury.   2988
ARCH-BYSHOP = 3*1
 Suf. He ha's, and we shall see him | For it, an Arch-byshop.   1921
 Install'd Lord Arch-byshop of Canterbury.   2313
 When by the Arch-byshop of Canterbury,   2507
 Den. Sir, I haue brought my Lord the Arch-byshop, | As you
 commanded me.   2867
ARCH-HERETIQUE = 1
 A most Arch-Heretique, a Pestilence   2824
ARCH-ONE = 1
 An Heretique, an Arch-one; *Cranmer*, one   1960
ARDE = 1
 Nor. 'Twixt Guynes and Arde,   48
ARE *see also* th'are, w'are, y'are, you'r = 118*12
ARGUE = 2
 Wee are too open heere to argue this: 1024
 Schollers allow'd freely to argue for her.   1160
ARGUMENTS = 1
 And that (without delay) their Arguments | Be now produc'd, and
 heard.   1423
ARIPENING *see* ripening
ARISE = 3
 King. Arise, and take place by vs; halfe your Suit   335
 Wol. So much fairer | And spotlesse, shall mine Innocence arise,   2194
 King. Pray you arise | My good and gracious Lord of Canterburie: 2887
ARMES = 4*3
 The Noble Spirits to Armes, they did performe   79
 Enter Brandon, a Sergeant at Armes before him, and | two or three of the
 Guard.   276
 Kin. And once more in mine armes I bid him welcome,   1146
 accompanyed with a Sergeant at Armes, bearing a   1341
 Lay kissing in your Armes, Lord Cardinall.   2189
 his Coate of Armes, and on his head he wore a Gilt Copper | Crowne.   2427
 Our King ha's all the Indies in his Armes,   2459
ARMY = 1
 An Army cannot rule 'em.   3337
AROLLING *see* rowling
AROSE = 1
 Had the full view of, such a noyse arose,   2491
ARRAIGNMENT = *1
 Enter Buckingham from his Arraignment, Tipstaues before   889
ARREST = 1
 Arrest thee of High Treason, in the name | Of our most Soueraigne
 King.   282
ARRESTED = 1
 For after the stout Earle Northumberland | Arrested him at Yorke, and
 brought him forward   2565

ARRIUD = 1
Cardinall *Campeius* is arriu'd, and lately, | As all thinke for this busines. 1013
ARROGANCE = 1
Can ye endure to heare this Arrogance? 2169
ARROGANCIE = 1
Is cramm'd with Arrogancie, Spleene, and Pride. 1470
ART *l.*1118 1500 2138 2330 = 4, 2
In sweet Musicke is such Art, 1630
So excellent in Art, and still so rising, 2620
ARTHUR = 1
And Widdow to Prince *Arthur.* 1917
ARTICLES = 3*1
The Articles o'th' Combination drew 245
Produce the grand summe of his sinnes, the Articles 2186
*Nor. Those Articles, my Lord, are in the Kings hand: 2192
Some of these Articles, and out they shall. 2199
AS = 156*8
Such Noble Scoenes, as draw the Eye to flow 5
The Subiect will deserue it. Such as giue 8
As Foole, and Fight is, beside forfeyting 20
Therefore, for Goodnesse sake, and as you are knowne 24
Be sad, as we would make ye. Thinke ye see 26
As they were Liuing: Thinke you see them Great, 28
In their Embracement, as they grew together, | Which had they, 51
As Cherubins, all gilt: the Madams too, 67
Was to them, as a Painting. Now this Maske 70
As presence did present them: Him in eye, 74
Nor. As I belong to worship, and affect 84
Nor. As you guesse: 94
To whom as great a Charge, as little Honor 128
They shall abound as formerly. 135
Me as his abiect obiect, at this instant 197
As you would to your Friend. 207
And proofes as cleere as Founts in *Iuly,* when 228
*Buck. To th'King Ile say't, & make my vouch as strong 232
As shore of Rocke: attend. This holy Foxe, 233
As he is subtile, and as prone to mischiefe, 235
As able to perform't) his minde, and place 236
Only to shew his pompe, as well in France, 238
As here at home, suggests the King our Master 239
As himselfe pleas'd; and they were ratified 246
As he cride thus let be, to as much end, 247
**As giue a Crutch to th'dead. But our Count-Cardinall 248
(Which as I take it, is a kinde of Puppie 251
Deales with our Cardinal, and as I troa 260
(As soone he shall by me) that thus the Cardinall 267
Does buy and sell his Honour as he pleases, 268
Abur. As the Duke said, 299
Most bitterly on you, as putter on | Of these exactions: yet the King, our Maister 351
As rau'nous Fishes doe a Vessell follow 414
Not ours, or not allow'd; what worst, as oft 418
That once were his, and is become as blacke, 462
As if besmear'd in hell. Sit by Vs, you shall heare 463
As to the Tower, I thought; I would haue plaid 545
(As he made semblance of his duty) would | Haue put his knife into him. 549

AS *cont.*

His Father, by as much as a performance | Do's an irresolute purpose.	561
L.Ch. As farre as I see, all the good our English	576
Pertaining thereunto; as Fights and Fire-workes,	605
An honest Country Lord as I am, beaten	625
A hand as fruitfull as the Land that feeds vs,	643
and diuers other Ladies, & Gentlemen, as Guests	663
One care abroad: hee would haue all as merry:	671
As first, good Company, good wine, good welcome, | Can make good people.	672
San. As easie as a downe bed would affoord it.	689
But he would bite none, iust as I doe now,	702
And hither make, as great Embassadors | From forraigne Princes.	742
*Hoboyes. Enter King and others as Maskers, habited like	753
Wish him ten faddom deepe: This Duke as much	886
Euen as the Axe falls, if I be not faithfull.	902
And as the long diuorce of Steele fals on me,	918
Buck. Sir *Thomas Louell,* I as free forgiue you	925
As I would be forgiuen: I forgiue all.	926
And fit it with such furniture as suites | The Greatnesse of his Person.	944
This from a dying man receiue as certaine:	971
Cardinall *Campeius* is arriu'd, and lately, | As all thinke for this busines.	1013
As I am made without him, so Ile stand,	1086
It from the bearer, 'tis a sufferance, panging | As soule and bodies seuering.	1218
Old as I am, to Queene it: but I pray you,	1246
As from a blushing Handmaid, to his Highnesse;	1289
*vnder him as Iudges. The Queene takes place some di-|stance	1346
As I saw it inclin'd? When was the houre	1381
That longer you desire the Court, as well	1417
For your owne quiet, as to rectifie | What is vnsetled in the King.	1418
And worthily my Falsehood, yea, as much	1456
As you haue done my Truth. If he know	1457
I say, set on. | *Exeunt, in manner as they enter'd.*	1613
Enter Queene and her Women as at worke.	1616
Euer sprung; as Sunne and Showers,	1625
They should bee good men, their affaires as righteous:	1643
Could speake this with as free a Soule as I doe.	1656
As not to know the Language I haue liu'd in:	1667
Offers, as I doe, in a signe of peace, | His Seruice, and his Counsell. | *Queen.* To betray me.	1691
They are (as all my other comforts) far hence | In mine owne Countrey Lords.	1718
They swell and grow, as terrible as stormes.	1801
A Soule as euen as a Calme; Pray thinke vs,	1803
As yours was, put into you, euer casts	1808
*Such doubts as false Coine from it. The King loues you,	1809
I should be glad to heare such Newes as this | Once euery houre.	1855
As I would wish mine Enemy.	1860
Is posted as the Agent of our Cardinall, | To second all his plot. I do assure you,	1903
As I requir'd: and wot you what I found	1985
(As I will lend you cause) my doing well, | With my well saying.	2022
Does pay the Act of it, as i'th'contrary	2057
That as my hand ha's open'd Bounty to you,	2059
As 'twer in Loues particular, be more | To me your Friend, then any.	2064
Abound, as thicke as thought could make 'em, and	2071

AS *cont.*

As doth a Rocke against the chiding Flood,	2073
He parted Frowning from me, as if Ruine	2085
The Letter (as I liue) with all the Businesse	2101
As if it fed ye, and how sleeke and wanton	2126
You haue as little Honestie, as Honor,	2160
My Lord of Norfolke, as you are truly Noble,	2182
As you respect the common good, the State	2183
And then he fals as I do. I haue ventur'd	2259
This day was view'd in open, as his Queene,	2317
And when I am forgotten, as I shall be,	2347
As let 'em haue their rights, they are euer forward	2389
head, bearing a long white Wand, as High Steward. With	2434
Sir, as I haue a Soule, she is an Angell;	2458
2 Good Sir, speake it to vs? | 3 As well as I am able. The rich streame	2481
As the shrowdes make at Sea, in a stiffe Tempest,	2492
As lowd, and to as many Tunes. Hats, Cloakes,	2493
As holy Oyle, *Edward* Confessors Crowne,	2509
Something I can command. As I walke thither, | Ile tell ye more.	2544
Did'st thou not tell me *Griffith*, as thou lead'st mee,	2556
As a man sorely tainted, to his Answer,	2567
His Promises, were as he then was, Mighty:	2596
But his performance, as he is now, Nothing:	2597
But, to those men that sought him, sweet as Summer.	2612
But such an honest Chronicler as *Griffith*.	2630
(as it were by inspiration) she makes (in her sleepe) signes of	2654
As you wish Christian peace to soules departed,	2748
(As they say Spirits do) at midnight, haue	2787
Louell. Now Sir, you speake of two | The most remark'd i'th'Kingdome: as for *Cromwell,*	2810
Den. Sir, I haue brought my Lord the Arch-byshop, | As you commanded me.	2867
Might corrupt mindes procure, Knaues as corrupt	2933
Of as great Size. Weene you of better lucke,	2936
And do as I haue bid you. *Exit Cranmer.*	2959
Acquainted with this stranger; 'tis as like you, | As Cherry, is to Cherry.	2975
Cran. 'Tis *Buts.* | The Kings Physitian, as he past along	3003
At least good manners; as not thus to suffer	3028
Seate being left void aboue him, as for Canterburies Seate. Cromwell at lower end, as Secretary.	3038
	3041
Of the whole State; as of late dayes our neighbours,	3077
I make as little doubt as you doe conscience,	3116
At Chamber dore? and one, as great as you are?	3210
Power, as he was a Counsellour to try him,	3213
Not as a Groome: There's some of ye, I see,	3214
As I haue made ye one Lords, one remaine:	3254
Man. Pray Sir be patient; 'tis as much impossible,	3269
To scatter 'em, as 'tis to make 'em sleepe	3271
We may as well push against Powles as stirre 'em.	3273
As much as one sound Cudgell of foure foote,	3276
As if we kept a Faire heere? Where are these Porters?	3328
Cham. As I liue, | If the King blame me for't; Ile lay ye all	3338
That mould vp such a mighty Piece as this is,	3396
Nor shall this peace sleepe with her: But as when	3410
As great in admiration as her selfe.	3413
Shall Star-like rise, as great in fame as she was,	3417

ASAPH = *1
  Rochester, and S.(aint) Asaph: Next them, with some small 1337
ASHER-HOUSE = 1
  To Asher-house, my Lord of Winchesters, 2114
ASHES = 3
  (Now in his Ashes) Honor: Peace be with him. 2633
  Her Ashes new create another Heyre, 3412
  Who, from the sacred Ashes of her Honour 3416
ASKD = 1
  Ere it was ask'd. But when the way was made 263
ASKE = 5
  Aske God for Temp'rance, that's th'appliance onely | Which your
  disease requires. 193
  The other moity ere you aske is giuen, 337
  A Woman of lesse Place might aske by Law; 1159
  You aske with such a Violence, the King 2131
  2 May I be bold to aske what that containes, | That Paper in your hand. 2394
ASKING = 2
  For not bestowing on him at his asking, 1017
  An. My good Lord, | Not your demand; it values not your asking: 1266
ASLEEP = 1
  Grif. She is asleep: Good wench, let's sit down quiet, 2640
ASLEEPE = 1
  Killing care, & griefe of heart, | Fall asleepe, or hearing dye. 1631
ASPECT = 2
  That sweet Aspect of Princes, and their ruine, 2270
  'Tis his Aspect of Terror. All's not well. 2881
ASPIRE = 1
  There is betwixt that smile we would aspire too, 2269
ASSEMBLED = 1
  Yea, the elect o'th'Land, who are assembled 1415
ASSEMBLY = 2
  Of this so Noble and so faire assembly, 760
  You hold a faire Assembly; you doe well Lord: 790
ASSENT = 2
  Haue at you. | First, that without the Kings assent or knowledge, 2206
  The Kings late Scruple, by the maine assent 2413
ASSISTANTS = 1
  To eminent Assistants; but Spider-like 111
ASSURANCE = 1
  No Iudge indifferent, nor no more assurance 1371
ASSURE = 3
  The Beauty of this Kingdome Ile assure you. 640
  Is posted as the Agent of our Cardinall, | To second all his plot. I do
  assure you, 1903
  1 Neuer greater, | Nor Ile assure you better taken Sir. 2392
ASSUREDLY = 1
  I am not worthy yet to weare: I shall assuredly. 2669
AST = 1
  (Domestickes to you) serue your will, as't please 1474
ASUNDER = 1
  And Corne shall flye asunder. For I know 2909
AT = 69*10
ATTACH = 1
  Bran. Here is a warrant from | The King, t'attach Lord *Mountacute,*
  and the Bodies 302

ATTACHD = 2
    For France hath flaw'd the League, and hath attach'd   151
    To sheath his knife in vs: he is attach'd,   564
ATTEMPT = 1
    Barre his accesse to'th'King, neuer attempt   1846
ATTEND = 7
    Who should attend on him? He makes vp the File   126
    As shore of Rocke: attend. This holy Foxe,   233
    Shall shine at full vpon them. Some attend him. | *All rise, and Tables*
    remou'd.   748
    Attend him heere this Morning.   1936
    Cran. It is my dutie | T'attend your Highnesse pleasure.   2885
    But their pleasures | Must be fulfill'd, and I attend with patience.   3012
    With all the Vertues that attend the good,   3397
ATTENDANCE = 1
    To dance attendance on their Lordships pleasures,   3030
ATTENDANTS = 2
    Attendants stand in conuenient order about the Stage.   1350
    Exit Queene, and her Attendants.   1496
ATTENDS = 1
    Den. He attends your Highnesse pleasure. | *King.* Bring him to Vs.   2872
ATTENDURE = 1
    1. Tis likely, | By all coniectures: First *Kildares* Attendure;   872
ATTENTION = 1
    I will be bold with time and your attention: 1535
ATTURNEY = 1
    The Kings Atturney on the contrary,   842
AUAUNT = 1
    To giue her the auaunt, it is a pitty | Would moue a Monster.   1211
AUDIENCE = *1
    *and fight for bitten Apples, that no Audience but the   3319
AUDIT = 1
    To keepe your earthly Audit, sure in that   2010
AUGHT *see also* ought = 1
    And proue it too, against mine Honor, aught;   1393
AUGMENT = 1
    In seeming to augment it, wasts it: be aduis'd;   218
AUNCESTRY = 1
    For being not propt by Auncestry, whose grace   108
AUNT = 1
    Vnder pretence to see the Queene his Aunt,   253
AUOW = 1
    Of which there is not one, I dare auow   2734
AUOYD = 1
    King. Auoyd the Gallery. *Louel seemes to stay.*   2877
AUTHORITY = 3
    And on all sides th'Authority allow'd,   1355
    *Where's your Commission? Lords, words cannot carrie | Authority so
    weighty.   2117
    And the strong course of my Authority,   3083
AUTHORS = 1
    I feare, too many curses on their heads | That were the Authors.   985
AWAY = 1
    The pennance lyes on you; if these faire Ladies | Passe away frowning.   706
AWAY = 1
    The least rub in your fortunes, fall away   975

AWAY = 12
Ile vndertake may see away their shilling   13
They may *Cum Priuilegio*, wee away   612
1. Whether away so fast? | 2. O, God saue ye: 821
Turne me away: and let the fowl'st Contempt   1396
Shee's going away. | *Kin.* Call her againe.   1486
You'l part away disgrac'd.   1727
Is stolne away to Rome, hath 'tane no leaue,   1901
Cromwel, I charge thee, fling away Ambition,   2355
I caus'd you write, yet sent away? | *Pat.* No Madam.   2717
Cast none away: That I shall cleere my selfe,   3114
Come Lords, we trifle time away: I long   3252
Go breake among the preasse, and finde away out   3345
AXE = 2*1
him, the Axe with the edge towards him, Halberds on each   890
Euen as the Axe falls, if I be not faithfull.   902
Whil'st your great Goodnesse, out of holy pitty, | Absolu'd him with an
Axe.   2151
AY *see* I
AYD = 1
And neuer seeke for ayd out of himselfe: yet see,   453
AYME = 2
Car. Madam, you wander from the good | We ayme at.   1771
The cheefe ayme of his Honour, and to strengthen   3187
AYMST = 1
Let all the ends thou aym'st at, be thy Countries,   2362
AYRD = 1
This world had ayr'd them. Hence I tooke a thought,   1560
AYRE = 2
The Ayre will drinke the Sap. To euery County   434
Card. There's fresher ayre my Lord, | In the next Chamber.   810
BACKE = 11
The Backe is Sacrifice to th'load; They say   381
Of bringing backe the Prisoner.   827
For more then blushing comes to: If your backe   1252
I know your backe will beare a Dutchesse. Say,   1321
Gent.Vsh. Madam, you are cald backe.   1489
Made to the Queene to call backe her Appeale | She intends vnto his
Holinesse.   1605
About the giuing backe the Great Seale to vs,   2247
And with the same full State pac'd backe againe   2514
Gent. within. Come backe: what meane you?   2962
Lady. Ile not come backe, the tydings that I bring   2963
When they passe backe from the Christening?   3333
BACKES = 1
Buc. O many | Haue broke their backes with laying Mannors on 'em   136
BAD = 3
The Kings eyes, that so long haue slept vpon | This bold bad man.   1075
He did it with a Serious minde: a heede | Was in his countenance. You
he bad   1934
Bad me enioy it, with the Place, and Honors   2133
BADE *see* bad
BAITING = 1
And heere ye lye baiting of Bombards, when   3342
BANISHD = 2
Alas, ha's banish'd me his Bed already,   1751
Banish'd the Kingdome. *Patience*, is that Letter   2716

BANISTER = 1
  Flying for succour to his Seruant *Banister*,   955
BANKET = 3
  Should finde a running Banket, ere they rested,   681
  You haue now a broken Banket, but wee'l mend it.   750
  Card. Sir *Thomas Louell*, is the Banket ready | I'th' Priuy Chamber? |
  Lou. Yes, my Lord.   804
BANQUET = 1*1
  Inuite me to a Banquet, whose bright faces   2665
  *these three dayes; besides the running Banquet of two | Beadles, that is
  to come.   3323
BAPTISME = 1
  That is, a faire young Maid that yet wants Baptisme,   3233
BAR = 2
  Came to the Bar; where, to his accusations   839
  1. When he was brought agen to th' Bar, to heare   860
BAREHEADED = *1
  each a Siluer Crosse: Then a Gentleman Vsher bare-| headed,   1340
BARGE = 3
  My Barge stayes; | Your Lordship shall along: Come, good Sir *Thomas*, 654
  For so they seeme; th'haue left their Barge and landed,   741
  Vaux. Prepare there, | The Duke is comming: See the Barge be ready; 942
BARKE = 2
  From euery Tree, lop, barke, and part o'th' Timber: 432
  Barke when their fellowes doe. By some of these   1526
BARONS = 1
  1 They that beare | The Cloath of Honour ouer her, are foure Barons |
  Of the Cinque-Ports.   2462
BARRE = 1
  Barre his accesse to'th'King, neuer attempt   1846
BASE = 3
  Yet I am richer then my base Accusers,   950
  Enuy and base opinion set against 'em,   1660
  They are too thin, and base to hide offences,   3194
BASENESSE = 1
  There is no primer basenesse.   400
BAWDY = 1
  That come to heare a Merry, Bawdy Play,   15
BAYES = *2
  Bayes, and golden Vizards on their faces, Branches of Bayes 2645
BAYON = 1
  By th'Bishop of *Bayon*, then French Embassador,   1539
BE *see also* maybe = 172*10
BEADLES = 1
  *these three dayes; besides the running Banquet of two | Beadles, that is
  to come.   3323
BEAMES = 1
  Cast thousand beames vpon me, like the Sun?   2666
BEARE = 17*2
  That beare a Weighty, and a Serious Brow,   3
  Not vs'd to toyle, did almost sweat to beare   68
  Bran. Nay, he must beare you company. The King   296
  Most pestilent to th'hearing, and to beare 'em,   380
  (Out of the great respect they beare to beauty)   762
  2. After all this, how did he beare himselfe?   859
  And by that name must dye; yet Heauen beare witnes, 900
  The Law I beare no mallice for my death,   903

BEARE *cont.*
My Lord, youle beare vs company? | *Cham.* Excuse me,　　1094
What thinke you of a Dutchesse? Haue you limbs | To beare that load
of Title?　　1247
Cham. You beare a gentle minde, & heau'nly blessings　　1273
I know your backe will beare a Dutchesse. Say,　　1321
But that you shall sustaine moe new disgraces, | With these you beare
alreadie.　　1831
King. Good my Lord, | *You are full of Heauenly stuffe, and beare the
Inuentory　　2005
I beare i'th'State: and Nature does require　　2016
Wol. So farewell, to the little good you beare me.　　2251
Beare witnesse, all that haue not hearts of Iron,　　2339
1 They that beare | The Cloath of Honour ouer her, are foure Barons |
Of the Cinque-Ports.　　2462
Must beare the same proportion, and not euer　　2930
BEARER = 1
It from the bearer, 'tis a sufferance, panging | As soule and bodies
seuering.　　1218
BEARES = 3
Lou. That Churchman | Beares a bounteous minde indeed,　　641
And beares his blushing Honors thicke vpon him:　　2255
Who's that that beares the Scepter? | 1 Marquesse Dorset,　　2448
BEARING = 3*11
distance, followes a Gentleman bearing the Purse, with the　　1338
great Seale, and a Cardinals Hat: Then two Priests, bea-| ring　　1339
accompanyed with a Sergeant at Armes, bearing a　　1341
Siluer Mace: Then two Gentlemen bearing two great　　1342
Bearing a State of mighty moment in't,　　1582
Bearing the Kings will from his mouth expressely?　　2120
5 Maior of London, bearing the Mace. Then Garter, in　　2426
6 Marquesse Dorset, bearing a Scepter of Gold, on his head,　　2429
*bearing the Rod of Siluer with the Doue, Crowned with an| Earles
Coronet. Collars of Esses.*　　2431
head, bearing a long white Wand, as High Steward. With　　2434
wrought with Flowers bearing the Queenes Traine.　　2442
Staffe, Duke of Suffolke, two Noblemen, bearing great　　3356
Noblemen bearing a Canopy, vnder which the Dutchesse of　　3358
Norfolke, Godmother, bearing the Childe richly habited in　　3359
BEATE = 1
No new deuice to beate this from his Braines?　　2097
BEATEN = 2
An honest Country Lord as I am, beaten　　625
Her Foes shake like a Field of beaten Corne,　　3401
BEAUTIE = 1
For Vertue, and true Beautie of the Soule,　　2736
BEAUTY = 6
The Beauty of this Kingdome Ile assure you.　　640
Into our presence, where this heauen of beauty　　747
(Out of the great respect they beare to beauty)　　762
King. The fairest hand I euer touch'd: O Beauty,　　771
Beauty and Honour in her are so mingled,　　1294
The Beauty of her Person to the People.　　2488
BECAME = 1
Became the next dayes master, till the last　　61
BECAUSE = 1*2
Cham. Because they speak no English, thus they praid　　758

BECAUSE   *cont.*

Because all those things you haue done of late	2238
Gard. My Lord, because we haue busines of more mo-|(ment,	3100

BECOME = 5

That once were his, and is become as blacke,	462
Eu'n to the Hall, to heare what shall become | Of the great Duke of Buckingham.	823
What will become of me now, wretched Lady?	1782
But I beseech you, what's become of *Katherine*	2404
Become a Churchman, better then Ambition:	3112

BECOMES = 1

Then but once thinke his place becomes thee not.	3202

BECOMMING = 1

Cham. It was a gentle businesse, and becomming	1269

BED = 6

San. As easie as a downe bed would affoord it.	689
Alas, ha's banish'd me his Bed already,	1751
So went to bed; where eagerly his sicknesse	2578
You must not leaue me yet. I must to bed,	2759
Lou. I must to him too | Before he go to bed. Ile take my leaue.	2781
Prythee to bed, and in thy Prayres remember	2857

BEDFELLOW = 1

So sweet a Bedfellow? But Conscience, Conscience;	1198

BED-CHAMBER = 1

Crom. To his owne hand, in's Bed-chamber.	1930

BEE *l.**1033 1643 2451 *3296 = 2*2

BEEN *l.*580 = 1

BEENE *see also* bene, bin *l.**347 544 1302 1389 1540 1703 2046 2403 2495 3125 *3381 = 9*2

BEET = 1

You may then spare that time. | *Car.* Bee't so, proceed.	1356

BEFORE *see also* 'fore = 25*6

Or ha's giuen all before, and he begins | A new Hell in himselfe.	121
*Enter Cardinall Wolsey, the Purse borne before him, certaine	175
Enter Brandon, a Sergeant at Armes before him, and | *two or three of the Guard.*	276
To you that choak'd it. Let be cald before vs	324
Sur. Not long before your Highnesse sped to France,	497
That neuer see 'em pace before, the Spauen	584
passe directly before the Cardinall and gracefully sa-|*lute him.*	755
*Enter Buckingham from his Arraignment, Tipstaues before	889
*'em from me, with this reason: his maister would bee seru'd be-|fore	1033
a Subiect, if not before the King, which stop'd our mouthes | *Sir.*	1034
Lie like one lumpe before him, to be fashion'd | Into what pitch he please.	1082
In this mans place before him? | *Wol.* Yes, he was.	1173
This compel'd fortune: haue your mouth fild vp, | Before you open it.	1307
A yeare before. It is not to be question'd,	1404
Wol. Be patient yet. | *Qu.* I will, when you are humble; Nay before,	1431
Remoue these Thoughts from you. The which before	1461
Before you all, Appeale vnto the Pope,	1479
(*Katherine* our Queene) before the primest Creature | That's Parragon'd o'th' World.	1599
3 *Lord* Chancellor, *with Purse and Mace before him.*	2424
I neuer saw before. Great belly'd women,	2496
And make 'em reele before 'em. No man liuing	2499
If well, he stept before me happily | For my example.	2562

BEFORE *cont.*
Enter Gardiner Bishop of Winchester, a Page with a Torch | before him,
met by Sir Thomas Louell.   2769
Lou. I must to him too | Before he go to bed. Ile take my leaue.   2781
Our Reasons layd before him, hath commanded   2829
Suff. Sir, I did neuer win of you before.   2839
This Morning come before vs, where I know   2898
You do appeare before them. If they shall chance   2948
*There make before them. Looke, the goodman weeps: 2955
To mow 'em downe before me: but if I spar'd any   3281
Kin. O Lord Archbishop | Thou hast made me now a man, neuer before   3435
BEGAN = 1
And Doctors learn'd. First I began in priuate,   1573
BEGET = *1
*Christian Conscience this one Christening will beget a   3295
BEGGER = 1
Made it a Foole, and Begger. The two Kings   72
BEGGERLY = 1
(Am yet a Courtier beggerly) nor could   1303
BEGGERS = 1
Not wake him in his slumber. A Beggers booke, | Out-worths a Nobles
blood.   190
BEGGES = 1
Bestow your Councels on me. She now begges   1821
BEGGING = 1
I haue beene begging sixteene yeares in Court   1302
BEGINS = 1
Or ha's giuen all before, and he begins | A new Hell in himselfe.   121
BEHAUIOUR = 2
Hath my behauiour giuen to your displeasure,   1374
To vse so rude behauiour. Go too, kneele.   2686
BEHELD = 1
Beheld them when they lighted, how they clung   50
BEHIND = *1
*stil, when sodainly a File of Boyes behind 'em, loose shot,   3314
BEHINDE = 1
And leaue me heere in wretchednesse, behinde ye?   2659
BEHOLD = 4
2. Let's stand close and behold him.   895
1 You come to take your stand heere, and behold   2381
To sit heere at this present, and behold   3057
(But few now liuing can behold that goodnesse)   3391
BEHOLDING = 4
I am beholding to you: cheere your neighbours: 719
I should haue beene beholding to your Paper: 2403
May be beholding to a Subiect; I   3228
And you good Brethren, I am much beholding: 3442
BEING *l.*75 81 108 204 498 529 539 *542 547 956 1325 1602 2624 2896
2925 *3038 3104 3336 = 16*2
BELEEUD = 2
Being now seene, possible enough, got credit | That *Beuis* was beleeu'd.   81
It forg'd him some designe, which being beleeu'd   529
BELEEUE = 10*1
Their Money out of hope they may beleeue,   9
Of this Commission? I beleeue, not any.   428
Touch me alike: th'are breath I not beleeue in.   1088
Camp. Beleeue me, there's an ill opinion spread then,   1177

BELEEUE *cont.*

Or God will punish me. I do beleeue | (Induc'd by potent
Circumstances) that   1433
Beleeue me she ha's had much wrong. Lord Cardinall,   1671
Nor. Beleeue it, this is true.   1857
Sur. Ha's the King this? | *Suf.* Beleeue it.   1872
Almost in Christendome: shortly (I beleeue)   1913
2 A Royall Traine beleeue me: These I know: 2447
Beleeue me Sir, she is the goodliest Woman   2489
BELL = 1
Worse then the Sacring Bell, when the browne Wench   2188
BELLYD = 1
I neuer saw before. Great belly'd women,   2496
BELONG = 2*1
Nor. As I belong to worship, and affect   84
Within. Good M.(aster) Porter I belong to th' Larder.   3262
Port. Belong to th' Gallowes, and be hang'd ye Rogue: 3263
BELONGS = 1
No great offence belongs too't, giue your Friend   2785
BELOUD = 1
Euer belou'd and louing, may his Rule be;   936
BELOW = 1*1
each side the Court in manner of a Consistory: Below them   1348
His Thinkings are below the Moone, not worth | His serious
considering.   1999
BENE *l.*1354 1377 1390 2041 2934 = 5
BENEFICIALL = 1
Take vp the Rayes o'th'beneficiall Sun, | And keepe it from the Earth.   104
BENEFIT = 1
That is new trim'd; but benefit no further   415
BENEFITS = 1
When these so Noble benefits shall proue   454
BESEECH = 7
Yes, heartily beseech you.   523
Louell. I doe beseech your Grace, for charity   922
Are all I can returne. 'Beseech your Lordship,   1287
Beseech you Sir, to spare me, till I may   1408
His Highnesse shall speake in, I do beseech   1462
But I beseech you, what's become of *Katherine*   2404
Dare bite the best. I doe beseech your, Lordships,   3093
BESEECHING = 1
Beseeching him to giue her vertuous breeding.   2725
BESHREW = 1
Old.L. Beshrew me, I would, | And venture Maidenhead for't, and so
would you   1232
BESIDE = 2
As Foole, and Fight is, beside forfeyting   20
Beside that of the Iewell-House, is made Master   2812
BESIDES = 1*1
The King ha's sent me otherwhere: Besides   1096
*these three dayes; besides the running Banquet of two | Beadles, that is
to come.   3323
BESIEGE = *1
*great *Toole*, come to Court, the women so besiege vs?   3293
BESMEARD = 1
As if besmear'd in hell. Sit by Vs, you shall heare   463

BEST = 15*2
  Equall in lustre, were now best, now worst   73
  Haue not the power to muzzle him, therefore best   189
  King. My life it selfe, and the best heart of it,   321
  Then vainly longing. What we oft doe best,   416
  For our best Act: if we shall stand still,   420
  Who's best in fauour. Let the Musicke knock it. | *Exeunt with*
  Trumpets.   817
  They were young and handsome, and of the best breed in the   1030
  Kin. I, and the best she shall haue; and my fauour   1161
  To him that does best, God forbid els: Cardinall,   1162
  Old L. Our content | Is our best hauing.   1228
  *(Well worthy the best Heyre o'th' World) should not   1562
  Of your best Graces, in your minde; the which   2007
  (With thee, and all thy best parts bound together)   2146
  The best perswasions to the contrary   2950
  And want of wisedome, you that best should teach vs,   3061
  Dare bite the best. I doe beseech your, Lordships,   3093
  All the best men are ours; for 'tis ill hap,   3462
BESTOW = 3
  And to bestow your pitty on me; for   1368
  Bestow your Councels on me. She now begges   1821
  But par'd my present Hauings, to bestow | My Bounties vpon you.   2031
BESTOWING = 2
  For not bestowing on him at his asking,   1017
  (Which was a sinne) yet in bestowing, Madam,   2614
BETRAID = 1
  Being distrest; was by that wretch betraid,   956
BETRAY = 2
  Nor to betray you any way to sorrow;   1680
  Offers, as I doe, in a signe of peace, | His Seruice, and his Counsell. |
  Queen. To betray me.   1691
BETTER = 15
  Abusing better men then they can be   606
  I thinke would better please 'em: by my life,   682
  An. Oh Gods will, much better | She ne're had knowne pompe; though't
  be temporall,   1215
  I sweare, tis better to be lowly borne,   1224
  A better Wife, let him in naught be trusted,   1499
  Both for your Honour better, and your Cause: 1725
  Within these fortie houres, Surrey durst better | Haue burnt that
  Tongue, then saide so.   2140
  How to liue better. For your stubborne answer   2246
  1 Neuer greater, | Nor Ile assure you better taken Sir.   2392
  Shee's a good Creature, and sweet-Ladie do's | Deserue our better
  wishes.   2801
  Of as great Size. Weene you of better lucke,   2936
  None better in my Kingdome. Get you gone,   2958
  And our consent, for better tryall of you,   3102
  Become a Churchman, better then Ambition: 3112
  By all that's holy, he had better starue,   3201
BETWEEN = *1
  *Between vs & the Emperor (the Queens great Nephew)   1058
BETWEENE = 6
  The Peace betweene the French and vs, not valewes | The Cost that did
  conclude it.   142
  Pray sit betweene these Ladies.   695

BETWEENE *cont.*

A buzzing of a Separation | Betweene the King and *Katherine?*   999
Betweene the King and you, and to deliuer   1683
A League betweene his Highnesse, and *Ferrara.*   2221
Enter Katherine Dowager, sicke, lead betweene Griffith,   2548
BETWIXT *see also* 'twixt = 6
Betwixt you, and the Cardinall. I aduise you   162
His feares were that the Interview betwixt   256
Come pat betwixt too early, and too late   1304
Haue blowne this Coale, betwixt my Lord, and me;   1437
There is betwixt that smile we would aspire too,   2269
The cause betwixt her, and this great offender.   3190
BEUIS = 1
Being now seene, possible enough, got credit | That *Beuis* was beleeu'd.   81
BEUY = 1
In all this Noble Beuy, has brought with her   670
BEWAILING = 1
Sur. Thy Ambition | (Thou Scarlet sinne) robb'd this bewailing Land   2142
BEWARE = 1
Beware you loose it not: For vs (if you please   1810
BEYOND = 6
Beyond thoughts Compasse, that former fabulous Storie   80
His will is most malignant, and it stretches | Beyond you to your
friends.   482
One that ne're dream'd a Ioy, beyond his pleasure;   1768
Beyond all mans endeauors. My endeauors,   2043
But farre beyond my depth: my high-blowne Pride   2262
O *Cromwell,* | The King ha's gone beyond me: All my Glories   2321
BID = 6*1
Things to strike Honour sad. Bid him recount   465
(Tell you the Duke) shall prosper, bid him striue   515
Kin. And once more in mine armes I bid him welcome,   1146
Kath. Bid the Musicke leaue, | They are harsh and heauy to me.
Musicke ceases.   2672
And do as I haue bid you. *Exit Cranmer.*   2959
Bid ye so farre forget your selues? I gaue ye   3212
If they hold, when their Ladies bid 'em clap. | FINIS.   3463
BIDS = 1
Cran. Let me speake Sir, | For Heauen now bids me; and the words I
vtter,   3384
BIGGE = 1
Shall lessen this bigge looke. | *Exeunt Cardinall, and his Traine.*   186
BIGGER = *1
Man. The Spoones will be the bigger Sir: There is   3298
BILLOWES = 1
Euen the Billowes of the Sea,   1628
BIN *l.*1764 *2473 2495 = 2*1
BIRD = 2
The Rod, and Bird of Peace, and all such Emblemes   2510
The Bird of Wonder dyes, the Mayden Phoenix,   3411
BISHOP see also B.Lin., byshop = 4*1
Scribes in the habite of Doctors; after them, the Bishop of   1335
By th'Bishop of *Bayon,* then French Embassador,   1539
Ere a determinate resolution, hee | (I meane the Bishop) did require a
respite,   1543
Enter Gardiner Bishop of Winchester, a Page with a Torch | before him,
met by Sir Thomas Louell.   2769

BISHOP cont.

Bishop of *Winchester*. But know I come not | 3192

BISHOPS = 1*4

  *Canterbury alone; after him, the Bishops of Lincolne, Ely, | 1336
  *from the King. The Bishops place themselues on | 1347
  *the Scribes. The Lords sit next the Bishops. The rest of the | 1349
  You maim'd the Iurisdiction of all Bishops. | 2209
  * Pearle, Crowned. On each side her, the Bishops of London, | and
  Winchester, | 2439

BITE = 2

  But he would bite none, iust as I doe now, | 702
  Dare bite the best. I doe beseech your, Lordships, | 3093

BITES = 1

  Is in his braine: He bites his lip, and starts, | 1975

BITS = *1

  *But stop their mouthes with stubborn Bits & spurre 'em, | 3071

BITTEN = *1

  *and fight for bitten Apples, that no Audience but the | 3319

BITTER = 3

  Is only bitter to him, only dying: | 916
  To leaue, a thousand fold more bitter, then | 1209
  Old L. How tasts it? Is it bitter? Forty pence, no: | 1310

BITTERLY = 1

  Most bitterly on you, as putter on | Of these exactions: yet the King,
  our Maister | 351

BLACK = *1

  *Which makes my whit'st part, black. The will of Heau'n | 293

BLACKE = 3

  That once were his, and is become as blacke, | 462
  He had a blacke mouth that said other of him. | 646
  No blacke Enuy shall make my Graue. | 929

BLACK-FRYERS = 1

  For such receipt of Learning, is Black-Fryers: | 1194

BLADDERS = 1

  Like little wanton Boyes that swim on bladders: | 2260

BLAMD = 1

  You that are blam'd for it alike with vs, | 368

BLAME = 3

  I cannot blame his Conscience. | 2461
  Deserue we no more Reuerence? | *Grif*. You are too blame, | 2683
  Cham. As I liue, | If the King blame me for't; Ile lay ye all | 3338

BLESS = *1

  *Bless me, what a fry of Fornication is at dore? On my | 3294

BLESSE = 8

  Will blesse the King: and is not this course pious? | 1069
  Some Spirit put this paper in the Packet, | To blesse your eye withall. | 1993
  Car. Heauen forgiue me, | Euer God blesse your Highnesse. | 2003
  Is your displeasure with the King. | *Card*. God blesse him. | 2301
  2 Heauen blesse thee, | Thou hast the sweetest face I euer look'd on. | 2456
  Both now, and euer blesse her: 'Tis a Gyrle | 2972
  She shall be lou'd and fear'd. Her owne shall blesse her; | 3400
  *To all the Plaines about him: Our Childrens Children | Shall see this,
  and blesse Heauen. | 3425

BLESSED = 4

  Thou fall'st a blessed Martyr. | 2364
  His blessed part to Heauen, and slept in peace. | 2584
  Kath. No? Saw you not euen now a blessed Troope | 2664

BLESSED *cont.*
Fly o're thy Royall head, and shade thy person | Vnder their blessed
wings. 2965
BLESSEDNESSE = 2
And found the Blessednesse of being little. 2624
So shall she leaue her Blessednesse to One, 3414
BLESSES = 1
To taint that honour euery good Tongue blesses; 1679
BLESSING = 2
Will fall some blessing to this Land, which shall | In it be memoriz'd. 1892
With this Kisse, take my Blessing: God protect thee, 3378
BLESSINGS = 6*1
Shall cry for blessings on him. May he liue 934
If the King please: his Curses and his blessings 1087
Which, to say sooth, are Blessings; and which guifts 1238
Cham. You beare a gentle minde, & heau'nly blessings 1273
When he ha's run his course, and sleepes in Blessings, 2309
The dewes of Heauen fall thicke in Blessings on her, 2724
Vpon this Land a thousand thousand Blessings, 3389
BLEST = 3
Vpward of twenty years, and haue bene blest 1390
Out of this world. Tell him in death I blest him 2756
He's honest on mine Honor. Gods blest Mother, 2956
BLEW = 1
Ye blew the fire that burnes ye: now haue at ye. 3180
BLIN = 1
BLINDE = 1
That blinde Priest, like the eldest Sonne of Fortune, 1052
BLISTRED = 1
Short blistred Breeches, and those types of Trauell; 609
BLOOD = 6
Not wake him in his slumber. A Beggers booke, | Out-worths a Nobles
blood. 190
For then, my guiltlesse blood must cry against 'em. 909
The Spaniard tide by blood and fauour to her, 1137
If this salute my blood a iot; it faints me | To thinke what followes. 1326
Thou should'st feele | My Sword i'th'life blood of thee else. My Lords, 2167
And by those claime their greatnesse; not by Blood. 3409
BLOODY = 1
Thou hast a cruell Nature and a bloody. 3198
BLOSSOMES = 1
The tender Leaues of hopes, to morrow Blossomes, 2254
BLOUD = *1
*And with that bloud will make 'em one day groane for't. 952
BLOW = *1
*like a Morter-piece to blow vs. There was a Habberda-|shers 3305
BLOWNE = 3
Haue blowne this Coale, betwixt my Lord, and me; 1437
That I haue blowne this Coale: I do deny it, 1453
But farre beyond my depth: my high-blowne Pride 2262
BLUSH = 2
Now, if you can blush, and crie guiltie Cardinall, | You'l shew a little
Honestie. 2200
Wol. Speake on Sir, | I dare your worst Obiections: If I blush, 2202
BLUSHING = 3
For more then blushing comes to: If your backe 1252
As from a blushing Handmaid, to his Highnesse; 1289

BLUSHING *cont.*
  And beares his blushing Honors thicke vpon him: 2255
BODIES = 2
  Bran. Here is a warrant from | The King, t'attach Lord *Mountacute,*
  and the Bodies   302
  It from the bearer, 'tis a sufferance, panging | As soule and bodies
  seuering.   1218
BODY = 3
  I meane who set the Body, and the Limbes | Of this great Sport
  together?   92
  Of his owne body he was ill, and gaue | The Clergy ill .example.   2598
  Kin. Body a me: where is it? | *Butts.* There my Lord: 3019
BOHUN = 1
  And Duke of *Buckingham*: now, poore *Edward Bohun*;   949
BOLD = 9*2
  *Is nam'd, your warres in France: this makes bold mouths,   393
  **Card.* Stand forth, & with bold spirit relate what you   468
  You few that lou'd me, | And dare be bold to weepe for *Buckingham,*   913
  The Kings eyes, that so long haue slept vpon | This bold bad man.   1075
  Kin. Ye are too bold: 1112
  I will be bold with time and your attention: 1535
  Ambassador to the Emperor, you made bold | To carry into Flanders,
  the Great Seale.   2216
  2 May I be bold to aske what that containes, | That Paper in your hand.   2394
  2 A bold braue Gentleman. That should bee | The Duke of Suffolke.   2451
  Gard. I shall remember this bold Language. | *Crom.* Doe.   3137
  Remember your bold life too.   3139
BOLDLY = 2
  Out with it boldly: Truth loues open dealing.   1663
  You shall know many dare accuse you boldly,   3105
BOLDNED = 1
  In tempting of your patience, but am boldned   388
BOLDNESSE = 1
  Will make my boldnesse, manners. Now good Angels   2964
BOMBARDS = 1
  And heere ye lye baiting of Bombards, when   3342
BOND = 2
  My bond to Wedlocke, or my Loue and Dutie   1394
  Should, notwithstanding that your bond of duty,   2063
BONES = 2
  For Truths-sake, and his Conscience; that his bones,   2308
  Is come to lay his weary bones among ye: 2576
BOOKE = 1
  Not wake him in his slumber. A Beggers booke, | Out-worths a Nobles
  blood.   190
BOORD = 2
  The Honourable Boord of Councell, out | Must fetch him in, he Papers.   130
  To morrow Morning to the Councell Boord   2830
BOOTLESSE = 1
  To pleade your Cause. It shall be therefore bootlesse,   1416
BORDEAUX *see* Burdeux
BORE = 1
  Zeale and obedience he still bore your Grace,   1688
BORES = 1
  He bores me with some tricke; He's gone to'th'King: 198
BORNE = 2*4
  **Enter Cardinall Wolsey, the Purse borne before him, certaine*   175

BORNE *cont.*
I sweare, tis better to be lowly borne,	1224
Borne out of your Dominions: hauing heere	1370
*The Queene of earthly Queenes: Shee's Noble borne;	1505
*8 *A* Canopy, *borne by foure of the* Cinque-Ports, *vnder it*	2437
a Mantle, &c. Traine borne by a Lady: Then followes	3360

BOSOME = 3
Thither he darts it. Bosome vp my counsell,	172
The bosome of my Conscience, enter'd me;	1549
Our cause, that she should lye i'th'bosome of	1958

BOTH = 16
Still him in praise, and being present both,	75
Cardinall in his passage, fixeth his eye on Buck-|ingham, and	
Buckingham on him,| both full of disdaine.	177
Or Wolfe, or both (for he is equall rau'nous	234
Yet thus farre we are one in Fortunes; both	967
Cham. Good day to both your Graces.	1041
Both of his truth and him (which was too farre)	1690
My Lords, I thanke you both for your good wills,	1694
Both for your Honour better, and your Cause:	1725
Queen. Ye tell me what ye wish for both, my ruine:	1729
Both. You may command vs Sir. *Exeunt.*	2546
Both in his words, and meaning. He was neuer	2594
Haue follow'd both my Fortunes, faithfully,	2733
Both now, and euer blesse her: 'Tis a Gyrle	2972
Both of my Life and Office, I haue labour'd,	3081
Both in his priuate Conscience, and his place,	3088
I shall both finde your Lordship, Iudge and Iuror,	3109

BOUGHT = 1
She should haue bought her Dignities so deere. *Exeunt*	1823

BOUND = 6
To Nature none more bound; his trayning such,	451
Of all these eares (for where I am rob'd and bound,	1511
If you are bound to vs, or no. What say you?	2039
(With thee, and all thy best parts bound together)	2146
But that I am bound in Charitie against it.	2191
Gard. Dread Soueraigne, | How much are we bound to Heauen,	3182

BOUNTEOUS = 1*1
Lou. That Churchman | Beares a bounteous minde indeed,	641
*They loue and doate on: call him bounteous *Buckingham,* | The Mirror	
of all courtesie.	887

BOUNTIES = 1
But par'd my present Hauings, to bestow | My Bounties vpon you.	2031

BOUNTY = 1
That as my hand ha's open'd Bounty to you,	2059

BOW = 2
Bow themselues when he did sing.	1623
My Legges like loaden Branches bow to'th'Earth,	2553

BOWD = 1*1
Old.L. Tis strange; a threepence bow'd would hire me	1245
Then rose againe, and bow'd her to the people:	2506

BOWLE = 1
Let me haue such a Bowle may hold my thankes,	716

BOWLES = *1
standing Bowles for the Christening Guifts: Then foure	3357

BOY = 5
Cannot vouchsafe this burthen, tis too weake | Euer to get a Boy.	1253

BOY *cont.*
  Gard. It's one a clocke Boy, is't not. | *Boy.* It hath strooke.   2771
  Say I, and of a boy. | *Lady.* I, I my Liege,   2969
  And of a louely Boy: the God of heauen   2971
  This honest man, wait like a lowsie Foot-boy   3209
BOY = 1
BOYES = 5*1
  Like little wanton Boyes that swim on bladders: 2260
  The Queene is comming. *Ho-boyes.*   2420
  Promises Boyes heereafter. Sir, your Queen | Desires your Visitation,
  and to be   2973
  Wait else at doore: a fellow Councellor | 'Mong Boyes, Groomes, and
  Lackeyes.   3010
  Who holds his State at dore 'mongst Purseuants, | Pages, and
  Foot-boyes.   3022
  *stil, when sodainly a File of Boyes behind 'em, loose shot,   3314
BRA = 2
BRAINE = 2
  Is in his braine: He bites his lip, and starts,   1975
  Your Braine, and euery Function of your power,   2062
BRAINES = 2
  Our owne Braines, and the Opinion that we bring   21
  No new deuice to beate this from his Braines?   2097
BRAKE = 1
  'Tis but the fate of Place, and the rough Brake   410
BRAN = 3
BRANCHES = 2*1
  My Legges like loaden Branches bow to'th'Earth,   2553
  Bayes, and golden Vizards on their faces, Branches of Bayes   2645
  And like a Mountaine Cedar, reach his branches,   3424
BRANDED = 1
  A Woman (I dare say without Vainglory) | Neuer yet branded with
  Suspition?   1760
BRANDON see also Bra., Bran. = 1
  Enter Brandon, a Sergeant at Armes before him, and | two or three of the
  Guard.   276
BRANDON = 1
BRASIER = *1
  *a fellow somewhat neere the doore, he should be a Brasi-|er   3299
BRASSE = 1
  Grif. Noble Madam: | Mens euill manners, liue in Brasse, their Vertues   2600
BRAUE = 1
  2 A bold braue Gentleman. That should bee | The Duke of Suffolke.   2451
BREACH = 3
  Dashing the Garment of this Peace, aboaded | The sodaine breach on't.   148
  Malice ne're meant: Our breach of Duty this way,   1109
  How euer, yet there is no great breach, when it comes   2532
BREAKE = 5
  Did breake ith'wrenching. | *Norf.* Faith, and so it did.   242
  And breake the foresaid peace. Let the King know   266
  My comfort comes along: breake vp the Court;   1612
  Should the approach of this wilde Riuer breake, | And stand vnshaken
  yours.   2074
  Go breake among the preasse, and finde away out   3345
BREAKES = 1
  Language vnmannerly; yea, such which breakes   354

BREAKFAST = 1
And after this, and then to Breakfast with | What appetite you haue.   2079
BREAST = 2
Another spread on's breast, mounting his eyes,   558
The region of my Breast, which forc'd such way,   1551
BREATH = 2
He would Kisse you Twenty with a breath.   703
Touch me alike: th'are breath I not beleeue in.   1088
BREECHES = 1
Short blistred Breeches, and those types of Trauell;   609
BREED = 2*1
Breed him some preiudice; for from this League,   258
*They were young and handsome, and of the best breed in the   1030
Card. Noble Lady, | I am sorry my integrity should breed,   1674
BREEDING = 1
Beseeching him to giue her vertuous breeding.   2725
BREST = 2
Strikes his brest hard, and anon, he casts   1979
Take notice Lords, he ha's a Loyall brest,   2077
BRETHREN = 2
I her fraile sonne, among'st my Brethren mortall, | Must giue my
tendance to.   2018
And you good Brethren, I am much beholding: 3442
BRIEFE = 1
To steale from Spirituall leysure, a briefe span   2009
BRIGHT = 3
I haste now to my Setting. I shall fall | Like a bright exhalation in the
Euening,   2105
Inuite me to a Banquet, whose bright faces   2665
Where euer the bright Sunne of Heauen shall shine,   3421
BRING = 11
Our owne Braines, and the Opinion that we bring   21
A long time out of play, may bring his plaine song,   626
To bring my whole Cause 'fore his Holinesse,   1480
The Cordiall that ye bring a wretched Lady?   1738
Bring me a constant woman to her Husband,   1767
Will bring me off againe. What's this? To th' Pope?   2100
Ye appeare in euery thing may bring my ruine?   2127
Den. He attends your Highnesse pleasure. | King. Bring him to Vs.   2872
I should haue tane some paines, to bring together   2918
Lady. Ile not come backe, the tydings that I bring   2963
Which Time shall bring to ripenesse: She shall be,   3390
BRINGING = 1
Of bringing backe the Prisoner.   827
BRINGS = 1
All his trickes founder, and he brings his Physicke   1877
BRITAINE = 1
Made Britaine, India: Euery man that stood,   65
BROACH = 1
Did broach this busines to your Highnes, or   1514
BROILING = *1
*1 God saue you Sir. Where haue you bin broiling?   2473
BROKE = 3
Buc. O many | Haue broke their backes with laying Mannors on 'em   136
A thing Inspir'd, and not consulting, broke   146
At length broke vnder me, and now ha's left me   2263

BROKEN = 3
   You haue now a broken Banket, but wee'l mend it.   750
   An old man, broken with the stormes of State,   2575
   Haue broken with the King, who hath so farre   2826
BROOME = *1
   *length they came to th' broome staffe to me, I defide 'em   3313
BROTHER = 3
   I will haue none so neere els. Learne this Brother,   1189
   To make your house our Towre: you, a Brother of vs   2903
   Gard. With a true heart, | And Brother; loue I doe it.   3244
BROTHERS = 1*2
   Norf. What's the cause? | *Cham.* It seemes the Marriage with his
   Brothers Wife   1045
   Sometimes our Brothers Wife. This respite shooke   1548
   *their deare Brothers are able to endure. I haue some of   3321
BROTHER-CARDINALS = 1
   The heads of all thy Brother-Cardinals,   2145
BROUGHT = 9*2
   Sur. He was brought to this,   490
   In all this Noble Beuy, has brought with her   670
   To him brought *viua voce* to his face;   845
   1. When he was brought agen to th' Bar, to heare   860
   Car. If your Grace | Could but be brought to know, our Ends are
   honest,   1790
   Was still inscrib'd: in which you brought the King | To be your Seruant.   2212
   Of Lords, and Ladies, hauing brought the Queene   2483
   For after the stout Earle Northumberland | Arrested him at Yorke, and
   brought him forward   2565
   And brought me Garlands (*Griffith*) which I feele   2668
   Den. Sir, I haue brought my Lord the Arch-byshop, | As you
   commanded me.   2867
   A Councell Table brought in with Chayres and Stooles, and   3035
BROW = 1
   That beare a Weighty, and a Serious Brow,   3
BROWNE = 1
   Worse then the Sacring Bell, when the browne Wench   2188
BUC = 10*1
BUCK = 11*3
BUCKINGHAM see also Buc., Buck. = 14*3
   the Duke of Buckingham, and the Lord | Aburgauenny.   36
   Cardinall in his passage, fixeth his eye on Buck-|ingham, and
   Buckingham on him, | both full of disdaine.   177
   Car. Well, we shall then know more, & Buckingham   185
   Sergeant. Sir, | My Lord the Duke of *Buckingham*, and Earle   279
   I am the shadow of poore *Buckingham*,   313
   Queen. I am sorry, that the Duke of *Buckingham* | Is run in your
   displeasure.   447
   Most like a carefull Subiect haue collected | Out of the Duke of
   Buckingham.   469
   Eu'n to the Hall, to heare what shall become | Of the great Duke of
   Buckingham.   823
   *They loue and doate on: call him bounteous *Buckingham*, | The Mirror
   of all courtesie.   887
   Enter Buckingham from his Arraignment, Tipstaues before   889
   You few that lou'd me, | And dare be bold to weepe for *Buckingham*,   913
   And if he speake of *Buckingham*; pray tell him,   931
   And Duke of *Buckingham*: now, poore *Edward Bohun*;   949

BUCKINGHAM cont.

My noble Father *Henry* of *Buckingham,*	953
Of Noble Buckingham, my Father-in-Law,	2144
The Duke of Buckingham came from his Triall.	2384

BUCKINGHAM = 1
BUCKINGHAMS = 2

Car. The Duke of *Buckinghams* Surueyor? Ha?	180
That Gentleman of *Buckinghams,* in person,	325

BUDDED = 1

Nor. Which is budded out,	150

BUILD = 1

Nor build their euils on the graues of great men;	908

BULKE = 1

That such a Keech can with his very bulke	103

BULLEN see also An.B., An.Bul. = 6

longer Table for the Guests. Then Enter Anne Bullen,	662
Choose Ladies, King and An Bullen.	770
Enter Anne Bullen, and an old Lady.	1201
My King is tangled in affection, to | A Creature of the Queenes, Lady Anne Bullen.	1870
Anne Bullen? No: Ile no *Anne Bullens* for him,	1942
There's more in't then faire Visage. *Bullen?*	1943

BULLENS = 3

Sir *Thomas Bullens* Daughter, the Viscount *Rochford,*	798
Anne Bullen? No: Ile no *Anne Bullens* for him,	1942
No, wee'l no *Bullens*: Speedily I wish	1944

BULMER = 1

Sur. Being at *Greenwich,* | After your Highnesse had reprou'd the Duke | About Sir *William Bulmer.*	539

BURDEN = 2

O 'tis a burden *Cromwel,* 'tis a burden	2290

BURDEUX = 1

Our Merchants goods at Burdeux.	152

BURNES = 2

This Candle burnes not cleere, 'tis I must snuffe it,	1954
Ye blew the fire that burnes ye: now haue at ye.	3180

BURNT = 1

Within these fortie houres, Surrey durst better | Haue burnt that Tongue, then saide so.	2140

BURTHEN = 4

Cannot vouchsafe this burthen, tis too weake | Euer to get a Boy.	1253
The burthen of my sorrowes, fall vpon ye.	1743
Willing to leaue their burthen: Reach a Chaire,	2554
Suf. God safely quit her of her Burthen, and	2853

BUSIE = 1

Kin. We are busie; goe.	1125

BUSINES = 9*1

The busines present. Tis his Highnes pleasure | You shall to th' Tower.	289
Cardinall *Campeius* is arriu'd, and lately, | As all thinke for this busines.	1013
Norf. Let's in; | And with some other busines, put the King	1091
There ye shall meete about this waighty busines.	1195
Did broach this busines to your Highnes, or	1514
Haue wish'd the sleeping of this busines, neuer desir'd	1529
Our Daughter *Mary*: I'th' Progresse of this busines,	1542
Queen. Pray their Graces | To come neere: what can be their busines	1639
I know my life so euen. If your busines	1661
Gard. My Lord, because we haue busines of more mo-|(ment,	3100

BUSINESSE = 21
One certes, that promises no Element | In such a businesse.   95
Buc. Why all this Businesse | Our Reuerend Cardinall carried.   158
Norf. How holily he workes in all his businesse,   1056
Is businesse of Estate; in which, we come | To know your Royall
  pleasure.   1110
Go too; Ile make ye know your times of businesse: 1113
In the vnpartiall iudging of this Businesse.   1154
Cham. It was a gentle businesse, and becomming   1269
Of euery Realme, that did debate this Businesse,   1406
Vpon this businesse my appearance make, | In any of their Courts.   1494
Either for such men, or such businesse;   1702
To trust vs in your businesse) we are ready | To vse our vtmost Studies,
  in your seruice.   1811
Nor. This same *Cranmer*'s | A worthy Fellow, and hath tane much
  paine | In the Kings businesse.   1918
To thinke vpon the part of businesse, which   2015
Car. What should this meane? | *Sur.* The Lord increase this businesse.   2033
The Letter (as I liue) with all the Businesse   2101
2 'Tis all my businesse. At our last encounter,   2383
The Princesse Dowager? How goes her businesse?   2405
Some touch of your late businesse: Affaires that walke   2786
In them a wilder Nature, then the businesse | That seekes dispatch by
  day.   2788
Chan. Speake to the businesse, M.(aster) Secretary;   3042
'Has businesse at his house; for all shall stay: 3447
BUT *l.*59 76 111 118 139 222 225 226 *248 254 263 371 372 375 388 405
  410 415 512 525 543 577 578 592 653 680 *684 702 750 763 779 826 837
  854 857 864 904 905 947 977 1001 1006 1020 1123 1129 1168 1198 1246
  *1261 1296 1427 1469 1517 1525 1528 1530 1591 1594 1596 1644 1681
  1696 1711 1736 1741 1749 1776 *1781 1791 1800 1831 1876 1888 1889
  1894 1908 1916 1998 2031 2050 2191 2193 2250 2262 2306 2341 2344
  2354 2370 2385 2404 2411 2502 2521 2559 2595 2597 2612 2630 *2690
  2700 2711 2735 2741 2797 2803 2840 2844 2900 2995 3012 3058 *3071
  3104 3118 3151 3171 3185 3192 3197 3200 3202 3206 3230 *3265 3281
  *3291 *3319 3335 3391 3410 3431 3452 = 125*9
BUTCHERS = *1
  Buc. This Butchers Curre is venom'd-mouth'd, and I   188
BUTS = 5
  Enter Doctor Buts.   2998
  I came this way so happily. The King | Shall vnderstand it presently.
  Exit Buts   3001
  Cran. 'Tis *Buts.* | The Kings Physitian, as he past along   3003
  Enter the King, and Buts, at a Windowe | aboue.   3014
  King. What's that *Buts*?   3017
BUTS = 2
BUTTS see also Buts. = 1
  By holy *Mary* (*Butts*) there's knauery;   3032
BUTTS = 2
BUY = 1
  Does buy and sell his Honour as he pleases,   268
BUYES = 1
  A guift that heauen giues for him, which buyes | A place next to the
  King,   114
BUZ = 1
  Suf. No, no: | There be moe Waspes that buz about his Nose,   1898

BUZZING = 1
   A buzzing of a Separation | Betweene the King and *Katherine*?   999
BY = 111*14
BYR = 1
   And haue an houre of hearing, and by'r Lady | Held currant Musicke
too.   627
BYSHOP = 1
   Lou. This is about that, which the Byshop spake, | I am happily come
hither.   2874
BYSHOP = 3*1
   Suf. He ha's, and we shall see him | For it, an Arch-byshop.   1921
   Install'd Lord Arch-byshop of Canterbury.   2313
   When by the Arch-byshop of Canterbury,   2507
   Den. Sir, I haue brought my Lord the Arch-byshop, | As you
commanded me.   2867
BYSHOPS = 1
   2 What two Reuerend Byshops | Were those that went on each side of
the Queene?   2523
BYT = 1
   Disdainfull to be tride by't; tis not well.   1485
BYTH = 1
   To his owne portion? And what expence by'th'houre   1969
CAKES = *1
   *Do you looke for Ale, and Cakes heere, you rude | Raskalls?   3267
CALD = 3
   To you that choak'd it. Let be cald before vs   324
   Gent.Vsh. Madam, you are cald backe.   1489
   When you are cald returne. Now the Lord helpe,   1491
CALL = 9*2
   Call him to present tryall: if he may   565
   *They loue and doate on: call him bounteous *Buckingham,* | The Mirror
of all courtesie.   887
   Prethee call *Gardiner* to me, my new Secretary.   1163
   He was from thence discharg'd? Sir, call to minde,   1388
   Shee's going away. | *Kin.* Call her againe.   1486
   Made to the Queene to call backe her Appeale | She intends vnto his
Holinesse.   1605
   I dare now call mine owne. O *Cromwel, Cromwel,*   2369
   1 Sir, | You must no more call it Yorke-place, that's past: 2516
   Grif. Madam, we are heere. | *Kath.* It is not you I call for,   2660
   Call in more women. When I am dead, good Wench,   2760
   *(When Heauen shal call her from this clowd of darknes)   3415
CALLD = 4
   Chalkes Successors their way; nor call'd vpon   109
   Her Coronation. *Katherine* no more | Shall be call'd Queene, but
Princesse Dowager,   1915
   'Tis now the Kings, and call'd White-Hall. | 3 I know it: 2519
   Cran. Why? | *Keep.* Your Grace must waight till you be call'd for.   2996
CALLING = 2
   You signe your Place, and Calling, in full seeming,   1468
   But reuerence to your calling, makes me modest.   3118
CALME = 1
   A Soule as euen as a Calme; Pray thinke vs,   1803
CALS = 1
   1. O, this is full of pitty; Sir, it cals   984

CALUMNIOUS = 1
There's none stands vnder more calumnious tongues, | Then I my selfe,
poore man.   2910
CAM = *1
CAME = 10*2
(For twas indeed his colour, but he came   254
Came to the Bar; where, to his accusations   839
When I came hither, I was Lord High Constable,   948
*Then marke th'inducement. Thus it came; giue heede | (too't: 1536
Sur. How came | His practises to light?   1861
And came to th'eye o'th'King, wherein was read   1866
The Duke of Buckingham came from his Triall.   2384
Came to the Altar, where she kneel'd, and Saint-like   2504
Kath. Alas poore man. | *Grif.* At last, with easie Rodes, he came to
Leicester,   2570
Whether so late? | *Lou.* Came you from the King, my Lord?   2777
I came this way so happily. The King | Shall vnderstand it presently.
Exit Buts   3001
*length they came to th' broome staffe to me, I defide 'em   3313
CAMP = 10*3
CAMPEIUS see also Cam., Camp. = 4
Cardinall *Campeius* is arriu'd, and lately, | As all thinke for this busines. 1013
Enter Wolsey and Campeius with a Commission.   1115
This iust and learned Priest, Cardnall *Campeius*,   1144
Will make this sting the sooner. Cardinall *Campeius*,   1900
CAMPIAN = 1
Enter the two Cardinalls, Wolsey & Campian.   1645
CAN *l.*6 32 103 118 206 531 537 606 673 *745 988 1136 1193 1287 1392
1640 1711 1732 1754 1844 2050 2154 2158 2163 2169 2200 2278 2356
2406 2544 2766 2926 3078 3115 3391 3450 = 35*1
CANDLE = 1
This Candle burnes not cleere, 'tis I must snuffe it,   1954
CANNONS = 1
Vnlesse wee sweepe 'em from the dore with Cannons,   3270
CANNOT = 13*1
Abur. I cannot tell | What Heauen hath giuen him: let some Grauer eye 116
(Who cannot erre) he did it. Now this followes,   250
We cannot feele too little, heare too much.   467
An.B. You cannot shew me.   730
There cannot be those numberlesse offences   927
Gainst me, that I cannot take peace with: 928
I be not found a Talker. | *Wol.* Sir, you cannot;   1121
But this cannot continue.   1129
*Where's your Commission? Lords, words cannot carrie | Authority so
weighty.   2117
Sur. This cannot saue you: 2197
I cannot blame his Conscience.   2461
You cannot with such freedome purge your selfe,   2899
Keep. Yes, my Lord: | But yet I cannot helpe you.   2994
To me you cannot reach. You play the Spaniell,   3195
CANNOT = 1
The offer of this time, I cannot promise,   1830
CANNOT = 5
Cannot vouchsafe this burthen, tis too weake | Euer to get a Boy.   1253
Cannot stand vnder them. If you omit   1829
Giues way to vs) I much feare. If you cannot   1845
Suff. Nay, my Lord, | That cannot be; you are a Counsellor,   3097

CANNOT *cont.*
An Army cannot rule 'em. 3337
CANOPY = *2
   *8 *A* Canopy, *borne by foure of the* Cinque-Ports, *vnder it* 2437
   Noblemen bearing a Canopy, vnder which the Dutchesse of 3358
CANST *l.*536 1619 = 2
CANTERBURIE = 1
   King. Pray you arise | My good and gracious Lord of Canterburie: 2887
CANTERBURIES = *1
   Seate being left void aboue him, as for Canterburies Seate. 3038
CANTERBURY = 9*3
   Canterbury alone; after him, the Bishops of Lincolne, Ely, 1336
   Kin. I then mou'd you, | My Lord of *Canterbury*, and got your leaue 1587
   Install'd Lord Arch-byshop of Canterbury. 2313
   Of Canterbury, accompanied with other 2407
   When by the Arch-byshop of Canterbury, 2507
   King. Ha? Canterbury? | *Den.* I my good Lord. 2869
   King. Stand vp, good Canterbury, 2912
   Enter Cranmer, Archbyshop of Canterbury. 2988
   The high promotion of his Grace of *Canterbury*, 3021
   Crom. Please your Honours, | The chiefe cause concernes his Grace of
   Canterbury. 3044
   *Be friends for shame my Lords: My Lord of *Canterbury* 3231
   *Of thee, which sayes thus: Doe my Lord of *Canterbury* 3250
CAP = 1
   And dare vs with his Cap, like Larkes. 2173
CAP = 5
CAPABLE = 1
   In our owne natures fraile, and capable 3059
CAPACITY = 1
   (Sauing your mincing) the capacity | Of your soft Chiuerell Conscience,
   would receiue, 1239
CAPUCHIUS see also Cap. = 2
   Enter Lord Capuchius. 2692
   My Royall Nephew, and your name *Capuchius.* | *Cap.* Madam the
   same. Your Seruant. 2695
CAR = 3
   Of the Dukes Confessor, *Iohn de la Car,* 304
   Iohn de la Car, my Chaplaine, a choyce howre 508
   Sir *Gilbert Pecke* his Chancellour, and *Iohn Car,* 847
CAR = 21*3
CARD = 30*4
CARDERS = 1
   The Spinsters, Carders, Fullers, Weauers, who 361
CARDINAL = 1
   Deales with our Cardinal, and as I troa 260
CARDINALL see also Car., Card. = 46*7
   Of the right Reuerend Cardinall of Yorke. 99
   Buc. Why all this Businesse | Our Reuerend Cardinall carried. 158
   Betwixt you, and the Cardinall. I aduise you 162
   Enter Cardinall Wolsey, the Purse borne before him, certaine 175
   Cardinall in his passage, fixeth his eye on Buck-|ingham, and
   Buckingham on him, | *both full of disdaine.* 177
   Shall lessen this bigge looke. | *Exeunt Cardinall, and his Traine.* 186
   Buck. Pray giue me fauour Sir: This cunning Cardinall 244
   *As giue a Crutch to th'dead. But our Count-Cardinall 248
   (As soone he shall by me) that thus the Cardinall 267

CARDINALL cont.

Buck. My Surueyor is falce: The ore-great *Cardinall*	311
the *Nobles, and Sir Thomas Louell: the Cardinall*	318
Of all their Loyalties; wherein, although | My good Lord Cardinall,	
they vent reproches	349
Kin. Taxation? | Wherein? and what Taxation? My Lord Cardinall,	366
Lord *Aburgany*, to whom by oth he menac'd | Reuenge vpon the	
Cardinall.	477
Queen. My learn'd Lord *Cardinall*, | Deliuer all with Charity.	484
Hoboies. A small Table vnder a State for the Cardinall, a	661
San. Sir *Thomas Louell*, had the Cardinall	679
Hoboyes. Enter Cardinall Wolsey, and takes his State.	710
passe directly before the Cardinall and gracefully sa-|lute him.	755
Kin. Ye haue found him Cardinall,	789
You are a Churchman, or Ile tell you Cardinall,	791
*Good my Lord Cardinal: I haue halfe a dozen healths,	814
2. Certainly, | The Cardinall is the end of this.	870
The King will venture at it. Either the Cardinall,	1009
Cardinall *Campeius* is arriu'd, and lately, | As all thinke for this busines.	1013
1. Tis the Cardinall; | And meerely to reuenge him on the Emperour,	1015
That she should feele the smart of this: the Cardinall	1021
Norf. Tis so; | This is the Cardinals doing: The King-Cardinall,	1050
Who's there? my good Lord Cardinall? O my *Wolsey*,	1116
Cardinall of *Yorke*, are ioyn'd with me their Seruant,	1153
To him that does best, God forbid els: Cardinall,	1162
Euen of your selfe Lord Cardinall. | *Wol.* How? of me?	1178
Qu. Lord Cardinall, to you I speake. | *Wol.* Your pleasure, Madam.	1425
Kin. My Lord Cardinall, | I doe excuse you; yea, vpon mine Honour,	1521
Beleeue me she ha's had much wrong. Lord Cardinall,	1671
Vpon my Soule two reuerend Cardinall Vertues:	1735
But Cardinall Sins, and hollow hearts I feare ye:	1736
And force them with a Constancy, the Cardinall	1828
How that the Cardinall did intreat his Holinesse	1867
Will make this sting the sooner. Cardinall *Campeius*,	1900
Is posted as the Agent of our Cardinall, | To second all his plot. I do	
assure you,	1903
The Cardinall. | *Nor.* Obserue, obserue, hee's moody.	1926
Does he rake this together? Now my Lords, | Saw you the Cardinall?	1971
King takes his Seat, whispers Louell, who goes | to the Cardinall.	2001
Exit King, frowning vpon the Cardinall, the Nobles | throng after him	
smiling, and whispering.	2081
Nor. Heare the Kings pleasure Cardinall,	2110
Lay kissing in your Armes, Lord Cardinall.	2189
Now, if you can blush, and crie guiltie Cardinall, | You'l shew a little	
Honestie.	2200
Suf. Lord Cardinall, the Kings further pleasure is,	2237
So fare you well, my little good Lord Cardinall. | *Exeunt all but Wolsey.*	2249
For since the Cardinall fell, that Titles lost,	2518
That the great Childe of Honor, Cardinall *Wolsey* | Was dead?	2557
Grif. This Cardinall, | Though from an humble Stocke, vndoubtedly	2606

CARDINALLS = 1*2

of my Lord Cardinalls, by Commission, and maine power tooke	1032
place vnder the Cloth of State. The two Cardinalls sit	1345
Enter the two Cardinalls, Wolsey & Campian.	1645

CARDINALS = 8*4

Honor, and plenteous safety) that you reade | The Cardinals Malice,	
and his Potency	164

CARDINALS *cont.*
   **Cornets. Enter King Henry, leaning on the Cardinals shoul-| der,*   317
   The Cardinals and Sir *Thomas Louels* heads | Should haue gone off.   533
   Lou. To the Cardinals;   635
   Norf. Tis so; | This is the Cardinals doing: The King-Cardinall,   1050
   **great Seale, and a Cardinals Hat: Then two Priests, bea-| ring*   1339
   **Siluer Pillers: After them, side by side, the two Cardinals,*   1343
   Kin. I may perceiue | These Cardinals trifle with me: I abhorre   1607
   **Gent.* And't please your Grace, the two great Cardinals | Wait in the
   presence.   1635
   Suf. The Cardinals Letters to the Pope miscarried,   1865
   Sur. But will the King | Digest this Letter of the Cardinals?   1894
   The heads of all thy Brother-Cardinals,   2145
CARDNALL = 4
   The Cardnall instantly will finde imployment,   882
   This iust and learned Priest, Cardnall *Campeius,*   1144
   I speake my good Lord Cardnall, to this point;   1532
   Into your owne hands (Card'nall) by Extortion: 2178
CARE = 9*1
   Thankes you for this great care: I stood i'th' leuell   322
   Kin. Things done well, | And with a care, exempt themselues from feare: 424
   I put it to your care.   438
   One care abroad: hee would haue all as merry: 671
   **care I had, I saw well chosen, ridden, and furnish'd.*   1029
   Vse vs, and it: My good Lord, haue great care,   1120
   That's Christian care enough: for liuing Murmurers,   1185
   Killing care, & griefe of heart, | *Fall asleepe, or hearing dye.*   1631
   My Lords, I care not (so much I am happy | Aboue a number) if my
   actions   1657
   And Princely Care, fore-seeing those fell Mischiefes,   2828
CAREFULL = 1
   Most like a carefull Subiect haue collected | Out of the Duke of
   Buckingham.   469
CARNARUANSHIRE = 1
   Would for *Carnaruanshire,* although there long'd   1260
CARPD = 1
   In feare our motion will be mock'd, or carp'd at,   421
CARRIAGE = 1*1
   *Grow from the Kings Acquaintance, by this Carriage.   1798
   For honestie, and decent Carriage | A right good Husband (let him be a
   Noble)   2737
CARRIE = *1
   *Where's your Commission? Lords, words cannot carrie | Authority so
   weighty.   2117
CARRIED = 2
   Buc. Why all this Businesse | Our Reuerend Cardinall carried.   158
   And like her true Nobility, she ha's | Carried her selfe towards me.   1506
CARRIES = 2
   I take it, she that carries vp the Traine,   2466
   The Iustice and the Truth o'th' question carries   2931
CARRY = 3
   Should without issue dye; hee'l carry it so   474
   Ambassador to the Emperor, you made bold | To carry into Flanders,
   the Great Seale.   2216
   Still in thy right hand, carry gentle Peace   2360

CARRYING = *1
    *their Dancing vanish, carrying the Garland with them. | The Musicke
    continues.   2656
CASE = 1
    That in this case of Iustice, my Accusers,   3094
CASSADO = 1
    Sur. Item, You sent a large Commission | To Gregory de Cassado, to
    conclude   2218
CAST = 5
    Your Colts tooth is not cast yet? | L.San. No my Lord,   630
    Cast her faire eyes to Heauen, and pray'd deuoutly.   2505
    Cast thousand beames vpon me, like the Sun?   2666
    How earnestly he cast his eyes vpon me: 3005
    Cast none away: That I shall cleere my selfe,   3114
CASTLES = 1
    To forfeit all your Goods, Lands, Tenements, | Castles, and whatsoeuer,
    and to be   2242
CASTS = 2
    As yours was, put into you, euer casts   1808
    Strikes his brest hard, and anon, he casts   1979
CATCH = 1
    And am right glad to catch this good occasion   2907
CATCHING = 1
    L.San. Tis time to giue 'em Physicke, their diseases | Are growne so
    catching.   614
CAUGHT = *1
    *That they haue caught the King: and who knowes yet   1295
CAUSD = 2
    Suf. That out of meere Ambition, you haue caus'd   2222
    I caus'd you write, yet sent away? | Pat. No Madam.   2717
CAUSE = 19*2
    He neuer was so womanish, the cause | He may a little grieue at.   868
    Norf. What's the cause? | *Cham. It seemes the Marriage with his
    Brothers Wife   1045
    In what haue I offended you? What cause   1373
    To pleade your Cause. It shall be therefore bootlesse,   1416
    To bring my whole Cause 'fore his Holinesse,   1480
    The full cause of our comming. | Queen. Speake it heere.   1652
    *A strange Tongue makes my cause more strange, suspiti- | (ous: 1668
    (Like free and honest men) our iust opinions, | And comforts to our
    cause.   1684
    Let me haue time and Councell for my Cause: 1705
    Queen. How Sir? | *Camp. Put your maine cause into the Kings
    protection,   1722
    Both for your Honour better, and your Cause: 1725
    Put my sicke cause into his hands, that hates me?   1750
    Vpon what cause wrong you? Alas, our Places,   1793
    Ha's left the cause o'th'King vnhandled, and   1902
    Our cause, that she should lye i'th'bosome of   1958
    (As I will lend you cause) my doing well, | With my well saying.   2022
    His Noble Iurie, and foule Cause can witnesse.   2158
    Cause the Musitians play me that sad note   2636
    Crom. Please your Honours, | The chiefe cause concernes his Grace of
    Canterbury.   3044
    By vertue of that Ring, I take my cause   3162
    The cause betwixt her, and this great offender.   3190

CAUTION = 1
   And prest in with this Caution. First, me thought   1553
CEASES = 1
   Kath. Bid the Musicke leaue, | They are harsh and heauy to me.
   Musicke ceases.   2672
CEDAR = 1
   And like a Mountaine Cedar, reach his branches,   3424
CELEBRATION = 1
   In Celebration of this day with Shewes, | Pageants, and Sights of Honor.   2390
CELESTIALL *see* coelestiall
CENSURE = 2
   Durst wagge his Tongue in censure, when these Sunnes   77
   Forgetting (like a good man) your late Censure   1689
CENSURERS = 1
   To cope malicious Censurers, which euer,   413
CEREMONY = 2
   1. Ile saue you | That labour Sir. All's now done but the Ceremony   825
   2 You saw the Ceremony? | 3 That I did.   2477
CERTAINE = 7*3
   **Enter Cardinall Wolsey, the Purse borne before him, certaine*   175
   'Twould proue the verity of certaine words   505
   This from a dying man receiue as certaine: 971
   Fresher then e're it was; and held for certaine   1008
   We are a Queene (or long haue dream'd so) certaine   1428
   Scruple, and pricke, on certaine Speeches vtter'd   1538
   10 Certaine Ladies or Countesses, with plaine Circlets of | Gold, without
   Flowers.   2443
   **Dance: and at certaine Changes, the first two hold a spare*   2647
   Pray heauen he found not my disgrace: for certaine   3006
   Cham. Tis now too certaine; | How much more is his Life in value with
   him?   3173
CERTAINLY = 1
   2. Certainly, | The Cardinall is the end of this.   870
CERTES = 1
   One certes, that promises no Element | In such a businesse.   95
CHAFED = 1
   Leap'd from his Eyes. So lookes the chafed Lyon   2086
CHAFFD = 1
   Nor. What are you chaff'd?   192
CHAFFE = 1
   Most throughly to be winnowed, where my Chaffe   2908
CHAIRE = 2*1
   **The Queene makes no answer, rises out of her Chaire,*   1364
   In a rich Chaire of State, opposing freely   2487
   Willing to leaue their burthen: Reach a Chaire,   2554
CHALKES = 1
   Chalkes Successors their way; nor call'd vpon   109
CHALLENGD = 1
   (For so they phrase 'em) by their Heralds challeng'd   78
CHALLENGE = 1
   You are mine Enemy, and make my Challenge,   1435
CHAM = 22*6
CHAMBER = 6
   Buck. An vntimely Ague | Staid me a Prisoner in my Chamber, when   44
   Card. Sir *Thomas Louell*, is the Banket ready | I'th' Priuy Chamber? |
   Lou. Yes, my Lord.   804
   Card. There's fresher ayre my Lord, | In the next Chamber.   810

CHAMBER *cont.*

Into your priuate Chamber; we shall giue you	1651
Crom. To his owne hand, in's Bed-chamber.	1930
At Chamber dore? and one, as great as you are?	3210

CHAMBERLAINE *see also Cham., L.Ch., L.Cham.* = 14*3

Enter L.(ord) Chamberlaine and L.(ord) Sandys.	570
Enter L.(ord) Chamberlaine L.(ord) Sands, and Louell.	674
Card. Good Lord Chamberlaine, | *Go, giue 'em welcome; you can speake the French tongue	744
Shepheards, vsher'd by the Lord Chamberlaine. They	754
Card. Say, Lord *Chamberlaine,* | They haue done my poore house grace:	766
Kin. My Lord Chamberlaine, | Prethee come hither, what faire Ladie's that?	795
Enter Lord Chamberlaine, reading this Letter.	1027
Enter to the Lord Chamberlaine, the Dukes of Nor-|folke and Suffolke.	1038
Norf. Well met my Lord *Chamberlaine.*	1040
Norfolke. Thankes my good Lord *Chamberlaine.*	1099
Exit Lord Chamberlaine, and the King drawes the Curtaine | and sits reading pensiuely.	1100
Enter Lord Chamberlaine.	1263
And say I spoke with you. | *Exit Lord Chamberlaine.*	1298
Enter the Duke of Norfolke, Duke of Suffolke, Lord Surrey, | and Lord Chamberlaine.	1825
Enter to Woolsey, the Dukes of Norfolke and Suffolke, the | Earle of Surrey, and the Lord Chamberlaine.	2108
Duke of Suffolke, Duke of Norfolke, Surrey, Lord Cham-|berlaine,	3039
Enter Lord Chamberlaine.	3325

CHAMBERS = 2

Buck. All the whole time | I was my Chambers Prisoner.	55
Drum and Trumpet, Chambers dischargd.	731

CHAMBLET = 1

Por. You i'th'Chamblet, get vp o'th' raile,	3351

CHAN = 4

CHANCE = 2

If I chance to talke a little wilde, forgiue me:	698
You do appeare before them. If they shall chance	2948

CHANCELLOR = 2

Crom. The next is, that Sir *Thomas Moore* is chosen | Lord Chancellor, in your place.	2303
3 *Lord* Chancellor, *with Purse and Mace before him.*	2424

CHANCELLOUR *see also Chan.* = 1*1

Sir *Gilbert Pecke* his Chancellour, and *Iohn Car,*	847
placed vnder the State. Enter Lord Chancellour, places	3036

CHANGES = *2

Dance: and at certaine Changes, the first two hold a spare	2647
in their Changes, and holding the Garland ouer her	2651

CHAPLAINE = 2

Iohn de la Car, my Chaplaine, a choyce howre	508
My Chaplaine to no Creature liuing, but	512

CHAPLAINES = *1

The whole Realme, by your teaching & your Chaplaines	3064

CHAPPELL = 1

Going to Chappell: and the voyce is now | Onely about her Corronation.	2318

CHARGD = 1

Of a full-charg'd confederacie, and giue thankes	323

CHARGE = 8
To whom as great a Charge, as little Honor   128
You charge not in your spleene a Noble person,   521
Place you that side, Ile take the charge of this: 691
Then giue my Charge vp to Sir *Nicholas Vaux*,   940
Yea, the whole Consistorie of Rome. You charge me,   1452
Out of the Kings protection. This is my Charge.   2244
Cromwel, I charge thee, fling away Ambition,   2355
Once more my Lord of *Winchester*, I charge you | Embrace, and loue
this man.   3242
CHARGES = 1
But that till further Triall, in those Charges   2900
CHARGING = 1
In charging you with matters, to commit you: 2949
CHARITIE = 1
But that I am bound in Charitie against it.   2191
CHARITY = 6
Queen. My learn'd Lord *Cardinall*, | Deliuer all with Charity.   484
Louell. I doe beseech your Grace, for charity   922
Haue stood to Charity, and displayd th'effects   1445
I haue more Charity. But say I warn'd ye;   1741
Giue him a little earth for Charity.   2577
And yet with Charity. He was a man   2588
CHARLES = 5
To th'old dam Treason) *Charles* the Emperour,   252
King. Charles, I will play no more to night,   2837
King. But little *Charles*, | Nor shall not when my Fancies on my play. 2840
King. 'Tis midnight *Charles*,   2856
King. Charles good night. *Exit Suffolke.*   2864
CHARTREUX = 2
Bra. A Monke o'th' *Chartreux.* | *Buck.* O *Michaell Hopkins?* | *Bra.* He. 308
Kin. What was that *Henton?* | *Sur.* Sir, a *Chartreux* Fryer,   492
CHASTE = 2
The Modell of our chaste loues: his yong daughter,   2723
I was a chaste Wife, to my Graue: Embalme me,   2763
CHAYRE = 1
That Chayre stand empty: But we all are men   3058
CHAYRES = *1
A Councell Table brought in with Chayres and Stooles, and   3035
CHEEFE = 1
The cheefe ayme of his Honour, and to strengthen   3187
CHEEKES = *1
*In their faire cheekes my Lord, then wee shall haue 'em, | Talke vs to
silence.   723
CHEERE = 2
I am beholding to you: cheere your neighbours: 719
The trap is laid for me. | *King.* Be of good cheere,   2944
CHERISH = 1
Loue thy selfe last, cherish those hearts that hate thee;   2358
CHERRY = 2
Acquainted with this stranger; 'tis as like you, | As Cherry, is to Cherry. 2975
CHERUBINS = 1
As Cherubins, all gilt: the Madams too,   67
CHIDING = 1
As doth a Rocke against the chiding Flood,   2073

CHIEFE = 1
   Crom. Please your Honours, | The chiefe cause concernes his Grace of
   Canterbury.   3044
CHILD = 3
   If it conceiu'd a male-child by me, should   1556
   This happy Child, did I get any thing.   3437
   To see what this Child does, and praise my Maker.   3440
CHILDE = 1*1
   That the great Childe of Honor, Cardinall *Wolsey* | Was dead?   2557
   Norfolke, Godmother, bearing the Childe richly habited in   3359
CHILDISH = 1
   Out of our easinesse and childish pitty   3073
CHILDREN = 1*1
   With many Children by you. If in the course   1391
   *To all the Plaines about him: Our Childrens Children | Shall see this,
   and blesse Heauen.   3425
CHILDRENS = *1
   *To all the Plaines about him: Our Childrens Children | Shall see this,
   and blesse Heauen.   3425
CHINE = 1
   Let me ne're hope to see a Chine againe,   3284
CHIUERELL = 1
   (Sauing your mincing) the capacity | Of your soft Chiuerell Conscience,
   would receiue,   1239
CHOAKD = 1
   To you that choak'd it. Let be cald before vs   324
CHOICE = 1
   Wol. You haue heere Lady, | (And of your choice) these Reuerend
   Fathers, men   1412
CHOLLER = 2
   And let your Reason with your Choller question   201
   And somthing spoke in choller, ill, and hasty: 863
CHOOSE = 1
   Choose Ladies, King and An Bullen.   770
CHOSEN = 3*1
   To ranke our chosen Truth with such a show   19
   care I had, I saw well chosen, ridden, and furnish'd.   1029
   Crom. The next is, that Sir *Thomas Moore* is chosen | Lord Chancellor,
   in your place.   2303
   That were the Seruants to this chosen Infant,   3419
CHOYCE = 2
   Iohn de la Car, my Chaplaine, a choyce howre   508
   By all your good leaues Gentlemen; heere Ile make | My royall choyce.   787
CHOYSEST = 1
   With all the choysest Musicke of the Kingdome,   2512
CHRISTENDOME = 4
   That sure th'haue worne out Christendome: how now?   588
   Your scruple to the voyce of Christendome: 1135
   Almost in Christendome: shortly (I beleeue)   1913
   That Christendome shall euer speake his Vertue.   2621
CHRISTENING = 2*2
   *Christian Conscience this one Christening will beget a   3295
   When they passe backe from the Christening?   3333
   Th'are come already from the Christening,   3344
   standing Bowles for the Christening Guifts: Then foure 3357
CHRISTENINGS = *1
   *Ile scratch your heads; you must be seeing Christenings? 3266

CHRISTIAN = 6*1
  (I meane the learned ones in Christian Kingdomes)   1140
  That's Christian care enough: for liuing Murmurers,   1185
  Is this your Christian Councell? Out vpon ye.   1730
  You haue Christian warrant for 'em, and no doubt   2129
  As you wish Christian peace to soules departed,   2748
  To haue this young one made a Christian.   3253
  *Christian Conscience this one Christening will beget a   3295
CHRISTIANS = 1
  But those that sought it, I could wish more Christians: 905
CHRONICLER = 1
  But such an honest Chronicler as *Griffith.*   2630
CHRONICLES = 1
  The Chronicles of my doing: Let me say,   409
CHURCH = 1
  One that in all obedience, makes the Church   3186
CHURCHMAN = 3
  Lou. That Churchman | Beares a bounteous minde indeed, 641
  You are a Churchman, or Ile tell you Cardinall,   791
  Become a Churchman, better then Ambition: 3112
CHURCHMENS = 1
  If ye be any thing but Churchmens habits)   1749
CINQUE-PORTS = 1*1
  *8 *A* Canopy, *borne by foure of the* Cinque-Ports, *vnder it* 2437
  1 They that beare | The Cloath of Honour ouer her, are foure Barons |
  Of the Cinque-Ports.   2462
CIRCLETS = *1
  *10 *Certaine* Ladies *or* Countesses, *with plaine Circlets of* | *Gold, without*
  Flowers.   2443
CIRCUMSTANCES = 1
  Or God will punish me. I do beleeue | (Induc'd by potent
  Circumstances) that   1433
CITED *see* cyted
CITIZENS = 1
  2 'Tis well: The Citizens | I am sure haue shewne at full their Royall
  minds,   2387
CITY = 1
  They'l say tis naught. Others to heare the City   3454
CLAD = *1
  clad in white Robes, wearing on their heades Garlands of 2644
CLAIME = 2
  1 Yes, 'tis the List | Of those that claime their Offices this day, 2396
  And by those claime their greatnesse; not by Blood.   3409
CLAIMES = 1
  The Duke of Suffolke is the first, and claimes   2399
CLAP = 2
  Clap round Fines for neglect: y'are lazy knaues,   3341
  If they hold, when their Ladies bid 'em clap. | FINIS.   3463
CLAPT = 2
  That's clapt vpon the Court Gate.   593
  The very thought of this faire Company, | Clapt wings to me. 676
CLEANE = 1
  Out of a forreigne wisedome, renouncing cleane   607
CLEARE = 2
  And thus farre cleare him.   1533
  W haue frighted with our Trumpets: so 'tis cleare,   3453

CLEERE = 4
And proofes as cleere as Founts in *Iuly*, when	228
By Darkning my cleere Sunne. My Lords farewell. *Exe.*	315
This Candle burnes not cleere, 'tis I must snuffe it,	1954
Cast none away: That I shall cleere my selfe,	3114

CLERGY = 1
| Of his owne body he was ill, and gaue \| The Clergy ill example. | 2598 |

CLERKES = 1
| The Tryall, iust and Noble. All the Clerkes, | 1139 |

CLIMBE = 1
| What 'tis you go about: to climbe steepe hilles | 202 |

CLINQUANT = 1
| All Clinquant all in Gold, like Heathen Gods | 63 |

CLOAKES = 1
| As lowd, and to as many Tunes. Hats, Cloakes, | 2493 |

CLOATH = 1
| 1 They that beare \| The Cloath of Honour ouer her, are foure Barons \| | |
| Of the Cinque-Ports. | 2462 |

CLOATHES = 1
| *L.Ch.* Death my Lord, \| Their cloathes are after such a Pagan cut too't, | 586 |

CLOCKE = 1
| *Gard.* It's one a clocke Boy, is't not. \| *Boy.* It hath strooke. | 2771 |

CLOSE = 5
2. Let's stand close and behold him.	895
The Trumpets sound: Stand close,	2419
Let 'em alone, and draw the Curtaine close:	3033
Keepe the dore close Sirha.	3288
Man. You great fellow, | Stand close vp, or Ile make your head ake.	3349

CLOTH = *1
| **place vnder the Cloth of State. The two Cardinalls sit* | 1345 |

CLOTHARIUS = 1
| To *Pepin* or *Clotharius*, they keepe State so. | 581 |

CLOTHIERS = 1
| The Clothiers all not able to maintaine | 359 |

CLOWD = 1*1
| Whose Figure euen this instant Clowd puts on, | 314 |
| *(When Heauen shal call her from this clowd of darknes) | 3415 |

CLUBBES = *1
| *and hit that Woman, who cryed out Clubbes, when I | 3309 |

CLUNG = 1
| Beheld them when they lighted, how they clung | 50 |

COALE = 2
| Haue blowne this Coale, betwixt my Lord, and me; | 1437 |
| That I haue blowne this Coale: I do deny it, | 1453 |

COASTS = *1
| *Sur.* Will this worke? \| **Cham.* The King in this perceiues him, how he | |
| coasts | 1874 |

COAT = 1
| *Sur.* By my Soule, \| Your long Coat (Priest) protects you, | 2165 |

COATE = 1*1
| *In a long Motley Coate, garded with Yellow,* | 17 |
| **his Coate of Armes, and on his head he wore a Gilt Copper \| Crowne.* | 2427 |

COELESTIALL = 1
| On that Coelestiall Harmony I go too. \| *Sad and solemne Musicke.* | 2638 |

COINE = 1*1
| **Such doubts as false Coine from it. The King loues you, | 1809 |
| Your holy-Hat to be stampt on the Kings Coine. | 2223 |

COLD = 4
Tongues spit their duties out, and cold hearts freeze	394
Two women plac'd together, makes cold weather:	693
And sleepe in dull cold Marble, where no mention	2348
And of an earthy cold? Marke her eyes?	2677

COLEBRAND = 1
Man. I am not *Sampson,* nor Sir *Guy,* nor *Colebrand,*	3280

COLLARS = 2
bearing the Rod of Siluer with the Doue, Crowned with an | Earles Coronet. Collars of Esses.	2431
him, the Duke of Norfolke, with the Rod of Marshalship, | a Coronet on his head. Collars of Esses.	2435

COLLECTED = 2
Most like a carefull Subiect haue collected | Out of the Duke of Buckingham.	469
Collected from his life. Ile startle you	2187

COLLEDGES = 1
Together with all famous Colledges	1912

COLOUR = 1
(For twas indeed his colour, but he came	254

COLTS = 1
Your Colts tooth is not cast yet? | *L.San.* No my Lord,	630

COMBINATION = 1
The Articles o'th' Combination drew	245

COMBUSTION = *1
*such a combustion in the State. I mist the Meteor once,	3308

COME = 40*5
I Come no more to make you laugh, Things now,	2
May heere finde Truth too. Those that come to see	10
That come to heare a Merry, Bawdy Play,	15
Liue where their prayers did: and it's come to passe,	396
Made suit to come in's presence; which if granted,	548
My Barge stayes; | Your Lordship shall along: Come, good Sir *Thomas,*	654
Kin. My Lord Chamberlaine, | Prethee come hither, what faire Ladie's that?	795
Buck. All good people, | You that thus farre haue come to pitty me;	896
Of my long weary life is come vpon me:	979
Is businesse of Estate; in which, we come | To know your Royall pleasure.	1110
Forthwith for what you come. Where's *Gardiner?*	1156
Kin. Come hither *Gardiner.* | *Walkes and whispers.*	1170
Come pat betwixt too early, and too late	1304
An. Come you are pleasant.	1314
Scri. Say, *Henry* K.(ing) of England, come into the Court.	1358
Scribe. Say, *Katherine* Queene of England, | Come into the Court.	1361
Crier. Katherine. Q.(ueene) of England, come into the Court.	1488
To weare our mortall State to come, with her,	1598
Queen. Pray their Graces | To come neere: what can be their busines	1639
We come not by the way of Accusation,	1678
While I shall haue my life. Come reuerend Fathers,	1820
(Not to come off) in his displeasure. | *Sur.* Sir,	1853
Card. Is he ready to come abroad? | *Crom.* I thinke by this he is.	1937
Imploy'd you where high Profits might come home,	2030
Haue euer come too short of my Desires,	2044
1 You come to take your stand heere, and behold	2381
Come Gentlemen, ye shall go my way, '	2542
Is come to lay his weary bones among ye:	2576

COME *cont.*

Lou. This is about that, which the Byshop spake, | I am happily come hither.	2874
Come, you and I must walke a turne together:	2889
Come, come, giue me your hand.	2891
This Morning come before vs, where I know	2898
It fits we thus proceed, or else no witnesse | Would come against you.	2904
Gent. within. Come backe: what meane you?	2962
Lady. Ile not come backe, the tydings that I bring	2963
Chan. Let him come in. | *Keep.* Your Grace may enter now.	3053
Bishop of *Winchester.* But know I come not	3192
Kin. Come, come my Lord, you'd spare your spoones;	3238
Come Lords, we trifle time away: I long	3252
*great *Toole*, come to Court, the women so besiege vs?	3293
*these three dayes; besides the running Banquet of two | Beadles, that is to come.	3323
Th'are come already from the Christening,	3344
All that are heere: Some come to take their ease,	3451

COMES = 6*5

*You'l finde it wholesome. Loe, where comes that Rock	173
*Comes through Commissions, which compels from each	390
And pardon comes: I shall anon aduise you	444
For more then blushing comes to: If your backe	1252
*No more to th' Crowne but that: Lo, who comes here?	1261
goes about the Court, comes to the King, and kneeles at | his Feete. Then speakes.	1365
My comfort comes along: breake vp the Court;	1612
The third day, comes a Frost; a killing Frost,	2256
How euer, yet there is no great breach, when it comes	2532
Kath. O my good Lord, that comfort comes too late,	2708
His Royall selfe in Iudgement comes to heare	3189

COMFORT = 7*2

My comfort comes along: breake vp the Court;	1612
Mend 'em for shame my Lords: Is this your comfort?	1737
*You'd feele more comfort. Why shold we (good Lady)	1792
Grif. She is going Wench. Pray, pray. | *Pati.* Heauen comfort her.	2678
And heartily entreats you take good comfort.	2707
Kath. O my good Lord, that comfort comes too late,	2708
Keepe comfort to you, and this Morning see	2947
All comfort, ioy in this most gracious Lady,	3371
This Oracle of comfort, ha's so pleas'd me,	3438

COMFORTING = 1

With comforting repose, and not for vs	2775

COMFORTLESSE = 1

The Queene is comfortlesse, and wee forgetfull	1328

COMFORTS = 3

(Like free and honest men) our iust opinions, | And comforts to our cause.	1684
They are (as all my other comforts) far hence | In mine owne Countrey Lords.	1718
But now I am past all Comforts heere, but Prayers.	2711

COMMAND = 4

He sent command to the Lord Mayor straight	1003
If I command him followes my appointment,	1188
Something I can command. As I walke thither, | Ile tell ye more.	2544
Both. You may command vs Sir. *Exeunt.*	2546

COMMANDED = 6
Gard. But to be commanded | For euer by your Grace, whose hand ha's
rais'd me.   1168
Let silence be commanded.   1352
Commanded Nature, that my Ladies wombe   1555
Our Reasons layd before him, hath commanded   2829
What you commanded me, but by her woman,   2844
*Den. Sir, I haue brought my Lord the Arch-byshop, | As you
commanded me.   2867
COMMANDING = 2
The Court of Rome commanding. You my Lord   1152
Obeying in commanding, and thy parts   1503
COMMANDS = 1
Who commands you | To render vp the Great Seale presently   2111
COMMEND = 2
Commend mee to his Grace: 930
And durst commend a secret to your eare   2791
COMMENDATIONS = 1*1
Sends you his Princely Commendations,   2706
*Kin. You were euer good at sodaine Commendations,   3191
COMMENDED = 1
Kath. In which I haue commended to his goodnesse   2722
COMMENDS = 1
Commends his good opinion of you, to you; and   1277
COMMING = 6
Vaux. Prepare there, | The Duke is comming: See the Barge be ready;   942
I doe not like their comming; now I thinke on't,   1642
The full cause of our comming. | *Queen.* Speake it heere.   1652
I am not such a Truant since my comming,   1666
The Queene is comming. *Ho-boyes.*   2420
They grow still too; from all Parts they are comming,   3327
COMMISSION = 8*2
Of this Commission? I beleeue, not any.   428
The force of this Commission: pray looke too't;   437
*of my Lord Cardinalls, by Commission, and maine power tooke   1032
Enter Wolsey and Campeius with a Commission.   1115
I tender my Commission; by whose vertue,   1151
Car. Whil'st our Commission from Rome is read,   1351
By a Commission from the Consistorie,   1451
**Where's your Commission? Lords, words cannot carrie | Authority so
weighty.   2117
Sur. Item, You sent a large Commission | To *Gregory de Cassado,* to
conclude   2218
Why, what a shame was this? Did my Commission   3211
COMMISSIONS = 1*2
**Are in great grieuance: There haue beene Commissions   347
**Comes through Commissions, which compels from each   390
Whom after vnder the Commissions Seale,   510
COMMIT = 1
In charging you with matters, to commit you: 2949
COMMITTED = 4
Sur. If (quoth he) I for this had beene committed,   544
And consequence of dread, that I committed   1583
The willing'st sinne I euer yet committed, | May be absolu'd in English.   1672
From hence you be committed to the Tower,   3103
COMMITTING = 1
Aboue all Princes, in committing freely   1134

COMMON = 3
Vaux, Sir Walter Sands, and common people, &c.   892
As you respect the common good, the State   2183
The common voyce I see is verified   3249
COMMONALTY = 1
To the loue o'th'Commonalty, the Duke | Shall gouerne England.   516
COMMONS = 1*1
*Of the Kings grace and pardon: the greeued Commons   441
2. All the Commons | Hate him perniciously, and o' my Conscience   884
COMMOTION = *1
Nor. My Lord, we haue | *Stood heere obseruing him. Some strange
Commotion   1973
COMMOTIONS = 1
Commotions, vprores, with a generall Taint   3076
COMMUNICATION = 1
But minister communication of | A most poore issue.   139
COMPANION = 1
To haue you therein my Companion.   2012
COMPANY = 6
Bran. Nay, he must beare you company. The King   296
As first, good Company, good wine, good welcome, | Can make good
people.   672
The very thought of this faire Company, | Clapt wings to me.   676
A noble Company: what are their pleasures?   757
My Lord, youle beare vs company? | *Cham.* Excuse me,   1094
For I must thinke of that, which company | Would not be friendly too. 2859
COMPASSE = 2
Beyond thoughts Compasse, that former fabulous Storie   80
Fall into'th'compasse of a Premunire;   2240
COMPELD = 2
Vnfit for other life, compeld by hunger   362
This compel'd fortune: haue your mouth fild vp, | Before you open it. 1307
COMPELS = *1
*Comes through Commissions, which compels from each   390
COMPLAINT = 2
On the complaint o'th'Tenants; take good heed   520
Giuen eare to our Complaint, of his great Grace,   2827
COMPLAINTS = 2
Norf. If you will now vnite in your Complaints,   1827
Greeuous complaints of you; which being consider'd,   2896
COMPLEAT = 1
Then euer they were faire. This man so compleat,   457
COMPLEATE = 1
She is a gallant Creature, and compleate   1890
COMPOUNDED = 1
What foure Thron'd ones could haue weigh'd | Such a compounded
one?   53
COMPTROLLERS = 1
For I was spoke to, with Sir *Henry Guilford* | This night to be
Comptrollers.   657
CONCEALE = 1
A strong faith to conceale it.   994
CONCEIT = 1
Cham. Lady; | I shall not faile t'approue the faire conceit   1291
CONCEIUD = 1
If it conceiu'd a male-child by me, should   1556

CONCEIUE = 1
Hardly conceiue of me. Let it be nois'd,   442
CONCEPTION = 1
This dangerous conception in this point,   480
CONCERNES = 1
Crom. Please your Honours, | The chiefe cause concernes his Grace of
Canterbury.   3044
CONCERNING = 2
Concerning the French Iourney. I replide,   501
Concerning his Imprisonment, was rather   3221
CONCLAUE = 1
And thanke the holy Conclaue for their loues,   1147
CONCLUDE = 2
The Peace betweene the French and vs, not valewes | The Cost that did
conclude it.   142
Sur. Item, You sent a large Commission | To *Gregory de Cassado*, to
conclude   2218
CONDEMND = 1
1. Yes truely is he, | And condemn'd vpon't.   833
CONDITION = 1
And those of true condition; That your Subiects   346
CONDITIONS = 1
Lou. They must either | (For so run the Conditions) leaue those
remnants   601
CONDUCT = 3
And pray receiue 'em Nobly, and conduct 'em   746
But leaue their Flockes, and vnder your faire Conduct   763
Lou. To th' water side I must conduct your Grace;   939
CONFEDERACIE = 1
Of a full-charg'd confederacie, and giue thankes   323
CONFERENCE = 2
I would your Grace would giue vs but an houre | Of priuate conference.   1123
The secret of your conference?   1265
CONFESSE = 4
Cham. Such a one, they all confesse   783
Must now confesse, if they haue any goodnesse,   1138
And if you may confesse it, say withall   2038
Car. My Soueraigne, I confesse your Royall graces   2040
CONFESSIONS = 2
Ile heare him his confessions iustifie,   326
Vrg'd on the Examinations, proofes, confessions   843
CONFESSOR = 3*1
Of the Dukes Confessor, *Iohn de la Car,*   304
His Confessor, who fed him euery minute | With words of Soueraignty.   494
*Lou. O that your Lordship were but now Confessor, | To one or two of
these.   684
Confessor to him, with that Diuell Monke, | *Hopkins,* that made this
mischiefe.   848
CONFESSORS = 1
As holy Oyle, *Edward* Confessors Crowne,   2509
CONFIDENCE = 1
To me, should vtter, with demure Confidence,   513
CONFIDENT = 1
2. I am confident; | You shall Sir: Did you not of late dayes heare   997
CONFINE = 1
Into our hands, and to Confine your selfe   2113

CONFIRMATION = 1
Cran. And let Heauen | Witnesse how deare, I hold this Confirmation. 3246
CONFIRME = 3
Is not my Friend. This to confirme my welcome, 713
That will vndoe her: To confirme this too, 1012
During my life; and to confirme his Goodnesse, 2134
CONFORMABLE = 1
At all times to your will conformable: 1378
CONGE = *1
or Palme in their hands. They first Conge vnto her, then 2646
CONIECTURES = 1
1. Tis likely, | By all coniectures: First *Kildares* Attendure; 872
CONIUNCTION = 1
Sur. Now all my ioy | Trace the Coniunction. 1883
CONSCIENCE = 21*3
2. All the Commons | Hate him perniciously, and o' my Conscience 884
And if I haue a Conscience, let it sincke me, 901
Ha's crept too neere his Conscience. 1047
Suff. No, his Conscience | Ha's crept too neere another Ladie. 1048
Dangers, doubts, wringing of the Conscience, 1060
The quiet of my wounded Conscience; 1117
So sweet a Bedfellow? But Conscience, Conscience; 1198
(Sauing your mincing) the capacity | Of your soft Chiuerell Conscience, would receiue, 1239
My Conscience first receiu'd a tendernes, 1537
The bosome of my Conscience, enter'd me; 1549
The wild Sea of my Conscience, I did steere 1567
I meant to rectifie my Conscience, which 1570
There's nothing I haue done yet o' my Conscience 1654
There (on my Conscience put vnwittingly) 1986
*(By what meanes got, I leaue to your owne conscience) 2225
A still, and quiet Conscience. The King ha's cur'd me, 2286
For Truths-sake, and his Conscience; that his bones, 2308
I cannot blame his Conscience. 2461
Lou. Me thinkes I could | Cry the Amen, and yet my Conscience sayes 2799
Both in his priuate Conscience, and his place, 3088
I make as little doubt as you doe conscience, 3116
*Christian Conscience this one Christening will beget a 3295
*by his face, for o' my conscience twenty of the Dog-|dayes 3300
CONSENT = 2
But by particular consent proceeded 1591
And our consent, for better tryall of you, 3102
CONSEQUENCE = 1
And consequence of dread, that I committed 1583
CONSIDER = 2
Together; To consider further, that | What his high Hatred would effect, wants not 166
For Goodnesse sake, consider what you do, 1796
CONSIDERATION = 1
Would giue it quicke consideration; for 399
CONSIDERD = 1
Greeuous complaints of you; which being consider'd, 2896
CONSIDERING = 1
His Thinkings are below the Moone, not worth | His serious considering. 1999
CONSIDERINGS = 1
That many maz'd considerings, did throng 1552

CONSISTORIE = 2
By a Commission from the Consistorie,   1451
Yea, the whole Consistorie of Rome. You charge me,   1452
CONSISTORY = *1
*each side the Court in manner of a Consistory: Below them   1348
CONSTABLE = 1
When I came hither, I was Lord High Constable,   948
CONSTANCY = 1
And force them with a Constancy, the Cardinall   1828
CONSTANT = 1
Bring me a constant woman to her Husband,   1767
CONSTRUCTION = 1
The mercifull construction of good women,   3459
CONSULTING = 1
A thing Inspir'd, and not consulting, broke   146
CONTAGIOUS = 1
To one mans Honour, this contagious sicknesse;   3074
CONTAINES = 1
2 May I be bold to aske what that containes, | That Paper in your hand.   2394
CONTEMPLATION = 1
His Contemplation were aboue the earth,   1996
CONTEMPT = 1
Turne me away: and let the fowl'st Contempt   1396
CONTENT = 4
To faire content, and you: None heere he hopes   669
And range with humble liuers in Content,   1225
Old L. Our content | Is our best hauing.   1228
Almost forgot my Prayres to content him?   1765
CONTENTED = 2
And Kingly Dignity, we are contented   1597
Your patience to you, and be well contented   2902
CONTENTS = 1
These are the whole Contents, and good my Lord,   2746
CONTINUALL = 1
Continuall Meditations, Teares, and Sorrowes,   2582
CONTINUE = 3
But this cannot continue.   1129
Continue in my Liking? Nay, gaue notice   1387
But he's a Learned man. May he continue   2306
CONTINUES = 1
*their Dancing vanish, carrying the Garland with them. | The Musicke
continues.   2656
CONTRADICTED = 1
I euer contradicted your Desire?   1382
CONTRARIE = 1
In the Diuorce, his contrarie proceedings | Are all vnfolded: wherein he
appeares,   1858
CONTRARY = 3
The Kings Atturney on the contrary,   842
Does pay the Act of it, as i'th'contrary   2057
The best perswasions to the contrary   2950
CONTRIBUTION = 1
A trembling Contribution; why we take   431
CONUAID = 1
You be conuaid to th' Tower a Prisoner;   3146
CONUENIENT = 2
The most conuenient place, that I can thinke of   1193

CONUENIENT *cont.*
  Attendants stand in conuenient order about the Stage.   1350
CONUENTED = 1
  He be conuented. He's a ranke weed Sir *Thomas*,   2831
CONUERTING = 1
  For sure there's no conuerting of 'em: now   624
COPE = 1
  To cope malicious Censurers, which euer,   413
COPPER = *1
  his Coate of Armes, and on his head he wore a Gilt Copper | Crowne.   2427
CORD = 1
  The Master-cord on's heart.   1966
CORDIALL = 1
  The Cordiall that ye bring a wretched Lady?   1738
CORNE = 2
  And Corne shall flye asunder. For I know   2909
  Her Foes shake like a Field of beaten Corne,   3401
CORNER = 1
  Deserues a Corner: would all other Women   1655
CORNETS = 1*1
  Cornets. Enter King Henry, leaning on the Cardinals shoul- | der,   317
  Trumpets, Sennet, and Cornets.   1333
CORONALL = *2
  a Demy Coronall of Gold. With him, the Earle of Surrey,   2430
  9 The Olde Dutchesse of Norfolke, *in a Coronall of Gold,*   2441
CORONATION = 4
  Suf. There's order giuen for her Coronation: 1887
  Her Coronation. *Katherine* no more | Shall be call'd Queene, but
  Princesse Dowager,   1915
  By custome of the Coronation.   2398
  The Order of the Coronation.   2421
CORONET = 2*1
  bearing the Rod of Siluer with the Doue, Crowned with an | Earles
  Coronet. Collars of Esses.   2431
  7 Duke of Suffolke, *in his Robe of Estate, his Coronet on his*   2433
  him, the Duke of Norfolke, *with the Rod of Marshalship, | a Coronet on*
  his head. Collars of Esses.   2435
CORONETS = 1
  2 Their Coronets say so. These are Starres indeed, | And sometimes
  falling ones.   2469
CORRECT = 1
  (Not you) correct him. My heart weepes to see him | So little, of his
  great Selfe.   2234
CORRONATION = 2
  Going to Chappell: and the voyce is now | Onely about her
  Corronation.   2318
  The Lady *Anne*, passe from her Corronation.   2382
CORRUPT = 5
  Wee see each graine of grauell; I doe know | To be corrupt and
  treasonous.   229
  Not well dispos'd, the minde growing once corrupt,   455
  Heauen is aboue all yet; there sits a Iudge, | That no King can corrupt.   1731
  Might corrupt mindes procure, Knaues as corrupt   2933
CORRUPTION = 2
  Corruption wins not more then Honesty.   2359
  To keepe mine Honor, from Corruption,   2629

COST = 1
   The Peace betweene the French and vs, not valewes | The Cost that did
   conclude it.   142
COSTLY = 1
   To this last costly Treaty: Th'enteruiew,   240
COUENT = 1
   With all his Couent, honourably receiu'd him;   2573
COUETOUS = 1
   More couetous of Wisedome, and faire Vertue   3394
COULD *l.*53 271 459 761 854 905 1204 1303 1315 1504 1656 1791 2041
   2071 *2190 2475 2500 2569 2626 2741 2799 2843 3117 3277 = 23*1
COUNCEL = *1
   Cham. Heauen keep me from such councel: tis most true   1070
COUNCELL = 14*1
   The Honourable Boord of Councell, out | Must fetch him in, he Papers.   130
   That they had gather'd a wise Councell to them   1405
   Let me haue time and Councell for my Cause: 1705
   That any English man dare giue me Councell?   1712
   Is this your Christian Councell? Out vpon ye.   1730
   Either of King or Councell, when you went   2215
   And one already of the Priuy Councell.   2539
   Sir (I may tell it you) I thinke I haue | Incenst the Lords o'th'Councell,
   that he is   2821
   To morrow Morning to the Councell Boord   2830
   Haue mou'd Vs, and our Councell, that you shall   2897
   That was sent to me from the Councell, pray'd me   2990
   A Councell Table brought in with Chayres and Stooles, and   3035
   Why are we met in Councell?   3043
   Cranmer approches the Councell Table.   3055
   And wisedome of my Councell; but I finde none: 3206
COUNCELLOR = 1
   Wait else at doore: a fellow Councellor | 'Mong Boyes, Groomes, and
   Lackeyes.   3010
COUNCELLOUR = 1
   One *Gilbert Pecke*, his Councellour.   305
COUNCELLOURS = 1
   Their very noses had been Councellours   580
COUNCELS = 2
   Where you are liberall of your loues and Councels,   972
   Bestow your Councels on me. She now begges   1821
COUNSAILE = 2
   Be by my Friends in Spaine, aduis'd; whose Counsaile   1409
   The daringst Counsaile which I had to doubt,   1584
COUNSELL = 4
   Thither he darts it. Bosome vp my counsell,   172
   Offers, as I doe, in a signe of peace, | His Seruice, and his Counsell. |
   Queen. To betray me.   1691
   Camp. I would your Grace | Would leaue your greefes, and take my
   Counsell.   1720
   Holy and Heauenly thoughts still Counsell her: 3399
COUNSELLOR = 1
   Suff. Nay, my Lord, | That cannot be; you are a Counsellor,   3097
COUNSELLOUR = 1
   Power, as he was a Counsellour to try him,   3213
COUNSELS = 1
   He counsels a Diuorce, a losse of her   1063

COUNT = 1
I would not be a young Count in your way,   1251
COUNTENANCE = 2
Yea, subiect to your Countenance: Glad, or sorry,   1380
He did it with a Serious minde: a heede | Was in his countenance. You
he bad   1934
COUNTERFEIT = 1
Cham. This is the Kings Ring. | *Sur.* 'Tis no counterfeit.   3165
COUNTESSES = 1*1
  *10 *Certaine* Ladies *or* Countesses, *with plaine Circlets of| Gold, without
  Flowers.*   2443
  1 It is, and all the rest are Countesses.   2468
COUNTREY = 1
They are (as all my other comforts) far hence | In mine owne Countrey
Lords.   1718
COUNTRIES = 1
Let all the ends thou aym'st at, be thy Countries,   2362
COUNTRY = 1
An honest Country Lord as I am, beaten   625
COUNTY = 1
The Ayre will drinke the Sap. To euery County   434
COUNT-CARDINALL = *1
*As giue a Crutch to th'dead. But our Count-Cardinall   248
COURSE = 7
That he would please to alter the Kings course,   265
Will blesse the King: and is not this course pious?   1069
With many Children by you. If in the course   1391
And did entreate your Highnes to this course, | Which you are running
heere.   1585
Of what course Mettle ye are molded, Enuy,   2124
When he ha's run his course, and sleepes in Blessings,   2309
And the strong course of my Authority,   3083
COURSES = 2
So many courses of the Sun enthroaned,   1207
Follow your enuious courses, men of Malice;   2128
COURT = 13*6
That's clapt vpon the Court Gate.   593
That fill the Court with quarrels, talke, and Taylors.   596
And farre enough from Court too.   883
The Court of Rome commanding. You my Lord   1152
I haue beene begging sixteene yeares in Court   1302
each side the Court in manner of a Consistory: Below them   1348
Scri. Say, *Henry* K.(ing) of England, come into the Court.   1358
Scribe. Say, *Katherine* Queene of England, | Come into the Court.   1361
*goes about the Court, comes to the King, and kneeles at| his Feete.
Then speakes.*   1365
That longer you desire the Court, as well   1417
Crier. Katherine. Q.(ueene) of England, come into the Court.   1488
I left no Reuerend Person in this Court;   1590
That we adiourne this Court till further day;   1603
My comfort comes along: breake vp the Court;   1612
The Hopes of Court, my Hopes in Heauen do dwell. | *Exeunt.*   2375
Held a late Court at Dunstable; sixe miles off   2409
Which is to'th Court, and there ye shall be my Guests: 2543
*you take the Court for Parish Garden: ye rude Slaues, | leaue your
gaping.   3260
*great *Toole*, come to Court, the women so besiege vs?   3293

COURTESIE = 1
   *They loue and doate on: call him bounteous *Buckingham,* | The Mirror
   of all courtesie.   887
COURTIER = 2
   To thinke an English Courtier may be wise, | And neuer see the *Louure.*   599
   (Am yet a Courtier beggerly) nor could   1303
COURTS = 1
   Vpon this businesse my appearance make, | In any of their Courts.   1494
COW = 1
   And that I would not for a Cow, God saue her.   3285
CRAB-TREE = *1
   *Is this a place to roare in? Fetch me a dozen Crab-tree   3264
CRACKE = 1
   (Though all the world should cracke their duty to you,   2069
CRACKT = *1
   *And with what zeale? For now he has crackt the League   1057
CRADLE = 2
   Was fashion'd to much Honor. From his Cradle   2608
   Though in her Cradle; yet now promises   3388
CRAMMD = 1
   Is cramm'd with Arrogancie, Spleene, and Pride.   1470
CRAN = 17*4
CRANMER see also Cran. = 11*1
   My learn'd and welbeloued Seruant *Cranmer,*   1610
   Norf. But my Lord | When returnes *Cranmer?*   1908
   An Heretique, an Arch-one; *Cranmer,* one   1960
   What more? | *Crom.* That *Cranmer* is return'd with welcome;   2311
   2 He of Winchester | Is held no great good louer of the Archbishops, |
   The vertuous *Cranmer.*   2528
   Cranmer will finde a Friend will not shrinke from him.   2533
   Till *Cranmer, Cromwel,* her two hands, and shee | Sleepe in their
   Graues.   2808
   Enter Cranmer and Denny.   2876
   And do as I haue bid you. *Exit Cranmer.*   2959
   Enter Cranmer, Archbyshop of Canterbury.   2988
   Cranmer approches the Councell Table.   3055
   Garter, Cranmer, Duke of Norfolke with his Marshals   3355
CRANMERS = 1
   Nor. This same *Cranmer*'s | A worthy Fellow, and hath tane much
   paine | In the Kings businesse.   1918
CRAUE = 1
   Craue leaue to view these Ladies, and entreat   764
CRAWLD = 1
   Hath crawl'd into the fauour of the King, | And is his Oracle.   1961
CREATE = 1
   Her Ashes new create another Heyre,   3412
CREATURE = 5
   My Chaplaine to no Creature liuing, but   512
   (*Katherine* our Queene) before the primest Creature | That's Parragon'd
   o'th' World.   1599
   My King is tangled in affection, to | A Creature of the Queenes, Lady
   Anne Bullen.   1870
   She is a gallant Creature, and compleate   1890
   Shee's a good Creature, and sweet-Ladie do's | Deserue our better
   wishes.   2801
CREATURES = 1
   Follow such Creatures. That you may, faire Lady   1274

CREDIT = 1
Wol. This, and all else | This talking Lord can lay vpon my credit,   2153
CREDIT = 1
Being now seene, possible enough, got credit | That *Beuis* was beleeu'd.   81
CREEDE = 1
Suff. For me, my Lords, | I loue him not, nor feare him, there's my
Creede: 1084
CREPT = 2
Ha's crept too neere his Conscience.   1047
Suff. No, his Conscience | Ha's crept too neere another Ladie.   1048
CRIDE = 2
As he cride thus let be, to as much end,   247
Hitting a grosser quality, is cride vp   419
CRIE = 1
Now, if you can blush, and crie guiltie Cardinall, | You'l shew a little
Honestie.   2200
CRIER = 2*1
CROM = 21
CROMWEL = 9
O 'tis a burden *Cromwel*, 'tis a burden   2290
Vpon my smiles. Go get thee from me *Cromwel*,   2326
With what a sorrow *Cromwel* leaues his Lord.   2340
Card. *Cromwel*, I did not thinke to shed a teare   2343
Let's dry our eyes: And thus farre heare me *Cromwel*,   2346
Cromwel, I charge thee, fling away Ambition,   2355
I dare now call mine owne. O *Cromwel, Cromwel*,   2369
Till *Cranmer, Cromwel*, her two hands, and shee | Sleepe in their
Graues.   2808
CROMWELL see also Crom. = 11*1
Enter Wolsey and Cromwell.   1925
Car. The Packet Cromwell, | Gau't you the King?   1928
Card. Leaue me a while. *Exit Cromwell.*   1939
Enter Cromwell, standing amazed.   2274
Why how now *Cromwell?*   2275
Neuer so truly happy, my good *Cromwell*,   2283
O *Cromwell,* | The King ha's gone beyond me: All my Glories   2321
Thy hopefull seruice perish too. Good *Cromwell*   2333
*Thy Gods, and Truths. Then if thou fall'st (O *Cromwell*)   2363
2 Who may that be, I pray you. | 3 *Thomas Cromwell*,   2534
Louell. Now Sir, you speake of two | The most remark'd i'th'Kingdome:
as for *Cromwell*,   2810
Cromwell at lower end, as Secretary.   3041
CROOKED = 1
Enuy, and crooked malice, nourishment;   3092
CROSSE = 2*1
each a Siluer Crosse: Then a Gentleman Vsher bare-| headed,   1340
Fit for a Foole to fall by: What crosse Diuell   2094
Suf. Who dare crosse 'em,   2119
CROWD = 1
3 Among the crowd i'th'Abbey, where a finger   2474
CROWNE = 6*1
For high feats done to'th'Crowne; neither Allied   110
Kin. Speake on; | How grounded hee his Title to the Crowne   486
*No more to th' Crowne but that: Lo, who comes here?   1261
He said he did, and with his deed did Crowne   2027
his Coate of Armes, and on his head he wore a Gilt Copper | Crowne.   2427
As holy Oyle, *Edward* Confessors Crowne,   2509

CROWNE *cont.*
And yet no day without a deed to Crowne it.   3430
CROWNED = *2
*bearing the Rod of Siluer with the Doue, Crowned with an | Earles
Coronet. Collars of Esses.*   2431
Pearle, Crowned. On each side her, the Bishops of London, | and
Winchester,   2439
CRUELL = 3
2. I thinke | You haue hit the marke; but is't not cruell,   1019
Out of the gripes of cruell men, and giue it   3163
Thou hast a cruell Nature and a bloody.   3198
CRUELTY = 1
For what they haue beene: 'tis a cruelty, | To load a falling man.   3125
CRUTCH = *1
*As giue a Crutch to th'dead. But our Count-Cardinall   248
CRY = 7
Buc. Ile to the King, | And from a mouth of Honor, quite cry downe   208
For then, my guiltlesse blood must cry against 'em.   909
Shall cry for blessings on him. May he liue   934
Cham. Now God incense him, | And let him cry Ha, lowder.   1906
Lou. Me thinkes I could | Cry the Amen, and yet my Conscience sayes   2799
Gard. Good M.(aster) Secretary, | I cry your Honour mercie; you may
worst | Of all this Table say so.   3127
Abus'd extreamly, and to cry that's witty,   3455
CRYDE = 1
The King cry'de Ha, at this.   1905
CRYDE = 1
Was cry'de incompareable; and th'ensuing night   71
CRYED = *1
*and hit that Woman, who cryed out Clubbes, when I   3309
CRYING = 1*1
A noyse within crying roome for the Queene, vsher'd by the   329
To pray for her? What is she crying out?   2849
CUCKOLD = 1
He or shee, Cuckold or Cuckold-maker: 3283
CUCKOLD-MAKER = 1
He or shee, Cuckold or Cuckold-maker: 3283
CUDGELL = 1
As much as one sound Cudgell of foure foote,   3276
CUM = 1
They may *Cum Priuilegio*, wee away   612
CUNNING = *2
Buck. Pray giue me fauour Sir: This cunning Cardinall   244
*T'oppose your cunning. Y'are meek, & humble-mouth'd   1467
CURD = 2
A still, and quiet Conscience. The King ha's cur'd me,   2286
That gentle Physicke giuen in time, had cur'd me: 2710
CURE = 6
San. For my little Cure, | Let me alone.   708
Thou art a cure fit for a King; you'r welcome   1118
It lies to cure me, and the Cure is to   1460
We are to Cure such sorrowes, not to sowe 'em.   1795
I sent the King? Is there no way to cure this?   2096
CURRANT = 1
And haue an houre of hearing, and by'r Lady | Held currant Musicke
too.   627

CURRE = *1
*Buc. This Butchers Curre is venom'd-mouth'd, and I   188
CURRES = 1
Why they are so; but like to Village Curres,   1525
CURSE = 1
To me, aboue this wretchednesse? All your Studies | Make me a Curse,
like this.   1755
CURSES = 3
Allegeance in them; their curses now   395
I feare, too many curses on their heads | That were the Authors.   985
If the King please: his Curses and his blessings   1087
CURTAINE = 1*1
*Exit Lord Chamberlaine, and the King drawes the Curtaine | and sits
reading pensiuely.   1100
Let 'em alone, and draw the Curtaine close: 3033
CURTSIES = 1*1
And to be iudg'd by him. | She Curtsies to the King, and offers to
depart.   1481
*Curtsies. Then the two that held the Garland, deli-|uer   2649
CUSTOME = 1
By custome of the Coronation.   2398
CUSTOMES = 1
L.San. New customes, | Though they be neuer so ridiculous,   573
CUSTOMS = *1
*1 I thanke you Sir: Had I not known those customs,   2402
CUT = 1
L.Ch. Death my Lord, | Their cloathes are after such a Pagan cut too't,   586
CYTED = 1
She was often cyted by them, but appear'd not: 2411
DAGGER = 1
He stretch'd him, and with one hand on his dagger,   557
DAILY = 1
Showr'd on me daily, haue bene more then could   2041
DAINTY = 1
Kin. By Heauen she is a dainty one. Sweet heart,   800
DAM = 1
To th'old dam Treason) Charles the Emperour,   252
DAMAGE = 1
It can do me no damage; adding further,   531
DANCE = 2*2
Till now I neuer knew thee. | Musicke, Dance.   772
*Dance: and at certaine Changes, the first two hold a spare   2647
To dance attendance on their Lordships pleasures,   3030
*'em in Limbo Patrum, and there they are like to dance   3322
DANCING = 1*1
Card. Your Grace | I feare, with dancing is a little heated.   807
*their Dancing vanish, carrying the Garland with them. | The Musicke
continues.   2656
DANGER = 4
Daring th'euent too th'teeth, are all in vprore, | And danger serues
among them.   364
To the Kings danger: presently, the Duke   503
I weigh'd the danger which my Realmes stood in   1564
You take a Precepit for no leape of danger,   2940
DANGEROUS = 3*1
This dangerous conception in this point,   480
*The Monke might be deceiu'd, and that 'twas dangerous   527

DANGEROUS *cont.*
  Diuers and dangerous; which are Heresies;   3066
  When we first put this dangerous stone a rowling,   3168
DANGERS = 1
  Dangers, doubts, wringing of the Conscience,   1060
DARE = 20
  More then I dare make faults.   912
  You few that lou'd me, | And dare be bold to weepe for *Buckingham*,   913
  And euery true heart weepes for't. All that dare   1072
  Kin. Who's there I say? How dare you thrust your | (selues   1105
  That any English man dare giue me Councell?   1712
  A Woman (I dare say without Vainglory) | Neuer yet branded with
  Suspition?   1760
  Qu. My Lord, | I dare not make my selfe so guiltie,   1773
  Suf. Who dare crosse 'em,   2119
  I dare, and must deny it. Now I feele   2123
  Dare mate a sounder man then Surrie can be, | And all that loue his
  follies.   2163
  And dare vs with his Cap, like Larkes.   2173
  Wol. Speake on Sir, | I dare your worst Obiections: If I blush,   2202
  Then my Weake-hearted Enemies, dare offer.   2298
  I dare now call mine owne. O *Cromwel, Cromwel,*   2369
  Of which there is not one, I dare auow   2734
  Is the Kings hand, and tongue, and who dare speak | One syllable
  against him?   2816
  Gard. Yes, yes, Sir *Thomas,* | There are that Dare, and I my selfe haue
  ventur'd   2818
  Dare bite the best. I doe beseech your, Lordships,   3093
  And by that vertue no man dare accuse you.   3099
  You shall know many dare accuse you boldly,   3105
DARES = 1
  Hee, that dares most, but wag his finger at thee.   3200
DARING = 2
  Daring th'euent too th'teeth, are all in vprore, | And danger serues
  among them.   364
  Vpon the daring Huntsman that has gall'd him: 2087
DARINGST = 1
  The daringst Counsaile which I had to doubt,   1584
DARKNES = *1
  *(When Heauen shal call her from this clowd of darknes)   3415
DARKNING = 1
  By Darkning my cleere Sunne. My Lords farewell. *Exe.*   315
DARTS = 1
  Thither he darts it. Bosome vp my counsell,   172
DASHING = 1
  Dashing the Garment of this Peace, aboaded | The sodaine breach on't.   148
DAUGHTER = 7
  Sir *Thomas Bullens* Daughter, the Viscount *Rochford,*   798
  The daughter of a King, my drops of teares,   1429
  Our Daughter *Mary:* I'th' Progresse of this busines,   1542
  Whether our Daughter were legitimate,   1546
  A Knights Daughter | To be her Mistris Mistris? The Queenes, Queene?   1952
  The Modell of our chaste loues: his yong daughter,   2723
  A Queene, and Daughter to a King enterre me.   2765
DAY = 22*2
  A Man may weepe vpon his Wedding day.   33
  To one aboue it selfe. Each following day   60

DAY *cont.*

Made former Wonders, it's. To day the French,	62
Sur. First, it was vsuall with him; euery day	472
Let him not seek't of vs: By day and night	567
I haue this day receiu'd a Traitors iudgement,	899
*And with that bloud will make 'em one day groane for't.	952
Cham. Good day to both your Graces.	1041
*Turnes what he list. The King will know him one day.	1053
The French Kings Sister. Heauen will one day open	1074
That we adiourne this Court till further day;	1603
This is the state of Man; to day he puts forth	2253
The third day, comes a Frost; a killing Frost,	2256
This day was view'd in open, as his Queene,	2317
In Celebration of this day with Shewes, | Pageants, and Sights of Honor.	2390
1 Yes, 'tis the List | Of those that claime their Offices this day,	2396
Bin loose, this day they had beene lost. Such ioy	2495
In them a wilder Nature, then the businesse | That seekes dispatch by day.	2788
To speake my minde of him: and indeed this day,	2820
Butts. I thinke your Highnesse saw this many a day.	3018
On May-day Morning, which will neuer be:	3272
And yet no day without a deed to Crowne it.	3430
She will be sicke els. This day, no man thinke	3446
This Little-One shall make it Holy-day. *Exeunt.*	3448

DAYES = 5*1

Became the next dayes master, till the last	61
2. I am confident; | You shall Sir: Did you not of late dayes heare	997
Of the whole State; as of late dayes our neighbours,	3077
*these three dayes; besides the running Banquet of two | Beadles, that is to come.	3323
In her dayes, Euery Man shall eate in safety,	3404
An aged Princesse; many dayes shall see her,	3429

DAYLY = 2

In doing dayly wrongs. I could say more,	3117
In dayly thankes; that gaue vs such a Prince;	3184

DE *l.*304 508 2219 = 3

DEAD = 3*1

*As giue a Crutch to th'dead. But our Count-Cardinall	248
The Graue does to th' dead: For her Male Issue,	1558
That the great Childe of Honor, Cardinall *Wolsey* | Was dead?	2557
Call in more women. When I am dead, good Wench,	2760

DEALES = 1

Deales with our Cardinal, and as I troa	260

DEALING = 1

Out with it boldly: Truth loues open dealing.	1663

DEARE = 3*1

So deare in heart, not to deny her that	1158
That holy duty out of deare respect,	3188
Cran. And let Heauen | Witnesse how deare, I hold this Confirmation.	3246
*their deare Brothers are able to endure. I haue some of	3321

DEATH = 10

L.Ch. Death my Lord, | Their cloathes are after such a Pagan cut too't,	586
2. I doe not thinke he feares death. | 1. Sure he does not,	866
The Law I beare no mallice for my death,	903
Your Master wed me to: nothing but death | Shall e're diuorce my Dignities.	1776

DEATH *cont.*

After his Patients death; the King already | Hath married the faire
Lady. | *Sur.* Would he had. 1878
Which euer ha's, and euer shall be growing, | Till death (that Winter)
kill it. 2052
Grif. How do's your Grace? | *Kath.* O *Griffith*, sicke to death: 2551
Kath. After my death, I wish no other Herald, 2627
Out of this world. Tell him in death I blest him 2756
Almost each pang, a death. | *King.* Alas good Lady. 2851

DEBATE = 1
Of euery Realme, that did debate this Businesse, 1406

DEBATING = 1
Who had beene hither sent on the debating 1540

DECEIUD = *1
*The Monke might be deceiu'd, and that 'twas dangerous 527

DECENT = 1
For honestie, and decent Carriage | A right good Husband (let him be a
Noble) 2737

DECEYUD = 1
Will be deceyu'd. For gentle Hearers, know 18

DECLARE = 1
That it shall please you to declare in hearing 1510

DECLINE = 1
A great man should decline. Nay, and you weep | I am falne indeed. 2279

DEDICATES = 1
Salutes ye all; This Night he dedicates 668

DEED = 3
That I gainsay my Deed, how may he wound, 1455
He said he did, and with his deed did Crowne 2027
And yet no day without a deed to Crowne it. 3430

DEEDE = 1
And 'tis a kinde of good deede to say well, 2025

DEEDS = 1
And yet words are no deeds. My Father lou'd you, 2026

DEEMD = *1
*Who deem'd our Marriage lawful. Wherefore I humbly 1407

DEEME = 1
I deeme you an ill Husband, and am glad 2011

DEEPE = 3
2. That tricke of State | Was a deepe enuious one, 877
Wish him ten faddom deepe: This Duke as much 886
So deepe suspition, where all faith was meant; 1677

DEERE = 1
She should haue bought her Dignities so deere. *Exeunt* 1823

DEERELY = 2
To loue her for her Mothers sake, that lou'd him, | Heauen knowes how
deerely. 2728
The vpper *Germany* can deerely witnesse: 3078

DEEREST = 1
By that you loue the deerest in this world, 2747

DEFACERS = 1
Defacers of a publique peace then I doe: 3089

DEFEAT = 1
Many sharpe reasons to defeat the Law. 841

DEFIDE = *1
*length they came to th' broome staffe to me, I defide 'em 3313

DELAY = 2
    Without delay; and the pretence for this   392
    And that (without delay) their Arguments | Be now produc'd, and
    heard.   1423
DELIGHTS = 1
    Not for delights: Times to repayre our Nature   2774
DELIUER = 7*2
    Queen. My learn'd Lord *Cardinall*, | Deliuer all with Charity.   484
    Kin. Deliuer this with modesty to th' Queene. | *Exit Gardiner.*   1191
    In our long absence: pray doe not deliuer,   1329
    Betweene the King and you, and to deliuer   1683
    Curtsies. Then the two that held the Garland, deli-|uer   2649
    head. Which done, they deliuer the same Garland to the   2652
    Kath. Sir, I most humbly pray you to deliuer   2719
    Lou. I could not personally deliuer to her   2843
    Deliuer them, and your Appeale to vs   2954
DELIUERANCE = 1
    Norf. We had need pray, | And heartily, for our deliuerance;   1078
DELIUERD = 1*1
    King. Now by thy lookes | I gesse thy Message. Is the Queene deliuer'd?   2967
    *deliuer'd such a showre of Pibbles, that I was faine to   3315
DEMAND = 2
    Saint *Laurence Poultney*, did of me demand   499
    An. My good Lord, | Not your demand; it values not your asking: 1266
DEMURE = 1
    To me, should vtter, with demure Confidence,   513
DEMY = *1
    a Demy Coronall of Gold. With him, the Earle of Surrey,   2430
DEN = 2*1
DENNY see also Den. = 4
    Enter Sir Anthony Denny.   2866
    King. 'Tis true: where is he *Denny*?   2871
    Enter Cranmer and Denny.   2876
    Ha? I haue said. Be gone. | What? *Exeunt Louell and Denny.*   2878
DENY = 4
    So deare in heart, not to deny her that   1158
    That I haue blowne this Coale: I do deny it,   1453
    I dare, and must deny it. Now I feele   2123
    I haue a Suite which you must not deny mee.   3232
DENYDE = 1
    Free pardon to each man that has deny'de   436
DEPART = 1
    And to be iudg'd by him. | *She Curtsies to the King, and offers to*
    depart.   1481
DEPARTED = 1
    As you wish Christian peace to soules departed,   2748
DEPTH = 1
    But farre beyond my depth: my high-blowne Pride   2262
DEPTHS = 1
    And sounded all the Depths, and Shoales of Honor,   2351
DEPUTIE = 1
    You sent me Deputie for Ireland,   2148
DEPUTY = 1
    Then Deputy of Ireland, who remou'd | Earle *Surrey*, was sent thither,
    and in hast too,   874
DERIUD = 1
    That had to him deriu'd your Anger, did I   1386

DESERTS = 1
Found his deserts. How innocent I was   2156
DESERUE = 8*1
The Subiect will deserue it. Such as giue   8
Cam. Your Grace must needs deserue all strangers loues,   1149
2 He will deserue more. | 3 Yes without all doubt.   2540
Deserue we no more Reuerence? | *Grif.* You are too blame,   2683
I hope she will deserue well; and a little   2727
(And now I should not lye) but will deserue   2735
Shee's a good Creature, and sweet-Ladie do's | Deserue our better
wishes.   2801
This good man (few of you deserue that Title)   3208
In such an honour: how may I deserue it,   3236
DESERUES = 2
Deserues a Corner: would all other Women   1655
What he deserues of you and me, I know: 1843
DESERUING = 1
And well deseruing? yet I know her for   1956
DESIGNE = 1
It forg'd him some designe, which being beleeu'd   529
DESIR'D = 4
And pau'd with gold: the Emperor thus desir'd,   264
Of diuers witnesses, which the Duke desir'd   844
Haue wish'd the sleeping of this busines, neuer desir'd   1529
In the great'st humblenesse, and desir'd your Highnesse | Most heartily
to pray for her.   2846
DESIRE = 5
Sir, I desire you do me Right and Iustice,   1367
I euer contradicted your Desire?   1382
That longer you desire the Court, as well   1417
You do desire to know wherefore | I sent for you.   2883
That when I am in Heauen, I shall desire   3439
DESIRES = 2
Haue euer come too short of my Desires,   2044
Promises Boyes heereafter. Sir, your Queen | Desires your Visitation,
and to be   2973
DESPAIRES = 1
Feares, and despaires, and all these for his Marriage.   1061
DESPERATE = 2
And lack of other meanes, in desperate manner   363
(Though he be growne so desperate to be honest)   1714
DESPIS'D = 1
Of our despis'd Nobilitie, our Issues,   2184
DESPISE = *1
Car. How much me thinkes, I could despise this man,   2190
DESTRUCTION = 1
And woe your owne destruction.   2941
DETERMINATE = 1
Ere a determinate resolution, hee | (I meane the Bishop) did require a
respite,   1543
DETERMINES = 1
Is pleas'd you shall to th'Tower, till you know | How he determines
further.   297
DETESTS = 1
A man that more detests, more stirres against,   3087
DEUICE = 2
The net has falne vpon me, I shall perish | Vnder deuice, and practise.   285

DEUICE *cont.*
No new deuice to beate this from his Braines? 2097
DEUILL *see* diuell
DEUILS *see* diuels
DEUISD = 1
They are deuis'd by you, or else you suffer | Too hard an exclamation. 382
DEUM = 1
Together sung *Te Deum.* So she parted, 2513
DEUOUTLY = 1
Cast her faire eyes to Heauen, and pray'd deuoutly. 2505
DEW = 2
(Which Gods dew quench) therefore, I say againe, 1438
The dew o'th'Verdict with it; at what ease 2932
DEWES = 2
His dewes fall euery where. 644
The dewes of Heauen fall thicke in Blessings on her, 2724
DID *l.*68 74 79 90 91 138 143 242 243 250 396 499 559 859 998 1386 1406
1514 1544 1552 1567 1571 1575 1581 1585 1623 1839 1867 1869 1933
1934 1995 2027 2070 2343 2478 2618 2779 2839 3211 3279 *3303
3437 = 43*1
DIDE *see also* dy'de = 2
That he ran mad, and dide. 1183
Or di'de where they were made, or shortly after 1559
DIDST = 1
Did'st thou not tell me *Griffith*, as thou lead'st mee, 2556
DIE *see* dye
DIES *see* dyes
DIFFERENCE = 3
Nor. Like it your Grace, | The State takes notice of the priuate
difference 160
There's difference in no persons. 211
How you stand minded in the waighty difference 1682
DIGEST = 1
Sur. But will the King | Digest this Letter of the Cardinals? 1894
DIGESTION = 1
A good digestion to you all; and once more 751
DIGNITIES = 4
Your Master wed me to: nothing but death | Shall e're diuorce my
Dignities. 1776
She should haue bought her Dignities so deere. *Exeunt* 1823
You haue for Dignities, to the meere vndooing 2227
A peace aboue all earthly Dignities, 2285
DIGNITY = 2
The dignity of your Office; is the poynt | Of my Petition. 342
And Kingly Dignity, we are contented 1597
DILATORY = 1
This dilatory sloth, and trickes of Rome. 1609
DIMME = 1
(For so I will) mine eyes grow dimme. Farewell 2757
DIRECT = 1
More stronger to direct you then your selfe; 220
DIRECTLY = 1*1
For when they hold 'em, you would sweare directly 579
passe directly before the Cardinall and gracefully sa-| lute him. 755
DISCERNER = 1
'Twas said they saw but one, and no Discerner 76

DISCHARGD = 2
Drum and Trumpet, Chambers dischargd. 731
He was from thence discharg'd? Sir, call to minde, 1388
DISCHARGE = 1
He did discharge a horrible Oath, whose tenor 559
DISCHARGED = *1
*was his Nose discharged against mee; hee stands there 3304
DISCIPLES = 1
And his Disciples onely enuy at, 3179
DISCONTENTED = 1
Nor. He's discontented. 1946
DISCOUERS = 1
That's the plaine truth; your painted glosse discouers 3120
DISCOURSER = 1
Would by a good Discourser loose some life, 86
DISCRETION = 2
Nor. All this was ordred by the good Discretion 98
Was it discretion Lords, to let this man, 3207
DISDAINE = 1
*Cardinall in his passage, fixeth his eye on Buck-|ingham, and
Buckingham on him, | both full of disdaine.* 177
DISDAINFULL = 1
Disdainfull to be tride by't; tis not well. 1485
DISEASE = 1
Aske God for Temp'rance, that's th'appliance onely | Which your
disease requires. 193
DISEASES = 1
L.San. Tis time to giue 'em Physicke, their diseases | Are growne so
catching. 614
DISGRACD = 1
You'l part away disgrac'd. 1727
DISGRACE = 1
Pray heauen he found not my disgrace: for certaine 3006
DISGRACES = 2
But that you shall sustaine moe new disgraces, | With these you beare
alreadie. 1831
How eagerly ye follow my Disgraces 2125
DISHONOUR = 1
Pronounce dishonour of her; by my life, 1205
DISLIKE = 2
Euer in feare to kindle your Dislike, 1379
For no dislike i'th' world against the person 1593
DISPATCH = 1
In them a wilder Nature, then the businesse | That seekes dispatch by
day. 2788
DISPERSE = 2
To stop the rumor; and allay those tongues | That durst disperse it. 1004
Sing, and disperse 'em if thou canst: leaue working. 1619
DISPLAYD = 1
Haue stood to Charity, and displayd th'effects 1445
DISPLEASURE = 4
Queen. I am sorry, that the Duke of *Buckingham* | Is run in your
displeasure. 447
Hath my behauiour giuen to your displeasure, 1374
(Not to come off) in his displeasure. | *Sur.* Sir, 1853
Is your displeasure with the King. | *Card.* God blesse him. 2301

DISPOSD = 1
  Not well dispos'd, the minde growing once corrupt,   455
DISPOSING = 1
  Buc. All was Royall, | To the disposing of it nought rebell'd,   88
DISPOSITION = 1
  Of disposition gentle, and of wisedome,   1446
DISTANCE = 1 *2
  *distance, followes a Gentleman bearing the Purse, with the   1338
  *vnder him as Iudges. The Queene takes place some di-| stance   1346
  A distance from her; while her Grace sate downe   2485
DISTINCTLY = 1
  Distinctly his full Function: who did guide,   91
DISTRACTION = 1
  Car. Madam, this is a meere distraction,   1744
DISTREST = 1
  Being distrest; was by that wretch betraid,   956
DISTRIBUTE = 1
  (You see the poore remainder) could distribute,   3277
DISTURBE = 1
  You'l finde a most vnfit time to disturbe him: 1097
DIUELL = 8
  Buc. The diuell speed him: No mans Pye is freed   100
  If not from Hell? The Diuell is a Niggard,   120
  Buc. Why the Diuell, | Vpon this French going out, tooke he vpon him   123
  L.San. The Diuell fiddle 'em, | I am glad they are going,   622
  Confessor to him, with that Diuell Monke, | *Hopkins,* that made this
  mischiefe.   848
  Fit for a Foole to fall by: What crosse Diuell   2094
  Against this man, whose honesty the Diuell   3178
  Diuell was amongst 'em I thinke surely.   3317
DIUELS = 1
  I told my Lord the Duke, by th'Diuels illusions   526
DIUERS = 3
  and diuers other Ladies, & Gentlemen, as Guests   663
  Of diuers witnesses, which the Duke desir'd   844
  Diuers and dangerous; which are Heresies;   3066
DIUES = 1
  He diues into the Kings Soule, and there scatters   1059
DIUORCD = 1
  Of all these Learned men, she was diuorc'd,   2414
DIUORCE = 7
  And as the long diuorce of Steele fals on me,   918
  He counsels a Diuorce, a losse of her   1063
  Yet if that quarrell. Fortune, do diuorce   1217
  Your Master wed me to: nothing but death | Shall e're diuorce my
  Dignities.   1776
  In the Diuorce, his contrarie proceedings | Are all vnfolded: wherein he
  appeares,   1858
  To stay the Iudgement o'th'Diuorce; for if   1868
  Haue satisfied the King for his Diuorce,   1911
DO *l.*102 132 214 531 1217 1367 1422 1433 1443 *1447 1453 1462 1478
  1796 1813 1818 1844 1869 1904 2066 2121 2259 2307 2375 2674 2687
  2714 2750 2787 2883 2895 2948 2959 *3267 3286 = 33*2
DOATE = *1
  **They loue and doate on: call him bounteous *Buckingham,* | The Mirror
  of all courtesie.   887

DOCTOR = 1*1
  *Camp. My Lord of Yorke, was not one Doctor Pace   1172
  Enter Doctor Buts.   2998
DOCTORS = 1*1
  *Scribes in the habite of Doctors; after them, the Bishop of   1335
  And Doctors learn'd. First I began in priuate,   1573
DOCTRINE = 1
  Sparing would shew a worse sinne, then ill Doctrine,   649
DOE l.229 261 274 414 416 530 702 761 790 866 922 992 996 1054 1130
1255 1282 1329 1331 1522 1526 1557 1642 1656 1691 3025 3085 3089
3093 3116 3131 3138 3170 3245 *3250 *3259 3289 3290 3335 3343
3461 = 39*2
DOES l.268 867 1162 1278 1558 1948 1971 2016 2057 2281 2712 2825 3204
3440 = 14
DOGDAYES = *1
  *by his face, for o' my conscience twenty of the Dog-|dayes   3300
DOING = 5
  The Chronicles of my doing: Let me say,   409
  Norf. Tis so;| This is the Cardinals doing: The King-Cardinall,   1050
  She neuer knew harme-doing: Oh, now after   1206
  (As I will lend you cause) my doing well,| With my well saying.   2022
  In doing dayly wrongs. I could say more,   3117
DOMESTICKES = 1
  (Domestickes to you) serue your will, as't please   1474
DOMINIONS = 1
  Borne out of your Dominions: hauing heere   1370
DONE l.39 110 249 294 300 424 426 767 826 904 982 1457 1654 1769 2238
*2652 2934 3052 3142 3336 3456 = 20*1
DOORE = 5*1
  Enter the Duke of Norfolke at one doore. At the other,   35
  at one Doore; at an other Doore enter| Sir Henry Guilford.   664
  Shut doore vpon me, and so giue me vp   1397
  Wait else at doore: a fellow Councellor| 'Mong Boyes, Groomes, and
  Lackeyes.   3010
  *a fellow somewhat neere the doore, he should be a Brasi-|er   3299
DOORES = 1
  Enter two Gentlemen at seuerall Doores.   820
DORE = 5*1
  Who holds his State at dore 'mongst Purseuants,| Pages, and
  Foot-boyes.   3022
  And at the dore too, like a Post with Packets: 3031
  At Chamber dore? and one, as great as you are?   3210
  Vnlesse wee sweepe 'em from the dore with Cannons,   3270
  Keepe the dore close Sirha.   3288
  *Bless me, what a fry of Fornication is at dore? On my   3294
DORSET = 1*3
  *6 Marquesse Dorset, bearing a Scepter of Gold, on his head,   2429
  Who's that that beares the Scepter?| 1 Marquesse Dorset,   2448
  *Duchesse of Norfolke, and Lady Marquesse Dorset? will| these please
  you?   3240
  *the Marchionesse Dorset, the other Godmother, and La-|dies.   3361
DOS l.562 2551 2801 = 3
DOTH l.358 2073 = 2
DOUBLE = 1
  He would say vntruths, and be euer double   2593
DOUBLED = 1
  Shall still be doubled on her. Truth shall Nurse her,   3398

DOUBLETS = 1
(Doublets, I thinke) flew vp, and had their Faces   2494
DOUBT = 8*1
   L.Cham. No doubt hee's Noble;   645
   1. At his returne, | No doubt he will requite it; this is noted   879
   What may it be? you doe not doubt my faith Sir?   992
   The daringst Counsaile which I had to doubt,   1584
   You haue Christian warrant for 'em, and no doubt   2129
   *The King shall know it, and (no doubt) shal thanke you.   2248
   2 He will deserue more. | 3 Yes without all doubt.   2540
   I make as little doubt as you doe conscience,   3116
   Great store of roome no doubt, left for the Ladies,   3332
DOUBTED = 1
   Said, 'twas the feare indeed, and that he doubted   504
DOUBTS = 1*1
   Dangers, doubts, wringing of the Conscience,   1060
   *Such doubts as false Coine from it. The King loues you,   1809
DOUE = *1
   *bearing the Rod of Siluer with the Doue, Crowned with an| Earles
   Coronet. Collars of Esses.*   2431
DOWAGER = 4
   Respecting this our Marriage with the Dowager,   1547
   Her Coronation. *Katherine* no more | Shall be call'd Queene, but
   Princesse Dowager,   1915
   The Princesse Dowager? How goes her businesse?   2405
   Enter Katherine Dowager, sicke, lead betweene Griffith,   2548
DOWN = 1
   Grif. She is asleep: Good wench, let's sit down quiet,   2640
DOWNE = 9*1
   Shone downe the English; and to morrow, they   64
   Buc. Ile to the King, | And from a mouth of Honor, quite cry downe   208
   Sent downe among 'em, which hath flaw'd the heart   348
   Haue got a speeding tricke to lay downe Ladies.   620
   San. As easie as a downe bed would affoord it.   689
   Card. There was the waight that pull'd me downe.   2320
   A distance from her; while her Grace sate downe   2485
   Good man sit downe: Now let me see the proudest   3199
   To mow 'em downe before me: but if I spar'd any   3281
   *But knock 'em downe by th' dozens? Is this More fields   3291
DOZEN = *2
   *Good my Lord Cardinall: I haue halfe a dozen healths,   814
   *Is this a place to roare in? Fetch me a dozen Crab-tree   3264
DOZENS = *1
   *But knock 'em downe by th' dozens? Is this More fields   3291
DRAW = 3*2
   Such Noble Scoenes, as draw the Eye to flow   5
   (But pouerty could neuer draw 'em from me)   2741
   Let 'em alone, and draw the Curtaine close: 3033
   *might see from farre, some forty Truncheoners draw to   3310
   *draw mine Honour in, and let 'em win the Worke, the   3316
DRAWES = *1
   *Exit Lord Chamberlaine, and the King drawes the Curtaine| and sits
   reading pensiuely.*   1100
DRAWING = 1
   Out of his Selfe-drawing Web. O giues vs note,   112
DRAWNE = 2
   Of all that world of Wealth I haue drawne together   2091

DRAWNE *cont.*
　How long her face is drawne? How pale she lookes,　　　2676
DREAD = 4
　And consequence of dread, that I committed　　　1583
　Cran. Most dread Liege, | The good I stand on, is my Truth and
　Honestie:　　　2921
　Gard. Dread Soueraigne, | How much are we bound to Heauen,　　　3182
　Chan. Thus farre | My most dread Soueraigne, may it like your Grace,　　3218
DREAMD = 2
　We are a Queene (or long haue dream'd so) certaine　　　1428
　One that ne're dream'd a Ioy, beyond his pleasure;　　　1768
DREAME = 1
　To lead 'em once againe, and then let's dreame　　　816
DREAMES = 1
　Grif. I am most ioyfull Madam, such good dreames | Possesse your
　Fancy.　　　2670
DREW = 1
　The Articles o'th' Combination drew　　　245
DRINKE = 2
　The Ayre will drinke the Sap. To euery County　　　434
　To drinke to these faire Ladies, and a measure　　　815
DRIUES = 1
　Of my alleadged reasons, driues this forward:　　　1595
DROP = 1
　An. So much the more | Must pitty drop vpon her; verily　　　1222
DROPD = 1
　My heart drop'd Loue, my powre rain'd Honor, more　　　2060
DROPS = 1
　The daughter of a King, my drops of teares,　　　1429
DRUM = 1
　Drum and Trumpet, Chambers dischargd.　　　731
DRY = 1
　Let's dry our eyes: And thus farre heare me *Cromwel*,　　　2346
DUCHESSE = *1
　*Duchesse of *Norfolke*, and Lady Marquesse *Dorset*? will | these please
　you?　　　3240
DUELY = 1
　Are not words duely hallowed; nor my Wishes　　　1285
DUKE = 34*6
　Enter the Duke of Norfolke at one doore. At the other,　　　35
　the Duke of Buckingham, and the Lord | Aburgauenny.　　　36
　Car. The Duke of *Buckinghams* Surueyor? Ha?　　　180
　Sergeant. Sir, | My Lord the Duke of *Buckingham*, and Earle　　　279
　Abur. As the Duke said,　　　299
　Duke of Norfolke. Enter the Queene, Norfolke and　　　330
　Queen. I am sorry, that the Duke of *Buckingham* | Is run in your
　displeasure.　　　447
　Most like a carefull Subiect haue collected | Out of the Duke of
　Buckingham.　　　469
　The Duke being at the Rose, within the Parish　　　498
　To the Kings danger: presently, the Duke　　　503
　(Tell you the Duke) shall prosper, bid him striue　　　515
　To the loue o'th'Commonalty, the Duke | Shall gouerne England.　　　516
　I told my Lord the Duke, by th'Diuels illusions　　　526
　Sur. Being at *Greenwich*, | After your Highnesse had reprou'd the
　Duke | About Sir *William Bulmer.*　　　539
　The Duke retein'd him his. But on: what hence?　　　543

HENRY 8

DUKE *cont.*
Sur. After the Duke his Father, with the knife 556
Eu'n to the Hall, to heare what shall become | Of the great Duke of
Buckingham. 823
1. Ile tell you in a little. The great Duke 838
Of diuers witnesses, which the Duke desir'd 844
Wish him ten faddom deepe: This Duke as much 886
Vaux. Prepare there, | The Duke is comming: See the Barge be ready; 942
And Duke of *Buckingham*: now, poore *Edward Bohun*; 949
I haue done; and God forgiue me. | *Exeunt Duke and Traine.* 982
2. If the Duke be guiltlesse, 987
And Marriage 'twixt the Duke of *Orleance,* and 1541
Enter the Duke of Norfolke, Duke of Suffolke, Lord Surrey, | *and Lord*
Chamberlaine. 1825
Remembrance of my Father-in-Law, the Duke, | To be reueng'd on
him. 1835
I answer, is most false. The Duke by Law 2155
The Duke of Buckingham came from his Triall. 2384
The Duke of Suffolke is the first, and claimes 2399
To be high Steward; Next the Duke of Norfolke, 2400
7 Duke of Suffolke, in his Robe of Estate, his Coronet on his 2433
**him, the Duke of* Norfolke, *with the Rod of Marshalship,* | *a Coronet on*
his head. Collars of Esses. 2435
2 A bold braue Gentleman. That should bee | The Duke of Suffolke. 2451
Gar. I did Sir *Thomas,* and left him at Primero | With the Duke of
Suffolke. 2779
**Duke of Suffolke, Duke of Norfolke, Surrey, Lord Cham-* | *berlaine,* 3039
**Garter, Cranmer, Duke of Norfolke with his Marshals* 3355
**Staffe, Duke of Suffolke, two Noblemen, bearing great* 3356
DUKES = 4
Of the Dukes Confessor, *Iohn de la Car,* 304
Queen. If I know you well, | You were the Dukes Surueyor, and lost
your Office 518
Enter to the Lord Chamberlaine, the Dukes of Nor- | *folke and Suffolke.* 1038
Enter to Woolsey, the Dukes of Norfolke and Suffolke, the | *Earle of*
Surrey, and the Lord Chamberlaine. 2108
DULL = 1
And sleepe in dull cold Marble, where no mention 2348
DULY = 1
That they may haue their wages, duly paid 'em, 2742
DUNSTABLE = 1
Held a late Court at Dunstable; sixe miles off 2409
DURING = 1
During my life; and to confirme his Goodnesse, 2134
DURST = 4
Durst wagge his Tongue in censure, when these Sunnes 77
To stop the rumor; and allay those tongues | That durst disperse it. 1004
Within these fortie houres, Surrey durst better | Haue burnt that
Tongue, then saide so. 2140
And durst commend a secret to your eare 2791
DUTCHES = 1
It shall be to the Dutches of Alanson, 1940
DUTCHESSE = 3*2
What thinke you of a Dutchesse? Haue you limbs | To beare that load
of Title? 1247
I know your backe will beare a Dutchesse. Say, 1321
9 The Olde Dutchesse of Norfolke, *in a Coronall of Gold,* 2441

76

DUTCHESSE *cont.*

Is that old Noble Lady, Dutchesse of Norfolke.	2467
Noblemen bearing a Canopy, vnder which the Dutchesse of	3358

DUTIE = 2

My bond to Wedlocke, or my Loue and Dutie	1394
Cran. It is my dutie | T'attend your Highnesse pleasure.	2885

DUTIES = 1

Tongues spit their duties out, and cold hearts freeze	394

DUTY = 7

(As he made semblance of his duty) would | Haue put his knife into him.	549
(If I but knew him) with my loue and duty	779
Malice ne're meant: Our breach of Duty this way,	1109
Should, notwithstanding that your bond of duty,	2063
(Though all the world should cracke their duty to you,	2069
Appeare in formes more horrid) yet my Duty,	2072
That holy duty out of deare respect,	3188

DWARFISH = 1

Shew'd like a Mine. Their Dwarfish Pages were	66

DWELL = 3

Dwell in his Musings, but I am affraid	1998
The Hopes of Court, my Hopes in Heauen do dwell. | *Exeunt.*	2375
When I shall dwell with Wormes, and my poore name	2715

DYDE = 2

Kath. Pre'thee good *Griffith*, tell me how he dy'de.	2561
Then man could giue him; he dy'de, fearing God.	2626

DYE = 5

Buck. It will helpe me nothing | To plead mine Innocence; for that dye is on me	291
Should without issue dye; hee'l carry it so	474
And by that name must dye; yet Heauen beare witnes,	900
Killing care, & griefe of heart, | *Fall asleepe, or hearing dye.*	1631
Would I had knowne no more: But she must dye,	3431

DYES = 1

The Bird of Wonder dyes, the Mayden Phoenix,	3411

DYING = 2

Is only bitter to him, only dying:	916
This from a dying man receiue as certaine:	971

EACH = 9*6

To one aboue it selfe. Each following day	60
Order gaue each thing view. The Office did	90
Peepe through each part of him: whence ha's he that,	119
Wee see each graine of grauell; I doe know | To be corrupt and treasonous.	229
*Comes through Commissions, which compels from each	390
To each incensed Will: I would your Highnesse	398
And sticke them in our Will. Sixt part of each?	430
Free pardon to each man that has deny'de	436
him, the Axe with the edge towards him, Halberds on each	890
each a Siluer Crosse: Then a Gentleman Vsher bare-|headed,	1340
each side the Court in manner of a Consistory: Below them	1348
Pearle, Crowned. On each side her, the Bishops of London, | *and* Winchester,	2439
2 What two Reuerend Byshops | Were those that went on each side of the Queene?	2523
Almost each pang, a death. | *King.* Alas good Lady.	2851
Gardiner, seat themselues in Order on each side.	3040

EAGERLY = 2
How eagerly ye follow my Disgraces 2125
So went to bed; where eagerly his sicknesse 2578
EARE = 3
Out of the paine you suffer'd, gaue no eare too't. 2560
And durst commend a secret to your eare 2791
Giuen eare to our Complaint, of his great Grace, 2827
EARES = 2
Of all these eares (for where I am rob'd and bound, 1511
To some eares vnrecounted. But my Lords 1889
EARLE = 6*1
Sergeant. Sir, | My Lord the Duke of *Buckingham,* and Earle 279
Then Deputy of Ireland, who remou'd | Earle *Surrey,* was sent thither,
and in hast too, 874
*Enter to Woolsey, the Dukes of Norfolke and Suffolke, the | Earle of
Surrey, and the Lord Chamberlaine.* 2108
He to be Earle Marshall: you may reade the rest. 2401
a Demy Coronall of Gold. With him, the Earle of Surrey, 2430
And that the Earle of Surrey, with the Rod. 2450
For after the stout Earle Northumberland | Arrested him at Yorke, and
brought him forward 2565
EARLES = 1
*bearing the Rod of Siluer with the Doue, Crowned with an | Earles
Coronet. Collars of Esses.* 2431
EARLY = 1
Come pat betwixt too early, and too late 1304
EARNEST = 1
Meane while, must be an earnest motion 1604
EARNESTLY = 1
How earnestly he cast his eyes vpon me: 3005
EARTH = 4
Take vp the Rayes o'th'beneficiall Sun, | And keepe it from the Earth. 104
Qu. Would I had neuer trod this English Earth, 1779
Giue him a little earth for Charity. 2577
Vpon this naughty Earth? Go too, go too, 2939
EARTH = 1
My Legges like loaden Branches bow to'th'Earth, 2553
EARTH = 1
His Contemplation were aboue the earth, 1996
EARTHLY = 3*1
Nor. Then you lost | The view of earthly glory: Men might say 57
*The Queene of earthly Queenes: Shee's Noble borne; 1505
To keepe your earthly Audit, sure in that 2010
A peace aboue all earthly Dignities, 2285
EARTHY = 1
And of an earthy cold? Marke her eyes? 2677
EASE = 3
So now (me thinkes) I feele a little ease. 2555
The dew o'th'Verdict with it; at what ease 2932
All that are heere: Some come to take their ease, 3451
EASIE = 5
San. I would I were, | They should finde easie pennance. 686
Lou. Faith how easie? 688
San. As easie as a downe bed would affoord it. 689
And when he thinkes, good easie man, full surely 2257
Kath. Alas poore man. | *Grif.* At last, with easie Rodes, he came to
Leicester, 2570

EASINESSE = 1
Out of our easinesse and childish pitty   3073
EATE = 1
In her dayes, Euery Man shall eate in safety,   3404
EDGE = 1*1
Hath a sharpe edge: It's long, and't may be saide   170
*him, the Axe with the edge towards him, Halberds on each   890
EDWARD = 2
And Duke of Buckingham: now, poore Edward Bohun;   949
As holy Oyle, Edward Confessors Crowne,   2509
EFFECT = 2
Together; To consider further, that | What his high Hatred would effect,
wants not   166
And the late Marriage made of none effect: 2415
EFFECTS = 1
Haue stood to Charity, and displayd th'effects   1445
EGO = 1
Nor. Then, That in all you writ to Rome, or else | To Forraigne
Princes, Ego & Rex meus   2210
EGYPT = 1
For all the mud in Egypt; haue you heard it?   1313
EIGHT see also 8. = 3
Henry the Eight, Life, Honour, Name and all   962
About the houre of eight, which he himselfe   2580
The Famous History of the Life of | King HENRY the Eight.   3465
EITHER = 6
Lou. They must either | (For so run the Conditions) leaue those
remnants   601
Was either pittied in him, or forgotten.   858
The King will venture at it. Either the Cardinall,   1009
Either for such men, or such businesse;   1702
Either of King or Councell, when you went   2215
That had a head to hit, either young or old,   3282
ELDEST = 1
That blinde Priest, like the eldest Sonne of Fortune,   1052
ELECT = 1
Yea, the elect o'th'Land, who are assembled   1415
ELEMENT = 1
One certes, that promises no Element | In such a businesse.   95
ELIZABETH = 2
Long, and euer happie, to the high and Mighty | Princesse of England
Elizabeth.   3366
What is her Name? | Cran. Elizabeth.   3375
ELS = 4
To him that does best, God forbid els: Cardinall,   1162
I will haue none so neere els. Learne this Brother,   1189
Soueraigne and Pious els, could speake thee out)   1504
She will be sicke els. This day, no man thinke   3446
ELSE = 11
They are deuis'd by you, or else you suffer | Too hard an exclamation.   382
We shall be late else, which I would not be,   656
Suff. Pray God he doe, | Hee'l neuer know himselfe else.   1054
Wol. This, and all else | This talking Lord can lay vpon my credit,   2153
Thou should'st feele | My Sword i'th'life blood of thee else. My Lords,   2167
Nor. Then, That in all you writ to Rome, or else | To Forraigne
Princes, Ego & Rex meus   2210
I were malicious else.   2605

ELSE *cont.*

It fits we thus proceed, or else no witnesse | Would come against you.	2904
Haue more, or else vnsay't: and now, while 'tis hot,	2985
Wait else at doore: a fellow Councellor | 'Mong Boyes, Groomes, and Lackeyes.	3010
Ile pecke you o're the pales else. *Exeunt.*	3352

ELY = *1

Canterbury alone; after him, the Bishops of Lincolne, Ely,	1336

EM = 54*11

(For so they phrase 'em) by their Heralds challeng'd	78
Buc. O many | Haue broke their backes with laying Mannors on 'em	136
Sent downe among 'em, which hath flaw'd the heart	348
Most pestilent to th'hearing, and to beare 'em,	380
(Nay let 'em be vnmanly) yet are follow'd.	575
For when they hold 'em, you would sweare directly	579
That neuer see 'em pace before, the Spauen	584
A Spring-halt rain'd among 'em.	585
L.San. Tis time to giue 'em Physicke, their diseases | Are growne so catching.	614
L.San. The Diuell fiddle 'em, | I am glad they are going,	622
For sure there's no conuerting of'em: now	624
I thinke would better please 'em: by my life,	682
My Lord *Sands*, you are one will keepe 'em waking:	694
*In their faire cheekes my Lord, then wee shall haue 'em, | Talke vs to silence.	723
Card. Good Lord Chamberlaine, | *Go, giue 'em welcome; you can speake the French tongue	744
And pray receiue 'em Nobly, and conduct 'em	746
An houre of Reuels with 'em.	765
For which I pay 'em a thousand thankes,	768
And pray 'em take their pleasures.	769
Card. Pray tell 'em thus much from me:	776
There should be one amongst'em by his person	777
To lead 'em once againe, and then let's dreame	816
(Be what they will) I heartily forgiue'em;	906
Yet let 'em looke they glory not in mischiefe;	907
For then, my guiltlesse blood must cry against 'em.	909
*And with that bloud will make 'em one day groane for't.	952
'em from me, with this reason: his maister would bee seru'd be-|fore	1033
These newes are euery where, euery tongue speaks 'em,	1071
Sing, and disperse 'em if thou canst: leaue working.	1619
Were tri'de by eu'ry tongue, eu'ry eye saw 'em,	1659
Enuy and base opinion set against 'em,	1660
Mend 'em for shame my Lords: Is this your comfort?	1737
We are to Cure such sorrowes, not to sowe 'em.	1795
Abound, as thicke as thought could make 'em, and	2071
Suf. Who dare crosse 'em,	2119
You haue Christian warrant for 'em, and no doubt	2129
As let 'em haue their rights, they are euer forward	2389
And make 'em reele before 'em. No man liuing	2499
And sure those men are happy that shall haue 'em.	2739
(But pouerty could neuer draw 'em from me)	2741
That they may haue their wages, duly paid 'em,	2742
'Tis well there's one aboue 'em yet; I had thought	3026
They had parted so much honesty among 'em,	3027
Let 'em alone, and draw the Curtaine close:	3033
Pace 'em not in their hands to make 'em gentle;	3070

EM *cont.*
*But stop their mouthes with stubborn Bits & spurre 'em, 3071
*staues, and strong ones; these are but switches to 'em: 3265
Vnlesse wee sweepe 'em from the dore with Cannons, 3270
To scatter 'em, as 'tis to make 'em sleepe 3271
We may as well push against Powles as stirre'em. 3273
To mow 'em downe before me: but if I spar'd any 3281
*But knock 'em downe by th' dozens? Is this More fields 3291
*length they came to th' broome staffe to me, I defide 'em 3313
*stil, when sodainly a File of Boyes behind 'em, loose shot, 3314
*draw mine Honour in, and let 'em win the Worke, the 3316
Diuell was amongst 'em I thinke surely. 3317
*'em in *Limbo Patrum*, and there they are like to dance 3322
An Army cannot rule 'em. 3337
Let none thinke Flattery; for they'l finde'em Truth. 3386
For such a one we shew'd 'em: If they smile, 3460
If they hold, when their Ladies bid 'em clap. | FINIS. 3463
EMBALLING = 1
You'ld venture an emballing: I my selfe 1259
EMBALME = 1
I was a chaste Wife, to my Graue: Embalme me, 2763
EMBASSADOR = 1
By th'Bishop of *Bayon*, then French Embassador, 1539
EMBASSADORS = 1
And hither make, as great Embassadors | From forraigne Princes. 742
EMBLEMES = 1
The Rod, and Bird of Peace, and all such Emblemes 2510
EMBRACE = 2
Make me no more adoe, but all embrace him; 3230
Once more my Lord of *Winchester*, I charge you | Embrace, and loue
this man. 3242
EMBRACEMENT = 1
In their Embracement, as they grew together, | Which had they, 51
EMINENCE = 1
Affected Eminence, Wealth, Soueraignty; 1237
EMINENT = 1
To eminent Assistants; but Spider-like 111
EMPEROR = 3*1
And pau'd with gold: the Emperor thus desir'd, 264
*Between vs & the Emperor (the Queens great Nephew) 1058
Ambassador to the Emperor, you made bold | To carry into Flanders,
the Great Seale. 2216
If my sight faile not, | You should be Lord Ambassador from the
Emperor, 2693
EMPEROUR = 3
To th'old dam Treason) *Charles* the Emperour, 252
Which I doe well; for I am sure the Emperour 261
1. Tis the Cardinall; | And meerely to reuenge him on the Emperour, 1015
EMPLOYD *see* imploy'd
EMPLOYMENT *see* imployment
EMPTY = 1*1
*More worth, then empty vanities: yet Prayers & Wishes 1286
That Chayre stand empty: But we all are men 3058
ENCOUNTER = 1
2 'Tis all my businesse. At our last encounter, 2383
END = 14*1
As he cride thus let be, to as much end, 247

END *cont.*

The lag end of their lewdnesse, and be laugh'd at.	613
Card. What warlike voyce, | And to what end is this? Nay, Ladies, feare not;	735
2. Certainly, | The Cardinall is the end of this.	870
Goe with me like good Angels to my end,	917
And when old Time shall lead him to his end,	937
Who vndertakes you to your end.	941
Heauen ha's an end in all: yet, you that heare me,	970
Looke into these affaires, see this maine end,	1073
From any priuate malice in his end,	2157
They say in great Extremity, and fear'd | Shee'l with the Labour, end.	2793
himselfe at the vpper end of the Table, on the left hand: A	3037
Cromwell at lower end, as Secretary.	3041
Might goe one way, and safely; and the end	3084
You are so mercifull. I see your end,	3110

ENDEAUORS = 2

Beyond all mans endeauors. My endeauors,	2043

ENDLESSE = 1

Gart. Heauen | From thy endlesse goodnesse, send prosperous life,	3364

ENDS = 5

Nor. Surely Sir, | There's in him stuffe, that put's him to these ends:	106
Car. If your Grace | Could but be brought to know, our Ends are honest,	1790
Yet fill'd with my Abilities: Mine owne ends	2045
For mine owne ends, (Indeed to gaine the Popedome,	2092
Let all the ends thou aym'st at, be thy Countries,	2362

ENDURANCE *see* indurance

ENDURE = 2*1

Can ye endure to heare this Arrogance?	2169
To endure more Miseries, and greater farre	2297
*their deare Brothers are able to endure. I haue some of	3321

ENEMIES = 5

That you haue many enemies, that know not	1524
Then my Weake-hearted Enemies, dare offer.	2298
Haue left me naked to mine Enemies.	2372
If they shall faile, I with mine Enemies	2923
Your Enemies are many, and not small; their practises	2929

ENEMY = 3

He were mine Enemy? What Friend of mine,	1385
You are mine Enemy, and make my Challenge,	1435
As I would wish mine Enemy.	1860

ENGLAND = 10*2

Selfe-mettle tyres him: Not a man in England	205
England and France, might through their amity	257
To the loue o'th'Commonalty, the Duke | Shall gouerne England.	516
Old.L. In faith, for little England	1258
Scri. Say, *Henry* K.(ing) of England, come into the Court.	1358
Crier. Henry King of England, &c. | *King.* Heere.	1359
Scribe. Say, *Katherine* Queene of England, | Come into the Court.	1361
Crier. Katherine Queene of England, &c.	1363
Crier. Katherine. Q.(ueene) of England, come into the Court.	1488
Your hopes and friends are infinite. | *Queen.* In England,	1709
Long, and euer happie, to the high and Mighty | Princesse of England *Elizabeth.*	3366
Cran. She shall be to the happinesse of England,	3428

ENGLISH = 8*2
Shone downe the English; and to morrow, they   64
I say againe there is no English Soule   219
L.Ch. As farre as I see, all the good our English   576
To thinke an English Courtier may be wise, | And neuer see the *Louure.*   599
**Cham.* Because they speak no English, thus they praid   758
*Pray speake in English; heere are some will thanke you,   1669
The willing'st sinne I euer yet committed, | May be absolu'd in English.   1672
That any English man dare giue me Councell?   1712
Qu. Would I had neuer trod this English Earth,   1779
I thanke ye heartily: So shall this Lady, | When she ha's so much
English.   3382
ENIOY = 1
Bad me enioy it, with the Place, and Honors   2133
ENOUGH = 4
Being now seene, possible enough, got credit | That *Beuis* was beleeu'd.   81
And farre enough from Court too.   883
That's Christian care enough: for liuing Murmurers,   1185
Sur. Sharpe enough, | Lord for thy Iustice.   1949
ENROLD = 1
Who was enrold 'mongst wonders; and when we   458
ENSUDE = 1
This pausingly ensu'de; neither the King, nor's Heyres   514
ENSUING = 2
Was cry'de incompareable; and th'ensuing night   71
Of an ensuing euill, if it fall, | Greater then this.   989
ENTER = 47*8
Enter the Duke of Norfolke at one doore. At the other,   35
**Enter Cardinall Wolsey, the Purse borne before him, certaine*   175
*Enter Brandon, a Sergeant at Armes before him, and | two or three of the
Guard.*   276
**Cornets. Enter King Henry, leaning on the Cardinals shoul-| der,*   317
Duke of Norfolke. Enter the Queene, Norfolke and   330
Enter Surueyor.   446
Enter L.(ord) Chamberlaine and L.(ord) Sandys.   570
Enter Sir Thomas Louell.   590
longer Table for the Guests. Then Enter Anne Bullen,   662
at one Doore; at an other Doore enter | Sir Henry Guilford.   664
Enter L.(ord) Chamberlaine L.(ord) Sands, and Louell.   674
Hoboyes. Enter Cardinall Wolsey, and takes his State.   710
Enter a Seruant.   738
**Hoboyes. Enter King and others as Maskers, habited like*   753
Enter two Gentlemen at seuerall Doores.   820
**Enter Buckingham from his Arraignment, Tipstaues before*   889
Enter Lord Chamberlaine, reading this Letter.   1027
Enter to the Lord Chamberlaine, the Dukes of Nor-| folke and Suffolke.   1038
Enter Wolsey and Campeius with a Commission.   1115
Enter Gardiner.   1165
Enter Anne Bullen, and an old Lady.   1201
Enter Lord Chamberlaine.   1263
**Enter two Vergers, with short siluer wands; next them two*   1334
Enter Queene and her Women as at worke.   1616
Enter a Gentleman. | Queen. How now?   1633
Enter the two Cardinalls, Wolsey & Campian.   1645
*Enter the Duke of Norfolke, Duke of Suffolke, Lord Surrey, | and Lord
Chamberlaine.*   1825
Enter Wolsey and Cromwell.   1925

ENTER *cont.*
   Enter King, reading of a Scedule. 1964
   Enter to Woolsey, the Dukes of Norfolke and Suffolke, the | Earle of
   Surrey, and the Lord Chamberlaine. 2108
   Enter Cromwell, standing amazed. 2274
   Enter two Gentlemen, meeting one another. 2378
   Enter a third Gentleman. 2472
   Enter Katherine Dowager, sicke, lead betweene Griffith, 2548
   The Vision. | *Enter solemnely tripping one after another, sixe
   Personages, 2642
   Saw ye none enter since I slept? | *Grif.* None Madam. 2662
   Enter a Messenger. 2680
   Enter Lord Capuchius. 2692
   Enter Gardiner Bishop of Winchester, a Page with a Torch | before him,
   met by Sir Thomas Louell. 2769
   Enter King and Suffolke. 2836
   Enter Sir Anthony Denny. 2866
   Enter Cranmer and Denny. 2876
   Enter Olde Lady. 2961
   Enter Cranmer, Archbyshop of Canterbury. 2988
   Enter Keeper. 2993
   Enter Doctor Buts. 2998
   Enter the King, and Buts, at a Windowe | aboue. 3014
   *placed vnder the State. Enter Lord Chancellour, places 3036
   Chan. Let him come in. | *Keep.* Your Grace may enter now. 3053
   Enter the Guard. 3155
   Enter King frowning on them, takes his Seate. 3181
   Noyse and Tumult within: Enter Porter and | his man. 3257
   Enter Lord Chamberlaine. 3325
   *Enter Trumpets sounding: Then two Aldermen, L.(ord) Maior, 3354
   Flourish. Enter King and Guard. 3368
ENTERD = 2
   The bosome of my Conscience, enter'd me; 1549
   I say, set on. | *Exeunt, in manner as they enter'd.* 1613
ENTERRE = 1
   A Queene, and Daughter to a King enterre me. 2765
ENTERUIEW = 1
   To this last costly Treaty: Th'enteruiew, 240
ENTHROANED = 1
   So many courses of the Sun enthroaned, 1207
ENTRANCE = *1
   *Kath. Admit him entrance *Griffith.* But this Fellow 2690
ENTREAT *see also* intreat = 2
   Craue leaue to view these Ladies, and entreat 764
   Mes. I humbly do entreat your Highnesse pardon, 2687
ENTREATE = 1
   And did entreate your Highnes to this course, | Which you are running
   heere. 1585
ENTREATIES *see* intreaties
ENTREATS = 1
   And heartily entreats you take good comfort. 2707
ENTRING = 1
   His Grace is entring. Nay, you must not freeze, 692
ENUIDE = 1
   Camp. They will not sticke to say, you enuide him; 1180
ENUIOUS = 3
   2. That tricke of State | Was a deepe enuious one, 877

ENUIOUS *cont.*
Follow your enuious courses, men of Malice;   2128
To silence enuious Tongues. Be iust, and feare not;   2361
ENUY = 7
No blacke Enuy shall make my Graue.   929
Who can be angry now? What Enuy reach you?   1136
Enuy and base opinion set against 'em,   1660
You turne the good we offer, into enuy.   1745
Of what course Mettle ye are molded, Enuy,   2124
Enuy, and crooked malice, nourishment;   3092
And his Disciples onely enuy at,   3179
EPILOGVE = 1
THE EPILOGVE. | *Tis ten to one, this Play can neuer please*   3449
EQUALL = 3*1
Equall in lustre, were now best, now worst   73
Or Wolfe, or both (for he is equall rau'nous   234
Kin. Two equall men: The Queene shall be acquain-|(ted   1155
Of equall Friendship and Proceeding. Alas Sir: 1372
ERE = 7
Paid ere he promis'd, whereby his Suit was granted   262
Ere it was ask'd. But when the way was made   263
The other moity ere you aske is giuen,   337
Should finde a running Banket, ere they rested,   681
Fresher then e're it was; and held for certaine   1008
Ere a determinate resolution, hee | (I meane the Bishop) did require a
respite,   1543
Your Master wed me to: nothing but death | Shall e're diuorce my
Dignities.   1776
ERGA = *1
Card. Tanta est erga te mentis integritas Regina serenissima.   1664
ERRE = 1
(Who cannot erre) he did it. Now this followes,   250
ESCAPES = *1
*Whose Honor Heauen shield from soile; euen he escapes | (not   353
ESSES = 2
*bearing the Rod of Siluer with the Doue, Crowned with an | Earles
Coronet. Collars of Esses.*   2431
*him, the Duke of Norfolke, with the Rod of Marshalship, | a Coronet on
his head. Collars of Esses.*   2435
EST *l.*1664 = *1
ESTATE = 2*1
Is businesse of Estate; in which, we come | To know your Royall
pleasure.   1110
*7 Duke of Suffolke, *in his Robe of Estate, his Coronet on his*   2433
Th'estate of my poore Queene. Leaue me alone,   2858
ESTATES = 1
By this, so sicken'd their Estates, that neuer   134
ESTEEME = 1
A man in much esteeme with th'King, and truly   2536
ETCETERA *see* &c.
ETERNALL = 1
They promis'd me eternall Happinesse,   2667
EUEN = 8*1
Whose Figure euen this instant Clowd puts on,   314
*Whose Honor Heauen shield from soile; euen he escapes | (not   353
Euen as the Axe falls, if I be not faithfull.   '   902
That Angels loue good men with: Euen of her,   1067

EUEN *cont.*
 Euen of your selfe Lord Cardinall. | *Wol.* How? of me?   1178
 Euen the Billowes of the Sea,   1628
 I know my life so euen. If your busines   1661
 A Soule as euen as a Calme; Pray thinke vs,   1803
 Kath. No? Saw you not euen now a blessed Troope   2664
EUENING = 1
 I haste now to my Setting. I shall fall | Like a bright exhalation in the
 Euening,   2105
EUENT = 1
 Daring th'euent too th'teeth, are all in vprore, | And danger serues
 among them.   364
EUER = 52*2
 Healthfull, and euer since a fresh Admirer | Of what I saw there.   42
 To cope malicious Censurers, which euer,   413
 Then euer they were faire. This man so compleat,   457
 King. The fairest hand I euer touch'd: O Beauty,   771
 (And generally) who euer the King fauours,   881
 If euer any malice in your heart   923
 Euer belou'd and louing, may his Rûle be;   936
 For euer from the World. I had my Tryall,   964
 Gard. But to be commanded | For euer by your Grace, whose hand ha's
 rais'd me.   1168
 So good a Lady, that no Tongue could euer   1204
 Haue (too) a Womans heart, which euer yet   1236
 Cannot vouchsafe this burthen, tis too weake | Euer to get a Boy.   1253
 Euer in feare to kindle your Dislike,   1379
 I euer contradicted your Desire?   1382
 Wol. I do professe | You speake not like your selfe: who euer yet   1443
 I will not tarry: no, nor euer more   1493
 At once, and fully satisfide) whether euer I   1513
 Induce you to the question on't: or euer   1516
 But will you be more iustifi'de? You euer   1528
 Euer sprung; as Sunne and Showers,   1625
 The willing'st sinne I euer yet committed, | May be absolu'd in English.   1672
 As yours was, put into you, euer casts   1808
 Matter against him, that for euer marres | The Hony of his Language.
 No, he's setled   1851
 Car. Heauen forgiue me, | Euer God blesse your Highnesse.   2003
 *Car. And euer may your Highnesse yoake together,   2021
 Haue euer come too short of my Desires,   2044
 Which euer ha's, and euer shall be growing, | Till death (that Winter)
 kill it.   2052
 Car. I do professe, | That for your Highnesse good, I euer labour'd   2066
 Toward the King, my euer Roiall Master,   2162
 Of a rude streame, that must for euer hide me.   2265
 In that one woman, I haue lost for euer.   2323
 No Sun, shall euer vsher forth mine Honors,   2324
 For euer, and for euer shall be yours.   2342
 As let 'em haue their rights, they are euer forward   2389
 2 Heauen blesse thee, | Thou hast the sweetest face I euer look'd on.   2456
 That euer lay by man: which when the people   2490
 How euer, yet there is no great breach, when it comes   2532
 Of an vnbounded stomacke, euer ranking   2589
 He would say vntruths, and be euer double   2593
 He was most Princely: Euer witnesse for him   2615
 That Christendome shall euer speake his Vertue.   2621

EUER   *cont.*
  Kath. So may he euer do, and euer flourish, 2714
  Must beare the same proportion, and not euer 2930
  Both now, and euer blesse her: 'Tis a Gyrle 2972
  Was euer to doe well: nor is there liuing, 3085
  How euer faulty, yet should finde respect 3124
  Kin. You were euer good at sodaine Commendations, 3191
  A shrewd turne, and hee's your friend for euer: 3251
  Long, and euer happie, to the high and Mighty | Princesse of England
  Elizabeth. 3366
  Heauen euer laid vp to make Parents happy, | May hourely fall vpon
  ye. 3372
  Where euer the bright Sunne of Heauen shall shine, 3421
EUERMORE = 1
  Haue beene mine so, that euermore they pointed 2046
EUERY = 18
  Made Britaine, India: Euery man that stood, 65
  Buc. Euery man, | After the hideous storme that follow'd, was 144
  From euery Tree, lop, barke, and part o'th' Timber: 432
  The Ayre will drinke the Sap. To euery County 434
  Let there be Letters writ to euery Shire, 440
  Sur. First, it was vsuall with him; euery day 472
  His Confessor, who fed him euery minute | With words of Soueraignty. 494
  His dewes fall euery where. 644
  These newes are euery where, euery tongue speaks 'em, 1071
  And euery true heart weepes for't. All that dare 1072
  Of euery Realme, that did debate this Businesse, 1406
  Euery thing that heard him play, 1627
  To taint that honour euery good Tongue blesses; 1679
  I should be glad to heare such Newes as this | Once euery houre. 1855
  Your Braine, and euery Function of your power, 2062
  Ye appeare in euery thing may bring my ruine? 2127
  In her dayes, Euery Man shall eate in safety, 3404
EUERYONE *see* eu'ry
EUERYTHING *see* euery, eu'ry
EUERYWHERE *see* euery
EUIDENCE = 1
  And so his Peeres vpon this euidence, 855
EUILL = 3
  Was, were he euill vs'd, he would outgoe 560
  Of an ensuing euill, if it fall, | Greater then this. 989
  Grif. Noble Madam: | Mens euill manners, liue in Brasse, their Vertues 2600
EUILS = 1
  Nor build their euils on the graues of great men; 908
EUN = 1
  Eu'n to the Hall, to heare what shall become | Of the great Duke of
  Buckingham. 823
EURY = 3*1
  In Honor, Honesty, the tract of eu'ry thing, 85
  Kin. Lead in your Ladies eu'ry one: Sweet Partner, 812
  Were tri'de by eu'ry tongue, eu'ry eye saw 'em, 1659
EXACTION = 2
  Kin. Still Exaction: | The nature of it, in what kinde let's know, 384
  Is this Exaction? 386
EXACTIONS = 2
  Most bitterly on you, as putter on | Of these exactions: yet the King,
  our Maister 351

EXACTIONS *cont.*
Perforce be their acquaintance. These exactions 378
EXAMINATION = 1
Where's his Examination? | *Secr.* Heere so please you. 181
EXAMINATIONS = 1
Vrg'd on the Examinations, proofes, confessions 843
EXAMPLE = 3
Things done without example, in their issue 426
If well, he stept before me happily | For my example. 2562
Of his owne body he was ill, and gaue | The Clergy ill example. 2598
EXAMPLES = 1
They are set heere for examples. | *L.Cham.* True, they are so; 651
EXCEEDING = 2
San. O very mad, exceeding mad, in loue too; 701
Exceeding wise, faire spoken, and perswading: 2610
EXCELLENCE = 1
Of her that loues him with that excellence, 1066
EXCELLENT = 2
A Prince most Prudent; of an excellent 1400
So excellent in Art, and still so rising, 2620
EXCLAMATION = 1
They are deuis'd by you, or else you suffer | Too hard an exclamation. 382
EXCUSD = 1
The Queene is put in anger; y'are excus'd: 1527
EXCUSE = 3
My Lord, youle beare vs company? | *Cham.* Excuse me, 1094
Kin. My Lord Cardinall, | I doe excuse you; yea, vpon mine Honour, 1521
To let my tongue excuse all. What was purpos'd 3220
EXE = 1
By Darkning my cleere Sunne. My Lords farewell. *Exe.* 315
EXECUTE = 1
Brandon. Your Office Sergeant: execute it. 278
EXECUTION = 1
'Tis like a Pardon after Execution; 2709
EXEMPT = 1
Kin. Things done well, | And with a care, exempt themselues from feare: 424
EXEUNT see also Exe. = 19*1
Shall lessen this bigge looke. | *Exeunt Cardinall, and his Traine.* 186
Hee's Traytor to th' height. *Exeunt.* 568
L.San. I am your Lordships. *Exeunt.* 659
Who's best in fauour. Let the Musicke knock it. | *Exeunt with Trumpets.* 817
I haue done; and God forgiue me. | *Exeunt Duke and Traine.* 982
Let's thinke in priuate more. *Exeunt.* 1025
Exeunt Norfolke and Suffolke. 1132
O 'tis a tender place, and I must leaue her. *Exeunt.* 1199
Old L. What doe you thinke me --- *Exeunt.* 1331
I say, set on. | *Exeunt, in manner as they enter'd.* 1613
She should haue bought her Dignities so deere. *Exeunt* 1823
So fare you well, my little good Lord Cardinall. | *Exeunt all but Wolsey.* 2249
The Hopes of Court, my Hopes in Heauen do dwell. | *Exeunt.* 2375
Exeunt, first passing ouer the Stage in Order and State, and | then, A great Flourish of Trumpets. 2445
Both. You may command vs Sir. *Exeunt.* 2546
I can no more. | *Exeunt leading Katherine.* 2766
Ha? I haue said. Be gone. | What? *Exeunt Louell and Denny.* 2878
So I grow stronger, you more Honour gaine. *Exeunt.* 3255

EXEUNT cont.
Ile pecke you o're the pales else. *Exeunt.*   3352
This Little-One shall make it Holy-day. *Exeunt.*   3448
EXHALATION = 1
I haste now to my Setting. I shall fall | Like a bright exhalation in the
Euening,   2105
EXIT = 13*1
Further in the proceeding. *Exit Secret.(ary)*   445
*Exit Lord Chamberlaine, and the King drawes the Curtaine | and sits
reading pensiuely.*   1100
Kin. Deliuer this with modesty to th' Queene. | *Exit Gardiner.*   1191
And say I spoke with you. | *Exit Lord Chamberlaine.*   1298
Exit Queene, and her Attendants.   1496
Card. Leaue me a while. *Exit Cromwell.*   1939
*Exit King, frowning vpon the Cardinall, the Nobles | throng after him
smiling, and whispering.*   2081
Let me ne're see againe. *Exit Messeng.*   2691
I hinder you too long: Good night, Sir *Thomas.* | *Exit Gardiner and
Page.*   2833
King. Charles good night. *Exit Suffolke.*   2864
And do as I haue bid you. *Exit Cranmer.*   2959
Ile to the Queene. *Exit King.*   2980
Ile put it to the issue. *Exit Ladie.*   2986
I came this way so happily. The King | Shall vnderstand it presently.
Exit Buts   3001
EXPECT = 1
Gard. What other, | Would you expect? You are strangely troublesome: 3152
EXPECTED = 1
All the expected good w'are like to heare.   3457
EXPENCE = 1
To his owne portion? And what expence by'th'houre   1969
EXPRESSELY = 1
Bearing the Kings will from his mouth expressely?   2120
EXTEND = 1
It reaches farre, and where 'twill not extend,   171
EXTORTION = 1
Into your owne hands (Card'nall) by Extortion: 2178
EXTREAMLY = 2
With such an Agony, he sweat extreamly,   862
Abus'd extreamly, and to cry that's witty,   3455
EXTREMITY = 1
They say in great Extremity, and fear'd | Shee'l with the Labour, end.   2793
EYE = 9
Such Noble Scoenes, as draw the Eye to flow   5
As presence did present them: Him in eye,   74
Abur. I cannot tell | What Heauen hath giuen him: let some Grauer eye   116
*Cardinall in his passage, fixeth his eye on Buck-|ingham, and
Buckingham on him, | both full of disdaine.*   177
Buc. I read in's looks | Matter against me, and his eye reuil'd   195
Were tri'de by eu'ry tongue, eu'ry eye saw 'em,   1659
And came to th'eye o'th'King, wherein was read   1866
His eye against the Moone: in most strange Postures   1980
Some Spirit put this paper in the Packet, | To blesse your eye withall.   1993
EYES = 8
Another spread on's breast, mounting his eyes,   558
The Kings eyes, that so long haue slept vpon | This bold bad man.   1075
Leap'd from his Eyes. So lookes the chafed Lyon   2086

EYES *cont.*

Let's dry our eyes: And thus farre heare me *Cromwel*,   2346
Cast her faire eyes to Heauen, and pray'd deuoutly.   2505
And of an earthy cold? Marke her eyes?   2677
(For so I will) mine eyes grow dimme. Farewell   2757
How earnestly he cast his eyes vpon me: 3005
FABULOUS = 1
Beyond thoughts Compasse, that former fabulous Storie   80
FACE = 6*1
A fit or two o'th' face, (but they are shrewd ones)   578
To him brought *viua voce* to his face;   845
2 Heauen blesse thee, | Thou hast the sweetest face I euer look'd on.   2456
How long her face is drawne? How pale she lookes,   2676
Be what they will, may stand forth face to face,   3095
*by his face, for o' my conscience twenty of the Dog- | dayes   3300
FACES = 2*2
*Ye haue Angels Faces; but Heauen knowes your hearts.   1781
(Doublets, I thinke) flew vp, and had their Faces   2494
Bayes, and golden Vizards on their faces, Branches of Bayes   2645
Inuite me to a Banquet, whose bright faces   2665
FACULTIES = 1
My faculties nor person, yet will be   408
FADDOM = 1
Wish him ten faddom deepe: This Duke as much   886
FAILD = 1
That had the King in his last Sicknesse faild,   532
FAILE = 6
Vpon our faile; to this poynt hast thou heard him, | At any time speake
ought?   488
Cham. Lady; | I shall not faile t'approue the faire conceit   1291
By this my Issues faile, and that gaue to me   1565
If my sight faile not, | You should be Lord Ambassador from the
Emperor,   2693
If they shall faile, I with mine Enemies   2923
Faile not to vse, and with what vehemencie   2951
FAINE = 1*1
1. The same, | All these accus'd him strongly, which he faine   852
*deliuer'd such a showre of Pibbles, that I was faine to   3315
FAINTS = 1
If this salute my blood a iot; it faints me | To thinke what followes.   1326
FAIRE = 22*2
Then euer they were faire. This man so compleat,   457
To faire content, and you: None heere he hopes   669
The very thought of this faire Company, | Clapt wings to me.   676
They are a sweet society of faire ones.   683
The pennance lyes on you; if these faire Ladies | Passe away frowning.   706
Card. Y'are welcome my faire Guests; that noble Lady   711
*In their faire cheekes my Lord, then wee shall haue 'em, | Talke vs to
silence.   723
Of this so Noble and so faire assembly,   760
But leaue their Flockes, and vnder your faire Conduct   763
You hold a faire Assembly; you doe well Lord: 790
Kin. My Lord Chamberlaine, | Prethee come hither, what faire Ladie's
that?   795
To drinke to these faire Ladies, and a measure   815
You that haue so faire parts of Woman on you,   1235
Follow such Creatures. That you may, faire Lady   1274

FAIRE *cont.*
Cham. Lady; | I shall not faile t'approue the faire conceit 1291
After his Patients death; the King already | Hath married the faire
Lady. | *Sur.* Would he had. 1878
There's more in't then faire Visage. *Bullen?* 1943
Cast her faire eyes to Heauen, and pray'd deuoutly. 2505
Ty'de all the Kingdome. Symonie, was faire play, 2591
Exceeding wise, faire spoken, and perswading: 2610
And faire purgation to the world then malice, | I'm sure in me. 3223
That is, a faire young Maid that yet wants Baptisme, 3233
As if we kept a Faire heere? Where are these Porters? 3328
More couetous of Wisedome, and faire Vertue 3394
FAIRELY = 4
Cham. Well said my Lord: | So now y'are fairely seated: Gentlemen, 704
King. Fairely answer'd: | A Loyall, and obedient Subiect is 2054
Would I were fairely out on't. 3175
To let the Troope passe fairely; or Ile finde 3346
FAIRER = 1
Wol. So much fairer | And spotlesse, shall mine Innocence arise, 2194
FAIREST = 1
King. The fairest hand I euer touch'd: O Beauty, 771
FAITH = 10
Did breake ith'wrenching. | *Norf.* Faith, and so it did. 242
Louell. Faith my Lord, | I heare of none but the new Proclamation, 591
The faith they haue in Tennis and tall Stockings, 608
Lou. Faith how easie? 688
San. By my faith, | *And thanke your Lordship: by your leaue sweet
Ladies, 696
What may it be? you doe not doubt my faith Sir? 992
A strong faith to conceale it. 994
Old.L. In faith, for little England 1258
So deepe suspition, where all faith was meant; 1677
(If there be faith in men) meant for his Tryall, 3222
FAITHFULL = 2
Euen as the Axe falls, if I be not faithfull. 902
Your faithfull friends o'th' Suburbs? We shall haue 3331
FAITHFULLY = 1
Haue follow'd both my Fortunes, faithfully, 2733
FAITHLESSE = 1
A most vnnaturall and faithlesse Seruice. 969
FALCE = *1
Buck. My Surueyor is falce: The ore-great *Cardinall* 311
FALL = 16
May (if they thinke it well) let fall a Teare, 7
His dewes fall euery where. 644
The least rub in your fortunes, fall away 975
Of an ensuing euill, if it fall, | Greater then this. 989
Will haue his will, and she must fall. | 1. 'Tis wofull. 1022
Killing care, & griefe of heart, | Fall asleepe, or hearing dye. 1631
The burthen of my sorrowes, fall vpon ye. 1743
Will fall some blessing to this Land, which shall | In it be memoriz'd. 1892
Fit for a Foole to fall by: What crosse Diuell 2094
I haste now to my Setting. I shall fall | Like a bright exhalation in the
Euening, 2105
Fall into'th'compasse of a Premunire; 2240
Marke but my Fall, and that that Ruin'd me: 2354
The dewes of Heauen fall thicke in Blessings on her, 2724

FALL *cont.*

Cran. God, and your Maiesty | Protect mine innocence, or I fall into   2942

'Twold fall vpon our selues.   3169

Heauen euer laid vp to make Parents happy, | May hourely fall vpon

ye.   3372

FALLES = 2

And when he falles, he falles like Lucifer, | Neuer to hope againe.   2272

FALLING = 3

Cham. O my Lord, | Presse not a falling man too farre: 'tis Vertue: 2231

2 Their Coronets say so. These are Starres indeed, | And sometimes

falling ones.   2469

For what they haue beene: 'tis a cruelty, | To load a falling man.   3125

FALLS = 2

Euen as the Axe falls, if I be not faithfull.   902

That when the greatest stroake of Fortune falls   1068

FALLST = 1*1

*Thy Gods, and Truths. Then if thou fall'st (O *Cromwell*)   2363

Thou fall'st a blessed Martyr.   2364

FALNE = 4

The net has falne vpon me, I shall perish | Vnder deuice, and practise.   285

With me, a poore weake woman, falne from fauour?   1641

A great man should decline. Nay, and you weep | I am falne indeed.   2279

I am a poore falne man, vnworthy now   2327

FALS = 2

And as the long diuorce of Steele fals on me,   918

And then he fals as I do. I haue ventur'd   2259

FALSE = 3*1

For speaking false in that; thou art alone   1500

And all such false Professors. Would you haue me   1747

*Such doubts as false Coine from it. The King loues you,   1809

I answer, is most false. The Duke by Law   2155

FALSEHOOD = 1

And worthily my Falsehood, yea, as much   1456

FAME = 2

To tell your Grace: That hauing heard by fame   759

Shall Star-like rise, as great in fame as she was,   3417

FAMOUS = 3

Together with all famous Colledges   1912

The other (though vnfinish'd) yet so Famous,   2619

The Famous History of the Life of | King HENRY the Eight.   3465

FANCIES = 1

King. But little *Charles,* | Nor shall not when my Fancies on my play.   2840

FANCY = 2

An. Good Lady, | Make your selfe mirth with your particular fancy,   1323

Grif. I am most ioyfull Madam, such good dreames | Possesse your

Fancy.   2670

FAR = 1

They are (as all my other comforts) far hence | In mine owne Countrey

Lords.   1718

FARE = 2

O my Lord *Aburgany*: Fare you well.   295

So fare you well, my little good Lord Cardinall. | *Exeunt all but Wolsey.*   2249

FAREWELL = 10*1

By Darkning my cleere Sunne. My Lords farewell. *Exe.*   315

*Farewell; and when you would say somthing that is sad, | Speake how

I fell.   980

I writ too's Holinesse. Nay then, farewell: 2102

FAREWELL *cont.*

Farewell Nobilitie: let his Grace go forward,	2172
Wol. So farewell, to the little good you beare me.	2251
Farewell? A long farewell to all my Greatnesse.	2252
Crom. Good Sir, haue patience. | *Card.* So I haue. Farewell	2373
(For so I will) mine eyes grow dimme. Farewell	2757
My Lord. *Griffith* farewell. Nay *Patience,*	2758
Farewell all Physicke: and what followes then?	3075

FARRE = 21*1

Buc. Oh you go farre.	83
It reaches farre, and where 'twill not extend,	171
For this to ruminate on this so farre, vntill	528
L.Ch. As farre as I see, all the good our English	576
And farre enough from Court too.	883
Buck. All good people, | You that thus farre haue come to pitty me;	896
Yet thus farre we are one in Fortunes; both	967
For you, or any: how farre I haue proceeded,	1449
Or how farre further (Shall) is warranted	1450
And thus farre cleare him.	1533
Kin. I haue spoke long, be pleas'd your selfe to say | How farre you	
satisfide me.	1578
Both of his truth and him (which was too farre)	1690
Farre from his succour; from the King, from all	2149
Cham. O my Lord, | Presse not a falling man too farre: 'tis Vertue:	2231
But farre beyond my depth: my high-blowne Pride	2262
To endure more Miseries, and greater farre	2297
Let's dry our eyes: And thus farre heare me *Cromwel,*	2346
Yet thus farre *Griffith,* giue me leaue to speake him,	2587
Haue broken with the King, who hath so farre	2826
Bid ye so farre forget your selues? I gaue ye	3212
Chan. Thus farre | My most dread Soueraigne, may it like your Grace,	3218
*might see from farre, some forty Truncheoners draw to	3310

FASHION = 1

Cap. By Heauen I will, | Or let me loose the fashion of a man.	2751

FASHIOND = 2

Lie like one lumpe before him, to be fashion'd | Into what pitch he	
please.	1082
Was fashion'd to much Honor. From his Cradle	2608

FAST = 3

1. Whether away so fast? | 2. O, God saue ye:	821
Springs out into fast gate, then stops againe,	1978
To make great hast. All fast? What meanes this? Hoa?	2991

FATE = 2

'Tis but the fate of Place, and the rough Brake	410
For any suit of pounds: and you, (oh fate)	1305

FATHER = 11*2

The Part my Father meant to act vpon	546
Sur. After the Duke his Father, with the knife	556
His Father, by as much as a performance | Do's an irresolute purpose.	561
I had it from my Father.	699
Least he should helpe his Father.	876
My noble Father *Henry* of *Buckingham,*	953
A little happier then my wretched Father:	966
The King your Father, was reputed for	1399
My Father, King of Spaine, was reckon'd one	1402
And yet words are no deeds. My Father lou'd you,	2026
To whom he gaue these words. O Father Abbot,	2574

FATHER *cont.*
*thousand, here will bee Father, God-father, and all to-|gether.   3296
FATHERS = 5
My Fathers losse; like a most Royall Prince   959
Wol. You haue heere Lady, | (And of your choice) these Reuerend
Fathers, men   1412
By all the Reuerend Fathers of the Land,   1572
While I shall haue my life. Come reuerend Fathers,   1820
Learned, and Reuerend Fathers of his Order,   2408
FATHER-IN-LAW = 2
Remembrance of my Father-in-Law, the Duke, | To be reueng'd on
him.   1835
Of Noble Buckingham, my Father-in-Law,   2144
FAULT = 2
Ladies you are not merry; Gentlemen, | Whose fault is this?   720
That might haue mercie on the fault, thou gau'st him: 2150
FAULTS = 3
More then I dare make faults.   912
His faults lye open to the Lawes, let them   2233
Kath. So may he rest, | His Faults lye gently on him: 2585
FAULTY = 1
How euer faulty, yet should finde respect   3124
FAUORS = 1
You haue by Fortune, and his Highnesse fauors,   1471
FAUOUR = 8*2
**Buck.* Pray giue me fauour Sir: This cunning Cardinall   244
Who's best in fauour. Let the Musicke knock it. | *Exeunt with*
Trumpets.   817
The Spaniard tide by blood and fauour to her,   1137
Kin. I, and the best she shall haue; and my fauour   1161
* *Wol.* Giue me your hand: much ioy & fauour to you;   1166
With me, a poore weake woman, falne from fauour?   1641
Hath crawl'd into the fauour of the King, | And is his Oracle.   1961
Long in his Highnesse fauour, and do Iustice   2307
A man of his Place, and so neere our fauour   3029
By your good fauour, too sharpe; Men so Noble,   3123
FAUOURER = 1
Crom. Why my Lord? | *Gard.* Doe not I know you for a Fauourer   3130
FAUOURS = 2
(And generally) who euer the King fauours,   881
Is that poore man, that hangs on Princes fauours?   2268
FEARD = 3
Are to be fear'd. Haue you a President   427
They say in great Extremity, and fear'd | Shee'l with the Labour, end.   2793
She shall be lou'd and fear'd. Her owne shall blesse her;   3400
FEARE = 22*1
Our necessary actions, in the feare   412
In feare our motion will be mock'd, or carp'd at,   421
Kin. Things done well, | And with a care, exempt themselues from feare: 424
Men feare the French would proue perfidious   502
Said, 'twas the feare indeed, and that he doubted   504
Card. What warlike voyce, | And to what end is this? Nay, Ladies, feare
not;   735
Card. Your Grace | I feare, with dancing is a little heated.   807
Kin. I feare too much.   809
I feare, too many curses on their heads | That were the Authors.   985

FEARE *cont.*

*I feare he will indeede; well, let him haue them; hee | will haue all I
thinke.   1036
Suff. For me, my Lords, | I loue him not, nor feare him, there's my
Creede: 1084
Euer in feare to kindle your Dislike,   1379
(More neere my Life I feare) with my weake wit;   1698
But Cardinall Sins, and hollow hearts I feare ye: 1736
Giues way to vs) I much feare. If you cannot   1845
Nor. O feare him not, | His spell in that is out: the King hath found   1849
I feare the Story of his Anger. 'Tis so: 2089
To silence enuious Tongues. Be iust, and feare not;   2361
For feare we wake her. Softly, gentle *Patience.*   2641
Being of those Vertues vacant. I feare nothing | What can be said
against me.   2925
More then (I feare) you are prouided for.   3106
And sleepe an Act or two; but those we feare   3452
Which wee haue not done neither; that I feare   3456

FEAREFULL = 1
    Cran. I am fearefull: Wherefore frownes he thus?   2880

FEARES = 8
    His feares were that the Interview betwixt   256
    2. I doe not thinke he feares death. | 1. Sure he does not,   866
    Feares, and despaires, and all these for his Marriage.   1061
    Wol. Madam, | You wrong the Kings loue with these feares,   1707
    Camp. Your feares are worse.   1757
    With these weake Womens feares. A Noble Spirit   1807
    More pangs, and feares then warres, or women haue;   2271
    Mens prayers then would seeke you, not their feares.   3136

FEARING = 2
    And fearing he would rise (he was so vertuous)   1181
    Then man could giue him; he dy'de, fearing God.   2626

FEAST = 1
    To Yorke-Place, where the Feast is held.   2515

FEATHER = 1
    Of Foole and Feather, that they got in France,   603

FEATS = 1
    For high feats done to'th'Crowne; neither Allied   110

FEATURE = 1
    In minde and feature. I perswade me, from her   1891

FED = 3
    His Confessor, who fed him euery minute | With words of Soueraignty.   494
    2. That was hee | That fed him with his Prophecies.   850
    As if it fed ye, and how sleeke and wanton   2126

FEE = 1
    And fee my Friends in Rome.) O Negligence!   2093

FEEDS = 1
    A hand as fruitfull as the Land that feeds vs,   643

FEELE = 11*1
    We cannot feele too little, heare too much.   467
    That she should feele the smart of this: the Cardinall   1021
    I then did feele full sicke, and yet not well,   1571
    For her sake that I haue beene, for I feele   1703
    *Youl'd feele more comfort. Why shold we (good Lady)   1792
    I dare, and must deny it. Now I feele   2123
    Thou should'st feele | My Sword i'th'life blood of thee else. My Lords,   2167
    I feele my heart new open'd. Oh how wretched   2267

FEELE *cont.*
I know my selfe now, and I feele within me,   2284
(Out of a Fortitude of Soule, I feele)   2296
So now (me thinkes) I feele a little ease.   2555
And brought me Garlands (*Griffith*) which I feele   2668
FEETE = 2
places himselfe vnder the Kings feete on | his right side.   319
**goes about the Court, comes to the King, and kneeles at | his Feete.*
Then speakes.   1365
FELL = 10*2
But he fell to himselfe againe, and sweetly,   864
And without Tryall, fell; Gods peace be with him.   957
Fell by our Seruants, by those Men we lou'd most: 968
**Farewell; and when you would say somthing that is sad, | Speake how
I fell.*   980
By that sinne fell the Angels: how can man then   2356
To a prepar'd place in the Quire, fell off   2484
For since the Cardinall fell, that Titles lost,   2518
He fell sicke sodainly, and grew so ill | He could not sit his Mule.   2568
Ipswich and Oxford: one of which, fell with him,   2617
And Princely Care, fore-seeing those fell Mischiefes,   2828
**till her pinck'd porrenger fell off her head, for kindling*   3307
**was quartered; they fell on, I made good my place; at*   3312
FELLOW = 10*2
A noyse of Targets: Or to see a Fellow   16
By your prescription: but this top-proud fellow,   225
A French Song, and a Fiddle, ha's no Fellow.   621
I find him a fit fellow.   1164
For he would needs be vertuous. That good Fellow,   1187
Nor. This same *Cranmer*'s | A worthy Fellow, and hath tane much
paine | In the Kings businesse.   1918
And from this Fellow? If we liue thus tamely,   2170
Mes. And't like your Grace --- | *Kath.* You are a sawcy Fellow,   2681
* *Kath.* Admit him entrance *Griffith.* But this Fellow   2690
Wait else at doore: a fellow Councellor | 'Mong Boyes, Groomes, and
Lackeyes.   3010
**a fellow somewhat neere the doore, he should be a Brasi- | er*   3299
Man. You great fellow, | Stand close vp, or Ile make your head ake.   3349
FELLOWES = 4
This *Ipswich* fellowes insolence; or proclaime,   210
His Noble Friends and Fellowes; whom to leaue   915
Barke when their fellowes doe. By some of these   1526
These lazy knaues? Y'haue made a fine hand fellowes?   3329
FELLOWSHIP = 1
And all the Fellowship I hold now with him   1753
FELT = 2
Or felt the Flatteries that grow vpon it: 1780
For then, and not till then, he felt himselfe,   2623
FERDINAND = 1
And vnmatch'd Wit, and Iudgement. *Ferdinand*   1401
FERRARA = 1
A League betweene his Highnesse, and *Ferrara.*   2221
FETCH = 1*1
The Honourable Boord of Councell, out | Must fetch him in, he Papers.   130
**Is this a place to roare in? Fetch me a dozen Crab-tree*   3264
FEW = 6
Queen. I am solicited not by a few,   345

FEW *cont.*
But few now giue so great ones: 653
You few that lou'd me, | And dare be bold to weepe for *Buckingham,* 913
Of our flesh, few are Angels; out of which frailty 3060
This good man (few of you deserue that Title) 3208
(But few now liuing can behold that goodnesse) 3391
FIDDLE = 2
A French Song, and a Fiddle, ha's no Fellow. 621
L.San. The Diuell fiddle 'em, | I am glad they are going, 622
FIE *see* fye
FIELD = 2
That once was Mistris of the Field, and flourish'd, 1788
Her Foes shake like a Field of beaten Corne, 3401
FIELDS = *1
*But knock 'em downe by th' dozens? Is this More fields 3291
FIERCE = 1
To do in these fierce Vanities? I wonder, 102
FIGHT = 1*1
As Foole, and Fight is, beside forfeyting 20
*and fight for bitten Apples, that no Audience but the 3319
FIGHTS = 1
Pertaining thereunto; as Fights and Fire-workes, 605
FIGURE = 1
Whose Figure euen this instant Clowd puts on, 314
FILD = 1
This compel'd fortune: haue your mouth fild vp, | Before you open it. 1307
FILE = 2*1
Who should attend on him? He makes vp the File 126
Pertaines to th'State; and front but in that File 372
*stil, when sodainly a File of Boyes behind 'em, loose shot, 3314
FILL = 2
That fill the Court with quarrels, talke, and Taylors. 596
Goodnesse and he, fill vp one Monument. 938
FILLD = 1
Yet fill'd with my Abilities: Mine owne ends 2045
FILLING = 1
Toward the King first, then his Lawes, in filling 3063
FIND = 4*1
Find out, and he will take it. | *Card.* Let me see then, 785
I find him a fit fellow. 1164
**Queen.* Your Graces find me heere part of a Houswife, 1647
Pray Heauen the King may neuer find a heart 3090
And ye shall find me thankfull. Lead the way Lords, 3444
FINDE = 19*1
May heere finde Truth too. Those that come to see 10
*You'l finde it wholesome. Loe, where comes that Rock 173
Almost with rauish'd listning, could not finde 459
Finde mercy in the Law, 'tis his; if none, 566
Should finde a running Banket, ere they rested, 681
San. I would I were, | They should finde easie pennance. 686
The Cardnall instantly will finde imployment, 882
You'l finde a most vnfit time to disturbe him: 1097
Camp. Madam, you'l finde it so: | You wrong your Vertues 1805
I finde at such proud Rate, that it out-speakes | Possession of a Subiect. 1990
Car. Till I finde more then will, or words to do it, 2121
In time will finde their fit Rewards. That Seale 2130
Cranmer will finde a Friend will not shrinke from him. 2533

FINDE *cont.*

   Gard. The fruite she goes with | I pray for heartily, that it may finde   2795
I shall both finde your Lordship, Iudge and Iuror,   3109
How euer faulty, yet should finde respect   3124
And wisedome of my Councell; but I finde none: 3206
Go breake among the preasse, and finde away out   3345
To let the Troope passe fairely; or Ile finde   3346
Let none thinke Flattery; for they'l finde'em Truth.   3386
FINDES = 1
Since Vertue findes no friends) a Wife, a true one?   1759
FINE = 1
These lazy knaues? Y'haue made a fine hand fellowes?   3329
FINES = 1
Clap round Fines for neglect: y'are lazy knaues,   3341
FINGER = 5
From his Ambitious finger. What had he   101
Then layes his finger on his Temple: straight   1977
3 Among the crowd i'th'Abbey, where a finger   2474
The King will suffer but the little finger | Of this man to be vex'd?   3171
Hee, that dares most, but wag his finger at thee.   3200
FINIS *l.*3464 = 1
FIRE = 4
The fire that mounts the liquor til't run ore,   217
Or but allay the fire of passion.   222
Ile turne to sparkes of fire.   1430
Ye blew the fire that burnes ye: now haue at ye.   3180
FIREDRAKE = *1
*vnder the Line, they need no other pennance: that Fire-|Drake   3302
FIRE-WORKES = 1
Pertaining thereunto; as Fights and Fire-workes,   605
FIRST = 20*3
   The First and Happiest Hearers of the Towne,   25
Requires slow pace at first. Anger is like   203
Sur. First, it was vsuall with him; euery day   472
As first, good Company, good wine, good welcome, | Can make good
people.   672
San. The red wine first must rise   722
1. Tis likely, | By all coniectures: First *Kildares* Attendure;   872
Who first rais'd head against Vsurping *Richard,*   954
'Tis sweet at first t'acquire. After this Processe.   1210
My Conscience first receiu'd a tendernes,   1537
And prest in with this Caution. First, me thought   1553
And Doctors learn'd. First I began in priuate,   1573
How vnder my oppression I did reeke | When I first mou'd you.   1575
Lin. So please your Highnes, | The question did at first so stagger me,   1580
Crom. Presently | He did vnseale them, and the first he view'd,   1932
Haue at you. | First, that without the Kings assent or knowledge,   2206
The Duke of Suffolke is the first, and claimes   2399
*Exeunt, first passing ouer the Stage in Order and State, and | then, A
great Flourish of Trumpets.*   2445
or Palme in their hands. They first Conge vnto her, then   2646
Dance: and at certaine Changes, the first two hold a spare   2647
With me, since first you knew me.   2699
Cap. Noble Lady, | First mine owne seruice to your Grace, the next   2702
Toward the King first, then his Lawes, in filling   3063
When we first put this dangerous stone a rowling,   3168

FISH = 1
A very fresh Fish heere; fye, fye, fye vpon   1306
FISHES = 1
As rau'nous Fishes doe a Vessell follow   414
FIT = 8
A fit or two o'th' face, (but they are shrewd ones)   578
And fit it with such furniture as suites | The Greatnesse of his Person.   944
Thou art a cure fit for a King; you'r welcome   1118
I find him a fit fellow.   1164
It's fit this Royall Session do proceed,   1422
The last fit of my Greatnesse; good your Graces   1704
Fit for a Foole to fall by: What crosse Diuell   2094
In time will finde their fit Rewards. That Seale   2130
FITNESSE = 1
Camp. So please your Highnes, | The Queene being absent, 'tis a
needfull fitnesse,   1601
FITS = 1
It fits we thus proceed, or else no witnesse | Would come against you.   2904
FIUE *see* 5.
FIXD = 1
And so stand fix'd. Peace, Plenty, Loue, Truth, Terror,   3418
FIXETH = 1
*Cardinall in his passage, fixeth his eye on Buck-|ingham, and
Buckingham on him, | both full of disdaine.*   177
FIXT = 1
And fixt on Spirituall obiect, he should still   1997
FLANDERS = 1
Ambassador to the Emperor, you made bold | To carry into Flanders,
the Great Seale.   2216
FLATTERIES = 1
Or felt the Flatteries that grow vpon it: 1780
FLATTERY = 2
To heare such flattery now, and in my presence   3193
Let none thinke Flattery; for they'l finde 'em Truth.   3386
FLAWD = 2
For France hath flaw'd the League, and hath attach'd   151
Sent downe among 'em, which hath flaw'd the heart   348
FLESH = 1
Of our flesh, few are Angels; out of which frailty   3060
FLEW = 1
(Doublets, I thinke) flew vp, and had their Faces   2494
FLING = 1
Cromwel, I charge thee, fling away Ambition,   2355
FLOCKES = 1
But leaue their Flockes, and vnder your faire Conduct   763
FLOOD = 1
As doth a Rocke against the chiding Flood,   2073
FLOURISH = 5
1 A liuely Flourish of Trumpets. | 2 Then, two Iudges.   2422
*Exeunt, first passing ouer the Stage in Order and State, and | then, A
great Flourish of Trumpets.*   2445
Kath. So may he euer do, and euer flourish,   2714
Flourish. Enter King and Guard.   3368
Shall be, and make new Nations. He shall flourish,   3423
FLOURISHD = 1
That once was Mistris of the Field, and flourish'd,   1788

FLOW = 3
Such Noble Scoenes, as draw the Eye to flow   5
Whom from the flow of gall I name not, but   226
Seemes to flow from him? How, i'th'name of Thrift   1970
FLOWERS = 4
To his Musicke, Plants and Flowers   1624
wrought with Flowers bearing the Queenes Traine.   2442
*10 Certaine Ladies or Countesses, with plaine Circlets of | Gold, without
Flowers.   2443
With Maiden Flowers, that all the world may know   2762
FLOWING = 1
Doe's purpose honour to you no lesse flowing,   1278
FLUNG = 1
Would haue flung from him; but indeed he could not; 854
FLY = 1
Fly o're thy Royall head, and shade thy person | Vnder their blessed
wings.   2965
FLYE = 1
And Corne shall flye asunder. For I know   2909
FLYING = 1
Flying for succour to his Seruant *Banister,*   955
FOE = 2
Norf. Be aduis'd; | Heat not a Furnace for your foe so hot 212
I hold my most malicious Foe, and thinke not | At all a Friend to truth. 1441
FOES = 1
Her Foes shake like a Field of beaten Corne,   3401
FOLD = 1
To leaue, a thousand fold more bitter, then   1209
FOLLIES = 1
Dare mate a sounder man then Surrie can be, | And all that loue his
follies.   2163
FOLLOW = 5
Ile follow, and out-stare him. | *Nor.* Stay my Lord,   199
As rau'nous Fishes doe a Vessell follow   414
Follow such Creatures. That you may, faire Lady   1274
How eagerly ye follow my Disgraces   2125
Follow your enuious courses, men of Malice;   2128
FOLLOWD = 5
And follow'd with the generall throng, and sweat   29
Buc. Euery man, | After the hideous storme that follow'd, was 144
(Nay let 'em be vnmanly) yet are follow'd.   575
2 But what follow'd? | 3 At length, her Grace rose, and with modest
paces   2502
Haue follow'd both my Fortunes, faithfully,   2733
FOLLOWES = 7*2
(Who cannot erre) he did it. Now this followes,   250
If I command him followes my appointment,   1188
If this salute my blood a iot; it faints me | To thinke what followes. 1326
*distance, followes a Gentleman bearing the Purse, with the 1338
Be gladded in't by me. Then followes, that   1563
Well Sir, what followes?   2865
And am right sorrie to repeat what followes.   2893
Farewell all Physicke: and what followes then?   3075
*a Mantle, &c. Traine borne by a Lady: Then followes 3360
FOLLOWING = 1
To one aboue it selfe. Each following day   60

FONDNESSE = 1
Bin (out of fondnesse) superstitious to him?   1764
FOOLE = 5
As Foole, and Fight is, beside forfeyting   20
Made it a Foole, and Begger. The two Kings   72
Of Foole and Feather, that they got in France,   603
There's places of rebuke. He was a Foole;   1186
Fit for a Foole to fall by: What crosse Diuell   2094
FOOTE = 1
As much as one sound Cudgell of foure foote,   3276
FOOTING = 1
That little thought when she set footing heere,   1822
FOOT-BOY = 1
This honest man, wait like a lowsie Foot-boy   3209
FOOT-BOYES = 1
Who holds his State at dore 'mongst Purseuants, | Pages, and
Foot-boyes.   3022
FOR *l.*18 24 78 108 110 114 127 138 151 193 213 234 249 254 258 261 269
292 322 *329 358 362 368 392 399 403 420 453 528 544 579 594 602 624
651 657 *661 662 708 729 741 768 857 903 909 910 914 922 934 955 964
973 978 1002 1007 1008 1014 1017 *1028 *1031 *1057 1061 1079 1084
1114 1118 1128 1147 *1148 1156 1160 1169 1185 1187 1194 *1202 1214
1234 1244 1252 1257 1258 1260 1290 1305 1313 1317 1368 1399 1418
1436 1440 1449 1478 1500 1511 1517 1558 1593 1670 1694 1702 1703
1705 1711 1725 1726 1729 *1734 1737 1742 1786 1796 1810 1847 1851
1868 1882 1887 1911 1922 1942 1950 1956 2014 2048 2051 2067 2078
2092 2094 2129 2148 2227 2246 2265 2291 2308 2323 2335 2342 2412
2518 2563 2565 2577 2615 2623 2641 2661 2705 2728 2736 2737 2740
2757 2773 2774 2775 2796 2797 2811 2823 2838 2847 2849 2859 2884
2909 2940 2944 2982 2984 2997 3006 *3038 3065 3069 3102 3106 3125
3131 3141 *3144 3156 3197 3222 3227 3229 *3231 3234 3251 *3260
*3267 3285 *3300 *3307 *3319 3332 3341 3348 *3357 3385 3386 3447
3458 3460 3462 = 194*17
FORBEARE = 1
Cham. This is too much; | Forbeare for shame my Lords.   3140
FORBID = 2
To him that does best, God forbid els: Cardinall,   1162
The Lord forbid. | *Nor.* Marry Amen.   1896
FORCD = 2
The region of my Breast, which forc'd such way,   1551
In all my Miseries: But thou hast forc'd me   2344
FORCE = 3
The force of his owne merit makes his way   113
The force of this Commission: pray yelde too't;   437
And force them with a Constancy, the Cardinall   1828
FORE = 1
To bring my whole Cause 'fore his Holinesse,   1480
FORESAID = 1
And breake the foresaid peace. Let the King know   266
FORETOLD = 1
Foretold should be his last, full of Repentance,   2581
FOREUER *see* euer
FORE-RECITED = 1
The fore-recited practises, whereof   466
FORE-SEEING = 1
And Princely Care, fore-seeing those fell Mischiefes,   2828

FORE-SKIRT = 1
Is longer then his fore-skirt; by this time   1320
FORFEIT = 1
To forfeit all your Goods, Lands, Tenements, | Castles, and whatsoeuer,
and to be   2242
FORFEYTING = 1
As Foole, and Fight is, beside forfeyting   20
FORGD = 1
It forg'd him some designe, which being beleeu'd   529
FORGET = 1
Bid ye so farre forget your selues? I gaue ye   3212
FORGETFULL = 1
The Queene is comfortlesse, and wee forgetfull   1328
FORGETTING = 1
Forgetting (like a good man) your late Censure   1689
FORGIUE = 9
If I chance to talke a little wilde, forgiue me: 698
(Be what they will) I heartily forgiue'em;   906
Were hid against me, now to forgiue me frankly.   924
Buck. Sir *Thomas Louell,* I as free forgiue you   925
As I would be forgiuen: I forgiue all.   926
I haue done; and God forgiue me. | *Exeunt Duke and Traine.*   982
Qu. Do what ye will, my Lords: | And pray forgiue me;   1813
Car. Heauen forgiue me, | Euer God blesse your Highnesse.   2003
Sur. I forgiue him.   2236
FORGIUEN = 1
As I would be forgiuen: I forgiue all.   926
FORGO = 1
Crom. O my Lord, | Must I then leaue you? Must I needes forgo   2336
FORGOT = 1
Almost forgot my Prayres to content him?   1765
FORGOTTEN = 2
Was either pittied in him, or forgotten.   858
And when I am forgotten, as I shall be,   2347
FORMER = 2
Made former Wonders, it's. To day the French,   62
Beyond thoughts Compasse, that former fabulous Storie   80
FORMERLY = 1
They shall abound as formerly.   135
FORMES = 2
They turne to vicious formes, ten times more vgly   456
Appeare in formes more horrid) yet my Duty,   2072
FORNICATION = *1
*Bless me, what a fry of Fornication is at dore? On my   3294
FORRAIGNE = 3
And hither make, as great Embassadors | From forraigne Princes.   742
Kept him a forraigne man still, which so greeu'd him,   1182
Nor. Then, That in all you writ to Rome, or else | To Forraigne
Princes, *Ego & Rex meus*   2210
FORREIGNE = 1
Out of a forreigne wisedome, renouncing cleane   607
FORSAKE = 3
I must not yet forsake you: Let's be merry,   813
Yet are the Kings; and till my Soule forsake,   933
Pray for me, I must now forsake ye; the last houre   978
FORSOOTH = 2
And liue a Subiect? Nay forsooth, my Friends,   1715

FORSOOTH *cont.*
  Forsooth an Inuentòry, thus importing | The seuerall parcels of his
  Plate, his Treasure,   1987
FORT = 4*1
  2. I am sorry fort. | 1. So are a number more.   835
  *And with that bloud will make 'em one day groane for't.   952
  And euery true heart weepes for't. All that dare   1072
  Old.L. Beshrew me, I would, | And venture Maidenhead for't, and so
  would you   1232
  Cham. As I liue, | If the King blame me for't; Ile lay ye all   3338
FORTH = 4*1
  Card. Stand forth, & with bold spirit relate what you   468
  This is the state of Man; to day he puts forth   2253
  No Sun, shall euer vsher forth mine Honors,   2324
  Then lay me forth (although vnqueen'd) yet like   2764
  Be what they will, may stand forth face to face,   3095
FORTHWITH = 2
  Forthwith for what you come. Where's *Gardiner*?   1156
  I take it, by all voyces: That forthwith,   3145
FORTIE = 1
  Within these fortie houres, Surrey durst better | Haue burnt that
  Tongue, then saide so.   2140
FORTITUDE = 1
  (Out of a Fortitude of Soule, I feele)   2296
FORTUNE = 6
  That blinde Priest, like the eldest Sonne of Fortune,   1052
  That when the greatest stroake of Fortune falls   1068
  Yet if that quarrell. Fortune, do diuorce   1217
  This compel'd fortune: haue your mouth fild vp, | Before you open it. 1307
  You haue by Fortune, and his Highnesse fauors,   1471
  A way, if it take right, in spight of Fortune   2099
FORTUNES = 4
  Yet thus farre we are one in Fortunes; both   967
  The least rub in your fortunes, fall away   975
  Alas (poore Wenches) where are now your Fortunes?   1784
  Haue follow'd both my Fortunes, faithfully,   2733
FORTY = 1*1
  Old L. How tasts it? Is it bitter? Forty pence, no: 1310
  *might see from farre, some forty Truncheoners draw to   3310
FORWARD = 5
  Kin. Let him on: Goe forward.   524
  Of my alleadged reasons, driues this forward: 1595
  Farewell Nobilitie: let his Grace go forward,   2172
  As let 'em haue their rights, they are euer forward   2389
  For after the stout Earle Northumberland | Arrested him at Yorke, and
  brought him forward   2565
FOULE = 2
  His Noble Iurie, and foule Cause can witnesse.   2158
  But thus much, they are foule ones.   2193
FOUND = 13
  Kin. Ye haue found him Cardinall,   789
  2. Is he found guilty?   832
  Haue found him guilty of high Treason. Much   856
  Like water from ye, neuer found againe   976
  2. But that slander Sir, | Is found a truth now: for it growes agen 1006
  I be not found a Talker. | *Wol.* Sir, you cannot;   1121
  Nor. O feare him not, | His spell in that is out: the King hath found 1849

FOUND *cont.*
As I requir'd: and wot you what I found	1985
If what I now pronounce, you haue found true:	2037
Found his deserts. How innocent I was	2156
Found thee a way (out of his wracke) to rise in:	2352
And found the Blessednesse of being little.	2624
Pray heauen he found not my disgrace: for certaine	3006

FOUNDER = 1
All his trickes founder, and he brings his Physicke	1877

FOUNTS = 1
And proofes as cleere as Founts in *Iuly*, when	228

FOURE *see also* 4. = 3*3
What foure Thron'd ones could haue weigh'd | Such a compounded one?	53
*8 *A* Canopy, *borne by foure of the* Cinque-Ports, *vnder it*	2437
1 They that beare | The Cloath of Honour ouer her, are foure Barons | Of the Cinque-Ports.	2462
**Garland ouer her Head, at which the other foure make re-|uerend*	2648
As much as one sound Cudgell of foure foote,	3276
**standing Bowles for the Christening Guifts: Then foure*	3357

FOWLENESSE = 1
The fowlenesse is the punishment. I presume,	2058

FOWLST = 1
Turne me away: and let the fowl'st Contempt	1396

FOXE = 1
As shore of Rocke: attend. This holy Foxe,	233

FRAILE = 2
I her fraile sonne, among'st my Brethren mortall, | Must giue my tendance to.	2018
In our owne natures fraile, and capable	3059

FRAILTY = 1
Of our flesh, few are Angels; out of which frailty	3060

FRAME = 1
Queen. No, my Lord? | You know no more then others? But you frame	374

FRANCE = 7*1
Since last we saw in France?	40
For France hath flaw'd the League, and hath attach'd	151
Only to shew his pompe, as well in France,	238
England and France, might through their amity	257
*Is nam'd, your warres in France: this makes bold mouths,	393
Sur. Not long before your Highnesse sped to France,	497
L.Ch. Is't possible the spels of France should iuggle	571
Of Foole and Feather, that they got in France,	603

FRANKLY = 1
Were hid against me, now to forgiue me frankly.	924

FREE = 7*1
Free pardon to each man that has deny'de	436
Buck. Sir *Thomas Louell,* I as free forgiue you	925
Suff. And free vs from his slauery.	1077
*Haue their free voyces. Rome (the Nurse of Iudgement)	1141
That I am free of your Report, he knowes	1458
I free you from't: You are not to be taught	1523
Could speake this with as free a Soule as I doe.	1656
(Like free and honest men) our iust opinions, | And comforts to our cause.	1684

FREED = 1
Buc. The diuell speed him: No mans Pye is freed	100

FREEDOME = 1*1
*Card. Now Madam, may his Highnes liue in freedome,   552
You cannot with such freedome purge your selfe,   2899
FREELY = 6
Kin. Speake freely.   471
Or Gentleman that is not freely merry   712
Aboue all Princes, in committing freely   1134
Schollers allow'd freely to argue for her.   1160
In a rich Chaire of State, opposing freely   2487
And freely vrge against me.   3096
FREEZE = 3
Tongues spit their duties out, and cold hearts freeze   394
His Grace is entring. Nay, you must not freeze,   692
And the Mountaine tops that freeze,   1622
FRENCH = 9*1
Made former Wonders, it's. To day the French,   62
Buc. Why the Diuell, | Vpon this French going out, tooke he vpon him   123
The Peace betweene the French and vs, not valewes | The Cost that did
conclude it.   142
Concerning the French Iourney. I replide,   501
Men feare the French would proue perfidious   502
A French Song, and a Fiddle, ha's no Fellow.   621
Card. Good Lord Chamberlaine, | *Go, giue 'em welcome; you can
speake the French tongue   744
The French Kings Sister. Heauen will one day open   1074
By th'Bishop of Bayon, then French Embassador,   1539
The French Kings Sister; He shall marry her.   1941
FRENDED = 1
Not frended by his wish to your High person;   481
FRENDLESSE = 1
Alas, I am a Woman frendlesse, hopelesse.   1706
FRESH = 3
Healthfull, and euer since a fresh Admirer | Of what I saw there.   42
A very fresh Fish heere; fye, fye, fye vpon   1306
But 'tis so lately alter'd, that the old name | Is fresh about me.   2521
FRESHER = 2
Card. There's fresher ayre my Lord, | In the next Chamber.   810
Fresher then e're it was; and held for certaine   1008
FRESHLY = 1
Yet freshly pittied in our memories.   3079
FRET = *1
*Sur. I would 'twer somthing y would fret the string,   1965
FRIEND = 14
Will leaue vs neuer an vnderstanding Friend.   23
As you would to your Friend.   207
Is not my Friend. This to confirme my welcome,   713
He were mine Enemy? What Friend of mine,   1385
I hold my most malicious Foe, and thinke not | At all a Friend to truth.   1441
Or be a knowne friend 'gainst his Highnes pleasure,   1713
As 'twer in Loues particular, be more | To me your Friend, then any.   2064
Cranmer will finde a Friend will not shrinke from him.   2533
A worthy Friend. The King ha's made him | Master o'th'Iewell House,   2537
Stand these poore peoples Friend, and vrge the King | To do me this
last right.   2749
No great offence belongs too't, giue your Friend   2785
In vs thy Friend. Giue me thy hand, stand vp,   2914
You are alwayes my good Friend, if your will passe,   3108

FRIEND *cont.*
A shrewd turne, and hee's your friend for euer: 3251
FRIENDLY = 1
For I must thinke of that, which company | Would not be friendly too.   2859
FRIENDS = 3*1
His will is most malignant, and it stretches | Beyond you to your
friends.   482
Be sure you be not loose; for those you make friends,   973
Since Vertue findes no friends) a Wife, a true one?   1759
*Those we professe, Peace-makers, Friends, and Seruants.   1804
FRIENDS = 1
His Noble Friends and Fellowes; whom to leaue   915
FRIENDS = 8*1
Of thousand Friends: Then, in a moment, see   30
Or made it not mine too? Or which of your Friends   1383
Be by my Friends in Spaine, aduis'd; whose Counsaile   1409
Your hopes and friends are infinite. | *Queen.* In England,   1709
And liue a Subiect? Nay forsooth, my Friends,   1715
No Friends, no Hope, no Kindred weepe for me?   1786
And fee my Friends in Rome.) O Negligence!   2093
*Be friends for shame my Lords: My Lord of *Canterbury*   3231
Your faithfull friends o'th' Suburbs? We shall haue   3331
FRIENDSHIP = 1
Of equall Friendship and Proceeding. Alas Sir: 1372
FRIGHTED = 1
W^e *haue frighted with our Trumpets: so 'tis cleare,*   3453
FROM *l.*101 105 120 163 209 226 227 258 288 302 331 *353 *390 425 429
432 509 667 699 743 776 854 883 *889 964 971 976 991 *1033 *1070
1077 1081 *1093 1218 1289 1296 *1347 1351 1376 1388 1439 1451 1461
1641 1771 *1798 *1809 1891 *1945 1970 2009 2070 2085 2086 2097 2104
2115 2120 2149 2157 2170 2187 2287 2326 2382 2384 2410 2485 2526
2533 2607 2608 2629 2689 2694 2741 2778 2832 2842 2990 3103 3270
*3310 3327 3333 3344 3365 3408 *3415 3416 = 80*12
FROMT = 1
I free you from't: You are not to be taught   1523
FRONT = 1
Pertaines to th'State; and front but in that File   372
FROST = 2
The third day, comes a Frost; a killing Frost,   2256
FROWNES = 1
Cran. I am fearefull: Wherefore frownes he thus?   2880
FROWNING = 4
The pennance lyes on you; if these faire Ladies | Passe away frowning.   706
Exit King, frowning vpon the Cardinall, the Nobles | *throng after him*
smiling, and whispering.   2081
He parted Frowning from me, as if Ruine   2085
Enter King frowning on them, takes his Seate.   3181
FRUITE = 1
Gard. The fruite she goes with | I pray for heartily, that it may finde   2795
FRUITFULL = 1
A hand as fruitfull as the Land that feeds vs,   643
FRY = *1
*Bless me, what a fry of Fornication is at dore? On my   3294
FRYER = 1
Kin. What was that *Henton*? | *Sur.* Sir, a *Chartreux* Fryer,   492
FRYERS = 1
For such receipt of Learning, is Black-Fryers: 1194

FULFILLD = 2
　I will implore. If not, i'th'name of God | Your pleasure be fulfill'd.　　1410
　But their pleasures | Must be fulfill'd, and I attend with patience.　　3012
FULL = 19*1
　Sad, high, and working, full of State and Woe:　　4
　Distinctly his full Function: who did guide,　　91
　Cardinall in his passage, fixeth his eye on Buck-|ingham, and
　Buckingham on him, | both full of disdaine.　　177
　A full hot Horse, who being allow'd his way　　204
　Shall shine at full vpon them. Some attend him. | *All rise, and Tables*
　remou'd.　　748
　1. O, this is full of pitty; Sir, it cals　　984
　'Tis full of woe: yet I can giue you inckling　　988
　Full of sad thoughts and troubles.　　1044
　You signe your Place, and Calling, in full seeming,　　1468
　I then did feele full sicke, and yet not well,　　1571
　The full cause of our comming. | *Queen.* Speake it heere.　　1652
　Among my Maids, full little (God knowes) looking　　1701
　Haue I, with all my full Affections　　1762
　King. Good my Lord, | *You are full of Heauenly stuffe, and beare the
　Inuentory　　2005
　And from that full Meridian of my Glory,　　2104
　And when he thinkes, good easie man, full surely　　2257
　2 'Tis well: The Citizens | I am sure haue shewne at full their Royall
　minds,　　2387
　Had the full view of, such a noyse arose,　　2491
　And with the same full State pac'd backe againe　　2514
　Foretold should be his last, full of Repentance,　　2581
FULLERS = 1
　The Spinsters, Carders, Fullers, Weauers, who　　361
FULLY = 1
　At once, and fully satisfide) whether euer I　　1513
FULL-CHARGD = 1
　Of a full-charg'd confederacie, and giue thankes　　323
FUNCTION = 2
　Distinctly his full Function: who did guide,　　91
　Your Braine, and euery Function of your power,　　2062
FURNACE = 1
　Norf. Be aduis'd; | Heat not a Furnace for your foe so hot　　212
FURNISH = 2
　That he may furnish and instruct great Teachers,　　452
　To furnish Rome, and to prepare the wayes　　2226
FURNISHD = 1*1
　care I had, I saw well chosen, ridden, and furnish'd.　　1029
　My *Wolsey*, see it furnish'd, O my Lord,　　1196
FURNITURE = 1
　And fit it with such furniture as suites | The Greatnesse of his Person.　　944
FURTHER = 16
　Together; To consider further, that | What his high Hatred would effect,
　wants not　　166
　Is pleas'd you shall to th'Tower, till you know | How he determines
　further.　　297
　Card. And for me, | I haue no further gone in this, then by　　403
　That is new trim'd; but benefit no further　　415
　Further in the proceeding. *Exit Secret.(ary)*　　445
　It can do me no damage; adding further,　　531
　There's mischiefe in this man; canst thou say further?　　536

FURTHER *cont.*

For further life in this world I ne're hope,	910
Or how farre further (Shall) is warranted	1450
That we adiourne this Court till further day;	1603
Till you heare further from his Highnesse. | *Car.* Stay:	2115
Suf. Lord Cardinall, the Kings further pleasure is,	2237
O'th'Rolles, and the Kings Secretary. Further Sir,	2813
But that till further Triall, in those Charges	2900
Your selfe, and your Accusers, and to haue heard you | Without	
indurance further.	2919
There to remaine till the Kings further pleasure	3147

FUTURE = 1

Neglect him not; make vse now, and prouide | For thine owne future	
safety.	2334

FYE = 3

A very fresh Fish heere; fye, fye, fye vpon	1306

GAINE = 2

For mine owne ends, (Indeed to gaine the Popedome,	2092
So I grow stronger, you more Honour gaine. *Exeunt.*	3255

GAINSAY = 1

That I gainsay my Deed, how may he wound,	1455

GAINST = 2

Gainst me, that I cannot take peace with:	928
Or be a knowne friend 'gainst his Highnes pleasure,	1713

GAIT *see* gate

GALL = 1

Whom from the flow of gall I name not, but	226

GALLANT = 1

She is a gallant Creature, and compleate	1890

GALLANTS = 1

L.Cham. What is't for? | *Lou.* The reformation of our trauel'd Gallants,	594

GALLD = 1

Vpon the daring Huntsman that has gall'd him:	2087

GALLERY = 1

King. Auoyd the Gallery. *Louel seemes to stay.*	2877

GALLOWES = *1

**Port.* Belong to th' Gallowes, and be hang'd ye Rogue:	3263

GAMSTER = 1

An.B. You are a merry Gamster | My Lord *Sands.*	725

GAP = 1

Stands in the gap and Trade of moe Preferments,	2814

GAPING = 1

*you take the Court for Parish Garden: ye rude Slaues, | leaue your	
gaping.	3260

GAR = 1

GARD = 19*2

GARDED = 1

In a long Motley Coate, garded with Yellow,	17

GARDEN = *1

*you take the Court for Parish Garden: ye rude Slaues, | leaue your	
gaping.	3260

GARDINER *see also Gar., Gard.* = 8*1

Forthwith for what you come. Where's *Gardiner?*	1156
Prethee call *Gardiner* to me, my new Secretary.	1163
Enter Gardiner.	1165
Kin. Come hither *Gardiner.* | *Walkes and whispers.*	1170
Kin. Deliuer this with modesty to th' Queene. | *Exit Gardiner.*	1191

GARDINER cont.
  3 *Stokeley* and *Gardiner*, the one of Winchester,   2525
  Enter Gardiner Bishop of Winchester, a Page with a Torch | before him,
  met by Sir Thomas Louell.   2769
  I hinder you too long: Good night, Sir *Thomas.* | *Exit Gardiner and*
  Page.   2833
  *Gardiner, seat themselues in Order on each side.   3040
GARLAND = *5
  *Garland ouer her Head, at which the other foure make re-|uerend   2648
  *Curtsies. Then the two that held the Garland, deli-|uer   2649
  *in their Changes, and holding the Garland ouer her   2651
  *head. Which done, they deliuer the same Garland to the   2652
  *their Dancing vanish, carrying the Garland with them. | The Musicke
  continues.   2656
GARLANDS = 1*1
  *clad in white Robes, wearing on their heades Garlands of   2644
  And brought me Garlands (*Griffith*) which I feele   2668
GARMENT = 1
  Dashing the Garment of this Peace, aboaded | The sodaine breach on't.   148
GART = 1
GARTER see also Gart. = *3
  *5 Maior of London, *bearing the Mace. Then* Garter, *in*   2426
  *Garter, Cranmer, Duke of Norfolke with his Marshals   3355
  *The Troope passe once about the Stage, and Gar-|ter speakes.   3362
GATE = 2
  That's clapt vpon the Court Gate.   593
  Springs out into fast gate, then stops againe,   1978
GATHERD = 1
  That they had gather'd a wise Councell to them   1405
GAUE = 12
  Order gaue each thing view. The Office did   90
  Continue in my Liking? Nay, gaue notice   1387
  By this my Issues faile, and that gaue to me   1565
  (Mine, and your Master) with his owne hand, gaue me: 2132
  Ti'de it by Letters Patents. Now, who'll take it? | *Sur.* The King that
  gaue it.   2135
  Out of the paine you suffer'd, gaue no eare too't.   2560
  To whom he gaue these words. O Father Abbot,   2574
  He gaue his Honors to the world agen,   2583
  Of his owne body he was ill, and gaue | The Clergy ill example.   2598
  Crom. My mind gaue me, | In seeking tales and Informations   3176
  In dayly thankes; that gaue vs such a Prince;   3184
  Bid ye so farre forget your selues? I gaue ye   3212
GAUST = 1
  That might haue mercie on the fault, thou gau'st him: 2150
GAUT = 1
  Car. The Packet Cromwell, | Gau't you the King?   1928
GENERALL = 6
  And follow'd with the generall throng, and sweat   29
  Into a generall Prophesie; That this Tempest   147
  S.Hen.Guilf. Ladyes, | A generall welcome from his Grace   666
  One generall Tongue vnto vs. This good man,   1143
  1 'Tis very true. But that time offer'd sorrow, | This generall ioy.   2385
  Commotions, vprores, with a generall Taint   3076
GENERALLY = 1
  (And generally) who euer the King fauours,   881

GENT = 2*1
GENTLE = 9*1
 Will be deceyu'd. For gentle Hearers, know   18
 Cham. It was a gentle businesse, and becomming   1269
 *Cham. You beare a gentle minde, & heau'nly blessings 1273
 Of disposition gentle, and of wisedome,   1446
 I know you haue a Gentle, Noble temper,   1802
 Still in thy right hand, carry gentle Peace   2360
 For feare we wake her. Softly, gentle *Patience.*   2641
 That gentle Physicke giuen in time, had cur'd me: 2710
 With gentle Trauaile, to the gladding of | Your Highnesse with an
 Heire.   2854
 Pace 'em not in their hands to make 'em gentle;   3070
GENTLEMAN see also Gent., Gent.Vsh., 1., 2., 3. = 10*3
 That Gentleman of *Buckinghams,* in person,   325
 The Gentleman is Learn'd, and a most rare Speaker, 450
 (This was his Gentleman in trust) of him   464
 Or Gentleman that is not freely merry   712
 *distance, followes a Gentleman bearing the Purse, with the 1338
 *each a Siluer Crosse: Then a Gentleman Vsher bare-| headed, 1340
 Enter a Gentleman. | Queen. How now?   1633
 2 A bold braue Gentleman. That should bee | The Duke of Suffolke. 2451
 Enter a third Gentleman.   2472
 her Gentleman Vsher, and Patience| her Woman.   2549
 A Gentleman sent from the King, to see you.   2689
 Gard. But Sir, Sir, | Heare me Sir *Thomas,* y'are a Gentleman 2803
 *Cran. I hope I am not too late, and yet the Gentleman 2989
GENTLEMEN = 9*1
 and diuers other Ladies, & Gentlemen, as Guests   663
 Cham. Well said my Lord: | So now y'are fairely seated: Gentlemen, 704
 Ladies you are not merry; Gentlemen, | Whose fault is this? 720
 By all your good leaues Gentlemen; heere Ile make | My royall choyce. 787
 And not to kisse you. A health Gentlemen, | Let it goe round. 802
 Enter two Gentlemen at seuerall Doores.   820
 *Siluer Mace: Then two Gentlemen bearing two great 1342
 (Whom if he liue, will scarse be Gentlemen)   2185
 Enter two Gentlemen, meeting one another.   2378
 Come Gentlemen, ye shall go my way,   2542
GENTLENESSE = 1
 (If thy rare qualities, sweet gentlenesse,   1501
GENTLEWOMAN = 1
 Car. The late Queenes Gentlewoman?   1951
GENTLY = 1
 Kath. So may he rest, | His Faults lye gently on him: 2585
GENTRY = 1
 Of all the Gentry; for the most part such   127
GENTVSH = 1
GERMANY = 1
 The vpper *Germany* can deerely witnesse: 3078
GESSE = 1
 King. Now by thy lookes | I gesse thy Message. Is the Queene deliuer'd? 2967
GET = 5
 Cannot vouchsafe this burthen, tis too weake | Euer to get a Boy. 1253
 Vpon my smiles. Go get thee from me *Cromwel,*   2326
 None better in my Kingdome. Get you gone,   2958
 Por. You i'th'Chamblet, get vp o'th' raile,   3351
 This happy Child, did I get any thing.   3437

GETS = 1
   Man. Alas I know not, how gets the Tide in?   3275
GETTING = 1
   And though he were vnsatisfied in getting,   2613
GIANT *see* gyant
GIFT *see* guift
GIFTS *see* guifts
GILBERT = 2
   One *Gilbert Pecke*, his Councellour.   305
   Sir *Gilbert Pecke* his Chancellour, and *Iohn Car,*   847
GILDE = 1
   Or gilde againe the Noble Troopes that waighted   2325
GILT = 1*1
   As Cherubins, all gilt: the Madams too,   67
   his Coate of Armes, and on his head he wore a Gilt Copper | Crowne.   2427
GIRLE *see* gyrle
GIUE = 27*5
   The Subiect will deserue it. Such as giue   8
   Buck. Pray giue me fauour Sir: This cunning Cardinall   244
   *As giue a Crutch to th'dead. But our Count-Cardinall   248
   Of a full-charg'd confederacie, and giue thankes   323
   Would giue it quicke consideration; for   399
   L.San. Tis time to giue 'em Physicke, their diseases | Are growne so
   catching.   614
   But few now giue so great ones: 653
   Card. Good Lord Chamberlaine, | *Go, giue 'em welcome; you can
   speake the French tongue   744
   Then giue my Charge vp to Sir *Nicholas Vaux,*   940
   And giue your hearts to; when they once perceiue   974
   'Tis full of woe: yet I can giue you inckling   988
   I would your Grace would giue vs but an houre | Of priuate conference.   1123
   Wol. Giue me your hand: much ioy & fauour to you;   1166
   To giue her the auaunt, it is a pitty | Would moue a Monster.   1211
   Shut doore vpon me, and so giue me vp   1397
   *Then marke th'inducement. Thus it came; giue heede | (too't: 1536
   Into your priuate Chamber; we shall giue you   1651
   That any English man dare giue me Councell?   1712
   To giue vp willingly that Noble Title   1775
   Sur. I am ioyfull | To meete the least occasion, that may giue me   1833
   I her fraile sonne, among'st my Brethren mortall, | Must giue my
   tendance to.   2018
   Giue him a little earth for Charity.   2577
   Yet thus farre *Griffith,* giue me leaue to speake him,   2587
   Then man could giue him; he dy'de, fearing God.   2626
   Beseeching him to giue her vertuous breeding.   2725
   No great offence belongs too't, giue your Friend   2785
   Come, come, giue me your hand.   2891
   In vs thy Friend. Giue me thy hand, stand vp,   2914
   They shall no more preuaile, then we giue way too: 2946
   King. Giue her an hundred Markes.   2979
   Out of the gripes of cruell men, and giue it   3163
   Into whose hand, I giue thy Life. | *Cran. Amen.*   3379
GIUEN = 10
   Abur. I cannot tell | What Heauen hath giuen him: let some Grauer eye   116
   Or ha's giuen all before, and he begins | A new Hell in himselfe.   121
   The other moity ere you aske is giuen,   337
   Wol. Your Grace ha's giuen a President of wisedome   1133

GIUEN *cont.*
Hath my behauiour giuen to your displeasure,   1374
Suf. There's order giuen for her Coronation: 1887
That gentle Physicke giuen in time, had cur'd me: 2710
If Heauen had pleas'd to haue giuen me longer life   2744
Giuen eare to our Complaint, of his great Grace,   2827
You would haue giuen me your Petition, that   2917
GIUES = 3
Out of his Selfe-drawing Web. O giues vs note,   112
A guift that heauen giues for him, which buyes | A place next to the
King.   114
Giues way to vs) I much feare. If you cannot   1845
GIUING = 1
About the giuing backe the Great Seale to vs,   2247
GLAD = 9
L.Cham. I'm glad 'tis there;   597
L.San. The Diuell fiddle 'em, | I am glad they are going,   622
Card. I am glad | Your Grace is growne so pleasant.   793
Yea, subiect to your Countenance: Glad, or sorry,   1380
I should be glad to heare such Newes as this | Once euery houre.   1855
I deeme you an ill Husband, and am glad   2011
Crom. I am glad your Grace, | Ha's made that right vse of it.   2292
And am right glad to catch this good occasion   2907
Cran. So. | *Buts.* This is a Peere of Malice: I am glad   2999
GLADDED = 1
Be gladded in't by me. Then followes, that   1563
GLADDING = 1
With gentle Trauaile, to the gladding of | Your Highnesse with an
Heire.   2854
GLASSE = 1
That swallowed so much treasure, and like a glasse   241
GLEANING = 1
Sur. Yes, that goodnesse | Of gleaning all the Lands wealth into one,   2176
GLISTRING = 1
Then to be perk'd vp in a glistring griefe, | And weare a golden sorrow.   1226
GLORIES = 1
O *Cromwell,* | The King ha's gone beyond me: All my Glories   2321
GLORY = 8
Those Sunnes of Glory, those two Lights of Men | Met in the vale of
Andren.   46
Nor. Then you lost | The view of earthly glory: Men might say   57
Yet let 'em looke they glory not in mischiefe;   907
And from that full Meridian of my Glory,   2104
This many Summers in a Sea of Glory,   2261
Vaine pompe, and glory of this World, I hate ye,   2266
Say *Wolsey,* that once trod the wayes of Glory,   2350
Cran. The greatest Monarch now aliue may glory   3235
GLOSSE = 1
That's the plaine truth; your painted glosse discouers   3120
GO = 13*1
Buc. Oh you go farre.   83
What 'tis you go about: to climbe steepe hilles   202
Card. Good Lord Chamberlaine, | *Go, giue 'em welcome; you can
speake the French tongue   744
Go too; Ile make ye know your times of businesse: 1113
Farewell Nobilitie: let his Grace go forward,   2172
Vpon my smiles. Go get thee from me *Cromwel,*   2326

GO *cont.*
That had not halfe a weeke to go, like Rammes   2497
Come Gentlemen, ye shall go my way,   2542
On that Coelestiall Harmony I go too. | *Sad and solemne Musicke.*   2638
To vse so rude behauiour. Go too, kneele.   2686
Lou. I must to him too | Before he go to bed. Ile take my leaue.   2781
Vpon this naughty Earth? Go too, go too,   2939
Go breake among the preasse, and finde away out   3345
GOD = 25*1
Aske God for Temp'rance, that's th'appliance onely | Which your
disease requires.   193
Queen. God mend all.   554
1. Whether away so fast? | 2. O, God saue ye: 821
I haue done; and God forgiue me. | *Exeunt Duke and Traine.*   982
Suff. Pray God he doe, | Hee'l neuer know himselfe else.   1054
Kin. Who's there? Ha? | *Norff.* Pray God he be not angry.   1103
To him that does best, God forbid els: Cardinall,   1162
An. Now I pray God, *Amen.*   1272
I will implore. If not, i'th'name of God | Your pleasure be fulfill'd.   1410
Or God will punish me. I do beleeue | (Induc'd by potent
Circumstances) that   1433
Haue to you, but with thankes to God for such   1517
Ye speake like honest men, (pray God ye proue so)   1695
Among my Maids, full little (God knowes) looking   1701
Cham. Now God incense him, | And let him cry Ha, lowder.   1906
Car. Heauen forgiue me, | Euer God blesse your Highnesse.   2003
Is your displeasure with the King. | *Card.* God blesse him.   2301
Had I but seru'd my God, with halfe the Zeale   2370
*1 God saue you Sir. Where haue you bin broiling?   2473
Then man could giue him; he dy'de, fearing God.   2626
Suf. God safely quit her of her Burthen, and   2853
Cran. God, and your Maiesty | Protect mine innocence, or I fall into   2942
And of a louely Boy: the God of heauen   2971
(God turne their hearts, I neuer sought their malice)   3008
And that I would not for a Cow, God saue her.   3285
With this Kisse, take my Blessing: God protect thee,   3378
God shall be truely knowne, and those about her,   3407
GODFATHER = 1
You must be Godfather, and answere for her.   3234
GODMOTHER = *2
Norfolke, Godmother, bearing the Childe richly habited in   3359
the Marchionesse Dorset, the other Godmother, and La-|dies.   3361
GODS = 7*1
All Clinquant all in Gold, like Heathen Gods   63
And lift my Soule to Heauen. | Lead on a Gods name.   920
And without Tryall, fell; Gods peace be with him.   957
An. Oh Gods will, much better | She ne're had knowne pompe; though't
be temporall,   1215
Against your Sacred Person; in Gods name   1395
(Which Gods dew quench) therefore, I say againe,   1438
*Thy Gods, and Truths. Then if thou fall'st (O *Cromwell*)   2363
He's honest on mine Honor. Gods blest Mother,   2956
GOD-FATHER = *1
*thousand, here will bee Father, God-father, and all to-|gether.   3296
GOE = 11
Buck. Sir, | I am thankfull to you, and Ile goe along   223
That Vertue must goe through: we must not stint   411

GOE *cont.*
Kin. Let him on: Goe forward.	524
And not to kisse you. A health Gentlemen, | Let it goe round.	802
Heare what I say, and then goe home and lose me.	898
Goe with me like good Angels to my end,	917
Kin. We are busie; goe.	1125
Kin. Goe thy wayes *Kate*,	1497
Vnder your hands and Seales; therefore goe on,	1592
Might goe one way, and safely; and the end	3084
Cran. For me? | Must I goe like a Traytor thither?	3156

GOES = 5*1
*goes about the Court, comes to the King, and kneeles at | his Feete. Then speakes.	1365
Then out it goes. What though I know her vertuous	1955
King takes his Seat, whispers Louell, who goes | to the Cardinall.	2001
The Princesse Dowager? How goes her businesse?	2405
Grif. Well, the voyce goes Madam,	2564
Gard. The fruite she goes with | I pray for heartily, that it may finde	2795

GOING = 6
Buc. Why the Diuell, | Vpon this French going out, tooke he vpon him	123
L.San. The Diuell fiddle 'em, | I am glad they are going,	622
L.Cham. Sir *Thomas*, | Whither were you a going?	633
Shee's going away. | *Kin.* Call her againe.	1486
Going to Chappell: and the voyce is now | Onely about her Corronation.	2318
Grif. She is going Wench. Pray, pray. | *Pati.* Heauen comfort her.	2678

GOLD = 4*3
All Clinquant all in Gold, like Heathen Gods	63
And pau'd with gold: the Emperor thus desir'd,	264
Hath shew'd him gold; my life is spand already:	312
*6 Marquesse Dorset, bearing a Scepter of Gold, on his head,	2429
*a Demy Coronall of Gold. With him, the Earle of Surrey,	2430
*9 The Olde Dutchesse of Norfolke, in a Coronall of Gold,	2441
*10 Certaine Ladies or Countesses, with plaine Circlets of | Gold, without Flowers.	2443

GOLDEN = 1*1
Then to be perk'd vp in a glistring griefe, | And weare a golden sorrow.	1226
*Bayes, and golden Vizards on their faces, Branches of Bayes	2645

GONE *see also* begone = 8*1
He bores me with some tricke; He's gone to'th'King:	198
Card. And for me, | I haue no further gone in this, then by	403
The Cardinals and Sir *Thomas Louels* heads | Should haue gone off.	533
Gone slightly o're loose steppes, and now are mounted	1472
Suf. Which of the Peeres | Haue vncontemn'd gone by him, or at least	1837
O *Cromwell*, | The King ha's gone beyond me: All my Glories	2321
*Kath. Spirits of peace, where are ye? Are ye all gone?	2658
Ha? I haue said. Be gone. | What? *Exeunt Louell and Denny.*	2878
None better in my Kingdome. Get you gone,	2958

GOOD = 105*13
Buckingham. | Good morrow, and well met. How haue ye done	38
Would by a good Discourser loose some life,	86
Nor. All this was ordred by the good Discretion	98
Of all their Loyalties; wherein, although | My good Lord Cardinall, they vent reproches	349
On the complaint o'th'Tenants; take good heed	520
L.Ch. As farre as I see, all the good our English	576
My Barge stayes; | Your Lordship shall along: Come, good Sir *Thomas,*	654

GOOD *cont.*

As first, good Company, good wine, good welcome, | Can make good people.	672
And to you all good health.	714
Card. Good Lord Chamberlaine, | *Go, giue 'em welcome; you can speake the French tongue	744
A good digestion to you all; and once more	751
By all your good leaues Gentlemen; heere Ile make | My royall choyce.	787
*Good my Lord Cardinall: I haue halfe a dozen healths,	814
Buck. All good people, | You that thus farre haue come to pitty me;	896
Goe with me like good Angels to my end,	917
But where they meane to sinke ye: all good people	977
1. Good Angels keepe it from vs:	991
To the good Queene, possest him with a scruple	1011
Cham. Good day to both your Graces.	1041
That Angels loue good men with: Euen of her,	1067
Norfolke. Thankes my good Lord *Chamberlaine.*	1099
Who's there? my good Lord Cardinall? O my *Wolsey,*	1116
Vse vs, and it: My good Lord, haue great care,	1120
One generall Tongue vnto vs. This good man,	1143
For he would needs be vertuous. That good Fellow,	1187
So good a Lady, that no Tongue could euer	1204
If you might please to stretch it. | *Anne.* Nay, good troth.	1241
L.Cham. Good morrow Ladies; what wer't worth to | (know	1264
An. My good Lord, | Not your demand; it values not your asking:	1266
The action of good women, there is hope | All will be well.	1270
Commends his good opinion of you, to you; and	1277
An. Good Lady, | Make your selfe mirth with your particular fancy,	1323
And take your good Grace from me? Heauen witnesse,	1376
Or touch of her good Person?	1520
I speake my good Lord Cardnall, to this point;	1532
Of the good Queene; but the sharpe thorny points	1594
They should bee good men, their affaires as righteous:	1643
Queen. O good my Lord, no Latin;	1665
To taint that honour euery good Tongue blesses;	1679
You haue too much good Lady: But to know	1681
Forgetting (like a good man) your late Censure	1689
My Lords, I thanke you both for your good wills,	1694
The last fit of my Greatnesse; good your Graces	1704
You turne the good we offer, into enuy.	1745
Car. Madam, you wander from the good | We ayme at.	1771
*You'l'd feele more comfort. Why shold we (good Lady)	1792
King. Good my Lord, | *You are full of Heauenly stuffe, and beare the Inuentory	2005
And 'tis a kinde of good deede to say well,	2025
To'th'good of your most Sacred Person, and	2047
Car. I do professe, | That for your Highnesse good, I euer labour'd	2066
As you respect the common good, the State	2183
So fare you well, my little good Lord Cardinall. | *Exeunt all but Wolsey.*	2249
Wol. So farewell, to the little good you beare me.	2251
And when he thinkes, good easie man, full surely	2257
Neuer so truly happy, my good *Cromwell,*	2283
Thy hopefull seruice perish too. Good *Cromwell*	2333
So good, so Noble, and so true a Master?	2338
Crom. Good Sir, haue patience. | *Card.* So I' haue. Farewell	2373
Where she remaines now sicke. | 2 Alas good Lady.	2417
2 Good Sir, speake it to vs? | 3 As well as I am able. The rich streame	2481

GOOD *cont.*

2 He of Winchester | Is held no great good louer of the Archbishops, |
The vertuous *Cranmer.* 2528
Kath. Pre'thee good *Griffith*, tell me how he dy'de. 2561
To heare me speake his good now? | *Kath.* Yes good *Griffith*, 2603
He was a Scholler, and a ripe, and good one: 2609
Vnwilling to out-liue the good that did it. 2618
I haue not long to trouble thee. Good *Griffith*, 2635
Grif. She is asleep: Good wench, let's sit down quiet, 2640
Grif. I am most ioyfull Madam, such good dreames | Possesse your
Fancy. 2670
And heartily entreats you take good comfort. 2707
Kath. O my good Lord, that comfort comes too late, 2708
How does his Highnesse? | *Cap.* Madam, in good health. 2712
For honestie, and decent Carriage | A right good Husband (let him be a
Noble) 2737
These are the whole Contents, and good my Lord, 2746
Call in more women. When I am dead, good Wench, 2760
*To waste these times. Good houre of night Sir *Thomas*: 2776
Good time, and liue: but for the Stocke Sir *Thomas*, 2797
Shee's a good Creature, and sweet-Ladie do's | Deserue our better
wishes. 2801
I hinder you too long: Good night, Sir *Thomas*. | *Exit Gardiner and
Page.* 2833
Lou. Many good nights, my Lord, I rest your seruant. 2835
Almost each pang, a death. | *King.* Alas good Lady. 2851
Suf. I wish your Highnesse | A quiet night, and my good Mistris will |
Remember in my Prayers. 2861
King. Charles good night. *Exit Suffolke.* 2864
King. Ha? Canterbury? | *Den.* I my good Lord. 2869
King. Pray you arise | My good and gracious Lord of Canterburie: 2887
Ah my good Lord, I greeue at what I speake, 2892
And am right glad to catch this good occasion 2907
King. Stand vp, good Canterbury, 2912
Cran. Most dread Liege, | The good I stand on, is my Truth and
Honestie: 2921
The trap is laid for me. | *King.* Be of good cheere, 2944
Will make my boldnesse, manners. Now good Angels 2964
At least good manners; as not thus to suffer 3028
Chan. My good Lord Archbishop, I'm very sorry 3056
Cran. My good Lords; Hitherto, in all the Progresse 3080
Cran. Ah my good Lord of *Winchester*: I thanke you, 3107
You are alwayes my good Friend, if your will passe, 3108
By your good fauour, too sharpe; Men so Noble, 3123
Gard. Good M.(aster) Secretary, | I cry your Honour mercie; you may
worst | Of all this Table say so. 3127
Cran. Stay good my Lords, | I haue a little yet to say. Looke there my
Lords, 3160
Not onely good and wise, but most religious: 3185
Kin. You were euer good at sodaine Commendations, 3191
Good man sit downe: Now let me see the proudest 3199
This good man (few of you deserue that Title) 3208
Kin. Good Man, those ioyfull teares shew thy true | (hearts, 3248
Within. Good M.(aster) Porter I belong to th' Larder. 3262
Port. I shall be with you presently, good M.(aster) *Puppy*, 3287
*was quartered; they fell on, I made good my place; at 3312
Cran. And to your Royall Grace, & the good Queen, 3369

GOOD *cont.*
  Kin. Thanke you good Lord Archbishop: 3374
  With all the Vertues that attend the good,   3397
  Good growes with her.   3403
  I thanke ye all. To you my good Lord Maior,   3441
  And you good Brethren, I am much beholding: 3442
  All the expected good w'are like to heare.   3457
  The mercifull construction of good women,   3459
GOODLIEST = 1
  Beleeue me Sir, she is the goodliest Woman   2489
GOODMAN = *1
  *There make before them. Looke, the goodman weeps: 2955
GOODNESSE = 13
  Therefore, for Goodnesse sake, and as you are knowne   24
  Goodnesse and he, fill vp one Monument.   938
  Must now confesse, if they haue any goodnesse,   1138
  For Goodnesse sake, consider what you do,   1796
  During my life; and to confirme his Goodnesse,   2134
  Whil'st your great Goodnesse, out of holy pitty, | Absolu'd him with an
  Axe.   2151
  Card. All Goodnesse | Is poyson to thy Stomacke.   2174
  Sur. Yes, that goodnesse | Of gleaning all the Lands wealth into one,   2176
  The goodnesse of your intercepted Packets   2179
  You writ to'th Pope, against the King: your goodnesse   2180
  Kath. In which I haue commended to his goodnesse   2722
  Gart. Heauen | From thy endlesse goodnesse, send prosperous life,   3364
  (But few now liuing can behold that goodnesse)   3391
GOODS = 2
  Our Merchants goods at Burdeux.   152
  To forfeit all your Goods, Lands, Tenements, | Castles, and whatsoeuer,
  and to be   2242
GOSSIPS = *1
  Kin. My Noble Gossips, y'haue beene too Prodigall;   3381
GOT = 6*1
  Being now seene, possible enough, got credit | That *Beuis* was beleeu'd.   81
  Haue got by the late Voyage, is but meerely   577
  Of Foole and Feather, that they got in France,   603
  Haue got a speeding tricke to lay downe Ladies.   620
  Kin. I then mou'd you, | My Lord of *Canterbury*, and got your leaue   1587
  *(By what meanes got, I leaue to your owne conscience)   2225
  Por. How got they in, and be hang'd?   3274
GOUERNE = 1
  To the loue o'th'Commonalty, the Duke | Shall gouerne England.   516
GOUERNMENT = 1
  Thy meeknesse Saint-like, Wife-like Gouernment,   1502
GRACE = 47*4
  Norf. I thanke your Grace: 41
  For being not propt by Auncestry, whose grace   108
  Nor. Like it your Grace, | The State takes notice of the priuate
  difference   160
  Car. Is he in person, ready? | *Secr.* I, please your Grace.   183
  *Of the Kings grace and pardon: the greeued Commons   441
  S.Hen.Guilf. Ladyes, | A generall welcome from his Grace   666
  His Grace is entring. Nay, you must not freeze,   692
  San. Your Grace is Noble,   715
  San. I told your Grace, they would talke anon.   732
  To tell your Grace: That hauing heard by fame   759

GRACE *cont.*
    Card. Say, Lord *Chamberlaine,* | They haue done my poore house grace: 766
    Card. My Lord. | *Cham.* Your Grace.   774
    There is indeed, which they would haue your Grace   784
    Card. I am glad | Your Grace is growne so pleasant.   793
    Cham. An't please your Grace,   797
    Card. Your Grace | I feare, with dancing is a little heated.   807
    Louell. I doe beseech your Grace, for charity   922
    Commend mee to his Grace: 930
    Lou. To th' water side I must conduct your Grace;   939
    I would your Grace would giue vs but an houre | Of priuate conference.   1123
    Wol. Your Grace ha's giuen a President of wisedome   1133
    *Cam. Your Grace must needs deserue all strangers loues,   1149
    Gard. But to be commanded | For euer by your Grace, whose hand ha's
rais'd me.   1168
    A Thousand pound a yeare, Annuall support, | Out of his Grace, he
addes.   1280
    And take your good Grace from me? Heauen witnesse,   1376
    Camp. His Grace | Hath spoken well, and iustly: Therefore Madam,   1420
    *Gent. And't please your Grace, the two great Cardinals | Wait in the
presence.   1635
    Zeale and obedience he still bore your Grace,   1688
    Camp. I would your Grace | Would leaue your greefes, and take my
Counsell.   1720
    Car. If your Grace | Could but be brought to know, our Ends are
honest,   1790
    Farewell Nobilitie: let his Grace go forward,   2172
    Crom. How does your Grace. | *Card.* Why well: 2281
    I humbly thanke his Grace: and from these shoulders   2287
    Crom. I am glad your Grace, | Ha's made that right vse of it.   2292
    A distance from her; while her Grace sate downe   2485
    2 But what follow'd? | 3 At length, her Grace rose, and with modest
paces   2502
    Grif. How do's your Grace? | *Kath.* O *Griffith,* sicke to death: 2551
    Grif. Yes Madam: but I thinke your Grace   2559
    Pati. Do you note | How much her Grace is alter'd on the sodaine?   2674
    Mes. And't like your Grace --- | *Kath.* You are a sawcy Fellow,   2681
    Cap. Noble Lady, | First mine owne seruice to your Grace, the next   2702
    My next poore Petition, | Is, that his Noble Grace would haue some
pittie   2730
    Giuen eare to our Complaint, of his great Grace,   2827
    Cran. Why? | *Keep.* Your Grace must waight till you be call'd for.   2996
    Buts. Ile shew your Grace the strangest sight.   3016
    The high promotion of his Grace of *Canterbury,*   3021
    Crom. Please your Honours, | The chiefe cause concernes his Grace of
Canterbury.   3044
    Chan. Let him come in. | *Keep.* Your Grace may enter now.   3053
    Sur. May it please your Grace; --- | *Kin.* No Sir, it doe's not please me,   3203
    Chan. Thus farre | My most dread Soueraigne, may it like your Grace,   3218
    *Cran. And to your Royall Grace, & the good Queen,   3369
GRACEFULLY = *1
    *passe directly before the Cardinall and gracefully sa- | *lute him.*   755
GRACES = 8*1
    Hath into monstrous habits put the Graces   461
    Cham. Good day to both your Graces.   1041
    Queen. Pray their Graces | To come neere: what can be their busines   1639
    *Queen. Your Graces find me heere part of a Housewife,   1647

GRACES *cont.*

The last fit of my Greatnesse; good your Graces	1704
Of your best Graces, in your minde; the which	2007
Car. My Soueraigne, I confesse your Royall graces	2040
The profit of the State. For your great Graces	2048
Then this pure Soule shall be. All Princely Graces	3395

GRACIOUS = 6

Norff. A gracious King, that pardons all offences	1108
You (gracious Madam) to vnthinke your speaking, | And to say so no more.	1463
Wol. Most gracious Sir, | In humblest manner I require your Highnes,	1508
Hee's louing and most gracious. 'Twill be much,	1724
King. Pray you arise | My good and gracious Lord of Canterburie:	2887
All comfort, ioy in this most gracious Lady,	3371

GRAINE = 1

Wee see each graine of grauell; I doe know | To be corrupt and treasonous.	229

GRAND = 1

Produce the grand summe of his sinnes, the Articles	2186

GRANTED = 2

Paid ere he promis'd, whereby his Suit was granted	262
Made suit to come in's presence; which if granted,	548

GRAUE = 4

No blacke Enuy shall make my Graue.	929
The Graue does to th' dead: For her Male Issue,	1558
Almost no Graue allow'd me? Like the Lilly	1787
I was a chaste Wife, to my Graue: Embalme me,	2763

GRAUELL = 1

Wee see each graine of grauell; I doe know | To be corrupt and treasonous.	229

GRAUER = 1

Abur. I cannot tell | What Heauen hath giuen him: let some Grauer eye	116

GRAUES = 2

Nor build their euils on the graues of great men;	908
Till *Cranmer, Cromwel*, her two hands, and shee | Sleepe in their Graues.	2808

GRAUITY = 1

And to such men of grauity and learning;	1699

GREAT = 38*8

As they were Liuing: Thinke you see them Great,	28
I meane who set the Body, and the Limbes | Of this great Sport together?	92
To whom as great a Charge, as little Honor	128
For this great Iourney. What did this vanity	138
Buck. My Surueyor is falce: The ore-great *Cardinall*	311
Thankes you for this great care: I stood i'th' leuell	322
*Are in great grieuance: There haue beene Commissions	347
That he may furnish and instruct great Teachers,	452
This night he makes a Supper, and a great one,	638
But few now giue so great ones:	653
And hither make, as great Embassadors | From forraigne Princes.	742
(Out of the great respect they beare to beauty)	762
Eu'n to the Hall, to heare what shall become | Of the great Duke of Buckingham.	823
1. Ile tell you in a little. The great Duke	838
Nor build their euils on the graues of great men;	908
*Between vs & the Emperor (the Queens great Nephew)	1058

GREAT *cont.*

Vse vs, and it: My good Lord, haue great care,	1120
*great Seale, and a Cardinals Hat: Then two Priests, bea-| ring	1339
*Siluer Mace: Then two Gentlemen bearing two great	1342
*Gent. And't please your Grace, the two great Cardinals | Wait in the presence.	1635
Yet will I adde an Honor; a great Patience.	1770
The profit of the State. For your great Graces	2048
Who commands you | To render vp the Great Seale presently	2111
Whil'st your great Goodnesse, out of holy pitty, | Absolu'd him with an Axe.	2151
Ambassador to the Emperor, you made bold | To carry into Flanders, the Great Seale.	2216
(Not you) correct him. My heart weepes to see him | So little, of his great Selfe.	2234
About the giuing backe the Great Seale to vs,	2247
A great man should decline. Nay, and you weep | I am falne indeed.	2279
*Exeunt, *first passing ouer the Stage in Order and State, and* | *then, A great Flourish of Trumpets.*	2445
I neuer saw before. Great belly'd women,	2496
2 He of Winchester | Is held no great good louer of the Archbishops, | The vertuous *Cranmer.*	2528
How euer, yet there is no great breach, when it comes	2532
That the great Childe of Honor, Cardinall *Wolsey* | Was dead?	2557
No great offence belongs too't, giue your Friend	2785
They say in great Extremity, and fear'd | Shee'l with the Labour, end.	2793
Giuen eare to our Complaint, of his great Grace,	2827
Of as great Size. Weene you of better lucke,	2936
To make great hast. All fast? What meanes this? Hoa?	2991
The cause betwixt her, and this great offender.	3190
At Chamber dore? and one, as great as you are?	3210
*great *Toole*, come to Court, the women so besiege vs?	3293
Great store of roome no doubt, left for the Ladies,	3332
Man. You great fellow, | Stand close vp, or Ile make your head ake.	3349
Staffe, Duke of Suffolke, two Noblemen, bearing great	3356
As great in admiration as her selfe.	3413
Shall Star-like rise, as great in fame as she was,	3417

GREATER = 4

Of an ensuing euill, if it fall, | Greater then this.	989
To endure more Miseries, and greater farre	2297
1 Neuer greater, | Nor Ile assure you better taken Sir.	2392
And to adde greater Honors to his Age	2625

GREATEST = 2

That when the greatest stroake of Fortune falls	1068
Cran. The greatest Monarch now aliue may glory	3235

GREATNESSE = 8

And fit it with such furniture as suites | The Greatnesse of his Person.	944
The last fit of my Greatnesse; good your Graces	1704
I haue touch'd the highest point of all my Greatnesse,	2103
Farewell? A long farewell to all my Greatnesse.	2252
His Greatnesse is a ripening, nippes his roote,	2258
Knowing she will not loose her wonted Greatnesse	2685
And by those claime their greatnesse; not by Blood.	3409
His Honour, and the greatnesse of his Name,	3422

GREATST = 1

In the great'st humblenesse, and desir'd your Highnesse | Most heartily to pray for her.	2846

GREEFES = 1
Camp. I would your Grace | Would leaue your greefes, and take my
Counsell.   1720
GREENWICH = 1
Sur. Being at *Greenwich,* | After your Highnesse had reprou'd the
Duke | About Sir *William Bulmer.*   539
GREEUD = 1
Kept him a forraigne man still, which so greeu'd him,   1182
GREEUE = 1
Ah my good Lord, I greeue at what I speake,   2892
GREEUED = *1
*Of the Kings grace and pardon: the greeued Commons   441
GREEUES = 1
Who greeues much for your weakenesse, and by me   2705
GREEUINGLY = 1
Nor. Greeuingly I thinke,   141
GREEUOUS = 2
Heard many greeuous, I do say my Lord   2895
Greeuous complaints of you; which being consider'd,   2896
GREGORY = 1
Sur. Item, You sent a large Commission | To *Gregory de Cassado,* to
conclude   2218
GREW = 2
In their Embracement, as they grew together, | Which had they,   51
He fell sicke sodainly, and grew so ill | He could not sit his Mule.   2568
GRIEFE = 3
Vnder your promis'd pardon. The Subiects griefe   389
Then to be perk'd vp in a glistring griefe, | And weare a golden sorrow. 1226
Killing care, & griefe of heart, | *Fall asleepe, or hearing dye.*   1631
GRIEUANCE = *1
*Are in great grieuance: There haue beene Commissions   347
GRIEUE = 2
He neuer was so womanish, the cause | He may a little grieue at.   868
Would it not grieue an able man to leaue   1197
GRIEUES = 1
Kin. It grieues many: 449
GRIF = 12
GRIFFITH see also Grif. = 10*1
Enter Katherine Dowager, sicke, lead betweene Griffith,   2548
Grif. How do's your Grace? | *Kath.* O *Griffith,* sicke to death: 2551
Did'st thou not tell me *Griffith,* as thou lead'st mee,   2556
Kath. Pre'thee good *Griffith,* tell me how he dy'de.   2561
Yet thus farre *Griffith,* giue me leaue to speake him,   2587
To heare me speake his good now? | *Kath.* Yes good *Griffith,*   2603
But such an honest Chronicler as *Griffith.*   2630
I haue not long to trouble thee. Good *Griffith,*   2635
And brought me Garlands (*Griffith*) which I feele   2668
**Kath.* Admit him entrance *Griffith.* But this Fellow   2690
My Lord. *Griffith* farewell. Nay *Patience,*   2758
GRIPD = 1
We liue not to be grip'd by meaner persons.   1190
GRIPES = 1
Out of the gripes of cruell men, and giue it   3163
GROANE = *1
*And with that bloud will make 'em one day groane for't.   952
GROANING = 1
Many a groaning throw: thus hulling in   1566

GROOME = 2
  An ordinary Groome is for such payment. 2982
  Not as a Groome: There's some of ye, I see, 3214
GROOMES = 1
  Wait else at doore: a fellow Councellor | 'Mong Boyes, Groomes, and
  Lackeyes. 3010
GROSSER = 1
  Hitting a grosser quality, is cride vp 419
GROUND = 2
  Stops on a sodaine, looles vpon the ground, 1976
  To th' ground, and all the World shall mourne her. 3434
GROUNDED = 1
  Kin. Speake on; | How grounded hee his Title to the Crowne 486
GROW = 7*1
  They that my trust must grow to, liue not heere, 1717
  Or felt the Flatteries that grow vpon it: 1780
  *Grow from the Kings Acquaintance, by this Carriage. 1798
  They swell and grow, as terrible as stormes. 1801
  (For so I will) mine eyes grow dimme. Farewell 2757
  So I grow stronger, you more Honour gaine. *Exeunt.* 3255
  They grow still too; from all Parts they are comming, 3327
  Shall then be his, and like a Vine grow to him; 3420
GROWES = 3
  2. But that slander Sir, | Is found a truth now: for it growes agen 1006
  My Soule growes sad with troubles, 1618
  Good growes with her. 3403
GROWING = 3
  Not well dispos'd, the minde growing once corrupt, 455
  Still growing in a Maiesty and pompe, the which 1208
  Which euer ha's, and euer shall be growing, | Till death (that Winter)
  kill it. 2052
GROWNE = 3
  L.San. Tis time to giue 'em Physicke, their diseases | Are growne so
  catching. 614
  Card. I am glad | Your Grace is growne so pleasant. 793
  (Though he be growne so desperate to be honest) 1714
GRUBBD = 1
  I wish it grubb'd vp now. 2798
GUARD = 5
  of the Guard, and two Secretaries with Papers: The 176
  Enter Brandon, a Sergeant at Armes before him, and | two or three of the
  Guard. 276
  Let some o'th' Guard be ready there. 3154
  Enter the Guard. 3155
  Flourish. Enter King and Guard. 3368
GUARDED *see* garded
GUESSE *see also* gesse = 2
  Nor. As you guesse: 94
  1. You may guesse quickly what. 831
GUEST = 1
  Your Lordship is a guest too. | *L.Cham.* O, 'tis true; 636
GUESTS = 3*1
  longer Table for the Guests. Then Enter Anne Bullen, 662
  and diuers other Ladies, & Gentlemen, as Guests 663
  Card. Y'are welcome my faire Guests; that noble Lady 711
  Which is to'th' Court, and there ye shall be my Guests: 2543

GUIDE = 1
Distinctly his full Function: who did guide, 91
GUIFT = 1
A guift that heauen giues for him, which buyes | A place next to the
King. 114
GUIFTS = 1*1
Which, to say sooth, are Blessings; and which guifts 1238
*standing Bowles for the Christening Guifts: Then foure 3357
GUILFORD see also S.Hen.Guilf. = 3
For I was spoke to, with Sir *Henry Guilford* | This night to be
Comptrollers. 657
at one Doore; at an other Doore enter | Sir Henry Guilford. 664
Cham. You are young Sir *Harry Guilford.* 678
GUILTIE = 2
Qu. My Lord, | I dare not make my selfe so guiltie, 1773
Now, if you can blush, and crie guiltie Cardinall, | You'l shew a little
Honestie. 2200
GUILTLESSE = 2
For then, my guiltlesse blood must cry against 'em. 909
2. If the Duke be guiltlesse, 987
GUILTY = 3
2. Is he found guilty? 832
He pleaded still not guilty, and alleadged 840
Haue found him guilty of high Treason. Much 856
GUY = 1
Man. I am not *Sampson*, nor Sir *Guy*, nor *Colebrand*, 3280
GUYNES = 1
Nor. 'Twixt Guynes and Arde, 48
GYANT = 1
Kin. A Gyant Traytor. 551
GYRLE = 2
Both now, and euer blesse her: 'Tis a Gyrle 2972
Said I for this, the Gyrle was like to him? Ile 2984
HA *l.*180 535 *1103 1107 1114 1905 1907 2848 2869 2878 3024 = 11*1, *1
*Lady. An hundred Markes? By this light, Ile ha more. 2981
HABBERDASHERS = *1
*like a Morter-piece to blow vs. There was a Habberda-|shers 3305
HABITE = *1
*Scribes in the habite of Doctors; after them, the Bishop of 1335
HABITED = *2
*Hoboyes. Enter King and others as Maskers, habited like 753
*Norfolke, Godmother, bearing the Childe richly habited in 3359
HABITS = 2
Hath into monstrous habits put the Graces 461
If ye be any thing but Churchmens habits) 1749
HACKT = 1
And though we leaue it with a roote thus hackt, 433
HAD *l.*52 101 511 532 540 544 580 646 679 699 964 *1029 1078 1216 1325
1386 1403 1405 1540 1554 1560 1584 1626 1671 1779 1880 2028 2205
2370 *2402 2491 2494 2495 2497 2508 2710 2744 2745 3026 3027 3046
3201 3205 3216 3282 3431 = 46*2
HAIRE = 1*1
Weigh'd not a haire of his. Plague of your policie, 2147
*the Queene in her Robe, in her haire, richly adorned with 2438
HALBERDS = *1
*him, the Axe with the edge towards him, Halberds on each 890

HALFE = 10*1
    King. Arise, and take place by vs; halfe your Suit   335
    Neuer name to vs; you haue halfe our power: 336
    But halfe my Lay-thoughts in him, some of these   680
    *Good my Lord Cardinall: I haue halfe a dozen healths,   814
    You met him halfe in Heauen: my vowes and prayers   932
    I will not wish ye halfe my miseries,   1740
    Had I but seru'd my God, with halfe the Zeale   2370
    To rest a while, some halfe an houre, or so,   2486
    That had not halfe a weeke to go, like Rammes   2497
    Keep. My Lord Archbishop: | And ha's done halfe an houre to know
      your pleasures.   3051
    Crom. Would you were halfe so honest: 3135
HALL = 2
    Eu'n to the Hall, to heare what shall become | Of the great Duke of
      Buckingham.   823
    'Tis now the Kings, and call'd White-Hall. | 3 I know it: 2519
HALLOWED = 1
    Are not words duely hallowed; nor my Wishes   1285
HALT = 1
    A Spring-halt rain'd among 'em.   585
HAND = 16*3
    He stretch'd him, and with one hand on his dagger,   557
    A hand as fruitfull as the Land that feeds vs,   643
    King. The fairest hand I euer touch'd: O Beauty,   771
    You are so Noble: To your Highnesse hand   1150
    * *Wol.* Giue me your hand: much ioy & fauour to you;   1166
    Gard. But to be commanded | For euer by your Grace, whose hand ha's
      rais'd me.   1168
    Crom. To his owne hand, in's Bed-chamber.   1930
    That as my hand ha's open'd Bounty to you,   2059
    On you, then any: So your Hand, and Heart,   2061
    (Mine, and your Master) with his owne hand, gaue me: 2132
    * *Nor.* Those Articles, my Lord, are in the Kings hand: 2192
    Still in thy right hand, carry gentle Peace   2360
    2 May I be bold to aske what that containes, | That Paper in your hand. 2394
    Is the Kings hand, and tongue, and who dare speak | One syllable
      against him?   2816
    Come, come, giue me your hand.   2891
    In vs thy Friend. Giue me thy hand, stand vp,   2914
    *himselfe at the vpper end of the Table, on the left hand: A   3037
    These lazy knaues? Y'haue made a fine hand fellowes?   3329
    Into whose hand, I giue thy Life. | *Cran. Amen.*   3379
HANDMAID = 1
    As from a blushing Handmaid, to his Highnesse;   1289
HANDS = 6*2
    Vnder your hands and Seales; therefore goe on,   1592
    Put my sicke cause into his hands, that hates me?   1750
    Into our hands, and to Confine your selfe   2113
    Into your owne hands (Card'nall) by Extortion: 2178
    *or Palme in their hands. They first Conge vnto her, then   2646
    *reioycing, and holdeth vp her hands to heauen. And so, in   2655
    Till Cranmer, Cromwel, her two hands, and shee | Sleepe in their
      Graues.   2808
    Pace 'em not in their hands to make 'em gentle;   3070
HANDSOME = *1
    *They were young and handsome, and of the best breed in the   1030

HANG = 2
Ile hang my head, and perish. 1789
And hang their heads with sorrow: 3402
HANGD = 1*1
*Port. Belong to th' Gallowes, and be hang'd ye Rogue: 3263
Por. How got they in, and be hang'd? 3274
HANGS = 1
Is that poore man, that hangs on Princes fauours? 2268
HAP = 1
All the best men are ours; for 'tis ill hap, 3462
HAPPEN = 2
(I would be all) against the worst may happen: 1648
Is onely my Obedience. What can happen 1754
HAPPEND = 1
2. Pray speake what ha's happen'd. 830
HAPPIE = 1
Long, and euer happie, to the high and Mighty | Princesse of England
Elizabeth. 3366
HAPPIER = 1
A little happier then my wretched Father: 966
HAPPIEST = 1
The First and Happiest Hearers of the Towne, 25
HAPPILY = 3
If well, he stept before me happily | For my example. 2562
Lou. This is about that, which the Byshop spake, | I am happily come
hither. 2874
I came this way so happily. The King | Shall vnderstand it presently.
Exit Buts 3001
HAPPINESSE = 3
His Ouerthrow, heap'd Happinesse vpon him: 2622
They promis'd me eternall Happinesse, 2667
Cran. She shall be to the happinesse of England, 3428
HAPPY = 8
That made me happy; at one stroake ha's taken 963
My Lords, I care not (so much I am happy | Aboue a number) if my
actions 1657
Suf. May you be happy in your wish my Lord, | For I professe you haue
it. 1881
Neuer so truly happy, my good Cromwell, 2283
2 Those men are happy, | And so are all, are neere her. 2464
And sure those men are happy that shall haue 'em. 2739
Heauen euer laid vp to make Parents happy, | May hourely fall vpon
ye. 3372
This happy Child, did I get any thing. 3437
HARD = 5
They are deuis'd by you, or else you suffer | Too hard an exclamation. 382
Old La. Hearts of most hard temper | Melt and lament for her. 1213
Our hard rul'd King. Againe, there is sprung vp 1959
Strikes his brest hard, and anon, he casts 1979
My mindes not on't, you are too hard for me. 2838
HARDLY = 1
Hardly conceiue of me. Let it be nois'd, 442
HARKE = 1
Ye should doe Seruice. Harke the Trumpets sound, 3343
HARMES = 1
Peep'd harmes that menac'd him. Priuily 259

HARME-DOING = 1
  She neuer knew harme-doing: Oh, now after   1206
HARMONY = 1
  On that Coelestiall Harmony I go too. | *Sad and solemne Musicke.*   2638
HARRY = 2
  Cham. You are young Sir *Harry Guilford.*   678
  Cham. Sweet Ladies will it please you sit; Sir *Harry*   690
HARSH = 1
  Kath. Bid the Musicke leaue, | They are harsh and heauy to me.
  Musicke ceases.   2672
HAS *see also* t'has *l.*119 249 285 436 621 670 830 963 970 1047 1049 *1057
  1064 1096 1126 1133 1157 1169 1498 1506 1671 1769 1819 1872 1921
  2052 2059 2077 2087 2090 2263 2286 2293 2309 2322 2459 2537 2960
  3046 3052 3383 3438 = 41*1, 5
  Or ha's giuen all before, and he begins | A new Hell in himselfe.   121
  L.San. He may my Lord, | Ha's wherewithall in him;   647
  Alas, ha's banish'd me his Bed already,   1751
  Ha's left the cause o'th'King vnhandled, and   1902
  'Has businesse at his house; for all shall stay: 3447
HAST *l.*488 2344 2457 2631 3198 3436 = 6, 4
  Then Deputy of Ireland, who remou'd | Earle *Surrey*, was sent thither,
  and in hast too,   874
  My hast made me vnmannerly. There is staying   2688
  It seemes you are in hast: and if there be   2784
  To make great hast. All fast? What meanes this? Hoa?   2991
HASTE *see also* hast = 1
  I haste now to my Setting. I shall fall | Like a bright exhalation in the
  Euening,   2105
HASTY = 1
  And somthing spoke in choller, ill, and hasty: 863
HAT = 1 *1
  *great Seale, and a Cardinals Hat: Then two Priests, bea-| ring   1339
  Your holy-Hat to be stampt on the Kings Coine.   2223
HATE = 4
  2. All the Commons | Hate him perniciously, and o' my Conscience 884
  Vaine pompe, and glory of this World, I hate ye,   2266
  Loue thy selfe last, cherish those hearts that hate thee;   2358
  This is of purpose laid by some that hate me,   3007
HATED = 1
  Whom I most hated Liuing, thou hast made mee   2631
HATES = 1
  Put my sicke cause into his hands, that hates me?   1750
HATH *l.*117 151 170 312 348 461 507 1142 1293 1354 1374 1421 1847
  1850 1879 1901 1919 1961 1968 2316 2772 2826 2829 = 24
HATRED = 1
  Together; To consider further, that | What his high Hatred would effect,
  wants not   166
HATS = 1
  As lowd, and to as many Tunes. Hats, Cloakes,   2493
HAUE *see also* ha, I'ue, th'haue, w'haue, y'haue *l.*39 53 133 137 189 336
  *347 360 379 404 427 469 534 545 550 577 582 608 617 620 627 632 671
  716 *723 750 767 784 789 *814 854 856 897 899 901 911 935 982 995
  1010 1020 1022 *1036 1037 1075 1120 1130 1138 *1141 *1148 1161 1189
  1235 1236 1247 1293 *1295 1302 1307 1313 1373 1377 1384 1389 1390
  1412 1428 1437 1445 1448 1449 1453 1457 1471 1517 1524 1529 1530
  1578 1654 1667 1681 1703 1705 1741 1747 1748 1758 1762 *1781 1802
  1815 1819 1820 1823 1838 1882 1911 1973 1981 2008 2012 2014 2020

HAUE *cont.*
  2029 2035 2037 2041 2044 2046 2068 2078 2080 2084 2091 2103 2129
  2141 2150 2160 2206 2222 *2224 2227 2238 2259 2271 2276 2294 2310
  2323 2329 2339 2341 2366 2372 2373 2374 2388 2389 2403 2458 *2473
  2635 2722 2731 2733 2739 2742 2744 2787 2819 2821 2826 *2867 2878
  2890 2894 2897 2917 2918 2919 2934 2959 2983 2985 3062 3081 *3100
  3125 3142 3161 3180 3217 3232 *3239 3253 3254 3289 *3292 *3321 3331
  3336 3432 3443 3456 = 172*16

HAUING = 5
  To tell your Grace: That hauing heard by fame   759
  His Highnesse, hauing liu'd so long with her, and she   1203
  Old L. Our content | Is our best hauing.   1228
  Borne out of your Dominions: hauing heere   1370
  Of Lords, and Ladies, hauing brought the Queene   2483

HAUINGS = 1
  But par'd my present Hauings, to bestow | My Bounties vpon you.   2031

HE *see also* o = 187*7

HEAD = 7*7
  Who first rais'd head against Vsurping *Richard*,   954
  Ile hang my head, and perish.   1789
  Sur. I had rather want those, then my head;   2205
  *his Coate of Armes, and on his head he wore a Gilt Copper| Crowne. 2427
  *6 Marquesse Dorset, *bearing a Scepter of Gold, on his head*,   2429
  *head, *bearing a long white Wand, as High Steward. With*   2434
  him, the Duke of Norfolke, *with the Rod of Marshalship*, | *a Coronet on*
  his head. Collars of Esses.   2435
  Garland ouer her Head, at which the other foure make re-|uerend 2648
  head. Which done, they deliuer the same Garland to the   2652
  Fly o're thy Royall head, and shade thy person | Vnder their blessed
  wings.   2965
  That had a head to hit, either young or old,   3282
  *did I hit three times on the head, and three times   3303
  *till her pinck'd porrenger fell off her head, for kindling   3307
  Man. You great fellow, | Stand close vp, or Ile make your head ake. 3349

HEADES = *1
  clad in white Robes, wearing on their heades Garlands of   2644

HEADS = 6*1
  The Cardinals and Sir *Thomas Louels* heads | Should haue gone off. 533
  I feare, too many curses on their heads | That were the Authors.   985
  Hung their heads, & then lay by.   1629
  The heads of all thy Brother-Cardinals,   2145
  *Ile scratch your heads; you must be seeing Christenings?   3266
  By th' heeles, and sodainly: and on your heads   3340
  And hang their heads with sorrow: 3402

HEALTH = 5
  And to you all good health.   714
  And not to kisse you. A health Gentlemen, | Let it goe round.   802
  Health to your Lordships.   1098
  Whose health and Royalty I pray for.   1290
  How does his Highnesse? | *Cap.* Madam, in good health.   2712

HEALTHFULL = 1
  Healthfull, and euer since a fresh Admirer | Of what I saw there.   42

HEALTHS = *1
  *Good my Lord Cardinall: I haue halfe a dozen healths,   814

HEAPD = 2
  Heap'd vpon me (poore Vndeseruer) I   2049
  His Ouerthrow, heap'd Happinesse vpon him: 2622

HEARD = 11

I'ue heard him vtter to his Sonne in Law, 476

Vpon our faile; to this poynt hast thou heard him, | At any time speake
ought? 488

To tell your Grace: That hauing heard by fame 759

For when the King once heard it, out of anger 1002

For all the mud in Egypt; haue you heard it? 1313

What heere y'haue heard to her. 1330

And that (without delay) their Arguments | Be now produc'd, and
heard. 1423

Euery thing that heard him play, 1627

Of me, more must be heard of: Say I taught thee; 2349

Heard many greeuous, I do say my Lord 2895

Your selfe, and your Accusers, and to haue heard you | Without
indurance further. 2919

HEARE = 27*1

That come to heare a Merry, Bawdy Play, 15

To heare this of him; and could wish he were | Somthing mistaken in't. 271

Ile heare him his confessions iustifie, 326

As if besmear'd in hell. Sit by Vs, you shall heare 463

We cannot feele too little, heare too much. 467

To heare from him a matter of some moment: 509

Louell. Faith my Lord, | I heare of none but the new Proclamation, 591

Eu'n to the Hall, to heare what shall become | Of the great Duke of
Buckingham. 823

1. When he was brought agen to th' Bar, to heare 860

Heare what I say, and then goe home and lose me. 898

Heauen ha's an end in all: yet, you that heare me, 970

2. I am confident; | You shall Sir: Did you not of late dayes heare 997

Car. Pray heare me. 1778

I should be glad to heare such Newes as this | Once euery houre. 1855

Nor. So I heare. | *Suf.* 'Tis so. 1923

*To heare from Rome. The Marchionesse of Penbroke? 1945

Nor. Heare the Kings pleasure Cardinall, 2110

Till you heare further from his Highnesse. | *Car.* Stay: 2115

Can ye endure to heare this Arrogance? 2169

Let's dry our eyes: And thus farre heare me *Cromwel,* 2346

To heare me speake his good now? | *Kath.* Yes good *Griffith,* 2603

Gard. But Sir, Sir, | Heare me Sir *Thomas,* y'are a Gentleman 2803

We shall heare more anon. 3034

His Royall selfe in Iudgement comes to heare 3189

To heare such flattery now, and in my presence 3193

Within. Do you heare M.(aster) Porter? 3286

They'l say tis naught. Others to heare the City 3454

All the expected good w'are like to heare. 3457

HEARERS = 2

Will be deceyu'd. For gentle Hearers, know 18

The First and Happiest Hearers of the Towne, 25

HEARES = 1

Suf. Maybe he heares the King | Does whet his Anger to him. 1947

HEARING = 4

Most pestilent to th'hearing, and to beare 'em, 380

And haue an houre of hearing, and by'r Lady | Held currant Musicke
too. 627

That it shall please you to declare in hearing 1510

Killing care, & griefe of heart, | Fall asleepe, or hearing dye. 1631

HEART = 20

(And take it from a heart, that wishes towards you	163
King. My life it selfe, and the best heart of it,	321
Sent downe among 'em, which hath flaw'd the heart	348
Kin. By Heauen she is a dainty one. Sweet heart,	800
If euer any malice in your heart	923
And euery true heart weepes for't. All that dare	1072
So deare in heart, not to deny her that	1158
Haue (too) a Womans heart, which euer yet	1236
With Meekenesse and Humilitie: but your Heart	1469
Killing care, & griefe of heart, | Fall asleepe, or hearing dye.	1631
He ha's my heart yet, and shall haue my Prayers	1819
The Master-cord on's heart.	1966
I haue kept you next my Heart, haue not alone	2029
My heart drop'd Loue, my powre rain'd Honor, more	2060
On you, then any: So your Hand, and Heart,	2061
(Not you) correct him. My heart weepes to see him | So little, of his great Selfe.	2234
I feele my heart new open'd. Oh how wretched	2267
(I speake it with a single heart, my Lords)	3086
Pray Heauen the King may neuer find a heart	3090
Gard. With a true heart, | And Brother; loue I doe it.	3244

HEARTED = 2

Then my Weake-hearted Enemies, dare offer.	2298
I sweare he is true-hearted, and a soule	2957

HEARTILY = 7

Yes, heartily beseech you.	523
(Be what they will) I heartily forgiue'em;	906
Norf. We had need pray, | And heartily, for our deliuerance;	1078
And heartily entreats you take good comfort.	2707
Gard. The fruite she goes with | I pray for heartily, that it may finde	2795
In the great'st humblenesse, and desir'd your Highnesse | Most heartily to pray for her.	2846
I thanke ye heartily: So shall this Lady, | When she ha's so much English.	3382

HEARTS = 9*1

Tongues spit their duties out, and cold hearts freeze	394
And giue your hearts to; when they once perceiue	974
Old La. Hearts of most hard temper | Melt and lament for her.	1213
But Cardinall Sins, and hollow hearts I feare ye:	1736
*Ye haue Angels Faces; but Heauen knowes your hearts.	1781
The hearts of Princes kisse Obedience,	1799
Beare witnesse, all that haue not hearts of Iron,	2339
Loue thy selfe last, cherish those hearts that hate thee;	2358
(God turne their hearts, I neuer sought their malice)	3008
Kin. Good Man, those ioyfull teares shew thy true | (hearts,	3248

HEAT = 1

Norf. Be aduis'd; | Heat not a Furnace for your foe so hot	212

HEATED = 1

Card. Your Grace | I feare, with dancing is a little heated.	807

HEATHEN = 1

All Clinquant all in Gold, like Heathen Gods	63

HEAUEN = 39*5

A guift that heauen giues for him, which buyes | A place next to the King.	114
Abur. I cannot tell | What Heauen hath giuen him: let some Grauer eye	116
The will of Heauen be done, and the Kings pleasure | By me obey'd.	300

HEAUEN *cont.*

*Whose Honor Heauen shield from soile; euen he escapes | (not	353
Into our presence, where this heauen of beauty	747
Kin. By Heauen she is a dainty one. Sweet heart,	800
And by that name must dye; yet Heauen beare witnes,	900
And lift my Soule to Heauen. | Lead on a Gods name.	920
You met him halfe in Heauen: my vowes and prayers	932
Heauen ha's an end in all: yet, you that heare me,	970
**Cham.* Heauen keep me from such councel: tis most true	1070
The French Kings Sister. Heauen will one day open	1074
Anne. No, not for all the riches vnder Heauen.	1244
And take your good Grace from me? Heauen witnesse,	1376
I stood not in the smile of Heauen, who had	1554
Heauen is aboue all yet; there sits a Iudge, | That no King can corrupt.	1731
*Ye haue Angels Faces; but Heauen knowes your hearts.	1781
Car. Heauen forgiue me, | Euer God blesse your Highnesse.	2003
My Prayres to heauen for you; my Loyaltie	2051
Too heauy for a man, that hopes for Heauen.	2291
And my Integrity to Heauen, is all,	2368
The Hopes of Court, my Hopes in Heauen do dwell. | *Exeunt.*	2375
2 Heauen blesse thee, | Thou hast the sweetest face I euer look'd on.	2456
Cast her faire eyes to Heauen, and pray'd deuoutly.	2505
His blessed part to Heauen, and slept in peace.	2584
**reioycing, and holdeth vp her hands to heauen. And so, in*	2655
Grif. She is going Wench. Pray, pray. | *Pati.* Heauen comfort her.	2678
The dewes of Heauen fall thicke in Blessings on her,	2724
To loue her for her Mothers sake, that lou'd him, | Heauen knowes how	
deerely.	2728
If Heauen had pleas'd to haue giuen me longer life	2744
Cap. By Heauen I will, | Or let me loose the fashion of a man.	2751
And of a louely Boy: the God of heauen	2971
Pray heauen he found not my disgrace: for certaine	3006
Pray Heauen the King may neuer find a heart	3090
Gard. Dread Soueraigne, | How much are we bound to Heauen,	3182
Cran. And let Heauen | Witnesse how deare, I hold this Confirmation.	3246
Gart. Heauen | From thy endlesse goodnesse, send prosperous life,	3364
Heauen euer laid vp to make Parents happy, | May hourely fall vpon	
ye.	3372
Cran. Let me speake Sir, | For Heauen now bids me; and the words I	
vtter,	3384
This Royall Infant, Heauen still moue about her;	3387
*(When Heauen shal call her from this clowd of darknes)	3415
Where euer the bright Sunne of Heauen shall shine,	3421
*To all the Plaines about him: Our Childrens Children | Shall see this,	
and blesse Heauen.	3425
That when I am in Heauen, I shall desire	3439

HEAUENLY = 1 *1

King. Good my Lord, | *You are full of Heauenly stuffe, and beare the	
Inuentory	2005
Holy and Heauenly thoughts still Counsell her:	3399

HEAUENS = 2

Take heed, for heauens sake take heed, least at once	1742
Nor. It's Heauens will,	1992

HEAUIEST = 1

What Newes abroad? | *Crom.* The heauiest, and the worst,	2299

HEAUN = 1 *2

*Which makes my whit'st part, black. The will of Heau'n	293

HEAUN *cont.*
  *Still met the King? Lou'd him next Heau'n? Obey'd him?   1763
  Suff. 'Tis the right Ring, by Heau'n: I told ye all,   3167
HEAUNLY = *1
  **Cham.* You beare a gentle minde, & heau'nly blessings   1273
HEAUNS = 1
  Wol. Heau'ns peace be with him: 1184
HEAUY = 2
  Too heauy for a man, that hopes for Heauen.   2291
  Kath. Bid the Musicke leaue, | They are harsh and heauy to me.
  Musicke ceases.   2672
HEDGES = 1
  And hedges his owne way. But in this point,   1876
HEE *l.*487 671 850 *1036 1543 *3304 = 4*2, 1
  Hee, that dares most, but wag his finger at thee.   3200
HEED = 4
  On the complaint o'th'Tenants; take good heed   520
  And spoyle your nobler Soule; I say, take heed;   522
  Take heed, for heauens sake take heed, least at once   1742
HEEDE = 1*1
  *Then marke th'inducement. Thus it came; giue heede | (too't: 1536
  He did it with a Serious minde: a heede | Was in his countenance. You
  he bad   1934
HEEL *l.*474 1055 = 2
HEELES = 1
  By th' heeles, and sodainly: and on your heads   3340
HEERE = 30*4
  We now present. Those that can Pitty, heere   6
  May heere finde Truth too. Those that come to see   10
  Where's his Examination? | *Secr.* Heere so please you.   181
  They are set heere for examples. | *L.Cham.* True, they are so;   651
  To faire content, and you: None heere he hopes   669
  This night to meet heere they could doe no lesse,   761
  By all your good leaues Gentlemen; heere Ile make | My royall choyce.   787
  Wee are too open heere to argue this: 1024
  A very fresh Fish heere; fye, fye, fye vpon   1306
  What heere y'haue heard to her.   1330
  Crier. Henry King of England, &c. | *King.* Heere.   1359
  Borne out of your Dominions: hauing heere   1370
  Wol. You haue heere Lady, | (And of your choice) these Reuerend
  Fathers, men   1412
  I do refuse you for my Iudge, and heere   1478
  Now present heere together: that's to say,   1569
  And did entreate your Highnes to this course, | Which you are running
  heere.   1585
  * *Queen.* Your Graces find me heere part of a Houswife,   1647
  The full cause of our comming. | *Queen.* Speake it heere.   1652
  *Pray speake in English; heere are some will thanke you,   1669
  They that my trust must grow to, liue not heere,   1717
  That little thought when she set footing heere,   1822
  Attend him heere this Morning.   1936
  Nor. My Lord, we haue | *Stood heere obseruing him. Some strange
  Commotion   1973
  1 You come to take your stand heere, and behold   2381
  And leaue me heere in wretchednesse, behinde ye?   2659
  Grif. Madam, we are heere. | *Kath.* It is not you I call for,   2660
  But now I am past all Comforts heere, but Prayers.   2711

HEERE *cont.*
Whose Minister you are, whiles heere he liu'd   2938
To sit heere at this present, and behold   3057
*Do you looke for Ale, and Cakes heere, you rude | Raskalls?   3267
Cham. Mercy o' me: what a Multitude are heere?   3326
As if we kept a Faire heere? Where are these Porters?   3328
And heere ye lye baiting of Bombards, when   3342
All that are heere: Some come to take their ease,   3451
HEEREAFTER = 1
Promises Boyes heereafter. Sir, your Queen | Desires your Visitation,
and to be   2973
HEERS = 1
Heer's to your Ladiship, and pledge it Madam: | For tis to such a thing.   728
HEES = 6
Hee's Traytor to th' height. *Exeunt.*   568
L.Cham. No doubt hee's Noble;   645
Hee's louing and most gracious. 'Twill be much,   1724
The Cardinall. | *Nor.* Obserue, obserue, hee's moody.   1926
Take him, and vse him well; hee's worthy of it.   3226
A shrewd turne, and hee's your friend for euer: 3251
HEIGHT = 1
Hee's Traytor to th' height. *Exeunt.*   568
HEIRE = 1
With gentle Trauaile, to the gladding of | Your Highnesse with an
Heire.   2854
HELD = 1
And haue an houre of hearing, and by'r Lady | Held currant Musicke
too.   627
HELD = 6*1
1. Yes, but it held not;   1001
Fresher then e're it was; and held for certaine   1008
Camp. Was he not held a learned man? | *Wol.* Yes surely.   1175
Held a late Court at Dunstable; sixe miles off   2409
To Yorke-Place, where the Feast is held.   2515
2 He of Winchester | Is held no great good louer of the Archbishops, |
The vertuous *Cranmer.*   2528
Curtsies. Then the two that held the Garland, deli-|uer   2649
HELL = 3
If not from Hell? The Diuell is a Niggard,   120
Or ha's giuen all before, and he begins | A new Hell in himselfe.   121
As if besmear'd in hell. Sit by Vs, you shall heare   463
HELPE = 4
Buck. It will helpe me nothing | To plead mine Innocence; for that dye
is on me   291
Least he should helpe his Father.   876
When you are cald returne. Now the Lord helpe,   1491
Keep. Yes, my Lord: | But yet I cannot helpe you.   2994
HENCE = 4
The Duke retein'd him his. But on: what hence?   543
This world had ayr'd them. Hence I tooke a thought,   1560
They are (as all my other comforts) far hence | In mine owne Countrey
Lords.   1718
From hence you be committed to the Tower,   3103
HENRY = 7*2
Cornets. Enter King Henry, leaning on the Cardinals shoul-|der,   317
For I was spoke to, with Sir *Henry Guilford* | This night to be
Comptrollers.   657

HENRY *cont.*

at one Doore; at an other Doore enter | *Sir Henry Guilford.*	664
My noble Father *Henry* of *Buckingham,*	953
Henry the Seauenth succeeding, truly pittying	958
Henry the Eight, Life, Honour, Name and all	962
**Scri.* Say, *Henry* K.(ing) of England, come into the Court.	1358
Crier. Henry King of England, &c. | *King.* Heere.	1359
The Famous History of the Life of | King HENRY the Eight.	3465

HENTON = 2

By a vaine Prophesie of *Nicholas Henton.*	491
Kin. What was that *Henton?* | *Sur.* Sir, a *Chartreux* Fryer,	492

HER *l.*332 333 670 799 1012 1063 1065 1066 1067 1137 1157 1158 1160
1199 1203 1205 1211 1214 1223 1293 1294 1330 *1364 1487 1496 1506
1507 1519 1520 1558 1598 1605 1616 1703 1767 1823 1887 1891 1915
1941 1953 1955 1956 2017 2018 2319 2382 2405 *2438 *2439 2463 2465
2485 2488 2503 2505 2506 2511 2549 2550 2641 *2646 *2648 *2651
*2654 *2655 2675 2676 2677 2679 2685 2724 2725 2728 2808 2843 2844
2845 2847 2849 *2850 2853 2972 2979 3190 3234 3285 *3307 *3311 3375
3387 3388 3392 3398 3399 3400 3401 3403 3404 3407 3408 3410 3412
3413 3414 *3415 3416 3429 3432 3434 = 103*15

HERALD = 1

Kath. After my death, I wish no other Herald,	2627

HERALDS = 1

(For so they phrase 'em) by their Heralds challeng'd	78

HERE = 4*2

As here at home, suggests the King our Master	239
To whisper *Wolsey*) here makes visitation,	255
Bran. Here is a warrant from | The King, t'attach Lord *Mountacute,* and the Bodies	302
We should take roote here, where we sit;	422
*No more to th' Crowne but that: Lo, who comes here?	1261
*thousand, here will bee Father, God-father, and all to-|gether.	3296

HERES = *1

**An.* Not for that neither; here's the pang that pinches.	1202

HERESIES = 1

Diuers and dangerous; which are Heresies;	3066

HERETIQUE = 2

An Heretique, an Arch-one; *Cranmer,* one	1960
A most Arch-Heretique, a Pestilence	2824

HERSELFE *see* selfe

HERTFORD = 1

Of *Hertford, Stafford* and *Northampton,* I	281

HES = 7

That he's Reuengefull; and I know, his Sword	169
He bores me with some tricke; He's gone to'th'King:	198
Matter against him, that for euer marres | The Hony of his Language. No, he's setled	1851
Nor. He's discontented.	1946
But he's a Learned man. May he continue	2306
He be conuented. He's a ranke weed Sir *Thomas,*	2831
He's honest on mine Honor. Gods blest Mother,	2956

HEYRE = 1*1

*(Well worthy the best Heyre o'th' World) should not	1562
Her Ashes new create another Heyre,	3412

HEYRES = 1

This pausingly ensu'de; neither the King, nor's Heyres	514

HID = 1
    Were hid against me, now to forgiue me frankly.   924
HIDE = 2
    Of a rude streame, that must for euer hide me.   2265
    They are too thin, and base to hide offences,   3194
HIDEOUS = 1
    Buc. Euery man, | After the hideous storme that follow'd, was   144
HIGH = 14*1
    Sad, high, and working, full of State and Woe: 4
    For high feats done to'th'Crowne; neither Allied   110
    Together; To consider further, that | What his high Hatred would effect,
    wants not   166
    Arrest thee of High Treason, in the name | Of our most Soueraigne
    King.   282
    Not frended by his wish to your High person;   481
    Haue found him guilty of high Treason. Much   856
    When I came hither, I was Lord High Constable,   948
    Perceiue I speake sincerely, and high notes   1275
    Your high profession Spirituall. That agen   1477
    Imploy'd you where high Profits might come home,   2030
    To be high Steward; Next the Duke of Norfolke,   2400
    head, bearing a long white Wand, as High Steward. With   2434
    1 'Tis the same: high Steward.   2453
    The high promotion of his Grace of *Canterbury,*   3021
    Long, and euer happie, to the high and Mighty | Princesse of England
    Elizabeth.   3366
HIGHEST = 1
    I haue touch'd the highest point of all my Greatnesse,   2103
HIGHNES = 7*1
    The busines present. Tis his Highnes pleasure | You shall to th' Tower.   289
    Card. Now Madam, may his Highnes liue in freedome,   552
    Wol. Most gracious Sir, | In humblest manner I require your Highnes,   1508
    Did broach this busines to your Highnes, or   1514
    Lin. So please your Highnes, | The question did at first so stagger me,   1580
    And did entreate your Highnes to this course, | Which you are running
    heere.   1585
    Camp. So please your Highnes, | The Queene being absent, 'tis a
    needfull fitnesse,   1601
    Or be a knowne friend 'gainst his Highnes pleasure,   1713
HIGHNESSE = 1
    To each incensed Will: I would your Highnesse   398
HIGHNESSE = 27*2
    Card. Please your Highnesse note   479
    Sur. Not long before your Highnesse sped to France,   497
    Sur. Being at *Greenwich,* | After your Highnesse had reprou'd the
    Duke | About Sir *William Bulmer.*   539
    One of her Highnesse women.   799
    Whom once more, I present vnto your Highnesse.   1145
    You are so Noble: To your Highnesse hand   1150
    His Highnesse, hauing liu'd so long with her, and she   1203
    As from a blushing Handmaid, to his Highnesse;   1289
    His Highnesse shall speake in, I do beseech   1462
    You haue by Fortune, and his Highnesse fauors,   1471
    Wols. Peace to your Highnesse.   1646
    Car. Heauen forgiue me, | Euer God blesse your Highnesse.   2003
    Car. And euer may your Highnesse yoake together,   2021
    Car. I do professe, | That for your Highnesse good, I euer labour'd   2066

HIGHNESSE *cont.*
Till you heare further from his Highnesse. | *Car.* Stay:	2115
A League betweene his Highnesse, and *Ferrara.*	2221
Long in his Highnesse fauour, and do Iustice	2307
We write in Water. May it please your Highnesse	2602
Mes. I humbly do entreat your Highnesse pardon,	2687
How does his Highnesse? | *Cap.* Madam, in good health.	2712
Kath. I thanke you honest Lord. Remember me | In all humilitie vnto his Highnesse:	2753
In the great'st humblenesse, and desir'd your Highnesse | Most heartily to pray for her.	2846
With gentle Trauaile, to the gladding of | Your Highnesse with an Heire.	2854
Suf. I wish your Highnesse | A quiet night, and my good Mistris will | Remember in my Prayers.	2861
Den. He attends your Highnesse pleasure. | *King.* Bring him to Vs.	2872
Cran. It is my dutie | T'attend your Highnesse pleasure.	2885
Cran. I humbly thanke your Highnesse,	2906
Butts. I thinke your Highnesse saw this many a day.	3018
*We will be short with you. 'Tis his Highnesse pleasure	3101

HIGH-BLOWNE = 1
But farre beyond my depth: my high-blowne Pride	2262

HILL = *1
*tribulation of Tower Hill, or the Limbes of Limehouse,	3320

HILLES = 1
What 'tis you go about: to climbe steepe hilles	202

HIM *l.*74 75 100 107 114 117 119 124 126 131 *175 179 189 190 199 205
258 259 271 274 276 312 326 333 464 465 472 476 488 494 509 515 524
529 543 550 557 565 567 646 648 680 748 757 779 789 845 846 848 851
853 854 856 858 885 886 *887 *890 895 916 931 932 934 937 957 1010
1011 1016 1017 *1036 *1053 1066 1082 1085 1086 1089 1090 *1093
1097 1126 1130 *1146 1162 1164 1173 1180 1182 1184 1188 *1336 *1346
1386 1454 1459 1481 1499 1533 1627 1690 1753 *1763 1764 1765 1836
1838 1844 1847 1849 1851 *1875 1906 1907 1921 1936 1942 1948 1970
*1974 1981 2078 2082 2087 2088 2098 2150 2152 2234 2236 2255 2302
2310 2329 2331 2334 2424 *2430 *2435 2533 2537 2566 2573 2577 2579
2586 2587 2611 2612 2615 2617 2622 2626 2633 *2690 2725 2728 2738
2756 2770 2779 2781 2815 2817 2820 2829 2832 2873 2983 2984 *3038
3053 3158 3159 3174 3213 3216 3225 3226 3227 3229 3230 *3301 *3306
3420 *3425 = 176*21

HIMSELFE = 13*1
Or ha's giuen all before, and he begins | A new Hell in himselfe.	121
As himselfe pleas'd; and they were ratified	246
places himselfe vnder the Kings feete on | his right side.	319
And neuer seeke for ayd out of himselfe: yet see,	453
2. After all this, how did he beare himselfe?	859
But he fell to himselfe againe, and sweetly,	864
Suff. Pray God he doe, | Hee'l neuer know himselfe else.	1054
The stampe of Noblenesse in any person | Out of himselfe?	1840
We haue seene him set himselfe.	1981
Car. It must be himselfe then. | *Sur.* Thou art a proud Traitor, Priest.	2137
About the houre of eight, which he himselfe	2580
Himselfe with Princes. One that by suggestion	2590
For then, and not till then, he felt himselfe,	2623
himselfe at the vpper end of the Table, on the left hand: A	3037

HINDER = 1
I hinder you too long: Good night, Sir *Thomas*. | *Exit Gardiner and
Page. 2833
HINDRED = 1
It to be stir'd; but oft haue hindred, oft 1530
HIPOCRISIE = 1
For all this spice of your Hipocrisie: 1234
HIRE = *1
Old.L. Tis strange; a threepence bow'd would hire me 1245
HIS *see also* in's, nor's, on's, too's *l.*33 77 91 101 103 112 113 118 129 165
167 168 169 177 181 187 190 196 197 204 236 238 253 254 256 262 268
269 289 305 320 326 327 331 391 451 460 462 464 473 475 476 481 482
487 494 532 543 549 550 *552 556 557 558 561 563 564 566 626 644 650
667 692 710 777 839 845 846 847 851 855 861 876 879 *889 915 930 935
936 937 945 955 961 1017 1022 *1033 *1046 1047 1048 1056 1061 1065
1077 1087 1128 1203 1277 1281 1289 1320 1366 1420 1462 1471 1480
1545 1606 1621 1624 1676 1687 1690 1692 1713 1750 1751 1752 1768
1818 1846 1850 1852 1853 1858 1862 1867 1876 1877 1878 1899 1904
1910 1911 1914 1930 1935 1948 1962 1969 1975 1977 1979 1980 1988
1996 1998 1999 2000 2001 2027 2028 2086 2089 2097 2115 2120 2132
2134 2147 2149 2156 2157 2158 2164 2172 2173 2186 2187 2221 2233
2235 2255 2258 2287 2307 2308 2309 2317 2332 2340 2352 2357 2384
2408 *2427 *2429 *2433 2436 2459 2461 2567 2569 2573 2576 2578 2581
2583 2584 2586 2592 2594 2596 2597 2598 2603 2608 2621 2622 2625
2633 2706 2712 2722 2723 2731 2754 2755 2827 2881 2960 3005 3021
3022 3029 3045 3063 3088 *3101 3174 3179 3181 3187 3189 3200 3202
3221 3222 3229 3258 *3300 *3304 *3355 3405 3406 3420 3422 3424
3447 = 253*14
HISTORY = 1
The Famous History of the Life of | King HENRY the Eight. 3465
HIT = 2*2
2. I thinke | You haue hit the marke; but is't not cruell, 1019
That had a head to hit, either young or old, 3282
*did I hit three times on the head, and three times 3303
*and hit that Woman, who cryed out Clubbes, when I 3309
HITHER = 6
And hither make, as great Embassadors | From forraigne Princes. 742
Kin. My Lord Chamberlaine, | Prethee come hither, what faire Ladie's
that? 795
When I came hither, I was Lord High Constable, 948
Kin. Come hither *Gardiner*. | *Walkes and whispers.* 1170
Who had beene hither sent on the debating 1540
Lou. This is about that, which the Byshop spake, | I am happily come
hither. 2874
HITHERTO = *1
Cran. My good Lords; Hitherto, in all the Progresse 3080
HITTING = 1
Hitting a grosser quality, is cride vp 419
HOA = 1
To make great hast. All fast? What meanes this? Hoa? 2991
HOBOIES = *1
Hoboies. A small Table vnder a State for the Cardinall, a 661
HOBOYES *see also* ho-boyes = 1*1
Hoboyes. Enter Cardinall Wolsey, and takes his State. 710
Hoboyes. Enter King and others as Maskers, habited like 753
HOLD = 8*1
For when they hold 'em, you would sweare directly 579

HOLD *cont.*

Let me haue such a Bowle may hold my thankes,	716
You hold a faire Assembly; you doe well Lord:	790
I hold my most malicious Foe, and thinke not | At all a Friend to truth.	1441
And all the Fellowship I hold now with him	1753
Dance: and at certaine Changes, the first two hold a spare	2647
Cran. And let Heauen | Witnesse how deare, I hold this Confirmation.	3246
A Marshallsey, shall hold ye play these two Monthes.	3347
If they hold, when their Ladies bid 'em clap. | FINIS.	3463

HOLDETH = *1

reioycing, and holdeth vp her hands to heauen. And so, in	2655

HOLDING = *1

in their Changes, and holding the Garland ouer her	2651

HOLDS = 1

Who holds his State at dore 'mongst Purseuants, | Pages, and Foot-boyes.	3022

HOLILY = 1

Norf. How holily he workes in all his businesse,	1056

HOLINESSE = 4

To bring my whole Cause 'fore his Holinesse,	1480
Made to the Queene to call backe her Appeale | She intends vnto his Holinesse.	1605
How that the Cardinall did intreat his Holinesse	1867
I writ too's Holinesse. Nay then, farewell:	2102

HOLLOW = 1

But Cardinall Sins, and hollow hearts I feare ye:	1736

HOLY = 10*1

As shore of Rocke: attend. This holy Foxe,	233
Spoke by a holy Monke, that oft, sayes he,	506
And thanke the holy Conclaue for their loues,	1147
Queen. The more shame for ye; holy men I thought ye,	1734
Car. Sir, | For Holy Offices I haue a time; a time	2013
Whil'st your great Goodnesse, out of holy pitty, | Absolu'd him with an Axe.	2151
As holy Oyle, *Edward* Confessors Crowne,	2509
By holy *Mary* (*Butts*) there's knauery;	3032
That holy duty out of deare respect,	3188
By all that's holy, he had better starue,	3201
Holy and Heauenly thoughts still Counsell her:	3399

HOLYDAME = 1

Prythee let's walke. Now by my Holydame,	2915

HOLY-DAY = 1

This Little-One shall make it Holy-day. *Exeunt.*	3448

HOLY-HAT = 1

Your holy-Hat to be stampt on the Kings Coine.	2223

HOME = 3

As here at home, suggests the King our Master	239
Heare what I say, and then goe home and lose me.	898
Imploy'd you where high Profits might come home,	2030

HONEST = 12

And vnderstand againe like honest men,	610
An honest Country Lord as I am, beaten	625
(Like free and honest men) our iust opinions, | And comforts to our cause.	1684
Ye speake like honest men, (pray God ye proue so)	1695
(Though he be growne so desperate to be honest)	1714

137

HONEST *cont.*

Car. If your Grace | Could but be brought to know, our Ends are
honest,   1790
(Out of thy honest truth) to play the Woman.   2345
But such an honest Chronicler as *Griffith.*   2630
Kath. I thanke you honest Lord. Remember me | In all humilitie vnto
his Highnesse: 2753
He's honest on mine Honor. Gods blest Mother,   2956
Crom. Would you were halfe so honest: 3135
This honest man, wait like a lowsie Foot-boy   3209
HONESTIE = 4

You haue as little Honestie, as Honor,   2160
Now, if you can blush, and crie guiltie Cardinall, | You'l shew a little
Honestie.   2200
For honestie, and decent Carriage | A right good Husband (let him be a
Noble)   2737
Cran. Most dread Liege, | The good I stand on, is my Truth and
Honestie: 2921
HONESTY = 4

In Honor, Honesty, the tract of eu'ry thing,   85
Corruption wins not more then Honesty.   2359
They had parted so much honesty among 'em,   3027
Against this man, whose honesty the Diuell   3178
HONOR = 19*2

In Honor, Honesty, the tract of eu'ry thing,   85
To whom as great a Charge, as little Honor   128
Honor, and plenteous safety) that you reade | The Cardinals Malice,
and his Potency   164
Buc. Ile to the King, | And from a mouth of Honor, quite cry downe   208
*Whose Honor Heauen shield from soile; euen he escapes | (not   353
And proue it too, against mine Honor, aught;   1393
You tender more your persons Honor, then   1476
Yet will I adde an Honor; a great Patience.   1770
Therein illustrated, the Honor of it   2056
My heart drop'd Loue, my powre rain'd Honor, more   2060
You haue as little Honestie, as Honor,   2160
A loade, would sinke a Nauy, (too much Honor.)   2289
And sounded all the Depths, and Shoales of Honor,   2351
In Celebration of this day with Shewes, | Pageants, and Sights of Honor.   2390
That the great Childe of Honor, Cardinall *Wolsey* | Was dead?   2557
Was fashion'd to much Honor. From his Cradle   2608
To keepe mine Honor, from Corruption,   2629
(Now in his Ashes) Honor: Peace be with him.   2633
Let me be vs'd with Honor; strew me ouer   2761
He's honest on mine Honor. Gods blest Mother,   2956
*To quench mine Honor; they would shame to make me   3009
HONORS = 5

Bad me enioy it, with the Place, and Honors   2133
And beares his blushing Honors thicke vpon him: 2255
No Sun, shall euer vsher forth mine Honors,   2324
He gaue his Honors to the world agen,   2583
And to adde greater Honors to his Age   2625
HONOUR = 23*1

Does buy and sell his Honour as he pleases,   268
Not vnconsidered leaue your Honour, nor   341
Things to strike Honour sad. Bid him recount   465
Henry the Eight, Life, Honour, Name and all   962

HONOUR *cont.*

Doe's purpose honour to you no lesse flowing,	1278
Beauty and Honour in her are so mingled,	1294
Kin. My Lord Cardinall, | I doe excuse you; yea, vpon mine Honour,	1521
The passages made toward it; on my Honour,	1531
To taint that honour euery good Tongue blesses;	1679
In such a poynt of weight, so neere mine Honour,	1697
Both for your Honour better, and your Cause:	1725
1 They that beare | The Cloath of Honour ouer her, are foure Barons | Of the Cinque-Ports.	2462
Is this the Honour they doe one another?	3025
To one mans Honour, this contagious sicknesse;	3074
Gard. Good M.(aster) Secretary, | I cry your Honour mercie; you may worst | Of all this Table say so.	3127
The cheefe ayme of his Honour, and to strengthen	3187
In such an honour: how may I deserue it,	3236
So I grow stronger, you more Honour gaine. *Exeunt.*	3255
*draw mine Honour in, and let 'em win the Worke, the	3316
Por. And't please your Honour, | We are but men; and what so many may doe,	3334
From her shall read the perfect way of Honour,	3408
Who, from the sacred Ashes of her Honour	3416
His Honour, and the greatnesse of his Name,	3422
I haue receiu'd much Honour by your presence,	3443

HONOURABLE = 2

The Honourable Boord of Councell, out | Must fetch him in, he Papers.	130
With all their honourable points of ignorance	604

HONOURABLY = 1

With all his Couent, honourably receiu'd him;	2573

HONOURD = 2

An. My honour'd Lord.	1300
Camp. Most honour'd Madam, | My Lord of Yorke, out of his Noble nature,	1686

HONOURS = 4

Restor'd me to my Honours: and out of ruines	960
From Princes into Pages: all mens honours	1081
That promises mo thousands: Honours traine	1319
Crom. Please your Honours, | The chiefe cause concernes his Grace of *Canterbury.*	3044

HONY = 1

Matter against him, that for euer marres | The Hony of his Language. No, he's setled	1851

HOODS = 1

But all Hoods, make not Monkes.	1644

HOPE = 10*2

Their Money out of hope they may beleeue,	9
Buck. So, so; | These are the limbs o'th' Plot: no more I hope.	306
For further life in this world I ne're hope,	910
The action of good women, there is hope | All will be well.	1270
No Friends, no Hope, no Kindred weepe for me?	1786
And when he falles, he falles like Lucifer, | Neuer to hope againe.	2272
Card. I hope I haue:	2294
(The Image of his Maker) hope to win by it?	2357
I hope she will deserue well; and a little	2727
**Cran.* I hope I am not too late, and yet the Gentleman	2989
Let me ne're hope to see a Chine againe,	3284
*her succour, which were the hope o'th' Strond where she	3311

HOPEFULL = 1
Thy hopefull seruice perish too. Good *Cromwell*   2333
HOPELESSE = 1
Alas, I am a Woman frendlesse, hopelesse.   1706
HOPES = 6
To faire content, and you: None heere he hopes   669
Your hopes and friends are infinite. | *Queen*. In England,   1709
The tender Leaues of hopes, to morrow Blossomes,   2254
Too heauy for a man, that hopes for Heauen.   2291
The Hopes of Court, my Hopes in Heauen do dwell. | *Exeunt*.   2375
HOPKINS = 2
Bra. A Monke o'th' *Chartreux*. | *Buck*. O *Michaell Hopkins*? | *Bra*. He.   308
Confessor to him, with that Diuell Monke, | *Hopkins*, that made this
mischiefe.   848
HORRIBLE = 1
He did discharge a horrible Oath, whose tenor   559
HORRID = 1
Appeare in formes more horrid) yet my Duty,   2072
HORSE = 1
A full hot Horse, who being allow'd his way   204
HORSEBACKE = 1
I was then present, saw them salute on Horsebacke,   49
HORSES = 1*1
My Lord, the Horses your Lordship sent for, with all the   1028
My Noble Lords; for those that tame wild Horses,   3069
HOT = 3
A full hot Horse, who being allow'd his way   204
Norf. Be aduis'd; | Heat not a Furnace for your foe so hot   212
Haue more, or else vnsay't: and now, while 'tis hot,   2985
HOURE = 11*1
His houre of speech, a minute: He, (my Lady)   460
And haue an houre of hearing, and by'r Lady | Held currant Musicke
too.   627
An houre of Reuels with 'em.   765
Pray for me, I must now forsake ye; the last houre   978
I would your Grace would giue vs but an houre | Of priuate conference. 1123
As I saw it inclin'd? When was the houre   1381
I should be glad to heare such Newes as this | Once euery houre.   1855
To his owne portion? And what expence by'th'houre   1969
To rest a while, some halfe an houre, or so,   2486
About the houre of eight, which he himselfe   2580
*To waste these times. Good houre of night Sir *Thomas*:   2776
Keep. My Lord Archbishop: | And ha's done halfe an houre to know
your pleasures.   3051
HOURELY = 1
Heauen euer laid vp to make Parents happy, | May hourely fall vpon
ye.   3372
HOURES = 3
Richly in two short houres. Onely they   14
Within these fortie houres, Surrey durst better | Haue burnt that
Tongue, then saide so.   2140
Gard. These should be houres for necessities,   2773
HOUSE = 6
Card. Say, Lord *Chamberlaine*, | They haue done my poore house grace: 766
To Asher-house, my Lord of Winchesters,   2114
A worthy Friend. The King ha's made him | Master o'th'Iewell House, 2537
Beside that of the Iewell-House, is made Master   2812

HOUSE *cont.*
   To make your house our Towre: you, a Brother of vs   2903
   'Has businesse at his house; for all shall stay: 3447
HOUSHOLD = 1
   Rich Stuffes and Ornaments of Houshold, which   1989
HOUSWIFE = *1
   Queen. Your Graces find me heere part of a Houswife,   1647
HOW = 63*3
   How soone this Mightinesse, meets Misery: 31
   Buckingham. | Good morrow, and well met. How haue ye done   38
   Beheld them when they lighted, how they clung   50
   Is pleas'd you shall to th'Tower, till you know | How he determines
   further.   297
   Kin. Speake on; | How grounded hee his Title to the Crowne   486
   Kin. How know'st thou this?   496
   That sure th'haue worne out Christendome: how now?   588
   Lou. Faith how easie?   688
   Cham. How now, what is't? | *Seru.* A noble troupe of Strangers,   739
   2. But pray how past it?   837
   2. After all this, how did he beare himselfe?   859
   *Farewell; and when you would say somthing that is sad, | Speake how
   I fell.   980
   Suff. How is the King imployd? | *Cham.* I left him priuate,   1042
   Norf. How holily he workes in all his businesse,   1056
   Suff. How sad he lookes; sure he is much afflicted.   1102
   Kin. Who's there I say? How dare you thrust your | (selues   1105
   Euen of your selfe Lord Cardinall. | *Wol.* How? of me?   1178
   An. How you doe talke;   1255
   Old L. How tasts it? Is it bitter? Forty pence, no: 1310
   For you, or any: how farre I haue proceeded,   1449
   Or how farre further (Shall) is warranted   1450
   That I gainsay my Deed, how may he wound,   1455
   How vnder my oppression I did reeke | When I first mou'd you.   1575
   Kin. I haue spoke long, be pleas'd your selfe to say | How farre you
   satisfide me.   1578
   Enter a Gentleman. | *Queen.* How now?   1633
   How you stand minded in the waighty difference   1682
   But how to make ye sodainly an Answere   1696
   Queen. How Sir? | *Camp.* Put your maine cause into the Kings
   protection,   1722
   How you may hurt your selfe: I, vtterly   1797
   Sur. How came | His practises to light?   1861
   Suf. Most strangely. | *Sur.* O how? how?   1863
   How that the Cardinall did intreat his Holinesse   1867
   Sur. Will this worke? | *Cham.* The King in this perceiues him, how he
   coasts   1874
   Seemes to flow from him? How, i'th'name of Thrift   1970
   What sodaine Anger's this? How haue I reap'd it?   2084
   How eagerly ye follow my Disgraces   2125
   As if it fed ye, and how sleeke and wanton   2126
   Found his deserts. How innocent I was   2156
   Car. How much me thinkes, I could despise this man,   2190
   How to liue better. For your stubborne answer   2246
   I feele my heart new open'd. Oh how wretched   2267
   Why how now *Cromwell?*   2275
   Crom. How does your Grace. | *Card.* Why well: 2281
   What, and how true thou art; he will aduance thee: 2330

HOW *cont.*

By that sinne fell the Angels: how can man then   2356
The Princesse Dowager? How goes her businesse?   2405
1 How was it? | 3 Well worth the seeing.   2479
How euer, yet there is no great breach, when it comes   2532
Grif. How do's your Grace? | *Kath.* O *Griffith*, sicke to death: 2551
Kath. Pre'thee good *Griffith*, tell me how he dy'de.   2561
Pati. Do you note | How much her Grace is alter'd on the sodaine?   2674
How long her face is drawne? How pale she lookes,   2676
How does his Highnesse? | *Cap.* Madam, in good health.   2712
To loue her for her Mothers sake, that lou'd him, | Heauen knowes how
deerely.   2728
King. How now my Lord?   2882
King. Know you not | *How your state stands i'th'world, with the whole
world?   2927
How earnestly he cast his eyes vpon me: 3005
How euer faulty, yet should finde respect   3124
Cham. Tis now too certaine; | How much more is his Life in value with
him?   3173
Gard. Dread Soueraigne, | How much are we bound to Heauen,   3182
In such an honour: how may I deserue it,   3236
Cran. And let Heauen | Witnesse how deare, I hold this Confirmation.   3246
Por. How gqt they in, and be hang'd?   3274
Man. Alas I know not, how gets the Tide in?   3275
HOWEUER *see* how
HOWRE = 2
Iohn de la Car, my Chaplaine, a choyce howre   508
Is this an howre for temporall affaires? Ha?   1114
HO-BOYES = 1
The Queene is comming. *Ho-boyes.*   2420
HULLING = 1
Many a groaning throw: thus hulling in   1566
HUMBLE = 5
And range with humble liuers in Content,   1225
I haue bene to you, a true and humble Wife,   1377
Wol. Be patient yet. | *Qu.* I will, when you are humble; Nay before,   1431
Grif. This Cardinall, | Though from an humble Stocke, vndoubtedly   2606
That am a poore and humble Subiect to you?   3237
HUMBLENESSE = 1
In the great'st humblenesse, and desir'd your Highnesse | Most heartily
to pray for her.   2846
HUMBLEST = 1
Wol. Most gracious Sir, | In humblest manner I require your Highnes,   1508
HUMBLE-MOUTHD = *1
*T'oppose your cunning. Y'are meek, & humble-mouth'd   1467
HUMBLY = 4*1
*Who deem'd our Marriage lawful. Wherefore I humbly   1407
I humbly thanke his Grace: and from these shoulders   2287
Mes. I humbly do entreat your Highnesse pardon,   2687
Kath. Sir, I most humbly pray you to deliuer   2719
Cran. I humbly thanke your Highnesse,   2906
HUMILITIE = 2
With Meekenesse and Humilitie: but your Heart   1469
Kath. I thanke you honest Lord. Remember me | In all humilitie vnto
his Highnesse: 2753
HUNDRED = 1*1
King. Giue her an hundred Markes.   2979

HUNDRED *cont.*
**Lady.* An hundred Markes? By this light, Ile ha more.   2981
HUNG = 2
  That like a Iewell, ha's hung twenty yeares   1064
  Hung their heads, & then lay by.   1629
HUNGER = 1
  Vnfit for other life, compeld by hunger   362
HUNTSMAN = 1
  Vpon the daring Huntsman that has gall'd him: 2087
HURT = 1
  How you may hurt your selfe: I, vtterly   1797.
HUSBAND = 3
  Bring me a constant woman to her Husband,   1767
  I deeme you an ill Husband, and am glad   2011
  For honestie, and decent Carriage | A right good Husband (let him be a
  Noble)   2737
HYPOCRISIE *see* hipocrisie
I = 525*28, 8
  Car. Is he in person, ready? | *Secr.* I, please your Grace.   183
  Louell. I marry, | There will be woe indeed Lords, the slye whorsons   618
  Kin. I, and the best she shall haue; and my fauour   1161
  How you may hurt your selfe: I, vtterly   1797
  King. Ha? Canterbury? | *Den.* I my good Lord.   2869
  Say I, and of a boy. | *Lady.* I, I my Liege,   2969
IADED = 1
  To be thus Iaded by a peece of Scarlet,   2171
IEMME = 1
  But from this Lady, may proceed a Iemme,   1296
IEWELL = 2
  That like a Iewell, ha's hung twenty yeares   1064
  A worthy Friend. The King ha's made him | Master o'th'Iewell House,   2537
IEWELL-HOUSE = 1
  Beside that of the Iewell-House, is made Master   2812
IF *l.*7 12 32 120 221 406 420 463 473 518 544 548 565 566 698 706 727 779
  901 902 923 931 987 989 *1034 1087 1130 1138 1188 1217 1241 1252
  1326 1391 1410 1454 1457 1501 1556 1619 1658 1661 1670 1726 1748
  1749 1790 1810 1815 1827 1829 1845 1868 1995 2037 2038 2039 2085
  2099 2126 2159 2170 2185 2200 2203 *2363 2562 2693 2744 2784 2923
  2948 2952 3072 3108 3222 3227 3281 3328 3339 3460 3463 = 80*2
IGNORANCE = 1
  With all their honourable points of ignorance   604
IGNORANT = 1
  Traduc'd by ignorant Tongues, which neither know   407
ILE *l.*13 32 199 208 224 *232 326 525 640 691 787 791 825 838 1086 1113
  1130 1297 1430 1789 1942 2187 2393 2545 2782 2963 2980 *2981 2984
  2986 3016 *3266 3339 3346 3350 3352 = 33*3, 1
  To lighten all this Ile. I'le to the King,   1297
ILL = 7*1
  Sparing would shew a worse sinne, then ill Doctrine,   649
  And somthing spoke in choller, ill, and hasty: 863
  Camp. Beleeue me, there's an ill opinion spread then,   1177
  I deeme you an ill Husband, and am glad   2011
  He fell sicke sodainly, and grew so ill | He could not sit his Mule.   2568
  Of his owne body he was ill, and gaue | The Clergy ill example.   2598
  All the best men are ours; for 'tis ill hap,   3462

ILLUSIONS = 1
  I told my Lord the Duke, by th'Diuels illusions   526
ILLUSTRATED = 1
  Therein illustrated, the Honor of it   2056
IM = 4
  L.Cham. I'm glad 'tis there;   597
  Chan. My good Lord Archbishop, I'm very sorry   3056
  But whatsoere thou tak'st me for; I'm sure   3197
  And faire purgation to the world then malice, | I'm sure in me.   3223
IMAGE = 1
  (The Image of his Maker) hope to win by it?   2357
IMPERIOUS = 1
  Or this imperious man will worke vs all   1080
IMPLORE = 1
  I will implore. If not, i'th'name of God | Your pleasure be fulfill'd.   1410
IMPLOYD = 2
  Suff. How is the King imployd? | *Cham.* I left him priuate,   1042
  Imploy'd you where high Profits might come home,   2030
IMPLOYMENT = 1
  The Cardnall instantly will finde imployment,   882
IMPORTING = 1
  Forsooth an Inuentory, thus importing | The seuerall parcels of his
  Plate, his Treasure,   1987
IMPOSSIBLE = 1
  Man. Pray Sir be patient; 'tis as much impossible,   3269
IMPRISONMENT = 1
  Concerning his Imprisment, was rather   3221
IN *see also* a, i' = 261*33
INCENSE = 1
  Cham. Now God incense him, | And let him cry Ha, lowder.   1906
INCENSED = 1
  To each incensed Will: I would your Highnesse   398
INCENST = 1
  Sir (I may tell it you) I thinke I haue | Incenst the Lords o'th'Councell,
  that he is   2821
INCKLING = 1
  'Tis full of woe: yet I can giue you inckling   988
INCLIND = 1
  As I saw it inclin'd? When was the houre   1381
INCOMPAREABLE = 1
  Was cry'de incompareable; and th'ensuing night   71
INCREASE = 1
  Car. What should this meane? | *Sur.* The Lord increase this businesse.   2033
INDEED = 13
  (For twas indeed his colour, but he came   254
  Said, 'twas the feare indeed, and that he doubted   504
  Louell. I marry, | There will be woe indeed Lords, the slye whorsons   618
  Lou. That Churchman | Beares a bounteous minde indeed,   641
  There is indeed, which they would haue your Grace   784
  2. Were you there? | 1. Yes indeed was I.   828
  Would haue flung from him; but indeed he could not;   854
  For mine owne ends, (Indeed to gaine the Popedome,   2092
  A great man should decline. Nay, and you weep | I am falne indeed.   2279
  Card. That's Newes indeed.   2314
  2 Their Coronets say so. These are Starres indeed, | And sometimes
  falling ones.   2469
  To speake my minde of him: and indeed this day,   2820

INDEED *cont.*
  Kin. Ha? 'Tis he indeed.   3024
INDEEDE = *1
  *I feare he will indeede; well, let him haue them; hee | will haue all I
  thinke.   1036
INDIA = 1
  Made Britaine, India: Euery man that stood,   65
INDIAN = *1
  *to muster in? Or haue wee some strange Indian with the   3292
INDIES = 1
  Our King ha's all the Indies in his Armes,   2459
INDIFFERENT = 1
  No Iudge indifferent, nor no more assurance   1371
INDUCD = 1
  Or God will punish me. I do beleeue | (Induc'd by potent
  Circumstances) that   1433
INDUCE = 1
  Induce you to the question on't: or euer   1516
INDUCEMENT = *1
  *Then marke th'inducement. Thus it came; giue heede | (too't: 1536
INDURANCE = 1
  Your selfe, and your Accusers, and to haue heard you | Without
  indurance further.   2919
INFANT = 2
  This Royall Infant, Heauen still moue about her;   3387
  That were the Seruants to this chosen Infant,   3419
INFECT = 2
  It would infect his Speech: That if the King   473
  That does infect the Land: with which, they moued   2825
INFECTING = 1
  Infecting one another, yea reciprocally,   237
INFINITE = 1
  Your hopes and friends are infinite. | *Queen.* In England,   1709
INFORMATIONS = 1
  Crom. My mind gaue me, | In seeking tales and Informations 3176
INFORMD = 1
  (For so we are inform'd) with new opinions,   3065
INIUSTICE = 1
  I haue no Spleene against you, nor iniustice   1448
INNOCENCE = 3
  Buck. It will helpe me nothing | To plead mine Innocence; for that dye
  is on me   291
  Wol. So much fairer | And spotlesse, shall mine Innocence arise, 2194
  Cran. God, and your Maiesty | Protect mine innocence, or I fall into 2942
INNOCENT = 1
  Found his deserts. How innocent I was   2156
INS = 5*1
  Buc. I read in's looks | Matter against me, and his eye reuil'd 195
  Made suit to come in's presence; which if granted,   548
  Any thing on him: for he hath a Witchcraft | Ouer the King in's
  Tongue.   1847
  Crom. To his owne hand, in's Bed-chamber.   1930
  King. It may well be, | There is a mutiny in's minde. This morning, 1982
  *now reigne in's Nose; all that stand about him are   3301
INSCRIBD = 1
  Was still inscrib'd: in which you brought the King | To be your Seruant. 2212

INSIDE = 1
  Card. Look'd he o'th'inside of the Paper?   1931
INSOLENCE = 1
  This *Ipswich* fellowes insolence; or proclaime,   210
INSPIRATION = *1
  (as it were by inspiration) she makes (in her sleepe) signes of   2654
INSPIRD = 1
  A thing Inspir'd, and not consulting, broke   146
INSTALLD = 1
  Install'd Lord Arch-byshop of Canterbury.   2313
INSTANT = 2
  Me as his abiect obiect, at this instant   197
  Whose Figure euen this instant Clowd puts on,   314
INSTANTLY = 1
  The Cardnall instantly will finde imployment,   882
INSTRUCT = 2
  That he may furnish and instruct great Teachers,   452
  Th'occasion shall instruct you. If intreaties   2952
INT = 4
  To heare this of him; and could wish he were | Somthing mistaken in't.   271
  Be gladded in't by me. Then followes, that   1563
  Bearing a State of mighty moment in't,   1582
  There's more in't then faire Visage. *Bullen?*   1943
INTEGRITAS = *1
  Card. Tanta est erga te mentis integritas Regina serenissima.   1664
INTEGRITY = 5
  Of singular Integrity, and Learning;   1414
  Card. Noble Lady, | I am sorry my integrity should breed,   1674
  And my Integrity to Heauen, is all,   2368
  Thy Truth, and thy Integrity is rooted   2913
  More out of Malice then Integrity,   3215
INTELLIGENCE = 1
  From sincere motions, by Intelligence,   227
INTEND = 1
  To make that onely true, we now intend,   22
INTENDS = 1
  Made to the Queene to call backe her Appeale | She intends vnto his
  Holinesse.   1605
INTER *see* enterre
INTERCEPTED = 1
  The goodnesse of your intercepted Packets   2179
INTERCESSION = 1
  That through our Intercession, this Reuokement   443
INTERPRETERS = 1
  By sicke Interpreters (once weake ones) is   417
INTERUIEW *see also* enteruiew = 1
  His feares were that the Interview betwixt   256
INTO *l.*118 147 461 550 572 747 1059 1073 1081 1083 1106 1119 *1358
  1362 *1488 1651 *1723 1745 1746 1750 1808 1961 1978 2113 2177 2178
  2217 2240 2943 3379 = 27*3
INTREAT = 1
  How that the Cardinall did intreat his Holinesse   1867
INTREATIES = 1
  Th'occasion shall instruct you. If intreaties   2952
INUENTORY = 2*1
  Forsooth an Inuentory, thus importing | The seuerall parcels of his
  Plate, his Treasure,   1987

INUENTORY *cont.*

King. Good my Lord, | *You are full of Heauenly stuffe, and beare the
Inuentory   2005
There take an Inuentory of all I haue,   2366
INUITE = 1
Inuite me to a Banquet, whose bright faces   2665
INUITED = 1
Inuited by your Noble selfe, hath sent   1142
INUMERABLE = *1
Sur. Then, That you haue sent inumerable substance,   2224
IOHN = 3
Of the Dukes Confessor, *Iohn de la Car*,   304
Iohn de la Car, my Chaplaine, a choyce howre   508
Sir *Gilbert Pecke* his Chancellour, and *Iohn Car*,   847
IOT = 1
If this salute my blood a iot; it faints me | To thinke what followes.   1326
IOURNEY = 2
For this great Iourney. What did this vanity   138
Concerning the French Iourney. I replide,   501
IOY = 6*1
Wol. Giue me your hand: much ioy & fauour to you;   1166
One that ne're dream'd a Ioy, beyond his pleasure;   1768
Sur. Now all my ioy | Trace the Coniunction.   1883
1 'Tis very true. But that time offer'd sorrow, | This generall ioy.   2385
Could not be wedg'd in more: I am stifled | With the meere ranknesse
of their ioy.   2475
Bin loose, this day they had beene lost. Such ioy   2495
All comfort, ioy in this most gracious Lady,   3371
IOYFULL = 2*1
Sur. I am ioyfull | To meete the least occasion, that may giue me   1833
Grif. I am most ioyfull Madam, such good dreames | Possesse your
Fancy.   2670
Kin. Good Man, those ioyfull teares shew thy true | (hearts,   3248
IOYND = 1
Cardinall of *Yorke*, are ioyn'd with me their Seruant,   1153
IPSWICH = 2
This *Ipswich* fellowes insolence; or proclaime,   210
Ipswich and Oxford: one of which, fell with him,   2617
IRELAND = 2
Then Deputy of Ireland, who remou'd | Earle *Surrey*, was sent thither,
and in hast too,   874
You sent me Deputie for Ireland,   2148
IRON = 1
Beare witnesse, all that haue not hearts of Iron,   2339
IRRESOLUTE = 1
His Father, by as much as a performance | Do's an irresolute purpose.   561
IS *see also* all's, anger's, *Cranmer*'s, fancies, heer's, hee's, here's, he's, it's,
ladie's, mindes, queens, shee's, that's, there's, ther's, 'tis, titles, what's,
where's, who's = 183*8
ISLE *see* ile
ISSUE = 5
But minister communication of | A most poore issue.   139
Things done without example, in their issue   426
Should without issue dye; hee'l carry it so   474
The Graue does to th' dead: For her Male Issue,   1558
Ile put it to the issue. *Exit Ladie.*   2986

ISSUES = 2

By this my Issues faile, and that gaue to me	1565
Of our despis'd Nobilitie, our Issues,	2184

IST = 6

Abur. Is it therefore | Th'Ambassador is silenc'd? | *Nor.* Marry is't.	153
L.Ch. Is't possible the spels of France should iuggle	571
L.Cham. What is't for? | *Lou.* The reformation of our trauel'd Gallants,	594
Cham. How now, what is't? | *Seru.* A noble troupe of Strangers,	739
2. I thinke | You haue hit the marke; but is't not cruell,	1019
Gard. It's one a clocke Boy, is't not. | *Boy.* It hath strooke.	2771

IT *see also* and't, an't, as't, bee't, by't, for't, from't, gau't, in't, is't, on't, open't, perform't, say't, seek't, 't, tak't, though't, til't, too't, vnsay't, vpon't = 178*9

ITEM = 1

Sur. Item, You sent a large Commission | To *Gregory de Cassado*, to conclude	2218

ITH = 17*1

Did breake ith'wrenching. | *Norf.* Faith, and so it did.	242
Thankes you for this great care: I stood i'th' leuell	322
Card. Sir *Thomas Louell*, is the Banket ready | I'th' Priuy Chamber? | *Lou.* Yes, my Lord.	804
I will implore. If not, i'th'name of God | Your pleasure be fulfill'd.	1410
That man i'th' world, who shall report he ha's	1498
Our Daughter *Mary*: I'th' Progresse of this busines,	1542
For no dislike i'th' world against the person	1593
Our cause, that she should lye i'th'bosome of	1958
Seemes to flow from him? How, i'th'name of Thrift	1970
I beare i'th'State: and Nature does require	2016
Does pay the Act of it, as i'th'contrary	2057
Thou should'st feele | My Sword i'th'life blood of thee else. My Lords,	2167
3 Among the crowd i'th'Abbey, where a finger	2474
His owne Opinion was his Law. I'th'presence	2592
Louell. Now Sir, you speake of two | The most remark'd i'th'Kingdome: as for *Cromwell*,	2810
King. Know you not | *How your state stands i'th'world, with the whole world?	2927
Gard. Receiue him, | And see him safe i'th' Tower.	3158
Por. You i'th'Chamblet, get vp o'th' raile,	3351

ITS = 6

Made former Wonders, it's. To day the French,	62
Hath a sharpe edge: It's long, and't may be saide	170
Liue where their prayers did: and it's come to passe,	396
It's fit this Royall Session do proceed,	1422
Nor. It's Heauens will,	1992
Gard. It's one a clocke Boy, is't not. | *Boy.* It hath strooke.	2771

ITSELFE *see* selfe

IUDGD = 1

And to be iudg'd by him. | *She Curtsies to the King, and offers to depart.*	1481

IUDGE = 8

I should iudge now vnhappily.	792
No Iudge indifferent, nor no more assurance	1371
You shall not be my Iudge. For it is you	1436
Refuse you for my Iudge, whom yet once more	1440
I do refuse you for my Iudge, and heere	1478
Heauen is aboue all yet; there sits a Iudge, | That no King can corrupt.	1731
I shall both finde your Lordship, Iudge and Iuror,	3109

IUDGE *cont.*
To a most Noble Iudge, the King my Maister.   3164
IUDGEMENT = 6*1
His Knell rung out, his Iudgement, he was stir'd   861
I haue this day receiu'd a Traitors iudgement,   899
*Haue their free voyces. Rome (the Nurse of Iudgement)   1141
And vnmatch'd Wit, and Iudgement. *Ferdinand*   1401
This was a Iudgement on me, that my Kingdome   1561
To stay the Iudgement o'th'Diuorce; for if   1868
His Royall selfe in Iudgement comes to heare   3189
IUDGES = 2*1
By learned approbation of the Iudges: If I am   406
vnder him as Iudges. The Queene takes place some di-| stance   1346
1 *A liuely Flourish of Trumpets.* | 2 *Then, two Iudges.*   2422
IUDGING = 1
In the vnpartiall iudging of this Businesse.   1154
IUE = 1
I'ue heard him vtter to his Sonne in Law,   476
IUGGLE = 1
L.Ch. Is't possible the spels of France should iuggle   571
IULY = 1
And proofes as cleere as Founts in *Iuly*, when   228
IURIE = 1
His Noble Iurie, and foule Cause can witnesse.   2158
IURISDICTION = 1
You maim'd the Iurisdiction of all Bishops.   2209
IUROR = 1
I shall both finde your Lordship, Iudge and Iuror,   3109
IUST = 5
But he would bite none, iust as I doe now,   702
The Tryall, iust and Noble. All the Clerkes,   1139
This iust and learned Priest, Cardnall *Campeius,*   1144
(Like free and honest men) our iust opinions, | And comforts to our cause.   1684
To silence enuious Tongues. Be iust, and feare not;   2361
IUSTICE = 9
T'has done vpon the premises, but Iustice: 904
Sir, I desire you do me Right and Iustice,   1367
To the sharp'st kinde of Iustice. Please you, Sir,   1398
Stubborne to Iustice, apt to accuse it, and   1484
(If you haue any Iustice, any Pitty,   1748
Sur. Sharpe enough, | Lord for thy Iustice.   1949
Long in his Highnesse fauour, and do Iustice   2307
The Iustice and the Truth o'th' question carries   2931
That in this case of Iustice, my Accusers,   3094
IUSTIFIDE = 1
But will you be more iustifi'de? You euer   1528
IUSTIFIE = 1
Ile heare him his confessions iustifie,   326
IUSTLY = 1
Camp. His Grace | Hath spoken well, and iustly: Therefore Madam,   1420
KATE = 1
Kin. Goe thy wayes *Kate,*   1497
KATH = 15*3
KATHERINE see also Kath. = 8*1
A buzzing of a Separation | Betweene the King and *Katherine?*   999
Scribe. Say, *Katherine* Queene of England, | Come into the Court.   1361

KATHERINE cont.
   Crier. Katherine Queene of England, &c.   1363
   **Crier. Katherine.* Q.(ueene) of England, come into the Court.   1488
   (*Katherine* our Queene) before the primest Creature | That's Parragon'd
   o'th' World.   1599
   Her Coronation. *Katherine* no more | Shall be call'd Queene, but
   Princesse Dowager,   1915
   But I beseech you, what's become of *Katherine*   2404
   Enter Katherine Dowager, sicke, lead betweene Griffith,   2548
   I can no more. | *Exeunt leading Katherine.*   2766
KEECH = 1
   That such a Keech can with his very bulke   103
KEEP = *2
   **Cham.* Heauen keep me from such councel: tis most true   1070
   **Que.* What need you note it? pray you keep your way,   1490
KEEP = 5
KEEPE = 8
   Take vp the Rayes o'th'beneficiall Sun, | And keepe it from the Earth.   104
   To *Pepin* or *Clotharius*, they keepe State so.   581
   My Lord *Sands*, you are one will keepe 'em waking: 694
   1. Good Angels keepe it from vs: 991
   To keepe your earthly Audit, sure in that   2010
   To keepe mine Honor, from Corruption, ·   2629
   Keepe comfort to you, and this Morning see   2947
   Keepe the dore close Sirha.   3288
KEEPER see also Keep. = 1
   Enter Keeper.   2993
KEPT = 3
   Kept him a forraigne man still, which so greeu'd him,   1182
   I haue kept you next my Heart, haue not alone   2029
   As if we kept a Faire heere? Where are these Porters?   3328
KILDARES = 1
   1. Tis likely, | By all coniectures: First *Kildares* Attendure;   872
KILL = 1
   Which euer ha's, and euer shall be growing, | Till death (that Winter)
   kill it.   2052
KILLING = 2
   Killing care, & griefe of heart, | *Fall asleepe, or hearing dye.*   1631
   The third day, comes a Frost; a killing Frost,   2256
KIMBOLTON *see* Kymmalton
KIN = 39*10
KINDE = 5
   (Which as I take it, is a kinde of Puppie   251
   Kin. Still Exaction: | The nature of it, in what kinde let's know,   384
   An. I doe not know | What kinde of my obedience, I should tender;   1282
   To the sharp'st kinde of Iustice. Please you, Sir,   1398
   And 'tis a kinde of good deede to say well,   2025
KINDLE = 1
   Euer in feare to kindle your Dislike,   1379
KINDLING = *1
   *till her pinck'd porrenger fell off her head, for kindling   3307
KINDRED = 1
   No Friends, no Hope, no Kindred weepe for me?   1786
KING see also Kin. = 98*15
   A guift that heauen giues for him, which buyes | A place next to the
   King.   114
   (Without the priuity o'th'King) t'appoint   125

KING cont.

He bores me with some tricke; He's gone to'th'King:	198
Buc. Ile to the King, | And from a mouth of Honor, quite cry downe	208
Buck. To th'King Ile say't, & make my vouch as strong	232
As here at home, suggests the King our Master	239
And breake the foresaid peace. Let the King know	266
Arrest thee of High Treason, in the name | Of our most Soueraigne King.	282
Bran. Nay, he must beare you company. The King	296
Bran. Here is a warrant from | The King, t'attach Lord *Mountacute,* and the Bodies	302
Cornets. Enter King Henry, leaning on the Cardinals shoul-|der,	317
Suffolke: she kneels. King riseth from his State,	331
Most bitterly on you, as putter on | Of these exactions: yet the King, our Maister	351
It would infect his Speech: That if the King	473
This pausingly ensu'de; neither the King, nor's Heyres	514
That had the King in his last Sicknesse faild,	532
Hoboyes. Enter King and others as Maskers, habited like	753
Choose Ladies, King and An Bullen.	770
(And generally) who euer the King fauours,	881
Nor will I sue, although the King haue mercies	911
A buzzing of a Separation | Betweene the King and *Katherine?*	999
For when the King once heard it, out of anger	1002
The King will venture at it. Either the Cardinall,	1009
a Subiect, if not before the King, which stop'd our mouthes | Sir.	1034
Suff. How is the King imployd? | *Cham.* I left him priuate,	1042
*Turnes what he list. The King will know him one day.	1053
And out of all these, to restore the King,	1062
Will blesse the King: and is not this course pious?	1069
If the King please: his Curses and his blessings	1087
Norf. Let's in; | And with some other busines, put the King	1091
The King ha's sent me otherwhere: Besides	1096
Exit Lord Chamberlaine, and the King drawes the Curtaine | and sits reading pensiuely.	1100
Norff. A gracious King, that pardons all offences	1108
Thou art a cure fit for a King; you'r welcome	1118
The King hath of you. I haue perus'd her well,	1293
*That they haue caught the King: and who knowes yet	1295
To lighten all this Ile. I'le to the King,	1297
two Noblemen, with the Sword and Mace. The King takes	1344
from the King. The Bishops place themselues on	1347
Scri. Say, *Henry* K.(ing) of England, come into the Court.	1358
Crier. Henry King of England, &c. | *King.* Heere.	1359
goes about the Court, comes to the King, and kneeles at | his Feete. Then speakes.	1365
The King your Father, was reputed for	1399
My Father, King of Spaine, was reckon'd one	1402
For your owne quiet, as to rectifie | What is vnsetled in the King.	1418
The daughter of a King, my drops of teares,	1429
The King is present: If it be knowne to him,	1454
And to be iudg'd by him. | *She Curtsies to the King, and offers to depart.*	1481
Wherein he might the King his Lord aduertise,	1545
Betweene the King and you, and to deliuer	1683
Heauen is aboue all yet; there sits a Iudge, | That no King can corrupt.	1731
*Still met the King? Lou'd him next Heau'n? Obey'd him?	1763

KING cont.

*Such doubts as false Coine from it. The King loues you,	1809
Barre his accesse to'th'King, neuer attempt	1846
Any thing on him: for he hath a Witchcraft │ Ouer the King in's	
Tongue.	1847
Nor. O feare him not, │ His spell in that is out: the King hath found	1849
And came to th'eye o'th'King, wherein was read	1866
My King is tangled in affection, to │ A Creature of the Queenes, Lady	
Anne Bullen.	1870
Sur. Ha's the King this? │ *Suf.* Beleeue it.	1872
Sur. Will this worke? │ **Cham.* The King in this perceiues him, how he	
coasts	1874
After his Patients death; the King already │ Hath married the faire	
Lady. │ *Sur.* Would he had.	1878
Sur. But will the King │ Digest this Letter of the Cardinals?	1894
Ha's left the cause o'th'King vnhandled, and	1902
The King cry'de Ha, at this.	1905
Haue satisfied the King for his Diuorce,	1911
Car. The Packet Cromwell, │ Gau't you the King?	1928
Suf. Maybe he heares the King │ Does whet his Anger to him.	1947
Our hard rul'd King. Againe, there is sprung vp	1959
Hath crawl'd into the fauour of the King, │ And is his Oracle.	1961
Enter King, reading of a Scedule.	1964
Suf. The King, the King.	1967
King takes his Seat, whispers Louell, who goes │ to the Cardinall.	2001
Exit King, frowning vpon the Cardinall, the Nobles │ throng after him	
smiling, and whispering.	2081
I sent the King? Is there no way to cure this?	2096
You aske with such a Violence, the King	2131
Ti'de it by Letters Patents. Now, who'll take it? │ *Sur.* The King that	
gaue it.	2135
Farre from his succour; from the King, from all	2149
Toward the King, my euer Roiall Master,	2162
You writ to'th Pope, against the King: your goodnesse	2180
When the King knowes my Truth.	2196
Was still inscrib'd: in which you brought the King │ To be your Seruant.	2212
Either of King or Councell, when you went	2215
*The King shall know it, and (no doubt) shal thanke you.	2248
A still, and quiet Conscience. The King ha's cur'd me,	2286
Is your displeasure with the King. │ *Card.* God blesse him.	2301
Crom. Last, that the Lady *Anne,* │ Whom the King hath in secrecie long	
married,	2315
O *Cromwell,* │ The King ha's gone beyond me: All my Glories	2321
To be thy Lord, and Master. Seeke the King	2328
The King shall haue my seruice; but my prayres	2341
Serue the King: And prythee leade me in:	2365
I seru'd my King: he would not in mine Age	2371
Our King ha's all the Indies in his Armes,	2459
A man in much esteeme with th'King, and truly	2536
A worthy Friend. The King ha's made him │ Master o'th'Iewell House,	2537
A Gentleman sent from the King, to see you.	2689
This to my Lord the King. │ *Cap.* Most willing Madam.	2720
Stand these poore peoples Friend, and vrge the King │ To do me this	
last right.	2749
A Queene, and Daughter to a King enterre me.	2765
Whether so late? │ *Lou.* Came you from the King, my Lord?	2777
Haue broken with the King, who hath so farre	2826

KING cont.
   Enter King and Suffolke.   2836
   Ile to the Queene. *Exit King.*   2980
   I came this way so happily. The King | Shall vnderstand it presently.
   Exit Buts   3001
   Enter the King, and Buts, at a Windowe | aboue.   3014
   Toward the King first, then his Lawes, in filling   3063
   Pray Heauen the King may neuer find a heart   3090
   To a most Noble Iudge, the King my Maister.   3164
   The King will suffer but the little finger | Of this man to be vex'd?   3171
   Enter King frowning on them, takes his Seate.   3181
   Cham. As I liue, | If the King blame me for't; Ile lay ye all   3338
   Flourish. Enter King and Guard.   3368
   The Famous History of the Life of | King HENRY the Eight.   3465
KING = 33
KINGDOME = 11
   The Beauty of this Kingdome Ile assure you.   640
   Most learned Reuerend Sir, into our Kingdome,   1119
   This was a Iudgement on me, that my Kingdome   1561
   Shipwrack'd vpon a Kingdome, where no Pitty,   1785
   Of all the Kingdome. Many more there are,   2228
   By your power Legatine within this Kingdome,   2239
   With all the choysest Musicke of the Kingdome,   2512
   Ty'de all the Kingdome. Symonie, was faire play,   2591
   Banish'd the Kingdome. *Patience*, is that Letter   2716
   Louell. Now Sir, you speake of two | The most remark'd i'th'Kingdome:
   as for *Cromwell,*   2810
   None better in my Kingdome. Get you gone,   2958
KINGDOMES = 1
   (I meane the learned ones in Christian Kingdomes)   1140
KINGLY = 1
   And Kingly Dignity, we are contented   1597
KINGS = 32*4
   Made it a Foole, and Begger. The two Kings   72
   That he would please to alter the Kings course,   265
   The will of Heauen be done, and the Kings pleasure | By me obey'd.   300
   places himselfe vnder the Kings feete on | his right side.   319
   *Of the Kings grace and pardon: the greeued Commons   441
   To the Kings danger: presently, the Duke   503
   The Kings Atturney on the contrary,   842
   Yet are the Kings; and till my Soule forsake,   933
   He diues into the Kings Soule, and there scatters   1059
   The French Kings Sister. Heauen will one day open   1074
   The Kings eyes, that so long haue slept vpon | This bold bad man.   1075
   You are the Kings now.   1167
   Tane of your many vertues; the Kings Maiesty   1276
   Wol. Madam, | You wrong the Kings loue with these feares,   1707
   Queen. How Sir? | *Camp.* Put your maine cause into the Kings
   protection,   1722
   *Grow from the Kings Acquaintance, by this Carriage.   1798
   Nor. This same *Cranmer*'s | A worthy Fellow, and hath tane much
   paine | In the Kings businesse.   1918
   The French Kings Sister; He shall marry her.   1941
   Nor. Heare the Kings pleasure Cardinall,   2110
   Bearing the Kings will from his mouth expressely?   2120
   Nor. Those Articles, my Lord, are in the Kings hand: 2192
   Haue at you. | First, that without the Kings assent or knowledge,   2206

KINGS *cont.*

Without the Kings will, or the States allowance,	2220
Your holy-Hat to be stampt on the Kings Coine.	2223
Suf. Lord Cardinall, the Kings further pleasure is,	2237
Out of the Kings protection. This is my Charge.	2244
To the last peny, 'tis the Kings. My Robe,	2367
The Kings late Scruple, by the maine assent	2413
'Tis now the Kings, and call'd White-Hall. | 3 I know it:	2519
Newly preferr'd from the Kings Secretary: | The other London.	2526
The Kings request, that I would visit you,	2704
O'th'Rolles, and the Kings Secretary. Further Sir,	2813
Is the Kings hand, and tongue, and who dare speak | One syllable against him?	2816
Cran. 'Tis *Buts.* | The Kings Physitian, as he past along	3003
There to remaine till the Kings further pleasure	3147
Cham. This is the Kings Ring. | *Sur.* 'Tis no counterfeit.	3165

KING-CARDINALL = 1

Norf. Tis so; | This is the Cardinals doing: The King-Cardinall,	1050

KINSMEN = 1

Abur. I do know | Kinsmen of mine, three at the least, that haue	132

KISSE = 4

He would Kisse you Twenty with a breath.	703
And not to kisse you. A health Gentlemen, | Let it goe round.	802
The hearts of Princes kisse Obedience,	1799
With this Kisse, take my Blessing: God protect thee,	3378

KISSES = 1

takes her vp, kisses and placeth | her by him.	332

KISSING = 1

Lay kissing in your Armes, Lord Cardinall.	2189

KNAUERY = 1

By holy *Mary* (*Butts*) there's knauery;	3032

KNAUES = 3

Might corrupt mindes procure, Knaues as corrupt	2933
These lazy knaues? Y'haue made a fine hand fellowes?	3329
Clap round Fines for neglect: y'are lazy knaues,	3341·

KNEELD = 1

Came to the Altar, where she kneel'd, and Saint-like	2504

KNEELE = 2

Queen. Nay, we must longer kneele; I am a Suitor.	334
To vse so rude behauiour. Go too, kneele.	2686

KNEELES = *1

*goes about the Court, comes to the King, and kneeles at | his Feete. Then speakes.	1365

KNEELS = 1

Suffolke: she kneels. King riseth from his State,	331

KNELL = 2

His Knell rung out, his Iudgement, he was stir'd	861
I nam'd my Knell; whil'st I sit meditating	2637

KNEW = 7

Till now I neuer knew thee. | *Musicke, Dance.*	772
(If I but knew him) with my loue and duty	779
That neuer knew what Truth meant: I now seale it;	951
I knew him, and I know him: so I leaue him	1089
She neuer knew harme-doing: Oh, now after	1206
Haue I not stroue to loue, although I knew	1384
With me, since first you knew me.	2699

KNIFE = 3
(As he made semblance of his duty) would | Haue put his knife into
him.   549
Sur. After the Duke his Father, with the knife   556
To sheath his knife in vs: he is attach'd,   564
KNIGHTS = 1
A Knights Daughter | To be her Mistris Mistris? The Queenes, Queene?   1952
KNOCK = 1*1
Who's best in fauour. Let the Musicke knock it. | *Exeunt with
Trumpets.*   817
*But knock 'em downe by th' dozens? Is this More fields   3291
KNOW = 58*3
Will be deceyu'd. For gentle Hearers, know   18
Abur. I do know | Kinsmen of mine, three at the least, that haue   132
A Minister in his Power. You know his Nature,   168
That he's Reuengefull; and I know, his Sword   169
Car. Well, we shall then know more, & *Buckingham*   185
And lose by ouer-running: know you not,   216
Wee see each graine of grauell; I doe know | To be corrupt and
treasonous.   229
And breake the foresaid peace. Let the King know   266
Is pleas'd you shall to th'Tower, till you know | How he determines
further.   297
Know you of this Taxation?   369
Card. Please you Sir, | I know but of a single part in ought   370
Queen. No, my Lord? | You know no more then others? But you frame   374
To those which would not know them, and yet must   377
Kin. Still Exaction: | The nature of it, in what kinde let's know,   384
Traduc'd by ignorant Tongues, which neither know   407
Queen. If I know you well, | You were the Dukes Surueyor, and lost
your Office   518
*Turnes what he list. The King will know him one day.   1053
Suff. Pray God he doe, | Hee'l neuer know himselfe else.   1054
I knew him, and I know him: so I leaue him   1089
Is businesse of Estate; in which, we come | To know your Royall
pleasure.   1110
Go too; Ile make ye know your times of businesse: 1113
Wol. I know your Maiesty, ha's alwayes lou'd her   1157
L.Cham. Good morrow Ladies; what wer't worth to | (know   1264
An. I doe not know | What kinde of my obedience, I should tender;   1282
I know your backe will beare a Dutchesse. Say,   1321
As you haue done my Truth. If he know   1457
That you haue many enemies, that know not   1524
Prethee returne, with thy approch: I know,   1611
I know my life so euen. If your busines   1661
As not to know the Language I haue liu'd in: 1667
You haue too much good Lady: But to know   1681
In truth I know not. I was set at worke,   1700
Car. If your Grace | Could but be brought to know, our Ends are
honest,   1790
I know you haue a Gentle, Noble temper,   1802
You know I am a Woman, lacking wit   1816
What he deserues of you and me, I know: 1843
Then out it goes. What though I know her vertuous   1955
And well deseruing? yet I know her for   1956
I know 'twill stirre him strongly; yet I know   2098
(I meane your malice) know, Officious Lords,   2122

KNOW *cont.*
*The King shall know it, and (no doubt) shal thanke you.   2248
I know my selfe now, and I feele within me,   2284
(I know his Noble Nature) not to let   2332
2 A Royall Traine beleeue me: These I know: 2447
'Tis now the Kings, and call'd White-Hall. | 3 I know it: 2519
With Maiden Flowers, that all the world may know   2762
Of mine owne way. I know you Wise, Religious,   2805
(For so I know he is, they know he is)   2823
You do desire to know wherefore | I sent for you.   2883
This Morning come before vs, where I know   2898
And Corne shall flye asunder. For I know   2909
King. Know you not | *How your state stands i'th'world, with the whole
world?   2927
Who waites there? Sure you know me?   2992
Keep. My Lord Archbishop: | And ha's done halfe an houre to know
your pleasures.   3051
You shall know many dare accuse you boldly,   3105
Crom. Why my Lord? | *Gard.* Doe not I know you for a Fauourer   3130
Bishop of *Winchester.* But know I come not   3192
Man. Alas I know not, how gets the Tide in?   3275
And say twill doe; I know within a while,   3461
KNOWES = 5*2
*That they haue caught the King: and who knowes yet   1295
That I am free of your Report, he knowes   1458
Among my Maids, full little (God knowes) looking   1701
*Ye haue Angels Faces; but Heauen knowes your hearts.   1781
When the King knowes my Truth.   2196
3 All the Land knowes that: 2531
To loue her for her Mothers sake, that lou'd him, | Heauen knowes how
deerely.   2728
KNOWING = 1
Knowing she will not loose her wonted Greatnesse   2685
KNOWLEDGE = 3
Haue at you. | First, that without the Kings assent or knowledge,   2206
Suf. Then, that without the knowledge   2214
Gard. Ha's he had knowledge of it? | *Crom.* Yes.   3046
KNOWN = *1
*1 I thanke you Sir: Had I not known those customs,   2402
KNOWNE = 8
Therefore, for Goodnesse sake, and as you are knowne   24
Things that are knowne alike, which are not wholsome   376
An. Oh Gods will, much better | She ne're had knowne pompe; though't
be temporall,   1215
The King is present: If it be knowne to him,   1454
Or be a knowne friend 'gainst his Highnes pleasure,   1713
Be knowne vnto vs: are you all agreed Lords.   3148
God shall be truely knowne, and those about her,   3407
Would I had knowne no more: But she must dye,   3431
KNOWST = 1
Kin. How know'st thou this?   496
KYMMALTON = 1
Since which, she was remou'd to Kymmalton,   2416
L = 4*1
LA *l.*304 508 = 2
LA = 1

LABOR = *1
*Much waightier then this worke. The Queens in Labor 2792
LABOUR = 3
The Pride vpon them, that their very labour 69
1. Ile saue you | That labour Sir. All's now done but the Ceremony 825
They say in great Extremity, and fear'd | Shee'l with the Labour, end. 2793
LABOURD = 2
Car. I do professe, | That for your Highnesse good, I euer labour'd 2066
Both of my Life and Office, I haue labour'd, 3081
LACK = 1
And lack of other meanes, in desperate manner 363
LACKEYES = 1
Wait else at doore: a fellow Councellor | 'Mong Boyes, Groomes, and
Lackeyes. 3010
LACKING = 1
You know I am a Woman, lacking wit 1816
LADIE = 3
Suff. No, his Conscience | Ha's crept too neere another Ladie. 1048
Shee's a good Creature, and sweet-Ladie do's | Deserue our better
wishes. 2801
Ile put it to the issue. *Exit Ladie.* 2986
LADIES = 7*2
L.Cham. What a losse our Ladies | Will haue of these trim vanities? 616
Haue got a speeding tricke to lay downe Ladies. 620
Card. What warlike voyce, | And to what end is this? Nay, Ladies, feare
not; 735
Craue leaue to view these Ladies, and entreat 764
Choose Ladies, King and An Bullen. 770
Commanded Nature, that my Ladies wombe 1555
*10 *Certaine* Ladies *or* Countesses, *with plaine Circlets of* | *Gold, without
Flowers.* 2443
Of Lords, and Ladies, hauing brought the Queene 2483
**the Marchionesse Dorset, the other Godmother, and La-* | *dies.* 3361
LADIES = 1
To drinke to these faire Ladies, and a measure 815
LADIES = 9*3
To many Lords and Ladies; there will be 639
and diuers other Ladies, & Gentlemen, as Guests 663
Cham. Sweet Ladies will it please you sit; Sir *Harry* 690
Pray sit betweene these Ladies. 695
San. By my faith, | *And thanke your Lordship: by your leaue sweet
Ladies, 696
The pennance lyes on you; if these faire Ladies | Passe away frowning. 706
Ladies you are not merry; Gentlemen, | Whose fault is this? 720
Kin. My Lord Chamberlaine, | Prethee come hither, what faire Ladie's
that? 795
Kin. Lead in your Ladies eu'ry one: Sweet Partner, 812
L.Cham. Good morrow Ladies; what wer't worth to | (know 1264
Great store of roome no doubt, left for the Ladies, 3332
If they hold, when their Ladies bid 'em clap. | FINIS. 3463
LADISHIP = 1
Heer's to your Ladiship, and pledge it Madam: | For tis to such a thing. 728
LADY see also L., La., Old.L. = 29*4
Kin. Lady mine proceed. 344
His houre of speech, a minute: He, (my Lady) 460
And haue an houre of hearing, and by'r Lady | Held currant Musicke
too. 627

LADY cont.
    *Card. Y'are welcome my faire Guests; that noble Lady   711
    Enter Anne Bullen, and an old Lady.   1201
    So good a Lady, that no Tongue could euer   1204
    Old L. Alas poore Lady, | Shee's a stranger now againe.   1220
    Follow such Creatures. That you may, faire Lady   1274
    Cham. Lady; | I shall not faile t'approue the faire conceit   1291
    But from this Lady, may proceed a Iemme,   1296
    There was a Lady once (tis an old Story)   1311
    An. Good Lady, | Make your selfe mirth with your particular fancy,   1323
    Wol. You haue heere Lady, | (And of your choice) these Reuerend
Fathers, men   1412
    A Royall Lady, spake one, the least word that might   1518
    Card. Noble Lady, | I am sorry my integrity should breed,   1674
    You haue too much good Lady: But to know   1681
    The Cordiall that ye bring a wretched Lady?   1738
    What will become of me now, wretched Lady?   1782
    *Youl'd feele more comfort. Why shold we (good Lady)   1792
    My King is tangled in affection, to | A Creature of the Queenes, Lady
Anne Bullen.   1870
    After his Patients death; the King already | Hath married the faire
Lady. | *Sur.* 'Would he had.   1878
    Crom. Last, that the Lady *Anne,* | Whom the King hath in secrecie long
married,   2315
    The Lady *Anne,* passe from her Corronation.   2382
    Where she remaines now sicke. | 2 Alas good Lady.   2417
    And more, and richer, when he straines that Lady,   2460
    Is that old Noble Lady, Dutchesse of Norfolke.   2467
    Cap. Noble Lady, | First mine owne seruice to your Grace, the next   2702
    Almost each pang, a death. | *King.* Alas good Lady.   2851
    Enter Olde Lady.   2961
    *Duchesse of *Norfolke,* and Lady Marquesse *Dorset?* will | these please
you?   3240
    **a Mantle, &c. Traine borne by a Lady: Then followes*   3360
    All comfort, ioy in this most gracious Lady,   3371
    I thanke ye heartily: So shall this Lady, | When she ha's so much
English.   3382
LADY = 2*1
LADYES = 1
    S.Hen.Guilf. Ladyes, | A generall welcome from his Grace   666
LAG = 1
    The lag end of their lewdnesse, and be laugh'd at.   613
LAID = 5
    Laid any scruple in your way, which might   1515
    Laid Nobly on her: which perform'd, the Quire   2511
    The trap is laid for me. | *King.* Be of good cheere,   2944
    This is of purpose laid by some that hate me,   3007
    Heauen euer laid vp to make Parents happy, | May hourely fall vpon
ye.   3372
LAME = 1
    And lame ones; one would take it,   583
LAMENT = 1
    Old La. Hearts of most hard temper | Melt and lament for her.   1213
LAND = 8
    A hand as fruitfull as the Land that feeds vs,   643
    Yea, the elect o'th'Land, who are assembled   1415
    By all the Reuerend Fathers of the Land,   1572

LAND *cont.*
  Will fall some blessing to this Land, which shall | In it be memoriz'd.   1892
  Sur. Thy Ambition | (Thou Scarlet sinne) robb'd this bewailing Land   2142
  3 All the Land knowes that: 2531
  That does infect the Land: with which, they moued   2825
  Vpon this Land a thousand thousand Blessings,   3389
LANDED = 1
  For so they seeme; th'haue left their Barge and landed,   741
LANDS = 2
  Sur. Yes, that goodnesse | Of gleaning all the Lands wealth into one,   2176
  To forfeit all your Goods, Lands, Tenements, | Castles, and whatsoeuer,
  and to be   2242
LANGUAGE = 5
  Language vnmannerly; yea, such which breakes   354
  As not to know the Language I haue liu'd in: 1667
  Matter against him, that for euer marres | The Hony of his Language.
  No, he's setled   1851
  He ha's strangled his Language in his teares.   2960
  Gard. I shall remember this bold Language. | *Crom.* Doe.   3137
LARDER = 1
  Within. Good M.(aster) Porter I belong to th' Larder.   3262
LARGE = 1
  Sur. Item, You sent a large Commission | To *Gregory de Cassado*, to
  conclude   2218
LARKE = *1
  *O're-mount the Larke: The Marchionesse of *Pembrooke*?   1316
LARKES = 1
  And dare vs with his Cap, like Larkes.   2173
LAST = 14*1
  Since last we saw in France?   40
  Became the next dayes master, till the last   61
  To this last costly Treaty: Th'enteruiew,   240
  That had the King in his last Sicknesse faild,   532
  Pray for me, I must now forsake ye; the last houre   978
  The last fit of my Greatnesse; good your Graces   1704
  Crom. Last, that the Lady *Anne*, | Whom the King hath in secrecie long
  married,   2315
  Loue thy selfe last, cherish those hearts that hate thee;   2358
  To the last peny, 'tis the Kings. My Robe,   2367
  2 'Tis all my businesse. At our last encounter,   2383
  Kath. Alas poore man. | *Grif.* At last, with easie Rodes, he came to
  Leicester,   2570
  Foretold should be his last, full of Repentance,   2581
  last two: who likewise obserue the same Order. At which   2653
  The last is for my men, they are the poorest,   2740
  Stand these poore peoples Friend, and vrge the King | To do me this
  last right.   2749
LASTING = 1
  There had made a lasting Spring.   1626
LATE = 14*2
  Haue got by the late Voyage, is but meerely   577
  We shall be late else, which I would not be,   656
  2. I am confident; | You shall Sir: Did you not of late dayes heare   997
  Come pat betwixt too early, and too late   1304
  Forgetting (like a good man) your late Censure   1689
  Car. The late Queenes Gentlewoman?   1951
  Because all those things you haue done of late   2238

LATE *cont.*

Held a late Court at Dunstable; sixe miles off	2409
The Kings late Scruple, by the maine assent	2413
And the late Marriage made of none effect:	2415
Kath. O my good Lord, that comfort comes too late,	2708
Whether so late? | *Lou.* Came you from the King, my Lord?	2777
Some touch of your late businesse: Affaires that walke	2786
I haue, and most vnwillingly of late	2894
Cran. I hope I am not too late, and yet the Gentleman	2989
Of the whole State; as of late dayes our neighbours,	3077

LATELY = 2

Cardinall *Campeius* is arriu'd, and lately, | As all thinke for this busines.	1013
But 'tis so lately alter'd, that the old name | Is fresh about me.	2521

LATIN = 1

Queen. O good my Lord, no Latin;	1665

LAUGH = 1

I Come no more to make you laugh, Things now,	2

LAUGHD = 1

The lag end of their lewdnesse, and be laugh'd at.	613

LAUGHT = 1

A woman lost among ye, laugh't at, scornd?	1739

LAURENCE = 1

Saint *Laurence Poultney*, did of me demand	499

LAW = 10

I'ue heard him vtter to his Sonne in Law,	476
Finde mercy in the Law, 'tis his; if none,	566
Many sharpe reasons to defeat the Law.	841
The Law I beare no mallice for my death,	903
A Woman of lesse Place might aske by Law;	1159
For if the tryall of the Law o'retake ye,	1726
Remembrance of my Father-in-Law, the Duke, | To be reueng'd on him.	1835
Of Noble Buckingham, my Father-in-Law,	2144
I answer, is most false. The Duke by Law	2155
His owne Opinion was his Law. I'th'presence	2592

LAWES = 4

We must not rend our Subiects from our Lawes,	429
By all the lawes of Warre y'are priuiledg'd.	737
His faults lye open to the Lawes, let them	2233
Toward the King first, then his Lawes, in filling	3063

LAWFUL = *1

*Who deem'd our Marriage lawful. Wherefore I humbly	1407

LAWFULL = 1

Proue but our Marriage lawfull, by my Life	1596

LAY = 11

He meant to lay vpon: and his owne Letter	129
Haue got a speeding tricke to lay downe Ladies.	620
Hung their heads, & then lay by.	1629
Wol. This, and all else | This talking Lord can lay vpon my credit,	2153
Lay kissing in your Armes, Lord Cardinall.	2189
From Ampthill, where the Princesse lay, to which	2410
That euer lay by man: which when the people	2490
Is come to lay his weary bones among ye:	2576
Then lay me forth (although vnqueen'd) yet like	2764
Lay all the weight ye can vpon my patience,	3115
Cham. As I liue, | If the King blame me for't; Ile lay ye all	3338

LAYD = 1
Our Reasons layd before him, hath commanded 2829
LAYES = 1
Then layes his finger on his Temple: straight 1977
LAYING = 1
Buc. O many | Haue broke their backes with laying Mannors on 'em 136
LAY-THOUGHTS = 1
But halfe my Lay-thoughts in him, some of these 680
LAZY = 2
These lazy knaues? Y'haue made a fine hand fellowes? 3329
Clap round Fines for neglect: y'are lazy knaues, 3341
LCH = 3
LCHAM = 8*1
LEAD = 5*1
Kin. Lead in your Ladies eu'ry one: Sweet Partner, 812
To lead 'em once againe, and then let's dreame 816
And lift my Soule to Heauen. | Lead on a Gods name. 920
And when old Time shall lead him to his end, 937
Enter Katherine Dowager, sicke, lead betweene Griffith, 2548
And ye shall find me thankfull. Lead the way Lords, 3444
LEADE = 1
Serue the King: And prythee leade me in: 2365
LEADING = 1
I can no more. | *Exeunt leading Katherine.* 2766
LEADST = 1
Did'st thou not tell me *Griffith,* as thou lead'st mee, 2556
LEAGUE = 3*1
For France hath flaw'd the League, and hath attach'd 151
Breed him some preiudice; for from this League, 258
*And with what zeale? For now he has crackt the League 1057
A League betweene his Highnesse, and *Ferrara.* 2221
LEANING = *1
Cornets. Enter King Henry, leaning on the Cardinals shoul-| der, 317
LEAPD = 1
Leap'd from his Eyes. So lookes the chafed Lyon 2086
LEAPE = 1
You take a Precepit for no leape of danger, 2940
LEARND = 4
The Gentleman is Learn'd, and a most rare Speaker, 450
Queen. My learn'd Lord *Cardinall,* | Deliuer all with Charity. 484
And Doctors learn'd. First I began in priuate, 1573
My learn'd and welbeloued Seruant *Cranmer,* 1610
LEARNE = 1
I will haue none so neere els. Learne this Brother, 1189
LEARNED = 1
Camp. Was he not held a learned man? | *Wol.* Yes surely. 1175
LEARNED = 1
(I meane the learned ones in Christian Kingdomes) 1140
LEARNED = 6
By learned approbation of the Iudges: If I am 406
Most learned Reuerend Sir, into our Kingdome, 1119
This iust and learned Priest, Cardnall *Campeius,* 1144
But he's a Learned man. May he continue 2306
Learned, and Reuerend Fathers of his Order, 2408
Of all these Learned men, she was diuorc'd, 2414
LEARNEDLY = 1
He spoke, and learnedly for life: But all 857

LEARNING = 4
    For such receipt of Learning, is Black-Fryers: 1194
    Of singular Integrity, and Learning;   1414
    And to such men of grauity and learning;   1699
    Those twinnes of Learning, that he rais'd in you,   2616
LEAST = 8
    Abur. I do know | Kinsmen of mine, three at the least, that haue   132
    Least he should helpe his Father.   876
    The least rub in your fortunes, fall away   975
    A Royall Lady, spake one, the least word that might   1518
    Take heed, for heauens sake take heed, least at once   1742
    Sur. I am ioyfull | To meete the least occasion, that may giue me   1833
    Suf. Which of the Peeres | Haue vncontemn'd gone by him, or at least   1837
    At least good manners; as not thus to suffer   3028
LEAUE = 28*3
    Will leaue vs neuer an vnderstanding Friend.   23
    Not vnconsidered leaue your Honour, nor   341
    And though we leaue it with a roote thus hackt,   433
    Lou. They must either | (For so run the Conditions) leaue those
    remnants   601
    San. By my faith, | *And thanke your Lordship: by your leaue sweet
    Ladies,   696
    But leaue their Flockes, and vnder your faire Conduct   763
    Craue leaue to view these Ladies, and entreat   764
    His Noble Friends and Fellowes; whom to leaue   915
    I knew him, and I know him: so I leaue him   1089
    Would it not grieue an able man to leaue   1197
    O 'tis a tender place, and I must leaue her. *Exeunt.*   1199
    To leaue, a thousand fold more bitter, then   1209
    And leaue me out on't. Would I had no being   1325
    Kin. I then mou'd you, | My Lord of *Canterbury*, and got your leaue   1587
    Sing, and disperse 'em if thou canst: leaue working.   1619
    Camp. I would your Grace | Would leaue your greefes, and take my
    Counsell.   1720
    Is stolne away to Rome, hath 'tane no leaue,   1901
    Card. Leaue me a while. *Exit Cromwell.*   1939
    *(By what meanes got, I leaue to your owne conscience)   2225
    Nor. And so wee'l leaue you to your Meditations   2245
    Crom. O my Lord, | Must I then leaue you? Must I needes forgo   2336
    Willing to leaue their burthen: Reach a Chaire,   2554
    Yet thus farre *Griffith*, giue me leaue to speake him,   2587
    And leaue me heere in wretchednesse, behinde ye?   2659
    Kath. Bid the Musicke leaue, | They are harsh and heauy to me.
    Musicke ceases.   2672
    You must not leaue me yet. I must to bed,   2759
    Lou. I must to him too | Before he go to bed. Ile take my leaue.   2781
    Th'estate of my poore Queene. Leaue me alone,   2858
    * *Port.* You'l leaue your noyse anon ye Rascals: doe   3259
    *you take the Court for Parish Garden: ye rude Slaues, | leaue your
    gaping.   3260
    So shall she leaue her Blessednesse to One,   3414
LEAUES = 3
    By all your good leaues Gentlemen; heere Ile make | My royall choyce.   787
    The tender Leaues of hopes, to morrow Blossomes,   2254
    With what a sorrow *Cromwel* leaues his Lord.   2340
LEFT = 9*2
    For so they seeme; th'haue left their Barge and landed,   741

LEFT *cont.*

Suff. How is the King imployd? | *Cham.* I left him priuate, 1042
I left no Reuerend Person in this Court; 1590
Marry this is yet but yong, and may be left 1888
Ha's left the cause o'th'King vnhandled, and 1902
At length broke vnder me, and now ha's left me 2263
Haue left me naked to mine Enemies. 2372
Gar. I did Sir *Thomas*, and left him at Primero | With the Duke of Suffolke. 2779
*himselfe at the vpper end of the Table, on the left hand: A 3037
*Seate being left void aboue him, as for Canterburies Seate. 3038
Great store of roome no doubt, left for the Ladies, 3332

LEGATE = 1
You wrought to be a Legate, by which power 2208

LEGATINE = 1
By your power Legatine within this Kingdome, 2239

LEGGES = 1
My Legges like loaden Branches bow to'th'Earth, 2553

LEGITIMATE = 1
Whether our Daughter were legitimate, 1546

LEGS = 1
L.San. They haue all new legs, 582

LEICESTER = 1
Kath. Alas poore man. | *Grif.* At last, with easie Rodes, he came to Leicester, 2570

LEND = 1
(As I will lend you cause) my doing well, | With my well saying. 2022

LENGTH = 2*1
At length broke vnder me, and now ha's left me 2263
2 But what follow'd? | 3 At length, her Grace rose, and with modest paces 2502
*length they came to th' broome staffe to me, I defide 'em 3313

LESSE = 4
This night to meet heere they could doe no lesse, 761
A Woman of lesse Place might aske by Law; 1159
Doe's purpose honour to you no lesse flowing, 1278
With lesse Allegeance in it. Men that make 3091

LESSEN = 1
Shall lessen this bigge looke. | *Exeunt Cardinall, and his Traine.* 186

LEST *see* least

LET = 49*2
May (if they thinke it well) let fall a Teare, 7
Abur. I cannot tell | What Heauen hath giuen him: let some Grauer eye 116
And let your Reason with your Choller question 201
As he cride thus let be, to as much end, 247
And breake the foresaid peace. Let the King know 266
To you that choak'd it. Let be cald before vs 324
The Chronicles of my doing: Let me say, 409
Let there be Letters writ to euery Shire, 440
Hardly conceiue of me. Let it be nois'd, 442
Kin. Let him on: Goe forward. 524
Let him not seek't of vs: By day and night 567
(Nay let 'em be vnmanly) yet are follow'd. 575
San. For my little Cure, | Let me alone. 708
Let me haue such a Bowle may hold my thankes, 716
Find out, and he will take it. | *Card.* Let me see then, 785
And not to kisse you. A health Gentlemen, | Let it goe round. 802

LET *cont.*

Who's best in fauour. Let the Musicke knock it. | *Exeunt with Trumpets.*	817
And if I haue a Conscience, let it sincke me,	901
Yet let 'em looke they glory not in mischiefe;	907
Buck. Nay, Sir *Nicholas*, | Let it alone; my State now will but mocke me.	946
1. Let me haue it: | I doe not talke much.	995
*I feare he will indeede; well, let him haue them; hee | will haue all I thinke.	1036
Let silence be commanded.	1352
Turne me away: and let the fowl'st Contempt	1396
A better Wife, let him in naught be trusted,	1499
Let me haue time and Councell for my Cause:	1705
Qu. Haue I liu'd thus long (let me speake my selfe,	1758
Cham. Now God incense him, | And let him cry Ha, lowder.	1906
Farewell Nobilitie: let his Grace go forward,	2172
His faults lye open to the Lawes, let them	2233
(I know his Noble Nature) not to let	2332
Let all the ends thou aym'st at, be thy Countries,	2362
As let 'em haue their rights, they are euer forward	2389
Let me ne're see againe. *Exit Messeng.*	2691
For honestie, and decent Carriage | A right good Husband (let him be a Noble)	2737
Cap. By Heauen I will, | Or let me loose the fashion of a man.	2751
Let me be vs'd with Honor; strew me ouer	2761
And let me tell you, it will ne're be well,	2806
Let 'em alone, and draw the Curtaine close:	3033
Chan. Let him come in. | *Keep.* Your Grace may enter now.	3053
Let some o'th' Guard be ready there.	3154
Good man sit downe: Now let me see the proudest	3199
Was it discretion Lords, to let this man,	3207
To let my tongue excuse all. What was purpos'd	3220
Cran. And let Heauen | Witnesse how deare, I hold this Confirmation.	3246
Let me ne're hope to see a Chine againe,	3284
*draw mine Honour in, and let 'em win the Worke, the	3316
Theres a trim rabble let in: are all these	3330
To let the Troope passe fairely; or Ile finde	3346
Cran. Let me speake Sir, | For Heauen now bids me; and the words I vtter,	3384
Let none thinke Flattery; for they'l finde 'em Truth.	3386

LETS = 9

Kin. Still Exaction: | The nature of it, in what kinde let's know,	384
I must not yet forsake you: Let's be merry,	813
To lead 'em once againe, and then let's dreame	816
2. Let's stand close and behold him.	895
Let's thinke in priuate more. *Exeunt.*	1025
Norf. Let's in; | And with some other busines, put the King	1091
Let's dry our eyes: And thus farre heare me *Cromwel*,	2346
Grif. She is asleep: Good wench, let's sit down quiet,	2640
Prythee let's walke. Now by my Holydame,	2915

LETTER = 4

He meant to lay vpon: and his owne Letter	129
Enter Lord Chamberlaine, reading this Letter.	1027
Sur. But will the King | Digest this Letter of the Cardinals?	1894
The Letter (as I liue) with all the Businesse	2101

LETTER = 1
Banish'd the Kingdome. *Patience*, is that Letter   2716
LETTERS = 4
Where this is question'd, send our Letters, with   435
Let there be Letters writ to euery Shire,   440
Suf. The Cardinals Letters to the Pope miscarried,   1865
Ti'de it by Letters Patents. Now, who'll take it? | *Sur.* The King that
gaue it.   2135
LEUELL = 1
Thankes you for this great care: I stood i'th' leuell   322
LEUIED = 1
The sixt part of his Substance, to be leuied   391
LEWDNESSE = 1
The lag end of their lewdnesse, and be laugh'd at.   613
LEYSURE = 1
To steale from Spirituall leysure, a briefe span   2009
LIBERALL = 2
Men of his way, should be most liberall,   650
Where you are liberall of your loues and Councels,   972
LIBERTY = 1
Bran. I am sorry, | To see you tane from liberty, to looke on   287
LIE *see also* lye = 1
Lie like one lumpe before him, to be fashion'd | Into what pitch he
please.   1082
LIEDGE = 2
Sur. I can my Liedge. | *Kin.* Proceed.   537
B.Lin. Very well my Liedge.   1577
LIEGE = 2
Cran. Most dread Liege, | The good I stand on, is my Truth and
Honestie: 2921
Say I, and of a boy. | *Lady.* I, I my Liege,   2969
LIES *see also* lyes = 1
It lies to cure me, and the Cure is to   1460
LIEST *see* lyest
LIFE = 27
Would by a good Discourser loose some life,   86
Hath shew'd him gold; my life is spand already: 312
King. My life it selfe, and the best heart of it,   321
Vnfit for other life, compeld by hunger   362
Kin. By my life, | This is against our pleasure.   401
I thinke would better please 'em: by my life,   682
He spoke, and learnedly for life: But all   857
For further life in this world I ne're hope,   910
Henry the Eight, Life, Honour, Name and all   962
Of my long weary life is come vpon me: 979
Pronounce dishonour of her; by my life,   1205
No other obligation? by my Life,   1318
Doe no more Offices of life too't; then   1557
Proue but our Marriage lawfull, by my Life   1596
I know my life so euen. If your busines   1661
(More neere my Life I feare) with my weake wit;   1698
While I shall haue my life. Come reuerend Fathers,   1820
During my life; and to confirme his Goodnesse,   2134
Thou should'st feele | My Sword i'th'life blood of thee else. My Lords,   2167
Collected from his life. Ile startle you   2187
If Heauen had pleas'd to haue giuen me longer life   2744
Both of my Life and Office, I haue labour'd,   3081

LIFE *cont.*
    Remember your bold life too.   3139
    Cham. Tis now too certaine; | How much more is his Life in value with
    him?   3173
    Gart. Heauen | From thy endlesse goodnesse, send prosperous life,   3364
    Into whose hand, I giue thy Life. | *Cran. Amen.*   3379
    The Famous History of the Life of | King HENRY the Eight.   3465
LIFT = 1
    And lift my Soule to Heauen. | Lead on a Gods name.   920
LIGHT = 1*1
    Sur. How came | His practises to light?   1861
    *Lady. An hundred Markes? By this light, Ile ha more.   2981
LIGHTED = 1
    Beheld them when they lighted, how they clung   50
LIGHTEN = 1
    To lighten all this Ile. I'le to the King,   1297
LIGHTS = 1
    Those Sunnes of Glory, those two Lights of Men | Met in the vale of
    Andren.   46
LIKE = 49*3
    All Clinquant all in Gold, like Heathen Gods   63
    Shew'd like a Mine. Their Dwarfish Pages were   66
    To eminent Assistants; but Spider-like   111
    Nor. Like it your Grace, | The State takes notice of the priuate
    difference   160
    Requires slow pace at first. Anger is like   203
    Can aduise me like you: Be to your selfe,   206
    That swallowed so much treasure, and like a glasse   241
    Most like a carefull Subiect haue collected | Out of the Duke of
    Buckingham.   469
    It was much like to doe: He answer'd, Tush,   530
    And vnderstand againe like honest men,   610
    *Hoboyes. Enter King and others as Maskers, habited like   753
    Goe with me like good Angels to my end,   917
    My Fathers losse; like a most Royall Prince   959
    Like water from ye, neuer found againe   976
    That blinde Priest, like the eldest Sonne of Fortune,   1052
    That like a Iewell, ha's hung twenty yeares   1064
    Lie like one lumpe before him, to be fashion'd | Into what pitch he
    please.   1082
    Wol. I do professe | You speake not like your selfe: who euer yet   1443
    Thy meekenesse Saint-like, Wife-like Gouernment,   1502
    And like her true Nobility, she ha's | Carried her selfe towards me.   1506
    Why they are so; but like to Village Curres,   1525
    I doe not like their comming; now I thinke on't,   1642
    (Like free and honest men) our iust opinions, | And comforts to our
    cause.   1684
    Forgetting (like a good man) your late Censure   1689
    Ye speake like honest men, (pray God ye proue so)   1695
    To me, aboue this wretchednesse? All your Studies | Make me a Curse,
    like this.   1755
    Almost no Graue allow'd me? Like the Lilly   1787
    I haste now to my Setting. I shall fall | Like a bright exhalation in the
    Euening,   2105
    And dare vs with his Cap, like Larkes.   2173
    Like little wanton Boyes that swim on bladders: 2260
    And when he falles, he falles like Lucifer, | Neuer to hope againe.   2272

LIKE *cont.*
That had not halfe a weeke to go, like Rammes 2497
Came to the Altar, where she kneel'd, and Saint-like 2504
My Legges like loaden Branches bow to'th'Earth, 2553
Cast thousand beames vpon me, like the Sun? 2666
Mes. And't like your Grace --- | *Kath.* You are a sawcy Fellow, 2681
'Tis like a Pardon after Execution; 2709
Then lay me forth (although vnqueen'd) yet like 2764
Acquainted with this stranger; 'tis as like you, | As Cherry, is to Cherry. 2975
Said I for this, the Gyrle was like to him? Ile 2984
And at the dore too, like a Post with Packets: 3031
Cran. For me? | Must I goe like a Traytor thither? 3156
This honest man, wait like a lowsie Foot-boy 3209
Chan. Thus farre | My most dread Soueraigne, may it like your Grace, 3218
*like a Morter-piece to blow vs. There was a Habberda-|shers 3305
*'em in *Limbo Patrum*, and there they are like to dance 3322
Her Foes shake like a Field of beaten Corne, 3401
Shall Star-like rise, as great in fame as she was, 3417
Shall then be his, and like a Vine grow to him; 3420
And like a Mountaine Cedar, reach his branches, 3424
All the expected good w'are like to heare. 3457
LIKELY = 1
1. Tis likely, | By all coniectures: First *Kildares* Attendure; 872
LIKEWISE = *1
*last two: who likewise obserue the same Order. At which 2653
LIKING = 1
Continue in my Liking? Nay, gaue notice 1387
LILLY = 2
Almost no Graue allow'd me? Like the Lilly 1787
A most vnspotted Lilly shall she passe 3433
LIMBES = 1*1
I meane who set the Body, and the Limbes | Of this great Sport
together? 92
*tribulation of Tower Hill, or the Limbes of Limehouse, 3320
LIMBO = *1
*'em in *Limbo Patrum*, and there they are like to dance 3322
LIMBS = 2
Buck. So, so; | These are the limbs o'th' Plot: no more I hope. 306
What thinke you of a Dutchesse? Haue you limbs | To beare that load
of Title? 1247
LIME = 1
With which the Lime will loade him. Th'Archbyshop 2815
LIMEHOUSE = *1
*tribulation of Tower Hill, or the Limbes of Limehouse, 3320
LIN = 1
LINCOLNE see also B.Lin., Lin. = 1*1
*Canterbury alone; after him, the Bishops of Lincolne, Ely, 1336
With you my Lord of *Lincolne*; you remember 1574
LINE = *1
*vnder the Line, they need no other pennance: that Fire-|Drake 3302
LION *see* lyon
LIP = 1
Is in his braine: He bites his lip, and starts, 1975
LIQUOR = 1
The fire that mounts the liquor til't run ore, 217
LIST = 1*1
*Turnes what he list. The King will know him one day. 1053

LIST *cont.*
1 Yes, 'tis the List | Of those that claime their Offices this day,   2396
LISTNING = 1
Almost with rauish'd listning, could not finde   459
LITTLE = 30*1
To whom as great a Charge, as little Honor   128
We cannot feele too little, heare too much.   467
If I chance to talke a little wilde, forgiue me: 698
San. For my little Cure, | Let me alone.   708
Card. Your Grace | I feare, with dancing is a little heated.   807
1. Ile tell you in a little. The great Duke   838
He neuer was so womanish, the cause | He may a little grieue at.   868
A little happier then my wretched Father: 966
An. No in truth. | *Old.L.* Then you are weakly made; plucke off a
little,   1249
Old.L. In faith, for little England   1258
Among my Maids, full little (God knowes) looking   1701
But little for my profit can you thinke Lords,   1711
That little thought when she set footing heere,   1822
You haue as little Honestie, as Honor,   2160
Now, if you can blush, and crie guiltie Cardinall, | You'l shew a little
Honestie.   2200
(Not you) correct him. My heart weepes to see him | So little, of his
great Selfe.   2234
So fare you well, my little good Lord Cardinall. | *Exeunt all but Wolsey.*   2249
Wol. So farewell, to the little good you beare me.   2251
Like little wanton Boyes that swim on bladders: 2260
Some little memory of me, will stirre him   2331
So now (me thinkes) I feele a little ease.   2555
Giue him a little earth for Charity.   2577
And found the Blessednesse of being little.   2624
I hope she will deserue well; and a little   2727
King. But little *Charles,* | Nor shall not when my Fancies on my play.   2840
Haue misdemean'd your selfe, and not a little: 3062
And with no little study, that my teaching   3082
I make as little doubt as you doe conscience,   3116
Crom. My Lord of *Winchester,* y'are a little,   3122
Cran. Stay good my Lords, | I haue a little yet to say. Looke there my
Lords,   3160
The King will suffer but the little finger | Of this man to be vex'd?   3171
LITTLE-ONE = 1
This Little-One shall make it Holy-day. *Exeunt.*   3448
LIUD = 4
His Highnesse, hauing liu'd so long with her, and she   1203
As not to know the Language I haue liu'd in: 1667
Qu. Haue I liu'd thus long (let me speake my selfe,   1758
Whose Minister you are, whiles heere he liu'd   2938
LIUE = 14*1
Liue where their prayers did: and it's come to passe,   396
Card. Now Madam, may his Highnes liue in freedome,   552
Shall cry for blessings on him. May he liue   934
We liue not to be grip'd by meaner persons.   1190
And liue a Subiect? Nay forsooth, my Friends,   1715
They that my trust must grow to, liue not heere,   1717
The Letter (as I liue) with all the Businesse   2101
And from this Fellow? If we liue thus tamely,   2170
(Whom if he liue, will scarse be Gentlemen)   2185

LIUE *cont.*
How to liue better. For your stubborne answer ... 2246
Grif. Noble Madam: | Mens euill manners, liue in Brasse, their Vertues ... 2600
Vnwilling to out-liue the good that did it. ... 2618
Good time, and liue: but for the Stocke Sir *Thomas*, ... 2797
Which ye shall neuer haue while I liue. ... 3217
Cham. As I liue, | If the King blame me for't; Ile lay ye all ... 3338
LIUELY = 1
1 *A liuely Flourish of Trumpets.* | 2 *Then, two Iudges.* ... 2422
LIUERS = 1
And range with humble liuers in Content, ... 1225
LIUING = 10
As they were Liuing: Thinke you see them Great, ... 28
My Chaplaine to no Creature liuing, but ... 512
That's Christian care enough: for liuing Murmurers, ... 1185
I am the most vnhappy Woman liuing. ... 1783
And make 'em reele before 'em. No man liuing ... 2499
No other speaker of my liuing Actions, ... 2628
Whom I most hated Liuing, thou hast made mee ... 2631
Was euer to doe well: nor is there liuing, ... 3085
(But few now liuing can behold that goodnesse) ... 3391
A Patterne to all Princes liuing with her, ... 3392
LO = 1*1
Buck. Lo you my Lord, ... 284
*No more to th' Crowne but that: Lo, who comes here? ... 1261
LOAD = 3
The Backe is Sacrifice to th'load; They say ... 381
What thinke you of a Dutchesse? Haue you limbs | To beare that load of Title? ... 1247
For what they haue beene: 'tis a cruelty, | To load a falling man. ... 3125
LOADE = 2
A loade, would sinke a Nauy, (too much Honor.) ... 2289
With which the Lime will loade him. Th'Archbyshop ... 2815
LOADEN = 1
My Legges like loaden Branches bow to'th'Earth, ... 2553
LODGD = 1
Lodg'd in the Abbey; where the reuerend Abbot ... 2572
LOE = *1
*You'l finde it wholesome. Loe, where comes that Rock ... 173
LOFTY = 1
Lofty, and sowre to them that lou'd him not: ... 2611
LONDON = 1*3
* *North.* When they were ready to set out for London, a man ... 1031
*5 Maior of London, *bearing the Mace. Then* Garter, *in* ... 2426
* *Pearle, Crowned. On each side her, the Bishops of* London, | *and* Winchester, ... 2439
Newly preferr'd from the Kings Secretary: | The other London. ... 2526
LONDONERS = 1
What was the speech among the Londoners, ... 500
LONG = 24*1
In a long Motley Coate, garded with Yellow, ... 17
Hath a sharpe edge: It's long, and't may be saide ... 170
Sur. Not long before your Highnesse sped to France, ... 497
A long time out of play, may bring his plaine song, ... 626
And as the long diuorce of Steele fals on me, ... 918
Of my long weary life is come vpon me: ... 979
The Kings eyes, that so long haue slept vpon | This bold bad man. ... 1075

LONG *cont.*

His Highnesse, hauing liu'd so long with her, and she	1203
In our long absence: pray doe not deliuer,	1329
We are a Queene (or long haue dream'd so) certaine	1428
Kin. I haue spoke long, be pleas'd your selfe to say | How farre you satisfide me.	1578
His Loue, too long ago. I am old my Lords,	1752
Qu. Haue I liu'd thus long (let me speake my selfe,	1758
Sur. By my Soule, | Your long Coat (Priest) protects you,	2165
Farewell? A long farewell to all my Greatnesse.	2252
Long in his Highnesse fauour, and do Iustice	2307
Crom. Last, that the Lady *Anne*, | Whom the King hath in secrecie long married,	2315
*head, bearing a long white Wand, as High Steward. With	2434
I haue not long to trouble thee. Good *Griffith,*	2635
How long her face is drawne? How pale she lookes,	2676
Vpon my wretched women, that so long	2732
Say his long trouble now is passing	2755
I hinder you too long: Good night, Sir *Thomas.* | *Exit Gardiner and Page.*	2833
Come Lords, we trifle time away: I long	3252
Long, and euer happie, to the high and Mighty | Princesse of England *Elizabeth.*	3366

LONGD = 1

Would for *Carnaruanshire*, although there long'd	1260

LONGER = 2

longer Table for the Guests. Then Enter Anne Bullen,	662
That longer you desire the Court, as well	1417

LONGER = 1

Is longer then his fore-skirt; by this time	1320

LONGER = 3

Queen. Nay, we must longer kneele; I am a Suitor.	334
Longer then I haue time to tell his yeares;	935
If Heauen had pleas'd to haue giuen me longer life	2744

LONGING = 2

The many to them longing, haue put off	360
Then vainly longing. What we oft doe best,	416

LOOKD = 3

Card. Look'd he o'th'inside of the Paper?	1931
2 Heauen blesse thee, | Thou hast the sweetest face I euer look'd on.	2456
What manner of man are you? My Lord, I look'd	2916

LOOKE = 7*2

Shall lessen this bigge looke. | *Exeunt Cardinall, and his Traine.*	186
Bran. I am sorry, | To see you tane from liberty, to looke on	287
The force of this Commission: pray looke too't;	437
Card. What's that? | *Cham.* Looke out there, some of ye.	733
Yet let 'em looke they glory not in mischiefe;	907
Looke into these affaires, see this maine end,	1073
*There make before them. Looke, the goodman weeps:	2955
Cran. Stay good my Lords, | I haue a little yet to say. Looke there my Lords,	3160
*Do you looke for Ale, and Cakes heere, you rude | Raskalls?	3267

LOOKES = 5

Suff. How sad he lookes; sure he is much afflicted.	1102
Stops on a sodaine, lookes vpon the ground,	1976
Leap'd from his Eyes. So lookes the chafed Lyon	2086
How long her face is drawne? How pale she lookes,	2676

LOOKES *cont.*
King. Now by thy lookes | I gesse thy Message. Is the Queene deliuer'd?   2967
LOOKING = 1
Among my Maids, full little (God knowes) looking   1701
LOOKS = 1
Buc. I read in's looks | Matter against me, and his eye reuil'd   195
LOOSE = 6*1
Would by a good Discourser loose some life,   86
Be sure you be not loose; for those you make friends,   973
Beware you loose it not: For vs (if you please   1810
Bin loose, this day they had beene lost. Such ioy   2495
Knowing she will not loose her wonted Greatnesse   2685
Cap. By Heauen I will, | Or let me loose the fashion of a man.   2751
*stil, when sodainly a File of Boyes behind 'em, loose shot,   3314
LOP = 1
From euery Tree, lop, barke, and part o'th' Timber: 432
LORD see also L.Ch., L.Cham., L.San. = 123*20
the Duke of Buckingham, and the Lord | *Aburgauenny.*   36
Buc. I pray you who, my Lord?   97
Ile follow, and out-stare him. | *Nor.* Stay my Lord,   199
Sergeant. Sir, | My Lord the Duke of *Buckingham*, and Earle   279
Buck. Lo you my Lord,   284
O my Lord *Aburgany*: Fare you well.   295
Bran. Here is a warrant from | The King, t'attach Lord *Mountacute*,
and the Bodies   302
Of all their Loyalties; wherein, although | My good Lord Cardinall,
they vent reproches   349
Kin. Taxation? | Wherein? and what Taxation? My Lord Cardinall,   366
Queen. No, my Lord? | You know no more then others? But you frame   374
Lord *Aburgany*, to whom by oth he menac'd | Reuenge vpon the
Cardinall.   477
Queen. My learn'd Lord *Cardinall*, | Deliuer all with Charity.   484
I told my Lord the Duke, by th'Diuels illusions   526
Enter L.(ord) Chamberlaine and L.(ord) Sandys.   570
L.Ch. Death my Lord, | Their cloathes are after such a Pagan cut too't,   586
Louell. Faith my Lord, | I heare of none but the new Proclamation,   591
An honest Country Lord as I am, beaten   625
L.Cham. Well said Lord *Sands*,   629
Your Colts tooth is not cast yet? | *L.San.* No my Lord,   630
L.San. He may my Lord, | Ha's wherewithall in him;   647
Enter L.(ord) Chamberlaine L.(ord) Sands, and Louell.   674
O my Lord, y'are tardy;   675
My Lord *Sands*, you are one will keepe 'em waking: 694
Cham. Well said my Lord: | So now y'are fairely seated: Gentlemen,
And saue me so much talking. | *Card.* My Lord *Sands*,   704
*In their faire cheekes my Lord, then wee shall haue 'em, | Talke vs to
silence.   717
   723
An.B. You are a merry Gamster | My Lord *Sands*.   725
Card. Good Lord Chamberlaine, | *Go, giue 'em welcome; you can
speake the French tongue   744
**Shepheards, vsher'd by the Lord Chamberlaine. They*   754
Card. Say, Lord *Chamberlaine*, | They haue done my poore house grace: 766
Card. My Lord. | *Cham.* Your Grace.   774
Cham. I will my Lord. | *Card.* What say they?   781
You hold a faire Assembly; you doe well Lord: 790
Kin. My Lord Chamberlaine, | Prethee come hither, what faire Ladie's
that?   795

LORD cont.

Card. Sir *Thomas Louell*, is the Banket ready | I'th' Priuy Chamber? |	
Lou. Yes, my Lord.	804
Card. There's fresher ayre my Lord, | In the next Chamber.	810
*Good my Lord Cardinall: I haue halfe a dozen healths,	814
When I came hither, I was Lord High Constable,	948
He sent command to the Lord Mayor straight	1003
Enter Lord Chamberlaine, reading this Letter.	1027
* *My Lord, the Horses your Lordship sent for, with all the*	1028
* *of my Lord Cardinalls, by Commission, and maine power tooke*	1032
Enter to the Lord Chamberlaine, the Dukes of Nor-|folke and Suffolke.	1038
Norf. Well met my Lord *Chamberlaine.*	1040
My Lord, youle beare vs company? | *Cham.* Excuse me,	1094
Norfolke. Thankes my good Lord *Chamberlaine.*	1099
* *Exit Lord Chamberlaine, and the King drawes the Curtaine | and sits*	
reading pensiuely.	1100
Who's there? my good Lord Cardinall? O my *Wolsey*,	1116
Vse vs, and it: My good Lord, haue great care,	1120
The Court of Rome commanding. You my Lord	1152
* *Camp.* My Lord of *Yorke*, was not one Doctor *Pace*	1172
Euen of your selfe Lord Cardinall. | *Wol.* How? of me?	1178
My *Wolsey*, see it furnish'd, O my Lord,	1196
Enter Lord Chamberlaine.	1263
An. My good Lord, | Not your demand; it values not your asking:	1266
And say I spoke with you. | *Exit Lord Chamberlaine.*	1298
An. My honour'd Lord.	1300
Qu. Lord Cardinall, to you I speake. | *Wol.* Your pleasure, Madam.	1425
Haue blowne this Coale, betwixt my Lord, and me;	1437
Queen. My Lord, My Lord, | I am a simple woman, much too weake	1465
When you are cald returne. Now the Lord helpe,	1491
Kin. My Lord Cardinall, | I doe excuse you; yea, vpon mine Honour,	1521
I speake my good Lord Cardnall, to this point;	1532
Wherein he might the King his Lord aduertise,	1545
With you my Lord of *Lincolne*; you remember	1574
Kin. I then mou'd you, | My Lord of *Canterbury*, and got your leaue	1587
Queen. O good my Lord, no Latin;	1665
Beleeue me she ha's had much wrong. Lord Cardinall,	1671
Camp. Most honour'd Madam, | My Lord of Yorke, out of his Noble	
nature,	1686
Qu. My Lord, | I dare not make my selfe so guiltie,	1773
Enter the Duke of Norfolke, Duke of Suffolke, Lord Surrey, | and Lord	
Chamberlaine.	1825
Suf. May you be happy in your wish my Lord, | For I professe you haue	
it.	1881
The Lord forbid. | *Nor.* Marry Amen.	1896
Norf. But my Lord | When returnes *Cranmer*?	1908
Sur. Sharpe enough, | Lord for thy Iustice.	1949
Nor. My Lord, we haue | *Stood heere obseruing him. Some strange	
Commotion	1973
King. Good my Lord, | *You are full of Heauenly stuffe, and beare the	
Inuentory	2005
Car. What should this meane? | *Sur.* The Lord increase this businesse.	2033
Enter to Woolsey, the Dukes of Norfolke and Suffolke, the | Earle of	
Surrey, and the Lord Chamberlaine.	2108
To Asher-house, my Lord of Winchesters,	2114
Car. Proud Lord, thou lyest:	2139
Wol. This, and all else | This talking Lord can lay vpon my credit,	2153

172

LORD cont.
If I lou'd many words, Lord, I should tell you,	2159
My Lord of Norfolke, as you are truly Noble,	2182
Lay kissing in your Armes, Lord Cardinall.	2189
*Nor. Those Articles, my Lord, are in the Kings hand:	2192
Cham. O my Lord,	Presse not a falling man too farre: 'tis Vertue:	2231
Suf. Lord Cardinall, the Kings further pleasure is,	2237
So fare you well, my little good Lord Cardinall.	*Exeunt all but Wolsey.*	2249
Crom. The next is, that Sir *Thomas Moore* is chosen	Lord Chancellor,	
in your place.	2303
Install'd Lord Arch-byshop of Canterbury.	2313
To be thy Lord, and Master. Seeke the King	2328
Crom. O my Lord,	Must I then leaue you? Must I needes forgo	2336
With what a sorrow *Cromwel* leaues his Lord.	2340
3 *Lord* Chancellor, *with Purse and Mace before him.*	2424
2 And that my Lord of Norfolke?	1 Yes.	2454
Enter Lord Capuchius.	2692
If my sight faile not,	You should be Lord Ambassador from the	
Emperor,	2693
Kath. O my Lord,	The Times and Titles now are alter'd strangely	2697
*Kath. O my good Lord, that comfort comes too late,	2708
This to my Lord the King.	*Cap.* Most willing Madam.	2720
These are the whole Contents, and good my Lord,	2746
Kath. I thanke you honest Lord. Remember me	In all humilitie vnto	
his Highnesse:	2753
My Lord. *Griffith* farewell. Nay *Patience,*	2758
Whether so late?	*Lou.* Came you from the King, my Lord?	2777
Lou. My Lord, I loue you;	2790
*Lou. Many good nights, my Lord, I rest your seruant.	2835
*Den. Sir, I haue brought my Lord the Arch-byshop,	As you	
commanded me.	2867
King. Ha? Canterbury?	*Den.* I my good Lord.	2869
King. How now my Lord?	2882
King. Pray you arise	My good and gracious Lord of Canterburie:	2887
Ah my good Lord, I greeue at what I speake,	2892
Heard many greeuous, I do say my Lord	2895
What manner of man are you? My Lord, I look'd	2916
Keep. Yes, my Lord:	But yet I cannot helpe you.	2994
Kin. Body a me: where is it?	*Butts.* There my Lord:	3019
*placed vnder the State. Enter Lord Chancellour, places	3036
Duke of Suffolke, Duke of Norfolke, Surrey, Lord Cham-| berlaine,	3039
Keep. My Lord Archbishop:	And ha's done halfe an houre to know	
your pleasures.	3051
Chan. My good Lord Archbishop, I'm very sorry	3056
Suff. Nay, my Lord,	That cannot be; you are a Counsellor,	3097
*Gard. My Lord, because we haue busines of more mo-|(ment,	3100
*Cran. Ah my good Lord of *Winchester*: I thanke you,	3107
'Tis my vndoing. Loue and meekenesse, Lord	3111
Gard. My Lord, my Lord, you are a Sectary,	3119
Crom. My Lord of *Winchester,* y'are a little,	3122
Crom. Why my Lord?	*Gard.* Doe not I know you for a Fauourer	3130
*Cham. Then thus for you my Lord, it stands agreed	3144
*Be friends for shame my Lords: My Lord of *Canterbury*	3231
*Kin. Come, come my Lord, you'd spare your spoones;	3238
Once more my Lord of *Winchester,* I charge you	Embrace, and loue	
this man.	3242
*Of thee, which sayes thus: Doe my Lord of *Canterbury*	3250

173

LORD cont.

Enter Lord Chamberlaine.	3325
*Enter Trumpets sounding: Then two Aldermen, L.(ord) Maior,	3354
Kin. Thanke you good Lord Archbishop:	3374
Kin. Stand vp Lord,	3377
Kin. O Lord Archbishop │ Thou hast made me now a man, neuer before	3435
I thanke ye all. To you my good Lord Maior,	3441

LORDS = 35*4

By Darkning my cleere Sunne. My Lords farewell. *Exe.*	315
Louell. I marry, │ There will be woe indeed Lords, the slye whorsons	618
To many Lords and Ladies; there will be	639
Suff. For me, my Lords, │ I loue him not, nor feare him, there's my	
Creede:	1084
*the Scribes. The Lords sit next the Bishops. The rest of the	1349
What are your pleasures with me, reuerent Lords?	1649
My Lords, I care not (so much I am happy │ Aboue a number) if my	
actions	1657
My Lords, I thanke you both for your good wills,	1694
But little for my profit can you thinke Lords,	1711
They are (as all my other comforts) far hence │ In mine owne Countrey	
Lords.	1718
Mend 'em for shame my Lords: Is this your comfort?	1737
His Loue, too long ago. I am old my Lords,	1752
And am I thus rewarded? 'Tis not well Lords.	1766
Qu. Do what ye will, my Lords: │ And pray forgiue me;	1813
Cham. My Lords, you speake your pleasures:	1842
To some eares vnrecounted. But my Lords	1889
Does he rake this together? Now my Lords, │ Saw you the Cardinall?	1971
Take notice Lords, he ha's a Loyall brest,	2077
**Where's your Commission? Lords, words cannot carrie │ Authority so	
weighty.	2117
(I meane your malice) know, Officious Lords,	2122
Thou should'st feele │ My Sword i'th'life blood of thee else. My Lords,	2167
Of Lords, and Ladies, hauing brought the Queene	2483
Sir (I may tell it you) I thinke I haue │ Incenst the Lords o'th'Councell,	
that he is	2821
Norf. Who waits there? │ *Keep.* Without my Noble Lords? │ *Gard.* Yes.	3048
My Noble Lords; for those that tame wild Horses,	3069
*Cran. My good Lords; Hitherto, in all the Progresse	3080
(I speake it with a single heart, my Lords)	3086
Cham. This is too much; │ Forbeare for shame my Lords.	3140
Be knowne vnto vs: are you all agreed Lords.	3148
But I must needs to th' Tower my Lords?	3151
Cran. Stay good my Lords, │ I haue a little yet to say. Looke there my	
Lords,	3160
Norf. Doe you thinke my Lords	3170
Was it discretion Lords, to let this man,	3207
Kin. Well, well my Lords respect him,	3225
**Be friends for shame my Lords: My Lord of *Canterbury*	3231
Come Lords, we trifle time away: I long	3252
As I haue made ye one Lords, one remaine:	3254
And ye shall find me thankfull. Lead the way Lords,	3444

LORDSHIP = 4*3

Your Lordship is a guest too. │ *L.Cham.* O, 'tis true;	636
My Barge stayes; │ Your Lordship shall along: Come, good Sir *Thomas,*	654
*Lou. O that your Lordship were but now Confessor, │ To one or two of	
these.	684

LORDSHIP *cont.*
  San. By my faith, | *And thanke your Lordship: by your leaue sweet
Ladies, 696
**My Lord, the Horses your Lordship sent for, with all the* 1028
Are all I can returne. 'Beseech your Lordship, 1287
I shall both finde your Lordship, Iudge and Iuror, 3109
LORDSHIPS = 4
  L.San. I am your Lordships. *Exeunt.* 659
Health to your Lordships. 1098
To dance attendance on their Lordships pleasures, 3030
Dare bite the best. I doe beseech your, Lordships, 3093
LOSE *see also* loose = 2
And lose by ouer-running: know you not, 216
Heare what I say, and then goe home and lose me. 898
LOSSE = 3
  L.Cham. What a losse our Ladies | Will haue of these trim vanities? 616
My Fathers losse; like a most Royall Prince 959
He counsels a Diuorce, a losse of her 1063
LOST = 7
  Nor. Then you lost | The view of earthly glory: Men might say 57
  Queen. If I know you well, | You were the Dukes Surueyor, and lost
your Office 518
About his necke, yet neuer lost her lustre; 1065
A woman lost among ye, laugh't at, scornd? 1739
In that one woman, I haue lost for euer. 2323
Bin loose, this day they had beene lost. Such ioy 2495
For since the Cardinall fell, that Titles lost, 2518
LOU = 14*3
LOUD = 8*1
You few that lou'd me, | And dare be bold to weepe for *Buckingham*, 913
Fell by our Seruants, by those Men we lou'd most: 968
  Wol. I know your Maiesty, ha's alwayes lou'd her 1157
*Still met the King? Lou'd him next Heau'n? Obey'd him? 1763
And yet words are no deeds. My Father lou'd you, 2026
If I lou'd many words, Lord, I should tell you, 2159
Lofty, and sowre to them that lou'd him not: 2611
To loue her for her Mothers sake, that lou'd him, | Heauen knowes how
deerely. 2728
She shall be lou'd and fear'd. Her owne shall blesse her; 3400
LOUE = 23*1
  Queen. Thanke your Maiesty | That you would loue your selfe, and in
that loue 339
To the loue o'th'Commonalty, the Duke | Shall gouerne England. 516
  San. O very mad, exceeding mad, in loue too; 701
(If I but knew him) with my loue and duty 779
*They loue and doate on: call him bounteous *Buckingham*, | The Mirror
of all courtesie. 887
That Angels loue good men with: Euen of her, 1067
  Suff. For me, my Lords, | I loue him not, nor feare him, there's my
Creede: 1084
Haue I not stroue to loue, although I knew 1384
My bond to Wedlocke, or my Loue and Dutie 1394
  Wol. Madam, | You wrong the Kings loue with these feares, 1707
His Loue, too long ago. I am old my Lords, 1752
So much they loue it. But to stubborne Spirits, 1800
My heart drop'd Loue, my powre rain'd Honor, more 2060

LOUE   *cont.*
  Dare mate a sounder man then Surrie can be, | And all that loue his
  follies. 2163
  Loue thy selfe last, cherish those hearts that hate thee; 2358
  To loue her for her Mothers sake, that lou'd him, | Heauen knowes how
  deerely. 2728
  By that you loue the deerest in this world, 2747
  Lou. My Lord, I loue you; 2790
  'Tis my vndoing. Loue and meekenesse, Lord 3111
  Am for his loue and seruice, so to him. 3229
  Once more my Lord of *Winchester,* I charge you | Embrace, and loue
  this man. 3242
  Gard. With a true heart, | And Brother; loue I doe it. 3244
  And so stand fix'd. Peace, Plenty, Loue, Truth, Terror, 3418
LOUEL = 2
  Now *Louel,* from the Queene what is the Newes. 2842
  King. Auoyd the Gallery. *Louel seemes to stay.* 2877
LOUELL see also Lou. = 12*2
  the Nobles, and Sir Thomas Louell: the Cardinall 318
  What newes, Sir *Thomas Louell?* 589
  Enter Sir *Thomas Louell.* 590
  Enter L.(ord) Chamberlaine L.(ord) Sands, and Louell. 674
  San. Sir *Thomas Louell,* had the Cardinall 679
  Card. Sir *Thomas Louell,* is the Banket ready | I'th' Priuy Chamber? |
  Lou. Yes, my Lord. 804
  *side, accompanied with Sir Thomas Louell, Sir Nicholas 891
  Buck. Sir *Thomas Louell,* I as free forgiue you 925
  King takes his Seat, whispers Louell, who goes | to the Cardinall. 2001
  Enter Gardiner Bishop of Winchester, a Page with a Torch | before him,
  met by Sir Thomas Louell. 2769
  Gard. Not yet Sir *Thomas Louell:* what's the matter? 2783
  'Twill not Sir *Thomas Louell,* tak't of me, 2807
  Ha? I haue said. Be gone. | What? *Exeunt Louell and Denny.* 2878
  King. Louell. | Lou. Sir. 2977
LOUELL = 4
LOUELS = 1
  The Cardinals and Sir *Thomas Louels* heads | Should haue gone off. 533
LOUELY = 1
  And of a louely Boy: the God of heauen 2971
LOUER = 1
  2 He of Winchester | Is held no great good louer of the Archbishops, |
  The vertuous *Cranmer.* 2528
LOUES = 6*2
  Where you are liberall of your loues and Councels, 972
  Of her that loues him with that excellence, 1066
  And thanke the holy Conclaue for their loues, 1147
  Cam. Your Grace must needs deserue all strangers loues, 1149
  Out with it boldly: Truth loues open dealing. 1663
  *Such doubts as false Coine from it. The King loues you, 1809
  As 'twer in Loues particular, be more | To me your Friend, then any. 2064
  The Modell of our chaste loues: his yong daughter, 2723
LOUING = 2
  Euer belou'd and louing, may his Rule be; 936
  Hee's louing and most gracious. 'Twill be much, 1724
LOUURE = 1
  To thinke an English Courtier may be wise, | And neuer see the *Louure.* 599

LOWD = 2
The sides of loyalty, and almost appeares | In lowd Rebellion. 355
As lowd, and to as many Tunes. Hats, Cloakes, 2493
LOWDER = 1
Cham. Now God incense him, | And let him cry Ha, lowder. 1906
LOWE = 1
Gone slightly o're lowe steppes, and now are mounted 1472
LOWER = 2
Patience, be neere me still, and set me lower, 2634
Cromwell at lower end, as Secretary. 3041
LOWLY = 1
I sweare, tis better to be lowly borne, 1224
LOWSIE = 1
This honest man, wait like a lowsie Foot-boy 3209
LOYALL = 2
King. Fairely answer'd: | A Loyall, and obedient Subiect is 2054
Take notice Lords, he ha's a Loyall brest, 2077
LOYALTIE = 2
My Prayres to heauen for you; my Loyaltie 2051
That in the way of Loyaltie, and Truth, 2161
LOYALTIES = 1
Of all their Loyalties; wherein, although | My good Lord Cardinall,
they vent reproches 349
LOYALTY = 1
The sides of loyalty, and almost appeares | In lowd Rebellion. 355
LSAN = 7
LUCIFER = 1
And when he falles, he falles like Lucifer, | Neuer to hope againe. 2272
LUCKE = 1
Of as great Size. Weene you of better lucke, 2936
LUMPE = 1
Lie like one lumpe before him, to be fashion'd | Into what pitch he
please. 1082
LUSTRE = 2
Equall in lustre, were now best, now worst 73
About his necke, yet neuer lost her lustre; 1065
LUTE = 2
Queen. Take thy Lute wench, 1617
SONG. | *Orpheus with his Lute made Trees,* 1620
LUTHERAN = 1
A spleeny Lutheran, and not wholsome to 1957
LYE = 5
Our cause, that she should lye i'th'bosome of 1958
His faults lye open to the Lawes, let them 2233
Kath. So may he rest, | His Faults lye gently on him: 2585
(And now I should not lye) but will deserue 2735
And heere ye lye baiting of Bombards, when 3342
LYES = 1
The pennance lyes on you; if these faire Ladies | Passe away frowning. 706
LYEST = 1
Car. Proud Lord, thou lyest: 2139
LYON = 1
Leap'd from his Eyes. So lookes the chafed Lyon 2086
MACE = 1*3
Siluer Mace: Then two Gentlemen bearing two great 1342
two Noblemen, with the Sword and Mace. The King takes 1344
3 *Lord* Chancellor, *with Purse and Mace before him.* 2424

MACE *cont.*
    *5 Maior of London, *bearing the Mace. Then* Garter, *in*   2426
MAD = 4
    An.Bul. Was he mad Sir?   700
    San. O very mad, exceeding mad, in loue too;   701
    That he ran mad, and dide.   1183
MADAM = 23*2
    **Card.* Now Madam, may his Highnes liue in freedome,   552
    Heer's to your Ladiship, and pledge it Madam: | For tis to such a thing.   728
    Camp. His Grace | Hath spoken well, and iustly: Therefore Madam,   1420
    Qu. Lord Cardinall, to you I speake. | *Wol.* Your pleasure, Madam.   1425
    *Ore-topping womans powre. Madam, you do me wrong   1447
    You (gracious Madam) to vnthinke your speaking, | And to say so no
    more.   1463
    Gent.Vsh. Madam, you are cald backe.   1489
    Queen. Would they speake with me? | *Gent.* They wil'd me say so
    Madam.   1637
    Wol. May it please you Noble Madam, to withdraw   1650
    Camp. Most honour'd Madam, | My Lord of Yorke, out of his Noble
    nature,   1686
    Wol. Madam, | You wrong the Kings loue with these feares,   1707
    Car. Madam, this is a meere distraction,   1744
    Car. Madam, you wander from the good | We ayme at.   1771
    Camp. Madam, you'l finde it so: | You wrong your Vertues   1805
    Grif. Yes Madam: but I thinke your Grace   2559
    Grif. Well, the voyce goes Madam,   2564
    Grif. Noble Madam: | Mens euill manners, liue in Brasse, their Vertues   2600
    (Which was a sinne) yet in bestowing, Madam,   2614
    Grif. Madam, we are heere. | *Kath.* It is not you I call for,   2660
    Saw ye none enter since I slept? | *Grif.* None Madam.   2662
    Grif. I am most ioyfull Madam, such good dreames | Possesse your
    Fancy.   2670
    My Royall Nephew, and your name *Capuchius.* | *Cap.* Madam the
    same. Your Seruant.   2695
    How does his Highnesse? | *Cap.* Madam, in good health.   2712
    I caus'd you write, yet sent away? | *Pat.* No Madam.   2717
    This to my Lord the King. | *Cap.* Most willing Madam.   2720
MADAMS = 1
    As Cherubins, all gilt: the Madams too,   67
MADE = 32*3
    Made former Wonders, it's. To day the French,   62
    Made Britaine, India: Euery man that stood,   65
    Made it a Foole, and Begger. The two Kings   72
    Ere it was ask'd. But when the way was made   263
    Made suit to come in's presence; which if granted,   548
    (As he made semblance of his duty) would | Haue put his knife into
    him.   549
    Confessor to him, with that Diuell Monke, | *Hopkins,* that made this
    mischiefe.   848
    Made my Name once more Noble. Now his Sonne,   961
    That made me happy; at one stroake ha's taken   963
    As I am made without him, so Ile stand,   1086
    To him that made him proud; the Pope.   1090
    An. No in truth. | **Old.L.* Then you are weakly made; plucke off a
    little,   1249
    Or made it not mine too? Or which of your Friends   1383
    The passages made toward it; on my Honour,   1531

MADE *cont.*

Yea, with a spitting power, and made to tremble	1550
Or di'de where they were made, or shortly after	1559
Made to the Queene to call backe her Appeale | She intends vnto his	
Holinesse.	1605
SONG. | *Orpheus with his Lute made Trees,*	1620
There had made a lasting Spring.	1626
King. Haue I not made you | The prime man of the State? I pray you	
tell me,	2035
Made me put this maine Secret in the Packet	2095
Ambassador to the Emperor, you made bold | To carry into Flanders,	
the Great Seale.	2216
Crom. I am glad your Grace, | Ha's made that right vse of it.	2292
And the late Marriage made of none effect:	2415
A worthy Friend. The King ha's made him | Master o'th'Iewell House,	2537
Whom I most hated Liuing, thou hast made mee	2631
My hast made me vnmannerly. There is staying	2688
Beside that of the Iewell-House, is made Master	2812
Lou. So said her woman, and that her suffrance made	2850
To haue this young one made a Christian.	3253
As I haue made ye one Lords, one remaine:	3254
I made no spare Sir. | *Port.* You did nothing Sir.	3278
*was quartered; they fell on, I made good my place; at	3312
These lazy knaues? Y'haue made a fine hand fellowes?	3329
Kin. O Lord Archbishop | Thou hast made me now a man, neuer before	3435

MAID = 1

That is, a faire young Maid that yet wants Baptisme,	3233

MAIDEN = 1

With Maiden Flowers, that all the world may know	2762

MAIDENHEAD = 2

Anne. By my troth, and Maidenhead, | I would not be a Queene.	1230
Old.L. Beshrew me, I would, | And venture Maidenhead for't, and so	
would you	1232

MAIDS = 1

Among my Maids, full little (God knowes) looking	1701

MAIESTIE = 1

Pray do my seruice to his Maiestie,	1818

MAIESTY = 6

Queen. Thanke your Maiesty | That you would loue your selfe, and in	
that loue	339
Wol. I know your Maiesty, ha's alwayes lou'd her	1157
Still growing in a Maiesty and pompe, the which	1208
Tane of your many vertues; the Kings Maiesty	1276
(And seruice to his Maiesty and you)	1676
Cran. God, and your Maiesty | Protect mine innocence, or I fall into	2942

MAIMD = 1

You maim'd the Iurisdiction of all Bishops.	2209

MAINE = 3*2

of my Lord Cardinalls, by Commission, and maine power tooke	1032
Looke into these affaires, see this maine end,	1073
Queen. How Sir? | *Camp.* Put your maine cause into the Kings	
protection,	1722
Made me put this maine Secret in the Packet	2095
The Kings late Scruple, by the maine assent	2413

MAINTAINE = 1

The Clothiers all not able to maintaine	359

MAIOR = 1*2
  *5 Maior of London, *bearing the Mace. Then* Garter, *in*   2426
  Enter Trumpets sounding: Then two Aldermen, L.(ord) Maior,   3354
  I thanke ye all. To you my good Lord Maior,   3441
MAISTER = 3*1
  And point by point the Treasons of his Maister, | He shall againe relate.   327
  Most bitterly on you, as putter on | Of these exactions: yet the King,
  our Maister   351
  'em from me, with this reason: his maister would bee seru'd be-|fore   1033
  To a most Noble Iudge, the King my Maister.   3164
MAKE = 40*5
  I Come no more to make you laugh, Things now,   2
  To make that onely true, we now intend,   22
  Be sad, as we would make ye. Thinke ye see   26
  Buck. To th'King Ile say't, & make my vouch as strong   232
  To make the Scepter his. These very words   475
  As first, good Company, good wine, good welcome, | Can make good
  people.   672
  San. Yes, if I make my play: 727
  And hither make, as great Embassadors | From forraigne Princes.   742
  By all your good leaues Gentlemen; heere Ile make | My royall choyce.   787
  More then I dare make faults.   912
  Make of your Prayers one sweet Sacrifice,   919
  No blacke Enuy shall make my Graue.   929
  *And with that bloud will make 'em one day groane for't.   952
  Be sure you be not loose; for those you make friends,   973
  Go too; Ile make ye know your times of businesse: 1113
  An. Good Lady, | Make your selfe mirth with your particular fancy,   1323
  You are mine Enemy, and make my Challenge,   1435
  Vpon this businesse my appearance make, | In any of their Courts.   1494
  To make this present Summons vnsolicited.   1589
  But all Hoods, make not Monkes.   1644
  But how to make ye sodainly an Answere   1696
  To me, aboue this wretchednesse? All your Studies | Make me a Curse,
  like this.   1755
  Qu. My Lord, | I dare not make my selfe so guiltie,   1773
  To make a seemely answer to such persons.   1817
  Will make this sting the sooner. Cardinall *Campeius,*   1900
  Abound, as thicke as thought could make 'em, and   2071
  Neglect him not; make vse now, and prouide | For thine owne future
  safety.   2334
  As the shrowdes make at Sea, in a stiffe Tempest,   2492
  And make 'em reele before 'em. No man liuing   2499
  Garland ouer her Head, at which the other foure make re-|uerend   2648
  To make your house our Towre: you, a Brother of vs   2903
  *There make before them. Looke, the goodman weeps: 2955
  Will make my boldnesse, manners. Now good Angels   2964
  To make great hast. All fast? What meanes this? Hoa?   2991
  *To quench mine Honor; they would shame to make me   3009
  Pace 'em not in their hands to make 'em gentle;   3070
  With lesse Allegeance in it. Men that make   3091
  I make as little doubt as you doe conscience,   3116
  Make me no more adoe, but all embrace him;   3230
  To scatter 'em, as 'tis to make 'em sleepe   3271
  Por. Make way there, for the Princesse.   3348
  Man. You great fellow, | Stand close vp, or Ile make your head ake.   3349

MAKE *cont.*
Heauen euer laid vp to make Parents happy, | May hourely fall vpon
ye.   3372
Shall be, and make new Nations. He shall flourish,   3423
This Little-One shall make it Holy-day. *Exeunt.*   3448
MAKER = 3
(The Image of his Maker) hope to win by it?   2357
He or shee, Cuckold or Cuckold-maker: 3283
To see what this Child does, and praise my Maker.   3440
MAKERS = *1
*Those we professe, Peace-makers, Friends, and Seruants.   1804
MAKES = 9*5
The force of his owne merit makes his way   113
Who should attend on him? He makes vp the File   126
To whisper *Wolsey*) here makes visitation,   255
*Which makes my whit'st part, black. The will of Heau'n   293
*Is nam'd, your warres in France: this makes bold mouths,   393
This night he makes a Supper, and a great one,   638
Two women plac'd together, makes cold weather: 693
And must needs say a Noble one; which makes me   965
The Queene makes no answer, rises out of her Chaire,   1364
*A strange Tongue makes my cause more strange, suspiti-|(ous: 1668
Then makes him nothing. I must reade this paper: 2088
(as it were by inspiration) she makes (in her sleepe) signes of   2654
But reuerence to your calling, makes me modest.   3118
One that in all obedience, makes the Church   3186
MAKINGS = 1
She had all the Royall makings of a Queene;   2508
MALE = 1
The Graue does to th' dead: For her Male Issue,   1558
MALE-CHILD = 1
If it conceiu'd a male-child by me, should   1556
MALICE = 13
Honor, and plenteous safety) that you reade | The Cardinals Malice,
and his Potency   164
If euer any malice in your heart   923
Or some about him neere, haue out of malice   1010
Malice ne're meant: Our breach of Duty this way,   1109
(I meane your malice) know, Officious Lords,   2122
Follow your enuious courses, men of Malice;   2128
From any priuate malice in his end,   2157
You are Potently oppos'd, and with a Malice   2935
Cran. So. | *Buts.* This is a Peere of Malice: I am glad   2999
(God turne their hearts, I neuer sought their malice)   3008
Enuy, and crooked malice, nourishment;   3092
More out of Malice then Integrity,   3215
And faire purgation to the world then malice, | I'm sure in me.   3223
MALICIOUS = 3
To cope malicious Censurers, which euer,   413
I hold my most malicious Foe, and thinke not | At all a Friend to truth.   1441
I were malicious else.   2605
MALIGNANT = 1
His will is most malignant, and it stretches | Beyond you to your
friends.   482
MALLICE = 1
The Law I beare no mallice for my death,   903

MAN = 58*4

A Man may weepe vpon his Wedding day.	33
Made Britaine, India: Euery man that stood,	65
Buc. Euery man, | After the hideous storme that follow'd, was	144
Selfe-mettle tyres him: Not a man in England	205
Free pardon to each man that has deny'de	436
Then euer they were faire. This man so compleat,	457
There's mischiefe in this man; canst thou say further?	536
And this man out of Prison.	553
1. Stay there Sir, | And see the noble ruin'd man you speake of.	893
This from a dying man receiue as certaine:	971
North. When they were ready to set out for London, a man	1031
The Kings eyes, that so long haue slept vpon | This bold bad man.	1075
Or this imperious man will worke vs all	1080
One generall Tongue vnto vs. This good man,	1143
*They haue sent me such a Man, I would haue wish'd for.	1148
Camp. Was he not held a learned man? | *Wol.* Yes surely.	1175
Kept him a forraigne man still, which so greeu'd him,	1182
Would it not grieue an able man to leaue	1197
That man i'th' world, who shall report he ha's	1498
Forgetting (like a good man) your late Censure	1689
That any English man dare giue me Councell?	1712
King. Haue I not made you | The prime man of the State? I pray you tell me,	2035
And no man see me more.	2107
Dare mate a sounder man then Surrie can be, | And all that loue his follies.	2163
Car. How much me thinkes, I could despise this man,	2190
Cham. O my Lord, | Presse not a falling man too farre: 'tis Vertue:	2231
This is the state of Man; to day he puts forth	2253
And when he thinkes, good easie man, full surely	2257
Is that poore man, that hangs on Princes fauours?	2268
A great man should decline. Nay, and you weep | I am falne indeed.	2279
Too heauy for a man, that hopes for Heauen.	2291
But he's a Learned man. May he continue	2306
I am a poore falne man, vnworthy now	2327
By that sinne fell the Angels: how can man then	2356
That euer lay by man: which when the people	2490
And make 'em reele before 'em. No man liuing	2499
A man in much esteeme with th'King, and truly	2536
As a man sorely tainted, to his Answer,	2567
Kath. Alas poore man. | *Grif.* At last, with easie Rodes, he came to Leicester,	2570
An old man, broken with the stormes of State,	2575
And yet with Charity. He was a man	2588
Then man could giue him; he dy'de, fearing God.	2626
Cap. By Heauen I will, | Or let me loose the fashion of a man.	2751
There's none stands vnder more calumnious tongues, | Then I my selfe, poore man.	2910
What manner of man are you? My Lord, I look'd	2916
A man of his Place, and so neere our fauour	3029
A man that more detests, more stirres against,	3087
And by that vertue no man dare accuse you.	3099
Where being but a priuate man againe,	3104
For what they haue beene: 'tis a cruelty, | To load a falling man.	3125
The King will suffer but the little finger | Of this man to be vex'd?	3171
Against this man, whose honesty the Diuell	3178

MAN *cont.*

Good man sit downe: Now let me see the proudest	3199
Was it discretion Lords, to let this man,	3207
This good man (few of you deserue that Title)	3208
This honest man, wait like a lowsie Foot-boy	3209
Once more my Lord of *Winchester,* I charge you | Embrace, and loue	
this man.	3242
*Kin. Good Man, those ioyfull teares shew thy true | (hearts,	3248
Noyse and Tumult within: Enter Porter and | *his man.*	3257
In her dayes, Euery Man shall eate in safety,	3404
Kin. O Lord Archbishop | Thou hast made me now a man, neuer before	3435
She will be sicke els. This day, no man thinke	3446

MAN = 5*1

MANNAGE = 1

Till they obey the mannage. If we suffer	3072

MANNER = 4*1

And lack of other meanes, in desperate manner	363
*each side the Court in manner of a Consistory: Below them	1348
Wol. Most gracious Sir, | In humblest manner I require your Highnes,	1508
I say, set on. | *Exeunt, in manner as they enter'd.*	1613
What manner of man are you? My Lord, I look'd	2916

MANNERS = 4

It is to see a Nobleman want manners.	2204
Grif. Noble Madam: | Mens euill manners, liue in Brasse, their Vertues	2600
Will make my boldnesse, manners. Now good Angels	2964
At least good manners; as not thus to suffer	3028

MANNORS = 1

Buc. O many | Haue broke their backes with laying Mannors on 'em	136

MANS = 4

Buc. The diuell speed him: No mans Pye is freed	100
In this mans place before him? | *Wol.* Yes, he was.	1173
Beyond all mans endeauors. My endeauors,	2043
To one mans Honour, this contagious sicknesse;	3074

MANTLE = *1

*a Mantle, &c. Traine borne by a Lady: Then followes	3360

MANY = 23*1

Buc. O many | Haue broke their backes with laying Mannors on 'em	136
The many to them longing, haue put off	360
Kin. It grieues many:	449
To many Lords and Ladies; there will be	639
Many sharpe reasons to defeat the Law.	841
I feare, too many curses on their heads | That were the Authors.	985
So many courses of the Sun enthroaned,	1207
Tane of your many vertues; the Kings Maiesty	1276
With many Children by you. If in the course	1391
The wisest Prince, that there had reign'd, by many	1403
That you haue many enemies, that know not	1524
That many maz'd considerings, did throng	1552
Many a groaning throw: thus hulling in	1566
If I lou'd many words, Lord, I should tell you,	2159
Of all the Kingdome. Many more there are,	2228
This many Summers in a Sea of Glory,	2261
As lowd, and to as many Tunes. Hats, Cloakes,	2493
*Lou. Many good nights, my Lord, I rest your seruant.	2835
Heard many greeuous, I do say my Lord	2895
Your Enemies are many, and not small; their practises	2929
Butts. I thinke your Highnesse saw this many a day.	3018

MANY *cont.*

You shall know many dare accuse you boldly,	3105
Por. And't please your Honour, | We are but men; and what so many	
may doe,	3334
An aged Princesse; many dayes shall see her,	3429

MARBLE = 1

And sleepe in dull cold Marble, where no mention	2348

MARCHIONESSE = 1*3

Then Marchionesse of *Pembrooke*; to which Title,	1279
*O're-mount the Larke: The Marchionesse of *Pembrooke*?	1316
*To heare from Rome. The Marchionesse of Penbroke?	1945
the Marchionesse Dorset, the other Godmother, and La-|dies.	3361

MARKE = 3*1

2. I thinke | You haue hit the marke; but is't not cruell,	1019
*Then marke th'inducement. Thus it came; giue heede | (too't:	1536
Marke but my Fall, and that that Ruin'd me:	2354
And of an earthy cold? Marke her eyes?	2677

MARKES = 1*1

King. Giue her an hundred Markes.	2979
Lady. An hundred Markes? By this light, Ile ha more.	2981

MARQUESSE = 1*2

*6 Marquesse Dorset, *bearing a Scepter of Gold, on his head,*	2429
Who's that that beares the Scepter? | 1 Marquesse Dorset,	2448
*Duchesse of *Norfolke*, and Lady Marquesse *Dorset*? will | these please	
you?	3240

MARRES = 1

Matter against him, that for euer marres | The Hony of his Language.	
No, he's setled	1851

MARRIAGE = 6*2

Norf. What's the cause? | *Cham.* It seemes the Marriage with his	
Brothers Wife	1045
Feares, and despaires, and all these for his Marriage.	1061
*Who deem'd our Marriage lawful. Wherefore I humbly	1407
And Marriage 'twixt the Duke of *Orleance*, and	1541
Respecting this our Marriage with the Dowager,	1547
Proue but our Marriage lawfull, by my Life	1596
His second Marriage shall be publishd, and	1914
And the late Marriage made of none effect:	2415

MARRIED = 3

Till this time Pompe was single, but now married	59
After his Patients death; the King already | Hath married the faire	
Lady. | *Sur.* Would he had.	1878
Crom. Last, that the Lady *Anne,* | Whom the King hath in secrecie long	
married,	2315

MARRY = 5

Abur. Is it therefore | Th'Ambassador is silenc'd? | *Nor.* Marry is't.	153
Louell. I marry, | There will be woe indeed Lords, the slye whorsons	618
Marry this is yet but yong, and may be left	1888
The Lord forbid. | *Nor.* Marry Amen.	1896
The French Kings Sister; He shall marry her.	1941

MARSHALL = 1

He to be Earle Marshall: you may reade the rest.	2401

MARSHALLSEY = 1

A Marshallsey, shall hold ye play these two Monthes.	3347

MARSHALS = *1

Garter, Cranmer, Duke of Norfolke with his Marshals	3355

MARSHALSHIP = *1
*him, the Duke of Norfolke, with the Rod of Marshalship, | a Coronet on
his head. Collars of Esses.   2435
MARTYR = 1
Thou fall'st a blessed Martyr.   2364
MARY = 2
Our Daughter Mary: I'th' Progresse of this busines,   1542
By holy Mary (Butts) there's knauery;   3032
MASKE = 1
Was to them, as a Painting. Now this Maske   70
MASKERS = *1
*Hoboyes. Enter King and others as Maskers, habited like   753
MASTER = 15*1
Became the next dayes master, till the last   61
As here at home, suggests the King our Master   239
Your Master wed me to: nothing but death | Shall e're diuorce my
Dignities.   1776
(Mine, and your Master) with his owne hand, gaue me: 2132
Toward the King, my euer Roiall Master,   2162
To be thy Lord, and Master. Seeke the King   2328
So good, so Noble, and so true a Master?   2338
A sure, and safe one, though thy Master mist it.   2353
A worthy Friend. The King ha's made him | Master o'th'Iewell House,   2537
Beside that of the Iewell-House, is made Master   2812
I meane in periur'd Witnesse, then your Master,   2937
Chan. Speake to the businesse, M.(aster) Secretary;   3042
Gard. Good M.(aster) Secretary, | I cry your Honour mercie; you may
worst | Of all this Table say so.   3127
Within. Good M.(aster) Porter I belong to th' Larder.   3262
Within. Do you heare M.(aster) Porter?   3286
*Port. I shall be with you presently, good M.(aster) Puppy,   3287
MASTER-CORD = 1
The Master-cord on's heart.   1966
MATE = 1
Dare mate a sounder man then Surrie can be, | And all that loue his
follies.   2163
MATTER = 3*1
Buc. I read in's looks | Matter against me, and his eye reuil'd   195
To heare from him a matter of some moment: 509
Matter against him, that for euer marres | The Hony of his Language.
No, he's setled   1851
*Gard. Not yet Sir Thomas Louell: what's the matter?   2783
MATTERS = 1
In charging you with matters, to commit you: 2949
MAY l.7 9 10 12 13 33 170 214 452 *552 565 599 612 626 647 716 831 869
934 936 992 1274 1296 1356 1408 1455 1607 1648 1650 1673 1797 1834
1881 1888 1982 *2021 2038 2127 2306 2310 2329 2394 2401 2534 2546
2585 2602 2714 2742 2762 2796 2821 3054 3067 3090 3095 3128 3203
3219 3228 3235 3236 3273 3335 3373 = 63*2
MAYBE = 1
Suf. Maybe he heares the King | Does whet his Anger to him.   1947
MAYDEN = 1
The Bird of Wonder dyes, the Mayden Phoenix,   3411
MAYOR = 1
He sent command to the Lord Mayor straight   1003
MAY-DAY = 1
On May-day Morning, which will neuer be: 3272

MAZD = 1
That many maz'd considerings, did throng   1552
ME *l*.45 196 197 198 206 *244 267 285 291 292 301 373 403 405 409 442
499 507 513 531 677 698 709 716 717 730 776 786 897 898 901 913 917
918 924 928 947 960 963 965 970 978 979 982 995 *1033 *1070 1084
1088 1095 1096 *1148 1153 1163 *1166 1169 *1177 1179 1232 *1245
1309 1325 1326 1331 1367 1368 1375 1376 1396 1397 1408 1433 1437
*1447 1452 1460 1492 1507 1534 1549 1553 1556 1561 1563 1565 1579
1581 1608 1637 1638 1641 *1647 1649 1662 1671 1693 1705 1712 1729
1746 1747 1750 1751 1755 1756 1758 1767 1776 1778 1782 1786 1787
1814 1821 1834 1843 1891 1939 1984 2003 2036 2041 2049 2065 2085
2090 2095 2100 2107 2132 2133 2148 2181 *2190 2251 2263 2265 2284
2286 2295 2320 2322 2326 2331 2344 2346 2349 2354 2365 2372 2447
2489 2522 2555 2556 2561 2562 2587 2603 2634 2636 2659 2665 2666
2667 2668 2673 2688 2691 2699 2701 2705 2710 2741 2743 2744 2750
2752 2753 2759 2761 2763 2764 2765 2799 2804 2806 2807 2838 2844
2858 2868 2891 2914 2917 2926 2944 2990 2992 3005 3007 *3009 3019
3096 3118 3156 3176 3195 3196 3197 3199 3204 3224 3230 *3264 3281
3284 3289 *3294 *3306 *3313 3326 3339 3384 3385 3436 3438
3444 = 221*15
MEANE = 11
I meane who set the Body, and the Limbes | Of this great Sport
together?   92
But where they meane to sinke ye: all good people   977
(I meane the learned ones in Christian Kingdomes)   1140
Ere a determinate resolution, hee | (I meane the Bishop) did require a
respite,   1543
Meane while, must be an earnest motion   1604
Car. What should this meane? | *Sur.* The Lord increase this businesse. 2033
Car. What should this meane?   2083
(I meane your malice) know, Officious Lords,   2122
I meane in periur'd Witnesse, then your Master,   2937
Gent. within. Come backe: what meane you?   2962
Would trye him to the vtmost, had ye meane,   3216
MEANER = 1
We liue not to be grip'd by meaner persons.   1190
MEANES = 3*1
And lack of other meanes, in desperate manner   363
*(By what meanes got, I leaue to your owne conscience)   2225
And able meanes, we had not parted thus.   2745
To make great hast. All fast? What meanes this? Hoa?   2991
MEANEWHILE *see* meane
MEANING = 1
Both in his words, and meaning. He was neuer   2594
MEANT = 8
He meant to lay vpon: and his owne Letter   129
The Part my Father meant to act vpon   546
That neuer knew what Truth meant: I now seale it;   951
Malice ne're meant: Our breach of Duty this way,   1109
I meant to rectifie my Conscience, which   1570
So deepe suspition, where all faith was meant;   1677
(But where he meant to Ruine) pittifull.   2595
(If there be faith in men) meant for his Tryall,   3222
MEASURE = 1
To drinke to these faire Ladies, and a measure   815
MEDITATING = 1
I nam'd my Knell; whil'st I sit meditating   2637

MEDITATIONS = 3
  Into my priuate Meditations? | Who am I? Ha?   1106
  Nor. And so wee'l leaue you to your Meditations   2245
  Continuall Meditations, Teares, and Sorrowes,   2582
MEE *l.*930 2556 2631 3232 *3304 = 4*1
MEEK = *1
  *T'oppose your cunning. Y'are meek, & humble-mouth'd   1467
MEEKENESSE = 2
  With Meekenesse and Humilitie: but your Heart   1469
  'Tis my vndoing. Loue and meekenesse, Lord   3111
MEEKNESSE = 1
  Thy meeknesse Saint-like, Wife-like Gouernment,   1502
MEERE = 4
  Car. Madam, this is a meere distraction,   1744
  Suf. That out of meere Ambition, you haue caus'd   2222
  You haue for Dignities, to the meere vndooing   2227
  Could not be wedg'd in more: I am stifled | With the meere ranknesse
  of their ioy.   2475
MEERELY = 2
  Haue got by the late Voyage, is but meerely   577
  1. Tis the Cardinall; | And meerely to reuenge him on the Emperour,   1015
MEET = 1
  This night to meet heere they could doe no lesse,   761
MEETE = 2
  There ye shall meete about this waighty busines.   1195
  Sur. I am ioyfull | To meete the least occasion, that may giue me   1833
MEETING = 1
  Enter two Gentlemen, meeting one another.   2378
MEETS = 1
  How soone this Mightinesse, meets Misery: 31
MELT = 1
  Old La. Hearts of most hard temper | Melt and lament for her.   1213
MEMORIE = 1
  I thanke my Memorie, I yet remember   2198
MEMORIES = 1
  Yet freshly pittied in our memories.   3079
MEMORIZD = 1
  Will fall some blessing to this Land, which shall | In it be memoriz'd.   1892
MEMORY = 1
  Some little memory of me, will stirre him   2331
MEN = 31*2
  Those Sunnes of Glory, those two Lights of Men | Met in the vale of
  Andren.   46
  Nor. Then you lost | The view of earthly glory: Men might say   57
  Men feare the French would proue perfidious   502
  Men into such strange mysteries?   572
  Abusing better men then they can be   606
  And vnderstand againe like honest men,   610
  Men of his way, should be most liberall,   650
  Nor build their euils on the graues of great men;   908
  Fell by our Seruants, by those Men we lou'd most: 968
  That Angels loue good men with: Euen of her,   1067
  **Kin.* Two equall men: The Queene shall be acquain- | (ted   1155
  Wol. You haue heere Lady, | (And of your choice) these Reuerend
  Fathers, men   1412
  They should bee good men, their affaires as righteous: 1643

MEN *cont.*

(Like free and honest men) our iust opinions, | And comforts to our
cause.   1684
Ye speake like honest men, (pray God ye proue so)   1695
And to such men of grauity and learning;   1699
Either for such men, or such businesse;   1702
Queen. The more shame for ye; holy men I thought ye,   1734
Follow your enuious courses, men of Malice;   2128
Of all these Learned men, she was diuorc'd,   2414
2 Those men are happy, | And so are all, are neere her.   2464
But, to those men that sought him, sweet as Summer.   2612
And sure those men are happy that shall haue 'em.   2739
The last is for my men, they are the poorest,   2740
That Chayre stand empty: But we all are men   3058
With lesse Allegeance in it. Men that make   3091
To men that vnderstand you, words and weaknesse.   3121
By your good fauour, too sharpe; Men so Noble,   3123
Out of the gripes of cruell men, and giue it   3163
I had thought, I had had men of some vnderstanding,   3205
(If there be faith in men) meant for his Tryall,   3222
Por. And't please your Honour, | We are but men; and what so many
may doe,   3334
All the best men are ours; for 'tis ill hap,   3462
MENACD = 2
Peep'd harmes that menac'd him. Priuily   259
Lord *Aburgany*, to whom by oth he menac'd | Reuenge vpon the
Cardinall.   477
MEND = 3
Queen. God mend all.   554
You haue now a broken Banket, but wee'l mend it.   750
Mend 'em for shame my Lords: Is this your comfort?   1737
MENS = 4
From Princes into Pages: all mens honours   1081
Suf. My Amen too't. | *Nor.* All mens.   1885
Grif. Noble Madam: | Mens euill manners, liue in Brasse, their Vertues 2600
Mens prayers then would seeke you, not their feares.   3136
MENTION = 1
And sleepe in dull cold Marble, where no mention   2348
MENTIS = *1
Card. Tanta est erga te mentis integritas Regina serenissima.   1664
MERCHANTS = 1
Our Merchants goods at Burdeux.   152
MERCIE = 2
That might haue mercie on the fault, thou gau'st him: 2150
Gard. Good M.(aster) Secretary, | I cry your Honour mercie; you may
worst | Of all this Table say so.   3127
MERCIES = 1
Nor will I sue, although the King haue mercies   911
MERCIFULL = 2
You are so mercifull. I see your end,   3110
The mercifull construction of good women,   3459
MERCY = 4
Finde mercy in the Law, 'tis his; if none,   566
Weary, and old with Seruice, to the mercy   2264
All. We are. | *Cran.* Is there no other way of mercy,   3149
Cham. Mercy o' me: what a Multitude are heere?   3326

MERIDIAN = 1
And from that full Meridian of my Glory,   2104
MERIT = 1
The force of his owne merit makes his way   113
MERRY = 8
That come to heare a Merry, Bawdy Play,   15
And if you can be merry then, Ile say,   32
One care abroad: hee would haue all as merry: 671
Or Gentleman that is not freely merry   712
Ladies you are not merry; Gentlemen, | Whose fault is this?   720
An.B. You are a merry Gamster | My Lord *Sands.*   725
I must not yet forsake you: Let's be merry,   813
The merry Songs of Peace to all his Neighbours.   3406
MES = 2
MESSAGE = 2
I sent your Message, who return'd her thankes   2845
King. Now by thy lookes | I gesse thy Message. Is the Queene deliuer'd?   2967
MESSENG = 1
Let me ne're see againe. *Exit Messeng.*   2691
MESSENGER see also Mes. = 1
Enter a Messenger.   2680
MET = 7*1
Buckingham. | Good morrow, and well met. How haue ye done   38
Those Sunnes of Glory, those two Lights of Men | Met in the vale of
Andren.   46
You met him halfe in Heauen: my vowes and prayers   932
Norf. Well met my Lord *Chamberlaine.*   1040
*Still met the King? Lou'd him next Heau'n? Obey'd him?   1763
1 Y'are well met once againe. | 2 So are you.   2379
Enter Gardiner Bishop of Winchester, a Page with a Torch | before him,
met by Sir Thomas Louell.   2769
Why are we met in Councell?   3043
METEOR = *1
*such a combustion in the State. I mist the Meteor once,   3308
METHINKES *see* thinkes
METHOUGHT *see* thought
METTLE = 2
Selfe-mettle tyres him: Not a man in England   205
Of what course Mettle ye are molded, Enuy,   2124
MEUS = 1
Nor. Then, That in all you writ to Rome, or else | To Forraigne
Princes, *Ego & Rex meus*   2210
MICHAELL = 1
Bra. A Monke o'th' *Chartreux.* | *Buck.* O *Michaell Hopkins?* | *Bra.* He.   308
MIDNIGHT = 2
(As they say Spirits do) at midnight, haue   2787
King. 'Tis midnight *Charles,*   2856
MIGHT *l.*58 257 *527 1159 1241 1515 1518 1545 2030 2150 2933 3084
*3310 = 11*2
MIGHTINESSE = 1
How soone this Mightinesse, meets Misery: 31
MIGHTY = 4
Bearing a State of mighty moment in't,   1582
His Promises, were as he then was, Mighty: 2596
Long, and euer happie, to the high and Mighty | Princesse of England
Elizabeth.   3366
That mould vp such a mighty Piece as this is,   3396

MILES = 1
Held a late Court at Dunstable; sixe miles off   2409
MINCING = 1
(Sauing your mincing) the capacity | Of your soft Chiuerell Conscience,
would receiue,   1239
MIND = 1
Crom. My mind gaue me, | In seeking tales and Informations   3176
MINDE = 1
He did it with a Serious minde: a heede | Was in his countenance. You
he bad   1934
MINDE = *1
Cham. You beare a gentle minde, & heau'nly blessings   1273
MINDE = 8
As able to perform't) his minde, and place   236
Not well dispos'd, the minde growing once corrupt,   455
Lou. That Churchman | Beares a bounteous minde indeed,   641
He was from thence discharg'd? Sir, call to minde,   1388
In minde and feature. I perswade me, from her   1891
King. It may well be, | There is a mutiny in's minde. This morning,   1982
Of your best Graces, in your minde; the which   2007
To speake my minde of him: and indeed this day,   2820
MINDED = 1
How you stand minded in the waighty difference   1682
MINDES = 2
My mindes not on't, you are too hard for me.   2838
Might corrupt mindes procure, Knaues as corrupt   2933
MINDS = 1
2 'Tis well: The Citizens | I am sure haue shewne at full their Royall
minds,   2387
MINE *l.*133 344 *1146 1383 1385 1393 1435 1522 1697 1719 1860 2045
2046 2068 2092 2132 2324 2369 2371 2372 2629 2703 2757 2805 2943
2956 *3009 *3316 = 26*3, 1
Shew'd like a Mine. Their Dwarfish Pages were   66
MINE *l.*2195 = 1
MINE *l.*292 2923 = 2
MINGLED = 1
Beauty and Honour in her are so mingled,   1294
MINISTER = 3
But minister communication of | A most poore issue.   139
A Minister in his Power. You know his Nature,   168
Whose Minister you are, whiles heere he liu'd   2938
MINUTE = 2
His houre of speech, a minute: He, (my Lady)   460
His Confessor, who fed him euery minute | With words of Soueraignty.   494
MIRROR = 1
*They loue and doate on: call him bounteous *Buckingham,* | The Mirror
of all courtesie.   887
MIRTH = 1
An. Good Lady, | Make your selfe mirth with your particular fancy,   1323
MISCARRIED = 1
Suf. The Cardinals Letters to the Pope miscarried,   1865
MISCHIEFE = 4
As he is subtile, and as prone to mischiefe,   235
There's mischiefe in this man; canst thou say further?   536
Confessor to him, with that Diuell Monke, | *Hopkins,* that made this
mischiefe.   848
Yet let 'em looke they glory not in mischiefe;   907

MISCHIEFES = 1
And Princely Care, fore-seeing those fell Mischiefes,   2828
MISDEMEAND = 1
Haue misdemean'd your selfe, and not a little: 3062
MISERIES = 3
I will not wish ye halfe my miseries,   1740
To endure more Miseries, and greater farre   2297
In all my Miseries: But thou hast forc'd me   2344
MISERY = 1
How soone this Mightinesse, meets Misery: 31
MISFORTUNES = 1
Crom. I haue no power to speake Sir. | *Car.* What, amaz'd | At my
misfortunes? Can thy Spirit wonder   2276
MIST = 1*1
A sure, and safe one, though thy Master mist it.   2353
*such a combustion in the State. I mist the Meteor once,   3308
MISTAKEN = 1
To heare this of him; and could wish he were | Somthing mistaken in't.   271
MISTAKES = 1
Camp. Your rage mistakes vs.   1733
MISTRIS = 6
Our Mistris Sorrowes we were pittying.   1268
If you speake truth, for their poore Mistris sake;   1670
That once was Mistris of the Field, and flourish'd,   1788
A Knights Daughter | To be her Mistris Mistris? The Queenes, Queene?   1952
Suf. I wish your Highnesse | A quiet night, and my good Mistris will |
Remember in my Prayers.   2861
MO = 1
That promises mo thousands: Honours traine   1319
MOCKD = 1
In feare our motion will be mock'd, or carp'd at,   421
MOCKE = 1
Buck. Nay, Sir *Nicholas,* | Let it alone; my State now will but mocke
me.   946
MODELL = 1
The Modell of our chaste loues: his yong daughter,   2723
MODEST = 3
2 But what follow'd? | 3 At length, her Grace rose, and with modest
paces   2502
She is yong, and of a Noble modest Nature,   2726
But reuerence to your calling, makes me modest.   3118
MODESTIE = 1
With thy Religious Truth, and Modestie,   2632
MODESTY = 2
Kin. Deliuer this with modesty to th' Queene. | *Exit Gardiner.*   1191
Win straying Soules with modesty againe,   3113
MOE = 3
But that you shall sustaine moe new disgraces, | With these you beare
alreadie.   1831
Suf. No, no: | There be moe Waspes that buz about his Nose,   1898
Stands in the gap and Trade of moe Preferments,   2814
MOITY = 1
The other moity ere you aske is giuen,   337
MOLDED = 1
Of what course Mettle ye are molded, Enuy,   2124
MOMENT = 3*1
Of thousand Friends: Then, in a moment, see   30

HENRY 8

MOMENT cont.
To heare from him a matter of some moment:	509
Bearing a State of mighty moment in't,	1582
*Gard. My Lord, because we haue busines of more mo-	(ment,	3100

MONARCH = 1
| Cran. The greatest Monarch now aliue may glory | 3235 |

MONEY = 1
| *Their Money out of hope they may beleeue,* | 9 |

MONG = 1
| Wait else at doore: a fellow Councellor | 'Mong Boyes, Groomes, and Lackeyes. | 3010 |

MONGST = 2
| Who was enrold 'mongst wonders; and when we | 458 |
| Who holds his State at dore 'mongst Purseuants, | Pages, and Foot-boyes. | 3022 |

MONKE = 3*1
Bra. A Monke o'th' *Chartreux.*	Buck. O *Michaell Hopkins?*	Bra. He.	308
Spoke by a holy Monke, that oft, sayes he,	506
*The Monke might be deceiu'd, and that 'twas dangerous	527
Confessor to him, with that Diuell Monke,	*Hopkins*, that made this mischiefe.	848

MONKES = 1
| But all Hoods, make not Monkes. | 1644 |

MONSIEURS = 1
| Now I would pray our Monsieurs | 598 |

MONSTER = 1
| To giue her the auaunt, it is a pitty | Would moue a Monster. | 1211 |

MONSTROUS = 1
| Hath into monstrous habits put the Graces | 461 |

MONTHES = 1
| A Marshallsey, shall hold ye play these two Monthes. | 3347 |

MONUMENT = 1
| Goodnesse and he, fill vp one Monument. | 938 |

MOODY = 1
| The Cardinall. | Nor. Obserue, obserue, hee's moody. | 1926 |

MOONE = 2
| His eye against the Moone: in most strange Postures | 1980 |
| His Thinkings are below the Moone, not worth | His serious considering. | 1999 |

MOORE = 1
| Crom. The next is, that Sir *Thomas Moore* is chosen | Lord Chancellor, in your place. | 2303 |

MORE see also mo, moe = 68*11
I Come no more to make you laugh, Things now,	2
*Car. Well, we shall then know more, & *Buckingham*	185
More stronger to direct you then your selfe;	220
Buck. So, so;	These are the limbs o'th' Plot: no more I hope.	306
Queen. No, my Lord?	You know no more then others? But you frame	374
To Nature none more bound; his trayning such,	451
They turne to vicious formes, ten times more vgly	456
*Kin. Ther's somthing more would out of thee; what	(say'st?	555
A good digestion to you all; and once more	751
More worthy this place then my selfe, to whom	778
2. I am sorry fort.	1. So are a number more.	835
But those that sought it, I could wish more Christians:	905
More then I dare make faults.	912
Made my Name once more Noble. Now his Sonne,	961

MORE *cont.*

Let's thinke in priuate more. *Exeunt.*	1025
Whom once more, I present vnto your Highnesse.	1145
Kin. And once more in mine armes I bid him welcome,	1146
To leaue, a thousand fold more bitter, then	1209
An. So much the more | Must pitty drop vpon her; verily	1222
For more then blushing comes to: If your backe	1252
*No more to th' Crowne but that: Lo, who comes here?	1261
More then my All, is Nothing: Nor my Prayers	1284
*More worth, then empty vanities: yet Prayers & Wishes	1286
No Iudge indifferent, nor no more assurance	1371
Refuse you for my Iudge, whom yet once more	1440
You (gracious Madam) to vnthinke your speaking, | And to say so no	
more.	1463
You tender more your persons Honor, then	1476
I will not tarry: no, nor euer more	1493
But will you be more iustifi'de? You euer	1528
Doe no more Offices of life too't; then	1557
*A strange Tongue makes my cause more strange, suspiti-|(ous:	1668
(More neere my Life I feare) with my weake wit;	1698
Queen. The more shame for ye; holy men I thought ye,	1734
I haue more Charity. But say I warn'd ye;	1741
*Youl'd feele more comfort. Why shold we (good Lady)	1792
Her Coronation. *Katherine* no more | Shall be call'd Queene, but	
Princesse Dowager,	1915
There's more in't then faire Visage. *Bullen?*	1943
Showr'd on me daily, haue bene more then could	2041
My heart drop'd Loue, my powre rain'd Honor, more	2060
As 'twer in Loues particular, be more | To me your Friend, then any.	2064
More then mine owne: that am, haue, and will be	2068
Appeare in formes more horrid) yet my Duty,	2072
And no man see me more.	2107
Car. Till I finde more then will, or words to do it,	2121
Of all the Kingdome. Many more there are,	2228
More pangs, and feares then warres, or women haue;	2271
To endure more Miseries, and greater farre	2297
What more? | *Crom.* That *Cranmer* is return'd with welcome;	2311
Of me, more must be heard of: Say I taught thee;	2349
Corruption wins not more then Honesty.	2359
And more, and richer, when he straines that Lady,	2460
2 No more of that.	2471
Could not be wedg'd in more: I am stifled | With the meere ranknesse	
of their ioy.	2475
1 Sir, | You must no more call it Yorke-place, that's past:	2516
2 He will deserue more. | 3 Yes without all doubt.	2540
Something I can command. As I walke thither, | Ile tell ye more.	2544
Deserue we no more Reuerence? | *Grif.* You are too blame,	2683
Call in more women. When I am dead, good Wench,	2760
I can no more. | *Exeunt leading Katherine.*	2766
King. Charles, I will play no more to night,	2837
There's none stands vnder more calumnious tongues, | Then I my selfe,	
poore man.	2910
They shall no more preuaile, then we giue way too:	2946
Lady. An hundred Markes? By this light, Ile ha more.	2981
I will haue more, or scold it out of him.	2983
Haue more, or else vnsay't: and now, while 'tis hot,	2985
We shall heare more anon.	3034

MORE *cont.*

A man that more detests, more stirres against,	3087
Gard. My Lord, because we haue busines of more mo-|(ment,	3100
More then (I feare) you are prouided for.	3106
In doing dayly wrongs. I could say more,	3117
Cham. Tis now too certaine;| How much more is his Life in value with him?	3173
More out of Malice then Integrity,	3215
Make me no more adoe, but all embrace him;	3230
Once more my Lord of *Winchester,* I charge you | Embrace, and loue this man.	3242
So I grow stronger, you more Honour gaine. *Exeunt.*	3255
*But knock 'em downe by th' dozens? Is this More fields	3291
More couetous of Wisedome, and faire Vertue	3394
Would I had knowne no more: But she must dye,	3431

MORNING = 6

Attend him heere this Morning.	1936
King. It may well be, | There is a mutiny in's minde. This morning,	1982
To morrow Morning to the Councell Boord	2830
This Morning come before vs, where I know	2898
Keepe comfort to you, and this Morning see	2947
On May-day Morning, which will neuer be:	3272

MORROW = 4*1

Buckingham. | Good morrow, and well met. How haue ye done	38
Shone downe the English; and to morrow, they	64
L.Cham. Good morrow Ladies; what wer't worth to | (know	1264
The tender Leaues of hopes, to morrow Blossomes,	2254
To morrow Morning to the Councell Boord	2830

MORTALL = 2

To weare our mortall State to come, with her,	1598
I her fraile sonne, among'st my Brethren mortall, | Must giue my tendance to.	2018

MORTER-PIECE = *1

*like a Morter-piece to blow vs. There was a Habberda-|shers	3305

MOST = 47*1

Of all the Gentry; for the most part such	127
But minister communication of | A most poore issue.	139
Arrest thee of High Treason, in the name | Of our most Soueraigne King.	282
Most bitterly on you, as putter on | Of these exactions: yet the King, our Maister	351
Most pestilent to th'hearing, and to beare 'em,	380
The Gentleman is Learn'd, and a most rare Speaker,	450
Most like a carefull Subiect haue collected | Out of the Duke of *Buckingham.*	469
His will is most malignant, and it stretches | Beyond you to your friends.	482
Men of his way, should be most liberall,	650
In all the rest shew'd a most Noble patience.	865
My Fathers losse; like a most Royall Prince	959
Fell by our Seruants, by those Men we lou'd most:	968
A most vnnaturall and faithlesse Seruice.	969
Cham. Heauen keep me from such councel: tis most true	1070
You'l finde a most vnfit time to disturbe him:	1097
Most learned Reuerend Sir, into our Kingdome,	1119
The most conuenient place, that I can thinke of	1193
Old La. Hearts of most hard temper | Melt and lament for her.	1213

MOST *cont.*

I am a most poore Woman, and a Stranger,	1369
A Prince most Prudent; of an excellent	1400
I hold my most malicious Foe, and thinke not | At all a Friend to truth.	1441
Wol. Most gracious Sir, | In humblest manner I require your Highnes,	1508
Camp. Most honour'd Madam, | My Lord of Yorke, out of his Noble nature,	1686
Hee's louing and most gracious. 'Twill be much,	1724
And to that Woman (when she has done most)	1769
I am the most vnhappy Woman liuing.	1783
Suf. Most strangely. | *Sur.* O how? how?	1863
His eye against the Moone: in most strange Postures	1980
To'th'good of your most Sacred Person, and	2047
I answer, is most false. The Duke by Law	2155
Since you prouoke me, shall be most notorious.	2181
He was most Princely: Euer witnesse for him	2615
Whom I most hated Liuing, thou hast made mee	2631
Grif. I am most ioyfull Madam, such good dreames | Possesse your Fancy.	2670
Kath. Sir, I most humbly pray you to deliuer	2719
This to my Lord the King. | *Cap.* Most willing Madam.	2720
Louell. Now Sir, you speake of two | The most remark'd i'th'Kingdome: as for *Cromwell,*	2810
A most Arch-Heretique, a Pestilence	2824
In the great'st humblenesse, and desir'd your Highnesse | Most heartily to pray for her.	2846
I haue, and most vnwillingly of late	2894
Most throughly to be winnowed, where my Chaffe	2908
Cran. Most dread Liege, | The good I stand on, is my Truth and Honestie:	2921
To a most Noble Iudge, the King my Maister.	3164
Not onely good and wise, but most religious:	3185
Hee, that dares most, but wag his finger at thee.	3200
Chan. Thus farre | My most dread Soueraigne, may it like your Grace,	3218
All comfort, ioy in this most gracious Lady,	3371
A most vnspotted Lilly shall she passe	3433

MOTHER = 1

He's honest on mine Honor. Gods blest Mother,	2956

MOTHERS = 1

To loue her for her Mothers sake, that lou'd him, | Heauen knowes how deerely.	2728

MOTION = 2

In feare our motion will be mock'd, or carp'd at,	421
Meane while, must be an earnest motion	1604

MOTIONS = 1

From sincere motions, by Intelligence,	227

MOTLEY = 1

In a long Motley Coate, garded with Yellow,	17

MOUD = 4

Now, what mou'd me too't,	1534
How vnder my oppression I did reeke | When I first mou'd you.	1575
Kin. I then mou'd you, | My Lord of *Canterbury,* and got your leaue	1587
Haue mou'd Vs, and our Councell, that you shall	2897

MOUE = 2

To giue her the auaunt, it is a pitty | Would moue a Monster.	1211
This Royall Infant, Heauen still moue about her;	3387

MOUED = 1
That does infect the Land: with which, they moued   2825
MOULD = 1
That mould vp such a mighty Piece as this is,   3396
MOUNT = *1
*O're-mount the Larke: The Marchionesse of *Pembrooke*?   1316
MOUNTACUTE = 1
Bran. Here is a warrant from | The King, t'attach Lord *Mountacute,*
and the Bodies   302
MOUNTAINE = 2
And the Mountaine tops that freeze,   1622
And like a Mountaine Cedar, reach his branches,   3424
MOUNTED = 1
Gone slightly o're lowe steppes, and now are mounted   1472
MOUNTING = 1
Another spread on's breast, mounting his eyes,   558
MOUNTS = 1
The fire that mounts the liquor til't run ore,   217
MOURNE = 1
To th' ground, and all the World shall mourne her.   3434
MOUTH = 5
Buc. Ile to the King, | And from a mouth of Honor, quite cry downe   208
He had a blacke mouth that said other of him.   646
This compel'd fortune: haue your mouth fild vp, | Before you open it.   1307
Bearing the Kings will from his mouth expressely?   2120
Which since they are of you, and odious, | I will not taint my mouth
with.   2229
MOUTHD = *2
*Buc. This Butchers Curre is venom'd-mouth'd, and I   188
*T'oppose your cunning. Y'are meek, & humble-mouth'd   1467
MOUTHES = *2
a Subiect, if not before the King, which stop'd our mouthes | Sir.   1034
*But stop their mouthes with stubborn Bits & spurre 'em,   3071
MOUTHS = *1
*Is nam'd, your warres in France: this makes bold mouths,   393
MOW = 1
To mow 'em downe before me: but if I spar'd any   3281
MUCH = 41 *4
That swallowed so much treasure, and like a glasse   241
As he cride thus let be, to as much end,   247
Queen. I am much too venturous   387
We cannot feele too little, heare too much.   467
It was much like to doe: He answer'd, Tush,   530
His Father, by as much as a performance | Do's an irresolute purpose.   561
And saue me so much talking. | *Card.* My Lord *Sands,*   717
Card. Pray tell 'em thus much from me: 776
Kin. I feare too much.   809
Haue found him guilty of high Treason. Much   856
Wish him ten faddom deepe: This Duke as much   886
1. Let me haue it: | I doe not talke much.   995
*From these sad thoughts, that work too much vpon him: 1093
Suff. How sad he lookes; sure he is much afflicted.   1102
* *Wol.* Giue me your hand: much ioy & fauour to you;   1166
An. Oh Gods will, much better | She ne're had knowne pompe; though't
be temporall,   1215
An. So much the more | Must pitty drop vpon her; verily   1222
And worthily my Falsehood, yea, as much   1456

MUCH *cont.*

Queen. My Lord, My Lord, | I am a simple woman, much too weake   1465
My Lords, I care not (so much I am happy | Aboue a number) if my
actions   1657
Beleeue me she ha's had much wrong. Lord Cardinall,   1671
You haue too much good Lady: But to know   1681
Hee's louing and most gracious. 'Twill be much,   1724
So much they loue it. But to stubborne Spirits,   1800
Giues way to vs) I much feare. If you cannot   1845
Nor. This same *Cranmer*'s | A worthy Fellow, and hath tane much
paine | In the Kings businesse.   1918
*Car. How much me thinkes, I could despise this man,   2190
But thus much, they are foule ones.   2193
Wol. So much fairer | And spotlesse, shall mine Innocence arise,   2194
A loade, would sinke a Nauy, (too much Honor.)   2289
A man in much esteeme with th'King, and truly   2536
Was fashion'd to much Honor. From his Cradle   2608
Pati. Do you note | How much her Grace is alter'd on the sodaine?   2674
Who greeues much for your weaknesse, and by me   2705
*Much waightier then this worke. The Queens in Labor   2792
They had parted so much honesty among 'em,   3027
Cham. This is too much; | Forbeare for shame my Lords.   3140
Cham. Tis now too certaine; | How much more is his Life in value with
him?   3173
Gard. Dread Soueraigne, | How much are we bound to Heauen,   3182
I will say thus much for him, if a Prince   3227
Man. Pray Sir be patient; 'tis as much impossible,   3269
As much as one sound Cudgell of foure foote,   3276
I thanke ye heartily: So shall this Lady, | When she ha's so much
English.   3382
And you good Brethren, I am much beholding: 3442
I haue receiu'd much Honour by your presence,   3443

MUD = 1

For all the mud in Egypt; haue you heard it?   1313

MULE = 1

He fell sicke sodainly, and grew so ill | He could not sit his Mule.   2568

MULTITUDE = 1

Cham. Mercy o' me: what a Multitude are heere?   3326

MURMURERS = 1

That's Christian care enough: for liuing Murmurers,   1185

MUSICKE = 11

And haue an houre of hearing, and by'r Lady | Held currant Musicke
too.   627
Till now I neuer knew thee. | *Musicke, Dance.*   772
Who's best in fauour. Let the Musicke knock it. | *Exeunt with
Trumpets.*   817
To his Musicke, Plants and Flowers   1624
In sweet Musicke is such Art,   1630
4 Quirristers *singing.* Musicke.   2425
With all the choysest Musicke of the Kingdome,   2512
On that Coelestiall Harmony I go too. | *Sad and solemne Musicke.*   2638
**their Dancing vanish, carrying the Garland with them. | The Musicke
continues.*   2656
Kath. Bid the Musicke leaue, | They are harsh and heauy to me.
Musicke ceases.   2672

MUSINGS = 1

Dwell in his Musings, but I am affraid   1998

MUSITIANS = 1

Cause the Musitians play me that sad note	2636

MUST = 55*2

The Honourable Boord of Councell, out | Must fetch him in, he Papers.	130
Bran. Nay, he must beare you company. The King	296
Queen. Nay, we must longer kneele; I am a Suitor.	334
To those which would not know them, and yet must	377
That Vertue must goe through: we must not stint	411
We must not rend our Subiects from our Lawes,	429
Lou. They must either | (For so run the Conditions) leaue those remnants	601
His Grace is entring. Nay, you must not freeze,	692
San. The red wine first must rise	722
I must not yet forsake you: Let's be merry,	813
And by that name must dye; yet Heauen beare witnes,	900
For then, my guiltlesse blood must cry against 'em.	909
Lou. To th' water side I must conduct your Grace;	939
And must needs say a Noble one; which makes me	965
Pray for me, I must now forsake ye; the last houre	978
Will haue his will, and she must fall. | 1. 'Tis wofull.	1022
Must now confesse, if they haue any goodnesse,	1138
Cam. Your Grace must needs deserue all strangers loues,	1149
O 'tis a tender place, and I must leaue her. *Exeunt.*	1199
An. So much the more | Must pitty drop vpon her; verily	1222
Your selfe pronounce their Office. I must tell you,	1475
There must I be vnloos'd, although not there	1512
Meane while, must be an earnest motion	1604
They that must weigh out my afflictions,	1716
They that my trust must grow to, liue not heere,	1717
This Candle burnes not cleere, 'tis I must snuffe it,	1954
I her fraile sonne, among'st my Brethren mortall, | Must giue my tendance to.	2018
Then makes him nothing. I must reade this paper:	2088
I dare, and must deny it. Now I feele	2123
Car. It must be himselfe then. | *Sur.* Thou art a proud Traitor, Priest.	2137
Of a rude streame, that must for euer hide me.	2265
Crom. O my Lord, | Must I then leaue you? Must I needes forgo	2336
Of me, more must be heard of: Say I taught thee;	2349
1 Sir, | You must no more call it Yorke-place, that's past:	2516
You must not leaue me yet. I must to bed,	2759
Lou. I must to him too | Before he go to bed. Ile take my leaue.	2781
And we must root him out. From your Affaires	2832
For I must thinke of that, which company | Would not be friendly too.	2859
Come, you and I must walke a turne together:	2889
Which will require your Answer, you must take	2901
Must beare the same proportion, and not euer	2930
Cran. Why? | *Keep.* Your Grace must waight till you be call'd for.	2996
But their pleasures | Must be fulfill'd, and I attend with patience.	3012
Gard. Which Reformation must be sodaine too	3068
But I must needs to th' Tower my Lords?	3151
Cran. For me? | Must I goe like a Traytor thither?	3156
I haue a Suite which you must not deny mee.	3232
You must be Godfather, and answere for her.	3234
*Ile scratch your heads; you must be seeing Christenings?	3266
Would I had knowne no more: But she must dye,	3431
She must, the Saints must haue her; yet a Virgin,	3432
Ye must all see the Queene, and she must thanke ye,	3445

MUSTER = *1
*to muster in? Or haue wee some strange Indian with the   3292
MUTINY = 1
King. It may well be, | There is a mutiny in's minde. This morning,   1982
MUZZLE = 1
Haue not the power to muzzle him, therefore best   189
MY *l.*45 56 97 172 200 *232 280 284 *293 295 *311 312 315 321 343 350
367 374 379 401 408 409 460 484 508 512 525 526 537 *542 546 586 591
631 647 654 675 680 682 694 696 699 704 708 *711 713 716 718 *723
726 727 767 774 778 779 781 788 795 806 810 *814 885 903 909 917 920
929 932 933 940 947 950 953 959 960 961 964 966 979 992 *1028 *1032
1040 1084 1085 1094 1099 1106 1116 1117 1120 1151 1152 1161 1163
*1172 1188 1196 1205 1230 1259 1266 1283 1284 1285 1288 1300 1318
1326 1374 1387 1394 1402 1409 1429 1435 1436 1437 1439 1440 1441
1455 1456 1457 1465 1478 1480 1492 1494 1521 1531 1532 1537 1549
1551 1555 1561 1564 1565 1567 1570 1574 1575 1577 1588 1595 1596
1610 1612 1618 1654 1657 1658 1661 1665 1666 *1668 1675 1687 1694
1698 1701 1704 1705 1711 1715 1716 1717 1718 1721 1729 1735 1737
1740 1743 1750 1752 1754 1758 1762 1765 1773 1774 1777 1789 1813
1815 1818 1819 1820 1835 1842 1870 1881 1883 1885 1889 1908 1971
1973 1986 2005 2012 2018 2019 2022 2023 2026 2028 2029 2031 2032
2040 2042 2043 2044 2045 2051 2059 2060 2072 2093 2103 2104 2105
2114 2125 2127 2134 2144 2154 2162 2165 2168 2182 *2192 2196 2198
2205 2230 2231 2234 2244 2249 2252 2262 2267 2278 2283 2284 2298
2322 2326 2336 2341 2344 2354 2367 2368 2370 2371 2375 2383 2454
2500 2542 2543 2553 2563 2627 2628 2637 2688 2693 2695 2697 *2708
2715 2720 2730 2732 2733 2740 2746 2758 2763 2778 2782 2790 2800
2819 2820 *2835 2838 2841 2858 2862 2863 *2867 2870 2882 2885 2888
2892 2895 2908 2911 2915 2916 2922 2924 2958 2964 2970 2994 3006
3020 3049 3051 3056 3069 *3080 3081 3082 3083 3086 3094 3097 *3100
*3107 3108 3111 3114 3115 3119 3122 3130 3141 *3144 3151 3160 3161
3162 3164 3170 3176 3193 3206 3211 3219 3220 3225 *3231 *3238 3242
*3250 *3294 *3300 *3312 3370 3378 *3381 3440 3441 = 356*27
MYSELFE *see* selfe
MYSTERIES = 1
Men into such strange mysteries?   572
NAKED = 1
Haue left me naked to mine Enemies.   2372
NAMD = 1*1
*Is nam'd, your warres in France: this makes bold mouths,   393
I nam'd my Knell; whil'st I sit meditating   2637
NAME = 15
Whom from the flow of gall I name not, but   226
Arrest thee of High Treason, in the name | Of our most Soueraigne
King.   282
Neuer name to vs; you haue halfe our power: 336
And by that name must dye; yet Heauen beare witnes,   900
And lift my Soule to Heauen. | Lead on a Gods name.   920
Made my Name once more Noble. Now his Sonne,   961
Henry the Eight, Life, Honour, Name and all   962
Against your Sacred Person; in Gods name   1395
I will implore. If not, i'th'name of God | Your pleasure be fulfill'd.   1410
Seemes to flow from him? How, i'th'name of Thrift   1970
But 'tis so lately alter'd, that the old name | Is fresh about me.   2521
My Royall Nephew, and your name *Capuchius.* | *Cap.* Madam the
same. Your Seruant.   2695
When I shall dwell with Wormes, and my poore name   2715

NAME *cont.*
What is her Name? | *Cran. Elizabeth.* 3375
His Honour, and the greatnesse of his Name, 3422
NATIONS = 1
Shall be, and make new Nations. He shall flourish, 3423
NATURE = 11
A Minister in his Power. You know his Nature, 168
Kin. Still Exaction: | The nature of it, in what kinde let's know, 384
To Nature none more bound; his trayning such, 451
Commanded Nature, that my Ladies wombe 1555
Camp. Most honour'd Madam, | My Lord of Yorke, out of his Noble nature, 1686
I beare i'th'State: and Nature does require 2016
(I know his Noble Nature) not to let 2332
She is yong, and of a Noble modest Nature, 2726
Not for delights: Times to repayre our Nature 2774
In them a wilder Nature, then the businesse | That seekes dispatch by day. 2788
Thou hast a cruell Nature and a bloody. 3198
NATURES = 1
In our owne natures fraile, and capable 3059
NAUGHT *see also* nought = 2
A better Wife, let him in naught be trusted, 1499
They'l say tis naught. Others to heare the City 3454
NAUGHTY = 1
Vpon this naughty Earth? Go too, go too, 2939
NAUY = 1
A loade, would sinke a Nauy, (too much Honor.) 2289
NAY = 14
Bran. Nay, he must beare you company. The King 296
Queen. Nay, we must longer kneele; I am a Suitor. 334
(Nay let 'em be vnmanly) yet are follow'd. 575
His Grace is entring. Nay, you must not freeze, 692
Card. What warlike voyce, | And to what end is this? Nay, Ladies, feare not; 735
Buck. Nay, Sir *Nicholas,* | Let it alone; my State now will but mocke me. 946
If you might please to stretch it. | *Anne.* Nay, good troth. 1241
Continue in my Liking? Nay, gaue notice 1387
Wol. Be patient yet. | *Qu.* I will, when you are humble; Nay before, 1431
And liue a Subiect? Nay forsooth, my Friends, 1715
I writ too's Holinesse. Nay then, farewell: 2102
A great man should decline. Nay, and you weep | I am falne indeed. 2279
My Lord. *Griffith* farewell. Nay *Patience,* 2758
Suff. Nay, my Lord, | That cannot be; you are a Counsellor, 3097
NECESSARY = 1
Our necessary actions, in the feare 412
NECESSITIES = 1
Gard. These should be houres for necessities, 2773
NECKE = 1
About his necke, yet neuer lost her lustre; 1065
NEED = 2*2
Norf. We had need pray, | And heartily, for our deliuerance; 1078
King. What's the need? | It hath already publiquely bene read, 1353
*Que. What need you note it? pray you keep your way, 1490
*vnder the Line, they need no other pennance: that Fire-| Drake 3302

NEEDES = 1
Crom. O my Lord, | Must I then leaue you? Must I needes forgo　　2336
NEEDFULL = 1
Camp. So please your Highnes, | The Queene being absent, 'tis a
needfull fitnesse,　　1601
NEEDS = 3*1
And must needs say a Noble one; which makes me　　965
Cam. Your Grace must needs deserue all strangers loues,　　1149
For he would needs be vertuous. That good Fellow,　　1187
But I must needs to th' Tower my Lords?　　3151
NEERE = 10*2
Or some about him neere, haue out of malice　　1010
Ha's crept too neere his Conscience.　　1047
Suff. No, his Conscience | Ha's crept too neere another Ladie.　　1048
I will haue none so neere els. Learne this Brother,　　1189
Queen. Pray their Graces | To come neere: what can be their busines　　1639
In such a poynt of weight, so neere mine Honour,　　1697
(More neere my Life I feare) with my weake wit;　　1698
2 Those men are happy, | And so are all, are neere her.　　2464
Patience, be neere me still, and set me lower,　　2634
A man of his Place, and so neere our fauour　　3029
*a fellow somewhat neere the doore, he should be a Brasi-|er　　3299
*Wife of small wit, neere him, that rail'd vpon me,　　3306
NEGLECT = 2
Neglect him not; make vse now, and prouide | For thine owne future
safety.　　2334
Clap round Fines for neglect: y'are lazy knaues,　　3341
NEGLECTED = 1
Strangely neglected? When did he regard　　1839
NEGLIGENCE = 1
And fee my Friends in Rome.) O Negligence!　　2093
NEIGHBOURS = 3
I am beholding to you: cheere your neighbours:　　719
Of the whole State; as of late dayes our neighbours,　　3077
The merry Songs of Peace to all his Neighbours.　　3406
NEITHER = 4*1
For high feats done to'th'Crowne; neither Allied　　110
Traduc'd by ignorant Tongues, which neither know　　407
This pausingly ensu'de; neither the King, nor's Heyres　　514
An. Not for that neither; here's the pang that pinches.　　1202
Which wee haue not done neither; that I feare　　3456
NEPHEW = 1*1
*Between vs & the Emperor (the Queens great Nephew)　　1058
My Royall Nephew, and your name *Capuchius.* | *Cap.* Madam the
same. Your Seruant.　　2695
NERE = 7
For further life in this world I ne're hope,　　910
Malice ne're meant: Our breach of Duty this way,　　1109
An. Oh Gods will, much better | She ne're had knowne pompe; though't
be temporall,　　1215
One that ne're dream'd a Ioy, beyond his pleasure;　　1768
Let me ne're see againe. *Exit Messeng.*　　2691
And let me tell you, it will ne're be well,　　2806
Let me ne're hope to see a Chine againe,　　3284
NET = 1
The net has falne vpon me, I shall perish | Vnder deuice, and practise.　　285

NEUER *see also* ne're = 33

Will leaue vs neuer an vnderstanding Friend.	23
By this, so sicken'd their Estates, that neuer	134
Neuer name to vs; you haue halfe our power:	336
And neuer seeke for ayd out of himselfe: yet see,	453
L.San. New customes, | Though they be neuer so ridiculous,	573
That neuer see 'em pace before, the Spauen	584
To thinke an English Courtier may be wise, | And neuer see the *Louure.*	599
Till now I neuer knew thee. | *Musicke, Dance.*	772
He neuer was so womanish, the cause | He may a little grieue at.	868
That neuer knew what Truth meant: I now seale it;	951
Like water from ye, neuer found againe	976
Suff. Pray God he doe, | Hee'l neuer know himselfe else.	1054
About his necke, yet neuer lost her lustre;	1065
She neuer knew harme-doing: Oh, now after	1206
Haue wish'd the sleeping of this busines, neuer desir'd	1529
A Woman (I dare say without Vainglory) | Neuer yet branded with Suspition?	1760
Qu. Would I had neuer trod this English Earth,	1779
Barre his accesse to 'th'King, neuer attempt	1846
And when he falles, he falles like Lucifer, | Neuer to hope againe.	2272
Neuer so truly happy, my good *Cromwell,*	2283
(That Sun, I pray may neuer set) I haue told him,	2329
1 Neuer greater, | Nor Ile assure you better taken Sir.　　　.	2392
I neuer saw before. Great belly'd women,	2496
Both in his words, and meaning. He was neuer	2594
(But pouerty could neuer draw 'em from me)	2741
Suff. Sir, I did neuer win of you before.	2839
(God turne their hearts, I neuer sought their malice)	3008
Pray Heauen the King may neuer find a heart	3090
Which ye shall neuer haue while I liue.	3217
On May-day Morning, which will neuer be:	3272
And all that shall succeed: *Saba* was neuer	3393
Kin. O Lord Archbishop | Thou hast made me now a man, neuer before	3435
THE EPILOGVE. | *Tis ten to one, this Play can neuer please*	3449

NEW = 13

Or ha's giuen all before, and he begins | A new Hell in himselfe.	121
That is new trim'd; but benefit no further	415
L.San. New customes, | Though they be neuer so ridiculous,	573
L.San. They haue all new legs,	582
Louell. Faith my Lord, | I heare of none but the new Proclamation,	591
Prethee call *Gardiner* to me, my new Secretary.	1163
But that you shall sustaine moe new disgraces, | With these you beare alreadie.	1831
No new deuice to beate this from his Braines?	2097
I feele my heart new open'd. Oh how wretched	2267
(For so we are inform'd) with new opinions,	3065
Of this new Sect? ye are not sound.	3132
Her Ashes new create another Heyre,	3412
Shall be, and make new Nations. He shall flourish,	3423

NEWES = 7

What newes, Sir *Thomas Louell*?	589
These newes are euery where, euery tongue speaks 'em,	1071
I should be glad to heare such Newes as this | Once euery houre.	1855
What Newes abroad? | *Crom.* The heauiest, and the worst,	2299
Card. That's Newes indeed.	2314
Now *Louel*, from the Queene what is the Newes.	2842

NEWES *cont.*
I haue Newes to tell you. 2890
NEWLY = 1
Newly preferr'd from the Kings Secretary: | The other London. 2526
NEXT = 8*5
Became the next dayes master, till the last 61
A guift that heauen giues for him, which buyes | A place next to the
King. 114
Card. There's fresher ayre my Lord, | In the next Chamber. 810
Enter two Vergers, with short siluer wands; next them two 1334
Rochester, and S.(aint) Asaph: Next them, with some small 1337
the Scribes. The Lords sit next the Bishops. The rest of the 1349
*Still met the King? Lou'd him next Heau'n? Obey'd him? 1763
I haue kept you next my Heart, haue not alone 2029
Crom. The next is, that Sir *Thomas Moore* is chosen | Lord Chancellor,
in your place. 2303
To be high Steward; Next the Duke of Norfolke, 2400
the same to the other next two, who obserue the same or-| der 2650
Cap. Noble Lady, | First mine owne seruice to your Grace, the next 2702
My next poore Petition, | Is, that his Noble Grace would haue some
pittie 2730
NICHOLAS = 3*1
By a vaine Prophesie of *Nicholas Henton.* 491
side, accompanied with Sir Thomas Louell, Sir Nicholas 891
Then giue my Charge vp to Sir *Nicholas Vaux,* 940
Buck. Nay, Sir *Nicholas,* | Let it alone; my State now will but mocke
me. 946
NIGGARD = 1
If not from Hell? The Diuell is a Niggard, 120
NIGHT = 10*1
Was cry'de incompareable; and th'ensuing night 71
Let him not seek't of vs: By day and night 567
This night he makes a Supper, and a great one, 638
For I was spoke to, with Sir *Henry Guilford* | This night to be
Comptrollers. 657
Salutes ye all; This Night he dedicates 668
This night to meet heere they could doe no lesse, 761
*To waste these times. Good houre of night Sir *Thomas*: 2776
I hinder you too long: Good night, Sir *Thomas.* | *Exit Gardiner and
Page.* 2833
King. Charles, I will play no more to night, 2837
Suf. I wish your Highnesse | A quiet night, and my good Mistris will |
Remember in my Prayers. 2861
King. Charles good night. *Exit Suffolke.* 2864
NIGHTS = 1*1
Pursu'd him still, and three nights after this, 2579
Lou. Many good nights, my Lord, I rest your seruant. 2835
NINE *see* 9.
NIPPES = 1
His Greatnesse is a ripening, nippes his roote, 2258
NO *l.*2 76 95 100 211 219 273 307 374 375 400 404 415 512 531 621 624
631 645 *758 761 880 903 929 1048 1126 1204 1244 1249 *1261 1278
1310 1318 1325 *1364 1371 1448 1464 1493 1557 1590 1593 1665 1732
1759 1785 1786 1787 1852 1898 1901 1915 1942 1944 2026 2039 2096
2097 2107 2129 *2248 2276 2324 2348 2471 2499 2517 2529 2532 2560
2627 2628 2664 2683 2718 2766 2785 2837 2904 2940 2946 2953 3082

NO *cont.*
3099 3150 3166 3204 3230 3278 *3302 *3319 3332 3430 3431
3446 = 95*6
NOBILITIE = 2
Farewell Nobilitie: let his Grace go forward,   2172
Of our despis'd Nobilitie, our Issues,   2184
NOBILITY = 1
And like her true Nobility, she ha's | Carried her selfe towards me.   1506
NOBLE = 43*4
Such Noble Scoenes, as draw the Eye to flow   5
The very Persons of our Noble Story,   27
The Noble Spirits to Armes, they did performe   79
When these so Noble benefits shall proue   454
You charge not in your spleene a Noble person,   521
L.Cham. No doubt hee's Noble;   645
In all this Noble Beuy, has brought with her   670
Card. Y'are welcome my faire Guests; that noble Lady   711
San. Your Grace is Noble,   715
Cham. How now, what is't? | *Seru.* A noble troupe of Strangers,   739
A noble Company: what are their pleasures?   757
Of this so Noble and so faire assembly,   760
In all the rest shew'd a most Noble patience.   865
1. Stay there Sir, | And see the noble ruin'd man you speake of.   893
His Noble Friends and Fellowes; whom to leaue   915
My noble Father *Henry* of *Buckingham,*   953
Made my Name once more Noble. Now his Sonne,   961
And must needs say a Noble one; which makes me   965
The Tryall, iust and Noble. All the Clerkes,   1139
Inuited by your Noble selfe, hath sent   1142
You are so Noble: To your Highnesse hand   1150
*The Queene of earthly Queenes: Shee's Noble borne;   1505
Wol. May it please you Noble Madam, to withdraw   1650
Card. Noble Lady, | I am sorry my integrity should breed,   1674
Camp. Most honour'd Madam, | My Lord of Yorke, out of his Noble
nature,   1686
To giue vp willingly that Noble Title   1775
I know you haue a Gentle, Noble temper,   1802
With these weake Womens feares. A Noble Spirit   1807
Of Noble Buckingham, my Father-in-Law,   2144
His Noble Iurie, and foule Cause can witnesse.   2158
My Lord of Norfolke, as you are truly Noble,   2182
Or gilde againe the Noble Troopes that waighted   2325
(I know his Noble Nature) not to let   2332
So good, so Noble, and so true a Master?   2338
Is that old Noble Lady, Dutchesse of Norfolke.   2467
Grif. Noble Madam: | Mens euill manners, liue in Brasse, their Vertues 2600
Cap. Noble Lady, | First mine owne seruice to your Grace, the next 2702
She is yong, and of a Noble modest Nature,   2726
My next poore Petition, | Is, that his Noble Grace would haue some
pittie   2730
For honestie, and decent Carriage | A right good Husband (let him be a
Noble)   2737
Norf. Who waits there? | *Keep.* Without my Noble Lords? | *Gard.* Yes. 3048
My Noble Lords; for those that tame wild Horses,   3069
By your good fauour, too sharpe; Men so Noble,   3123
To a most Noble Iudge, the King my Maister.   3164
*You shall haue two noble Partners with you: the old   3239

NOBLE *cont.*
My Noble Partners, and my selfe thus pray   3370
*Kin. My Noble Gossips, y'haue beene too Prodigall;   3381
NOBLEMAN = 1
It is to see a Nobleman want manners.   2204
NOBLEMEN = *3
*two Noblemen, with the Sword and Mace. The King takes   1344
*Staffe, Duke of Suffolke, two Noblemen, bearing great   3356
*Noblemen bearing a Canopy, vnder which the Dutchesse of   3358
NOBLENESSE = 1
The stampe of Noblenesse in any person | Out of himselfe?   1840
NOBLER = 1
And spoyle your nobler Soule; I say, take heed;   522
NOBLES = 3
Not wake him in his slumber. A Beggers booke, | Out-worths a Nobles
blood.   190
the Nobles, and Sir Thomas Louell: the Cardinall   318
*Exit King, frowning vpon the Cardinall, the Nobles | throng after him
smiling, and whispering.*   2081
NOBLY = 3
And pray receiue 'em Nobly, and conduct 'em   746
King. 'Tis Nobly spoken: 2076
Laid Nobly on her: which perform'd, the Quire   2511
NOISD = 1
Hardly conceiue of me. Let it be nois'd,   442
NONE = 14
To Nature none more bound; his trayning such,   451
Finde mercy in the Law, 'tis his; if none,   566
Louell. Faith my Lord, | I heare of none but the new Proclamation,   591
To faire content, and you: None heere he hopes   669
But he would bite none, iust as I doe now,   702
I will haue none so neere els. Learne this Brother,   1189
And the late Marriage made of none effect: 2415
Saw ye none enter since I slept? | *Grif.* None Madam.   2662
There's none stands vnder more calumnious tongues, | Then I my selfe,
poore man.   2910
None better in my Kingdome. Get you gone,   2958
Cast none away: That I shall cleere my selfe,   3114
And wisedome of my Councell; but I finde none: 3206
Let none thinke Flattery; for they'l finde'em Truth.   3386
NOR *l.*109 341 408 632 908 911 1085 1284 1285 1303 1371 1448 1493 1680
2393 2841 3085 3280 3410 = 20
NOR = 26*1
NORF = 16
NORFF = 4
NORFOLKE see also Nor., Norf., Norff. = *1
*9 The Olde Dutchesse of Norfolke, *in a Coronall of Gold,*   2441
NORFOLKE = 1
2 And that my Lord of Norfolke? | 1 Yes.   2454
NORFOLKE = 10*5
Enter the Duke of Norfolke at one doore. At the other,   35
Duke of Norfolke. Enter the Queene, Norfolke and   330
Enter to the Lord Chamberlaine, the Dukes of Nor- | folke and Suffolke.   1038
Exeunt Norfolke and Suffolke.   1132
*Enter the Duke of Norfolke, Duke of Suffolke, Lord Surrey, | and Lord
Chamberlaine.*   1825

NORFOLKE *cont.*
Enter to Woolsey, the Dukes of Norfolke and Suffolke, the | Earle of
Surrey, and the Lord Chamberlaine.   2108
My Lord of Norfolke, as you are truly Noble,   2182
To be high Steward; Next the Duke of Norfolke,   2400
*him, the Duke of Norfolke, with the Rod of Marshalship, | a Coronet on
his head. Collars of Esses.   2435
Is that old Noble Lady, Dutchesse of Norfolke.   2467
*Duke of Suffolke, Duke of Norfolke, Surrey, Lord Cham-| berlaine,   3039
*Duchesse of Norfolke, and Lady Marquesse Dorset? will | these please
you?   3240
*Garter, Cranmer, Duke of Norfolke with his Marshals   3355
*Norfolke, Godmother, bearing the Childe richly habited in   3359
NORFOLKE = 1
NORS = 1
This pausingly ensu'de; neither the King, nor's Heyres   514
NORTH = *1
*North. When they were ready to set out for London, a man   1031
NORTHAMPTON = 1
Of *Hertford, Stafford* and *Northampton,* I   281
NORTHUMBERLAND = 1
For after the stout Earle Northumberland | Arrested him at Yorke, and
brought him forward   2565
NOSE = 1*2
Suf. No, no: | There be moe Waspes that buz about his Nose,   1898
*now reigne in's Nose; all that stand about him are   3301
*was his Nose discharged against mee; hee stands there   3304
NOSES = 1
Their very noses had been Councellours   580
NOT *l.*68 108 120 142 146 167 171 189 190 205 213 216 226 231 273 341
345 354 357 359 376 377 405 411 418 428 429 455 459 481 497 521 567
630 632 656 692 712 713 720 736 802 813 840 854 866 867 902 907 973
992 996 998 1001 1017 1020 *1034 1069 1085 1088 1104 1121 1127 1128
1158 *1172 1175 1180 1190 1197 *1202 1231 *1243 1244 1251 1256 1267
1282 1285 1292 1312 1322 1329 1383 1384 1404 1410 1436 1441 1444
1459 1485 1493 1512 1523 1524 1554 *1562 1571 1642 1644 1657 1666
1667 1678 1700 1717 1740 1766 1774 1795 1810 1849 1853 1954 1957
1999 2029 2035 2147 2230 2232 2234 2332 2334 2339 2343 2359 2361
2371 *2402 2411 2412 2475 2497 2533 2556 2569 2611 2623 2635 2661
2664 2669 2685 2693 2734 2735 2745 2759 2771 2774 2775 *2783 2807
2838 2841 2843 2860 2881 2924 2927 2929 2930 2951 2963 *2989 3006
3028 3062 3067 3070 3131 3132 3133 3134 3136 3185 3192 3202 3204
3214 3232 3275 3280 3285 3336 3409 3456 = 184*8
NOTE = 5*1
Out of his Selfe-drawing Web. O giues vs note,   112
(Whereof my Soueraigne would haue note) they are   379
Card. Please your Highnesse note   479
*Que. What need you note it? pray you keep your way,   1490
Cause the Musitians play me that sad note   2636
Pati. Do you note | How much her Grace is alter'd on the sodaine?   2674
NOTED = 1
1. At his returne, | No doubt he will requite it; this is noted   879
NOTES = 1
Perceiue I speake sincerely, and high notes   1275
NOTHING = 10
Buck. It will helpe me nothing | To plead mine Innocence; for that dye
is on me   291

NOTHING *cont.*

More then my All, is Nothing: Nor my Prayers	1284
There's nothing I haue done yet o' my Conscience	1654
Quee. Ye turne me into nothing. Woe vpon ye,	1746
Your Master wed me to: nothing but death | Shall e're diuorce my Dignities.	1776
Can nothing render but Allegiant thankes,	2050
Then makes him nothing. I must reade this paper:	2088
But his performance, as he is now, Nothing:	2597
Being of those Vertues vacant. I feare nothing | What can be said against me.	2925
I made no spare Sir. | *Port.* You did nothing Sir.	3278

NOTICE = 3

Nor. Like it your Grace, | The State takes notice of the priuate difference	160
Continue in my Liking? Nay, gaue notice	1387
Take notice Lords, he ha's a Loyall brest,	2077

NOTORIOUS = 1

Since you prouoke me, shall be most notorious.	2181

NOTWITHSTANDING = 1

Should, notwithstanding that your bond of duty,	2063

NOUGHT = 1

Buc. All was Royall, | To the disposing of it nought rebell'd,	88

NOURISHMENT = 1

Enuy, and crooked malice, nourishment;	3092

NOW = 94*4

I Come no more to make you laugh, Things now,	2
We now present. Those that can Pitty, heere	6
To make that onely true, we now intend,	22
Till this time Pompe was single, but now married	59
Was to them, as a Painting. Now this Maske	70
Equall in lustre, were now best, now worst	73
Being now seene, possible enough, got credit | That *Beuis* was beleeu'd.	81
(Who cannot erre) he did it. Now this followes,	250
Allegeance in them; their curses now	395
Card. Now Madam, may his Highnes liue in freedome,	552
That sure th'haue worne out Christendome: how now?	588
Now I would pray our Monsieurs	598
For sure there's no conuerting of'em: now	624
But few now giue so great ones:	653
Lou. O that your Lordship were but now Confessor, | To one or two of these.	684
But he would bite none, iust as I doe now,	702
Cham. Well said my Lord: | So now y'are fairely seated: Gentlemen,	704
Cham. How now, what is't? | *Seru.* A noble troupe of Strangers,	739
You haue now a broken Banket, but wee'l mend it.	750
Till now I neuer knew thee. | *Musicke, Dance.*	772
I should iudge now vnhappily.	792
1. Ile saue you | That labour Sir. All's now done but the Ceremony	825
Were hid against me, now to forgiue me frankly.	924
Buck. Nay, Sir *Nicholas*, | Let it alone; my State now will but mocke me.	946
And Duke of *Buckingham*: now, poore *Edward Bohun*;	949
That neuer knew what Truth meant: I now seale it;	951
Made my Name once more Noble. Now his Sonne,	961
Pray for me, I must now forsake ye; the last houre	978
2. But that slander Sir, | Is found a truth now: for it growes agen	1006

NOW *cont.*

*And with what zeale? For now he has crackt the League	1057
Who can be angry now? What Enuy reach you?	1136
Must now confesse, if they haue any goodnesse,	1138
You are the Kings now.	1167
She neuer knew harme-doing: Oh, now after	1206
Old L. Alas poore Lady,	Shee's a stranger now againe.	1220
An. Now I pray God, *Amen.*	1272
And that (without delay) their Arguments	Be now produc'd, and heard.	1423
Gone slightly o're lowe steppes, and now are mounted	1472
When you are cald returne. Now the Lord helpe,	1491
Now, what mou'd me too't,	1534
Now present heere together: that's to say,	1569
Enter a Gentleman.	*Queen.* How now?	1633
I doe not like their comming; now I thinke on't,	1642
And all the Fellowship I hold now with him	1753
What will become of me now, wretched Lady?	1782
Alas (poore Wenches) where are now your Fortunes?	1784
Bestow your Councels on me. She now begges	1821
Norf. If you will now vnite in your Complaints,	1827
What we can do to him (though now the time	1844
Sur. Now all my ioy	Trace the Coniunction.	1883
Cham. Now God incense him,	And let him cry Ha, lowder.	1906
Does he rake this together? Now my Lords,	Saw you the Cardinall?	1971
You were now running o're: you haue scarse time	2008
If what I now pronounce, you haue found true:	2037
I haste now to my Setting. I shall fall	Like a bright exhalation in the Euening,	2105
I dare, and must deny it. Now I feele	2123
Ti'de it by Letters Patents. Now, who'll take it?	*Sur.* The King that gaue it.	2135
Now, if you can blush, and crie guiltie Cardinall,	You'l shew a little Honestie.	2200
At length broke vnder me, and now ha's left me	2263
Why how now *Cromwell?*	2275
I know my selfe now, and I feele within me,	2284
I am able now (me thinkes)	2295
Going to Chappell: and the voyce is now	Onely about her Corronation.	2318
I am a poore falne man, vnworthy now	2327
Neglect him not; make vse now, and prouide	For thine owne future safety.	2334
I dare now call mine owne. O *Cromwel, Cromwel,*	2369
Where she remaines now sicke.	2 Alas good Lady.	2417
'Tis now the Kings, and call'd White-Hall.	3 I know it:	2519
So now (me thinkes) I feele a little ease.	2555
But his performance, as he is now, Nothing:	2597
To heare me speake his good now?	*Kath.* Yes good *Griffith,*	2603
(Now in his Ashes) Honor: Peace be with him.	2633
Kath. No? Saw you not euen now a blessed Troope	2664
Kath. O my Lord,	The Times and Titles now are alter'd strangely	2697
But now I am past all Comforts heere, but Prayers.	2711
(And now I should not lye) but will deserue	2735
Say his long trouble now is passing	2755
I wish it grubb'd vp now.	2798

NOW *cont.*

Louell. Now Sir, you speake of two | The most remark'd i'th'Kingdome: as for *Cromwell*, 2810
Now *Louel*, from the Queene what is the Newes. 2842
King. How now my Lord? 2882
Prythee let's walke. Now by my Holydame, 2915
Will make my boldnesse, manners. Now good Angels 2964
King. Now by thy lookes | I gesse thy Message. Is the Queene deliuer'd? 2967
Both now, and euer blesse her: 'Tis a Gyrle 2972
Haue more, or else vnsay't: and now, while 'tis hot, 2985
Chan. Let him come in. | *Keep.* Your Grace may enter now. 3053
Cham. Tis now too certaine; | How much more is his Life in value with him? 3173
Ye blew the fire that burnes ye: now haue at ye. 3180
To heare such flattery now, and in my presence 3193
Good man sit downe: Now let me see the proudest 3199
Cran. The greatest Monarch now aliue may glory 3235
*now reigne in's Nose; all that stand about him are 3301
Cran. Let me speake Sir, | For Heauen now bids me; and the words I vtter, 3384
Though in her Cradle; yet now promises 3388
(But few now liuing can behold that goodnesse) 3391
Kin. O Lord Archbishop | Thou hast made me now a man, neuer before 3435

NOYSE = 3*2

A noyse of Targets: Or to see a Fellow 16
A noyse within crying roome for the Queene, vsher'd by the 329
Had the full view of, such a noyse arose, 2491
Noyse and Tumult within: Enter Porter and | his man. 3257
Port. You'l leaue your noyse anon ye Rascals: doe 3259

NUMBER = 2

2. I am sorry fort. | 1. So are a number more. 835
My Lords, I care not (so much I am happy | Aboue a number) if my actions 1657

NUMBERLESSE = 1

There cannot be those numberlesse offences 927

NURSE = 1*1

*Haue their free voyces. Rome (the Nurse of Iudgement) 1141
Shall still be doubled on her. Truth shall Nurse her, 3398

O *l*.136 295 309 637 675 *684 701 771 822 984 1116 1196 1199 1665 1849 1864 2093 2231 2290 2321 2336 *2363 2369 2552 2574 2697 *2708 3435 = 25*3, 4*1

Out of his Selfe-drawing Web. O giues vs note, 112
2. All the Commons | Hate him perniciously, and o' my Conscience 884
There's nothing I haue done yet o' my Conscience 1654
*by his face, for o' my conscience twenty of the Dog- | dayes 3300
Cham. Mercy o' me: what a Multitude are heere? 3326

OATH *see also* oth = 1

He did discharge a horrible Oath, whose tenor 559

OBEDIENCE = 8

This tractable obedience is a Slaue 397
An. I doe not know | What kinde of my obedience, I should tender; 1282
Vouchsafe to speake my thankes, and my obedience, 1288
That I haue beene your Wife, in this Obedience, 1389
Zeale and obedience he still bore your Grace, 1688
Is onely my Obedience. What can happen 1754
The hearts of Princes kisse Obedience, 1799
One that in all obedience, makes the Church 3186

OBEDIENT = 1
   King. Fairely answer'd: | A Loyall, and obedient Subiect is   2054
OBEY = 2
   Be done in this and all things: I obey.   294
   Till they obey the mannage. If we suffer   3072
OBEYD = 1*1
   The will of Heauen be done, and the Kings pleasure | By me obey'd.   300
   *Still met the King? Lou'd him next Heau'n? Obey'd him?   1763
OBEYING = 1
   Obeying in commanding, and thy parts   1503
OBIECT = 2
   Me as his abiect obiect, at this instant   197
   And fixt on Spirituall obiect, he should still   1997
OBIECTIONS = 1
   Wol. Speake on Sir, | I dare your worst Obiections: If I blush,   2202
OBLIGATION = 1
   No other obligation? by my Life,   1318
OBSERUE = 2*2
   The Cardinall. | *Nor.* Obserue, obserue, hee's moody.   1926
   *the same to the other next two, who obserue the same or-| der   2650
   *last two: who likewise obserue the same Order. At which   2653
OBSERUING = *1
   Nor. My Lord, we haue | *Stood heere obseruing him. Some strange
   Commotion   1973
OBSTINATE = 1
   Camp. The Queene is obstinate,   1483
OCCASION = 3
   Sur. I am ioyfull | To meete the least occasion, that may giue me   1833
   And am right glad to catch this good occasion   2907
   Th'occasion shall instruct you. If intreaties   2952
OCLOCKE *see* clocke
ODIOUS = 1
   Which since they are of you, and odious, | I will not taint my mouth
   with.   2229
OF *see also* a, o' = 485*64
OFF *l.*360 534 *1250 1375 1853 2100 2409 2484 *3307 = 7*2
OFFENCE = 1
   No great offence belongs too't, giue your Friend   2785
OFFENCES = 3
   There cannot be those numberlesse offences   927
   Norff. A gracious King, that pardons all offences   1108
   They are too thin, and base to hide offences,   3194
OFFENDED = 1
   In what haue I offended you? What cause   1373
OFFENDER = 1
   The cause betwixt her, and this great offender.   3190
OFFER = 3
   You turne the good we offer, into enuy.   1745
   The offer of this time, I cannot promise,   1830
   Then my Weake-hearted Enemies, dare offer.   2298
OFFERD = 1
   1 'Tis very true. But that time offer'd sorrow, | This generall ioy.   2385
OFFERS = 2
   And to be iudg'd by him. | *She Curtsies to the King, and offers to
   depart.*   1481
   Offers, as I doe, in a signe of peace, | His Seruice, and his Counsell. |
   Queen. To betray me.   1691

OFFICE = 7
Order gaue each thing view. The Office did	90
Brandon. Your Office Sergeant: execute it.	278
The dignity of your Office; is the poynt | Of my Petition.	342
Queen. If I know you well, | You were the Dukes Surueyor, and lost your Office	518
Your selfe pronounce their Office. I must tell you,	1475
His word vpon you. Since I had my Office,	2028
Both of my Life and Office, I haue labour'd,	3081

OFFICES = 3
Doe no more Offices of life too't; then	1557
Car. Sir, | For Holy Offices I haue a time; a time	2013
1 Yes, 'tis the List | Of those that claime their Offices this day,	2396

OFFICIOUS = 1
(I meane your malice) know, Officious Lords,	2122

OFT = 5
Then vainly longing. What we oft doe best,	416
Not ours, or not allow'd; what worst, as oft	418
Spoke by a holy Monke, that oft, sayes he,	506
It to be stir'd; but oft haue hindred, oft	1530

OFTEN = 1
She was often cyted by them, but appear'd not:	2411

OH *see also* O *l.*83 1206 1215 1305 2267 = 5
OILE *see* oyle
OLD = 18*2
To th'old dam Treason) *Charles* the Emperour,	252
Or pack to their old Playfellowes; there, I take it,	611
And when old Time shall lead him to his end,	937
Enter Anne Bullen, and an old Lady.	1201
Old La. Hearts of most hard temper | Melt and lament for her.	1213
Old L. Alas poore Lady, | Shee's a stranger now againe.	1220
Old L. Our content | Is our best hauing.	1228
**Old L.* Yes troth, & troth; you would not be a Queene?	1243
Old as I am, to Queene it: but I pray you,	1246
Old L. How tasts it? Is it bitter? Forty pence, no:	1310
There was a Lady once (tis an old Story)	1311
Old L. What doe you thinke me --- *Exeunt.*	1331
His Loue, too long ago. I am old my Lords,	1752
Weary, and old with Seruice, to the mercy	2264
Is that old Noble Lady, Dutchesse of Norfolke.	2467
In the old time of Warre, would shake the prease	2498
But 'tis so lately alter'd, that the old name | Is fresh about me.	2521
An old man, broken with the stormes of State,	2575
*You shall haue two noble Partners with you: the old	3239
That had a head to hit, either young or old,	3282

OLDE = 1*1
*9 *The* Olde Dutchesse of Norfolke, *in a Coronall of Gold,*	2441
Enter Olde Lady.	2961

OLDL = 4*2
OMIT = 1
Cannot stand vnder them. If you omit	1829

ON = 70*15
ONCE = 19*3
By sicke Interpreters (once weake ones) is	417
Not well dispos'd, the minde growing once corrupt,	455
That once were his, and is become as blacke,	462
A good digestion to you all; and once more	751

ONCE *cont.*
To lead 'em once againe, and then let's dreame	816
Made my Name once more Noble. Now his Sonne,	961
And giue your hearts to; when they once perceiue	974
For when the King once heard it, out of anger	1002
Whom once more, I present vnto your Highnesse.	1145
*Kin. And once more in mine armes I bid him welcome,	1146
There was a Lady once (tis an old Story)	1311
Refuse you for my Iudge, whom yet once more	1440
At once, and fully satisfide) whether euer I	1513
Take heed, for heauens sake take heed, least at once	1742
That once was Mistris of the Field, and flourish'd,	1788
I should be glad to heare such Newes as this | Once euery houre.	1855
Say *Wolsey,* that once trod the wayes of Glory,	2350
1 Y'are well met once againe. | 2 So are you.	2379
Then but once thinke his place becomes thee not.	3202
Once more my Lord of *Winchester,* I charge you | Embrace, and loue	
this man.	3242
*such a combustion in the State. I mist the Meteor once,	3308
* The Troope passe once about the Stage, and Gar-| ter speakes.	3362

ONE *see also* 1. = 61*6
Enter the Duke of Norfolke at one doore. At the other,	35
What foure Thron'd ones could haue weigh'd | Such a compounded	
one?	53
To one aboue it selfe. Each following day	60
'Twas said they saw but one, and no Discerner	76
One certes, that promises no Element | In such a businesse.	95
Infecting one another, yea reciprocally,	237
One *Gilbert Pecke,* his Councellour.	305
He stretch'd him, and with one hand on his dagger,	557
And lame ones; one would take it,	583
This night he makes a Supper, and a great one,	638
at one Doore; at an other Doore enter | *Sir Henry Guilford.*	664
One care abroad: hee would haue all as merry:	671
*Lou. O that your Lordship were but now Confessor, | To one or two of	
these.	684
My Lord *Sands,* you are one will keepe 'em waking:	694
There should be one amongst'em by his person	777
Cham. Such a one, they all confesse	783
One of her Highnesse women.	799
Kin. By Heauen she is a dainty one. Sweet heart,	800
*Kin. Lead in your Ladies eu'ry one: Sweet Partner,	812
2. That tricke of State | Was a deepe enuious one,	877
Make of your Prayers one sweet Sacrifice,	919
Goodnesse and he, fill vp one Monument.	938
**And with that bloud will make 'em one day groane for't.	952
That made me happy; at one stroake ha's taken	963
And must needs say a Noble one; which makes me	965
Yet thus farre we are one in Fortunes; both	967
**Turnes what he list. The King will know him one day.	1053
The French Kings Sister. Heauen will one day open	1074
Lie like one lumpe before him, to be fashion'd | Into what pitch he	
please.	1082
Norff. If it doe, Ile venture one; haue at him. | *Suff.* I another.	1130
One generall Tongue vnto vs. This good man,	1143
*Camp. My Lord of *Yorke,* was not one Doctor *Pace*	1172
My Father, King of Spaine, was reckon'd one	1402

ONE *cont.*

A Royall Lady, spake one, the least word that might	1518
Since Vertue findes no friends) a Wife, a true one?	1759
One that ne're dream'd a Ioy, beyond his pleasure;	1768
An Heretique, an Arch-one; *Cranmer,* one	1960
Sur. Yes, that goodnesse	Of gleaning all the Lands wealth into one,	2176
In that one woman, I haue lost for euer.	2323
A sure, and safe one, though thy Master mist it.	2353
Enter two Gentlemen, meeting one another.	2378
Could say this is my wife there, all were wouen	So strangely in one	
peece.	2500
3 *Stokeley* and *Gardiner,* the one of Winchester,	2525
And one already of the Priuy Councell.	2539
Himselfe with Princes. One that by suggestion	2590
He was a Scholler, and a ripe, and good one:	2609
Ipswich and Oxford: one of which, fell with him,	2617
The Vision.	*Enter solemnely tripping one after another, sixe*	
Personages,	2642
Of which there is not one, I dare auow	2734
Gard. It's one a clocke Boy, is't not.	*Boy.* It hath strooke.	2771
Is the Kings hand, and tongue, and who dare speak	One syllable	
against him?	2816
Is this the Honour they doe one another?	3025
'Tis well there's one aboue 'em yet; I had thought	3026
To one mans Honour, this contagious sicknesse;	3074
Might goe one way, and safely; and the end	3084
One that in all obedience, makes the Church	3186
At Chamber dore? and one, as great as you are?	3210
To haue this young one made a Christian.	3253
As I haue made ye one Lords, one remaine:	3254
As much as one sound Cudgell of foure foote,	3276
*Christian Conscience this one Christening will beget a	3295
So shall she leaue her Blessednesse to One,	3414
This Little-One shall make it Holy-day. *Exeunt.*	3448
THE EPILOGVE.	*Tis ten to one, this Play can neuer please*	3449
For such a one we shew'd 'em: If they smile,	3460

ONELY = 10

Onely a show or two, and so agree,	11
Richly in two short houres. Onely they	14
To make that onely true, we now intend,	22
Aske God for Temp'rance, that's th'appliance onely	Which your	
disease requires.	193
Or sit State-Statues onely.	423
Is onely my Obedience. What can happen	1754
Going to Chappell: and the voyce is now	Onely about her	
Corronation.	2318
And his Disciples onely enuy at,	3179
Not onely good and wise, but most religious:	3185
For this Play at this time, is onely in	3458

ONES = 9*1

What foure Thron'd ones could haue weigh'd	Such a compounded	
one?	53
By sicke Interpreters (once weake ones) is	417
A fit or two o'th' face, (but they are shrewd ones)	578
And lame ones; one would take it,	583
But few now giue so great ones:	653
They are a sweet society of faire ones.	683

ONES *cont.*

(I meane the learned ones in Christian Kingdomes) 1140
But thus much, they are foule ones. 2193
2 Their Coronets say so. These are Starres indeed, | And sometimes
falling ones. 2469
*staues, and strong ones; these are but switches to 'em: 3265

ONLY = 3
Only to shew his pompe, as well in France, 238
Is only bitter to him, only dying: 916

ONS = 2
Another spread on's breast, mounting his eyes, 558
The Master-cord on's heart. 1966

ONT = 6
Dashing the Garment of this Peace, aboaded | The sodaine breach on't. 148
And leaue me out on't. Would I had no being 1325
Induce you to the question on't: or euer 1516
I doe not like their comming; now I thinke on't, 1642
My mindes not on't, you are too hard for me. 2838
Would I were fairely out on't. 3175

OPEN = 6
Wee are too open heere to argue this: 1024
The French Kings Sister. Heauen will one day open 1074
This compel'd fortune: haue your mouth fild vp, | Before you open it. 1307
Out with it boldly: Truth loues open dealing. · 1663
His faults lye open to the Lawes, let them 2233
This day was view'd in open, as his Queene, 2317

OPEND = 2
That as my hand ha's open'd Bounty to you, 2059
I feele my heart new open'd. Oh how wretched 2267

OPENT = 1
For you haue seene him open't. Read o're this, 2078

OPINION = 4*1
Our owne Braines, and the Opinion that we bring 21
Camp. Beleeue me, there's an ill opinion spread then, 1177
Commends his good opinion of you, to you; and 1277
Enuy and base opinion set against 'em, 1660
His owne Opinion was his Law. I'th'presence 2592

OPINIONS = 3
(Like free and honest men) our iust opinions, | And comforts to our
cause. 1684
Suf. He is return'd in his Opinions, which 1910
(For so we are inform'd) with new opinions, 3065

OPPOSD = 1
You are Potently oppos'd, and with a Malice 2935

OPPOSE = *1
*T'oppose your cunning. Y'are meek, & humble-mouth'd 1467

OPPOSING = 1
In a rich Chaire of State, opposing freely 2487

OPPRESSION = 1
How vnder my oppression I did reeke | When I first mou'd you. 1575

OR *l.*11 16 121 210 222 234 277 382 418 421 423 578 581 611 685 712 791
858 1010 1080 1380 1383 1394 1428 1433 1449 1450 1514 1516 1520
1559 1632 1702 1713 1780 1838 2039 2121 2207 2210 2215 2220 2271
2325 *2443 2486 *2646 2752 2904 2943 2983 2985 3282 3283 *3292
*3320 3346 3350 3452 = 59*4

ORACLE = 2
Hath crawl'd into the fauour of the King, | And is his Oracle. 1961

ORACLE *cont.*
This Oracle of comfort, ha's so pleas'd me,   3438
ORDER = 5*4
   Order gaue each thing view. The Office did   90
   Attendants stand in conuenient order about the Stage.   1350
   Suf. There's order giuen for her Coronation: 1887
   Learned, and Reuerend Fathers of his Order,   2408
   The Order of the Coronation.   2421
   Exeunt, first passing ouer the Stage in Order and State, and |
   great Flourish of Trumpets.   2445
   the same to the other next two, who obserue the same or-| der 2650
   last two: who likewise obserue the same Order. At which   2653
   Gardiner, seat themselues in Order on each side.   3040
ORDINARY = 1
   An ordinary Groome is for such payment.   2982
ORDRED = 1
   Nor. All this was ordred by the good Discretion   98
ORE = 7
   The fire that mounts the liquor til't run ore,   217
   Gone slightly o're lowe steppes, and now are mounted   1472
   You were now running o're: you haue scarse time   2008
   For you haue seene him open't. Read o're this,   2078
   Will triumph o're my person, which I waigh not,   2924
   Fly o're thy Royall head, and shade thy person | Vnder their blessed
   wings.   2965
   Ile pecke you o're the pales else. *Exeunt.*   3352
ORETAKE = 1
   For if the tryall of the Law o'retake ye,   1726
ORE-GREAT = *1
   Buck. My Surueyor is falce: The ore-great *Cardinall*   311
ORE-MOUNT = *1
   *O're-mount the Larke: The Marchionesse of *Pembrooke*?*   1316
ORE-TOPPING = *1
   Ore-topping womans powre. Madam, you do me wrong   1447
ORLEANCE = 1
   And Marriage 'twixt the Duke of *Orleance*, and   1541
ORNAMENTS = 1
   Rich Stuffes and Ornaments of Houshold, which   1989
ORPHANTS = 1
   May haue a Tombe of Orphants teares wept on him.   2310
ORPHEUS = 1
   SONG. | *Orpheus with his Lute made Trees,*   1620
OTH = 24*2
   Take vp the Rayes o'th'beneficiall Sun, | And keepe it from the Earth.   104
   (Without the priuity o'th'King) t'appoint   125
   The Articles o'th' Combination drew   245
   Buck. So, so; | These are the limbs o'th' Plot: no more I hope.   306
   Bra. A Monke o'th' *Chartreux.* | *Buck.* O *Michaell Hopkins?* | *Bra.* He.   308
   From euery Tree, lop, barke, and part o'th' Timber: 432
   Lord *Aburgany*, to whom by oth he menac'd | Reuenge vpon the
   Cardinall.   477
   To the loue o'th'Commonalty, the Duke | Shall gouerne England.   516
   On the complaint o'th'Tenants; take good heed   520
   A fit or two o'th' face, (but they are shrewd ones)   578
   Yea, the elect o'th'Land, who are assembled   1415
   *(Well worthy the best Heyre o'th' World) should not   1562

OTH *cont.*

(*Katherine* our Queene) before the primest Creature | That's Parragon'd o'th' World.	1599
And came to th'eye o'th'King, wherein was read	1866
To stay the Iudgement o'th'Diuorce; for if	1868
Ha's left the cause o'th'King vnhandled, and	1902
Card. Look'd he o'th'inside of the Paper?	1931
A worthy Friend. The King ha's made him | Master o'th'Iewell House,	2537
O'th'Rolles, and the Kings Secretary. Further Sir,	2813
Sir (I may tell it you) I thinke I haue | Incenst the Lords o'th'Councell, that he is	2821
The Iustice and the Truth o'th' question carries	2931
The dew o'th'Verdict with it; at what ease	2932
Let some o'th' Guard be ready there.	3154
*her succour, which were the hope o'th' Strond where she	3311
Your faithfull friends o'th' Suburbs? We shall haue	3331
Por. You i'th'Chamblet, get vp o'th' raile,	3351

OTHER = 18*4

Enter the Duke of Norfolke at one doore. At the other,	35
The other moity ere you aske is giuen,	337
Vnfit for other life, compeld by hunger	362
And lack of other meanes, in desperate manner	363
He had a blacke mouth that said other of him.	646
and diuers other Ladies, & Gentlemen, as Guests	663
at one Doore; at an other Doore enter | *Sir Henry Guilford.*	664
Norf. Let's in; | And with some other busines, put the King	1091
No other obligation? by my Life,	1318
Deserues a Corner: would all other Women	1655
They are (as all my other comforts) far hence | In mine owne Countrey Lords.	1718
Of Canterbury, accompanied with other	2407
Newly preferr'd from the Kings Secretary: | The other London.	2526
The other (though vnfinish'd) yet so Famous,	2619
Kath. After my death, I wish no other Herald,	2627
No other speaker of my liuing Actions,	2628
**Garland ouer her Head, at which the other foure make re-|uerend*	2648
**the same to the other next two, who obserue the same or-|der*	2650
All. We are. | *Cran.* Is there no other way of mercy,	3149
Gard. What other, | Would you expect? You are strangely troublesome:	3152
**vnder the Line, they need no other pennance: that Fire-|Drake*	3302
**the Marchionesse Dorset, the other Godmother, and La-|dies.*	3361

OTHERS = 3*1

Where others tell steps with me.	373
Queen. No, my Lord? | You know no more then others? But you frame	374
**Hoboyes. Enter King and others as Maskers, habited like*	753
They'l say tis naught. Others to heare the City	3454

OTHERWHERE = 1

The King ha's sent me otherwhere: Besides	1096

OUER *see also* ore = 4*3

Any thing on him: for he hath a Witchcraft | Ouer the King in's Tongue.	1847
**Exeunt, *first passing ouer the Stage in Order and State, and* | *then, A great Flourish of Trumpets.*	2445
1 They that beare | The Cloath of Honour ouer her, are foure Barons | Of the Cinque-Ports.	2462
**Garland ouer her Head, at which the other foure make re-|uerend*	2648
**in their Changes, and holding the Garland ouer her*	2651

OUER   *cont.*
And something ouer to remember me by.   2743
Let me be vs'd with Honor; strew me ouer   2761
OUERTHROW = 1
His Ouerthrow, heap'd Happinesse vpon him: 2622
OUER-RUNNING = 1
And lose by ouer-running: know you not,   216
OUGHT = 2
Card. Please you Sir, | I know but of a single part in ought   370
Vpon our faile; to this poynt hast thou heard him, | At any time speake
ought?   488
OUI see wee
OUR *see also* by'r *l.*19 21 27 152 159 239 *248 260 283 336 352 402 412
420 421 429 430 435 443 488 576 595 598 616 747 968 *1034 1079 1109
1119 1228 1229 1268 1329 1351 *1407 1542 1546 1547 1548 1596 1598
1599 1652 1684 1685 1791 1793 1794 1812 1903 1958 1959 2113 2184
2346 2383 2459 2723 2774 2802 2827 2829 2897 2903 3029 3059 3060
3073 3077 3079 3102 3169 *3425 3453 = 73*4
OURS = 2
Not ours, or not allow'd; what worst, as oft   418
All the best men are ours; for 'tis ill hap,   3462
OURSELUES *see* selues
OUT *l.*9 112 124 130 150 394 453 470 553 *555 588 607 626 734 762 785
801 861 960 1002 1010 *1031 1062 1281 1325 *1364 1370 1504 1662
1663 1687 1716 1730 1764 1841 1850 1955 1978 2151 2199 2222 2244
2288 2296 2345 2352 2560 2756 2832 2849 2983 3060 3073 3163 3175
3188 3215 *3309 3345 = 55*4
OUTGOE = 1
Was, were he euill vs'd, he would outgoe   560
OUT-LIUE = 1
Vnwilling to out-liue the good that did it.   2618
OUT-RUNNE = 1
That it do sindge your selfe. We may out-runne   214
OUT-SPEAKES = 1
I finde at such proud Rate, that it out-speakes | Possession of a Subiect.   1990
OUT-STARE = 1
Ile follow, and out-stare him. | *Nor.* Stay my Lord,   199
OUT-WORTHS = 1
Not wake him in his slumber. A Beggers booke, | Out-worths a Nobles
blood.   190
OWNE = 24*1
Our owne Braines, and the Opinion that we bring   21
The force of his owne merit makes his way   113
He meant to lay vpon: and his owne Letter   129
And for his owne aduantage. | *Norf.* I am sorry   269
For your owne quiet, as to rectifie | What is vnsetled in the King.   1418
They are (as all my other comforts) far hence | In mine owne Countrey
Lords.   1718
And hedges his owne way. But in this point,   1876
Crom. To his owne hand, in's Bed-chamber.   1930
To his owne portion? And what expence by'th'houre   1969
Yet fill'd with my Abilities: Mine owne ends   2045
More then mine owne: that am, haue, and will be   2068
For mine owne ends, (Indeed to gaine the Popedome,   2092
(Mine, and your Master) with his owne hand, gaue me: 2132
Into your owne hands (Card'nall) by Extortion: 2178
*(By what meanes got, I leaue to your owne conscience)   2225

OWNE *cont.*

Neglect him not; make vse now, and prouide | For thine owne future safety.   2334

I dare now call mine owne. O *Cromwel, Cromwel,*   2369

His owne Opinion was his Law. I'th'presence   2592

Of his owne body he was ill, and gaue | The Clergy ill example.   2598

Cap. Noble Lady, | First mine owne seruice to your Grace, the next   2702

Of mine owne way. I know you Wise, Religious,   2805

And woe your owne destruction.   2941

In our owne natures fraile, and capable   3059

She shall be lou'd and fear'd. Her owne shall blesse her;   3400

Vnder his owne Vine what he plants; and sing   3405

OXFORD = 1

Ipswich and Oxford: one of which, fell with him,   2617

OYLE = 1

As holy Oyle, *Edward* Confessors Crowne,   2509

PACD = 1

And with the same full State pac'd backe againe   2514

PACE = 3*1

Requires slow pace at first. Anger is like   203

That neuer see 'em pace before, the Spauen   584

Camp. My Lord of *Yorke,* was not one Doctor *Pace*   1172

Pace 'em not in their hands to make 'em gentle;   3070

PACES = 1

2 But what follow'd? | 3 At length, her Grace rose, and with modest paces   2502

PACK = 1

Or pack to their old Playfellowes; there, I take it,   611

PACKET = 3

Car. The Packet Cromwell, | Gau't you the King?   1928

Some Spirit put this paper in the Packet, | To blesse your eye withall.   1993

Made me put this maine Secret in the Packet   2095

PACKETS = 2

The goodnesse of your intercepted Packets   2179

And at the dore too, like a Post with Packets: 3031

PAGAN = 1

L.Ch. Death my Lord, | Their cloathes are after such a Pagan cut too't,   586

PAGE = 2

Enter Gardiner Bishop of Winchester, a Page with a Torch | *before him, met by Sir Thomas Louell.*   2769

I hinder you too long: Good night, Sir *Thomas.* | *Exit Gardiner and Page.*   2833

PAGEANTS = 1

In Celebration of this day with Shewes, | Pageants, and Sights of Honor.   2390

PAGES = 3

Shew'd like a Mine. Their Dwarfish Pages were   66

From Princes into Pages: all mens honours   1081

Who holds his State at dore 'mongst Purseuants, | Pages, and Foot-boyes.   3022

PAID = 2

Paid ere he promis'd, whereby his Suit was granted   262

That they may haue their wages, duly paid 'em,   2742

PAINE = 2

Nor. This same *Cranmer's* | A worthy Fellow, and hath tane much paine | In the Kings businesse.   1918

Out of the paine you suffer'd, gaue no eare too't.   2560

PAINES = 1
I should haue tane some paines, to bring together   2918
PAINTED = 1
That's the plaine truth; your painted glosse discouers   3120
PAINTING = 1
Was to them, as a Painting. Now this Maske   70
PALE = 1
How long her face is drawne? How pale she lookes,   2676
PALES = 1
Ile pecke you o're the pales else. *Exeunt.*   3352
PALME = *1
or Palme in their hands. They first Conge vnto her, then   2646
PANG = 1*1
An. Not for that neither; here's the pang that pinches.   1202
Almost each pang, a death. | *King.* Alas good Lady.   2851
PANGING = 1
It from the bearer, 'tis a sufferance, panging | As soule and bodies
seuering.   1218
PANGS = 1
More pangs, and feares then warres, or women haue;   2271
PAPER = 5
Card. Look'd he o'th'inside of the Paper?   1931
Then makes him nothing. I must reade this paper: 2088
This paper ha's vndone me: 'Tis th' Accompt   2090
2 May I be bold to aske what that containes, | That Paper in your hand.   2394
I should haue beene beholding to your Paper: 2403
PAPER = 1
Some Spirit put this paper in the Packet, | To blesse your eye withall.   1993
PAPERS = 3
The Honourable Boord of Councell, out | Must fetch him in, he Papers.   130
of the Guard, and two Secretaries with Papers: The   176
Papers of State he sent me, to peruse   1984
PARCELS = 1
Forsooth an Inuentory, thus importing | The seuerall parcels of his
Plate, his Treasure,   1987
PARD = 1
But par'd my present Hauings, to bestow | My Bounties vpon you.   2031
PARDON = 5*1
Vnder your promis'd pardon. The Subiects griefe   389
Free pardon to each man that has deny'de   436
*Of the Kings grace and pardon: the greeued Commons   441
And pardon comes: I shall anon aduise you   444
Mes. I humbly do entreat your Highnesse pardon,   2687
'Tis like a Pardon after Execution;   2709
PARDONS = 1
Norff. A gracious King, that pardons all offences   1108
PARENTS = 1
Heauen euer laid vp to make Parents happy, | May hourely fall vpon
ye.   3372
PARISH = 1*1
The Duke being at the Rose, within the Parish   498
*you take the Court for Parish Garden: ye rude Slaues, | leaue your
gaping.   3260
PARRAGOND = 1
(*Katherine* our Queene) before the primest Creature | That's Parragon'd
o'th' World.   1599

PART = 10*2

Peepe through each part of him: whence ha's he that,	119
Of all the Gentry; for the most part such	127
*Which makes my whit'st part, black. The will of Heau'n	293
Card. Please you Sir, │ I know but of a single part in ought	370
The sixt part of his Substance, to be leuied	391
And sticke them in our Will. Sixt part of each?	430
From euery Tree, lop, barke, and part o'th' Timber:	432
The Part my Father meant to act vpon	546
Queen. Your Graces find me heere part of a Houswife,	1647
You'l part away disgrac'd.	1727
To thinke vpon the part of businesse, which	2015
His blessed part to Heauen, and slept in peace.	2584

PARTED = 4

He parted Frowning from me, as if Ruine	2085
Together sung *Te Deum.* So she parted,	2513
And able meanes, we had not parted thus.	2745
They had parted so much honesty among 'em,	3027

PARTICULAR = 3

An. Good Lady, │ Make your selfe mirth with your particular fancy,	1323
But by particular consent proceeded	1591
As 'twer in Loues particular, be more │ To me your Friend, then any.	2064

PARTNER = *1

Kin. Lead in your Ladies eu'ry one: Sweet Partner,	812

PARTNERS = 1*1

*You shall haue two noble Partners with you: the old	3239
My Noble Partners, and my selfe thus pray	3370

PARTS = 4

You that haue so faire parts of Woman on you,	1235
Obeying in commanding, and thy parts	1503
(With thee, and all thy best parts bound together)	2146
They grow still too; from all Parts they are comming,	3327

PASSAGE = 1

Cardinall in his passage, fixeth his eye on Buck-│ingham, and Buckingham on him,│ both full of disdaine.	177

PASSAGES = 1

The passages made toward it; on my Honour,	1531

PASSE = 9*2

The Play may passe: If they be still, and willing,	12
Liue where their prayers did: and it's come to passe,	396
The pennance lyes on you; if these faire Ladies │ Passe away frowning.	706
passe directly before the Cardinall and gracefully sa-│lute him.	755
They vexe me past my patience, pray you passe on;	1492
The Lady *Anne,* passe from her Corronation.	2382
You are alwayes my good Friend, if your will passe,	3108
When they passe backe from the Christening?	3333
To let the Troope passe fairely; or Ile finde	3346
The Troope passe once about the Stage, and Gar-│ter speakes.	3362
A most vnspotted Lilly shall she passe	3433

PASSED *see* past

PASSING = 1*1

Exeunt, first passing ouer the Stage in Order and State, and│ then, A great Flourish of Trumpets.	2445
Say his long trouble now is passing	2755

PASSION = 1

Or but allay the fire of passion.	222

PAST = 6
A single voice, and that not past me, but	405
2. But pray how past it?	837
They vexe me past my patience, pray you passe on;	1492
1 Sir, | You must no more call it Yorke-place, that's past:	2516
But now I am past all Comforts heere, but Prayers.	2711
Cran. 'Tis *Buts.* | The Kings Physitian, as he past along	3003

PAT = 1
Come pat betwixt too early, and too late	1304

PAT = 1
PATENTS = 1
Ti'de it by Letters Patents. Now, who'll take it? | *Sur.* The King that gaue it.	2135

PATI = 2
PATIENCE see also Pat., Pati. = 13
In tempting of your patience, but am boldned	388
In all the rest shew'd a most Noble patience.	865
They vexe me past my patience, pray you passe on;	1492
Yet will I adde an Honor; a great Patience.	1770
Crom. Good Sir, haue patience. | *Card.* So I haue. Farewell	2373
her Gentleman Vsher, and Patience | *her Woman.*	2549
Patience, be neere me still, and set me lower,	2634
For feare we wake her. Softly, gentle *Patience.*	2641
Banish'd the Kingdome. *Patience*, is that Letter	2716
My Lord. *Griffith* farewell. Nay *Patience*,	2758
Your patience to you, and be well contented	2902
But their pleasures | Must be fulfill'd, and I attend with patience.	3012
Lay all the weight ye can vpon my patience,	3115

PATIENT = 2
Wol. Be patient yet. | *Qu.* I will, when you are humble; Nay before,	1431
Man. Pray Sir be patient; 'tis as much impossible,	3269

PATIENTS = 1
After his Patients death; the King already | Hath married the faire Lady. | *Sur.* Would he had.	1878

PATRUM = *1
*'em in *Limbo Patrum*, and there they are like to dance	3322

PATTERNE = 1
A Patterne to all Princes liuing with her,	3392

PAUD = 1
And pau'd with gold: the Emperor thus desir'd,	264

PAUSINGLY = 1
This pausingly ensu'de; neither the King, nor's Heyres	514

PAY = 2
For which I pay 'em a thousand thankes,	768
Does pay the Act of it, as i'th'contrary	2057

PAYMENT = 1
An ordinary Groome is for such payment.	2982

PEACE = 19*1
The Peace betweene the French and vs, not valewes | The Cost that did conclude it.	142
Dashing the Garment of this Peace, aboaded | The sodaine breach on't.	148
Abur. A proper Title of a Peace, and purchas'd | At a superfluous rate.	156
And breake the foresaid peace. Let the King know	266
Gainst me, that I cannot take peace with:	928
And without Tryall, fell; Gods peace be with him.	957
Wol. Heau'ns peace be with him:	1184
Wols. Peace to your Highnesse.	1646

PEACE *cont.*
  Offers, as I doe, in a signe of peace, | His Seruice, and his Counsell. |
  Queen. To betray me.   1691
  A peace aboue all earthly Dignities,   2285
  Still in thy right hand, carry gentle Peace   2360
  The Rod, and Bird of Peace, and all such Emblemes   2510
  His blessed part to Heauen, and slept in peace.   2584
  (Now in his Ashes) Honor: Peace be with him.   2633
  Kath. Spirits of peace, where are ye? Are ye all gone?   2658
  As you wish Christian peace to soules departed,   2748
  Defacers of a publique peace then I doe: 3089
  The merry Songs of Peace to all his Neighbours.   3406
  Nor shall this peace sleepe with her: But as when   3410
  And so stand fix'd. Peace, Plenty, Loue, Truth, Terror,   3418
PEACE-MAKERS = *1
  *Those we professe, Peace-makers, Friends, and Seruants.   1804
PEARLE = *1
  Pearle, Crowned. On each side her, the Bishops of London, | *and*
  Winchester,   2439
PECKE = 3
  One *Gilbert Pecke,* his Councellour.   305
  Sir *Gilbert Pecke* his Chancellour, and *Iohn Car,*   847
  Ile pecke you o're the pales else. *Exeunt.*   3352
PEECE = 2
  To be thus Iaded by a peece of Scarlet,   2171
  Could say this is my wife there, all were wouen | So strangely in one
  peece.   2500
PEEPD = 1
  Peep'd harmes that menac'd him. Priuily   259
PEEPE = 1
  Peepe through each part of him: whence ha's he that,   119
PEERE = 1
  Cran. So. | *Buts.* This is a Peere of Malice: I am glad   2999
PEERES = 2
  And so his Peeres vpon this euidence,   855
  Suf. Which of the Peeres | Haue vncontemn'd gone by him, or at least   1837
PEMBROOKE = 1*1
  Then Marchionesse of *Pembrooke;* to which Title,   1279
  *O're-mount the Larke: The Marchionesse of *Pembrooke?*   1316
PENBROKE = *1
  *To heare from Rome. The Marchionesse of Penbroke?   1945
PENCE = 1
  Old L. How tasts it? Is it bitter? Forty pence, no: 1310
PENNANCE = 2*1
  San. I would I were, | They should finde easie pennance.   686
  The pennance lyes on you; if these faire Ladies | Passe away frowning.   706
  *vnder the Line, they need no other pennance: that Fire-|Drake   3302
PENSIUELY = 1
  *Exit Lord Chamberlaine, and the King drawes the Curtaine | and sits
  reading pensiuely.*   1100
PENY = 1
  To the last peny, 'tis the Kings. My Robe,   2367
PEOPLE = 7
  As first, good Company, good wine, good welcome, | Can make good
  people.   672
  Vaux, Sir Walter Sands, and common people, &c.   892
  Buck. All good people, | You that thus farre haue come to pitty me;   896

PEOPLE *cont.*
<table>
<tr><td>But where they meane to sinke ye: all good people</td><td>977</td></tr>
<tr><td>The Beauty of her Person to the People.</td><td>2488</td></tr>
<tr><td>That euer lay by man: which when the people</td><td>2490</td></tr>
<tr><td>Then rose againe, and bow'd her to the people:</td><td>2506</td></tr>
</table>

PEOPLES = 1
Stand these poore peoples Friend, and vrge the King | To do me this last right.   2749

PEPIN = 1
To *Pepin* or *Clotharius*, they keepe State so.   581

PERCEIUE = 4
<table>
<tr><td>And giue your hearts to; when they once perceiue</td><td>974</td></tr>
<tr><td>Perceiue I speake sincerely, and high notes</td><td>1275</td></tr>
<tr><td>*Kin.* I may perceiue | These Cardinals trifle with me: I abhorre</td><td>1607</td></tr>
<tr><td>It did take place, I do (quoth he) perceiue</td><td>1869</td></tr>
</table>

PERCEIUES = *1
Sur. Will this worke? | *Cham.* The King in this perceiues him, how he coasts   1874

PERFECT = 1
From her shall read the perfect way of Honour,   3408

PERFIDIOUS = 1
Men feare the French would proue perfidious   502

PERFORCE = 2
<table>
<tr><td>Perforce be their acquaintance. These exactions</td><td>378</td></tr>
<tr><td>Her times of preseruation, which perforce</td><td>2017</td></tr>
</table>

PERFORMANCE = 2
<table>
<tr><td>His Father, by as much as a performance | Do's an irresolute purpose.</td><td>561</td></tr>
<tr><td>But his performance, as he is now, Nothing:</td><td>2597</td></tr>
</table>

PERFORMD = 1
Laid Nobly on her: which perform'd, the Quire   2511

PERFORME = 1
The Noble Spirits to Armes, they did performe   79

PERFORMT = 1
As able to perform't) his minde, and place   236

PERILS = 1
And throw it from their Soule, though perils did   2070

PERIOD = 1
Kin. There's his period,   563

PERISH = 3
<table>
<tr><td>The net has falne vpon me, I shall perish | Vnder deuice, and practise.</td><td>285</td></tr>
<tr><td>Ile hang my head, and perish.</td><td>1789</td></tr>
<tr><td>Thy hopefull seruice perish too. Good *Cromwell*</td><td>2333</td></tr>
</table>

PERIURD = 1
I meane in periur'd Witnesse, then your Master,   2937

PERKD = 1
Then to be perk'd vp in a glistring griefe, | And weare a golden sorrow.   1226

PERMIT = 1
Hath sent to me, wishing me to permit   507

PERNICIOUS = 1
And not reform'd, may proue pernicious.   3067

PERNICIOUSLY = 1
2. All the Commons | Hate him perniciously, and o' my Conscience   884

PERSON = 16
<table>
<tr><td>*Car.* Is he in person, ready? | *Secr.* I, please your Grace.</td><td>183</td></tr>
<tr><td>That Gentleman of *Buckinghams*, in person,</td><td>325</td></tr>
<tr><td>My faculties nor person, yet will be</td><td>408</td></tr>
<tr><td>Not frended by his wish to your High person;</td><td>481</td></tr>
</table>

PERSON *cont.*

You charge not in your spleene a Noble person,	521
There should be one amongst'em by his person	777
And fit it with such furniture as suites | The Greatnesse of his Person.	944
Against your Sacred Person; in Gods name	1395
Or touch of her good Person?	1520
I left no Reuerend Person in this Court;	1590
For no dislike i'th' world against the person	1593
The stampe of Noblenesse in any person | Out of himselfe?	1840
To'th'good of your most Sacred Person, and	2047
The Beauty of her Person to the People.	2488
Will triumph o're my person, which I waigh not,	2924
Fly o're thy Royall head, and shade thy person | Vnder their blessed wings.	2965

PERSONAGES = *1

The Vision. \| **Enter solemnely tripping one after another, sixe Personages,* | 2642 |

PERSONALLY = 1

Lou. I could not personally deliuer to her | 2843 |

PERSONS = 5

The very Persons of our Noble Story,	27
There's difference in no persons.	211
We liue not to be grip'd by meaner persons.	1190
You tender more your persons Honor, then	1476
To make a seemely answer to such persons.	1817

PERSWADE = 1

In minde and feature. I perswade me, from her | 1891 |

PERSWADING = 1

Exceeding wise, faire spoken, and perswading: | 2610 |

PERSWASIONS = 1

The best perswasions to the contrary | 2950 |

PERTAINES = 1

Pertaines to th'State; and front but in that File | 372 |

PERTAINING = 1

Pertaining thereunto; as Fights and Fire-workes, | 605 |

PERUSD = 1

The King hath of you. I haue perus'd her well, | 1293 |

PERUSE = 1

Papers of State he sent me, to peruse | 1984 |

PESTILENCE = 1

A most Arch-Heretique, a Pestilence | 2824 |

PESTILENT = 1

Most pestilent to th'hearing, and to beare 'em, | 380 |

PETITION = 3

The dignity of your Office; is the poynt | Of my Petition.	342
My next poore Petition, | Is, that his Noble Grace would haue some pittie	2730
You would haue giuen me your Petition, that	2917

PHOENIX = 1

The Bird of Wonder dyes, the Mayden Phoenix, | 3411 |

PHRASE = 1

(For so they phrase 'em) by their Heralds challeng'd | 78 |

PHYSICKE = 4

L.San. Tis time to giue 'em Physicke, their diseases | Are growne so catching.	614
All his trickes founder, and he brings his Physicke	1877
That gentle Physicke giuen in time, had cur'd me:	2710

PHYSICKE *cont.*
Farewell all Physicke: and what followes then?   3075
PHYSITIAN = 1
Cran. 'Tis *Buts.* | The Kings Physitian, as he past along   3003
PIBBLES = *1
*deliuer'd such a showre of Pibbles, that I was faine to   3315
PIE *see* pye
PIECE *see also* peece = 1*1
*like a Morter-piece to blow vs. There was a Habberda-|shers   3305
That mould vp such a mighty Piece as this is,   3396
PIECES = 1
Not being torne a pieces, we haue done: 3336
PIERCE = 1
Pierce into that, but I can see his Pride   118
PILES = 1
King. What piles of wealth hath he accumulated   1968
PILLERS = 1*1
Siluer Pillers: After them, side by side, the two Cardinals,   1343
These ruin'd Pillers, out of pitty, taken   2288
PINCHES = *1
An. Not for that neither; here's the pang that pinches.   1202
PINCKD = *1
*till her pinck'd porrenger fell off her head, for kindling   3307
PIOUS = 2
Will blesse the King: and is not this course pious?   1069
Soueraigne and Pious els, could speake thee out)   1504
PITCH = 1
Lie like one lumpe before him, to be fashion'd | Into what pitch he
please.   1082
PITTIE = 1
My next poore Petition, | Is, that his Noble Grace would haue some
pittie   2730
PITTIED = 2
Was either pittied in him, or forgotten.   858
Yet freshly pittied in our memories.   3079
PITTIFULL = 1
(But where he meant to Ruine) pittifull.   2595
PITTY = 11
We now present. Those that can Pitty, heere   6
Buck. All good people, | You that thus farre haue come to pitty me;   896
1. O, this is full of pitty; Sir, it cals   984
To giue her the auaunt, it is a pitty | Would moue a Monster.   1211
An. So much the more | Must pitty drop vpon her; verily   1222
And to bestow your pitty on me; for   1368
(If you haue any Iustice, any Pitty,   1748
Shipwrack'd vpon a Kingdome, where no Pitty,   1785
Whil'st your great Goodnesse, out of holy pitty, | Absolu'd him with an
Axe.   2151
These ruin'd Pillers, out of pitty, taken   2288
Out of our easinesse and childish pitty   3073
PITTYING = 2
Henry the Seauenth succeeding, truly pittying   958
Our Mistris Sorrowes we were pittying.   1268
PLACD = 1
Two women plac'd together, makes cold weather: 693

PLACE = 21*5

A guift that heauen giues for him, which buyes | A place next to the King.	114
As able to perform't) his minde, and place	236
King. Arise, and take place by vs; halfe your Suit	335
'Tis but the fate of Place, and the rough Brake	410
Place you that side, Ile take the charge of this:	691
More worthy this place then my selfe, to whom	778
I would not be so sicke though for his place:	1128
A Woman of lesse Place might aske by Law;	1159
In this mans place before him? | *Wol.* Yes, he was.	1173
The most conuenient place, that I can thinke of	1193
O 'tis a tender place, and I must leaue her. *Exeunt.*	1199
*place vnder the Cloth of State. The two Cardinalls sit	1345
*vnder him as Iudges. The Queene takes place some di-|stance	1346
*from the King. The Bishops place themselues on	1347
You signe your Place, and Calling, in full seeming,	1468
It did take place, I do (quoth he) perceiue	1869
Bad me enioy it, with the Place, and Honors	2133
Crom. The next is, that Sir *Thomas Moore* is chosen | Lord Chancellor, in your place.	2303
To a prepar'd place in the Quire, fell off	2484
To Yorke-Place, where the Feast is held.	2515
1 Sir, | You must no more call it Yorke-place, that's past:	2516
A man of his Place, and so neere our fauour	3029
Both in his priuate Conscience, and his place,	3088
Then but once thinke his place becomes thee not.	3202
**Is this a place to roare in? Fetch me a dozen Crab-tree	3264
**was quartered; they fell on, I made good my place; at	3312

PLACED = *1

*placed vnder the State. Enter Lord Chancellour, places	3036

PLACES = 3*1

places himselfe vnder the Kings feete on | his right side.	319
There's places of rebuke. He was a Foole;	1186
Vpon what cause wrong you? Alas, our Places,	1793
*placed vnder the State. Enter Lord Chancellour, places	3036

PLACETH = 1

takes her vp, kisses and placeth | her by him.	332

PLAGUE = 1

Weigh'd not a haire of his. Plague of your policie,	2147

PLAID = 1

As to the Tower, I thought; I would haue plaid	545

PLAINE = 2*1

A long time out of play, may bring his plaine song,	626
*10 Certaine Ladies or Countesses, with plaine Circlets of | Gold, without Flowers.	2443
That's the plaine truth; your painted glosse discouers	3120

PLAINES = *1

**To all the Plaines about him: Our Childrens Children | Shall see this, and blesse Heauen.	3425

PLANTS = 2

To his Musicke, Plants and Flowers	1624
Vnder his owne Vine what he plants; and sing	3405

PLATE = 1

Forsooth an Inuentory, thus importing | The seuerall parcels of his Plate, his Treasure,	1987

PLAY = 14

The Play may passe: If they be still, and willing,	12
That come to heare a Merry, Bawdy Play,	15
A long time out of play, may bring his plaine song,	626
San. Yes, if I make my play:	727
Euery thing that heard him play,	1627
(Out of thy honest truth) to play the Woman.	2345
Ty'de all the Kingdome. Symonie, was faire play,	2591
Cause the Musitians play me that sad note	2636
King. Charles, I will play no more to night,	2837
King. But little *Charles,* | Nor shall not when my Fancies on my play.	2840
To me you cannot reach. You play the Spaniell,	3195
A Marshallsey, shall hold ye play these two Monthes.	3347
THE EPILOGVE. | *Tis ten to one, this Play can neuer please*	3449
For this Play at this time, is onely in	3458

PLAYFELLOWES = 1

Or pack to their old Playfellowes; there, I take it,	611

PLAYHOUSE = *1

* Por. These are the youths that thunder at a Playhouse,	3318

PLEAD = 1

Buck. It will helpe me nothing | To plead mine Innocence; for that dye is on me	291

PLEADE = 1

To pleade your Cause. It shall be therefore bootlesse,	1416

PLEADED = 1

He pleaded still not guilty, and alleadged	840

PLEASANT = 2

Card. I am glad | Your Grace is growne so pleasant.	793
An. Come you are pleasant.	1314

PLEASD = 5

As himselfe pleas'd; and they were ratified	246
Is pleas'd you shall to th'Tower, till you know | How he determines further.	297
Kin. I haue spoke long, be pleas'd your selfe to say | How farre you satisfide me.	1578
If Heauen had pleas'd to haue giuen me longer life	2744
This Oracle of comfort, ha's so pleas'd me,	3438

PLEASE = 25*1

Where's his Examination? | *Secr.* Heere so please you.	181
Car. Is he in person, ready? | *Secr.* I, please your Grace.	183
That he would please to alter the Kings course,	265
Card. Please you Sir, | I know but of a single part in ought	370
Card. Please your Highnesse note	479
I thinke would better please 'em: by my life,	682
Cham. Sweet Ladies will it please you sit; Sir *Harry*	690
Cham. An't please your Grace,	797
Lie like one lumpe before him, to be fashion'd | Into what pitch he please.	1082
If the King please: his Curses and his blessings	1087
If you might please to stretch it. | *Anne.* Nay, good troth.	1241
To the sharp'st kinde of Iustice. Please you, Sir,	1398
(Domestickes to you) serue your will, as't please	1474
That it shall please you to declare in hearing	1510
Lin. So please your Highnes, | The question did at first so stagger me,	1580
Camp. So please your Highnes, | The Queene being absent, 'tis a needfull fitnesse,	1601

PLEASE *cont.*
  *Gent. And't please your Grace, the two great Cardinals | Wait in the
presence.   1635
  Wol. May it please you Noble Madam, to withdraw   1650
  Beware you loose it not: For vs (if you please   1810
  We write in Water. May it please your Highnesse   2602
  Crom. Please your Honours, | The chiefe cause concernes his Grace of
Canterbury.   3044
  Sur. May it please your Grace; ---| *Kin.* No Sir, it doe's not please me,   3203
  *Duchesse of *Norfolke*, and Lady Marquesse *Dorset*? will | these please
you?   3240
  Por. And't please your Honour, | We are but men; and what so many
may doe,   3334
  THE EPILOGVE. | *Tis ten to one, this Play can neuer please*   3449
PLEASES = 1
  Does buy and sell his Honour as he pleases,   268
PLEASURE = 14*1
  The busines present. Tis his Highnes pleasure | You shall to th' Tower.   289
  The will of Heauen be done, and the Kings pleasure | By me obey'd.   300
  Kin. By my life, | This is against our pleasure.   401
  Is businesse of Estate; in which, we come | To know your Royall
pleasure.   1110
  I will implore. If not, i'th'name of God | Your pleasure be fulfill'd.   1410
  Qu. Lord Cardinall, to you I speake. | *Wol.* Your pleasure, Madam.   1425
  Or be a knowne friend 'gainst his Highnes pleasure,   1713
  One that ne're dream'd a Ioy, beyond his pleasure;   1768
  Nor. Heare the Kings pleasure Cardinall,   2110
  Suf. Lord Cardinall, the Kings further pleasure is,   2237
  But I pray you, | What is your pleasure with me?   2700
  Den. He attends your Highnesse pleasure. | *King.* Bring him to Vs.   2872
  Cran. It is my dutie | T'attend your Highnesse pleasure.   2885
  *We will be short with you. 'Tis his Highnesse pleasure   3101
  There to remaine till the Kings further pleasure   3147
PLEASURES = 7
  A noble Company: what are their pleasures?   757
  And pray 'em take their pleasures.   769
  What are your pleasures with me, reuerent Lords?   1649
  Cham. My Lords, you speake your pleasures: 1842
  But their pleasures | Must be fulfill'd, and I attend with patience.   3012
  To dance attendance on their Lordships pleasures,   3030
  Keep. My Lord Archbishop: | And ha's done halfe an houre to know
your pleasures.   3051
PLEDGE = 1
  Heer's to your Ladiship, and pledge it Madam: | For tis to such a thing.   728
PLENTEOUS = 1
  Honor, and plenteous safety) that you reade | The Cardinals Malice,
and his Potency   164
PLENTY = 1
  And so stand fix'd. Peace, Plenty, Loue, Truth, Terror,   3418
PLOT = 2
  Buck. So, so; | These are the limbs o'th' Plot: no more I hope.   306
  Is posted as the Agent of our Cardinall, | To second all his plot. I do
assure you,   1903
PLUCKE = *1
  An. No in truth. | **Old.L.* Then you are weakly made; plucke off a
little,   1249

POINT = 6
 And point by point the Treasons of his Maister, | He shall againe relate. 327
 This dangerous conception in this point, 480
 I speake my good Lord Cardnall, to this point; 1532
 And hedges his owne way. But in this point, 1876
 I haue touch'd the highest point of all my Greatnesse, 2103
POINTED = 1
 Haue beene mine so, that euermore they pointed 2046
POINTS = 2
 With all their honourable points of ignorance 604
 Of the good Queene; but the sharpe thorny points 1594
POLICIE = 1
 Weigh'd not a haire of his. Plague of your policie, 2147
POMPE = 5
 Till this time Pompe was single, but now married 59
 Only to shew his pompe, as well in France, 238
 Still growing in a Maiesty and pompe, the which 1208
 An. Oh Gods will, much better | She ne're had knowne pompe; though't
 be temporall, 1215
 Vaine pompe, and glory of this World, I hate ye, 2266
POORE = 20
 But minister communication of | A most poore issue. 139
 I am the shadow of poore *Buckingham,* 313
 Card. Say, Lord *Chamberlaine,* | They haue done my poore house grace: 766
 And Duke of *Buckingham*: now, poore *Edward Bohun*; 949
 Old L. Alas poore Lady, | Shee's a stranger now againe. 1220
 I am a most poore Woman, and a Stranger, 1369
 With me, a poore weake woman, falne from fauour? 1641
 If you speake truth, for their poore Mistris sake; 1670
 Alas (poore Wenches) where are now your Fortunes? 1784
 Heap'd vpon me (poore Vndeseruer) I 2049
 Is that poore man, that hangs on Princes fauours? 2268
 I am a poore falne man, vnworthy now 2327
 Kath. Alas poore man. | *Grif.* At last, with easie Rodes, he came to
 Leicester, 2570
 When I shall dwell with Wormes, and my poore name 2715
 My next poore Petition, | Is, that his Noble Grace would haue some
 pittie 2730
 Stand these poore peoples Friend, and vrge the King | To do me this
 last right. 2749
 Th'estate of my poore Queene. Leaue me alone, 2858
 There's none stands vnder more calumnious tongues, | Then I my selfe,
 poore man. 2910
 That am a poore and humble Subiect to you? 3237
 (You see the poore remainder) could distribute, 3277
POOREST = 1
 The last is for my men, they are the poorest, 2740
POPE = 5
 To him that made him proud; the Pope. 1090
 Before you all, Appeale vnto the Pope, 1479
 Suf. The Cardinals Letters to the Pope miscarried, 1865
 Will bring me off againe. What's this? *To th' Pope*? 2100
 You writ to'th Pope, against the King: your goodnesse 2180
POPEDOME = 1
 For mine owne ends, (Indeed to gaine the Popedome, 2092
POR = 5*1

PORRENGER = *1
  *till her pinck'd porrenger fell off her head, for kindling   3307
PORT = 1*3
PORTER see also Por., Port. = 3
  Noyse and Tumult within: Enter Porter and | his man.   3257
  Within. Good M.(aster) Porter I belong to th' Larder.   3262
  Within. Do you heare M.(aster) Porter?   3286
PORTERS = 1
  As if we kept a Faire heere? Where are these Porters?   3328
PORTION = 1
  To his owne portion? And what expence by'th'houre   1969
PORTS = 1*1
  *8 *A* Canopy, *borne by foure of the* Cinque-Ports, *vnder it*   2437
  1 They that beare | The Cloath of Honour ouer her, are foure Barons |
  Of the Cinque-Ports.   2462
POSSESSE = 1
  Grif. I am most ioyfull Madam, such good dreames | Possesse your
  Fancy.   2670
POSSESSION = 1
  I finde at such proud Rate, that it out-speakes | Possession of a Subiect.   1990
POSSEST = 1
  To the good Queene, possest him with a scruple   1011
POSSIBLE = 2
  Being now seene, possible enough, got credit | That *Beuis* was beleeu'd.   81
  L.Ch. Is't possible the spels of France should iuggle   571
POST = 1
  And at the dore too, like a Post with Packets: 3031
POSTED = 1
  Is posted as the Agent of our Cardinall, | To second all his plot. I do
  assure you,   1903
POSTURES = 1
  His eye against the Moone: in most strange Postures   1980
POTENCY = 1
  Honor, and plenteous safety) that you reade | The Cardinals Malice,
  and his Potency   164
POTENT = 1
  Or God will punish me. I do beleeue | (Induc'd by potent
  Circumstances) that   1433
POTENTLY = 1
  You are Potently oppos'd, and with a Malice   2935
POUERTY = 1
  (But pouerty could neuer draw 'em from me)   2741
POULTNEY = 1
  Saint *Laurence Poultney*, did of me demand   499
POUND = 1
  A Thousand pound a yeare, Annuall support, | Out of his Grace, he
  addes.   1280
POUNDS = 2
  For any suit of pounds: and you, (oh fate)   1305
  A thousand pounds a yeare, for pure respect?   1317
POWER = 9*1
  A Minister in his Power. You know his Nature,   168
  Haue not the power to muzzle him, therefore best   189
  Neuer name to vs; you haue halfe our power: 336
  of my Lord Cardinalls, by Commission, and maine power tooke   1032
  Yea, with a spitting power, and made to tremble   1550
  Your Braine, and euery Function of your power,   2062

POWER *cont.*

You wrought to be a Legate, by which power	2208
By your power Legatine within this Kingdome,	2239
Crom. I haue no power to speake Sir. | *Car.* What, amaz'd | At my misfortunes? Can thy Spirit wonder	2276
Power, as he was a Counsellour to try him,	3213

POWLES = 1

We may as well push against Powles as stirre'em.	3273

POWRE = 1*1

*Ore-topping womans powre. Madam, you do me wrong	1447
My heart drop'd Loue, my powre rain'd Honor, more	2060

POWRES = 1

Where Powres are your Retainers, and your words	1473

POYNT = 3

The dignity of your Office; is the poynt | Of my Petition.	342
Vpon our faile; to this poynt hast thou heard him, | At any time speake ought?	488
In such a poynt of weight, so neere mine Honour,	1697

POYSON = 1

Card. All Goodnesse | Is poyson to thy Stomacke.	2174

PRACTISE = 1

The net has falne vpon me, I shall perish | Vnder deuice, and practise.	285

PRACTISES = 3

The fore-recited practises, whereof	466
Sur. How came | His practises to light?	1861
Your Enemies are many, and not small; their practises	2929

PRAID = *1

Cham. Because they speak no English, thus they praid	758

PRAISE = 2

Still him in praise, and being present both,	75
To see what this Child does, and praise my Maker.	3440

PRAY = 40*3

Buc. I pray you who, my Lord?	97
Buck. Pray giue me fauour Sir: This cunning Cardinall	244
The force of this Commission: pray looke too't;	437
Now I would pray our Monsieurs	598
Pray sit betweene these Ladies.	695
And pray receiue 'em Nobly, and conduct 'em	746
And pray 'em take their pleasures.	769
Card. Pray tell 'em thus about from me:	776
2. Pray speake what ha's happen'd.	830
2. But pray how past it?	837
And if he speake of *Buckingham*; pray tell him,	931
Pray for me, I must now forsake ye; the last houre	978
Suff. Pray God he doe, | Hee'l neuer know himselfe else.	1054
Norf. We had need pray, | And heartily, for our deliuerance;	1078
Kin. Who's there? Ha? | *Norff.* Pray God he be not angry.	1103
Old as I am, to Queene it: but I pray you,	1246
An. Now I pray God, *Amen.*	1272
Whose health and Royalty I pray for.	1290
In our long absence: pray doe not deliuer,	1329
Que. What need you note it? pray you keep your way,	1490
They vexe me past my patience, pray you passe on;	1492
Queen. Pray their Graces | To come neere: what can be their busines	1639
*Pray speake in English; heere are some will thanke you,	1669
Ye speake like honest men, (pray God ye proue so)	1695
Car. Pray heare me.	1778

PRAY *cont.*

A Soule as euen as a Calme; Pray thinke vs, ... 1803
Qu. Do what ye will, my Lords: [And pray forgiue me; 1813
Pray do my seruice to his Maiestie, ... 1818
King. Haue I not made you | The prime man of the State? I pray you
tell me, ... 2035
(That Sun, I pray may neuer set) I haue told him, ... 2329
2 Who may that be, I pray you. | 3 *Thomas Cromwell,* 2534
Grif. She is going Wench. Pray, pray. | *Pati.* Heauen comfort her. 2678
But I pray you, | What is your pleasure with me? 2700
Kath. Sir, I most humbly pray you to deliuer 2719
Gard. The fruite she goes with | I pray for heartily, that it may finde 2795
In the great'st humblenesse, and desir'd your Highnesse | Most heartily
to pray for her. 2846
To pray for her? What is she crying out? 2849
King. Pray you arise | My good and gracious Lord of Canterburie: 2887
Pray heauen he found not my disgrace: for certaine 3006
Pray Heauen the King may neuer find a heart 3090
Man. Pray Sir be patient; 'tis as much impossible, ... 3269
My Noble Partners, and my selfe thus pray 3370
PRAYD = 2
Cast her faire eyes to Heauen, and pray'd deuoutly. 2505
That was sent to me from the Councell, pray'd me 2990
PRAYERS = 8*1
Liue where their prayers did: and it's come to passe, ... 396
Make of your Prayers one sweet Sacrifice, ... 919
You met him halfe in Heauen: my vowes and prayers 932
More then my All, is Nothing: Nor my Prayers 1284
*More worth, then empty vanities: yet Prayers & Wishes 1286
He ha's my heart yet, and shall haue my Prayers 1819
But now I am past all Comforts heere, but Prayers. 2711
Suf. I wish your Highnesse | A quiet night, and my good Mistris will |
Remember in my Prayers. 2861
Mens prayers then would seeke you, not their feares. 3136
PRAYRES = 4
Almost forgot my Prayres to content him? 1765
My Prayres to heauen for you; my Loyaltie 2051
The King shall haue my seruice; but my prayres 2341
Prythee to bed, and in thy Prayres remember 2857
PREASE = 1
In the old time of Warre, would shake the prease 2498
PREASSE = 1
Go breake among the preasse, and finde away out 3345
PRECEPIT = 1
You take a Precepit for no leape of danger, ... 2940
PREFERMENTS = 1
Stands in the gap and Trade of moe Preferments, ... 2814
PREFERRD = 1
Newly preferr'd from the Kings Secretary: | The other London. 2526
PREIUDICE = 2
Breed him some preiudice; for from this League, ... 258
Be to the preiudice of her present State, ... 1519
PREMISES = 1
T'has done vpon the premises, but Iustice: 904
PREMUNIRE = 1
Fall into'th'compasse of a Premunire; 2240

PREPARD = 1
To a prepar'd place in the Quire, fell off 2484
PREPARE = 2
Vaux. Prepare there, | The Duke is comming: See the Barge be ready; 942
To furnish Rome, and to prepare the wayes 2226
PRESCRIPTION = 1
By your prescription: but this top-proud fellow, 225
PRESENCE = 7
As presence did present them: Him in eye, 74
Made suit to come in's presence; which if granted, 548
Into our presence, where this heauen of beauty 747
Gent. And't please your Grace, the two great Cardinals | Wait in the
presence. 1635
His owne Opinion was his Law. I'th'presence 2592
To heare such flattery now, and in my presence 3193
I haue receiu'd much Honour by your presence, 3443
PRESENT = 13
We now present. Those that can Pitty, heere 6
I was then present, saw them salute on Horsebacke, 49
As presence did present them: Him in eye, 74
Still him in praise, and being present both, 75
The busines present. Tis his Highnes pleasure | You shall to th' Tower. 289
Call him to present tryall: if he may 565
Whom once more, I present vnto your Highnesse. 1145
The King is present: If it be knowne to him, 1454
Be to the preiudice of her present State, 1519
Now present heere together: that's to say, 1569
To make this present Summons vnsolicited. 1589
But par'd my present Hauings, to bestow | My Bounties vpon you. 2031
To sit heere at this present, and behold 3057
PRESENTLY = 4*1
To the Kings danger: presently, the Duke 503
Crom. Presently | He did vnseale them, and the first he view'd, 1932
Who commands you | To render vp the Great Seale presently 2111
I came this way so happily. The King | Shall vnderstand it presently.
Exit Buts 3001
Port. I shall be with you presently, good M.(aster) *Puppy,* 3287
PRESERUATION = 1
Her times of preseruation, which perforce 2017
PRESIDENT = 2
Are to be fear'd. Haue you a President 427
Wol. Your Grace ha's giuen a President of wisedome 1133
PRESSE = 1
Cham. O my Lord, | Presse not a falling man too farre: 'tis Vertue: 2231
PREST = 1
And prest in with this Caution. First, me thought 1553
PRESUME = 1
The fowlenesse is the punishment. I presume, 2058
PRETENCE = 2
Vnder pretence to see the Queene his Aunt, 253
Without delay; and the pretence for this 392
PRETHEE = 4
Kin. My Lord Chamberlaine, | Prethee come hither, what faire Ladie's
that? 795
Prethee call *Gardiner* to me, my new Secretary. 1163
Prethee returne, with thy approch: I know, 1611
Kath. Pre'thee good *Griffith,* tell me how he dy'de. 2561

PREUAILE = 1
They shall no more preuaile, then we giue way too: 2946
PRICKE = 1
Scruple, and pricke, on certaine Speeches vtter'd 1538
PRIDE = 5
The Pride vpon them, that their very labour 69
Pierce into that, but I can see his Pride 118
Norff. This Priest ha's no pride in him? | *Suff.* Not to speake of: 1126
Is cramm'd with Arrogancie, Spleene, and Pride. 1470
But farre beyond my depth: my high-blowne Pride 2262
PRIEST = 5
That blinde Priest, like the eldest Sonne of Fortune, 1052
Norff. This Priest ha's no pride in him? | *Suff.* Not to speake of: 1126
This iust and learned Priest, Cardnall *Campeius,* 1144
Car. It must be himselfe then. | *Sur.* Thou art a proud Traitor, Priest. 2137
Sur. By my Soule, | Your long Coat (Priest) protects you, 2165
PRIESTS = *1
*great Seale, and a Cardinals Hat: Then two Priests, bea-|ring 1339
PRIMA *l.*34 819 1615 2377 2768 = 5
PRIME = 1
King. Haue I not made you | The prime man of the State? I pray you
tell me, 2035
PRIMER = 1
There is no primer basenesse. 400
PRIMERO = 1
Gar. I did Sir *Thomas,* and left him at Primero | With the Duke of
Suffolke. 2779
PRIMEST = 1
(*Katherine* our Queene) before the primest Creature | That's Parragon'd
o'th' World. 1599
PRIMUS *l.*34 = 1
PRINCE = 6
My Fathers losse; like a most Royall Prince 959
A Prince most Prudent; of an excellent 1400
The wisest Prince, that there had reign'd, by many 1403
And Widdow to Prince *Arthur.* 1917
In dayly thankes; that gaue vs such a Prince; 3184
I will say thus much for him, if a Prince 3227
PRINCELY = 4
He was most Princely: Euer witnesse for him 2615
Sends you his Princely Commendations, 2706
And Princely Care, fore-seeing those fell Mischiefes, 2828
Then this pure Soule shall be. All Princely Graces 3395
PRINCES = 9
And hither make, as great Embassadors | From forraigne Princes. 742
From Princes into Pages: all mens honours 1081
Aboue all Princes, in committing freely 1134
The hearts of Princes kisse Obedience, 1799
Nor. Then, That in all you writ to Rome, or else | To Forraigne
Princes, *Ego & Rex meus* 2210
Is that poore man, that hangs on Princes fauours? 2268
That sweet Aspect of Princes, and their ruine, 2270
Himselfe with Princes. One that by suggestion 2590
A Patterne to all Princes liuing with her, 3392
PRINCESSE = 6
Her Coronation. *Katherine* no more | Shall be call'd Queene, but
Princesse Dowager, 1915

PRINCESSE *cont.*
The Princesse Dowager? How goes her businesse?   2405
From Ampthill, where the Princesse lay, to which   2410
Por. Make way there, for the Princesse.   3348
Long, and euer happie, to the high and Mighty | Princesse of England
Elizabeth.   3366
An aged Princesse; many dayes shall see her,   3429
PRISON = 1
And this man out of Prison.   553
PRISONER = 4
Buck. An vntimely Ague | Staid me a Prisoner in my Chamber, when   44
Buck. All the whole time | I was my Chambers Prisoner.   55
Of bringing backe the Prisoner.   827
You be conuaid to th' Tower a Prisoner;   3146
PRIUATE = 10
Nor. Like it your Grace, | The State takes notice of the priuate
difference   160
Let's thinke in priuate more. *Exeunt.*   1025
Suff. How is the King imployd? | *Cham.* I left him priuate,   1042
Into my priuate Meditations? | Who am I? Ha?   1106
I would your Grace would giue vs but an houre | Of priuate conference.   1123
And Doctors learn'd. First I began in priuate,   1573
Into your priuate Chamber; we shall giue you   1651
From any priuate malice in his end,   2157
Both in his priuate Conscience, and his place,   3088
Where being but a priuate man againe,   3104
PRIUILEDGD = 1
By all the lawes of Warre y'are priuiledg'd.   737
PRIUILEGIO = 1
They may *Cum Priuilegio*, wee away   612
PRIUILY = 1
Peep'd harmes that menac'd him. Priuily   259
PRIUITY = 1
(Without the priuity o'th'King) t'appoint   125
PRIUY = 2
Card. Sir *Thomas Louell*, is the Banket ready | I'th' Priuy Chamber? |
Lou. Yes, my Lord.   804
And one already of the Priuy Councell.   2539
PROCEED = 6
Kin. Lady mine proceed.   344
Sur. I can my Liedge. | *Kin.* Proceed.   537
But from this Lady, may proceed a Iemme,   1296
You may then spare that time. | *Car.* Bee't so, proceed.   1356
It's fit this Royall Session do proceed,   1422
It fits we thus proceed, or else no witnesse | Would come against you.   2904
PROCEEDE = 1
That thus you should proceede to put me off,   1375
PROCEEDED = 2
For you, or any: how farre I haue proceeded,   1449
· But by particular consent proceeded   1591
PROCEEDING = 2
Further in the proceeding. *Exit Secret.(ary)*   445
Of equall Friendship and Proceeding. Alas Sir: 1372
PROCEEDINGS = 1
In the Diuorce, his contrarie proceedings | Are all vnfolded: wherein he
appeares,   1858

PROCESSE = 2
'Tis sweet at first t'acquire. After this Processe. 1210
And processe of this time, you can report, 1392
PROCLAIME = 1
This *Ipswich* fellowes insolence; or proclaime, 210
PROCLAMATION = 1
Louell. Faith my Lord, | I heare of none but the new Proclamation, 591
PROCURE = 1
Might corrupt mindes procure, Knaues as corrupt 2933
PRODIGALL = *1
Kin. My Noble Gossips, y'haue beene too Prodigall; 3381
PRODUCD = 1
And that (without delay) their Arguments | Be now produc'd, and
heard. 1423
PRODUCE = 1
Produce the grand summe of his sinnes, the Articles 2186
PROFESSE = 3*1
Wol. I do professe | You speake not like your selfe: who euer yet 1443
*Those we professe, Peace-makers, Friends, and Seruants. 1804
Suf. May you be happy in your wish my Lord, | For I professe you haue
it. 1881
Car. I do professe, | That for your Highnesse good, I euer labour'd 2066
PROFESSION = 2
Your high profession Spirituall. That agen 1477
The way of our Profession is against it; 1794
PROFESSORS = 1
And all such false Professors. Would you haue me 1747
PROFIT = 2
But little for my profit can you thinke Lords, 1711
The profit of the State. For your great Graces 2048
PROFITS = 1
Imploy'd you where high Profits might come home, 2030
PROGRESSE = 1*1
Our Daughter *Mary*: I'th' Progresse of this busines, 1542
Cran. My good Lords; Hitherto, in all the Progresse 3080
PROLOGVE = 1
THE PROLOGVE. 1
PROMISD = 3
Paid ere he promis'd, whereby his Suit was granted 262
Vnder your promis'd pardon. The Subiects griefe 389
They promis'd me eternall Happinesse, 2667
PROMISE = 1
The offer of this time, I cannot promise, 1830
PROMISES = 5
One certes, that promises no Element | In such a businesse. 95
That promises mo thousands: Honours traine 1319
His Promises, were as he then was, Mighty: 2596
Promises Boyes heereafter. Sir, your Queen | Desires your Visitation,
and to be 2973
Though in her Cradle; yet now promises 3388
PROMOTION = 1
The high promotion of his Grace of *Canterbury*, 3021
PRONE = 1
As he is subtile, and as prone to mischiefe, 235
PRONOUNCE = 4
I doe pronounce him in that very shape 274
Pronounce dishonour of her; by my life, 1205

PRONOUNCE   *cont.*
Your selfe pronounce their Office. I must tell you,   1475
If what I now pronounce, you haue found true: 2037
PROOFE = 1
He shall appeare in proofe.   275
PROOFES = 2
And proofes as cleere as Founts in *Iuly*, when   228
Vrg'd on the Examinations, proofes, confessions   843
PROPER = 1
Abur. A proper Title of a Peace, and purchas'd | At a superfluous rate.   156
PROPHECIES = 1
2. That was hee | That fed him with his Prophecies.   850
PROPHESIE = 2
Into a generall Prophesie; That this Tempest   147
By a vaine Prophesie of *Nicholas Henton.*   491
PROPORTION = 1
Must beare the same proportion, and not euer   2930
PROPT = 1
For being not propt by Auncestry, whose grace   108
PROSPER = 1
(Tell you the Duke) shall prosper, bid him striue   515
PROSPEROUS = 1
Gart. Heauen | From thy endlesse goodnesse, send prosperous life,   3364
PROTECT = 2
Cran. God, and your Maiesty | Protect mine innocence, or I fall into   2942
With this Kisse, take my Blessing: God protect thee,   3378
PROTECTION = 1*1
Queen. How Sir? | *Camp.* Put your maine cause into the Kings
protection,   1722
Out of the Kings protection. This is my Charge.   2244
PROTECTS = 1
Sur. By my Soule, | Your long Coat (Priest) protects you,   2165
PROUD = 5
By your prescription: but this top-proud fellow,   225
To him that made him proud; the Pope.   1090
I finde at such proud Rate, that it out-speakes | Possession of a Subiect.   1990
Car. It must be himselfe then. | *Sur.* Thou art a proud Traitor, Priest.   2137
Car. Proud Lord, thou lyest: 2139
PROUDEST = 1
Good man sit downe: Now let me see the proudest   3199
PROUE = 7
When these so Noble benefits shall proue   454
Men feare the French would proue perfidious   502
'Twould proue the verity of certaine words   505
And proue it too, against mine Honor, aught;   1393
Proue but our Marriage lawfull, by my Life   1596
Ye speake like honest men, (pray God ye proue so)   1695
And not reform'd, may proue pernicious.   3067
PROUIDE = 1
Neglect him not; make vse now, and prouide | For thine owne future
safety.   2334
PROUIDED = 1
More then (I feare) you are prouided for.   3106
PROUOKE = 1
Since you prouoke me, shall be most notorious.   2181
PRUDENT = 1
A Prince most Prudent; of an excellent   1400

PRYTHEE = 3
  Serue the King: And prythee leade me in: 2365
  Prythee to bed, and in thy Prayres remember   2857
  Prythee let's walke. Now by my Holydame,   2915
PUBLIQUE = 1
  Defacers of a publique peace then I doe: 3089
PUBLIQUELY = 1
  King. What's the need? | It hath already publiquely bene read,   1353
PUBLISHD = 1
  His second Marriage shall be publishd, and   1914
PULLD = 1
  Card. There was the waight that pull'd me downe.   2320
PUNISH = 1
  Or God will punish me. I do beleeue | (Induc'd by potent
  Circumstances) that   1433
PUNISHMENT = 1
  The fowlenesse is the punishment. I presume,   2058
PUPPIE = 1
  (Which as I take it, is a kinde of Puppie   251
PUPPY = *1
  **Port.* I shall be with you presently, good M.(aster) *Puppy,*   3287
PURCHASD = 1
  Abur. A proper Title of a Peace, and purchas'd | At a superfluous rate. 156
PURE = 2
  A thousand pounds a yeare, for pure respect?   1317
  Then this pure Soule shall be. All Princely Graces   3395
PURGATION = 1
  And faire purgation to the world then malice, | I'm sure in me. 3223
PURGE = 1
  You cannot with such freedome purge your selfe,   2899
PURPOSD = 2
  The Archbishopricke of *Toledo,* this is purpos'd.   1018
  To let my tongue excuse all. What was purpos'd   3220
PURPOSE = 3
  His Father, by as much as a performance | Do's an irresolute purpose. 561
  Doe's purpose honour to you no lesse flowing,   1278
  This is of purpose laid by some that hate me,   3007
PURPOSES = 1
  My studied purposes requite, which went   2042
PURSE = 1*2
  **Enter Cardinall Wolsey, the Purse borne before him, certaine* 175
  **distance, followes a Gentleman bearing the Purse, with the* 1338
  3 *Lord* Chancellor, *with Purse and Mace before him.*   2424
PURSEUANTS = 1
  Who holds his State at dore 'mongst Purseuants, | Pages, and
  Foot-boyes.   3022
PURSUD = 1
  Pursu'd him still, and three nights after this,   2579
PUSH = 1
  We may as well push against Powles as stirre'em.   3273
PUT = 14*1
  The many to them longing, haue put off   360
  I put it to your care.   438
  Hath into monstrous habits put the Graces   461
  (As he made semblance of his duty) would | Haue put his knife into
  him.   549
  Norf. Let's in; | And with some other busines, put the King   1091

PUT *cont.*

That thus you should proceede to put me off,	1375
The Queene is put in anger; y'are excus'd:	1527
Queen. How Sir?	*Camp.* Put your maine cause into the Kings	
protection,	1722
Put my sicke cause into his hands, that hates me?	1750
As yours was, put into you, euer casts	1808
There (on my Conscience put vnwittingly)	1986
Some Spirit put this paper in the Packet,	To blesse your eye withall.	1993
Made me put this maine Secret in the Packet	2095
Ile put it to the issue. *Exit Ladie.*	2986
When we first put this dangerous stone a rowling,	3168

PUTS = 3

Nor. Surely Sir,	There's in him stuffe, that put's him to these ends:	106
Whose Figure euen this instant Clowd puts on,	314
This is the state of Man; to day he puts forth	2253

PUTTER = 1

Most bitterly on you, as putter on	Of these exactions: yet the King,	
our Maister	351

PYE = 1

Buc. The diuell speed him: No mans Pye is freed	100

QU = 7

QUALITIES = 1

(If thy rare qualities, sweet gentlenesse,	1501

QUALITY = 1

Hitting a grosser quality, is cride vp	419

QUARRELL = 1

Yet if that quarrell. Fortune, do diuorce	1217

QUARRELS = 1

That fill the Court with quarrels, talke, and Taylors.	596

QUARTA *l.*1332 3353 = 2

QUARTA *l.*660 = 1

QUARTERED = *1

*was quartered; they fell on, I made good my place; at	3312

QUARTUS *l.*2377 = 1

QUE = *1

QUEE = 1

QUEEN = 1*2

Old L. Yes troth, & troth; you would not be a Queene?	1243
Promises Boyes heereafter. Sir, your Queen	Desires your Visitation,	
and to be	2973
Cran. And to your Royall Grace, & the good Queen,	3369

QUEEN = 20*2

QUEENE see also Qu., Que., Quee., Queen. = 33*7

Vnder pretence to see the Queene his Aunt,	253
*A noyse within crying roome for the Queene, vsher'd by the	329
Duke of Norfolke. Enter the Queene, Norfolke and	330
To the good Queene, possest him with a scruple	1011
Kin. Two equall men: The Queene shall be acquain-	(ted	1155
Kin. Deliuer this with modesty to th' Queene.	*Exit Gardiner.*	1191
Anne. By my troth, and Maidenhead,	I would not be a Queene.	1230
Old as I am, to Queene it: but I pray you,	1246
I sweare againe, I would not be a Queene,	For all the world.	1256
That would not be a Queene, that would she not	1312
The Queene is comfortlesse, and wee forgetfull	1328
*vnder him as Iudges. The Queene takes place some di-	stance	1346
Scribe. Say, *Katherine* Queene of England,	Come into the Court.	1361

HENRY 8

QUEENE cont.

Crier. Katherine Queene of England, &c.	1363
The Queene makes no answer, rises out of her Chaire,	1364
We are a Queene (or long haue dream'd so) certaine	1428
Camp. The Queene is obstinate,	1483
*Crier. Katherine. Q.(ueene) of England, come into the Court.	1488
Exit Queene, and her Attendants.	1496
*The Queene of earthly Queenes: Shee's Noble borne;	1505
The Queene is put in anger; y'are excus'd:	1527
Of the good Queene; but the sharpe thorny points	1594
(Katherine our Queene) before the primest Creature | That's Parragon'd o'th' World.	1599
Camp. So please your Highnes, | The Queene being absent, 'tis a needfull fitnesse,	1601
Made to the Queene to call backe her Appeale | She intends vnto his Holinesse.	1605
Enter Queene and her Women as at worke.	1616
Her Coronation. Katherine no more | Shall be call'd Queene, but Princesse Dowager,	1915
A Knights Daughter | To be her Mistris Mistris? The Queenes, Queene?	1952
This day was view'd in open, as his Queene,	2317
The Queene is comming. Ho-boyes.	2420
the Queene in her Robe, in her haire, richly adorned with	2438
Of Lords, and Ladies, hauing brought the Queene	2483
She had all the Royall makings of a Queene;	2508
2 What two Reuerend Byshops | Were those that went on each side of the Queene?	2523
A Queene, and Daughter to a King enterre me.	2765
Now Louel, from the Queene what is the Newes.	2842
Th'estate of my poore Queene. Leaue me alone,	2858
King. Now by thy lookes | I gesse thy Message. Is the Queene deliuer'd?	2967
Ile to the Queene. Exit King.	2980
Ye must all see the Queene, and she must thanke ye,	3445

QUEENES = 4*1

*The Queene of earthly Queenes: Shee's Noble borne;	1505
My King is tangled in affection, to | A Creature of the Queenes, Lady Anne Bullen.	1870
Car. The late Queenes Gentlewoman?	1951
A Knights Daughter | To be her Mistris Mistris? The Queenes, Queene?	1952
wrought with Flowers bearing the Queenes Traine.	2442

QUEENS = *2

*Between vs & the Emperor (the Queens great Nephew)	1058
*Much waightier then this worke. The Queens in Labor	2792

QUENCH = 2*1

If with the sap of reason you would quench,	221
(Which Gods dew quench) therefore, I say againe,	1438
*To quench mine Honor; they would shame to make me	3009

QUESTION = 4

And let your Reason with your Choller question	201
Induce you to the question on't: or euer	1516
Lin. So please your Highnes, | The question did at first so stgger me,	1580
The Iustice and the Truth o'th' question carries	2931

QUESTION'D = 2

Where this is question'd, send our Letters, with	435
A yeare before. It is not to be question'd,	1404

QUICKE = 1

Would giue it quicke consideration; for	399

240

QUICKLY = 1
1. You may guesse quickly what. 831
QUIET = 5
The quiet of my wounded Conscience; 1117
For your owne quiet, as to rectifie | What is vnsetled in the King. 1418
A still, and quiet Conscience. The King ha's cur'd me, 2286
Grif. She is asleep: Good wench, let's sit down quiet, 2640
Suf. I wish your Highnesse | A quiet night, and my good Mistris will |
Remember in my Prayers. 2861
QUINTUS *l.*2768 = 1
QUIRE = 2
To a prepar'd place in the Quire, fell off 2484
Laid Nobly on her: which perform'd, the Quire 2511
QUIRRISTERS = 1
4 Quirristers *singing.* Musicke. 2425
QUIT = 1
Suf. God safely quit her of her Burthen, and 2853
QUITE = 1
Buc. Ile to the King, | And from a mouth of Honor, quite cry downe 208
QUOTH = 2
Sur. If (quoth he) I for this had beene committed, 544
It did take place, I do (quoth he) perceiue 1869
RABBLE = 1
Theres a trim rabble let in: are all these 3330
RAGE = 1
Camp. Your rage mistakes vs. 1733
RAILD = *1
*Wife of small wit, neere him, that rail'd vpon me, 3306
RAILE = 1
Por. You i'th'Chamblet, get vp o'th' raile, 3351
RAIND = 2
A Spring-halt rain'd among 'em. 585
My heart drop'd Loue, my powre rain'd Honor, more 2060
RAISD = 3
Who first rais'd head against Vsurping *Richard,* 954
Gard. But to be commanded | For euer by your Grace, whose hand ha's
rais'd me. 1168
Those twinnes of Learning, that he rais'd in you, 2616
RAKE = 1
Does he rake this together? Now my Lords, | Saw you the Cardinall? 1971
RAMMES = 1
That had not halfe a weeke to go, like Rammes 2497
RAN = 1
That he ran mad, and dide. 1183
RANCKE = 1
Kin. Ha? What, so rancke? Ah, ha, 535
RANGE = 1
And range with humble liuers in Content, 1225
RANKE = 2
To ranke our chosen Truth with such a show 19
He be conuented. He's a ranke weed Sir *Thomas,* 2831
RANKING = 1
Of an vnbounded stomacke, euer ranking 2589
RANKNESSE = 1
Could not be wedg'd in more: I am stifled | With the meere ranknesse
of their ioy. 2475

RARE = 2
The Gentleman is Learn'd, and a most rare Speaker,   450
(If thy rare qualities, sweet gentlenesse,   1501
RASCALS = *1
*Port. You'l leaue your noyse anon ye Rascals: doe   3259
RASKALLS = 1
*Do you looke for Ale, and Cakes heere, you rude | Raskalls?   3267
RATE = 2
Abur. A proper Title of a Peace, and purchas'd | At a superfluous rate.   156
I finde at such proud Rate, that it out-speakes | Possession of a Subiect.   1990
RATHER = 2
Sur. I had rather want those, then my head;   2205
Concerning his Imprisonment, was rather   3221
RATIFIED = 1
As himselfe pleas'd; and they were ratified   246
RAUISHD = 1
Almost with rauish'd listning, could not finde   459
RAUNOUS = 2
Or Wolfe, or both (for he is equall rau'nous   234
As rau'nous Fishes doe a Vessell follow   414
RAYES = 1
Take vp the Rayes o'th'beneficiall Sun, | And keepe it from the Earth.   104
REACH = 4
Who can be angry now? What Enuy reach you?   1136
Willing to leaue their burthen: Reach a Chaire,   2554
To me you cannot reach. You play the Spaniell,   3195
And like a Mountaine Cedar, reach his branches,   3424
REACHES = 1
It reaches farre, and where 'twill not extend,   171
READ = 6
Buc. I read in's looks | Matter against me, and his eye reuil'd   195
Car. Whil'st our Commission from Rome is read,   1351
King. What's the need? | It hath already publiquely bene read,   1353
And came to th'eye o'th'King, wherein was read   1866
For you haue seene him open't. Read o're this,   2078
From her shall read the perfect way of Honour,   3408
READE = 3
Honor, and plenteous safety) that you reade | The Cardinals Malice,
and his Potency   164
Then makes him nothing. I must reade this paper: 2088
He to be Earle Marshall: you may reade the rest.   2401
READING = 3
Enter Lord Chamberlaine, reading this Letter.   1027
*Exit Lord Chamberlaine, and the King drawes the Curtaine | and sits
reading pensiuely.   1100
Enter King, reading of a Scedule.   1964
READY = 6*1
Car. Is he in person, ready? | Secr. I, please your Grace.   183
Card. Sir Thomas Louell, is the Banket ready | I'th' Priuy Chamber? |
Lou. Yes, my Lord.   804
Vaux. Prepare there, | The Duke is comming: See the Barge be ready;   942
*North. When they were ready to set out for London, a man   1031
To trust vs in your businesse) we are ready | To vse our vtmost Studies,
in your seruice.   1811
Card. Is he ready to come abroad? | Crom. I thinke by this he is.   1937
Let some o'th' Guard be ready there.   3154

REALME = 1*1
Of euery Realme, that did debate this Businesse,   1406
*The whole Realme, by your teaching & your Chaplaines   3064
REALMES = 1
I weigh'd the danger which my Realmes stood in   1564
REAPD = 1
What sodaine Anger's this? How haue I reap'd it?   2084
REASON = 2*1
And let your Reason with your Choller question   201
If with the sap of reason you would quench,   221
*'em from me, with this reason: his maister would bee seru'd be-|fore   1033
REASONS = 3
Many sharpe reasons to defeat the Law.   841
Of my alleadged reasons, driues this forward: 1595
Our Reasons layd before him, hath commanded   2829
REBELLD = 1
Buc. All was Royall, | To the disposing of it nought rebell'd,   88
REBELLION = 1
The sides of loyalty, and almost appeares | In lowd Rebellion.   355
REBUKE = 1
There's places of rebuke. He was a Foole;   1186
RECEIPT = 1
For such receipt of Learning, is Black-Fryers: 1194
RECEIUD = 4
I haue this day receiu'd a Traitors iudgement,   899
My Conscience first receiu'd a tendernes,   1537
With all his Couent, honourably receiu'd him;   2573
I haue receiu'd much Honour by your presence,   3443
RECEIUE = 4
And pray receiue 'em Nobly, and conduct 'em   746
This from a dying man receiue as certaine: 971
(Sauing your mincing) the capacity | Of your soft Chiuerell Conscience,
would receiue,   1239
Gard. Receiue him, | And see him safe i'th' Tower.   3158
RECIPROCALLY = 1
Infecting one another, yea reciprocally,   237
RECITED = 1
The fore-recited practises, whereof   466
RECKOND = 1
My Father, King of Spaine, was reckon'd one   1402
RECOUNT = 1
Things to strike Honour sad. Bid him recount   465
RECTIFIE = 2
For your owne quiet, as to rectifie | What is vnsetled in the King.   1418
I meant to rectifie my Conscience, which   1570
RED = 1
San. The red wine first must rise   722
REEKE = 1
How vnder my oppression I did reeke | When I first mou'd you.   1575
REELE = 1
And make 'em reele before 'em. No man liuing   2499
REFORMATION = 2
L.Cham. What is't for? | *Lou.* The reformation of our trauel'd Gallants, 594
Gard. Which Reformation must be sodaine too   3068
REFORMD = 1
And not reform'd, may proue pernicious.   3067

REFUSE = 2
Refuse you for my Iudge, whom yet once more   1440
I do refuse you for my Iudge, and heere   1478
REGARD = 1
Strangely neglected? When did he regard   1839
REGINA = *1
*Card. Tanta est erga te mentis integritas Regina serenissima.   1664
REGION = 1
The region of my Breast, which forc'd such way,   1551
REIGND = 1
The wisest Prince, that there had reign'd, by many   1403
REIGNE = *1
*now reigne in's Nose; all that stand about him are   3301
REIOYCING = *1
*reioycing, and holdeth vp her hands to heauen. And so, in   2655
RELATE = 1*1
And point by point the Treasons of his Maister, | He shall againe relate. 327
*Card. Stand forth, & with bold spirit relate what you   468
RELIGIOUS = 3
With thy Religious Truth, and Modestie,   2632
Of mine owne way. I know you Wise, Religious,   2805
Not onely good and wise, but most religious: 3185
REMAINDER = 1
(You see the poore remainder) could distribute,   3277
REMAINE = 2
There to remaine till the Kings further pleasure   3147
As I haue made ye one Lords, one remaine: 3254
REMAINES = 1
Where she remaines now sicke. | 2 Alas good Lady.   2417
REMARKD = 1
Louell. Now Sir, you speake of two | The most remark'd i'th'Kingdome:
as for Cromwell,   2810
REMEDY = 2
Toward this remedy, whereupon we are   1568
Will render you no remedy, this Ring   2953
REMEMBER = 8*1
*Kin. I remember of such a time, being my sworn ser- | (uant,   542
With you my Lord of Lincolne; you remember   1574
I thanke my Memorie, I yet remember   2198
And something ouer to remember me by.   2743
Kath. I thanke you honest Lord. Remember me | In all humilitie vnto
his Highnesse: 2753
Prythee to bed, and in thy Prayres remember   2857
Suf. I wish your Highnesse | A quiet night, and my good Mistris will |
Remember in my Prayers.   2861
Gard. I shall remember this bold Language. | Crom. Doe.   3137
Remember your bold life too.   3139
REMEMBRANCE = 1
Remembrance of my Father-in-Law, the Duke, | To be reueng'd on
him.   1835
REMNANTS = 1
Lou. They must either | (For so run the Conditions) leaue those
remnants   601
REMOUD = 3
Shall shine at full vpon them. Some attend him. | All rise, and Tables
remou'd.   748

REMOUD *cont.*
Then Deputy of Ireland, who remou'd | Earle *Surrey*, was sent thither,
and in hast too,   874
Since which, she was remou'd to Kymmalton,   2416
REMOUE = 1
Remoue these Thoughts from you. The which before   1461
REND = 1
We must not rend our Subiects from our Lawes,   429
RENDER = 3
Can nothing render but Allegiant thankes,   2050
Who commands you | To render vp the Great Seale presently   2111
Will render you no remedy, this Ring   2953
RENOUNCING = 1
Out of a forreigne wisedome, renouncing cleane   607
REPAYRE = 1
Not for delights: Times to repayre our Nature   2774
REPEAT = 2
Repeat your will, and take it.   338
And am right sorrie to repeat what followes.   2893
REPENTANCE = 1
Foretold should be his last, full of Repentance,   2581
REPLIDE = 1
Concerning the French Iourney. I replide,   501
REPORT = 3
And processe of this time, you can report,   1392
That I am free of your Report, he knowes   1458
That man i'th' world, who shall report he ha's   1498
REPOSE = 1
With comforting repose, and not for vs   2775
REPROCHES = 1
Of all their Loyalties; wherein, although | My good Lord Cardinall,
they vent reproches   349
REPROUD = 1
Sur. Being at *Greenwich,* | After your Highnesse had reprou'd the
Duke | About Sir *William Bulmer.*   539
REPUTED = 1
The King your Father, was reputed for   1399
REQUEST = 1
The Kings request, that I would visit you,   2704
REQUIRD = 1
As I requir'd: and wot you what I found   1985
REQUIRE = 3
Ere a determinate resolution, hee | (I meane the Bishop) did require a
respite,   1543
I beare i'th'State: and Nature does require   2016
Which will require your Answer, you must take   2901
REQUIRE = 1
Wol. Most gracious Sir, | In humblest manner I require your Highnes,   1508
REQUIRE = 1
2. This Secret is so weighty, 'twill require   993
REQUIRES = 2
Aske God for Temp'rance, that's th'appliance onely | Which your
disease requires.   193
Requires slow pace at first. Anger is like   203
REQUITE = 2
1. At his returne, | No doubt he will requite it; this is noted   879
My studied purposes requite, which went   2042

RESOLUTION = 1
Ere a determinate resolution, hee | (I meane the Bishop) did require a
respite,   1543
RESPECT = 6
(Out of the great respect they beare to beauty)   762
A thousand pounds a yeare, for pure respect?   1317
As you respect the common good, the State   2183
How euer faulty, yet should finde respect   3124
That holy duty out of deare respect,   3188
Kin. Well, well my Lords respect him,   3225
RESPECTING = 1
Respecting this our Marriage with the Dowager,   1547
RESPITE = 2
Ere a determinate resolution, hee | (I meane the Bishop) did require a
respite,   1543
Sometimes our Brothers Wife. This respite shooke   1548
REST = 5*2
In all the rest shew'd a most Noble patience.   865
**the Scribes. The Lords sit next the Bishops. The rest of the*   1349
He to be Earle Marshall: you may reade the rest.   2401
1 It is, and all the rest are Countesses.   2468
To rest a while, some halfe an houre, or so,   2486
Kath. So may he rest, | His Faults lye gently on him: 2585
**Lou.* Many good nights, my Lord, I rest your seruant.   2835
RESTED = 1
Should finde a running Banket, ere they rested,   681
RESTORD = 1
Restor'd me to my Honours: and out of ruines   960
RESTORE = 1
And out of all these, to restore the King,   1062
RETAINERS = 1
Where Powres are your Retainers, and your words   1473
RETEIND = 1
The Duke retein'd him his. But on: what hence?   543
RETURND = 3
Suf. He is return'd in his Opinions, which   1910
What more? | *Crom.* That *Cranmer* is return'd with welcome;   2311
I sent your Message, who return'd her thankes   2845
RETURNE = 4
1. At his returne, | No doubt he will requite it; this is noted   879
Are all I can returne. 'Beseech your Lordship,   1287
When you are cald returne. Now the Lord helpe,   1491
Prethee returne, with thy approch: I know,   1611
RETURNES = 1
Norf. But my Lord | When returnes *Cranmer*?   1908
REUELS = 1
An houre of Reuels with 'em.   765
REUENGD = 1
Remembrance of my Father-in-Law, the Duke, | To be reueng'd on
him.   1835
REUENGE = 2
Lord *Aburgany*, to whom by oth he menac'd | Reuenge vpon the
Cardinall.   477
1. Tis the Cardinall; | And meerely to reuenge him on the Emperour,   1015
REUENGEFULL = 1
That he's Reuengefull; and I know, his Sword   169

REUERENCE = 2
Deserue we no more Reuerence? | *Grif.* You are too blame,　　　　2683
But reuerence to your calling, makes me modest.　　　　3118
REUEREND = 11*1
Of the right Reuerend Cardinall of Yorke.　　　　99
Buc. Why all this Businesse | Our Reuerend Cardinall carried.　　　　158
Most learned Reuerend Sir, into our Kingdome,　　　　1119
Wol. You haue heere Lady, | (And of your choice) these Reuerend
Fathers, men　　　　1412
By all the Reuerend Fathers of the Land,　　　　1572
I left no Reuerend Person in this Court;　　　　1590
Vpon my Soule two reuerend Cardinall Vertues:　　　　1735
While I shall haue my life. Come reuerend Fathers,　　　　1820
Learned, and Reuerend Fathers of his Order,　　　　2408
2 What two Reuerend Byshops | Were those that went on each side of
the Queene?　　　　2523
Lodg'd in the Abbey; where the reuerend Abbot　　　　2572
Garland ouer her Head, at which the other foure make re-|uerend　　　　2648
REUERENT = 1
What are your pleasures with me, reuerent Lords?　　　　1649
REUILD = 1
Buc. I read in's looks | Matter against me, and his eye reuil'd　　　　195
REUOKEMENT = 1
That through our Intercession, this Reuokement　　　　443
REWARDED = 1
And am I thus rewarded? 'Tis not well Lords.　　　　1766
REWARDS = 1
In time will finde their fit Rewards. That Seale　　　　2130
REX = 1
Nor. Then, That in all you writ to Rome, or else | To Forraigne
Princes, *Ego & Rex meus*　　　　2210
RICH = 3
Rich Stuffes and Ornaments of Houshold, which　　　　1989
2 Good Sir, speake it to vs? | 3 As well as I am able. The rich streame　　　　2481
In a rich Chaire of State, opposing freely　　　　2487
RICHARD = 2
Th' Vsurper *Richard*, who being at *Salsbury*,　　　　547
Who first rais'd head against Vsurping *Richard*,　　　　954
RICHER = 2
Yet I am richer then my base Accusers,　　　　950
And more, and richer, when he straines that Lady,　　　　2460
RICHES = 1
Anne. No, not for all the riches vnder Heauen.　　　　1244
RICHLY = 1*2
Richly in two short houres. Onely they　　　　14
the Queene in her Robe, in her haire, richly adorned with　　　　2438
Norfolke, Godmother, bearing the Childe richly habited in　　　　3359
RIDDEN = *1
care I had, I saw well chosen, ridden, and furnish'd.　　　　1029
RIDICULOUS = 1
L.San. New customes, | Though they be neuer so ridiculous,　　　　573
RIGHT = 11
Of the right Reuerend Cardinall of Yorke.　　　　99
places himselfe vnder the Kings feete on| his right side.　　　　319
Sir, I desire you do me Right and Iustice,　　　　1367
A way, if it take right, in spight of Fortune　　　　2099
Crom. I am glad your Grace, | Ha's made that right vse of it.　　　　2292

RIGHT *cont.*

Still in thy right hand, carry gentle Peace   2360
For honestie, and decent Carriage | A right good Husband (let him be a
Noble)   2737
Stand these poore peoples Friend, and vrge the King | To do me this
last right.   2749
And am right sorrie to repeat what followes.   2893
And am right glad to catch this good occasion   2907
Suff. 'Tis the right Ring, by Heau'n: I told ye all,   3167
RIGHTEOUS = 1
They should bee good men, their affaires as righteous: 1643
RIGHTLY = 1
Wol. He tels you rightly.   1728
RIGHTS = 1
As let 'em haue their rights, they are euer forward   2389
RING = 4
Will render you no remedy, this Ring   2953
By vertue of that Ring, I take my cause   3162
Cham. This is the Kings Ring. | *Sur.* 'Tis no counterfeit.   3165
Suff. 'Tis the right Ring, by Heau'n: I told ye all,   3167
RIPE = 1
He was a Scholler, and a ripe, and good one: 2609
RIPENESSE = 1
Which Time shall bring to ripenesse: She shall be,   3390
RIPENING = 1
His Greatnesse is a ripening, nippes his roote,   2258
RISE = 5
San. The red wine first must rise   722
Shall shine at full vpon them. Some attend him. | *All rise, and Tables
remou'd.*   748
And fearing he would rise (he was so vertuous)   1181
Found thee a way (out of his wracke) to rise in: 2352
Shall Star-like rise, as great in fame as she was,   3417
RISES = *1
The Queene makes no answer, rises out of her Chaire,   1364
RISETH = 1
Suffolke: she kneels. King riseth from his State,   331
RISING = 1
So excellent in Art, and still so rising,   2620
RIUER = 1
Should the approach of this wilde Riuer breake, | And stand vnshaken
yours.   2074
ROARE = *1
*Is this a place to roare in? Fetch me a dozen Crab-tree   3264
ROBBD = 1
Sur. Thy Ambition | (Thou Scarlet sinne) robb'd this bewailing Land   2142
ROBD = 1
Of all these eares (for where I am rob'd and bound,   1511
ROBE = 1 *2
To the last peny, 'tis the Kings. My Robe,   2367
*7 Duke of Suffolke, *in his Robe of Estate, his Coronet on his*   2433
the Queene in her Robe, in her haire, richly adorned with   2438
ROBES = *1
clad in white Robes, wearing on their heades Garlands of   2644
ROCHESTER = *1
Rochester, and S.(aint) Asaph: Next them, with some small   1337

ROCHFORD = 1
Sir *Thomas Bullens* Daughter, the Viscount *Rochford,*   798
ROCK = *1
*You'l finde it wholesome. Loe, where comes that Rock   173
ROCKE = 2
As shore of Rocke: attend. This holy Foxe,   233
As doth a Rocke against the chiding Flood,   2073
ROD = 2*2
bearing the Rod of Siluer with the Doue, Crowned with an | Earles
Coronet. Collars of Esses.   2431
him, the Duke of Norfolke, with the Rod of Marshalship, | a Coronet on
his head. Collars of Esses.   2435
And that the Earle of Surrey, with the Rod.   2450
The Rod, and Bird of Peace, and all such Emblemes   2510
RODES = 1
Kath. Alas poore man. | *Grif.* At last, with easie Rodes, he came to
Leicester,   2570
ROGUE = *1
Port. Belong to th' Gallowes, and be hang'd ye Rogue: 3263
ROIALL = 1
Toward the King, my euer Roiall Master,   2162
ROLLES = 1
O'th'Rolles, and the Kings Secretary. Further Sir,   2813
ROME = 8*2
*Haue their free voyces. Rome (the Nurse of Iudgement)   1141
The Court of Rome commanding. You my Lord   1152
Car. Whil'st our Commission from Rome is read,   1351
Yea, the whole Consistorie of Rome. You charge me,   1452
This dilatory sloth, and trickes of Rome.   1609
Is stolne away to Rome, hath 'tane no leaue,   1901
*To heare from Rome. The Marchionesse of Penbroke?   1945
And fee my Friends in Rome.) O Negligence!   2093
Nor. Then, That in all you writ to Rome, or else | To Forraigne
Princes, *Ego & Rex meus*   2210
To furnish Rome, and to prepare the wayes   2226
ROOME = 1*1
A noyse within crying roome for the Queene, vsher'd by the   329
Great store of roome no doubt, left for the Ladies,   3332
ROOT = 1
And we must root him out. From your Affaires   2832
ROOTE = 3
We should take roote here, where we sit;   422
And though we leaue it with a roote thus hackt,   433
His Greatnesse is a ripening, nippes his roote,   2258
ROOTED = 1
Thy Truth, and thy Integrity is rooted   2913
ROSE = 3
The Duke being at the Rose, within the Parish   498
2 But what follow'd? | 3 At length, her Grace rose, and with modest
paces   2502
Then rose againe, and bow'd her to the people: 2506
ROUGH = 1
'Tis but the fate of Place, and the rough Brake   410
ROUND = 2
And not to kisse you. A health Gentlemen, | Let it goe round.   802
Clap round Fines for neglect: y'are lazy knaues,   3341

ROWLING = 1
When we first put this dangerous stone a rowling,   3168
ROYALL = 14*1
Buc. All was Royall, | To the disposing of it nought rebell'd,   88
By all your good leaues Gentlemen; heere Ile make | My royall choyce.   787
My Fathers losse; like a most Royall Prince   959
Is businesse of Estate; in which, we come | To know your Royall
pleasure.   1110
It's fit this Royall Session do proceed,   1422
A Royall Lady, spake one, the least word that might   1518
Car. My Soueraigne, I confesse your Royall graces   2040
2 'Tis well: The Citizens | I am sure haue shewne at full their Royall
minds,   2387
2 A Royall Traine beleeue me: These I know: 2447
She had all the Royall makings of a Queene;   2508
My Royall Nephew, and your name *Capuchius.* | *Cap.* Madam the
same. Your Seruant.   2695
Fly o're thy Royall head, and shade thy person | Vnder their blessed
wings.   2965
His Royall selfe in Iudgement comes to heare   3189
Cran. And to your Royall Grace, & the good Queen,   3369
This Royall Infant, Heauen still moue about her;   3387
ROYALTY = 1
Whose health and Royalty I pray for.   1290
RUB = 1
The least rub in your fortunes, fall away   975
RUDE = 2*2
Of a rude streame, that must for euer hide me.   2265
To vse so rude behauiour. Go too, kneele.   2686
*you take the Court for Parish Garden: ye rude Slaues, | leaue your
gaping.   3260
*Do you looke for Ale, and Cakes heere, you rude | Raskalls?   3267
RUIND = 3
1. Stay there Sir, | And see the noble ruin'd man you speake of.   893
These ruin'd Pillers, out of pitty, taken   2288
Marke but my Fall, and that that Ruin'd me: 2354
RUINE = 5
Queen. Ye tell me what ye wish for both, my ruine: 1729
He parted Frowning from me, as if Ruine   2085
Ye appeare in euery thing may bring my ruine?   2127
That sweet Aspect of Princes, and their ruine,   2270
(But where he meant to Ruine) pittifull.   2595
RUINES = 1
Restor'd me to my Honours: and out of ruines   960
RULD = 1
Our hard rul'd King. Againe, there is sprung vp   1959
RULE = 2
Euer belou'd and louing, may his Rule be;   936
An Army cannot rule 'em.   3337
RUMINATE = 1
For this to ruminate on this so farre, vntill   528
RUMOR = 1
To stop the rumor; and allay those tongues | That durst disperse it.   1004
RUN = 5
By violent swiftnesse that which we run at;   215
The fire that mounts the liquor til't run ore,   217

RUN *cont.*
   Queen. I am sorry, that the Duke of *Buckingham* | Is run in your
displeasure. 447
   Lou. They must either | (For so run the Conditions) leaue those
remnants 601
   When he ha's run his course, and sleepes in Blessings, 2309
RUNG = 1
   His Knell rung out, his Iudgement, he was stir'd 861
RUNNE = 1
   That it do sindge your selfe. We may out-runne 214
RUNNING = 4*1
   And lose by ouer-running: know you not, 216
   Should finde a running Banket, ere they rested, 681
   And did entreate your Highnes to this course, | Which you are running
heere. 1585
   You were now running o're: you haue scarse time 2008
   *these three dayes; besides the running Banquet of two | Beadles, that is
to come. 3323
SABA = 1
   And all that shall succeed: *Saba* was neuer 3393
SACRED = 3
   Against your Sacred Person; in Gods name 1395
   To'th'good of your most Sacred Person, and 2047
   Who, from the sacred Ashes of her Honour 3416
SACRIFICE = 2
   The Backe is Sacrifice to th'load; They say 381
   Make of your Prayers one sweet Sacrifice, 919
SACRING = 1
   Worse then the Sacring Bell, when the browne Wench 2188
SAD = 8*2
   Sad, high, and working, full of State and Woe: 4
   Be sad, as we would make ye. Thinke ye see 26
   Things to strike Honour sad. Bid him recount 465
   *Farewell; and when you would say somthing that is sad, | Speake how
I fell. 980
   Full of sad thoughts and troubles. 1044
   *From these sad thoughts, that work too much vpon him: 1093
   Suff. How sad he lookes; sure he is much afflicted. 1102
   My Soule growes sad with troubles, 1618
   Cause the Musitians play me that sad note 2636
   On that Coelestiall Harmony I go too. | *Sad and solemne Musicke.* 2638
SAFE = 2
   A sure, and safe one, though thy Master mist it. 2353
   Gard. Receiue him, | And see him safe i'th' Tower. 3158
SAFELY = 2
   Suf. God safely quit her of her Burthen, and 2853
   Might goe one way, and safely; and the end 3084
SAFETY = 3
   Honor, and plenteous safety) that you reade | The Cardinals Malice,
and his Potency 164
   Neglect him not; make vse now, and prouide | For thine owne future
safety. 2334
   In her dayes, Euery Man shall eate in safety, 3404
SAID = 12*1
   'Twas said they saw but one, and no Discerner 76
   Abur. As the Duke said, 299
   Said, 'twas the feare indeed, and that he doubted 504

SAID *cont.*

L.Cham. Well said Lord *Sands*,	629
He had a blacke mouth that said other of him.	646
Cham. Well said my Lord: | So now y'are fairely seated: Gentlemen,	704
King. You haue said well.	2020
King. 'Tis well said agen,	2024
He said he did, and with his deed did Crowne	2027
Lou. So said her woman, and that her suffrance made	2850
Ha? I haue said. Be gone. | What? *Exeunt Louell and Denny.*	2878
Being of those Vertues vacant. I feare nothing | What can be said	
against me.	2925
Said I for this, the Gyrle was like to him? Ile	2984

SAIDE = 2

Hath a sharpe edge: It's long, and't may be saide	170
Within these fortie houres, Surrey durst better | Haue burnt that	
Tongue, then saide so.	2140

SAINT = 1*1

Saint *Laurence Poultney*, did of me demand	499
Rochester, and S.(aint) Asaph: Next them, with some small	1337

SAINTS = 1

She must, the Saints must haue her; yet a Virgin,	3432

SAINT-LIKE = 2

Thy meeknesse Saint-like, Wife-like Gouernment,	1502
Came to the Altar, where she kneel'd, and Saint-like	2504

SAKE = 7

Therefore, for Goodnesse sake, and as you are knowne	24
If you speake truth, for their poore Mistris sake;	1670
For her sake that I haue beene, for I feele	1703
Take heed, for heauens sake take heed, least at once	1742
For Goodnesse sake, consider what you do,	1796
For Truths-sake, and his Conscience; that his bones,	2308
To loue her for her Mothers sake, that lou'd him, | Heauen knowes how	
deerely.	2728

SALSBURY = 1

Th' Vsurper *Richard*, who being at *Salsbury*,	547

SALUTE = 2*1

I was then present, saw them salute on Horsebacke,	49
passe directly before the Cardinall and gracefully sa-| lute him.	755
If this salute my blood a iot; it faints me | To thinke what followes.	1326

SALUTES = 1

Salutes ye all; This Night he dedicates	668

SAME = 6*4

1. The same, | All these accus'd him strongly, which he faine	852
Nor. This same *Cranmer*'s | A worthy Fellow, and hath tane much	
paine | In the Kings businesse.	1918
1 'Tis the same: high Steward.	2453
And with the same full State pac'd backe againe	2514
the same to the other next two, who obserue the same or-| der	2650
head. Which done, they deliuer the same Garland to the	2652
last two: who likewise obserue the same Order. At which	2653
My Royall Nephew, and your name *Capuchius.* | *Cap.* Madam the	
same. Your Seruant.	2695
Must beare the same proportion, and not euer	2930

SAMPSON = 1

Man. I am not *Sampson*, nor Sir *Guy*, nor *Colebrand*,	3280

SAN = 10

SANDS = 6
L.Cham. Well said Lord *Sands,*   629
Enter L.(ord) Chamberlaine L.(ord) Sands, and Louell.   674
My Lord *Sands,* you are one will keepe 'em waking: 694
And saue me so much talking. | *Card.* My Lord *Sands,*   717
An.B. You are a merry Gamster | My Lord *Sands.*   725
Vaux, Sir Walter Sands, and common people, &c.   892
SANDYS see also L.San., San. = 1
Enter L.(ord) Chamberlaine and L.(ord) Sandys.   570
SAP = 2
If with the sap of reason you would quench,   221
The Ayre will drinke the Sap. To euery County   434
SATE = 1
A distance from her; while her Grace sate downe   2485
SATISFIDE = 2
At once, and fully satisfide) whether euer I   1513
Kin. I haue spoke long, be pleas'd your selfe to say | How farre you
satisfide me.   1578
SATISFIED = 1
Haue satisfied the King for his Diuorce,   1911
SAUE = 5*1
And saue me so much talking. | *Card.* My Lord *Sands,*   717
1. Whether away so fast? | 2. O, God saue ye: 821
1. Ile saue you | That labour Sir. All's now done but the Ceremony   825
Sur. This cannot saue you: 2197
*1 God saue you Sir. Where haue you bin broiling?   2473
And that I would not for a Cow, God saue her.   3285
SAUING = 1
(Sauing your mincing) the capacity | Of your soft Chiuerell Conscience,
would receiue,   1239
SAW = 12*1
Since last we saw in France?   40
Healthfull, and euer since a fresh Admirer | Of what I saw there.   42
I was then present, saw them salute on Horsebacke,   49
'Twas said they saw but one, and no Discerner   76
care I had, I saw well chosen, ridden, and furnish'd.   1029
As I saw it inclin'd? When was the houre   1381
Were tri'de by eu'ry tongue, eu'ry eye saw 'em,   1659
Does he rake this together? Now my Lords, | Saw you the Cardinall?   1971
2 You saw the Ceremony? | 3 That I did.   2477
I neuer saw before. Great belly'd women,   2496
Saw ye none enter since I slept? | *Grif.* None Madam.   2662
Kath. No? Saw you not euen now a blessed Troope   2664
Butts. I thinke your Highnesse saw this many a day.   3018
SAWCY = 1
Mes. And't like your Grace ---| *Kath.* You are a sawcy Fellow,   2681
SAY = 46*2
And if you can be merry then, Ile say,   32
Nor. Then you lost | The view of earthly glory: Men might say   57
I say againe there is no English Soule   219
Norf. Say not treasonous.   231
The Backe is Sacrifice to th'load; They say   381
The Chronicles of my doing: Let me say,   409
And spoyle your nobler Soule; I say, take heed;   522
There's mischiefe in this man; canst thou say further?   536
Card. Say, Lord *Chamberlaine,* | They haue done my poore house grace: 766
Cham. I will my Lord. | *Card.* What say they?   781

SAY *cont.*

Heare what I say, and then goe home and lose me.	898
And must needs say a Noble one; which makes me	965
*Farewell; and when you would say somthing that is sad, | Speake how I fell.	980
Kin. Who's there I say? How dare you thrust your | (selues	1105
Camp. They will not sticke to say, you enuide him;	1180
Which, to say sooth, are Blessings; and which guifts	1238
And say I spoke with you. | *Exit Lord Chamberlaine.*	1298
I know your backe will beare a Dutchesse. Say,	1321
**Scri.* Say, *Henry* K.(ing) of England, come into the Court.	1358
Scribe. Say, *Katherine* Queene of England, | Come into the Court.	1361
(Which Gods dew quench) therefore, I say againe,	1438
You (gracious Madam) to vnthinke your speaking, | And to say so no more.	1463
Now present heere together: that's to say,	1569
Kin. I haue spoke long, be pleas'd your selfe to say | How farre you satisfide me.	1578
I say, set on. | *Exeunt, in manner as they enter'd.*	1613
Queen. Would they speake with me? | *Gent.* They wil'd me say so Madam.	1637
I haue more Charity. But say I warn'd ye;	1741
A Woman (I dare say without Vainglory) | Neuer yet branded with Suspition?	1760
And 'tis a kinde of good deede to say well,	2025
And if you may confesse it, say withall	2038
If you are bound to vs, or no. What say you?	2039
Of me, more must be heard of: Say I taught thee;	2349
Say *Wolsey,* that once trod the wayes of Glory,	2350
2 Their Coronets say so. These are Starres indeed, | And sometimes falling ones.	2469
Could say this is my wife there, all were wouen | So strangely in one peece.	2500
He would say vntruths, and be euer double	2593
Say his long trouble now is passing	2755
(As they say Spirits do) at midnight, haue	2787
They say in great Extremity, and fear'd | Shee'l with the Labour, end.	2793
Heard many greeuous, I do say my Lord	2895
Say I, and of a boy. | *Lady.* I, I my Liege,	2969
In doing dayly wrongs. I could say more,	3117
Gard. Good M.(aster) Secretary, | I cry your Honour mercie; you may worst | Of all this Table say so.	3127
Crom. Not sound? | *Gard.* Not sound I say.	3133
Cran. Stay good my Lords, | I haue a little yet to say. Looke there my Lords,	3160
I will say thus much for him, if a Prince	3227
They'l say tis naught. Others to heare the City	3454
And say twill doe; I know within a while,	3461

SAYES = 2*1

Spoke by a holy Monke, that oft, sayes he,	506
Lou. Me thinkes I could | Cry the Amen, and yet my Conscience sayes	2799
*Of thee, which sayes thus: Doe my Lord of *Canterbury*	3250

SAYING = 1

(As I will lend you cause) my doing well, | With my well saying.	2022

SAYST = 2

**Kin.* Ther's somthing more would out of thee; what | (say'st?	555
King. What say'st thou? Ha?	2848

SAYT = *1
*Buck. To th'King Ile say't, & make my vouch as strong   232
SCAENA l.569 = 1
SCARLET = 2
Sur. Thy Ambition | (Thou Scarlet sinne) robb'd this bewailing Land   2142
To be thus Iaded by a peece of Scarlet,   2171
SCARSE = 2
You were now running o're: you haue scarse time   2008
(Whom if he liue, will scarse be Gentlemen)   2185
SCATTER = 1
To scatter 'em, as 'tis to make 'em sleepe   3271
SCATTERS = 1
He diues into the Kings Soule, and there scatters   1059
SCEDULE = 1
Enter King, reading of a Scedule.   1964
SCENA l.819 1026 1200 1332 1615 1824 2377 2547 2987 3256 3353 = 11
SCENA l.2768 = 1
SCENA l.316 660 = 2
SCEPTER = 2*1
To make the Scepter his. These very words   475
*6 Marquesse Dorset, bearing a Scepter of Gold, on his head,   2429
Who's that that beares the Scepter? | 1 Marquesse Dorset,   2448
SCHOLLER = 1
He was a Scholler, and a ripe, and good one: 2609
SCHOLLERS = 1
Schollers allow'd freely to argue for her.   1160
SCOENA l.34 = 1
SCOENES = 1
Such Noble Scoenes, as draw the Eye to flow   5
SCOLD = 1
I will haue more, or scold it out of him.   2983
SCORND = 1
A woman lost among ye, laugh't at, scornd?   1739
SCRATCH = *1
*Ile scratch your heads; you must be seeing Christenings?   3266
SCRI = *1
SCRIBE see also Scri. = 1
SCRIBES = *2
*Scribes in the habite of Doctors; after them, the Bishop of   1335
*the Scribes. The Lords sit next the Bishops. The rest of the   1349
SCRUPLE = 5
To the good Queene, possest him with a scruple   1011
Your scruple to the voyce of Christendome: 1135
Laid any scruple in your way, which might   1515
Scruple, and pricke, on certaine Speeches vtter'd   1538
The Kings late Scruple, by the maine assent   2413
SEA = 4
The wild Sea of my Conscience, I did steere   1567
Euen the Billowes of the Sea,   1628
This many Summers in a Sea of Glory,   2261
As the shrowdes make at Sea, in a stiffe Tempest,   2492
SEALE = 6*1
Whom after vnder the Commissions Seale,   510
That neuer knew what Truth meant: I now seale it;   951
*great Seale, and a Cardinals Hat: Then two Priests, bea-| ring   1339
Who commands you | To render vp the Great Seale presently   2111

SEALE *cont.*

In time will finde their fit Rewards. That Seale   2130
Ambassador to the Emperor, you made bold | To carry into Flanders,
the Great Seale.   2216
About the giuing backe the Great Seale to vs,   2247

SEALES = 1

Vnder your hands and Seales; therefore goe on,   1592

SEAT = 1*1

King takes his Seat, whispers Louell, who goes | to the Cardinall.   2001
Gardiner, seat themselues in Order on each side.   3040

SEATE = 1*2

Seate being left void aboue him, as for Canterburies Seate.   3038
Enter King frowning on them, takes his Seate.   3181

SEATED = 1

Cham. Well said my Lord: | So now y'are fairely seated: Gentlemen,   704

SEAUENTH = 1

Henry the Seauenth succeeding, truly pittying   958

SECOND = 2

Is posted as the Agent of our Cardinall, | To second all his plot. I do
assure you,   1903
His second Marriage shall be publishd, and   1914

SECR = 2

SECRECIE = 1

Crom. Last, that the Lady *Anne,* | Whom the King hath in secrecie long
married,   2315

SECRET = 4

2. This Secret is so weighty, 'twill require   993
The secret of your conference?   1265
Made me put this maine Secret in the Packet   2095
And durst commend a secret to your eare   2791

SECRETARIES = 1

of the Guard, and two Secretaries with Papers: The   176

SECRETARY see also Secr. = 7

Further in the proceeding. *Exit Secret.(ary)*   445
Prethee call *Gardiner* to me, my new Secretary.   1163
Newly preferr'd from the Kings Secretary: | The other London.   2526
O'th'Rolles, and the Kings Secretary. Further Sir,   2813
Cromwell at lower end, as Secretary.   3041
Chan. Speake to the businesse, M.(aster) Secretary;   3042
Gard. Good M.(aster) Secretary, | I cry your Honour mercie; you may
worst | Of all this Table say so.   3127

SECT = 1

Of this new Sect? ye are not sound.   3132

SECTARY = 1

Gard. My Lord, my Lord, you are a Sectary,   3119

SECUNDA *l.*316 1026 1824 2547 2987 = 5

SECUNDUS *l.*819 = 1

SEE = 39*1

May heere finde Truth too. Those that come to see   10
Ile vndertake may see away their shilling   13
A noyse of Targets: Or to see a Fellow   16
Be sad, as we would make ye. Thinke ye see   26
As they were Liuing: Thinke you see them Great,   28
Of thousand Friends: Then, in a moment, see   30
Pierce into that, but I can see his Pride   118
Wee see each graine of grauell; I doe know | To be corrupt and
treasonous.   229

SEE   *cont.*
Vnder pretence to see the Queene his Aunt,   253
Bran. I am sorry, | To see you tane from liberty, to looke on   287
And neuer seeke for ayd out of himselfe: yet see,   453
L.Ch. As farre as I see, all the good our English   576
That neuer see 'em pace before, the Spauen   584
To thinke an English Courtier may be wise, | And neuer see the *Louure.*   599
Find out, and he will take it. | *Card.* Let me see then,   785
1. Stay there Sir, | And see the noble ruin'd man you speake of.   893
Vaux. Prepare there, | The Duke is comming: See the Barge be ready;   942
Looke into these affaires, see this maine end,   1073
My *Wolsey,* see it furnish'd, O my Lord,   1196
Old.L. Why this it is: See, see,   1301
Suf. He ha's, and we shall see him | For it, an Arch-byshop.   1921
And no man see me more.   2107
It is to see a Nobleman want manners.   2204
(Not you) correct him. My heart weepes to see him | So little, of his
great Selfe.   2234
A Gentleman sent from the King, to see you.   2689
Let me ne're see againe. *Exit Messeng.*   2691
Keepe comfort to you, and this Morning see   2947
You are so mercifull. I see your end,   3110
Gard. Receiue him, | And see him safe i'th' Tower.   3158
Good man sit downe: Now let me see the proudest   3199
Not as a Groome: There's some of ye, I see,   3211
The common voyce I see is verified   3240
(You see the poore remainder) could distribute,   3277
Let me ne're hope to see a Chine againe,   3284
*might see from farre, some forty Truncheoners draw to   3310
*To all the Plaines about him: Our Childrens Children | Shall see this,
and blesse Heauen.   3425
An aged Princesse; many dayes shall see her,   3429
To see what this Child does, and praise my Maker.   3440
Ye must all see the Queene, and she must thanke ye,   3445
SEEING = 2*1
1 How was it? | 3 Well worth the seeing.   2479
And Princely Care, fore-seeing those fell Mischiefes,   2828
*Ile scratch your heads; you must be seeing Christenings?   3266
SEEKE = 4
And neuer seeke for ayd out of himselfe: yet see,   453
Seeke me out, and that way I am Wife in;   1662
To be thy Lord, and Master. Seeke the King   2328
Mens prayers then would seeke you, not their feares.   3136
SEEKES = 1
In them a wilder Nature, then the businesse | That seekes dispatch by
day.   2788
SEEKING = 1
Crom. My mind gaue me, | In seeking tales and Informations   3176
SEEKT = 1
Let him not seek't of vs: By day and night   567
SEEME = 1
For so they seeme; th'haue left their Barge and landed,   741
SEEMELY = 1
To make a seemely answer to such persons.   1817
SEEMES = 3*1
Norf. What's the cause? | *Cham.* It seemes the Marriage with his
Brothers Wife   1045

SEEMES *cont.*
Seemes to flow from him? How, i'th'name of Thrift 1970
It seemes you are in hast: and if there be 2784
King. Auoyd the Gallery. *Louel seemes to stay.* 2877
SEEMING = 2
In seeming to augment it, wasts it: be aduis'd; 218
You signe your Place, and Calling, in full seeming, 1468
SEENE = 3
Being now seene, possible enough, got credit | That *Beuis* was beleeu'd. 81
We haue seene him set himselfe. 1981
For you haue seene him open't. Read o're this, 2078
SELFE = 33
To one aboue it selfe. Each following day 60
Which Actions selfe, was tongue too. 87
Can aduise me like you: Be to your selfe, 206
That it do sindge your selfe. We may out-runne 214
More stronger to direct you then your selfe; 220
King. My life it selfe, and the best heart of it, 321
Queen. Thanke your Maiesty | That you would loue your selfe, and in that loue 339
More worthy this place then my selfe, to whom 778
Inuited by your Noble selfe, hath sent 1142
Euen of your selfe Lord Cardinall. | *Wol.* How? of me? 1178
You'ld venture an emballing: I my selfe 1259
An. Good Lady, | Make your selfe mirth with your particular fancy, 1323
Wol. I do professe | You speake not like your selfe: who euer yet 1443
Your selfe pronounce their Office. I must tell you, 1475
And like her true Nobility, she ha's | Carried her selfe towards me. 1506
Kin. I haue spoke long, be pleas'd your selfe to say | How farre you satisfide me. 1578
Qu. Haue I liu'd thus long (let me speake my selfe, 1758
Qu. My Lord, | I dare not make my selfe so guiltie, 1773
How you may hurt your selfe: I, vtterly 1797
If I haue vs'd my selfe vnmannerly, 1815
Into our hands, and to Confine your selfe 2113
(Not you) correct him. My heart weepes to see him | So little, of his great Selfe. 2234
I know my selfe now, and I feele within me, 2284
Loue thy selfe last, cherish those hearts that hate thee; 2358
Gard. Yes, yes, Sir *Thomas,* | There are that Dare, and I my selfe haue ventur'd 2818
You cannot with such freedome purge your selfe, 2899
There's none stands vnder more calumnious tongues, | Then I my selfe, poore man. 2910
Your selfe, and your Accusers, and to haue heard you | Without indurance further. 2919
Haue misdemean'd your selfe, and not a little: 3062
Cast none away: That I shall cleere my selfe, 3114
His Royall selfe in Iudgement comes to heare 3189
My Noble Partners, and my selfe thus pray 3370
As great in admiration as her selfe. 3413
SELFE-DRAWING = 1
Out of his Selfe-drawing Web. O giues vs note, 112
SELFE-METTLE = 1
Selfe-mettle tyres him: Not a man in England 205
SELL = 1
Does buy and sell his Honour as he pleases, 268

SELUES = 3
   Kin. Who's there I say? How dare you thrust your | (selues   1105
   'Twold fall vpon our selues.   3169
   Bid ye so farre forget your selues? I gaue ye   3212
SEMBLANCE = 1
   (As he made semblance of his duty) would | Haue put his knife into
   him.   549
SEND = 2
   Where this is question'd, send our Letters, with   435
   Gart. Heauen | From thy endlesse goodnesse, send prosperous life,   3364
SENDS = 1
   Sends you his Princely Commendations,   2706
SENNET = 1
   Trumpets, Sennet, and Cornets.   1333
SENT = 16*3
   Sent downe among 'em, which hath flaw'd the heart   348
   Hath sent to me, wishing me to permit   507
   Then Deputy of Ireland, who remou'd | Earle *Surrey*, was sent thither,
   and in hast too,   874
   He sent command to the Lord Mayor straight   1003
   * My Lord, the Horses your Lordship sent for, with all the   1028
   The King ha's sent me otherwhere: Besides   1096
   Inuited by your Noble selfe, hath sent   1142
   *They haue sent me such a Man, I would haue wish'd for.   1148
   Who had beene hither sent on the debating   1540
   Papers of State he sent me, to peruse   1984
   I sent the King? Is there no way to cure this?   2096
   You sent me Deputie for Ireland,   2148
   Sur. Item, You sent a large Commission | To *Gregory de Cassado*, to
   conclude   2218
   * Sur. Then, That you haue sent inumerable substance,   2224
   A Gentleman sent from the King, to see you.   2689
   I caus'd you write, yet sent away? | *Pat.* No Madam.   2717
   I sent your Message, who return'd her thankes   2845
   You do desire to know wherefore | I sent for you.   2883
   That was sent to me from the Councell, pray'd me   2990
SEPARATION = 1
   A buzzing of a Separation | Betweene the King and *Katherine*?   999
SERENISSIMA = *1
   * Card. Tanta est erga te mentis integritas Regina serenissima.   1664
SERGEANT = 2*1
   Enter Brandon, a Sergeant at Armes before him, and | two or three of the
   Guard.   276
   Brandon. Your Office Sergeant: execute it.   278
   *accompanyed with a Sergeant at Armes, bearing a   1341
SERGEANT = 1
SERIOUS = 3
   That beare a Weighty, and a Serious Brow,   3
   He did it with a Serious minde: a heede | Was in his countenance. You
   he bad   1934
   His Thinkings are below the Moone, not worth | His serious
   considering.   1999
SERU = 1
SERUANT *see also Seru.* = 6*2
   *Kin. I remember of such a time, being my sworn ser- | (uant,   542
   Enter a Seruant.   738
   Flying for succour to his Seruant *Banister*,   955

SERUANT *cont.*
Cardinall of *Yorke*, are ioyn'd with me their Seruant,   1153
My learn'd and welbeloued Seruant *Cranmer*,   1610
Was still inscrib'd: in which you brought the King | To be your Seruant.   2212
My Royall Nephew, and your name *Capuchius*. | *Cap.* Madam the
same. Your Seruant.   2695
*Lou. Many good nights, my Lord, I rest your seruant.   2835
SERUANTS = 2*1
Fell by our Seruants, by those Men we lou'd most: 968
*Those we professe, Peace-makers, Friends, and Seruants.   1804
That were the Seruants to this chosen Infant,   3419
SERUD = 2*1
*'em from me, with this reason: his maister would bee seru'd be-|fore   1033
Had I but seru'd my God, with halfe the Zeale   2370
I seru'd my King: he would not in mine Age   2371
SERUE = 2
(Domestickes to you) serue your will, as't please   1474
Serue the King: And prythee leade me in: 2365
SERUES = 1
Daring th'euent too th'teeth, are all in vprore, | And danger serues
among them.   364
SERUICE = 11
A most vnnaturall and faithlesse Seruice.   969
(And seruice to his Maiesty and you)   1676
Offers, as I doe, in a signe of peace, | His Seruice, and his Counsell. |
Queen. To betray me.   1691
To trust vs in your businesse) we are ready | To vse our vtmost Studies,
in your seruice.   1811
Pray do my seruice to his Maiestie,   1818
Weary, and old with Seruice, to the mercy   2264
Thy hopefull seruice perish too. Good *Cromwell*   2333
The King shall haue my seruice; but my prayres   2341
Cap. Noble Lady, | First mine owne seruice to your Grace, the next   2702
Am for his loue and seruice, so to him.   3229
Ye should doe Seruice. Harke the Trumpets sound,   3343
SESSION = 1
It's fit this Royall Session do proceed,   1422
SET = 9*1
I meane who set the Body, and the Limbes | Of this great Sport
together?   92
They are set heere for examples. | *L. Cham.* True, they are so;   651
*North. When they were ready to set out for London, a man   1031
I say, set on. | *Exeunt, in manner as they enter'd.*   1613
Enuy and base opinion set against 'em,   1660
In truth I know not. I was set at worke,   1700
That little thought when she set footing heere,   1822
We haue seene him set himselfe.   1981
(That Sun, I pray may neuer set) I haue told him,   2329
Patience, be neere me still, and set me lower,   2634
SETLED = 1
Matter against him, that for euer marres | The Hony of his Language.
No, he's setled   1851
SETTING = 1
I haste now to my Setting. I shall fall | Like a bright exhalation in the
Euening,   2105
SEUEN *see* 7.

SEUERALL = 2
Enter two Gentlemen at seuerall Doores.   820
Forsooth an Inuentory, thus importing | The seuerall parcels of his
Plate, his Treasure,   1987
SEUERING = 1
It from the bearer, 'tis a sufferance, panging | As soule and bodies
seuering.   1218
SHADE = 1
Fly o're thy Royall head, and shade thy person | Vnder their blessed
wings.   2965
SHADOW = 1
I am the shadow of poore *Buckingham*,   313
SHAKE = 2
In the old time of Warre, would shake the prease   2498
Her Foes shake like a Field of beaten Corne,   3401
SHAL *l.**2248 *3415 = *2
SHALL *l.*135 *185 186 267 275 285 290 297 328 420 444 454 463 515 517
632 655 656 *723 748 823 929 934 937 998 *1155 1161 1195 1292 1416
1436 1450 1462 1498 1510 1651 1777 1819 1820 1831 1892 1914 1916
1921 1940 1941 2052 2105 2181 2195 2199 *2248 2324 2341 2342 2347
2542 2543 2621 2669 2715 2739 2841 2897 2909 2923 2946 2948 2952
3002 3034 3105 3109 3114 3137 3217 *3239 *3287 3331 3347 3382 3390
3393 3395 3398 3400 3404 3407 3408 3410 3414 3417 3420 3421 3423
3426 3428 3429 3433 3434 3439 3444 3447 3448 = 102*6
SHAME = 3*3
**Queen.* The more shame for ye; holy men I thought ye,   1734
Mend 'em for shame my Lords: Is this your comfort?   1737
*To quench mine Honor; they would shame to make me   3009
Cham. This is too much; | Forbeare for shame my Lords.   3140
Why, what a shame was this? Did my Commission   3211
*Be friends for shame my Lords: My Lord of *Canterbury*   3231
SHAPE = 1
I doe pronounce him in that very shape   274
SHARPE = 5
Hath a sharpe edge: It's long, and't may be saide   170
Many sharpe reasons to defeat the Law.   841
Of the good Queene; but the sharpe thorny points   1594
Sur. Sharpe enough, | Lord for thy Iustice.   1949
By your good fauour, too sharpe; Men so Noble,   3123
SHARPST = 1
To the sharp'st kinde of Iustice. Please you, Sir,   1398
SHE = 48*2
SHEATH = 1
To sheath his knife in vs: he is attach'd,   564
SHED = 1
Card. Cromwel, I did not thinke to shed a teare   2343
SHEE *l.*2808 3283 = 2
SHEEL = 1
They say in great Extremity, and fear'd | Shee'l with the Labour, end.   2793
SHEES = 3*1
Old L. Alas poore Lady, | Shee's a stranger now againe.   1220
Shee's going away. | *Kin.* Call her againe.   1486
*The Queene of earthly Queenes: Shee's Noble borne;   1505
Shee's a good Creature, and sweet-Ladie do's | Deserùe our better
wishes.   2801
SHENGUILF = 1

SHEPHEARDS = *1
  *Shepheards, vsher'd by the Lord Chamberlaine. They   754
SHEW = 5*1
  Only to shew his pompe, as well in France,   238
  Sparing would shew a worse sinne, then ill Doctrine,   649
  An.B. You cannot shew me.   730
  Now, if you can blush, and crie guiltie Cardinall, | You'l shew a little
  Honestie.   2200
  Buts. Ile shew your Grace the strangest sight.   3016
  Kin. Good Man, those ioyfull teares shew thy true | (hearts,   3248
SHEWD = 4
  Shew'd like a Mine. Their Dwarfish Pages were   66
  Hath shew'd him gold; my life is spand already: 312
  In all the rest shew'd a most Noble patience.   865
  For such a one we shew'd 'em: If they smile,   3460
SHEWES = 1
  In Celebration of this day with Shewes, | Pageants, and Sights of Honor.   2390
SHEWNE = 1
  2 'Tis well: The Citizens | I am sure haue shewne at full their Royall
  minds,   2387
SHIELD = *1
  *Whose Honor Heauen shield from soile; euen he escapes | (not   353
SHILLING = 1
  Ile vndertake may see away their shilling   13
SHINE = 2
  Shall shine at full vpon them. Some attend him. | *All rise, and Tables
  remou'd.*   748
  Where euer the bright Sunne of Heauen shall shine,   3421
SHIPWRACKD = 1
  Shipwrack'd vpon a Kingdome, where no Pitty,   1785
SHIRE = 1
  Let there be Letters writ to euery Shire,   440
SHOALES = 1
  And sounded all the Depths, and Shoales of Honor,   2351
SHOLD *l.*1792 = *1
SHONE = 1
  Shone downe the English; and to morrow, they   64
SHOOKE = 1
  Sometimes our Brothers Wife. This respite shooke   1548
SHORE = 1
  As shore of Rocke: attend. This holy Foxe,   233
SHORT = 4*2
  Richly in two short houres. Onely they   14
  Short blistred Breeches, and those types of Trauell;   609
  Enter two Vergers, with short siluer wands; next them two   1334
  Haue euer come too short of my Desires,   2044
  And to be short, for not Appearance, and   2412
  *We will be short with you. 'Tis his Highnesse pleasure   3101
SHORTLY = 2
  Or di'de where they were made, or shortly after   1559
  Almost in Christendome: shortly (I beleeue)   1913
SHOT = *1
  *stil, when sodainly a File of Boyes behind 'em, loose shot,   3314
SHOULD *l.*126 422 474 513 534 571 650 681 687 777 792 876 1021 1283
  1375 1556 *1562 1643 1675 1823 1855 1958 1997 2033 2063 2069 2074
  2083 2159 2279 2403 2451 2581 2694 2735 2773 2918 3061 3124 3290
  *3299 3343 = 40*2

SHOULDER = *1
  Cornets. Enter King Henry, leaning on the Cardinals shoul-|der,   317
SHOULDERS = 1
  I humbly thanke his Grace: and from these shoulders   2287
SHOULDST *l.*2167 = 1
SHOW *see also* shew = 2
  Onely a show or two, and so agree,   11
  To ranke our chosen Truth with such a show   19
SHOWD *see* shew'd
SHOWERS = 1
  Euer sprung; as Sunne and Showers,   1625
SHOWES *see* shewes
SHOWNE *see* shewne
SHOWRD = 1
  Showr'd on me daily, haue bene more then could   2041
SHOWRE = 1 *1
  I showre a welcome on yee: welcome all.   752
  *deliuer'd such a showre of Pibbles, that I was faine to   3315
SHREWD = 2
  A fit or two o'th' face, (but they are shrewd ones)   578
  A shrewd turne, and hee's your friend for euer: 3251
SHRINKE = 1
  Cranmer will finde a Friend will not shrinke from him.   2533
SHROWDES = 1
  As the shrowdes make at Sea, in a stiffe Tempest,   2492
SHUNNING = 1
  That I aduice your shunning.   174
SHUT = 1
  Shut doore vpon me, and so giue me vp   1397
SICKE = 9
  By sicke Interpreters (once weake ones) is   417
  I would not be so sicke though for his place: 1128
  I then did feele full sicke, and yet not well,   1571
  Put my sicke cause into his hands, that hates me?   1750
  Where she remaines now sicke. | 2 Alas good Lady.   2417
  Enter Katherine Dowager, sicke, lead betweene Griffith,   2548
  Grif. How do's your Grace? | *Kath.* O *Griffith,* sicke to death: 2551
  He fell sicke sodainly, and grew so ill | He could not sit his Mule.   2568
  She will be sicke els. This day, no man thinke   3446
SICKEND = 1
  By this, so sicken'd their Estates, that neuer   134
SICKNESSE = 3
  That had the King in his last Sicknesse faild,   532
  So went to bed; where eagerly his sicknesse   2578
  To one mans Honour, this contagious sicknesse;   3074
SIDE = 4 *6
  places himselfe vnder the Kings feete on | his right side.   319
  Place you that side, Ile take the charge of this: 691
  side, accompanied with Sir Thomas Louell, Sir Nicholas   891
  Lou. To th' water side I must conduct your Grace;   939
  Siluer Pillers: After them, side by side, the two Cardinals,   1343
  each side the Court in manner of a Consistory: Below them   1348
  Pearle, Crowned. On each side her, the Bishops of London, | *and*
  Winchester,   2439
  2 What two Reuerend Byshops | Were those that went on each side of
  the Queene?   2523
  Gardiner, seat themselues in Order on each side.   3040

SIDES = 2
The sides of loyalty, and almost appeares | In lowd Rebellion. 355
And on all sides th'Authority allow'd, 1355
SIGHT = 2
If my sight faile not, | You should be Lord Ambassador from the
Emperor, 2693
Buts. Ile shew your Grace the strangest sight. 3016
SIGHTS = 1
In Celebration of this day with Shewes, | Pageants, and Sights of Honor. 2390
SIGNE = 2
You signe your Place, and Calling, in full seeming, 1468
Offers, as I doe, in a signe of peace, | His Seruice, and his Counsell. |
Queen. To betray me. 1691
SIGNES = *1
(as it were by inspiration) she makes (in her sleepe) signes of 2654
SILENCD = 1
Abur. Is it therefore | Th'Ambassador is silenc'd? | *Nor.* Marry is't. 153
SILENCE = 3
*In their faire cheekes my Lord, then wee shall haue 'em, | Talke vs to
silence. 723
Let silence be commanded. 1352
To silence enuious Tongues. Be iust, and feare not; 2361
SILLABLE = 1
Buck. No, not a sillable: 273
SILUER = *5
Enter two Vergers, with short siluer wands; next them two 1334
each a Siluer Crosse: Then a Gentleman Vsher bare-| headed, 1340
Siluer Mace: Then two Gentlemen bearing two great 1342
Siluer Pillers: After them, side by side, the two Cardinals, 1343
*bearing the Rod of Siluer with the Doue, Crowned with an | Earles
Coronet. Collars of Esses.* 2431
SIMPLE = 1
Queen. My Lord, My Lord, | I am a simple woman, much too weake 1465
SINCE = 11
Since last we saw in France? 40
Healthfull, and euer since a fresh Admirer | Of what I saw there. 42
I am not such a Truant since my comming, 1666
Since Vertue findes no friends) a Wife, a true one? 1759
His word vpon you. Since I had my Office, 2028
Since you prouoke me, shall be most notorious. 2181
Which since they are of you, and odious, | I will not taint my mouth
with. 2229
Since which, she was remou'd to Kymmalton, 2416
For since the Cardinall fell, that Titles lost, 2518
Saw ye none enter since I slept? | *Grif.* None Madam. 2662
With me, since first you knew me. 2699
SINCERE = 1
From sincere motions, by Intelligence, 227
SINCERELY = 1
Perceiue I speake sincerely, and high notes 1275
SINCKE = 1
And if I haue a Conscience, let it sincke me, 901
SINDGE = 1
That it do sindge your selfe. We may out-runne 214
SING = 3
Sing, and djsperse 'em if thou canst: leaue working. 1619
Bow themselues when he did sing. 1623

SING *cont.*
Vnder his owne Vine what he plants; and sing   3405
SINGING = 1
4 Quirristers *singing. Musicke.*   2425
SINGLE = 4
Till this time Pompe was single, but now married   59
Card. Please you Sir, | I know but of a single part in ought   370
A single voice, and that not past me, but   405
(I speake it with a single heart, my Lords)   3086
SINGULAR = 1
Of singular Integrity, and Learning;   1414
SINKE = 2
But where they meane to sinke ye: all good people   977
A loade, would sinke a Nauy, (too much Honor.)   2289
SINNE = 5
Sparing would shew a worse sinne, then ill Doctrine,   649
The willing'st sinne I euer yet committed, | May be absolu'd in English.   1672
Sur. Thy Ambition | (Thou Scarlet sinne) robb'd this bewailing Land   2142
By that sinne fell the Angels: how can man then   2356
(Which was a sinne) yet in bestowing, Madam,   2614
SINNES = 1
Produce the grand summe of his sinnes, the Articles   2186
SINS = 1
But Cardinall Sins, and hollow hearts I feare ye: 1736
SIR *see also S.Hen.Guilf. l.*106 223 *244 279 318 370 493 533 541 589 590
633 655 657 665 678 679 690 700 798 804 826 847 *891 892 893 925 940
946 984 992 998 1006 *1034 1119 1122 1367 1372 1388 1398 1408 1427 1508
1722 1854 2013 2202 2276 2303 2373 2393 *2402 2458 *2473 2481 2489
2516 2546 2719 2770 *2776 2779 *2783 2797 2803 2804 2807 2810 2813
2818 2821 2831 2833 2839 2865 2866 *2867 2973 2978 3204 3269 3278
3279 3280 *3298 3384 = 78*10
SIRHA = 1
Keepe the dore close Sirha.   3288
SISTER = 2
The French Kings Sister. Heauen will one day open   1074
The French Kings Sister; He shall marry her.   1941
SIT = 10*2
We should take roote here, where we sit;   422
Or sit State-Statues onely.   423
As if besmear'd in hell. Sit by Vs, you shall heare   463
Cham. Sweet Ladies will it please you sit; Sir *Harry*   690
Pray sit betweene these Ladies.   695
place vnder the Cloth of State. The two Cardinalls sit   1345
the Scribes. The Lords sit next the Bishops. The rest of the   1349
He fell sicke sodainly, and grew so ill | He could not sit his Mule.   2568
I nam'd my Knell; whil'st I sit meditating   2637
Grif. She is asleep: Good wench, let's sit down quiet,   2640
To sit heere at this present, and behold   3057
Good man sit downe: Now let me see the proudest   3199
SITS = 2
*Exit Lord Chamberlaine, and the King drawes the Curtaine | and sits
reading pensiuely.*   1100
Heauen is aboue all yet; there sits a Iudge, | That no King can corrupt.   1731
SIXE *see also* 6. = 1*1
Held a late Court at Dunstable; sixe miles off   2409

SIXE *cont.*
   The Vision. | *Enter solemnely tripping one after another, sixe*
   Personages,   2642
SIXT = 2
   The sixt part of his Substance, to be leuied   391
   And sticke them in our Will. Sixt part of each?   430
SIXTEENE = 1
   I haue beene begging sixteene yeares in Court   1302
SIZE = 1
   Of as great Size. Weene you of better lucke,   2936
SKIRT = 1
   Is longer then his fore-skirt; by this time   1320
SLANDER = 1
   2. But that slander Sir, | Is found a truth now: for it growes agen   1006
SLAUE = 1
   This tractable obedience is a Slaue   397
SLAUERY = 1
   Suff. And free vs from his slauery.   1077
SLAUES = *1
   *you take the Court for Parish Garden: ye rude Slaues, | leaue your
   gaping.   3260
SLEEKE = 1
   As if it fed ye, and how sleeke and wanton   2126
SLEEPE = 5*1
   And sleepe in dull cold Marble, where no mention   2348
   (as it were by inspiration) she makes (in her sleepe) signes of   2654
   Till *Cranmer, Cromwel,* her two hands, and shee | Sleepe in their
   Graues.   2808
   To scatter 'em, as 'tis to make 'em sleepe   3271
   Nor shall this peace sleepe with her: But as when   3410
   And sleepe an Act or two; but those we feare   3452
SLEEPES = 1
   When he ha's run his course, and sleepes in Blessings,   2309
SLEEPING = 1
   Haue wish'd the sleeping of this busines, neuer desir'd   1529
SLEPT = 3
   The Kings eyes, that so long haue slept vpon | This bold bad man.   1075
   His blessed part to Heauen, and slept in peace.   2584
   Saw ye none enter since I slept? | *Grif.* None Madam.   2662
SLIGHTLY = 1
   Gone slightly o're lowe steppes, and now are mounted   1472
SLOTH = 1
   This dilatory sloth, and trickes of Rome.   1609
SLOW = 1
   Requires slow pace at first. Anger is like   203
SLUMBER = 1
   Not wake him in his slumber. A Beggers booke, | Out-worths a Nobles
   blood.   190
SLYE = 1
   Louell. I marry, | There will be woe indeed Lords, the slye whorsons   618
SMALL = 1*3
   Hoboies. A small Table vnder a State for the Cardinall, a   661
   Rochester, and S.(aint) Asaph: Next them, with some small   1337
   Your Enemies are many, and not small; their practises   2929
   Wife of small wit, neere him, that rail'd vpon me,   3306
SMART = 1
   That she should feele the smart of this: the Cardinall   1021

SMILE = 3
    I stood not in the smile of Heauen, who had   1554
    There is betwixt that smile we would aspire too,   2269
    For such a one we shew'd 'em: If they smile,   3460
SMILES = 1
    Vpon my smiles. Go get thee from me *Cromwel*,   2326
SMILING = 1
    Exit King, frowning vpon the Cardinall, the Nobles | throng after him
    smiling, and whispering.   2081
SNUFFE = 1
    This Candle burnes not cleere, 'tis I must snuffe it,   1954
SO *l*.11 78 134 182 213 241 243 306 454 457 474 528 535 574 581 602 615
    652 653 705 717 741 760 794 821 836 855 868 993 1050 1075 1086 1089
    1128 1150 1158 1181 1182 1189 1198 1204 1207 1222 1233 1235 1294
    1357 1397 1428 1464 1525 1580 1581 1601 1638 1657 1661 1677 1695
    1697 1714 1774 1800 1805 1823 1923 1924 2046 2061 2086 2089 2118
    2141 2194 2235 2245 2249 2251 2283 2338 2374 2380 2465 2469 2486
    2501 2513 2521 2555 2568 2578 2585 2619 2620 *2655 2686 2714 2732
    2757 2777 2823 2826 *2850 2999 3001 3027 3029 3065 3110 3123 3129
    3135 3212 3229 3255 *3293 3335 3382 3383 3414 3418 3438
    3453 = 125*3
SO *l*.1203 = 1
SOCIETY = 1
    They are a sweet society of faire ones.   683
SODAIN = 1
    Card. That's somewhat sodain.   2305
SODAINE = 5*1
    Dashing the Garment of this Peace, aboaded | The sodaine breach on't.   148
    Stops on a sodaine, lookes vpon the ground,   1976
    What sodaine Anger's this? How haue I reap'd it?   2084
    Pati. Do you note | How much her Grace is alter'd on the sodaine?   2674
    Gard. Which Reformation must be sodaine too   3068
    Kin. You were euer good at sodaine Commendations,   3191
SODAINLY = 3*1
    But how to make ye sodainly an Answere   1696
    He fell sicke sodainly, and grew so ill | He could not sit his Mule.   2568
    *stil, when sodainly a File of Boyes behind 'em, loose shot,   3314
    By th' heeles, and sodainly: and on your heads   3340
SOFT = 1
    (Sauing your mincing) the capacity | Of your soft Chiuerell Conscience,
    would receiue,   1239
SOFTLY = 1
    For feare we wake her. Softly, gentle *Patience.*   2641
SOILE = *1
    *Whose Honor Heauen shield from soile; euen he escapes | (not   353
SOLEMNE = 1
    On that Coelestiall Harmony I go too. | *Sad and solemne Musicke.*   2638
SOLEMNELY = *1
    *The Vision. | *Enter solemnely tripping one after another, sixe*
    Personages,   2642
SOLICITED = 1
    Queen. I am solicited not by a few,   345
SOLLEMNLY = 1
    He sollemnly had sworne, that what he spoke   511
SOME = 26*7
    Would by a good Discourser loose some life,   86
    Abur. I cannot tell | What Heauen hath giuen him: let some Grauer eye   116

SOME *cont.*

He bores me with some tricke; He's gone to'th'King:	198
Breed him some preiudice; for from this League,	258
To heare from him a matter of some moment:	509
It forg'd him some designe, which being beleeu'd	529
But halfe my Lay-thoughts in him, some of these	680
Card. What's that? | *Cham.* Looke out there, some of ye.	733
Shall shine at full vpon them. Some attend him. | *All rise, and Tables remou'd.*	748
Or some about him neere, haue out of malice	1010
Norf. Let's in; | And with some other busines, put the King	1091
Rochester, and S.(aint) Asaph: Next them, with some small	1337
vnder him as Iudges. The Queene takes place some di-|stance	1346
Barke when their fellowes doe. By some of these	1526
*Pray speake in English; heere are some will thanke you,	1669
To some eares vnrecounted. But my Lords	1889
Will fall some blessing to this Land, which shall | In it be memoriz'd.	1892
Nor. My Lord, we haue | *Stood heere obseruing him. Some strange Commotion	1973
Some Spirit put this paper in the Packet, | To blesse your eye withall.	1993
Some of these Articles, and out they shall.	2199
Some little memory of me, will stirre him	2331
To rest a while, some halfe an houre, or so,	2486
My next poore Petition, | Is, that his Noble Grace would haue some pittie	2730
Some touch of your late businesse: Affaires that walke	2786
I should haue tane some paines, to bring together	2918
This is of purpose laid by some that hate me,	3007
Let some o'th' Guard be ready there.	3154
I had thought, I had had men of some vnderstanding,	3205
Not as a Groome: There's some of ye, I see,	3214
*to muster in? Or haue wee some strange Indian with the	3292
*might see from farre, some forty Truncheoners draw to	3310
*their deare Brothers are able to endure. I haue some of	3321
All that are heere: Some come to take their ease,	3451

SOMETHING = 3

Nor. He is vex'd at something.	1963
Something I can command. As I walke thither, | Ile tell ye more.	2544
And something ouer to remember me by.	2743

SOMETIMES = 2

Sometimes our Brothers Wife. This respite shooke	1548
2 Their Coronets say so. These are Starres indeed, | And sometimes falling ones.	2469

SOMEWHAT = 1*1

Card. That's somewhat sodain.	2305
*a fellow somewhat neere the doore, he should be a Brasi-|er	3299

SOMTHING = 2*3

To heare this of him; and could wish he were | Somthing mistaken in't.	271
Kin. Ther's somthing more would out of thee; what | (say'st?	555
And somthing spoke in choller, ill, and hasty:	863
*Farewell; and when you would say somthing that is sad, | Speake how I fell.	980
Sur. I would 'twer somthing y would fret the string,	1965

SONG = 3

A French Song, and a Fiddle, ha's no Fellow.	621
A long time out of play, may bring his plaine song,	626
SONG. | *Orpheus with his Lute made Trees,*	1620

Full isolation

SONGS = 1
The merry Songs of Peace to all his Neighbours.   3406
SONNE = 4
I'ue heard him vtter to his Sonne in Law,   476
Made my Name once more Noble. Now his Sonne,   961
That blinde Priest, like the eldest Sonne of Fortune,   1052
I her fraile sonne, among'st my Brethren mortall, | Must giue my
tendance to.   2018
SOONE = 2
How soone this Mightinesse, meets Misery: 31
(As soone he shall by me) that thus the Cardinall   267
SOONER = 1
Will make this sting the sooner. Cardinall *Campeius,*   1900
SOOTH = 1
Which, to say sooth, are Blessings; and which guifts   1238
SORELY = 1
As a man sorely tainted, to his Answer,   2567
SORRIE = 1
And am right sorrie to repeat what followes.   2893
SORROW = 5
Then to be perk'd vp in a glistring griefe, | And weare a golden sorrow.   1226
Nor to betray you any way to sorrow;   1680
With what a sorrow *Cromwel* leaues his Lord.   2340
1 'Tis very true. But that time offer'd sorrow, | This generall ioy.   2385
And hang their heads with sorrow: 3402
SORROWES = 1
We are to Cure such sorrowes, not to sowe 'em.   1795
SORROWES = 3
Our Mistris Sorrowes we were pittying.   1268
The burthen of my sorrowes, fall vpon ye.   1743
Continuall Meditations, Teares, and Sorrowes,   2582
SORRY = 7
And for his owne aduantage. | *Norf.* I am sorry   269
Bran. I am sorry, | To see you tane from liberty, to looke on   287
Queen. I am sorry, that the Duke of *Buckingham* | Is run in your
displeasure.   447
2. I am sorry fort. | 1. So are a number more.   835
Yea, subiect to your Countenance: Glad, or sorry,   1380
Card. Noble Lady, | I am sorry my integrity should breed,   1674
Chan. My good Lord Archbishop, I'm very sorry   3056
SOUERAIGNE = 6
Arrest thee of High Treason, in the name | Of our most Soueraigne
King.   282
(Whereof my Soueraigne would haue note) they are   379
Soueraigne and Pious els, could speake thee out)   1504
Car. My Soueraigne, I confesse your Royall graces   2040
Gard. Dread Soueraigne, | How much are we bound to Heauen,   3182
Chan. Thus farre | My most dread Soueraigne, may it like your Grace,   3218
SOUERAIGNTY = 2
His Confessor, who fed him euery minute | With words of Soueraignty.   494
Affected Eminence, Wealth, Soueraignty;   1237
SOUGHT = 3
But those that sought it, I could wish more Christians: 905
But, to those men that sought him, sweet as Summer.   2612
(God turne their hearts, I neuer sought their malice)   3008
SOULE = 19
I say againe there is no English Soule   219

SOULE *cont.*

And spoyle your nobler Soule; I say, take heed;	522
Sur. On my Soule, Ile speake but truth.	525
And lift my Soule to Heauen. | Lead on a Gods name.	920
Yet are the Kings; and till my Soule forsake,	933
He diues into the Kings Soule, and there scatters	1059
It from the bearer, 'tis a sufferance, panging | As soule and bodies seuering.	1218
I vtterly abhorre; yea, from my Soule	1439
My Soule growes sad with troubles,	1618
Could speake this with as free a Soule as I doe.	1656
Vpon my Soule two reuerend Cardinall Vertues:	1735
A Soule as euen as a Calme; Pray thinke vs,	1803
And throw it from their Soule, though perils did	2070
Sur. By my Soule, | Your long Coat (Priest) protects you,	2165
(Out of a Fortitude of Soule, I feele)	2296
Sir, as I haue a Soule, she is an Angell;	2458
For Vertue, and true Beautie of the Soule,	2736
I sweare he is true-hearted, and a soule	2957
Then this pure Soule shall be. All Princely Graces	3395

SOULES = 2

As you wish Christian peace to soules departed,	2748
Win straying Soules with modesty againe,	3113

SOUND = 6

The Trumpets sound: Stand close,	2419
Of this new Sect? ye are not sound.	3132
Crom. Not sound? | *Gard.* Not sound I say.	3133
As much as one sound Cudgell of foure foote,	3276
Ye should doe Seruice. Harke the Trumpets sound,	3343

SOUNDED = 1

And sounded all the Depths, and Shoales of Honor,	2351

SOUNDER = 1

Dare mate a sounder man then Surrie can be, | And all that loue his follies.	2163

SOUNDING = *1

Enter Trumpets sounding: Then two Aldermen, L.(ord) Maior,	3354

SOWE = 1

We are to Cure such sorrowes, not to sowe 'em.	1795

SOWRE = 1

Lofty, and sowre to them that lou'd him not:	2611

SPAINE = 2

My Father, King of Spaine, was reckon'd one	1402
Be by my Friends in Spaine, aduis'd; whose Counsaile	1409

SPAKE = 2

A Royall Lady, spake one, the least word that might	1518
Lou. This is about that, which the Byshop spake, | I am happily come hither.	2874

SPAN = 1

To steale from Spirituall leysure, a briefe span	2009

SPAND = 1

Hath shew'd him gold; my life is spand already:	312

SPANIARD = 1

The Spaniard tide by blood and fauour to her,	1137

SPANIELL = 1

To me you cannot reach. You play the Spaniell,	3195

SPARD = 1

To mow 'em downe before me: but if I spar'd any	3281

SPARE = 3*2
  You may then spare that time. | *Car.* Bee't so, proceed.   1356
  Beseech you Sir, to spare me, till I may   1408
  **Dance:* and at certaine Changes, the first two hold a spare*   2647
  **Kin.* Come, come my Lord, you'd spare your spoones;   3238
  I made no spare Sir. | *Port.* You did nothing Sir.   3278
SPARING = 1
  Sparing would shew a worse sinne, then ill Doctrine,   649
SPARKES = 1
  Ile turne to sparkes of fire.   1430
SPAUEN = 1
  That neuer see 'em pace before, the Spauen   584
SPEAK = 1*1
  **Cham.* Because they speak no English, thus they praid   758
  Is the Kings hand, and tongue, and who dare speak | One syllable
  against him?   2816
SPEAKE = 35*2
  Kin. Speake freely.   471
  Kin. Speake on; | How grounded hee his Title to the Crowne   486
  Vpon our faile; to this poynt hast thou heard him, | At any time speake
  ought?   488
  Sur. On my Soule, Ile speake but truth.   525
  Card. Good Lord Chamberlaine, | *Go, giue 'em welcome; you can
  speake the French tongue   744
  2. Pray speake what ha's happen'd.   830
  1. Stay there Sir, | And see the noble ruin'd man you speake of.   893
  And if he speake of *Buckingham*; pray tell him,   931
  *Farewell; and when you would say somthing that is sad, | Speake how
  I fell.   980
  Norff. This Priest ha's no pride in him? | *Suff.* Not to speake of: 1126
  Perceiue I speake sincerely, and high notes   1275
  Vouchsafe to speake my thankes, and my obedience,   1288
  Qu. Lord Cardinall, to you I speake. | *Wol.* Your pleasure, Madam.   1425
  Wol. I do professe | You speake not like your selfe: who euer yet   1443
  His Highnesse shall speake in, I do beseech   1462
  Soueraigne and Pious els, could speake thee out)   1504
  I speake my good Lord Cardnall, to this point;   1532
  Queen. Would they speake with me? | *Gent.* They wil'd me say so
  Madam.   1637
  The full cause of our comming. | *Queen.* Speake it heere.   1652
  Could speake this with as free a Soule as I doe.   1656
  *Pray speake in English; heere are some will thanke you,   1669
  If you speake truth, for their poore Mistris sake;   1670
  Ye speake like honest men, (pray God ye proue so)   1695
  Qu. Haue I liu'd thus long (let me speake my selfe,   1758
  Cham. My Lords, you speake your pleasures: 1842
  Wol. Speake on Sir, | I dare your worst Obiections: If I blush,   2202
  Crom. I haue no power to speake Sir. | *Car.* What, amaz'd | At my
  misfortunes? Can thy Spirit wonder   2276
  2 Good Sir, speake it to vs? | 3 As well as I am able. The rich streame   2481
  Yet thus farre *Griffith*, giue me leaue to speake him,   2587
  To heare me speake his good now? | *Kath.* Yes good *Griffith*,   2603
  That Christendome shall euer speake his Vertue.   2621
  Louell. Now Sir, you speake of two | The most remark'd i'th'Kingdome:
  as for *Cromwell*,   2810
  To speake my minde of him: and indeed this day,   2820
  Ah my good Lord, I greeue at what I speake,   2892

SPEAKE *cont.*
Chan. Speake to the businesse, M.(aster) Secretary;   3042
(I speake it with a single heart, my Lords)   3086
Cran. Let me speake Sir, | For Heauen now bids me; and the words I
vtter,   3384
SPEAKER = 2
The Gentleman is Learn'd, and a most rare Speaker,   450
No other speaker of my liuing Actions,   2628
SPEAKES = 1
The Troope passe once about the Stage, and Gar-| ter speakes.   3362
SPEAKES = 1
I finde at such proud Rate, that it out-speakes | Possession of a Subiect. 1990
SPEAKES = 1
*goes about the Court, comes to the King, and kneeles at | his Feete.
Then speakes.*   1365
SPEAKEST = 1
Kin. Thou speakest wonders.   3427
SPEAKING = 2
You (gracious Madam) to vnthinke your speaking, | And to say so no
more.   1463
For speaking false in that; thou art alone   1500
SPEAKS = 1
These newes are euery where, euery tongue speaks 'em,   1071
SPED = 1
Sur. Not long before your Highnesse sped to France,   497
SPEECH = 3
His houre of speech, a minute: He, (my Lady)   460
It would infect his Speech: That if the King   473
What was the speech among the Londoners,   500
SPEECHES = 1
Scruple, and pricke, on certaine Speeches vtter'd   1538
SPEED = 1
Buc. The diuell speed him: No mans Pye is freed   100
SPEEDILY = 1
No, wee'l no *Bullens*: Speedily I wish   1944
SPEEDING = 1
Haue got a speeding tricke to lay downe Ladies.   620
SPELL = 1
Nor. O feare him not, | His spell in that is out: the King hath found 1849
SPELS = 1
L.Ch. Is't possible the spels of France should iuggle   571
SPICE = 1
For all this spice of your Hipocrisie: 1234
SPIDER-LIKE = 1
To eminent Assistants; but Spider-like   111
SPIGHT = 1
A way, if it take right, in spight of Fortune   2099
SPINSTERS = 1
The Spinsters, Carders, Fullers, Weauers, who   361
SPIRIT = 3*1
Card. Stand forth, & with bold spirit relate what you   468
With these weake Womens feares. A Noble Spirit   1807
Some Spirit put this paper in the Packet, | To blesse your eye withall. 1993
Crom. I haue no power to speake Sir. | *Car.* What, amaz'd | At my
misfortunes? Can thy Spirit wonder   2276
SPIRITS = 3*1
The Noble Spirits to Armes, they did performe   79

SPIRITS *cont.*

So much they loue it. But to stubborne Spirits,	1800
Kath. Spirits of peace, where are ye? Are ye all gone?	2658
(As they say Spirits do) at midnight, haue	2787

SPIRITUALL = 3

Your high profession Spirituall. That agen	1477
And fixt on Spirituall obiect, he should still	1997
To steale from Spirituall leysure, a briefe span	2009

SPIT = 1

Tongues spit their duties out, and cold hearts freeze	394

SPITTING = 1

Yea, with a spitting power, and made to tremble	1550

SPLEENE = 3

You charge not in your spleene a Noble person,	521
I haue no Spleene against you, nor iniustice	1448
Is cramm'd with Arrogancie, Spleene, and Pride.	1470

SPLEENY = 1

A spleeny Lutheran, and not wholsome to	1957

SPOKE = 7

Spoke by a holy Monke, that oft, sayes he,	506
He sollemnly had sworne, that what he spoke	511
For I was spoke to, with Sir *Henry Guilford* | This night to be Comptrollers.	657
He spoke, and learnedly for life: But all	857
And somthing spoke in choller, ill, and hasty:	863
And say I spoke with you. | *Exit Lord Chamberlaine.*	1298
Kin. I haue spoke long, be pleas'd your selfe to say | How farre you satisfide me.	1578

SPOKEN = 3

Camp. His Grace | Hath spoken well, and iustly: Therefore Madam,	1420
King. 'Tis Nobly spoken:	2076
Exceeding wise, faire spoken, and perswading:	2610

SPOONES = *2

Kin. Come, come my Lord, you'd spare your spoones;	3238
Man. The Spoones will be the bigger Sir: There is	3298

SPORT = 1

I meane who set the Body, and the Limbes | Of this great Sport together?	92

SPOTLESSE = 1

Wol. So much fairer | And spotlesse, shall mine Innocence arise,	2194

SPOYLE = 1

And spoyle your nobler Soule; I say, take heed;	522

SPREAD = 1*1

Another spread on's breast, mounting his eyes,	558
Camp. Beleeue me, there's an ill opinion spread then,	1177

SPRING = 1

There had made a lasting Spring.	1626

SPRINGS = 1

Springs out into fast gate, then stops againe,	1978

SPRING-HALT = 1

A Spring-halt rain'd among 'em.	585

SPRUNG = 2

Euer sprung; as Sunne and Showers,	1625
Our hard rul'd King. Againe, there is sprung vp	1959

SPURRE = *1

*But stop their mouthes with stubborn Bits & spurre 'em,	3071

STAFFE = *2
    *length they came to th' broome staffe to me, I defide 'em   3313
    *Staffe, Duke of Suffolke, two Noblemen, bearing great   3356
STAFFORD = 1
    Of Hertford, Stafford and Northampton, I   281
STAGE = 1*2
    Attendants stand in conuenient order about the Stage.   1350
    *Exeunt, first passing ouer the Stage in Order and State, and | then, A
    great Flourish of Trumpets.   2445
    *The Troope passe once about the Stage, and Gar-| ter speakes.   3362
STAGGER = 1
    Lin. So please your Highnes, | The question did at first so stagger me,   1580
STAID = 1
    Buck. An vntimely Ague | Staid me a Prisoner in my Chamber, when   44
STAMPE = 1
    The stampe of Noblenesse in any person | Out of himselfe?   1840
STAMPT = 1
    Your holy-Hat to be stampt on the Kings Coine.   2223
STAND = 18*2
    For our best Act: if we shall stand still,   420
    *Card. Stand forth, & with bold spirit relate what you   468
    2. Let's stand close and behold him.   895
    As I am made without him, so Ile stand,   1086
    Attendants stand in conuenient order about the Stage.   1350
    How you stand minded in the waighty difference   1682
    Cannot stand vnder them. If you omit   1829
    Should the approach of this wildè Riuer breake, | And stand vnshaken
    yours.   -   2074
    1 You come to take your stand heere, and behold   2381
    The Trumpets sound: Stand close,   2419
    Stand these poore peoples Friend, and vrge the King | To do me this
    last right.   2749
    King. Stand vp, good Canterbury,   2912
    In vs thy Friend. Giue me thy hand, stand vp,   2914
    Cran. Most dread Liege, | The good I stand on, is my Truth and
    Honestie: 2921
    That Chayre stand empty: But we all are men   3058
    Be what they will, may stand forth face to face,   3095
    *now reigne in's Nose; all that stand about him are   3301
    Man. You great fellow, | Stand close vp, or Ile make your head ake.   3349
    Kin. Stand vp Lord,   3377
    And so stand fix'd. Peace, Plenty, Loue, Truth, Terror,   3418
STANDING = 1*1
    Enter Cromwell, standing amazed.   2274
    *standing Bowles for the Christening Guifts: Then foure   3357
STANDS = 2*3
    Stands in the gap and Trade of moe Preferments,   2814
    There's none stands vnder more calumnious tongues, | Then I my selfe,
    poore man.   2910
    King. Know you not | *How your state stands i'th'world, with the whole
    world?   2927
    *Cham. Then thus for you my Lord, it stands agreed   3144
    *was his Nose discharged against mee; hee stands there   3304
STARE = 1
    Ile follow, and out-stare him. | Nor. Stay my Lord,   199

STARRES = 1
  2 Their Coronets say so. These are Starres indeed, | And sometimes
falling ones.   2469
STARTLE = 1
  Collected from his life. Ile startle you   2187
STARTS = 1
  Is in his braine: He bites his lip, and starts,   1975
STARUE = 1
  By all that's holy, he had better starue,   3201
STAR-LIKE = 1
  Shall Star-like rise, as great in fame as she was,   3417
STATE = 22*6
  Sad, high, and working, full of State and Woe: 4
  Nor. Like it your Grace, | The State takes notice of the priuate
difference   160
  Suffolke: she kneels. King riseth from his State,   331
  Pertaines to th'State; and front but in that File   372
  To *Pepin* or *Clotharius,* they keepe State so.   581
  Hoboies. A small Table vnder a State for the Cardinall, a   661
  Hoboyes. Enter Cardinall Wolsey, and takes his State.   710
  2. That tricke of State | Was a deepe enuious one,   877
  Buck. Nay, Sir *Nicholas,* | Let it alone; my State now will but mocke
me.   946
  place vnder the Cloth of State. The two Cardinalls sit   1345
  Be to the preiudice of her present State,   1519
  Bearing a State of mighty moment in't,   1582
  To weare our mortall State to come, with her,   1598
  Papers of State he sent me, to peruse   1984
  I beare i'th'State: and Nature does require   2016
  King. Haue I not made you | The prime man of the State? I pray you
tell me,   2035
  The profit of the State. For your great Graces   2048
  As you respect the common good, the State   2183
  This is the state of Man; to day he puts forth   2253
  Exeunt, first passing ouer the Stage in Order and State, and | then, *A
great Flourish of Trumpets.*   2445
  In a rich Chaire of State, opposing freely   2487
  And with the same full State pac'd backe againe   2514
  An old man, broken with the stormes of State,   2575
  King. Know you not | *How your state stands i'th'world, with the whole
world?   2927
  Who holds his State at dore 'mongst Purseuants, | Pages, and
Foot-boyes.   3022
  placed vnder the State. Enter Lord Chancellour, places   3036
  Of the whole State; as of late dayes our neighbours,   3077
  *such a combustion in the State. I mist the Meteor once,   3308
STATES = 1
  Without the Kings will, or the States allowance,   2220
STATE-STATUES = 1
  Or sit State-Statues onely.   423
STATUES = 1
  Or sit State-Statues onely.   423
STAUES = *1
  *staues, and strong ones; these are but switches to 'em: 3265
STAY = 7
  Ile follow, and out-stare him. | *Nor.* Stay my Lord,   199
  1. Stay there Sir, | And see the noble ruin'd man you speake of.   893

STAY *cont.*

To stay the Iudgement o'th'Diuorce; for if	1868
Till you heare further from his Highnesse. | *Car.* Stay:	2115
King. Auoyd the Gallery. *Louel seemes to stay.*	2877
Cran. Stay good my Lords, | I haue a little yet to say. Looke there my Lords,	3160
'Has businesse at his house; for all shall stay:	3447

STAYES = 1

My Barge stayes; | Your Lordship shall along: Come, good Sir *Thomas,*	654

STAYING = 1

My hast made me vnmannerly. There is staying	2688

STEALE = 1

To steale from Spirituall leysure, a briefe span	2009

STEELE = 1

And as the long diuorce of Steele fals on me,	918

STEEPE = 1

What 'tis you go about: to climbe steepe hilles	202

STEERE = 1

The wild Sea of my Conscience, I did steere	1567

STEPPES = 1

Gone slightly o're lowe steppes, and now are mounted	1472

STEPS = 1

Where others tell steps with me.	373

STEPT = 1

If well, he stept before me happily | For my example.	2562

STEWARD = 2*1

To be high Steward; Next the Duke of Norfolke,	2400
head, bearing a long white Wand, as High Steward. With	2434
1 'Tis the same: high Steward.	2453

STICKE = 2

And sticke them in our Will. Sixt part of each?	430
Camp. They will not sticke to say, you enuide him;	1180

STIFFE = 1

As the shrowdes make at Sea, in a stiffe Tempest,	2492

STIFLED = 1

Could not be wedg'd in more: I am stifled | With the meere ranknesse of their ioy.	2475

STIL = *1

*stil, when sodainly a File of Boyes behind 'em, loose shot,	3314

STILL = 19*1

The Play may passe: If they be still, and willing,	12
Still him in praise, and being present both,	75
Kin. Still Exaction: | The nature of it, in what kinde let's know,	384
For our best Act: if we shall stand still,	420
He pleaded still not guilty, and alleadged	840
Kept him a forraigne man still, which so greeu'd him,	1182
Still growing in a Maiesty and pompe, the which	1208
Zeale and obedience he still bore your Grace,	1688
*Still met the King? Lou'd him next Heau'n? Obey'd him?	1763
And fixt on Spirituall obiect, he should still	1997
Was still inscrib'd: in which you brought the King | To be your Seruant.	2212
A still, and quiet Conscience. The King ha's cur'd me,	2286
Still in thy right hand, carry gentle Peace	2360
Pursu'd him still, and three nights after this,	2579
So excellent in Art, and still so rising,	2620
Patience, be neere me still, and set me lower,	2634
They grow still too; from all Parts they are comming,	3327

STILL *cont.*
This Royall Infant, Heauen still moue about her;   3387
Shall still be doubled on her. Truth shall Nurse her,   3398
Holy and Heauenly thoughts still Counsell her: 3399
STING = 1
Will make this sting the sooner. Cardinall *Campeius*,   1900
STINT = 1
That Vertue must goe through: we must not stint   411
STIRD = 2
His Knell rung out, his Iudgement, he was stir'd   861
It to be stir'd; but oft haue hindred, oft   1530
STIRRE = 3
I know 'twill stirre him strongly; yet I know   2098
Some little memory of me, will stirre him   2331
We may as well push against Powles as stirre'em.   3273
STIRRES = 1
A man that more detests, more stirres against,   3087
STOCKE = 2
Grif. This Cardinall, | Though from an humble ,Stocke, vndoubtedly 2606
Good time, and liue: but for the Stocke Sir *Thomas,*   2797
STOCKINGS = 1
The faith they haue in Tennis and tall Stockings,   608
STOKELEY = 1
3 *Stokeley* and *Gardiner,* the one of Winchester,   2525
STOLNE = 1
Is stolne away to Rome, hath 'tane no leaue,   1901
STOMACKE = 2
Card. All Goodnesse | Is poyson to thy Stomacke.   2174
Of an vnbounded stomacke, euer ranking   2589
STONE = 1
When we first put this dangerous stone a rowling,   3168
STOOD = 5*1
Made Britaine, India: Euery man that stood,   65
Thankes you for this great care: I stood i'th' leuell   322
Haue stood to Charity, and displayd th'effects   1445
I stood not in the smile of Heauen, who had   1554
I weigh'd the danger which my Realmes stood in   1564
Nor. My Lord, we haue | *Stood heere obseruing him. Some strange
Commotion   1973
STOOLES = *1
A Councell Table brought in with Chayres and Stooles, and   3035
STOP = 1*1
To stop the rumor; and allay those tongues | That durst disperse it. 1004
*But stop their mouthes with stubborn Bits & spurre 'em,   3071
STOPD = *1
a Subiect, if not before the King, which stop'd our mouthes | Sir. 1034
STOPS = 2
Stops on a sodaine, lookes vpon the ground,   1976
Springs out into fast gate, then stops againe,   1978
STORE = 1
Great store of roome no doubt, left for the Ladies,   3332
STORIE = 1
Beyond thoughts Compasse, that former fabulous Storie   80
STORME = 1
Buc. Euery man, | After the hideous storme that follow'd, was   144
STORMES = 2
They swell and grow, as terrible as stormes.   1801

STORMES *cont.*

An old man, broken with the stormes of State,	2575

STORY = 3

The very Persons of our Noble Story,	27
There was a Lady once (tis an old Story)	1311
I feare the Story of his Anger. 'Tis so:	2089

STOUT = 1

For after the stout Earle Northumberland | Arrested him at Yorke, and brought him forward	2565

STRAIGHT = 2

He sent command to the Lord Mayor straight	1003
Then layes his finger on his Temple: straight	1977

STRAINES = 1

And more, and richer, when he straines that Lady,	2460

STRANGE = 3*5

Men into such strange mysteries?	572
Old.L. Tis strange; a threepence bow'd would hire me	1245
An. This is strange to me.	1309
*A strange Tongue makes my cause more strange, suspiti- | (ous:	1668
Nor. My Lord, we haue | *Stood heere obseruing him. Some strange Commotion	1973
His eye against the Moone: in most strange Postures	1980
*to muster in? Or haue wee some strange Indian with the	3292

STRANGELY = 5

Strangely neglected? When did he regard	1839
Suf. Most strangely. | *Sur.* O how? how?	1863
Could say this is my wife there, all were wouen | So strangely in one peece.	2500
Kath. O my Lord, | The Times and Titles now are alter'd strangely	2697
Gard. What other, | Would you expect? You are strangely troublesome:	3152

STRANGER = 3

Old L. Alas poore Lady, | Shee's a stranger now againe.	1220
I am a most poore Woman, and a Stranger,	1369
Acquainted with this stranger; 'tis as like you, | As Cherry, is to Cherry.	2975

STRANGERS = 1*1

Cham. How now, what is't? | *Seru.* A noble troupe of Strangers,	739
Cam. Your Grace must needs deserue all strangers loues,	1149

STRANGEST = 1

Buts. Ile shew your Grace the strangest sight.	3016

STRANGLED = 1

He ha's strangled his Language in his teares.	2960

STRAYING = 1

Win straying Soules with modesty againe,	3113

STREAME = 2

Of a rude streame, that must for euer hide me.	2265
2 Good Sir, speake it to vs? | 3 As well as I am able. The rich streame	2481

STRENGTHEN = 1

The cheefe ayme of his Honour, and to strengthen	3187

STRETCH = 1

If you might please to stretch it. | *Anne.* Nay, good troth.	1241

STRETCHD = 1

He stretch'd him, and with one hand on his dagger,	557

STRETCHES = 1

His will is most malignant, and it stretches | Beyond you to your friends.	482

STREW = 1

Let me be vs'd with Honor; strew me ouer	2761

STRIKE = 1
Things to strike Honour sad. Bid him recount   465
STRIKES = 1
Strikes his brest hard, and anon, he casts   1979
STRING = *1
*Sur. I would 'twer somthing y would fret the string,   1965
STRIUE = 1
(Tell you the Duke) shall prosper, bid him striue   · 515
STROAKE = 2
That made me happy; at one stroake ha's taken   963
That when the greatest stroake of Fortune falls   1068
STROND = *1
*her succour, which were the hope o'th' Strond where she   3311
STRONG = 2*2
*Buck. To th'King Ile say't, & make my vouch as strong   232
A strong faith to conceale it.   994
And the strong course of my Authority,   3083
*staues, and strong ones; these are but switches to 'em: 3265
STRONGER = 3
More stronger to direct you then your selfe;   220
Are you not stronger then you were?   1322
So I grow stronger, you more Honour gaine. *Exeunt.*   3255
STRONGLY = 2
1. The same, | All these accus'd him strongly, which he faine   852
I know 'twill stirre him strongly; yet I know   2098
STROOKE = 1
Gard. It's one a clocke Boy, is't not. | *Boy.* It hath strooke. 2771
STROUE = 1
Haue I not stroue to loue, although I knew   1384
STUBBORN = *1
*But stop their mouthes with stubborn Bits & spurre 'em,   3071
STUBBORNE = 3
Stubborne to Iustice, apt to accuse it, and   1484
So much they loue it. But to stubborne Spirits,   1800
How to liue better. For your stubborne answer   2246
STUDIED = 1
My studied purposes requite, which went   2042
STUDIES = 2
To me, aboue this wretchednesse? All your Studies | Make me a Curse,
like this.   1755
To trust vs in your businesse) we are ready | To vse our vtmost Studies,
in your seruice.   1811
STUDY = 1
And with no little study, that my teaching   3082
STUFFE = 1*1
Nor. Surely Sir, | There's in him stuffe, that put's him to these ends: 106
King. Good my Lord, | *You are full of Heauenly stuffe, and beare the
Inuentory   2005
STUFFES = 1
Rich Stuffes and Ornaments of Houshold, which   1989
STUMPE = 1
Nor shall not while I haue a stumpe.   632
SUBIECT = 8*1
The Subiect will deserue it. Such as giue   8
Most like a carefull Subiect haue collected | Out of the Duke of
Buckingham.   469
a Subiect, if not before the King, which stop'd our mouthes | Sir. 1034

SUBIECT *cont.*
Yea, subiect to your Countenance: Glad, or sorry,   1380
And liue a Subiect? Nay forsooth, my Friends,   1715
I finde at such proud Rate, that it out-speakes | Possession of a Subiect.   1990
King. Fairely answer'd: | A Loyall, and obedient Subiect is   2054
May be beholding to a Subiect; I   3228
That am a poore and humble Subiect to you?   3237
SUBIECTS = 3
And those of true condition; That your Subiects   346
Vnder your promis'd pardon. The Subiects griefe   389
We must not rend our Subiects from our Lawes,   429
SUBSTANCE = 1*1
The sixt part of his Substance, to be leuied   391
Sur. Then, That you haue sent inumerable substance,   2224
SUBTILE = 1
As he is subtile, and as prone to mischiefe,   235
SUBURBS = 1
Your faithfull friends o'th' Suburbs? We shall haue   3331
SUCCEED = 1
And all that shall succeed: *Saba* was neuer   3393
SUCCEEDING = 1
Henry the Seauenth succeeding, truly pittying   958
SUCCESSORS = 1
Chalkes Successors their way; nor call'd vpon   109
SUCCOUR = 2*1
Flying for succour to his Seruant *Banister*,   955
Farre from his succour; from the King, from all   2149
*her succour, which were the hope o'th' Strond where she   3311
SUCH = 46*6
Such Noble Scoenes, as draw the Eye to flow   5
The Subiect will deserue it. Such as giue   8
To ranke our chosen Truth with such a show   19
What foure Thron'd ones could haue weigh'd | Such a compounded
one?   53
One certes, that promises no Element | In such a businesse.   95
That such a Keech can with his very bulke   103
Of all the Gentry; for the most part such   127
Language vnmannerly; yea, such which breakes   354
To Nature none more bound; his trayning such,   451
Kin. I remember of such a time, being my sworn ser-|(uant,   542
Men into such strange mysteries?   572
L.Ch. Death my Lord, | Their cloathes are after such a Pagan cut too't,   586
Let me haue such a Bowle may hold my thankes,   716
Heer's to your Ladiship, and pledge it Madam: | For tis to such a thing.   728
Cham. Such a one, they all confesse   783
With such an Agony, he sweat extreamly,   862
And fit it with such furniture as suites | The Greatnesse of his Person.   944
Cham. Heauen keep me from such councel: tis most true   1070
*They haue sent me such a Man, I would haue wish'd for.   1148
For such receipt of Learning, is Black-Fryers: 1194
Follow such Creatures. That you may, faire Lady   1274
Haue to you, but with thankes to God for such   1517
The region of my Breast, which forc'd such way,   1551
In sweet Musicke is such Art,   1630
I am not such a Truant since my comming,   1666
In such a poynt of weight, so neere mine Honour,   1697
And to such men of grauity and learning;   1699

SUCH *cont.*

Either for such men, or such businesse;	1702
And all such false Professors. Would you haue me	1747
We are to Cure such sorrowes, not to sowe 'em.	1795
*Such doubts as false Coine from it. The King loues you,	1809
To make a seemely answer to such persons.	1817
I should be glad to heare such Newes as this | Once euery houre.	1855
I finde at such proud Rate, that it out-speakes | Possession of a Subiect.	1990
You aske with such a Violence, the King	2131
That therefore such a Writ be sued against you,	2241
Had the full view of, such a noyse arose,	2491
Bin loose, this day they had beene lost. Such ioy	2495
The Rod, and Bird of Peace, and all such Emblemes	2510
But such an honest Chronicler as *Griffith.*	2630
Grif. I am most ioyfull Madam, such good dreames | Possesse your Fancy.	2670
You cannot with such freedome purge your selfe,	2899
To sweare against you: Such things haue bene done.	2934
An ordinary Groome is for such payment.	2982
In dayly thankes; that gaue vs such a Prince;	3184
To heare such flattery now, and in my presence	3193
In such an honour: how may I deserue it,	3236
*such a combustion in the State. I mist the Meteor once,	3308
*deliuer'd such a showre of Pibbles, that I was faine to	3315
That mould vp such a mighty Piece as this is,	3396
For such a one we shew'd 'em: If they smile,	3460

SUDDEN *see* sodain, sodaine

SUDDENLY *see* sodainly

SUE = 1

| Nor will I sue, although the King haue mercies | 911 |

SUED = 1

| That therefore such a Writ be sued against you, | 2241 |

SUF = 19

SUFF = 11

SUFFER = 4

They are deuis'd by you, or else you suffer | Too hard an exclamation.	382
At least good manners; as not thus to suffer	3028
Till they obey the mannage. If we suffer	3072
The King will suffer but the little finger | Of this man to be vex'd?	3171

SUFFERANCE = 1

| It from the bearer, 'tis a sufferance, panging \| As soule and bodies seuering. | 1218 |

SUFFERD = 1

| Out of the paine you suffer'd, gaue no eare too't. | 2560 |

SUFFOLKE see also Suf., Suff. = 10*3

Suffolke: she kneels. King riseth from his State,	331
Enter to the Lord Chamberlaine, the Dukes of Nor-|folke and Suffolke.	1038
Exeunt Norfolke and Suffolke.	1132
Enter the Duke of Norfolke, Duke of Suffolke, Lord Surrey, | and Lord Chamberlaine.	1825
Enter to Woolsey, the Dukes of Norfolke and Suffolke, the | Earle of Surrey, and the Lord Chamberlaine.	2108
The Duke of Suffolke is the first, and claimes	2399
7 Duke of Suffolke, in his Robe of Estate, his Coronet on his	2433
2 A bold braue Gentleman. That should bee | The Duke of Suffolke.	2451
Gar. I did Sir *Thomas*, and left him at Primero | With the Duke of Suffolke.	2779

SUFFOLKE cont.

Enter King and Suffolke.	2836
King. Charles good night. *Exit Suffolke.*	2864
**Duke of Suffolke, Duke of Norfolke, Surrey, Lord Cham-|berlaine,*	3039
**Staffe, Duke of Suffolke, two Noblemen, bearing great*	3356

SUFFRANCE = *1

**Lou.* So said her woman, and that her suffrance made	2850

SUGGESTION = 1

Himselfe with Princes. One that by suggestion	2590

SUGGESTS = 1

As here at home, suggests the King our Master	239

SUIT = 4

Paid ere he promis'd, whereby his Suit was granted	262
King. Arise, and take place by vs; halfe your Suit	335
Made suit to come in's presence; which if granted,	548
For any suit of pounds: and you, (oh fate)	1305

SUITE = 1

I haue a Suite which you must not deny mee.	3232

SUITES = 1

And fit it with such furniture as suites | The Greatnesse of his Person.	944

SUITOR = 1

Queen. Nay, we must longer kneele; I am a Suitor.	334

SUMME = 1

Produce the grand summe of his sinnes, the Articles	2186

SUMMER = 1

But, to those men that sought him, sweet as Summer.	2612

SUMMERS = 1

This many Summers in a Sea of Glory,	2261

SUMMONS = 1

To make this present Summons vnsolicited.	1589

SUN = 5

Take vp the Rayes o'th'beneficiall Sun, | And keepe it from the Earth.	104
So many courses of the Sun enthroaned,	1207
No Sun, shall euer vsher forth mine Honors,	2324
(That Sun, I pray may neuer set) I haue told him,	2329
Cast thousand beames vpon me, like the Sun?	2666

SUNG = 1

Together sung *Te Deum.* So she parted,	2513

SUNNE = 3

By Darkning my cleere Sunne. My Lords farewell. *Exe.*	315
Euer sprung; as Sunne and Showers,	1625
Where euer the bright Sunne of Heauen shall shine,	3421

SUNNES = 2

Those Sunnes of Glory, those two Lights of Men | Met in the vale of Andren.	46
Durst wagge his Tongue in censure, when these Sunnes	77

SUPERFLUOUS = 1

Abur. A proper Title of a Peace, and purchas'd | At a superfluous rate.	156

SUPERSTITIOUS = 1

Bin (out of fondnesse) superstitious to him?	1764

SUPPER = 1

This night he makes a Supper, and a great one,	638

SUPPORT = 1

A Thousand pound a yeare, Annuall support, | Out of his Grace, he addes.	1280

SUR = 31*2

SURE = 13
  Which I doe well; for I am sure the Emperour 261
  That sure th'haue worne out Christendome: how now? 588
  For sure there's no conuerting of'em: now 624
  2. I doe not thinke he feares death. | 1. Sure he does not, 866
  Be sure you be not loose; for those you make friends, 973
  Suff. How sad he lookes; sure he is much afflicted. 1102
  To keepe your earthly Audit, sure in that 2010
  A sure, and safe one, though thy Master mist it. 2353
  2 'Tis well: The Citizens | I am sure haue shewne at full their Royall
  minds, 2387
  And sure those men are happy that shall haue 'em. 2739
  Who waites there? Sure you know me? 2992
  But whatsoere thou tak'st me for; I'm sure 3197
  And faire purgation to the world then malice, | I'm sure in me. 3223
SURELY = 4
  Nor. Surely Sir, | There's in him stuffe, that put's him to these ends: 106
  Camp. Was he not held a learned man? | *Wol.* Yes surely. 1175
  And when he thinkes, good easie man, full surely 2257
  Diuell was amongst 'em I thinke surely. 3317
SURRENDER = 1
  I would surrender it. *Whisper.* 780
SURREY see also Sur. = 5*2
  Then Deputy of Ireland, who remou'd | Earle *Surrey*, was sent thither,
  and in hast too, 874
  Enter the Duke of Norfolke, Duke of Suffolke, Lord Surrey, | and Lord
  Chamberlaine. 1825
  Enter to Woolsey, the Dukes of Norfolke and Suffolke, the | Earle of
  Surrey, and the Lord Chamberlaine. 2108
  Within these fortie houres, Surrey durst better | Haue burnt that
  Tongue, then saide so. 2140
  a Demy Coronall of Gold. With him, the Earle of Surrey, 2430
  And that the Earle of Surrey, with the Rod. 2450
  Duke of Suffolke, Duke of Norfolke, Surrey, Lord Cham-| berlaine, 3039
SURRIE = 1
  Dare mate a sounder man then Surrie can be, | And all that loue his
  follies. 2163
SURUEYOR see also Sur. = 4*1
  Car. The Duke of *Buckinghams* Surueyor? Ha? 180
  Buck. My Surueyor is falce: The ore-great *Cardinall* 311
  Enter Surueyor. 446
  Queen. If I know you well, | You were the Dukes Surueyor, and lost
  your Office 518
  At which appear'd against him, his Surueyor 846
SUSPITION = 2
  So deepe suspition, where all faith was meant; 1677
  A Woman (I dare say without Vainglory) | Neuer yet branded with
  Suspition? 1760
SUSPITIOUS = *1
  *A strange Tongue makes my cause more strange, suspiti-| (ous: 1668
SUSTAINE = 1
  But that you shall sustaine moe new disgraces, | With these you beare
  alreadie. 1831
SWALLOWED = 1
  That swallowed so much treasure, and like a glasse 241
SWEARE = 5
  For when they hold 'em, you would sweare directly 579

SWEARE cont.
I sweare, tis better to be lowly borne,	1224
I sweare againe, I would not be a Queene, | For all the world.	1256
To sweare against you: Such things haue bene done.	2934
I sweare he is true-hearted, and a soule	2957

SWEAT = 3
And follow'd with the generall throng, and sweat	29
Not vs'd to toyle, did almost sweat to beare	68
With such an Agony, he sweat extreamly,	862

SWEEPE = 1
Vnlesse wee sweepe 'em from the dore with Cannons,	3270

SWEET = 10*2
They are a sweet society of faire ones.	683
Cham. Sweet Ladies will it please you sit; Sir *Harry*	690
San. By my faith, | *And thanke your Lordship: by your leaue sweet Ladies,	696
Kin. By Heauen she is a dainty one. Sweet heart,	800
Kin. Lead in your Ladies eu'ry one: Sweet Partner,	812
Make of your Prayers one sweet Sacrifice,	919
So sweet a Bedfellow? But Conscience, Conscience;	1198
'Tis sweet at first t'acquire. After this Processe.	1210
(If thy rare qualities, sweet gentlenesse,	1501
In sweet Musicke is such Art,	1630
That sweet Aspect of Princes, and their ruine,	2270
But, to those men that sought him, sweet as Summer.	2612

SWEETEST = 1
2 Heauen blesse thee, | Thou hast the sweetest face I euer look'd on.	2456

SWEETLY = 1
But he fell to himselfe againe, and sweetly,	864

SWEET-LADIE = 1
Shee's a good Creature, and sweet-Ladie do's | Deserue our better wishes.	2801

SWELL = 1
They swell and grow, as terrible as stormes.	1801

SWIFTNESSE = 1
By violent swiftnesse that which we run at;	215

SWIM = 1
Like little wanton Boyes that swim on bladders:	2260

SWITCHES = *1
*staues, and strong ones; these are but switches to 'em:	3265

SWORD = 2*1
That he's Reuengefull; and I know, his Sword	169
two Noblemen, with the Sword and Mace. The King takes	1344
Thou should'st feele | My Sword i'th'life blood of thee else. My Lords,	2167

SWORN = *1
Kin. I remember of such a time, being my sworn ser-|(uant,	542

SWORNE = 1
He sollemnly had sworne, that what he spoke	511

SYLLABLE *see also* sillable = 1
Is the Kings hand, and tongue, and who dare speak | One syllable against him?	2816

SYMONIE = 1
Ty'de all the Kingdome. Symonie, was faire play,	2591

T = 5*1
(Without the priuity o'th'King) t'appoint	125
Bran. Here is a warrant from | The King, t'attach Lord *Mountacute*, and the Bodies	302

T *cont.*
    'Tis sweet at first t'acquire. After this Processe.   1210
    Cham. Lady; | I shall not faile t'approue the faire conceit   1291
    *T'oppose your cunning. Y'are meek, & humble-mouth'd   1467
    · *Cran.* It is my dutie | T'attend your Highnesse pleasure.   2885
TABLE = 3*3
    Hoboies. A small Table vnder a State for the Cardinall, a   661
    longer Table for the Guests. Then Enter Anne Bullen,   662
    A Councell Table brought in with Chayres and Stooles, and   3035
    himselfe at the vpper end of the Table, on the left hand: A   3037
    Cranmer approches the Councell Table.   3055
    Gard. Good M.(aster) Secretary, | I cry your Honour mercie; you may
    worst | Of all this Table say so.   3127
TABLES = 1
    Shall shine at full vpon them. Some attend him. | *All rise, and Tables*
    remou'd.   748
TAINT = 3
    To taint that honour euery good Tongue blesses;   1679
    Which since they are of you, and odious, | I will not taint my mouth
    with.   2229
    Commotions, vprores, with a generall Taint   3076
TAINTED = 1
    As a man sorely tainted, to his Answer,   2567
TAKE = 37*1
    Take vp the Rayes o'th'beneficiall Sun, | And keepe it from the Earth.   104
    (And take it from a heart, that wishes towards you   163
    (Which as I take it, is a kinde of Puppie   251
    King. Arise, and take place by vs; halfe your Suit   335
    Repeat your will, and take it.   338
    We should take roote here, where we sit;   422
    A trembling Contribution; why we take   431
    On the complaint o'th'Tenants; take good heed   520
    And spoyle your nobler Soule; I say, take heed;   522
    And lame ones; one would take it,   583
    Or pack to their old Playfellowes; there, I take it,   611
    Place you that side, Ile take the charge of this: 691
    And pray 'em take their pleasures.   769
    Find out, and he will take it. | *Card.* Let me see then,   785
    I were vnmannerly to take you out,   801
    Gainst me, that I cannot take peace with: 928
    And take your good Grace from me? Heauen witnesse,   1376
    Queen. Take thy Lute wench,   1617
    Camp. I would your Grace | Would leaue your greefes, and take my
    Counsell.   1720
    Take heed, for heauens sake take heed, least at once   1742
    It did take place, I do (quoth he) perceiue   1869
    Take notice Lords, he ha's a Loyall brest,   2077
    A way, if it take right, in spight of Fortune   2099
    Ti'de it by Letters Patents. Now, who'll take it? | *Sur.* The King that
    gaue it.   2135
    There take an Inuentory of all I haue,   2366
    1 You come to take your stand heere, and behold   2381
    I take it, she that carries vp the Traine,   2466
    And heartily entreats you take good comfort.   2707
    Lou. I must to him too | Before he go to bed. Ile take my leaue.   2781
    Which will require your Answer, you must take   2901
    You take a Precepit for no leape of danger,   2940

TAKE *cont.*

I take it, by all voyces: That forthwith,	3145
By vertue of that Ring, I take my cause	3162
Take him, and vse him well; hee's worthy of it.	3226
*you take the Court for Parish Garden: ye rude Slaues, | leaue your gaping.	3260
With this Kisse, take my Blessing: God protect thee,	3378
All that are heere: Some come to take their ease,	3451

TAKEN *see also* tane = 3

That made me happy; at one stroake ha's taken	963
These ruin'd Pillers, out of pitty, taken	2288
1 Neuer greater, | Nor Ile assure you better taken Sir.	2392

TAKES = 5*2

Nor. Like it your Grace, | The State takes notice of the priuate difference	160
takes her vp, kisses and placeth | her by him.	332
Hoboyes. Enter Cardinall Wolsey, and takes his State.	710
two Noblemen, with the Sword and Mace. The King takes	1344
vnder him as Iudges. The Queene takes place some di-|stance	1346
King takes his Seat, whispers Louell, who goes | to the Cardinall.	2001
Enter King frowning on them, takes his Seate.	3181

TAKST = 1

But whatsoere thou tak'st me for; I'm sure	3197

TAKT = 1

'Twill not Sir *Thomas Louell,* tak't of me,	2807

TALES = 1

Crom. My mind gaue me, | In seeking tales and Informations	3176

TALKE = 6

That fill the Court with quarrels, talke, and Taylors.	596
If I chance to talke a little wilde, forgiue me:	698
*In their faire cheekes my Lord, then wee shall haue 'em, | Talke vs to silence.	723
San. I told your Grace, they would talke anon.	732
1. Let me haue it: | I doe not talke much.	995
An. How you doe talke;	1255

TALKER = 1

I be not found a Talker. | *Wol.* Sir, you cannot;	1121

TALKING = 2

And saue me so much talking. | *Card.* My Lord *Sands,*	717
Wol. This, and all else | This talking Lord can lay vpon my credit,	2153

TALL = 1

The faith they haue in Tennis and tall Stockings,	608

TAME = 1

My Noble Lords; for those that tame wild Horses,	3069

TAMELY = 1

And from this Fellow? If we liue thus tamely,	2170

TANE = 5

Bran. I am sorry, | To see you tane from liberty, to looke on	287
Tane of your many vertues; the Kings Maiesty	1276
Is stolne away to Rome, hath 'tane no leaue,	1901
Nor. This same *Cranmer's* | A worthy Fellow, and hath tane much paine | In the Kings businesse.	1918
I should haue tane some paines, to bring together	2918

TANGLED = 1

My King is tangled in affection, to | A Creature of the Queenes, Lady *Anne Bullen.*	1870

TANTA = *1
*Card. Tanta est erga te mentis integritas Regina serenissima.   1664
TARDY = 1
O my Lord, y'are tardy;   675
TARGETS = 1
A noyse of Targets: Or to see a Fellow   16
TARRY = 1
I will not tarry: no, nor euer more   1493
TASTS = 1
Old L. How tasts it? Is it bitter? Forty pence, no: 1310
TAUGHT = 2
I free you from't: You are not to be taught   1523
Of me, more must be heard of: Say I taught thee;   2349
TAXATION = 3
Kin. Taxation? | Wherein? and what Taxation? My Lord Cardinall,   366
Know you of this Taxation?   369
TAXATIONS = 1
Norf. Not almost appeares, | It doth appeare; for, vpon these Taxations, 357
TAYLORS = 1
That fill the Court with quarrels, talke, and Taylors.   596
TE l.*1664 2513 = 1*1
TEACH = 1
And want of wisedome, you that best should teach vs,   3061
TEACHERS = 1
That he may furnish and instruct great Teachers,   452
TEACHING = 1*1
*The whole Realme, by your teaching & your Chaplaines   3064
And with no little study, that my teaching   3082
TEARE = 2
May (if they thinke it well) let fall a Teare,   7
Card. Cromwel, I did not thinke to shed a teare   2343
TEARES = 4*1
The daughter of a King, my drops of teares,   1429
May haue a Tombe of Orphants teares wept on him.   2310
Continuall Meditations, Teares, and Sorrowes,   2582
He ha's strangled his Language in his teares.   2960
*Kin. Good Man, those ioyfull teares shew thy true | (hearts,   3248
TEETH = 1
Daring th'euent too th'teeth, are all in vprore, | And danger serues
among them.   364
TELL = 21
Abur. I cannot tell | What Heauen hath giuen him: let some Grauer eye   116
Where others tell steps with me.   373
(Tell you the Duke) shall prosper, bid him striue   515
To tell your Grace: That hauing heard by fame   759
Card. Pray tell 'em thus much from me: 776
You are a Churchman, or Ile tell you Cardinall,   791
1. Ile tell you in a little. The great Duke   838
And if he speake of Buckingham; pray tell him,   931
Longer then I haue time to tell his yeares;   935
Your selfe pronounce their Office. I must tell you,   1475
Queen. Ye tell me what ye wish for both, my ruine: 1729
King. Haue I not made you | The prime man of the State? I pray you
tell me,   2035
If I lou'd many words, Lord, I should tell you,   2159
1 That I can tell you too. The Archbishop   2406
Something I can command. As I walke thither, | Ile tell ye more.   2544

TELL *cont.*
Did'st thou not tell me *Griffith*, as thou lead'st mee, 2556
Kath. Pre'thee good *Griffith*, tell me how he dy'de. 2561
Out of this world. Tell him in death I blest him 2756
And let me tell you, it will ne're be well, 2806
Sir (I may tell it you) I thinke I haue | Incenst the Lords o'th'Councell,
  that he is 2821
I haue Newes to tell you. 2890
TELS = 1
Wol. He tels you rightly. 1728
TEMPER = 2
Old La. Hearts of most hard temper | Melt and lament for her. 1213
I know you haue a Gentle, Noble temper, 1802
TEMPEST = 2
Into a generall Prophesie; That this Tempest 147
As the shrowdes make at Sea, in a stiffe Tempest, 2492
TEMPLE = 1
Then layes his finger on his Temple: straight 1977
TEMPORALL = 2
Is this an howre for temporall affaires? Ha? 1114
An. Oh Gods will, much better | She ne're had knowne pompe; though't
  be temporall, 1215
TEMPRANCE = 1
Aske God for Temp'rance, that's th'appliance onely | Which your
  disease requires. 193
TEMPTING = 1
In tempting of your patience, but am boldned 388
TEN *see also* 10. = 3
They turne to vicious formes, ten times more vgly 456
Wish him ten faddom deepe: This Duke as much 886
THE EPILOGVE. | *Tis ten to one, this Play can neuer please* 3449
TENANTS = 1
On the complaint o'th'Tenants; take good heed 520
TENDANCE = 1
I her fraile sonne, among'st my Brethren mortall, | Must giue my
  tendance to. 2018
TENDER = 1
I tender my Commission; by whose vertue, 1151
TENDER = 4
O 'tis a tender place, and I must leaue her. *Exeunt.* 1199
An. I doe not know | What kinde of my obedience, I should tender; 1282
You tender more your persons Honor, then 1476
The tender Leaues of hopes, to morrow Blossomes, 2254
TENDERNES = 1
My Conscience first receiu'd a tendernes, 1537
TENEMENTS = 1
To forfeit all your Goods, Lands, Tenements, | Castles, and whatsoeuer,
  and to be 2242
TENNIS = 1
The faith they haue in Tennis and tall Stockings, 608
TENOR = 1
He did discharge a horrible Oath, whose tenor 559
TERRIBLE = 1
They swell and grow, as terrible as stormes. 1801
TERROR = 2
'Tis his Aspect of Terror. All's not well. 2881
And so stand fix'd. Peace, Plenty, Loue, Truth, Terror, 3418

TERTIA *l.*569 1200 3256 = 3
TERTIUS *l.*1615 = 1
TH *see also* by'th, into'th, i'th, o'th, to'th = 35*7

Was cry'de incompareable; and th'ensuing night	71
Abur. Is it therefore | Th'Ambassador is silenc'd? | *Nor.* Marry is't.	153
Aske God for Temp'rance, that's th'appliance onely | Which your disease requires.	193
Buck. To th'King Ile say't, & make my vouch as strong	232
To this last costly Treaty: Th'enteruiew,	240
*As giue a Crutch to th'dead. But our Count-Cardinall	248
To th'old dam Treason) *Charles* the Emperour,	252
The busines present. Tis his Highnes pleasure | You shall to th' Tower.	289
Is pleas'd you shall to th'Tower, till you know | How he determines further.	297
Daring th'euent too th'teeth, are all in vprore, | And danger serues among them.	364
Pertaines to th'State; and front but in that File	372
Most pestilent to th'hearing, and to beare 'em,	380
The Backe is Sacrifice to th'load; They say	381
I told my Lord the Duke, by th'Diuels illusions	526
Th' Vsurper *Richard*, who being at *Salsbury*,	547
Hee's Traytor to th' height. *Exeunt.*	568
1. When he was brought agen to th' Bar, to heare	860
Lou. To th' water side I must conduct your Grace;	939
Kin. Deliuer this with modesty to th' Queene. | *Exit Gardiner.*	1191
*No more to th' Crowne but that: Lo, who comes here?	1261
And on all sides th'Authority allow'd,	1355
Haue stood to Charity, and displayd th'effects	1445
*Then marke th'inducement. Thus it came; giue heede | (too't:	1536
By th'Bishop of *Bayon*, then French Embassador,	1539
The Graue does to th' dead: For her Male Issue,	1558
And came to th'eye o'th'King, wherein was read	1866
This paper ha's vndone me: 'Tis th' Accompt	2090
Will bring me off againe. What's this? *To th' Pope?*	2100
Fall into'th'compasse of a Premunire;	2240
A man in much esteeme with th'King, and truly	2536
With which the Lime will loade him. Th'Archbyshop	2815
Th'estate of my poore Queene. Leaue me alone,	2858
Th'occasion shall instruct you. If intreaties	2952
You be conuaid to th' Tower a Prisoner;	3146
But I must needs to th' Tower my Lords?	3151
Within. Good M.(aster) Porter I belong to th' Larder.	3262
Port. Belong to th' Gallowes, and be hang'd ye Rogue:	3263
*But knock 'em downe by th' dozens? Is this More fields	3291
*length they came to th' broome staffe to me, I defide 'em	3313
By th' heeles, and sodainly: and on your heads	3340
To th' ground, and all the World shall mourne her.	3434

THAN *see* then
THANKE = 12*5

Norf. I thanke your Grace:	41
Queene. Thanke your Maiesty | That you would loue your selfe, and in that loue	339
San. By my faith, | *And thanke your Lordship: by your leaue sweet Ladies,	696
And thanke the holy Conclaue for their loues,	1147
*Pray speake in English; heere are some will thanke you,	1669
My Lords, I thanke you both for your good wills,	1694

THANKE *cont.*

I thanke my Memorie, I yet remember	2198
*The King shall know it, and (no doubt) shal thanke you.	2248
I humbly thanke his Grace: and from these shoulders	2287
*1 I thanke you Sir: Had I not known those customs,	2402
Kath. I thanke you honest Lord. Remember me | In all humilitie vnto his Highnesse:	2753
Cran. I humbly thanke your Highnesse,	2906
Cran. Ah my good Lord of *Winchester*: I thanke you,	3107
Kin. Thanke you good Lord Archbishop:	3374
I thanke ye heartily: So shall this Lady, | When she ha's so much English.	3382
I thanke ye all. To you my good Lord Maior,	3441
Ye must all see the Queene, and she must thanke ye,	3445

THANKES = 10

Thankes you for this great care: I stood i'th' leuell	322
Of a full-charg'd confederacie, and giue thankes	323
Let me haue such a Bowle may hold my thankes,	716
For which I pay 'em a thousand thankes,	768
Norfolke. Thankes my good Lord *Chamberlaine.*	1099
Vouchsafe to speake my thankes, and my obedience,	1288
Haue to you, but with thankes to God for such	1517
Can nothing render but Allegiant thankes,	2050
I sent your Message, who return'd her thankes	2845
In dayly thankes; that gaue vs such a Prince;	3184

THANKFULL = 2

Buck. Sir, | I am thankfull to you, and Ile goe along	223
And ye shall find me thankfull. Lead the way Lords,	3444

THARE = 2

Touch me alike: th'are breath I not beleeue in.	1088
Th'are come already from the Christening,	3344

THAS = 1

T'has done vpon the premises, but Iustice:	904

THAT *see also* y *l.*3 15 21 22 65 69 80 82 95 103 107 114 118 119 133 134
143 145 147 163 164 166 169 *173 174 214 215 217 241 256 259 265 267
274 292 324 325 340 346 368 372 376 405 411 415 436 443 447 452 462
473 492 504 506 511 *527 532 584 588 596 603 641 643 646 *684 691
*711 712 733 759 796 826 848 849 850 851 877 897 900 905 913 928 951
*952 956 963 970 *980 986 1005 1006 1012 1021 1052 1064 1066 1067
1068 1072 1075 1090 *1093 1108 1158 1162 1183 1187 1193 *1202 1204
1217 1235 1248 *1261 1274 *1295 1312 1319 1356 1375 1386 1389 1403
1405 1406 1417 1423 1427 1434 1453 1455 1458 1477 1498 1500 1510
1518 1524 1552 1555 1561 1563 1565 1583 1603 1622 1627 1662 1679
1703 1712 1716 1717 1732 1738 1750 1768 1769 1775 1780 1788 1822
1831 1834 1850 1851 1867 1899 1958 1990 2010 2046 2053 2059 2063
2067 2068 2087 2091 2104 2130 2136 2141 2150 2161 2164 2176 2191
2207 2210 2214 2222 *2224 2241 2260 2265 2268 2269 2270 2291 2293
2303 2308 2312 2315 2320 2323 2325 2329 2339 2350 2354 2356 2358
2385 2394 2395 2397 2406 2448 2450 2451 2454 2460 2462 2466 2467
2471 2478 2490 2497 2518 2521 2524 2531 2534 2557 2590 2611 2612
2616 2618 2621 2636 2638 *2649 2704 *2708 2710 2716 2728 2731 2732
2739 2742 2747 2762 2786 2789 2796 2812 2819 2822 2825 *2850 2859
2874 2897 2900 2917 2963 2990 3007 3017 3058 3061 3069 3082 3087
3091 3094 3098 3099 3114 3121 3145 3162 3180 3184 3186 3188 3200
3208 3233 3237 3282 3285 *3301 *3302 *3306 *3309 *3315 *3318 *3319
3324 3391 3393 3396 3397 3419 3439 3451 3456 = 300*22

THAT *l.*10 = 1
THAT *l.*6 = 1
THATS = 11
Aske God for Temp'rance, that's th'appliance onely | Which your
disease requires.   193
That's clapt vpon the Court Gate.   593
That's Christian care enough: for liuing Murmurers,   1185
Now present heere together: that's to say,   1569
(*Katherine* our Queene) before the primest Creature | That's Parragon'd
o'th' World.   1599
Card. That's somewhat sodain.   2305
Card. That's Newes indeed.   2314
1 Sir, | You must no more call it Yorke-place, that's past: 2516
That's the plaine truth; your painted glosse discouers   3120
By all that's holy, he had better starue,   3201
Abus'd extreamly, and to cry that's witty,   3455
THE *see also* th' = 735*134
THEAME = 1
Old.L. With your Theame, I could   1315
THEE *l.*282 *555 772 1504 2146 2168 2326 2330 2349 2352 2355 2358 2456
    2635 3200 3202 *3250 3378 = 16*2
THEIR *l.*9 13 51 66 69 78 109 134 137 257 349 378 394 395 396 426 580
    587 604 611 613 614 *723 741 757 763 769 908 985 *1141 1147 1153
    1423 1475 1495 1526 1629 1639 1640 1642 1643 1670 2069 2070 2130
    2270 2388 2389 2397 2469 2476 2494 2554 2601 *2644 *2645 *2646
    *2651 *2656 2742 2809 2929 2966 3008 3012 3030 3070 *3071 3136
    *3321 3402 3409 3451 3463 = 66*9
THEM *see also* 'em *l.*28 49 50 69 70 74 360 365 377 395 430 748 *1036
    *1334 *1335 *1337 *1343 *1348 1405 1560 1828 1829 1933 2233 2411
    2611 *2656 2788 2948 2954 *2955 3181 = 24*8
THEMSELUES = 2*2
Kin. Things done well, | And with a care, exempt themselues from feare: 424
from the King. The Bishops place themselues on   1347
Bow themselues when he did sing.   1623
Gardiner, seat themselues in Order on each side.   3040
THEN *l.*30 32 49 57 *185 220 375 404 416 457 606 649 662 *723 778 786
    816 874 898 909 912 935 940 950 966 990 1008 *1177 1209 1226 *1250
    1252 1279 1284 *1286 1320 1322 *1339 *1340 *1342 1356 1366 1476
    *1536 1539 1557 1563 1571 1587 1629 1943 1955 1977 1978 2041 2061
    2065 2068 2079 2088 2102 2121 2137 2141 2163 2188 2205 2210 2214
    *2224 2259 2271 2298 2337 2356 2359 *2363 2423 *2426 2446 2506 2596
    2623 2626 *2646 *2649 2764 2788 *2792 2911 2937 2946 3063 3075 3089
    3106 3112 3136 *3144 3202 3215 3223 *3354 *3357 *3360 3395
    3420 = 89*19
THENCE = 1
He was from thence discharg'd? Sir, call to minde,   1388
THERE *l.*43 219 *347 400 440 597 611 619 639 734 777 784 828 893 927
    942 1059 *1103 1105 1116 1195 1260 1270 1311 1403 1512 1626 1731
    1899 1959 1983 1986 2096 2228 2269 2320 2366 2500 2532 2543 2688
    2734 2784 2819 *2955 2992 3020 3048 3085 3147 3150 3154 3161 3222
    *3298 *3304 *3305 *3322 3348 = 53*7
THEREFORE = 9
Therefore, for Goodnesse sake, and as you are knowne   24
Abur. Is it therefore | Th'Ambassador is silenc'd? | *Nor.* Marry is't.   153
Haue not the power to muzzle him, therefore best   189
To pleade your Cause. It shall be therefore bootlesse,   1416
Camp. His Grace | Hath spoken well, and iustly: Therefore Madam,   1420

THEREFORE *cont.*
(Which Gods dew quench) therefore, I say againe,   1438
I am not of your wrong. Therefore in him   1459
Vnder your hands and Seales; therefore goe on,   1592
That therefore such a Writ be sued against you,   2241
THEREIN = 2
To haue you therein my Companion.   2012
Therein illustrated, the Honor of it   2056
THERES = 16*1
Nor. Surely Sir, | There's in him stuffe, that put's him to these ends: 106
There's difference in no persons.   211
There's mischiefe in this man; canst thou say further?   536
Kin. There's his period,   563
For sure there's no conuerting of'em: now   624
Card. There's fresher ayre my Lord, | In the next Chamber.   810
Suff. For me, my Lords, | I loue him not, nor feare him, there's my
Creede: 1084
Camp. Beleeue me, there's an ill opinion spread then,   1177
There's places of rebuke. He was a Foole;   1186
There's nothing I haue done yet o' my Conscience   1654
Suf. There's order giuen for her Coronation: 1887
There's more in't then faire Visage. *Bullen?*   1943
There's none stands vnder more calumnious tongues, | Then I my selfe,
poore man.   2910
'Tis well there's one aboue 'em yet; I had thought   3026
By holy *Mary* (*Butts*) there's knauery;   3032
Not as a Groome: There's some of ye, I see,   3214
Theres a trim rabble let in: are all these   3330
THEREUNTO = 1
Pertaining thereunto; as Fights and Fire-workes,   605
THERS = *1
Kin. Ther's somthing more would out of thee; what | (say'st?   555
THESE *l.*77 102 107 307 352 358 378 454 475 617 680 685 695 706 764 815
853 1061 1062 1071 1073 *1093 1413 1461 1511 1526 1608 1708 1807
1832 2140 2199 2287 2288 2414 2447 2469 2574 2746 2749 2773 *2776
3241 *3265 *3318 *3323 3328 3329 3330 3347 = 45*5
THEY *see also* th'are, th'haue = 94*15
THEYL = 2
Let none thinke Flattery; for they'l finde'em Truth.   3386
They'l say tis naught. Others to heare the City   3454
THHAUE = 2
That sure th'haue worne out Christendome: how now?   588
For so they seeme; th'haue left their Barge and landed,   741
THICKE = 3
Abound, as thicke as thought could make 'em, and   2071
And beares his blushing Honors thicke vpon him: 2255
The dewes of Heauen fall thicke in Blessings on her,   2724
THIN = 1
They are too thin, and base to hide offences,   3194
THINE = 1
Neglect him not; make vse now, and prouide | For thine owne future
safety.   2334
THING = 9
In Honor, Honesty, the tract of eu'ry thing,   85
Order gaue each thing view. The Office did   90
A thing Inspir'd, and not consulting, broke   146
Heer's to your Ladiship, and pledge it Madam: | For tis to such a thing.   728

THING *cont.*
  Euery thing that heard him play,   1627
  If ye be any thing but Churchmens habits)   1749
  Any thing on him: for he hath a Witchcraft | Ouer the King in's
    Tongue.   1847
  Ye appeare in euery thing may bring my ruine?   2127
  This happy Child, did I get any thing.   3437
THINGS = 8
  I Come no more to make you laugh, Things now,   2
  Be done in this and all things: I obey.   294
  Things that are knowne alike, which are not wholsome   376
  Kin. Things done well, | And with a care, exempt themselues from feare: 424
  Things done without example, in their issue   426
  Things to strike Honour sad. Bid him recount   465
  Because all those things you haue done of late   2238
  To sweare against you: Such things haue bene done.   2934
THINKE = 34
  May (if they thinke it well) let fall a Teare,   7
  Be sad, as we would make ye. Thinke ye see   26
  As they were Liuing: Thinke you see them Great,   28
  Nor. Greeuingly I thinke,   141
  To thinke an English Courtier may be wise, | And neuer see the *Louure.*   599
  I thinke would better please 'em: by my life,   682
  2. I doe not thinke he feares death. | 1. Sure he does not,   866
  Cardinall *Campeius* is arriu'd, and lately, | As all thinke for this busines.   1013
  2. I thinke | You haue hit the marke; but is't not cruell,   1019
  Let's thinke in priuate more. *Exeunt.*   1025
  *I feare he will indeede; well, let him haue them; hee | will haue all I
    thinke.   1036
  The most conuenient place, that I can thinke of   1193
  What thinke you of a Dutchesse? Haue you limbs | To beare that load
    of Title?   1247
  If this salute my blood a iot; it faints me | To thinke what followes.   1326
  Old L. What doe you thinke me --- *Exeunt.*   1331
  I hold my most malicious Foe, and thinke not | At all a Friend to truth.   1441
  I doe not like their comming; now I thinke on't,   1642
  But little for my profit can you thinke Lords,   1711
  A Soule as euen as a Calme; Pray thinke vs,   1803
  Card. Is he ready to come abroad? | *Crom.* I thinke by this he is.   1937
  King. If we did thinke   1995
  To thinke vpon the part of businesse, which   2015
  Card. Cromwel, I did not thinke to shed a teare   2343
  (Doublets, I thinke) flew vp, and had their Faces   2494
  Grif. Yes Madam: but I thinke your Grace   2559
  Sir (I may tell it you) I thinke I haue | Incenst the Lords o'th'Councell,
    that he is   2821
  For I must thinke of that, which company | Would not be friendly too.   2859
  Butts. I thinke your Highnesse saw this many a day.   3018
  Norf. Doe you thinke my Lords   3170
  And thinke with wagging of your tongue to win me: 3196
  Then but once thinke his place becomes thee not.   3202
  Diuell was amongst 'em I thinke surely.   3317
  Let none thinke Flattery; for they'l finde'em Truth.   3386
  She will be sicke els. This day, no man thinke   3446
THINKES = 4*1
  Car. How much me thinkes, I could despise this man,   2190
  And when he thinkes, good easie man, full surely   2257

THINKES *cont.*
  I am able now (me thinkes)   2295
  So now (me thinkes) I feele a little ease.   2555
  Lou. Me thinkes I could | Cry the Amen, and yet my Conscience sayes   2799
THINKING = 1
  Qu. Sir, I am about to weepe; but thinking that   1427
THINKINGS = 1
  His Thinkings are below the Moone, not worth | His serious
  considering.   1999
THIRD = 2
  The third day, comes a Frost; a killing Frost,   2256
  Enter a third Gentleman.   2472
THIS *l.*31 59 70 93 98 124 134 138 147 148 158 186 *188 197 210 225 233
  240 *244 249 250 258 271 294 314 322 369 386 392 *393 397 402 404
  428 435 437 443 457 464 480 488 490 496 514 528 536 544 553 638 640
  658 668 670 676 691 713 721 736 747 760 761 778 849 855 859 871 880
  886 899 910 971 984 990 993 1012 1014 1018 1021 1024 1027 *1033 1051
  1069 1073 1076 1080 1109 1114 1126 1129 1143 1144 1154 1173 1189
  1191 1195 1210 1234 1253 1296 1297 1301 1307 1309 1320 1326 1389
  1392 1406 1422 1437 1453 1494 1514 1529 1532 1542 1547 1548 1553
  1560 1561 1565 1568 1585 1589 1590 1595 1603 1609 1656 1730 1737
  1744 1755 1756 1779 *1798 1830 1855 1857 1872 1874 *1875 1876 1888
  1892 1895 1900 1905 1918 1936 1938 1954 1971 1983 1993 2033 2034
  2074 2078 2079 2083 2084 2088 2090 2095 2096 2097 2100 2143 2153
  2154 2169 2170 *2190 2197 2239 2244 2253 2261 2266 2317 2386 2390
  2397 2495 2500 2579 2606 *2690 2720 2747 2750 2756 *2792 2820 2874
  2898 2907 2939 2947 2953 2975 *2981 2984 2991 3000 3001 3007 3018
  3025 3057 3074 3094 3129 3132 3137 3140 3165 3168 3172 3178 3190
  3207 3208 3209 3211 3243 3247 3253 *3264 *3291 *3295 3371 3378 3382
  3387 3389 3395 3396 3410 *3415 3419 3426 3437 3438 3440 3446 3448
  3450 3458 = 243*14
THITHER = 4
  Thither he darts it. Bosome vp my counsell,   172
  Then Deputy of Ireland, who remou'd | Earle *Surrey*, was sent thither,
  and in hast too,   874
  Something I can command. As I walke thither, | Ile tell ye more.   2544
  Cran. For me? | Must I goe like a Traytor thither?   3156
THOMAS = 20*3
  the Nobles, and Sir Thomas Louell: the Cardinall   318
  The Cardinals and Sir *Thomas Louels* heads | Should haue gone off.   533
  What newes, Sir *Thomas Louell?*   589
  Enter Sir Thomas Louell.   590
  L.Cham. Sir *Thomas,* | Whither were you a going?   633
  My Barge stayes; | Your Lordship shall along: Come, good Sir *Thomas,* 654
  San. Sir *Thomas Louell,* had the Cardinall   679
  Sir *Thomas Bullens* Daughter, the Viscount *Rochford,*   798
  Card. Sir *Thomas Louell,* iś the Banket ready | I'th' Priuy Chamber? |
  Lou. Yes, my Lord.   804
  **side*, accompanied with Sir Thomas Louell, Sir Nicholas*   891
  Buck. Sir *Thomas Louell,* I as free forgiue you   925
  Crom. The next is, that Sir *Thomas Moore* is chosen | Lord Chancellor,
  in your place.   2303
  2 Who may that be, I pray you. | 3 *Thomas Cromwell,*   2534
  Enter Gardiner Bishop of Winchester, a Page with a Torch | *before him,*
  met by Sir Thomas Louell.   2769
  *To waste these times. Good houre of night Sir *Thomas*:   2776

THOMAS *cont.*
  Gar. I did Sir *Thomas*, and left him at Primero | With the Duke of
  Suffolke. 2779
  Gard. Not yet Sir *Thomas Louell*: what's the matter? 2783
  Good time, and liue: but for the Stocke Sir *Thomas*, 2797
  Gard. But Sir, Sir, | Heare me Sir *Thomas*, y'are a Gentleman 2803
  'Twill not Sir *Thomas Louell*, tak't of me, 2807
  Gard. Yes, yes, Sir *Thomas*, | There are that Dare, and I my selfe haue
  ventur'd 2818
  He be conuented. He's a ranke weed Sir *Thomas*, 2831
  I hinder you too long: Good night, Sir *Thomas*. | *Exit Gardiner and*
  Page. 2833
THORNY = 1
  Of the good Queene; but the sharpe thorny points 1594
THOSE *l.*6 10 46 346 377 602 609 905 927 968 973 1004 *1804 *2192 2205
  2238 2358 2397 *2402 2464 2524 2612 2616 2739 2828 2900 2925 3069
  *3248 3407 3409 3452 = 29*4
THOU *l.*488 496 536 1118 1500 1619 2138 2139 2143 2150 2167 2330 2344
  2362 *2363 2364 2457 2556 2631 2848 3197 3198 3427 3436 = 24*1
THOUGH = 13
  And though we leaue it with a roote thus hackt, 433
  L.San. New customes, | Though they be neuer so ridiculous, 573
  I would not be so sicke though for his place: 1128
  (Though he be growne so desperate to be honest) 1714
  What we can do to him (though now the time 1844
  Then out it goes. What though I know her vertuous 1955
  (Though all the world should cracke their duty to you, 2069
  And throw it from their Soule, though perils did 2070
  A sure, and safe one, though thy Master mist it. 2353
  Grif. This Cardinall, | Though from an humble Stocke, vndoubtedly 2606
  And though he were vnsatisfied in getting, 2613
  The other (though vnfinish'd) yet so Famous, 2619
  Though in her Cradle; yet now promises 3388
THOUGHT = 9*1
  As to the Tower, I thought; I would haue plaid 545
  The very thought of this faire Company, | Clapt wings to me. 676
  An. Oh Gods will, much better | She ne're had knowne pompe; though't
  be temporall, 1215
  And prest in with this Caution. First, me thought 1553
  This world had ayr'd them. Hence I tooke a thought, 1560
  Queen. The more shame for ye; holy men I thought ye, 1734
  That little thought when she set footing heere, 1822
  Abound, as thicke as thought could make 'em, and 2071
  'Tis well there's one aboue 'em yet; I had thought 3026
  I had thought, I had had men of some vnderstanding, 3205
THOUGHTS = 5*1
  Beyond thoughts Compasse, that former fabulous Storie 80
  But halfe my Lay-thoughts in him, some of these 680
  Full of sad thoughts and troubles. 1044
  *From these sad thoughts, that work too much vpon him: 1093
  Remoue these Thoughts from you. The which before 1461
  Holy and Heauenly thoughts still Counsell her: 3399
THOUSAND = 8*1
  Of thousand Friends: Then, in a moment, see 30
  For which I pay 'em a thousand thankes, 768
  To leaue, a thousand fold more bitter, then 1209

THOUSAND *cont.*

A Thousand pound a yeare, Annuall support, | Out of his Grace, he addes.	1280
A thousand pounds a yeare, for pure respect?	1317
Cast thousand beames vpon me, like the Sun?	2666
*thousand, here will bee Father, God-father, and all to-|gether.	3296
Vpon this Land a thousand thousand Blessings,	3389

THOUSANDS = 1

That promises mo thousands: Honours traine	1319

THREE *see also* 3. = 3*3

Abur. I do know | Kinsmen of mine, three at the least, that haue	132
Enter Brandon, a Sergeant at Armes before him, and | *two or three of the Guard.*	276
Pursu'd him still, and three nights after this,	2579
*did I hit three times on the head, and three times	3303
*these three dayes; besides the running Banquet of two | Beadles, that is to come.	3323

THREEPENCE = *1

Old.L. Tis strange; a threepence bow'd would hire me	1245

THRIFT = 1

Seemes to flow from him? How, i'th'name of Thrift	1970

THROND = 1

What foure Thron'd ones could haue weigh'd | Such a compounded one?	53

THRONG = 3

And follow'd with the generall throng, and sweat	29
That many maz'd considerings, did throng	1552
Exit King, frowning vpon the Cardinall, the Nobles | *throng after him smiling, and whispering.*	2081

THROUGH = 4*1

Peepe through each part of him: whence ha's he that,	119
England and France, might through their amity	257
*Comes through Commissions, which compels from each	390
That Vertue must goe through: we must not stint	411
That through our Intercession, this Reuokement	443

THROUGHLY = 1

Most throughly to be winnowed, where my Chaffe	2908

THROW = 2

Many a groaning throw: thus hulling in	1566
And throw it from their Soule, though perils did	2070

THRUST = 1

Kin. Who's there I say? How dare you thrust your | (selues	1105

THUNDER = *1

Por. These are the youths that thunder at a Playhouse,	3318

THUS = 25*4

As he cride thus let be, to as much end,	247
And pau'd with gold: the Emperor thus desir'd,	264
(As soone he shall by me) that thus the Cardinall	267
And though we leaue it with a roote thus hackt,	433
Cham. Because they speak no English, thus they praid	758
Card. Pray tell 'em thus much from me:	776
Buck. All good people, | You that thus farre haue come to pitty me;	896
Yet thus farre we are one in Fortunes; both	967
That thus you should proceede to put me off,	1375
And thus' farre cleare him.	1533
*Then marke th'inducement. Thus it came; giue heede | (too't:	1536
Many a groaning throw: thus hulling in	1566

THUS *cont.*
  Qu. Haue I liu'd thus long (let me speake my selfe,   1758
  And am I thus rewarded? 'Tis not well Lords.   1766
  Forsooth an Inuentory, thus importing | The seuerall parcels of his
  Plate, his Treasure,   1987
  And from this Fellow? If we liue thus tamely,   2170
  To be thus Iaded by a peece of Scarlet,   2171
  But thus much, they are foule ones.   2193
  Let's dry our eyes: And thus farre heare me *Cromwel,*   2346
  Yet thus farre *Griffith,* giue me leaue to speake him,   2587
  And able meanes, we had not parted thus.   2745
  Cran. I am fearefull: Wherefore frownes he thus?   2880
  It fits we thus proceed, or else no witnesse | Would come against you.   2904
  At least good manners; as not thus to suffer   3028
  Cham. Then thus for you my Lord, it stands agreed   3144
  Chan. Thus farre | My most dread Soueraigne, may it like your Grace,   3218
  I will say thus much for him, if a Prince   3227
  *Of thee, which sayes thus: Doe my Lord of *Canterbury*   3250
  My Noble Partners, and my selfe thus pray   3370
THY *l.*1497 1501 1502 1503 1611 1617 1950 2142 2145 2146 2175 2278
  2328 2333 2345 2353 2358 2360 2362 *2363 2632 2857 2913 2914 2965
  2967 2968 *3248 3365 3379 = 31*2
TIDE = 3
  The Spaniard tide by blood and fauour to her,   1137
  Ti'de it by Letters Patents. Now, who'll take it? | *Sur.* The King that
  gaue it.   2135
  Man. Alas I know not, how gets the Tide in?   3275
TIDINGS *see* tydings
TIED *see* ti'de, ty'de
TILL = 16*1
  Till this time Pompe was single, but now married   59
  Became the next dayes master, till the last   61
  Is pleas'd you shall to th'Tower, till you know | How he determines
  further.   297
  Till now I neuer knew thee. | *Musicke, Dance.*   772
  Yet are the Kings; and till my Soule forsake,   933
  Beseech you Sir, to spare me, till I may   1408
  That we adiourne this Court till further day;   1603
  Which euer ha's, and euer shall be growing, | Till death (that Winter)
  kill it.   2052
  Till you heare further from his Highnesse. | *Car.* Stay: 2115
  Car. Till I finde more then will, or words to do it,   2121
  For then, and not till then, he felt himselfe,   2623
  Till *Cranmer, Cromwel,* her two hands, and shee | Sleepe in their
  Graues.   2808
  But that till further Triall, in those Charges   2900
  Cran. Why? | *Keep.* Your Grace must waight till you be call'd for.   2996
  Till they obey the mannage. If we suffer   3072
  There to remaine till the Kings further pleasure   3147
  *till her pinck'd porrenger fell off her head, for kindling   3307
TILT = 1
  The fire that mounts the liquor til't run ore,   217
TIMBER = 1
  From euery Tree, lop, barke, and part o'th' Timber: 432
TIME = 13
  Buck. All the whole time | I was my Chambers Prisoner.   55
  Till this time Pompe was single, but now married   59

TIME *cont.*

    Vpon our faile; to this poynt hast thou heard him, | At any time speake
ought?   488

    L.San. Tis time to giue 'em Physicke, their diseases | Are growne so
catching.   614

    You'l finde a most vnfit time to disturbe him: 1097

    Is longer then his fore-skirt; by this time   1320

    You may then spare that time. | *Car.* Bee't so, proceed.   1356

    I will be bold with time and your attention: 1535

    You were now running o're: you haue scarse time   2008

    In time will finde their fit Rewards. That Seale   2130

    That gentle Physicke giuen in time, had cur'd me: 2710

    Come Lords, we trifle time away: I long   3252

    For this Play at this time, is onely in   3458

TIME = 1

    A long time out of play, may bring his plaine song,   · 626

TIME = 12*1

    Kin. I remember of such a time, being my sworn ser-|(uant,   542

    Longer then I haue time to tell his yeares;   935

    And when old Time shall lead him to his end,   937

    And processe of this time, you can report,   1392

    Let me haue time and Councell for my Cause: 1705

    The offer of this time, I cannot promise,   1830

    What we can do to him (though now the time   1844

    Car. Sir, | For Holy Offices I haue a time; a time   2013

    1 'Tis very true. But that time offer'd sorrow, | This generall ioy. 2385

    In the old time of Warre, would shake the prease   2498

    Good time, and liue: but for the Stocke Sir *Thomas*,   2797

    Which Time shall bring to ripenesse: She shall be,   3390

TIMES = 6*3

    They turne to vicious formes, ten times more vgly   456

    Go too; Ile make ye know your times of businesse: 1113

    At all times to your will conformable: 1378

    Her times of preseruation, which perforce   2017

    Kath. O my Lord, | The Times and Titles now are alter'd strangely 2697

    Not for delights: Times to repayre our Nature   2774

    *To waste these times. Good houre of night Sir *Thomas*: 2776

    *did I hit three times on the head, and three times   3303

TIPSTAUES = *1

    Enter Buckingham from his Arraignment, Tipstaues before 889

TIRES *see* tyres

TIS *l.*202 249 289 410 566 597 614 637 729 872 988 1015 1023 1050 *1070
1199 1210 1218 1224 *1245 1253 1311 1485 1602 1766 1924 1954 2024
2025 2076 2089 2090 2232 2290 2367 2383 2385 2387 2396 2453 2519
2521 2709 2856 2871 2881 2972 2975 2985 3003 3024 3026 *3101 3111
3125 3166 3167 3173 3269 3271 3450 3453 3454 3462 = 62*3

TITLE = 6

    Abur. A proper Title of a Peace, and purchas'd | At a superfluous rate. 156

    Kin. Speake on; | How grounded hee his Title to the Crowne   486

    What thinke you of a Dutchesse? Haue you limbs | To beare that load
of Title?   1247

    Then Marchionesse of *Pembrooke*; to which Title,   1279

    To giue vp willingly that Noble Title   1775

    This good man (few of you deserue that Title)   3208

TITLES = 2

    For since the Cardinall fell, that Titles lost,   2518

    Kath. O my Lord, | The Times and Titles now are alter'd strangely 2697

TO *see also* t', too = 539*29
TODAY *see* day
TOGETHER = 12*2
    In their Embracement, as they grew together, | Which had they,   51
    I meane who set the Body, and the Limbes | Of this great Sport
    together?   92
    Together; To consider further, that | What his high Hatred would effect,
    wants not   166
    Two women plac'd together, makes cold weather: 693
    Now present heere together: that's to say,   1569
    Together with all famous Colledges   1912
    Does he rake this together? Now my Lords, | Saw you the Cardinall?   1971
    Car. And euer may your Highnesse yoake together,   2021
    Of all that world of Wealth I haue drawne together   2091
    (With thee, and all thy best parts bound together)   2146
    Together sung *Te Deum.* So she parted,   2513
    Come, you and I must walke a turne together: 2889
    I should haue tane some paines, to bring together   2918
    *thousand, here will bee Father, God-father, and all to-|gether.   3296
TOLD = 4
    I told my Lord the Duke, by th'Diuels illusions   526
    San. I told your Grace, they would talke anon.   732
    (That Sun, I pray may neuer set) I haue told him,   2329
    Suff. 'Tis the right Ring, by Heau'n: I told ye all,   3167
TOLEDO = 1
    The Archbishopricke of *Toledo*, this is purpos'd.   1018
TOMBE = 1
    May haue a Tombe of Orphants teares wept on him.   2310
TOMORROW *see* morrow
TONGUE = 12*2
    Durst wagge his Tongue in censure, when these Sunnes   77
    Which Actions selfe, was tongue too.   87
    Card. Good Lord Chamberlaine, | *Go, giue 'em welcome; you can
    speake the French tongue   744
    These newes are euery where, euery tongue speaks 'em,   1071
    One generall Tongue vnto vs. This good man,   1143
    So good a Lady, that no Tongue could euer   1204
    Were tri'de by eu'ry tongue, eu'ry eye saw 'em,   1659
    *A strange Tongue makes my cause more strange, suspiti-|(ous: 1668
    To taint that honour euery good Tongue blesses;   1679
    Any thing on him: for he hath a Witchcraft | Ouer the King in's
    Tongue.   1847
    Within these fortie houres, Surrey durst better | Haue burnt that
    Tongue, then saide so.   2140
    Is the Kings hand, and tongue, and who dare speak | One syllable
    against him?   2816
    And thinke with wagging of your tongue to win me: 3196
    To let my tongue excuse all. What was purpos'd   3220
TONGUES = 5
    Tongues spit their duties out, and cold hearts freeze   394
    Traduc'd by ignorant Tongues, which neither know   407
    To stop the rumor; and allay those tongues | That durst disperse it.   1004
    To silence enuious Tongues. Be iust, and feare not;   2361
    There's none stands vnder more calumnious tongues, | Then I my selfe,
    poore man.   2910
TONIGHT *see* night

TOO = 56*4

May heere finde Truth too. Those that come to see	10
As Cherubins, all gilt: the Madams too,	67
Which Actions selfe, was tongue too.	87
Daring th'euent too th'teeth, are all in vprore, | And danger serues among them.	364
They are deuis'd by you, or else you suffer | Too hard an exclamation.	382
Queen. I am much too venturous	387
We cannot feele too little, heare too much.	467
And haue an houre of hearing, and by'r Lady | Held currant Musicke too.	627
Your Lordship is a guest too. | *L.Cham.* O, 'tis true;	636
San. O very mad, exceeding mad, in loue too;	701
Kin. I feare too much.	809
Then Deputy of Ireland, who remou'd | Earle *Surrey*, was sent thither, and in hast too,	874
And farre enough from Court too.	883
I feare, too many curses on their heads | That were the Authors.	985
That will vndoe her: To confirme this too,	1012
Wee are too open heere to argue this:	1024
Ha's crept too neere his Conscience.	1047
Suff. No, his Conscience | Ha's crept too neere another Ladie.	1048
*From these sad thoughts, that work too much vpon him:	1093
Kin. Ye are too bold:	1112
Go too; Ile make ye know your times of businesse:	1113
Haue (too) a Womans heart, which euer yet	1236
Cannot vouchsafe this burthen, tis too weake | Euer to get a Boy.	1253
Come pat betwixt too early, and too late	1304
Or made it not mine too? Or which of your Friends	1383
And proue it too, against mine Honor, aught;	1393
Queen. My Lord, My Lord, | I am a simple woman, much too weake	1465
You haue too much good Lady: But to know	1681
Both of his truth and him (which was too farre)	1690
His Loue, too long ago. I am old my Lords,	1752
Haue euer come too short of my Desires,	2044
Cham. O my Lord, | Presse not a falling man too farre: 'tis Vertue:	2231
There is betwixt that smile we would aspire too,	2269
A loade, would sinke a Nauy, (too much Honor.)	2289
Too heauy for a man, that hopes for Heauen.	2291
Thy hopefull seruice perish too. Good *Cromwell*	2333
1 That I can tell you too. The Archbishop	2406
On that Coelestiall Harmony I go too. | *Sad and solemne Musicke.*	2638
Deserue we no more Reuerence? | *Grif.* You are too blame,	2683
To vse so rude behauiour. Go too, kneele.	2686
Kath. O my good Lord, that comfort comes too late,	2708
Lou. I must to him too | Before he go to bed. Ile take my leaue.	2781
I hinder you too long: Good night, Sir *Thomas.* | *Exit Gardiner and Page.*	2833
My mindes not on't, you are too hard for me.	2838
For I must thinke of that, which company | Would not be friendly too.	2859
Vpon this naughty Earth? Go too, go too,	2939
They shall no more preuaile, then we giue way too:	2946
Cran. I hope I am not too late, and yet the Gentleman	2989
And at the dore too, like a Post with Packets:	3031
Gard. Which Reformation must be sodaine too	3068
By your good fauour, too sharpe; Men so Noble,	3123
Remember your bold life too.	3139

TOO *cont.*

Cham. This is too much; | Forbeare for shame my Lords.	3140
Cham. Tis now too certaine; | How much more is his Life in value with	
him?	3173
They are too thin, and base to hide offences,	3194
They grow still too; from all Parts they are comming,	3327
*Kin. My Noble Gossips, y'haue beene too Prodigall;	3381

TOOKE = 2*1

Buc. Why the Diuell, | Vpon this French going out, tooke he vpon him	123
*of my Lord Cardinalls, by Commission, and maine power tooke	1032
This world had ayr'd them. Hence I tooke a thought,	1560

TOOLE = *1

*great Toole, come to Court, the women so besiege vs?	3293

TOOS = 1

I writ too's Holinesse. Nay then, farewell:	2102

TOOT = 8

The force of this Commission: pray looke too't;	437
L.Ch. Death my Lord, | Their cloathes are after such a Pagan cut too't,	586
Now, what mou'd me too't,	1534
*Then marke th'inducement. Thus it came; giue heede | (too't:	1536
Doe no more Offices of life too't; then	1557
Suf. My Amen too't. | *Nor.* All mens.	1885
Out of the paine you suffer'd, gaue no eare too't.	2560
No great offence belongs too't, giue your Friend	2785

TOOTH = 1

Your Colts tooth is not cast yet? | *L.San.* No my Lord,	630

TOPPING = *1

*Ore-topping womans powre. Madam, you do me wrong	1447

TOPS = 1

And the Mountaine tops that freeze,	1622

TOP-PROUD = 1

By your prescription: but this top-proud fellow,	225

TORCH = 1

Enter Gardiner Bishop of Winchester, a Page with a Torch | before him,	
met by Sir Thomas Louell.	2769

TORNE = 1

Not being torne a pieces, we haue done:	3336

TOTH = 7

For high feats done to'th'Crowne; neither Allied	110
He bores me with some tricke; He's gone to'th'King:	198
Barre his accesse to'th'King, neuer attempt	1846
To'th'good of your most Sacred Person, and	2047
You writ to'th Pope, against the King: your goodnesse	2180
Which is to'th Court, and there ye shall be my Guests:	2543
My Legges like loaden Branches bow to'th'Earth,	2553

TOUCH = 3

Touch me alike: th'are breath I not beleeue in.	1088
Or touch of her good Person?	1520
Some touch of your late businesse: Affaires that walke	2786

TOUCHD = 2

King. The fairest hand I euer touch'd: O Beauty,	771
I haue touch'd the highest point of all my Greatnesse,	2103

TOWARD = 4

The passages made toward it; on my Honour,	1531
Toward this remedy, whereupon we are	1568
Toward the King, my euer Roiall Master,	2162
Toward the King first, then his Lawes, in filling	3063

TOWARDS = 2*1
(And take it from a heart, that wishes towards you 163
*him, the Axe with the edge towards him, Halberds on each 890
And like her true Nobility, she ha's | Carried her selfe towards me. 1506
TOWER = 7*1
The busines present. Tis his Highnes pleasure | You shall to th' Tower. 289
Is pleas'd you shall to th'Tower, till you know | How he determines
further. 297
As to the Tower, I thought; I would haue plaid 545
From hence you be committed to the Tower, 3103
You be conuaid to th' Tower a Prisoner; 3146
But I must needs to th' Tower my Lords? 3151
Gard. Receiue him, | And see him safe i'th' Tower. 3158
*tribulation of Tower Hill, or the Limbes of Limehouse, 3320
TOWNE = 1
The First and Happiest Hearers of the Towne, 25
TOWRE = 1
To make your house our Towre: you, a Brother of vs 2903
TOYLE = 1
Not vs'd to toyle, did almost sweat to beare 68
TRACE = 1
Sur. Now all my ioy | Trace the Coniunction. 1883
TRACT = 1
In Honor, Honesty, the tract of eu'ry thing, 85
TRACTABLE = 1
This tractable obedience is a Slaue 397
TRADE = 1
Stands in the gap and Trade of moe Preferments, 2814
TRADUCD = 1
Traduc'd by ignorant Tongues, which neither know 407
TRAINE = 6*1
Shall lessen this bigge looke. | Exeunt Cardinall, and his Traine. 186
I haue done; and God forgiue me. | Exeunt Duke and Traine. 982
That promises mo thousands: Honours traine 1319
wrought with Flowers bearing the Queenes Traine. 2442
2 A Royall Traine beleeue me: These I know: 2447
I take it, she that carries vp the Traine, 2466
*a Mantle, &c. Traine borne by a Lady: Then followes 3360
TRAITOR = 1
Car. It must be himselfe then. | Sur. Thou art a proud Traitor, Priest. 2137
TRAITORS = 1
I haue this day receiu'd a Traitors iudgement, 899
TRAP = 1
The trap is laid for me. | King. Be of good cheere, 2944
TRAUAILE = 1
With gentle Trauaile, to the gladding of | Your Highnesse with an
Heire. 2854
TRAUELD = 1
L.Cham. What is't for? | Lou. The reformation of our trauel'd Gallants, 594
TRAUELL = 1
Short blistred Breeches, and those types of Trauell; 609
TRAYNING = 1
To Nature none more bound; his trayning such, 451
TRAYTOR = 3
Kin. A Gyant Traytor. 551
Hee's Traytor to th' height. Exeunt. 568
Cran. For me? | Must I goe like a Traytor thither? 3156

TREASON = 3
    To th'old dam Treason) *Charles* the Emperour,   252
    Arrest thee of High Treason, in the name | Of our most Soueraigne
    King.   282
    Haue found him guilty of high Treason. Much   .   856
TREASONOUS = 2
    Wee see each graine of grauell; I doe know | To be corrupt and
    treasonous.   229
    Norf. Say not treasonous.   231
TREASONS = 1
    And point by point the Treasons of his Maister, | He shall againe relate.   327
TREASURE = 2
    That swallowed so much treasure, and like a glasse   241
    Forsooth an Inuentory, thus importing | The seuerall parcels of his
    Plate, his Treasure,   1987
TREATY = 1
    To this last costly Treaty: Th'enteruiew,   240
TREE = 1 *1
    From euery Tree, lop, barke, and part o'th' Timber: 432
    *Is this a place to roare in? Fetch me a dozen Crab-tree   3264
TREES = 1
    SONG. | *Orpheus with his Lute made Trees,*   1620
TREMBLE = 1
    Yea, with a spitting power, and made to tremble   1550
TREMBLING = 1
    A trembling Contribution; why we take   431
TRIALL = 2
    The Duke of Buckingham came from his Triall.   2384
    But that till further Triall, in those Charges   2900
TRIBULATION = *1
    *tribulation of Tower Hill, or the Limbes of Limehouse,   3320
TRICKE = 3
    He bores me with some tricke; He's gone to'th'King: 198
    Haue got a speeding tricke to lay downe Ladies.   620
    2. That tricke of State | Was a deepe enuious one,   877
TRICKES = 2
    This dilatory sloth, and trickes of Rome.   1609
    All his trickes founder, and he brings his Physicke   1877
TRIDE = 2
    Disdainfull to be tride by't; tis not well.   1485
    Were tri'de by eu'ry tongue, eu'ry eye saw 'em,   1659
TRIFLE = 2
    Kin. I may perceiue | These Cardinals trifle with me: I abhorre   1607
    Come Lords, we trifle time away: I long   3252
TRIM = 2
    L.Cham. What a losse our Ladies | Will haue of these trim vanities?   616
    Theres a trim rabble let in: are all these   3330
TRIMD = 1
    That is new trim'd; but benefit no further   415
TRIPPING = *1
    The Vision. | *Enter solemnely tripping one after another, sixe*
    Personages,   2642
TRIUMPH = 1
    Will triumph o're my person, which I waigh not,   2924
TROA = 1
    Deales with our Cardinal, and as I troa   260

TROD = 2
Qu. Would I had neuer trod this English Earth,   1779
Say *Wolsey*, that once trod the wayes of Glory,   2350
TROOPE = 2*1
Kath. No? Saw you not euen now a blessed Troope   2664
To let the Troope passe fairely; or Ile finde   3346
* *The Troope passe once about the Stage, and Gar-| ter speakes.*   3362
TROOPES = 1
Or gilde againe the Noble Troopes that waighted   2325
TROTH = 2*2
Anne. By my troth, and Maidenhead, | I would not be a Queene.   1230
If you might please to stretch it. | *Anne.* Nay, good troth.   1241
* *Old L.* Yes troth, & troth; you would not be a Queen?   1243
TROUBLE = 2
I haue not long to trouble thee. Good *Griffith*,   2635
Say his long trouble now is passing   2755
TROUBLES = 2
Full of sad thoughts and troubles.   1044
My Soule growes sad with troubles,   1618
TROUBLESOME = 1
Gard. What other, | Would you expect? You are strangely troublesome: 3152
TROUPE = 1
Cham. How now, what is't? | *Seru.* A noble troupe of Strangers,   739
TRUANT = 1
I am not such a Truant since my comming,   1666
TRUE = 16*2
To make that onely true, we now intend,   22
And those of true condition; That your Subiects   346
Your Lordship is a guest too. | *L.Cham.* O, 'tis true;   636
They are set heere for examples. | *L.Cham.* True, they are so;   651
* *Cham.* Heauen keep me from such councel: tis most true   1070
And euery true heart weepes for't. All that dare   1072
I haue bene to you, a true and humble Wife,   1377
And like her true Nobility, she ha's | Carried her selfe towards me.   1506
Since Vertue findes no friends) a Wife, a true one?   1759
Nor. Beleeue it, this is true)   1857
If what I now pronounce, you haue found true: 2037
What, and how true thou art; he will aduance thee: 2330
So good, so Noble, and so true a Master?   2338
1 'Tis very true. But that time offer'd sorrow, | This generall ioy.   2385
For Vertue, and true Beautie of the Soule,   2736
King. 'Tis true: where is he *Denny*?   2871
Gard. With a true heart, | And Brother; loue I doe it.   3244
* *Kin.* Good Man, those ioyfull teares shew thy true | (hearts,   3248
TRUELY = 2
1. Yes truely is he, | And condemn'd vpon't.   833
God shall be truely knowne, and those about her,   3407
TRUE-HEARTED = 1
I sweare he is true-hearted, and a soule   2957
TRULY = 4
Henry the Seauenth succeeding, truly pittying   958
My Lord of Norfolke, as you are truly Noble,   2182
Neuer so truly happy, my good *Cromwell*,   2283
A man in much esteeme with th'King, and truly   2536
TRUMPET = 1
Drum and Trumpet, Chambers dischargd.   731

TRUMPETS = 7*1
Who's best in fauour. Let the Musicke knock it. | *Exeunt with
  Trumpets.*   817
Trumpets, Sennet, and Cornets.   1333
The Trumpets sound: Stand close,   2419
1 *A liuely Flourish of Trumpets.* | 2 *Then, two Iudges.*   2422
Exeunt, first passing ouer the Stage in Order and State, and | *then, A
  great Flourish of Trumpets.*   2445
Ye should doe Seruice. Harke the Trumpets sound,   3343
Enter Trumpets sounding: Then two Aldermen, L.(ord) Maior,   3354
Whaue frighted with our Trumpets: so 'tis cleare,   3453
TRUNCHEONERS = *1
*might see from farre, some forty Truncheoners draw to   3310
TRUST = 3
(This was his Gentleman in trust) of him   464
They that my trust must grow to, liue not heere,   1717
To trust vs in your businesse) we are ready | To vse our vtmost Studies,
  in your seruice.   1811
TRUSTED = 1
A better Wife, let him in naught be trusted,   1499
TRUTH = 23
May heere finde Truth too. Those that come to see   10
To ranke our chosen Truth with such a show   19
Sur. On my Soule, Ile speake but truth.   525
That neuer knew what Truth meant: I now seale it;   951
2. But that slander Sir, | Is found a truth now: for it growes agen 1006
An. No in truth. | *Old.L.* Then you are weakly made; plucke off a
  little,   1249
I hold my most malicious Foe, and thinke not | At all a Friend to truth. 1441
As you haue done my Truth. If he know   1457
Out with it boldly: Truth loues open dealing.   1663
If you speake truth, for their poore Mistris sake;   1670
Both of his truth and him (which was too farre)   1690
In truth I know not. I was set at worke,   1700
That in the way of Loyaltie, and Truth,   2161
When the King knowes my Truth.   2196
(Out of thy honest truth) to play the Woman.   2345
With thy Religious Truth, and Modestie,   2632
Thy Truth, and thy Integrity is rooted   2913
Cran. Most dread Liege, | The good I stand on, is my Truth and
  Honestie: 2921
The Iustice and the Truth o'th' question carries   2931
That's the plaine truth; your painted glosse discouers   3120
Let none thinke Flattery; for they'l finde'em Truth.   3386
Shall still be doubled on her. Truth shall Nurse her,   3398
And so stand fix'd. Peace, Plenty, Loue, Truth, Terror,   3418
TRUTHS = *1
*Thy Gods, and Truths. Then if thou fall'st (O *Cromwell*)   2363
TRUTHS-SAKE = 1
For Truths-sake, and his Conscience; that his bones,   2308
TRY = 1
Power, as he was a Counsellour to try him,   3213
TRYALL = 7
Call him to present tryall: if he may   565
And without Tryall, fell; Gods peace be with him.   957
For euer from the World. I had my Tryall,   964
The Tryall, iust and Noble. All the Clerkes,   1139

TRYALL *cont.*

For if the tryall of the Law o'retake ye,	1726
And our consent, for better tryall of you,	3102
(If there be faith in men) meant for his Tryall,	3222

TRYE = 1

Would trye him to the vtmost, had ye meane,	3216

TUMULT = 1

*Noyse and Tumult within: Enter Porter and	his man.*	3257

TUNES = 1

As lowd, and to as many Tunes. Hats, Cloakes,	2493

TURNE = 8

They turne to vicious formes, ten times more vgly	456
Turne me away: and let the fowl'st Contempt	1396
Ile turne to sparkes of fire.	1430
You turne the good we offer, into enuy.	1745
Quee. Ye turne me into nothing. Woe vpon ye,	1746
Come, you and I must walke a turne together:	2889
(God turne their hearts, I neuer sought their malice)	3008
A shrewd turne, and hee's your friend for euer:	3251

TURNES = *1

*Turnes what he list. The King will know him one day.	1053

TUSH = 1

It was much like to doe: He answer'd, Tush,	530

TWAS = 3*1

'Twas said they saw but one, and no Discerner	76
(For twas indeed his colour, but he came	254
Said, 'twas the feare indeed, and that he doubted	504
*The Monke might be deceiu'd, and that 'twas dangerous	527

TWENTY = 3*1

He would Kisse you Twenty with a breath.	703
That like a Iewell, ha's hung twenty yeares	1064
Vpward of twenty years, and haue bene blest	1390
*by his face, for o' my conscience twenty of the Dog-|dayes	3300

TWER = 1*1

Sur. I would 'twer somthing y would fret the string,	1965
As 'twer in Loues particular, be more	To me your Friend, then any.	2064

TWILL = 6

It reaches farre, and where 'twill not extend,	171
2. This Secret is so weighty, 'twill require	993
Hee's louing and most gracious. 'Twill be much,	1724
I know 'twill stirre him strongly; yet I know	2098
'Twill not Sir *Thomas Louell,* tak't of me,	2807
And say twill doe; I know within a while,	3461

TWINNES = 1

Those twinnes of Learning, that he rais'd in you,	2616

TWIXT = 2

Nor. 'Twixt Guynes and Arde,	48
And Marriage 'twixt the Duke of *Orleance,* and	1541

TWO *see also* 2. = 19*18

Onely a show or two, and so agree,	11
Richly in two short houres. Onely they	14
Those Sunnes of Glory, those two Lights of Men	Met in the vale of Andren.	46
Made it a Foole, and Begger. The two Kings	72
of the Guard, and two Secretaries with Papers: The	176
*Enter Brandon, a Sergeant at Armes before him, and	two or three of the Guard.*	276

VAINLY = 1
Then vainly longing. What we oft doe best,   416
VALE = 1
Those Sunnes of Glory, those two Lights of Men | Met in the vale of
Andren.   46
VALEWES = 1
The Peace betweene the French and vs, not valewes | The Cost that did
conclude it.   142
VALUE = 1
Cham. Tis now too certaine; | How much more is his Life in value with
him?   3173
VALUES = 1
An. My good Lord, | Not your demand; it values not your asking: 1266
VANISH = *1
*their Dancing vanish, carrying the Garland with them. | The Musicke
continues.*   2656
VANITIES = 2*1
To do in these fierce Vanities? I wonder,   102
L.Cham. What a losse our Ladies | Will haue of these trim vanities?   616
*More worth, then empty vanities: yet Prayers & Wishes   1286
VANITY = 1
For this great Iourney. What did this vanity   138
VAUX = 2
Vaux, Sir Walter Sands, and common people, &c.   892
Then giue my Charge vp to Sir *Nicholas Vaux,*   940
VAUX = 1
VEHEMENCIE = 1
Faile not to vse, and with what vehemencie   2951
VENOMD-MOUTHD = *1
**Buc.* This Butchers Curre is venom'd-mouth'd, and I   188
VENT = 1
Of all their Loyalties; wherein, although | My good Lord Cardinall,
they vent reproches   349
VENTURD = 2
And then he fals as I do. I haue ventur'd   2259
Gard. Yes, yes, Sir *Thomas,* | There are that Dare, and I my selfe haue
ventur'd   2818
VENTURE = 3
The King will venture at it. Either the Cardinall,   1009
Norff. If it doe, Ile venture one; haue at him. | *Suff.* I another.   1130
You'ld venture an emballing: I my selfe   1259
VENTURE = 1
Old.L. Beshrew me, I would, | And venture Maidenhead for't, and so
would you   1232
VENTUROUS = 1
Queen. I am much too venturous   387
VERDICT = 1
The dew o'th'Verdict with it; at what ease   2932
VERGERS = *1
Enter two Vergers, with short siluer wands; next them two   1334
VERIFIED = 1
The common voyce I see is verified   3249
VERILY = 1
An. So much the more | Must pitty drop vpon her; verily   1222
VERITY = 1
'Twould proue the verity of certaine words   505

VERTUE = 9
That Vertue must goe through: we must not stint   411
I tender my Commission; by whose vertue,   1151
Since Vertue findes no friends) a Wife, a true one?   1759
Cham. O my Lord, | Presse not a falling man too farre: 'tis Vertue: 2231
That Christendome shall euer speake his Vertue.   2621
For Vertue, and true Beautie of the Soule,   2736
And by that vertue no man dare accuse you.   3099
By vertue of that Ring, I take my cause   3162
More couetous of Wisedome, and faire Vertue   3394
VERTUES = 6
Tane of your many vertues; the Kings Maiesty   1276
Vpon my Soule two reuerend Cardinall Vertues: 1735
Camp. Madam, you'l finde it so: | You wrong your Vertues   1805
Grif. Noble Madam: | Mens euill manners, liue in Brasse, their Vertues   2600
Being of those Vertues vacant. I feare nothing | What can be said
against me.   2925
With all the Vertues that attend the good,   3397
VERTUOUS = 5
And fearing he would rise (he was so vertuous)   1181
For he would needs be vertuous. That good Fellow,   1187
Then out it goes. What though I know her vertuous   1955
2 He of Winchester | Is held no great good louer of the Archbishops, |
The vertuous *Cranmer.*   2528
Beseeching him to giue her vertuous breeding.   2725
VERY = 12
The very Persons of our Noble Story,   27
The Pride vpon them, that their very labour   69
That such a Keech can with his very bulke   103
I doe pronounce him in that very shape   274
To make the Scepter his. These very words   475
Their very noses had been Councellours   580
The very thought of this faire Company, | Clapt wings to me.   676
San. O very mad, exceeding mad, in loue too;   701
A very fresh Fish heere; fye, fye, fye vpon   1306
B.Lin. Very well my Liedge.   1577
1 'Tis very true. But that time offer'd sorrow, | This generall ioy.   2385
Chan. My good Lord Archbishop, I'm very sorry   3056
VESSELL = 1
As rau'nous Fishes doe a Vessell follow   414
VEXD = 2
Nor. He is vex'd at something.   1963
The King will suffer but the little finger | Of this man to be vex'd?   3171
VEXE = 1
They vexe me past my patience, pray you passe on;   1492
VGLY = 1
They turne to vicious formes, ten times more vgly   456
VICIOUS = 1
They turne to vicious formes, ten times more vgly   456
VIEW = 4
Nor. Then you lost | The view of earthly glory: Men might say   57
Order gaue each thing view. The Office did   90
Craue leaue to view these Ladies, and entreat   764
Had the full view of, such a noyse arose,   2491
VIEWD = 2
Crom. Presently | He did vnseale them, and the first he view'd,   1932
This day was view'd in open, as his Queene,   2317

VILLAGE = 1
Why they are so; but like to Village Curres, 1525
VINE = 2
Vnder his owne Vine what he plants; and sing 3405
Shall then be his, and like a Vine grow to him; 3420
VIOLENCE = 1
You aske with such a Violence, the King 2131
VIOLENT = 1
By violent swiftnesse that which we run at; 215
VIRGIN = 1
She must, the Saints must haue her; yet a Virgin, 3432
VIRTUE see vertue
VIRTUES see vertues
VIRTUOUS see vertuous
VISAGE = 1
There's more in't then faire Visage. *Bullen?* 1943
VISCOUNT = 1
Sir *Thomas Bullens* Daughter, the Viscount *Rochford,* 798
VISION = 1
The Vision. | *Enter solemnely tripping one after another, sixe
Personages,* 2642
VISIT = 1
The Kings request, that I would visit you, 2704
VISITATION = 2
To whisper *Wolsey*) here makes visitation, 255
Promises Boyes heereafter. Sir, your Queen | Desires your Visitation,
and to be 2973
VIUA = 1
To him brought *viua voce* to his face; 845
VIZARDS = *1
Bayes, and golden Vizards on their faces, Branches of Bayes 2645
VNBOUNDED = 1
Of an vnbounded stomacke, euer ranking 2589
VNCONSIDERED = 1
Not vnconsidered leaue your Honour, nor 341
VNCONTEMND = 1
Suf. Which of the Peeres | Haue vncontemn'd gone by him, or at least 1837
VNDER = 14*7
Vnder pretence to see the Queene his Aunt, 253
The net has falne vpon me, I shall perish | Vnder deuice, and practise. 285
places himselfe vnder the Kings feete on | his right side. 319
Vnder your promis'd pardon. The Subiects griefe 389
Whom after vnder the Commissions Seale, 510
Hoboies. A small Table vnder a State for the Cardinall, a 661
But leaue their Flockes, and vnder your faire Conduct 763
Anne. No, not for all the riches vnder Heauen. 1244
place vnder the Cloth of State. The two Cardinalls sit 1345
vnder him as Iudges. The Queene takes place some di- | stance 1346
How vnder my oppression I did reeke | When I first mou'd you. 1575
Vnder your hands and Seales; therefore goe on, 1592
Cannot stand vnder them. If you omit 1829
At length broke vnder me, and now ha's left me 2263
8 A Canopy, borne by foure of the Cinque-Ports, *vnder it* 2437
There's none stands vnder more calumnious tongues, | Then I my selfe,
poore man. 2910
Fly o're thy Royall head, and shade thy person | Vnder their blessed
wings. 2965

VNDER   cont.

*placed vnder the State. Enter Lord Chancellour, places   3036
*vnder the Line, they need no other pennance: that Fire-|Drake   3302
*Noblemen bearing a Canopy, vnder which the Dutchesse of   3358
Vnder his owne Vine what he plants; and sing   3405
VNDERSTAND = 3
And vnderstand againe like honest men,   610
I came this way so happily. The King | Shall vnderstand it presently.
Exit Buts   3001
To men that vnderstand you, words and weaknesse.   3121
VNDERSTANDING = 2
Will leaue vs neuer an vnderstanding Friend.   23
I had thought, I had had men of some vnderstanding,   3205
VNDERTAKE = 1
Ile vndertake may see away their shilling   13
VNDERTAKES = 1
Who vndertakes you to your end.   941
VNDESERUER = 1
Heap'd vpon me (poore Vndeseruer) I   2049
VNDOE = 1
That will vndoe her: To confirme this too,   1012
VNDOING = 1
'Tis my vndoing. Loue and meekenesse, Lord   3111
VNDONE = 1
This paper ha's vndone me: 'Tis th' Accompt   2090
VNDOOING = 1
You haue for Dignities, to the meere vndooing   2227
VNDOUBTEDLY = 1
Grif. This Cardinall, | Though from an humble Stocke, vndoubtedly   2606
VNFINISHD = 1
The other (though vnfinish'd) yet so Famous,   2619
VNFIT = 2
Vnfit for other life, compeld by hunger   362
You'l finde a most vnfit time to disturbe him: 1097
VNFOLDED = 1
In the Diuorce, his contrarie proceedings | Are all vnfolded: wherein he
appeares,   1858
VNHANDLED = 1
Ha's left the cause o'th'King vnhandled, and   1902
VNHAPPILY = 1
I should iudge now vnhappily.   792
VNHAPPY = 1
I am the most vnhappy Woman liuing.   1783
VNITE = 1
Norf. If you will now vnite in your Complaints,   1827
VNLESSE = 1
Vnlesse wee sweepe 'em from the dore with Cannons,   3270
VNLOOSD = 1
There must I be vnloos'd, although not there   1512
VNMANLY = 1
(Nay let 'em be vnmanly) yet are follow'd.   575
VNMANNERLY = 4
Language vnmannerly; yea, such which breakes   354
I were vnmannerly to take you out,   801
If I haue vs'd my selfe vnmannerly,   1815
My hast made me vnmannerly. There is staying   2688

VNMATCHD = 1
And vnmatch'd Wit, and Iudgement. *Ferdinand*   1401
VNNATURALL = 1
A most vnnaturall and faithlesse Seruice.   969
VNPARTIALL = 1
In the vnpartiall iudging of this Businesse.   1154
VNQUEEND = 1
Then lay me forth (although vnqueen'd) yet like   2764
VNRECOUNTED = 1
To some eares vnrecounted. But my Lords   1889
VNSATISFIED = 1
And though he were vnsatisfied in getting,   2613
VNSAYT = 1
Haue more, or else vnsay't: and now, while 'tis hot,   2985
VNSEALE = 1
Crom. Presently | He did vnseale them, and the first he view'd,   1932
VNSETLED = 1
For your owne quiet, as to rectifie | What is vnsetled in the King.   1418
VNSHAKEN = 1
Should the approach of this wilde Riuer breake, | And stand vnshaken
yours.   2074
VNSOLICITED = 1
To make this present Summons vnsolicited.   1589
VNSPOTTED = 1
A most vnspotted Lilly shall she passe   3433
VNTHINKE = 1
You (gracious Madam) to vnthinke your speaking, | And to say so no
more.   1463
VNTILL = 1
For this to ruminate on this so farre, vntill   528
VNTIMELY = 1
Buck. An vntimely Ague | Staid me a Prisoner in my Chamber, when   44
VNTO = 6*1
One generall Tongue vnto vs. This good man,   1143
Whom once more, I present vnto your Highnesse.   1145
Before you all, Appeale vnto the Pope,   1479
Made to the Queene to call backe her Appeale | She intends vnto his
Holinesse.   1605
or Palme in their hands. They first Conge vnto her, then   2646
Kath. I thanke you honest Lord. Remember me | In all humilitie vnto
his Highnesse: 2753
Be knowne vnto vs: are you all agreed Lords.   3148
VNTRUTHS = 1
He would say vntruths, and be euer double   2593
VNWILLING = 1
Vnwilling to out-liue the good that did it.   2618
VNWILLINGLY = 1
I haue, and most vnwillingly of late   2894
VNWITTINGLY = 1
There (on my Conscience put vnwittingly)   1986
VNWORTHY = 1
I am a poore falne man, vnworthy now   2327
VOCE = 1
To him brought *viua voce* to his face;   845
VOICE = 1
A single voice, and that not past me, but   405

VOID = *1
   *Seate being left void aboue him, as for Canterburies Seate.   3038
VOUCH = *1
   *Buck. To th'King Ile say't, & make my vouch as strong   232
VOUCHSAFE = 2
   Cannot vouchsafe this burthen, tis too weake | Euer to get a Boy.   1253
   Vouchsafe to speake my thankes, and my obedience,   1288
VOWES = 1
   You met him halfe in Heauen: my vowes and prayers   932
VOYAGE = 1
   Haue got by the late Voyage, is but meerely   577
VOYCE = 5
   Card. What warlike voyce, | And to what end is this? Nay, Ladies, feare
   not;   735
   Your scruple to the voyce of Christendome: 1135
   Going to Chappell: and the voyce is now | Onely about her
   Corronation.   2318
   Grif. Well, the voyce goes Madam,   2564
   The common voyce I see is verified   3249
VOYCES = 1*1
   *Haue their free voyces. Rome (the Nurse of Iudgement)   1141
   I take it, by all voyces: That forthwith,   3145
VP = 24*1
   Take vp the Rayes o'th'beneficiall Sun, | And keepe it from the Earth.   104
   Who should attend on him? He makes vp the File   126
   Thither he darts it. Bosome vp my counsell,   172
   takes her vp, kisses and placeth | her by him.   332
   Hitting a grosser quality, is cride vp   419
   Goodnesse and he, fill vp one Monument.   938
   Then giue my Charge vp to Sir Nicholas Vaux,   940
   Then to be perk'd vp in a glistring griefe, | And weare a golden sorrow.   1226
   This compel'd fortune: haue your mouth fild vp, | Before you open it.   1307
   Shut doore vpon me, and so giue me vp   1397
   My comfort comes along: breake vp the Court;   1612
   To giue vp willingly that Noble Title   1775
   Our hard rul'd King. Againe, there is sprung vp   1959
   Who commands you | To render vp the Great Seale presently   2111
   I take it, she that carries vp the Traine,   2466
   (Doublets, I thinke) flew vp, and had their Faces   2494
   *reioycing, and holdeth vp her hands to heauen. And so, in   2655
   I wish it grubb'd vp now.   2798
   King. Stand vp, good Canterbury,   2912
   In vs thy Friend. Giue me thy hand, stand vp,   2914
   Man. You great fellow, | Stand close vp, or Ile make your head ake.   3349
   Por. You i'th'Chamblet, get vp o'th' raile,   3351
   Heauen euer laid vp to make Parents happy, | May hourely fall vpon
   ye.   3372
   Kin. Stand vp Lord,   3377
   That mould vp such a mighty Piece as this is,   3396
VPON = 46*1
   A Man may weepe vpon his Wedding day.   33
   The Pride vpon them, that their very labour   69
   Chalkes Successors their way; nor call'd vpon   109
   Buc. Why the Diuell, | Vpon this French going out, tooke he vpon him   123
   He meant to lay vpon: and his owne Letter   129
   The net has falne vpon me, I shall perish | Vnder deuice, and practise.   285

VPON *cont.*

Vpon our faile; to this poynt hast thou heard him, | At any time speake
ought?   488
The Part my Father meant to act vpon   546
That's clapt vpon the Court Gate.   593
Shall shine at full vpon them. Some attend him. | *All rise, and Tables
remou'd.*   748
And so his Peeres vpon this euidence,   855
T'has done vpon the premises, but Iustice: 904
Of my long weary life is come vpon me: 979
The Kings eyes, that so long haue slept vpon | This bold bad man.   1075
An. So much the more | Must pitty drop vpon her; verily   1222
A very fresh Fish heere; fye, fye, fye vpon   1306
Shut doore vpon me, and so giue me vp   1397
Vpon this businesse my appearance make, | In any of their Courts.   1494
Kin. My Lord Cardinall, | I doe excuse you; yea, vpon mine Honour, 1521
Is this your Christian Councell? Out vpon ye.   1730
Vpon my Soule two reuerend Cardinall Vertues: 1735
The burthen of my sorrowes, fall vpon ye.   1743
Quee. Ye turne me into nothing. Woe vpon ye,   1746
Or felt the Flatteries that grow vpon it: 1780
Shipwrack'd vpon a Kingdome, where no Pitty,   1785
Vpon what cause wrong you? Alas, our Places,   1793
Stops on a sodaine, lookes vpon the ground,   1976
To thinke vpon the part of businesse, which   2015
His word vpon you. Since I had my Office,   2028
But par'd my present Hauings, to bestow | My Bounties vpon you.   2031
Heap'd vpon me (poore Vndeseruer) I   2049
*Exit King, frowning vpon the Cardinall, the Nobles | throng after him
smiling, and whispering.*   2081
Vpon the daring Huntsman that has gall'd him: 2087
Wol. This, and all else | This talking Lord can lay vpon my credit, 2153
And beares his blushing Honors thicke vpon him: 2255
Vpon my smiles. Go get thee from me *Cromwel,*   2326
His Ouerthrow, heap'd Happinesse vpon him: 2622
Cast thousand beames vpon me, like the Sun?   2666
Vpon my wretched women, that so long   2732
Vpon this naughty Earth? Go too, go too,   2939
How earnestly he cast his eyes vpon me: 3005
Lay all the weight ye can vpon my patience,   3115
'Twold fall vpon our selues.   3169
*Wife of small wit, neere him, that rail'd vpon me,   3306
Heauen euer laid vp to make Parents happy, | May hourely fall vpon
ye.   3372
Vpon this Land a thousand thousand Blessings,   3389

VPON = 1

Lord *Aburgany,* to whom by oth he menac'd | Reuenge vpon the
Cardinall.   477

VPON = 1 *1

Norf. Not almost appeares, | It doth appeare; for, vpon these Taxations, 357
*From these sad thoughts, that work too much vpon him: 1093

VPONT = 1

1. Yes truely is he, | And condemn'd vpon't.   833

VPPER = 1 *1

*himselfe at the vpper end of the Table, on the left hand: A   3037
The vpper *Germany* can deerely witnesse: 3078

VPRORE = 1
  Daring th'euent too th'teeth, are all in vprore, | And danger serues
  among them. 364
VPRORES = 1
  Commotions, vprores, with a generall Taint 3076
VPWARD = 1
  Vpward of twenty years, and haue bene blest 1390
VRGD = 1
  Vrg'd on the Examinations, proofes, confessions 843
VRGE = 2
  Stand these poore peoples Friend, and vrge the King | To do me this
  last right. 2749
  And freely vrge against me. 3096
VS *see also* let's *l.*23 112 142 324 335 336 368 463 564 567 643 724 991
  *1058 1077 1080 1094 1120 1123 1143 1733 1803 1810 1811 1845 2039
  2173 2247 2481 2546 2775 2873 2897 2898 2903 2914 2954 3061 3148
  3184 *3293 *3305 = 39*3
VSD = 4
  Not vs'd to toyle, did almost sweat to beare 68
  Was, were he euill vs'd, he would outgoe 560
  If I haue vs'd my selfe vnmannerly, 1815
  Let me be vs'd with Honor; strew me ouer 2761
VSE = 7
  Vse vs, and it: My good Lord, haue great care, 1120
  To trust vs in your businesse) we are ready | To vse our vtmost Studies,
  in your seruice. 1811
  Crom. I am glad your Grace, | Ha's made that right vse of it. 2292
  Neglect him not; make vse now, and prouide | For thine owne future
  safety. 2334
  To vse so rude behauiour. Go too, kneele. 2686
  Faile not to vse, and with what vehemencie 2951
  Take him, and vse him well; hee's worthy of it. 3226
VSHER *see also Gent.Vsh.* = 2*1
  each a Siluer Crosse: Then a Gentleman Vsher bare-| headed, 1340
  No Sun, shall euer vsher forth mine Honors, 2324
  her Gentleman Vsher, and Patience | her Woman. 2549
VSHERD = *2
  A noyse within crying roome for the Queene, vsher'd by the 329
  * Shepheards, vsher'd by the Lord Chamberlaine. They* 754
VSUALL = 1
  Sur. First, it was vsuall with him; euery day 472
VSURPER = 1
  Th' Vsurper *Richard*, who being at *Salsbury*, 547
VSURPING = 1
  Who first rais'd head against Vsurping *Richard*, 954
VTMOST = 2
  To trust vs in your businesse) we are ready | To vse our vtmost Studies,
  in your seruice. 1811
  Would trye him to the vtmost, had ye meane, 3216
VTTER = 3
  I'ue heard him vtter to his Sonne in Law, 476
  To me, should vtter, with demure Confidence, 513
  Cran. Let me speake Sir, | For Heauen now bids me; and the words I
  vtter, 3384
VTTERD = 1
  Scruple, and pricke, on certaine Speeches vtter'd 1538

VTTERLY = 2
I vtterly abhorre; yea, from my Soule   1439
How you may hurt your selfe: I, vtterly   1797
WAG = 1
Hee, that dares most, but wag his finger at thee.   3200
WAGES = 1
That they may haue their wages, duly paid 'em,   2742
WAGGE = 1
Durst waggé his Tongue in censure, when these Sunnes   77
WAGGING = 1
And thinke with wagging of your tongue to win me: 3196
WAIGH = 1
Will triumph o're my person, which I waigh not,   2924
WAIGHT = 2
Card. There was the waight that pull'd me downe.   2320
Cran. Why? | *Keep.* Your Grace must waight till you be call'd for.   2996
WAIGHTED = 1
Or gilde againe the Noble Troopes that waighted   2325
WAIGHTIER = *1
*Much waightier then this worke. The Queens in Labor   2792
WAIGHTY = 2
There ye shall meete about this waighty busines.   1195
How you stand minded in the waighty difference   1682
WAIT *see also* waight = 3
Gent. And't please your Grace, the two great Cardinals | Wait in the
presence.   1635
Wait else at doore: a fellow Councellor | 'Mong Boyes, Groomes, and
Lackeyes.   3010
This honest man, wait like a lowsie Foot-boy   3209
WAITES = 1
Who waites there? Sure you know me?   2992
WAITS = 1
Norf. Who waits there? | *Keep.* Without my Noble Lords? | *Gard.* Yes.   3048
WAKE = 2
Not wake him in his slumber. A Beggers booke, | Out-worths a Nobles
blood.   190
For feare we wake her. Softly, gentle *Patience.*   2641
WAKING = 1
My Lord *Sands*, you are one will keepe 'em waking: 694
WALKE = 4
Something I can command. As I walke thither, | Ile tell ye more.   2544
Some touch of your late businesse: Affaires that walke   2786
Come, you and I must walke a turne together: 2889
Prythee let's walke. Now by my Holydame,   2915
WALKES = 1
Kin. Come hither *Gardiner.* | *Walkes and whispers.*   1170
WALTER = 1
Vaux, Sir Walter Sands, and common people, &c.   892
WAND = *1
*head, bearing a long white Wand, as High Steward. With   2434
WANDER = 1
Car. Madam, you wander from the good | We ayme at.   1771
WANDS = *1
*Enter two Vergers, with short siluer wands; next them two   1334
WANT = 3
It is to see a Nobleman want manners.   2204
Sur. I had rather want those, then my head;   2205

WANT *cont.*

And want of wisedome, you that best should teach vs,   3061
WANTON = 2

As if it fed ye, and how sleeke and wanton   2126
Like little wanton Boyes that swim on bladders: 2260
WANTS = 2

Together; To consider further, that | What his high Hatred would effect,
wants not   166
That is, a faire young Maid that yet wants Baptisme,   3233
WARE = 1

All the expected good w'are like to heare.   3457
WARLIKE = 1

Card. What warlike voyce, | And to what end is this? Nay, Ladies, feare
not;   735
WARND = 1

I haue more Charity. But say I warn'd ye;   1741
WARRANT = 2

Bran. Here is a warrant from | The King, t'attach Lord *Mountacute*,
and the Bodies   302
You haue Christian warrant for 'em, and no doubt   2129
WARRANTED = 1

Or how farre further (Shall) is warranted   1450
WARRE = 2

By all the lawes of Warre y'are priuiledg'd.   737
In the old time of Warre, would shake the prease   2498
WARRES = 1*1

*Is nam'd, your warres in France: this makes bold mouths,   393
More pangs, and feares then warres, or women haue;   2271
WAS *see also* 'twas = 83*5
WASPES = 1

Suf. No, no: | There be moe Waspes that buz about his Nose,   1898
WASTE = *1

*To waste these times. Good houre of night Sir *Thomas*:   2776
WASTS = 1

In seeming to augment it, wasts it: be aduis'd;   218
WATER = 3

Lou. To th' water side I must conduct your Grace;   939
Like water from ye, neuer found againe   976
We write in Water. May it please your Highnesse   2602
WAY = 28*1

Chalkes Successors their way; nor call'd vpon   109
The force of his owne merit makes his way   113
A full hot Horse, who being allow'd his way   204
Ere it was ask'd. But when the way was made   263
Men of his way, should be most liberall,   650
Malice ne're meant: Our breach of Duty this way,   1109
I would not be a young Count in your way,   1251
Que. What need you note it? pray you keep your way,   1490
Laid any scruple in your way, which might   1515
The region of my Breast, which forc'd such way,   1551
Seeke me out, and that way I am Wife in;   1662
We come not by the way of Accusation,   1678
Nor to betray you any way to sorrow;   1680
The way of our Profession is against it;   1794
Giues way to vs) I much feare. If you cannot   1845
And hedges his owne way. But in this point,   1876
I sent the King? Is there no way to cure this?   2096

WAY *cont.*

A way, if it take right, in spight of Fortune	2099
That in the way of Loyaltie, and Truth,	2161
Found thee a way (out of his wracke) to rise in:	2352
Come Gentlemen, ye shall go my way,	2542
Of mine owne way. I know you Wise, Religious,	2805
They shall no more preuaile, then we giue way too:	2946
I came this way so happily. The King	Shall vnderstand it presently.	
Exit Buts	3001
Might goe one way, and safely; and the end	3084
All. We are.	*Cran.* Is there no other way of mercy,	3149
Por. Make way there, for the Princesse.	3348
From her shall read the perfect way of Honour,	3408
And ye shall find me thankfull. Lead the way Lords,	3444

WAYES = 3

Kin. Goe thy wayes *Kate,*	1497
To furnish Rome, and to prepare the wayes	2226
Say *Wolsey,* that once trod the wayes of Glory,	2350

WE *see also* w'are, w'haue = 67*5

WEAKE = 6

By sicke Interpreters (once weake ones) is	417
Cannot vouchsafe this burthen, tis too weake	Euer to get a Boy.	1253
Queen. My Lord, My Lord,	I am a simple woman, much too weake	1465
With me, a poore weake woman, falne from fauour?	1641
(More neere my Life I feare) with my weake wit;	1698
With these weake Womens feares. A Noble Spirit	1807

WEAKE-HEARTED = 1

Then my Weake-hearted Enemies, dare offer.	2298

WEAKLY = *1

An. No in truth.	*Old.L.* Then you are weakly made; plucke off a little,	1249

WEAKNESSE = 2

Who greeues much for your weaknesse, and by me	2705
To men that vnderstand you, words and weaknesse.	3121

WEALTH = 4

Affected Eminence, Wealth, Soueraignty;	1237
King. What piles of wealth hath he accumulated	1968
Of all that world of Wealth I haue drawne together	2091
Sur. Yes, that goodnesse	Of gleaning all the Lands wealth into one,	2176

WEARE = 3

Then to be perk'd vp in a glistring griefe,	And weare a golden sorrow.	1226
To weare our mortall State to come, with her,	1598
I am not worthy yet to weare: I shall assuredly.	2669

WEARING = *1

clad in white Robes, wearing on their heades Garlands of	2644

WEARY = 3

Of my long weary life is come vpon me:	979
Weary, and old with Seruice, to the mercy	2264
Is come to lay his weary bones among ye:	2576

WEATHER = 1

Two women plac'd together, makes cold weather:	693

WEAUERS = 1

The Spinsters, Carders, Fullers, Weauers, who	361

WEB = 1

Out of his Selfe-drawing Web. O giues vs note,	112

WED = 1
 Your Master wed me to: nothing but death | Shall e're diuorce my
 Dignities.   1776
WEDDING = 1
 A Man may weepe vpon his Wedding day.   33
WEDGD = 1
 Could not be wedg'd in more: I am stifled | With the meere ranknesse
 of their ioy.   2475
WEDLOCKE = 1
 My bond to Wedlocke, or my Loue and Dutie   1394
WEE *l.*229 *723 1024 1328 3270 *3292 3456 = 5*2, 1
 They may *Cum Priuilegio,* wee away   612
WEED = 1
 He be conuented. He's a ranke weed Sir *Thomas,*   2831
WEEKE = 1
 That had not halfe a weeke to go, like Rammes   2497
WEEL = 3
 You haue now a broken Banket, but wee'l mend it.   750
 No, wee'l no *Bullens*: Speedily I wish   1944
 Nor. And so wee'l leaue you to your Meditations   2245
WEENE = 1
 Of as great Size. Weene you of better lucke,   2936
WEEP = 1
 A great man should decline. Nay, and you weep | I am falne indeed. 2279
WEEPE = 4
 A Man may weepe vpon his Wedding day.   33
 You few that lou'd me, | And dare be bold to weepe for *Buckingham,* 913
 Qu. Sir, I am about to weepe; but thinking that   1427
 No Friends, no Hope, no Kindred weepe for me?   1786
WEEPES = 2
 And euery true heart weepes for't. All that dare   1072
 (Not you) correct him. My heart weepes to see him | So little, of his
 great Selfe.   2234
WEEPS = *1
 *There make before them. Looke, the goodman weeps: 2955
WEIGH *see also* waigh = 1
 They that must weigh out my afflictions,   1716
WEIGHD = 3
 What foure Thron'd ones could haue weigh'd | Such a compounded
 one?   53
 I weigh'd the danger which my Realmes stood in   1564
 Weigh'd not a haire of his. Plague of your policie,   2147
WEIGHT *see also* waight = 2
 In such a poynt of weight, so neere mine Honour,   1697
 Lay all the weight ye can vpon my patience,   3115
WEIGHTIER *see* waightier
WEIGHTY *see also* waighty = 3
 That beare a Weighty, and a Serious Brow,   3
 2. This Secret is so weighty, 'twill require   993
 *Where's your Commission? Lords, words cannot carrie | Authority so
 weighty.   2117
WELBELOUED = 1
 My learn'd and welbeloued Seruant *Cranmer,*   1610
WELCOME = 7*3
 S.Hen.Guilf. Ladyes, | A generall welcome from his Grace   666
 As first, good Company, good wine, good welcome, | Can make good
 people.   672

WELCOME *cont.*
  *Card. Y'are welcome my faire Guests; that noble Lady   711
Is not my Friend. This to confirme my welcome,   713
  Card. Good Lord Chamberlaine, | **Go, giue 'em welcome; you can
speake the French tongue   744
I showre a welcome on yee: welcome all.   752
Thou art a cure fit for a King; you'r welcome   1118
  * Kin. And once more in mine armes I bid him welcome,   1146
What more? | *Crom.* That *Cranmer* is return'd with welcome;   2311
WELL = 47*4
  May (*if they thinke it well*) *let fall a Teare,*   7
Buckingham. | Good morrow, and well met. How haue ye done   38
*Car. Well, we shall then know more, & *Buckingham*   185
Only to shew his pompe, as well in France,   238
Has done this, and tis well: for worthy *Wolsey*   249
Which I doe well; for I am sure the Emperour   261
O my Lord *Aburgany*: Fare you well.   295
Kin. Things done well, | And with a care, exempt themselues from feare: 424
Not well dispos'd, the minde growing once corrupt,   455
Queen. If I know you well, | You were the Dukes Surueyor, and lost
your Office   518
L.Cham. Well said Lord *Sands,*   629
Cham. Well said my Lord: | So now y'are fairely seated: Gentlemen,   704
You hold a faire Assembly; you doe well Lord: 790
*care I had, I saw well chosen, ridden, and furnish'd.   1029
**I feare he will indeede; well, let him haue them; hee | will haue all I
thinke.   1036
Norf. Well met my Lord *Chamberlaine.*   1040
The action of good women, there is hope | All will be well.   1270
The King hath of you. I haue perus'd her well,   1293
That longer you desire the Court, as well   1417
Camp. His Grace | Hath spoken well, and iustly: Therefore Madam,   1420
Disdainfull to be tride by't; tis not well.   1485
**(Well worthy the best Heyre o'th' World) should not   1562
I then did feele full sicke, and yet not well,   1571
B.Lin. Very well my Liedge.   1577
And am I thus rewarded? 'Tis not well Lords.   1766
And well deseruing? yet I know her for   1956
King. It may well be, | There is a mutiny in's minde. This morning,   1982
King. You haue said well.   2020
(As I will lend you cause) my doing well, | With my well saying.   2022
King. 'Tis well said agen,   2024
And 'tis a kinde of good deede to say well,   2025
So fare you well, my little good Lord Cardinall. | *Exeunt all but Wolsey.*   2249
Crom. How does your Grace. | *Card.* Why well: 2281
1 Y'are well met once againe. | 2 So are you.   2379
2 'Tis well: The Citizens | I am sure haue shewne at full their Royall
minds,   2387
1 How was it? | 3 Well worth the seeing.   2479
2 Good Sir, speake it to vs? | 3 As well as I am able. The rich streame   2481
If well, he stept before me happily | For my example.   2562
Grif. Well, the voyce goes Madam,   2564
I hope she will deserue well; and a little   2727
And let me tell you, it will ne're be well,   2806
Well Sir, what followes?   2865
'Tis his Aspect of Terror. All's not well.   2881
Your patience to you, and be well contented   2902

WELL *cont.*
 'Tis well there's one aboue 'em yet; I had thought   3026
 Was euer to doe well: nor is there liuing,   3085
 Kin. Well, well my Lords respect him,   3225
 Take him, and vse him well; hee's worthy of it.   3226
 We may as well push against Powles as stirre'em.   3273
WENCH = 5
 Queen. Take thy Lute wench,   1617
 Worse then the Sacring Bell, when the browne Wench   2188
 Grif. She is asleep: Good wench, let's sit down quiet,   2640
 Grif. She is going Wench. Pray, pray. | *Pati.* Heauen comfort her.   2678
 Call in more women. When I am dead, good Wench,   2760
WENCHES = 1
 Alas (poore Wenches) where are now your Fortunes?   1784
WENT = 4
 My studied purposes requite, which went   2042
 Either of King or Councell, when you went   2215
 2 What two Reuerend Byshops | Were those that went on each side of
 the Queene?   2523
 So went to bed; where eagerly his sicknesse   2578
WEPT = 1
 May haue a Tombe of Orphants teares wept on him.   2310
WERE *see also* 'twer *l.*28 66 73 246 256 271 457 462 519 560 634 *684 686
 801 828 924 986 *1030 *1031 1268 1322 1385 1546 1559 1659 1996 2008
 2500 2524 2596 2605 2613 *2654 3135 3175 *3191 *3311 3419 = 32*6
WERT *l.**1264 = *1
WHAT *l.*43 53 101 117 138 167 192 202 367 385 416 418 *468 492 500 511
 535 543 *555 589 594 616 735 736 739 757 782 796 823 830 831 898 906
 951 992 *1053 *1057 1083 1136 1156 1247 *1264 1283 1327 1330 1331
 1373 1385 1419 *1490 1534 1640 1649 1729 1754 1782 1793 1796 1813
 1843 1844 1955 1968 1969 1985 2033 2037 2039 2080 2083 2084 2094
 2124 *2225 2277 2299 2311 2330 2340 2394 2502 2523 2701 2842 2844
 2848 2849 2865 2879 2892 2893 2916 2926 2932 2951 2962 2991 3075
 3095 3125 3152 3211 3220 3289 3290 *3294 3326 3335 3375 3405
 3440 = 104*8
WHATS = 6*1
 Card. What's that? | *Cham.* Looke out there, some of ye.   733
 Norf. What's the cause? | *Cham.* It seemes the Marriage with his
 Brothers Wife   1045
 King. What's the need? | It hath already publiquely bene read,   1353
 Will bring me off againe. What's this? *To th' Pope*?   2100
 But I beseech you, what's become of *Katherine*   2404
 Gard. Not yet Sir *Thomas Louell*: what's the matter?   2783
 King. What's that *Buts*?   3017
WHATSOERE = 1
 But whatsoere thou tak'st me for; I'm sure   3197
WHATSOEUER = 1
 To forfeit all your Goods, Lands, Tenements, | Castles, and whatsoeuer,
 and to be   2242
WHAUE = 1
 W^haue frighted with our Trumpets: so 'tis cleare,   3453
WHEN *l.*45 50 77 228 263 454 458 579 860 937 948 974 *980 1002 *1031
 1068 1381 1432 1491 1526 1576 1623 1769 1822 1839 1909 2188 2196
 2215 2257 2272 2309 2347 2460 2490 2507 2532 2715 2760 2841 3168
 *3309 *3314 3333 3342 3383 3410 *3415 3439 3463 = 45*5
WHENCE = 1
 Peepe through each part of him: whence ha's he that,   119

WHERE *l.*171 *173 373 396 422 435 644 747 839 972 977 1071 1473 1511
1559 1677 1784 1785 2030 2348 2410 2417 *2473 2474 2504 2515 2572
2578 2595 *2658 2871 2898 2908 3019 3104 *3311 3328 3421 = 34*4
WHEREBY = 1
Paid ere he promis'd, whereby his Suit was granted   262
WHEREFORE = 2*1
*Who deem'd our Marriage lawful. Wherefore I humbly   1407
Cran. I am fearefull: Wherefore frownes he thus?   2880
You do desire to know wherefore | I sent for you.   2883
WHEREIN = 5
Of all their Loyalties; wherein, although | My good Lord Cardinall,
they vent reproches   349
Kin. Taxation? | Wherein? and what Taxation? My Lord Cardinall,   366
Wherein he might the King his Lord aduertise,   1545
In the Diuorce, his contrarie proceedings | Are all vnfolded: wherein he
appeares,   1858
And came to th'eye o'th'King, wherein was read   1866
WHEREOF = 2
(Whereof my Soueraigne would haue note) they are   379
The fore-recited practises, whereof   466
WHERES = 2*1
Where's his Examination? | *Secr.* Heere so please you.   181
Forthwith for what you come. Where's *Gardiner?*   1156
*Where's your Commission? Lords, words cannot carrie | Authority so
weighty.   2117
WHEREUPON = 1
Toward this remedy, whereupon we are   1568
WHEREWITHALL = 1
L.San. He may my Lord, | Ha's wherewithall in him;   647
WHERE-EUER *see* euer
WHET = 1
Suf. Maybe he heares the King | Does whet his Anger to him.   1947
WHETHER = 4
1. Whether away so fast? | 2. O, God saue ye: 821
At once, and fully satisfide) whether euer I   1513
Whether our Daughter were legitimate,   1546
Whether so late? | *Lou.* Came you from the King, my Lord?   2777
WHICH *l.*52 87 114 150 194 215 251 261 *293 348 354 376 377 *390 407
413 529 548 656 768 784 844 846 853 965 *1034 1110 1182 1208 1236
1238 1279 1383 1438 1461 1515 1551 1564 1570 1584 1586 1690 1837
1892 1910 1989 2007 2015 2017 2042 2208 2212 2229 2410 2416
2490 2511 2543 2580 2614 2617 *2648 *2652 *2653 2668 2722 2734 2815
2825 2859 2874 2896 2901 2924 3060 3066 3068 3217 3232 *3250 3272
*3311 *3358 3390 3456 = 78*9
WHILE = 9
Nor shall not while I haue a stumpe.   632
Meane while, must be an earnest motion   1604
While I shall haue my life. Come reuerend Fathers,   1820
Card. Leaue me a while. *Exit Cromwell.*   1939
A distance from her; while her Grace sate downe   2485
To rest a while, some halfe an houre, or so,   2486
Haue more, or else vnsay't: and now, while 'tis hot,   2985
Which ye shall neuer haue while I liue.   3217
And say twill doe; I know within a while,   3461
WHILES = 1
Whose Minister you are, whiles heere he liu'd   2938

WHILST = 3
    Car. Whil'st our Commission from Rome is read,   1351
    Whil'st your great Goodnesse, out of holy pitty, | Absolu'd him with an
    Axe.   2151
    I nam'd my Knell; whil'st I sit meditating   2637
WHISPER = 2
    To whisper *Wolsey*) here makes visitation,   255
    I would surrender it. *Whisper.*   780
WHISPERING = 1
    Exit King, frowning vpon the Cardinall, the Nobles | throng after him
    smiling, and whispering.   2081
WHISPERS = 2
    Kin. Come hither *Gardiner.* | *Walkes and whispers.*   1170
    King takes his Seat, whispers Louell, who goes | to the Cardinall.   2001
WHITE = *2
    *head, bearing a long white Wand, as High Steward. With   2434
    *clad in white Robes, wearing on their heades Garlands of   2644
WHITE-HALL = 1
    'Tis now the Kings, and call'd White-Hall. | 3 I know it: 2519
WHITHER *see also* whether = 1
    L.Cham. Sir *Thomas,* | Whither were you a going?   633
WHITST = *1
    *Which makes my whit'st part, black. The will of Heau'n   293
WHO *l.*91 92 97 126 204 250 361 458 494 547 874 881 941 954 1107 1136
    *1261 *1295 *1407 1415 1444 1498 1540 1554 2001 2111 2119 2534
    *2650 *2653 2705 2816 2826 2845 2992 3022 3048 *3309 3416 = 33*6
WHOEUER *see* who
WHOLE = 5*2
    Buck. All the whole time | I was my Chambers Prisoner.   55
    Yea, the whole Consistorie of Rome. You charge me,   1452
    To bring my whole Cause 'fore his Holinesse,   1480
    These are the whole Contents, and good my Lord,   2746
    King. Know you not | *How your state stands i'th'world, with the whole
    world?   2927
    *The whole Realme, by your teaching & your Chaplaines   3064
    Of the whole State; as of late dayes our neighbours,   3077
WHOLESOME = *1
    *You'l finde it wholesome. Loe, where comes that Rock   173
WHOLL = 1
    Ti'de it by Letters Patents. Now, who'll take it? | *Sur.* The King that
    gaue it.   2135
WHOLSOME = 2
    Things that are knowne alike, which are not wholsome   376
    A spleeny Lutheran, and not wholsome to   1957
WHOM *l.*128 226 477 510 778 915 1145 1440 2185 2316 2574 2631 = 12
WHORSONS = 1
    Louell. I marry, | There will be woe indeed Lords, the slye whorsons   618
WHOS = 4*1
    Who's best in fauour. Let the Musicke knock it. | *Exeunt with*
    Trumpets.   817
    Kin. Who's there? Ha? | *Norff.* Pray God he be not angry.   1103
    Kin. Who's there I say? How dare you thrust your | (selues   1105
    Who's there? my good Lord Cardinall? O my *Wolsey,*   1116
    Who's that that beares the Scepter? | 1 Marquesse Dorset,   2448
WHOSE = 12*1
    For being not propt by Auncestry, whose grace   108
    Whose Figure euen this instant Clowd puts on,   314

WHOSE *cont.*
*Whose Honor Heauen shield from soile; euen he escapes | (not	353
He did discharge a horrible Oath, whose tenor	559
Ladies you are not merry; Gentlemen, | Whose fault is this?	720
I tender my Commission; by whose vertue,	1151
Gard. But to be commanded | For euer by your Grace, whose hand ha's	
rais'd me.	1168
Whose health and Royalty I pray for.	1290
Be by my Friends in Spaine, aduis'd; whose Counsaile	1409
Inuite me to a Banquet, whose bright faces	2665
Whose Minister you are, whiles heere he liu'd	2938
Against this man, whose honesty the Diuell	3178
Into whose hand, I giue thy Life. | *Cran. Amen.*	3379

WHY *l.*123 158 431 1301 1525 *1792 2275 2282 2996 3043 3130
3211 = 11*1
WIDDOW = 1
And Widdow to Prince *Arthur*.	1917

WIFE = 8*2
Norf. What's the cause? | *Cham.* It seemes the Marriage with his	
Brothers Wife	1045
I haue bene to you, a true and humble Wife,	1377
That I haue beene your Wife, in this Obedience,	1389
A better Wife, let him in naught be trusted,	1499
Sometimes our Brothers Wife. This respite shooke	1548
Seeke me out, and that way I am Wife in;	1662
Since Vertue findes no friends) a Wife, a true one?	1759
Could say this is my wife there, all were wouen | So strangely in one	
peece.	2500
I was a chaste Wife, to my Graue: Embalme me,	2763
*Wife of small wit, neere him, that rail'd vpon me,	3306

WIFE-LIKE = 1
Thy meeknesse Saint-like, Wife-like Gouernment,	1502

WILD = 3
The wild Sea of my Conscience, I did steere	1567
Queen. Would they speake with me? | *Gent.* They wil'd me say so	
Madam.	1637
My Noble Lords; for those that tame wild Horses,	3069

WILDE = 2
If I chance to talke a little wilde, forgiue me:	698
Should the approach of this wilde Riuer breake, | And stand vnshaken	
yours.	2074

WILDER = 1
In them a wilder Nature, then the businesse | That seekes dispatch by	
day.	2788

WILL *see also* hee'l, Ile, shee'l, they'l, 'twill, wee'l, who'll, you'l, youle *l.*8
18 23 291 408 421 434 617 619 639 690 694 781 785 880 882 906 911 947
*952 1009 1012 1022 *1036 1037 *1053 1069 1074 1080 1180 1189 1271
1321 1410 1432 1433 1493 1528 1535 *1669 1740 1770 1782 1813 1827
1874 1892 1894 1900 2022 2068 2100 2130 2185 2230 2330 2331 2533
2540 2685 2727 2735 2751 2757 2806 2815 2837 2862 2901 2924 2953
2964 2983 3095 *3101 3171 3227 *3240 3272 *3295 *3296 *3298 3446 =
75*9, 14*1
*Which makes my whit'st part, black. The will of Heau'n	293
The will of Heauen be done, and the Kings pleasure | By me obey'd.	300
Repeat your will, and take it.	338
To each incensed Will: I would your Highnesse	398
And sticke them in our Will. Sixt part of each?	430

WILL *cont.*
His will is most malignant, and it stretches | Beyond you to your
friends.   482
Will haue his will, and she must fall. | 1. 'Tis wofull.   1022
An. Oh Gods will, much better | She ne're had knowne pompe; though't
be temporall,   1215
At all times to your will conformable: 1378
(Domestickes to you) serue your will, as't please   1474
Nor. It's Heauens will,   1992
Bearing the Kings will from his mouth expressely?   2120
Car. Till I finde more then will, or words to do it,   2121
Without the Kings will, or the States allowance,   2220
You are alwayes my good Friend, if your will passe,   3108
WILLIAM = 1
Sur. Being at *Greenwich,* | After your Highnesse had reprou'd the
Duke | About Sir *William Bulmer.*   539
WILLING = 3
The Play may passe: If they be still, and willing,   12
Willing to leaue their burthen: Reach a Chaire,   2554
This to my Lord the King. | *Cap.* Most willing Madam.   2720
WILLINGLY = 1
To giue vp willingly that Noble Title   1775
WILLINGST = 1
The willing'st sinne I euer yet committed, | May be absolu'd in English. 1672
WILLS = 1
My Lords, I thanke you both for your good wills,   1694
WIN = 4*1
(The Image of his Maker) hope to win by it?   2357
Suff. Sir, I did neuer win of you before.   2839
Win straying Soules with modesty againe,   3113
And thinke with wagging of your tongue to win me: 3196
*draw mine Honour in, and let 'em win the Worke, the   3316
WINCHESTER = 7*1
*Pearle, Crowned. On each side her, the Bishops of London, | and
Winchester,*   2439
3 *Stokeley* and *Gardiner,* the one of Winchester,   2525
2 He of Winchester | Is held no great good louer of the Archbishops, |
The vertuous *Cranmer.*   2528
*Enter Gardiner Bishop of Winchester, a Page with a Torch | before him,
met by Sir Thomas Louell.*   2769
Cran. Ah my good Lord of *Winchester*: I thanke you,   3107
Crom. My Lord of *Winchester,* y'are a little,   3122
Bishop of *Winchester.* But know I come not   3192
Once more my Lord of *Winchester,* I charge you | Embrace, and loue
this man.   3242
WINCHESTERS = 1
To Asher-house, my Lord of Winchesters,   2114
WINDOWE = 1
Enter the King, and Buts, at a Windowe | aboue.   3014
WINE = 2
As first, good Company, good wine, good welcome, | Can make good
people.   672
San. The red wine first must rise   722
WINGS = 2
The very thought of this faire Company, | Clapt wings to me.   676
Fly o're thy Royall head, and shade thy person | Vnder their blessed
wings.   2965

WINNOWED = 1
Most throughly to be winnowed, where my Chaffe   2908
WINS = 1
Corruption wins not more then Honesty.   2359
WINTER = 1
Which euer ha's, and euer shall be growing, | Till death (that Winter)
kill it.   2052
WISE = 5
To thinke an English Courtier may be wise, | And neuer see the *Louure*.   599
That they had gather'd a wise Councell to them   1405
Exceeding wise, faire spoken, and perswading: 2610
Of mine owne way. I know you Wise, Religious,   2805
Not onely good and wise, but most religious: 3185
WISEDOME = 6
Out of a forreigne wisedome, renouncing cleane   607
Wol. Your Grace ha's giuen a President of wisedome   1133
Of disposition gentle, and of wisedome,   1446
And want of wisedome, you that best should teach vs,   3061
And wisedome of my Councell; but I finde none: 3206
More couetous of Wisedome, and faire Vertue   3394
WISEST = 1
The wisest Prince, that there had reign'd, by many   1403
WISH = 13
To heare this of him; and could wish he were | Somthing mistaken in't.   271
Not frended by his wish to your High person;   481
Wish him ten faddom deepe: This Duke as much   886
But those that sought it, I could wish more Christians: 905
Queen. Ye tell me what ye wish for both, my ruine: 1729
I will not wish ye halfe my miseries,   1740
As I would wish mine Enemy.   1860
Suf. May you be happy in your wish my Lord, | For I professe you haue
it.   1881
No, wee'l no *Bullens*: Speedily I wish   1944
Kath. After my death, I wish no other Herald,   2627
As you wish Christian peace to soules departed,   2748
I wish it grubb'd vp now.   2798
Suf. I wish your Highnesse | A quiet night, and my good Mistris will |
Remember in my Prayers.   2861
WISHD = 1*1
*They haue sent me such a Man, I would haue wish'd for.   1148
Haue wish'd the sleeping of this busines, neuer desir'd   1529
WISHES = 3*1
(And take it from a heart, that wishes towards you   163
Are not words duely hallowed; nor my Wishes   1285
*More worth, then empty vanities: yet Prayers & Wishes   1286
Shee's a good Creature, and sweet-Ladie do's | Deserue our better
wishes.   2801
WISHING = 1
Hath sent to me, wishing me to permit   507
WIT = 3*1
And vnmatch'd Wit, and Iudgement. *Ferdinand*   1401
(More neere my Life I feare) with my weake wit;   1698
You know I am a Woman, lacking wit   1816
*Wife of small wit, neere him, that rail'd vpon me,   3306
WITCHCRAFT = 1
Any thing on him: for he hath a Witchcraft | Ouer the King in's
Tongue.   1847

WITH = 158*29
WITHALL = 2
   Some Spirit put this paper in the Packet, | To blesse your eye withall.   1993
   And if you may confesse it, say withall   2038
WITHDRAW = 1
   Wol. May it please you Noble Madam, to withdraw   1650
WITHIN = 9*1
   A noyse within crying roome for the Queene, vsher'd by the   329
   The Duke being at the Rose, within the Parish   498
   Within these fortie houres, Surrey durst better | Haue burnt that
   Tongue, then saide so.   2140
   By your power Legatine within this Kingdome,   2239
   I know my selfe now, and I feele within me,   2284
   Gent. within. Come backe: what meane you?   2962
   Noyse and Tumult within: Enter Porter and | *his man.*   3257
   Within. Good M.(aster) Porter I belong to th' Larder.   3262
   Within. Do you heare M.(aster) Porter?   3286
   And say twill doe; I know within a while,   3461
WITHOUT = 16
   (Without the priuity o'th'King) t'appoint   125
   Without delay; and the pretence for this   392
   Things done without example, in their issue   426
   Should without issue dye; hee'l carry it so   474
   And without Tryall, fell; Gods peace be with him.   957
   As I am made without him, so Ile stand,   1086
   And that (without delay) their Arguments | Be now produc'd, and
   heard.   1423
   A Woman (I dare say without Vainglory) | Neuer yet branded with
   Suspition?   1760
   Haue at you. | First, that without the Kings assent or knowledge,   2206
   Suf. Then, that without the knowledge   2214
   Without the Kings will, or the States allowance,   2220
   10 Certaine Ladies *or* Countesses, *with plaine Circlets of* | *Gold, without*
   Flowers.   2443
   2 He will deserue more. | 3 Yes without all doubt.   2540
   Your selfe, and your Accusers, and to haue heard you | Without
   indurance further.   2919
   Norf. Who waits there? | *Keep.* Without my Noble Lords? | *Gard.* Yes.   3048
   And yet no day without a deed to Crowne it.   3430
WITNES = 1
   And by that name must dye; yet Heauen beare witnes,   900
WITNESSE = 8
   And take your good Grace from me? Heauen witnesse,   1376
   His Noble Iurie, and foule Cause can witnesse.   2158
   Beare witnesse, all that haue not hearts of Iron,   2339
   He was most Princely: Euer witnesse for him   2615
   It fits we thus proceed, or else no witnesse | Would come against you.   2904
   I meane in periur'd Witnesse, then your Master,   2937
   The vpper *Germany* can deerely witnesse: 3078
   Cran. And let Heauen | Witnesse how deare, I hold this Confirmation.   3246
WITNESSES = 1
   Of diuers witnesses, which the Duke desir'd   844
WITTY = 1
   Abus'd extreamly, and to cry that's witty,   3455
WOE = 5
   Sad, high, and working, full of State and Woe: 4
   Louell. I marry, | There will be woe indeed Lords, the slye whorsons   618

WOE *cont.*

'Tis full of woe: yet I can giue you inckling	988
Quee. Ye turne me into nothing. Woe vpon ye,	1746
And woe your owne destruction.	2941

WOFULL = 1

Will haue his will, and she must fall. | 1. 'Tis wofull.	1022

WOL = 19*1

WOLFE = 1

Or Wolfe, or both (for he is equall rau'nous	234

WOLS = 1

WOLSEY see also Wol., Wols. = 11*1

Enter Cardinall Wolsey, the Purse borne before him, certaine	175
Has done this, and tis well: for worthy *Wolsey*	249
To whisper *Wolsey*) here makes visitation,	255
Hoboyes. Enter Cardinall Wolsey, and takes his State.	710
Enter Wolsey and Campeius with a Commission.	1115
Who's there? my good Lord Cardinall? O my *Wolsey*,	1116
My *Wolsey*, see it furnish'd, O my Lord,	1196
Enter the two Cardinalls, Wolsey & Campian.	1645
Enter Wolsey and Cromwell.	1925
So fare you well, my little good Lord Cardinall. | *Exeunt all but Wolsey.*	2249
Say *Wolsey*, that once trod the wayes of Glory,	2350
That the great Childe of Honor, Cardinall *Wolsey* | Was dead?	2557

WOMAN = 8*1

A Woman of lesse Place might aske by Law;	1159
I am a most poore Woman, and a Stranger,	1369
Queen. My Lord, My Lord, | I am a simple woman, much too weake	1465
A Woman (I dare say without Vainglory) | Neuer yet branded with Suspition?	1760
Bring me a constant woman to her Husband,	1767
And to that Woman (when she has done most)	1769
I am the most vnhappy Woman liuing.	1783
What you commanded me, but by her woman,	2844
Lou. So said her woman, and that her suffrance made	2850

WOMAN = 1

her Gentleman Vsher, and Patience | her Woman.	2549

WOMAN = 8*1

You that haue so faire parts of Woman on you,	1235
With me, a poore weake woman, falne from fauour?	1641
Alas, I am a Woman frendlesse, hopelesse.	1706
A woman lost among ye, laugh't at, scornd?	1739
You know I am a Woman, lacking wit	1816
In that one woman, I haue lost for euer.	2323
(Out of thy honest truth) to play the Woman.	2345
Beleeue me Sir, she is the goodliest Woman	2489
*and hit that Woman, who cryed out Clubbes, when I	3309

WOMANISH = 1

He neuer was so womanish, the cause | He may a little grieue at.	868

WOMANS = 1*1

Haue (too) a Womans heart, which euer yet	1236
*Ore-topping womans powre. Madam, you do me wrong	1447

WOMBE = 1

Commanded Nature, that my Ladies wombe	1555

WOMEN = 10*1

Two women plac'd together, makes cold weather:	693
One of her Highnesse women.	799
The action of good women, there is hope | All will be well.	1270

WOMEN *cont.*
Enter Queene and her Women as at worke. 1616
Deserues a Corner: would all other Women 1655
More pangs, and feares then warres, or women haue; 2271
I neuer saw before. Great belly'd women, 2496
Vpon my wretched women, that so long 2732
Call in more women. When I am dead, good Wench, 2760
*great *Toole*, come to Court, the women so besiege vs? 3293
The mercifull construction of good women, 3459
WOMENS = 1
With these weake Womens feares. A Noble Spirit 1807
WONDER = 3
To do in these fierce Vanities? I wonder, 102
Crom. I haue no power to speake Sir. | *Car.* What, amaz'd | At my
misfortunes? Can thy Spirit wonder 2276
The Bird of Wonder dyes, the Mayden Phoenix, 3411
WONDERS = 3
Made former Wonders, it's. To day the French, 62
Who was enrold 'mongst wonders; and when we 458
Kin. Thou speakest wonders. 3427
WONTED = 1
Knowing she will not loose her wonted Greatnesse 2685
WOOE *see* woe
WOOLSEY = 1
Enter to Woolsey, the Dukes of Norfolke and Suffolke, the | Earle of
Surrey, and the Lord Chamberlaine. 2108
WORD = 3
Card. A word with you. 439
A Royall Lady, spake one, the least word that might 1518
His word vpon you. Since I had my Office, 2028
WORDS = 12*1
To make the Scepter his. These very words 475
His Confessor, who fed him euery minute | With words of Soueraignty. 494
'Twould proue the verity of certaine words 505
Are not words duely hallowed; nor my Wishes 1285
Where Powres are your Retainers, and your words 1473
And yet words are no deeds. My Father lou'd you, 2026
*Where's your Commission? Lords, words cannot carrie | Authority so
weighty. 2117
Car. Till I finde more then will, or words to do it, 2121
If I lou'd many words, Lord, I should tell you, 2159
To whom he gaue these words. O Father Abbot, 2574
Both in his words, and meaning. He was neuer 2594
To men that vnderstand you, words and weaknesse. 3121
Cran. Let me speake Sir, | For Heauen now bids me; and the words I
vtter, 3384
WORE = *1
*his Coate of Armes, and on his head he wore a Gilt Copper | Crowne. 2427
WORK = *1
*From these sad thoughts, that work too much vpon him: 1093
WORKE = 4*2
Or this imperious man will worke vs all 1080
Enter Queene and her Women as at worke. 1616
In truth I know not. I was set at worke, 1700
Sur. Will this worke? | *Cham.* The King in this perceiues him, how he
coasts 1874
*Much waightier then this worke. The Queens in Labor 2792

329

WORKE *cont.*

*draw mine Honour in, and let 'em win the Worke, the 3316
WORKES = 2

Pertaining thereunto; as Fights and Fire-workes, 605
Norf. How holily he workes in all his businesse, 1056
WORKING = 2

Sad, high, and working, full of State and Woe: 4
Sing, and disperse 'em if thou canst: leaue working. 1619
WORLD = 16*3

For further life in this world I ne're hope, 910
For euer from the World. I had my Tryall, 964
I sweare againe, I would not be a Queene, | For all the world. 1256
That man i'th' world, who shall report he ha's 1498
This world had ayr'd them. Hence I tooke a thought, 1560
*(Well worthy the best Heyre o'th' World) should not 1562
For no dislike i'th' world against the person 1593
(*Katherine* our Queene) before the primest Creature | That's Parragon'd
o'th' World. 1599
(Though all the world should cracke their duty to you, 2069
Of all that world of Wealth I haue drawne together 2091
Vaine pompe, and glory of this World, I hate ye, 2266
He gaue his Honors to the world agen, 2583
By that you loue the deerest in this world, 2747
Out of this world. Tell him in death I blest him 2756
With Maiden Flowers, that all the world may know 2762
King. Know you not | *How your state stands i'th'world, with the whole
world? 2927
And faire purgation to the world then malice, | I'm sure in me. 3223
To th' ground, and all the World shall mourne her. 3434
WORMES = 1

When I shall dwell with Wormes, and my poore name 2715
WORNE = 1

That sure th'haue worne out Christendome: how now? 588
WORSE = 3

Sparing would shew a worse sinne, then ill Doctrine, 649
Camp. Your feares are worse. 1757
Worse then the Sacring Bell, when the browne Wench 2188
WORSHIP = 1

Nor. As I belong to worship, and affect 84
WORST = 6

Equall in lustre, were now best, now worst 73
Not ours, or not allow'd; what worst, as oft 418
(I would be all) against the worst may happen: 1648
Wol. Speake on Sir, | I dare your worst Obiections: If I blush, 2202
What Newes abroad? | *Crom.* The heauiest, and the worst, 2299
Gard. Good M.(aster) Secretary, | I cry your Honour mercie; you may
worst | Of all this Table say so. 3127
WORTH = 2*2

L.Cham. Good morrow Ladies; what wer't worth to | (know 1264
*More worth, then empty vanities: yet Prayers & Wishes 1286
His Thinkings are below the Moone, not worth | His serious
considering. 1999
1 How was it? | 3 Well worth the seeing. 2479
WORTHILY = 1

And worthily my Falsehood, yea, as much 1456

WORTHS = 1
   Not wake him in his slumber. A Beggers booke, | Out-worths a Nobles
   blood.   190
WORTHY = 6*1
   Has done this, and tis well: for worthy *Wolsey*   249
   More worthy this place then my selfe, to whom   778
   *(Well worthy the best Heyre o'th' World) should not   1562
   Nor. This same *Cranmer*'s·| A worthy Fellow, and hath tane much
   paine | In the Kings businesse.   1918
   A worthy Friend. The King ha's made him | Master o'th'Iewell House,   2537
   I am not worthy yet to weare: I shall assuredly.   2669
   Take him, and vse him well; hee's worthy of it.   3226
WOT = 1
   As I requir'd: and wot you what I found   1985
WOUEN = 1
   Could say this is my wife there, all were wouen | So strangely in one
   peece.   2500
WOULD *see also* 'twold, 'twould, you'd, you'ld *l.*26 86 167 207 221 265
   340 377 379 398 399 473 502 545 549 *555 560 579 583 598 649 656 671
   682 686 689 702 703 732 780 784 854 926 *980 *1033 1123 1128 *1148
   1181 1187 1197 1212 1231 1232 1233 1240 *1243 *1245 1251 1256 1260
   1312 1325 1637 1648 1655 1720 1721 1747 1779 1860 1880 *1965 2269
   2289 2371 2498 2593 2704 2731 2860 2905 2917 *3009 3135 3136 3153
   3175 3216 3285 3289 3431 = 76*9
WOUND = 1
   That I gainsay my Deed, how may he wound,   1455
WOUNDED = 1
   The quiet of my wounded Conscience;   1117
WRACKE = 1
   Found thee a way (out of his wracke) to rise in: 2352
WRENCHING = 1
   Did breake ith'wrenching. | *Norf.* Faith, and so it did.   242
WRETCH = 1
   Being distrest; was by that wretch betraid,   956
WRETCHED = 5
   A little happier then my wretched Father: 966
   The Cordiall that ye bring a wretched Lady?   1738
   What will become of me now, wretched Lady?   1782
   I feele my heart new open'd. Oh how wretched   2267
   Vpon my wretched women, that so long   2732
WRETCHEDNESSE = 2
   To me, aboue this wretchednesse? All your Studies | Make me a Curse,
   like this.   1755
   And leaue me heere in wretchednesse, behinde ye?   2659
WRINGING = 1
   Dangers, doubts, wringing of the Conscience,   1060
WRIT = 5
   Let there be Letters writ to euery Shire,   440
   I writ too's Holinesse. Nay then, farewell: 2102
   You writ to'th Pope, against the King: your goodnesse   2180
   Nor. Then, That in all you writ to Rome, or else | To Forraigne
   Princes, *Ego & Rex meus*   2210
   That therefore such a Writ be sued against you,   2241
WRITE = 2
   We write in Water. May it please your Highnesse   2602
   I caus'd you write, yet sent away? | *Pat.* No Madam.   2717

WRONG = 5*1

*Ore-topping womans powre. Madam, you do me wrong	1447
I am not of your wrong. Therefore in him	1459
Beleeue me she ha's had much wrong. Lord Cardinall,	1671
Wol. Madam, | You wrong the Kings loue with these feares,	1707
Vpon what cause wrong you? Alas, our Places,	1793
Camp. Madam, you'l finde it so: | You wrong your Vertues	1805

WRONGS = 1

In doing dayly wrongs. I could say more,	3117

WROUGHT = 2

You wrought to be a Legate, by which power	2208
wrought with Flowers bearing the Queenes Traine.	2442

Y = *1

Sur. I would 'twer somthing y would fret the string,	1965

YARE = 8*2

O my Lord, y'are tardy;	675
Cham. Well said my Lord: | So now y'are fairely seated: Gentlemen,	704
Card. Y'are welcome my faire Guests; that noble Lady	711
By all the lawes of Warre y'are priuiledg'd.	737
*T'oppose your cunning. Y'are meek, & humble-mouth'd	1467
The Queene is put in anger; y'are excus'd:	1527
1 Y'are well met once againe. | 2 So are you.	2379
Gard. But Sir, Sir, | Heare me Sir *Thomas*, y'are a Gentleman	2803
Crom. My Lord of *Winchester*, y'are a little,	3122
Clap round Fines for neglect: y'are lazy knaues,	3341

YE *l.*26 39 668 734 789 822 976 977 978 1112 1113 1195 1695 1696 1726 1729 1730 *1734 1736 1738 1739 1740 1741 1743 1746 1749 *1781 1813 2124 2125 2126 2127 2169 2266 2542 2543 2545 2576 *2658 2659 2662 3115 3132 3167 3180 3212 3214 3216 3217 3254 *3259 *3260 *3263 3339 3342 3343 3347 3373 3382 3441 3444 3445 = 64*8

YEA = 9

Infecting one another, yea reciprocally,	237
Language vnmannerly; yea, such which breakes	354
Yea, subiect to your Countenance: Glad, or sorry,	1380
Yea, the elect o'th'Land, who are assembled	1415
I vtterly abhorre; yea, from my Soule	1439
Yea, the whole Consistorie of Rome. You charge me,	1452
And worthily my Falsehood, yea, as much	1456
Kin. My Lord Cardinall, | I doe excuse you; yea, vpon mine Honour,	1521
Yea, with a spitting power, and made to tremble	1550

YEARE = 3

A Thousand pound a yeare, Annuall support, | Out of his Grace, he addes.	1280
A thousand pounds a yeare, for pure respect?	1317
A yeare before. It is not to be question'd,	1404

YEARES = 3

Longer then I haue time to tell his yeares;	935
That like a Iewell, ha's hung twenty yeares	1064
I haue beene begging sixteene yeares in Court	1302

YEARS = 1

Vpward of twenty years, and haue bene blest	1390

YEE *l.*752 = 1

YELLOW = 1

In a long Motley Coate, garded with Yellow,	17

YES = 19*1

Yes, heartily beseech you.	523
San. Yes, if I make my play:	727

YES *cont.*

Card. Sir *Thomas Louell*, is the Banket ready | I'th' Priuy Chamber? |
Lou. Yes, my Lord.   804
2. Were you there? | 1. Yes indeed was I.   828
1. Yes truely is he, | And condemn'd vpon't.   833
1. Yes, but it held not;   1001
In this mans place before him? | *Wol.* Yes, he was.   1173
Camp. Was he not held a learned man? | *Wol.* Yes surely.   1175
**Old L.* Yes troth, & troth; you would not be a Queene?   1243
Sur. Yes, that goodnesse | Of gleaning all the Lands wealth into one,   2176
1 Yes, 'tis the List | Of those that claime their Offices this day,   2396
2 And that my Lord of Norfolke? | 1 Yes.   2454
2 He will deserue more. | 3 Yes without all doubt.   2540
Grif. Yes Madam: but I thinke your Grace   2559
To heare me speake his good now? | *Kath.* Yes good *Griffith*,   2603
Gard. Yes, yes, Sir *Thomas*, | There are that Dare, and I my selfe haue
ventur'd   2818
Keep. Yes, my Lord: | But yet I cannot helpe you.   2994
Gard. Ha's he had knowledge of it? | *Crom.* Yes.   3046
Norf. Who waits there? | *Keep.* Without my Noble Lords? | *Gard.* Yes.   3048

YET = 54*4

Most bitterly on you, as putter on | Of these exactions: yet the King,
our Maister   351
To those which would not know them, and yet must   377
My faculties nor person, yet will be   408
And neuer seeke for ayd out of himselfe: yet see,   453
(Nay let 'em be vnmanly) yet are follow'd.   575
Your Colts tooth is not cast yet? | *L.San.* No my Lord,   630
I must not yet forsake you: Let's be merry,   813
And by that name must dye; yet Heauen beare witnes,   900
Yet let 'em looke they glory not in mischiefe;   907
Yet are the Kings; and till my Soule forsake me,   933
Yet I am richer then my base Accusers,   950
Yet thus farre we are one in Fortunes; both   967
Heauen ha's an end in all: yet, you that heare me,   970
'Tis full of woe: yet I can giue you inckling   988
About his necke, yet neuer lost her lustre;   1065
Yet if that quarrell. Fortune, do diuorce   1217
Haue (too) a Womans heart, which euer yet   1236
*More worth, then empty vanities: yet Prayers & Wishes   1286
*That they haue caught the King: and who knowes yet   1295
(Am yet a Courtier beggerly) nor could   1303
Wol. Be patient yet. | *Qu.* I will, when you are humble; Nay before,   1431
Refuse you for my Iudge, whom yet once more   1440
Wol. I do professe | You speake not like your selfe: who euer yet   1443
I then did feele full sicke, and yet not well,   1571
There's nothing I haue done yet o' my Conscience   1654
The willing'st sinne I euer yet committed, | May be absolu'd in English.   1672
Heauen is aboue all yet; there sits a Iudge, | That no King can corrupt.   1731
A Woman (I dare say without Vainglory) | Neuer yet branded with
Suspition?   1760
Yet will I adde an Honor; a great Patience.   1770
He ha's my heart yet, and shall haue my Prayers   1819
Marry this is yet but yong, and may be left   1888
And well deseruing? yet I know her for   1956
And yet words are no deeds. My Father lou'd you,   2026
Yet fill'd with my Abilities: Mine owne ends   2045

YET *cont.*

Appeare in formes more horrid) yet my Duty,	2072
I know 'twill stirre him strongly; yet I know	2098
I thanke my Memorie, I yet remember	2198
How euer, yet there is no great breach, when it comes	2532
Yet thus farre *Griffith,* giue me leaue to speake him,	2587
And yet with Charity. He was a man	2588
(Which was a sinne) yet in bestowing, Madam,	2614
The other (though vnfinish'd) yet so Famous,	2619
I am not worthy yet to weare: I shall assuredly.	2669
I caus'd you write, yet sent away? | *Pat.* No Madam.	2717
You must not leaue me yet. I must to bed,	2759
Then lay me forth (although vnqueen'd) yet like	2764
*Gard. Not yet Sir *Thomas Louell*: what's the matter?	2783
Lou. Me thinkes I could | Cry the Amen, and yet my Conscience sayes	2799
*Cran. I hope I am not too late, and yet the Gentleman	2989
Keep. Yes, my Lord: | But yet I cannot helpe you.	2994
'Tis well there's one aboue 'em yet; I had thought	3026
Yet freshly pittied in our memories.	3079
How euer faulty, yet should finde respect	3124
Cran. Stay good my Lords, | I haue a little yet to say. Looke there my Lords,	3160
That is, a faire young Maid that yet wants Baptisme,	3233
Though in her Cradle; yet now promises	3388
And yet no day without a deed to Crowne it.	3430
She must, the Saints must haue her; yet a Virgin,	3432

YHAUE = 2*1

What heere y'haue heard to her.	1330
These lazy knaues? Y'haue made a fine hand fellowes?	3329
*Kin. My Noble Gossips, y'haue beene too Prodigall;	3381

YOAKE = *1

*Car. And euer may your Highnesse yoake together,	2021

YONG = 3

Marry this is yet but yong, and may be left	1888
The Modell of our chaste loues: his yong daughter,	2723
She is yong, and of a Noble modest Nature,	2726

YORKE = 4*1

Of the right Reuerend Cardinall of Yorke.	99
Cardinall of *Yorke,* are ioyn'd with me their Seruant,	1153
*Camp. My Lord of *Yorke,* was not one Doctor *Pace*	1172
Camp. Most honour'd Madam, | My Lord of Yorke, out of his Noble nature,	1686
For after the stout Earle Northumberland | Arrested him at Yorke, and brought him forward	2565

YORKE-PLACE = 2

To Yorke-Place, where the Feast is held.	2515
1 Sir, | You must no more call it Yorke-place, that's past:	2516

YOU *see also* y'are, y'haue = 389*29

YOUD = *1

*Kin. Come, come my Lord, you'd spare your spoones;	3238

YOUL = 4*2

**You'l finde it wholesome. Loe, where comes that Rock	173
You'l finde a most vnfit time to disturbe him:	1097
You'l part away disgrac'd.	1727
Camp. Madam, you'l finde it so: | You wrong your Vertues	1805
Now, if you can blush, and crie guiltie Cardinall, | You'l shew a little Honestie.	2200

YOUL *cont.*
  Port. You'l leaue your noyse anon ye Rascals: doe   3259
YOULD = 1*1
  You'ld venture an emballing: I my selfe   1259
  *Youl'd feele more comfort. Why shold we (good Lady)   1792
YOULE = 1
  My Lord, youle beare vs company? | *Cham.* Excuse me,   1094
YOUNG = 5*1
  Cham. You are young Sir *Harry Guilford.*   678
  They were young and handsome, and of the best breed in the   1030
  I would not be a young Count in your way,   1251
  That is, a faire young Maid that yet wants Baptisme,   3233
  To haue this young one made a Christian.   3253
  That had a head to hit, either young or old,   3282
YOUR *l.*41 160 174 184 194 201 206 207 213 214 220 225 278 335 338 339
340 341 342 346 388 389 *393 398 438 448 479 481 483 497 519 521 522
540 630 636 655 659 *684 *697 715 719 728 732 759 763 775 784 787
794 797 807 *812 919 922 923 939 941 972 974 975 *1028 1041 1098
1105 1111 1113 1123 1133 1135 1142 1145 *1149 1150 1157 *1166 1169
1178 1234 1239 1240 1251 1252 1265 1267 1276 1287 1307 1315 1321
1324 1368 1370 1374 1376 1378 1379 1380 1382 1383 1386 1389 1395
1399 1411 1413 1416 1418 1426 1444 1458 1459 1463 *1467 1468 1469
1473 1474 1475 1476 1477 *1490 1509 1514 1515 1535 1578 1580 1585
1588 1592 1601 *1635 1646 *1647 1649 1651 1661 1688 1689 1694 1704
1709 1720 1721 *1723 1725 1730 1733 1737 1755 1757 1776 *1781 1784
1790 1797 1806 1811 1812 1821 1827 1842 1881 1994 2004 2007 2010
*2021 2040 2047 2048 2061 2062 2063 2065 2067 2113 *2117 2122 2128
2132 2147 2151 2166 2178 2179 2180 2189 2203 2213 2223 ·*2225 2239
2242 2245 2246 2281 2292 2301 2304 2381 2395 2403 2551 2559 2602
2671 2681 2687 2695 2696 2701 2703 2705 2785 2786 2791 2832 *2835
2845 2846 2855 2861 2872 2886 2891 2899 2901 2902 2903 2906 2917
2919 *2928 2929 2937 2941 2942 2954 2973 2974 2997 3016 3018 3044
3052 3054 3062 *3064 3093 3108 3109 3110 3118 3120 3123 3128 3139
3196 3203 3212 3219 *3238 3251 *3259 3261 *3266 3331 3334 3340 3350
*3369 3443 = 259*25, 1
  Thou art a cure fit for a King; you'r welcome   1118
YOURS = 3
  As yours was, put into you, euer casts   1808
  Should the approach of this wilde Riuer breake, | And stand vnshaken
  yours.   2074
  For euer, and for euer shall be yours.   2342
YOURSELFE *see* selfe
YOURSELUES *see* selues
YOUTHS = *1
  Por. These are the youths that thunder at a Playhouse,   3318
ZEALE = 2*1
  *And with what zeale? For now he has crackt the League   1057
  Zeale and obedience he still bore your Grace,   1688
  Had I but seru'd my God, with halfe the Zeale   2370
& *l.*185 *232 *468 663 *1058 *1166 *1243 *1273 *1286 *1467 1629 1631
1645 2211 *3064 *3071 *3369 = 5*12
& C *l.*892 1359 1363 *3360 = 3*1
1 *l.*2422 = 1
1 = 32*2
10 = *1
  *10 *Certaine* Ladies *or* Countesses, *with plaine Circlets of* | *Gold, without*
  Flowers.   2443

```
2  l.2423 = 1
2 = 37
3  l.2424 = 1
3 = 10
4  l.2425 = 1
5 = *1
```
　　*5 Maior of London, *bearing the Mace. Then* Garter, *in*　　2426
```
6 = *1
```
　　*6 Marquesse Dorset, *bearing a Scepter of Gold, on his head,*　　2429
```
7 = *1
```
　　*7 Duke of Suffolke, *in his Robe of Estate, his Coronet on his*　　2433
```
8 = *1
```
　　*8 *A* Canopy, *borne by foure of the* Cinque-Ports, *vnder it*　　2437
```
9 = *1
```
　　*9 *The* Olde Dutchesse of Norfolke, *in a Coronall of Gold,*　　2441

B2